Introduction to

MICROECONOMICS

FOURTH EDITION

EDWIN G. DOLAN

Ph.D. Yale University

BVT

The publisher of affordable textbooks

BVT

The publisher of affordable textbooks

INTRODUCTION TO MICROECONOMICS, FOURTH EDITION

ISBN: 978-1-60229-961-0

Copyright © 2010 by BVT Publishing, LLC

PROJECT DEVELOPMENT MANAGER: Brae Buhnerkemper

PROJECT DEVELOPMENT ASSISTANT: Brandi Cornwell

MANAGING EDITOR: Joyce Bianchini

SENIOR DEVELOPMENT EDITOR: Rhonda Minnema

PHOTO RESEARCHER: Della Brackett

COVER DESIGN TEAM: Jason James
Brae Buhnerkemper
Dan Harvey
Della Bracket

ILLUSTRATIONS: Dan Harvey

TYPESETTER: Dan Harvey

TEXT AND COVER PRINTING: Quad/Graphics

SALES MANAGER: Robert Rappeport

MARKETING MANGER: Richard Schofield

PERMISSIONS COORDINATOR: Suzanne Schmidt

ART DIRECTOR: Linda Price

Table of Contents

PART 1   Introduction to Economics

CHAPTER *1*   3
THE ECONOMIC WAY OF THINKING

PART 2 Markets and Government

CHAPTER 4   97
CHOICE, MARKETS, AND GOVERNMENT

CHAPTER 5   119
CHOICES BY CONSUMERS

CHAPTER 6   147

THE ECONOMICS OF CLIMATE CHANGE AND ENVIRONMENTAL POLICY

CHAPTER 7   175
GLOBAL TRADE AND TRADE POLICY

PART 3   Economics of the Firm

CHAPTER 8   199
PRODUCTION AND COST

CHAPTER 9   231
SUPPLY UNDER PERFECT COMPETITION

CHAPTER *10*   257
THE THEORY OF MONOPOLY

CHAPTER *11*   283
INDUSTRIAL ORGANIZATION, MONOPOLISTIC COMPETITION, AND OLIGOPOLY

CHAPTER *12*   311

ANTITRUST AND REGULATION

PART 4 Factor Markets and Income Distribution

CHAPTER 13   331
PRICING IN RESOURCE MARKETS

CHAPTER 16   403

INCOME DISTRIBUTION AND POVERTY

Preface

THE TWO YEARS leading up to this fourth edition of *Introduction to Micro-economics* from BVT Publishing have seen unusually rapid changes in the economy. These changes are incorporated in major revisions of several parts of the book.

As in the past, this book has a special focus on the globalization of economic life. Now, more than ever before, changes in the world economy affect what happens in the United States, and vice versa. In part, this is reflected in the early position given to the discussion of global climate change and international trade (Chapters 6 and 7). Discussions of global issues are not confined to these two chapters, however. New examples and illustrations from many parts of the world are found throughout the text.

Environmental economics is one of the areas in which change has been most rapid. Accordingly, Chapter 6, which covers climate change and environmental policy, is almost completely rewritten to incorporate both the latest scientific findings and the current policy initiatives. A new appendix covers the thorny issue of weighing the costs and benefits of economic decisions, effects of which stretch over a time horizon of hundreds of years.

The topics of income distribution and poverty are also of increasing importance. The early 2000s saw striking new trends in income distribution. The onset of worldwide recession after 2007 has made the issue of poverty, both at home and abroad, even more important than in the past. Extensive new material on these topics is found in Chapter 16.

Users who teach both micro- and macroeconomics sometimes find that it is harder to cover the wide diversity of microeconomic topics in a single semester than the more tightly integrated material of macroeconomics. In an effort to rebalance the micro and macro courses, there are two places where this fourth edition of *Introduction to Microeconomics* combines chapters that were previously separated. The result is a streamlined, sixteen-chapter outline and a book that is significantly shorter than before.

One such change occurs in Chapter 12, where issues of institutional economics and entrepreneurship, previously covered in a separate chapter, are now folded into the discussion of antitrust and regulatory policy. Another similar reorganization occurs in Chapter 13, which covers pricing in resource markets. As in earlier editions, this chapter begins with a general discussion of supply and demand in input markets, but now the number of figures and degree of detail is reduced to simplify the basic model. Following the general introduction, separate sections deal with applications to markets for labor, capital, and natural resources. Two chapters from previous editions are, thereby, combined into one.

As always, I thank the entire publishing and editorial staff of BVT Publishing for their highly professional support. They are a pleasure to work with, and I hope that all students and instructors who use this book benefit as much as I have from their unique and innovative approach to textbook publishing.

Features of This Edition

- *State of the art pedagogy*: An abundance of case studies introduce and illustrate the subject matter of every chapter.
- *Integrated international economics:* As the world economy itself comes closer together, international economics must be more closely integrated into the principles course. Accordingly, topics relating to international economics are not exclusively confined to Chapter 7, which outlines the theory of international trade. In addition, numerous examples and cases drawn from international economic experience are included throughout the book.

Supplements for Instructors

1. **Study Guide.** The Study Guide has hands-on applications and self-testing programs. Students can gain an advantage by reinforcing their reading and lecture notes with the following study guide features:

- *Where You're Going:* The objectives and terms for each chapter are recapped to tie concepts together.

- *Walking Tour:* The "Walking Tour" section provides a narrative summary of the chapter and incorporates questions on key points. Answers are given in the margin.

- *Hands On:* Geographical and numerical exercises clarify concepts and better prepare students for tests and quizzes.

- *Economics in the News:* A news item illustrates how concepts covered in the chapter could appear in the real world. Questions and answers reinforce the concepts.

- *Questions for Review:* These questions and answers follow the key chapter concepts, preparing students for the self-test.

- *Self-Test:* Extra test preparation increases a student's understanding and ability to succeed.

- *Careers in Economics:* Formerly an appendix in the text, this material provides students with an understanding of where the study of economics could lead them.

2. **Instructor's Manual.** The expanded Instructor's Manual contains material that can be easily included in lectures. The manual also includes all of its traditional elements, including instructional objectives, lecture notes, and suggestions.

3. **Test Bank.** The accompanying Test Bank has been expanded to include 150 questions per chapter in a variety of formats, including multiple choice, true/false, and essay questions.

4. **PowerPoints.** This edition is accompanied by a greatly expanded set of PowerPoint slides. Beginning with this edition, the slides for each chapter include coverage of all graphical material in the text, sometimes supplemented by additional material, as well.

5. **Customize This Book.** If you have additional material you'd like to add (handouts, lecture notes, syllabus, etc.) or simply rearrange and delete content, BVT Publishing's custom publishing division can help you modify this book's content, to produce a book that satisfies your specific instructional needs. BVT Publishing has the only custom publishing division that puts your material exactly where you want it to go, easily and seamlessly. Please visit www.bvtpublishing.com or call us at 1-800-646-7782 for more information on BVT Publishing's Custom Publishing Program.

Supplements for Students

BVT Publishing is pleased to provide students with a free, comprehensive online tutorial which can be found at www.bvtstudents.com. This website offers the following:

1. **eBook editions.** Save time, money and paper by purchasing an eBook version of this text directly from our convenient online store, located on our student website.

2. **Shopping Cart.** For the student's convenience and pocketbook, the student website also contains a shopping cart where they have the added option of purchasing the traditional paper textbook directly from the publisher if they prefer.

3. **Self Testing.** Students can test their knowledge of this book's content on our student website. The Self Test questions are designed to help improve students' mastery of the information in the book.

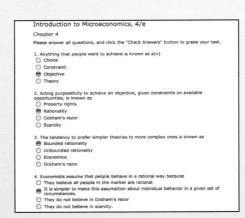 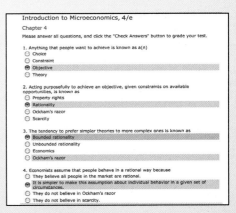

4. **Flash Cards.** The Flash Cards are an easy way for students to spot-check their understanding of common and important terms, as well as effectively retain the information.

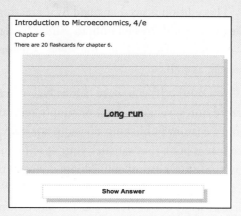 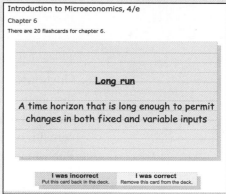

5. **Chapter Summaries.** The Chapter Summaries are another tool designed to give the students an overview of each chapter's content, further aiding the students in content comprehension and retention.

About the Author

EDWIN G. DOLAN was born in Oklahoma and grew up in a small town in Oregon. He attended Earlham College and Indiana University, where he majored in Russian Studies as an undergraduate and later earned a Masters degree from Indiana University's Russian and East-European Institute. After earning a doctorate in economics from Yale University, he taught at Dartmouth College, the University of Chicago, George Mason University, and Gettysburg College.

In 1971, he published his first book, TANSTAAFL: The Economic Strategy for Environmental Crisis, which, although long out of print, continues to be cited as a classic in its field. That slim volume was followed by a number of other textbooks covering principles of economics, money and banking, and problems of microeconomic policy. Combined world-wide sales of these books total more than a million copies.

As economic and political changes accelerated in the Soviet Union during the Gorbachev era, Professor Dolan returned to his early interest in Russia and Eastern Europe. He began teaching in Moscow in 1990. In 1993, he and his wife founded the American Institute of Business and Economics, an independent, not-for-profit MBA program that continues operation to this day. Since leaving Moscow in 2001, he has taught global macroeconomics, managerial economics, money and banking, and other courses in Latvia, Hungary, Croatia, Bulgaria, the Czech Republic, and Estonia. When not lecturing abroad, he makes his home in Washington's San Juan Islands, where he is active in the Community Education program of Skagit Valley College. Hobbies include tennis, horseback riding, woodworking, and bridge.

PART 1

Introduction to Economics

CHAPTER *1*

The Economic Way of Thinking

After reading this chapter, you will understand the following:

1. What is the subject matter of economics?
2. Four fundamental economic choices:
   – What will an economy produce?
   – How will goods and services be produced?
   – Who will produce which goods and services?
   – For whom will goods be produced?
3. How are economic choices coordinated?
4. How do economists use theory, graphs, and data in their work?

Scarcity

A situation in which there is not enough of a resource to meet all of everyone's wants

I T WAS A turbulent year for the world economy. In the first half of the year, oil prices rose to a record high, as did prices for a range of other commodities from wheat and corn to gold. Later in the year, prices of these same commodities fell sharply. At the same time other prices—those for housing in many countries, the prices of stocks traded on the New York Stock Exchange, and the exchange rate of the dollar against the euro—also displayed unprecedented volatility. Many factors lay behind these swings in prices—the weather in Australia, political events in Venezuela, a presidential election in the United States, and the onset of a global financial crisis. How can we understand all of these complex, yet interrelated, events?

This chapter will take the first steps toward a systematic way of thinking about the economy by introducing a few big ideas that apply to events in all markets, in all countries, at all times. The biggest of all the ideas that underlie this economic way of thinking is **scarcity**. Scarcity means any situation in which there is not enough of something to fill everyone's wants. For example, corn grown in the U.S. Midwest is scarce because there is not enough of it to fully meet the competing needs of Chinese consumers, who want to eat more corn-fed pork as they become wealthier, and U.S. drivers, who are burning more corn-based ethanol in their cars. The scarcity of corn affects people's choices about how to use not only corn but also other scarce goods. The effects on markets for wheat and oil are relatively direct. The effects on exchange rates and stock markets are not quite so easy to trace, but they are no less important. Scarcity and the way people deal with it are the central topics of **economics**, which is commonly defined as the social science that seeks to understand the choices people make in using scarce resources to meet their wants.

Economics, as its definition makes clear, is a study not of things or money or wealth but of *people*. Economics is about people because scarcity itself is a human phenomenon. Deposits of crude oil lay undisturbed in the ground for millions of years before they became the object of human wants. Only at that point did they become scarce in the sense that economists understand the term.

The focus on the human dimension of scarcity and choice is part of what makes economics a social science. In addition, economics is a social science because people do not attempt to solve the problem of scarcity in isolation. Instead, they can meet their wants much more effectively by trading with one another. As they trade, each person gives up something of value to others in such a way that each person gains from the exchange. Some economists think exchange is even more important than scarcity as a defining characteristic of economics.[1]

The wide range of topics covered by economics can be divided into two main branches. The example of corn prices is an application from **microeconomics**. The prefix *micro*, meaning "small," indicates that this branch of economics deals with the choices of small economic units such as households, firms, and government agencies. Although microeconomics studies individual behavior, its scope can be worldwide, as when it focuses on global trade in goods such as cars and crude oil.

Economics also has another branch, known as **macroeconomics**. The prefix *macro*, meaning "large," indicates that this branch deals with larger-scale economic phenomena. Typical problems in macroeconomics include how to maintain conditions in which people who want jobs can find them, how to protect the economy against the distortions caused by widespread price increases (inflation), and how to provide for a continued increase in living standards over time. Choices studied by macroeconomics include those made by governments—for example, choices among alternative policies concerning taxes, expenditures, budget deficits, and the financial system. However, because macroeconomic phenomena like inflation represent the end result of millions of individual choices regarding the prices of particular goods and services, macroeconomics ultimately rests on a microeconomic foundation.

Whether one is dealing with microeconomics or macroeconomics, whether with domestic or international economic relationships—all economic analysis comes down to a special way of thinking about how people interact with one another as they choose how to use scarce resources.

What? How? Who? For Whom?

Among the most important economic choices people make are those concerning what goods will be produced, how they will be produced, who will do which jobs, and for

---

Economics

The social science that seeks to understand the choices people make in using scarce resources to meet their wants

Microeconomics

The branch of economics that studies the choices of individual units—including households, business firms, and government agencies

Macroeconomics

The branch of economics that studies large-scale economic phenomena, particularly inflation, unemployment, and economic growth

whom the results of production will be available. Each of these choices is made necessary because of scarcity, and each can be used to introduce a key element of the economic way of thinking.

Deciding What to Produce: Opportunity Cost

The first choice is that of what goods to produce. Although the number of goods and services that could be produced in any real economy is immense, the basic concept of choice can be illustrated with an economy in which there are just two alternative goods. Suppose these goods are cars and education. For many students, going without a car (or driving a used car instead of a new one) is a sacrifice that must be made in order to get a college education. The same trade-off faced by an individual student is also faced by the economy as a whole: Not enough cars and education can be produced to satisfy everyone's wants. Somehow it must be decided how much of each good to produce.

The impossibility of producing as much of everything as people want reflects a scarcity of the productive resources that are used to make all goods. Many scarce productive resources must be combined to make even the simplest of goods. For example, making a car requires steel, glass, paint, welding machines, land for factories, and the labor of autoworkers. For convenience, all the various productive resources can be grouped into three basic categories called **factors of production**: labor, capital, and natural resources. **Labor** includes all of the productive contributions made by people working with their minds and muscles. **Capital** includes all the productive inputs created by people—including tools, machinery, buildings, and intangible items, such as computer software. **Natural resources** include anything that can be used as a productive input in its natural state—for example, farmland, building sites, forests, and mineral deposits.

Productive resources that are used to satisfy one want cannot be used to satisfy another at the same time. Steel, concrete, and building sites used for automobile factories cannot also be used for classrooms. People who are employed as teachers cannot spend the same time working on an automobile assembly line. Even the time students spend in class and studying for tests represents use of a factor of production that could otherwise be used as labor in an auto plant. Whenever the inputs to production have more than one possible use, producing one good means forgoing the opportunity to produce something else instead. Economists express this basic truth by saying that everything has an **opportunity cost**. The opportunity cost of a good or service is its cost in terms of the forgone opportunity to pursue the best possible alternative activity with the same time or resources.

In our two-good economy, the opportunity cost of producing a college graduate can be stated in terms of the number of cars that could have been produced by using the same labor, capital, and natural resources. Suppose that the opportunity cost of educating a college graduate is four Toyota Camrys. Such a ratio (graduates per car or cars per graduate) is a useful way to express opportunity cost when only two goods are involved. More typically, though, we deal with situations in which there are many goods. Having more of one means giving up a little bit of many others.

In an economy with many goods, opportunity costs can be expressed in terms of a common unit of measurement, money. For example, rather than saying that a college

Factors of production

The basic inputs of labor, capital, and natural resources used in producing all goods and services

Labor

The contributions to production made by people working with their minds and muscles

Capital

All means of production that are created by people—including tools, industrial equipment, and structures

Natural resources

Anything that can be used as a productive input in its natural state, such as farmland, building sites, forests, and mineral deposits

Opportunity cost

The cost of a good or service measured in terms of the forgone opportunity to pursue the best possible alternative activity with the same time or resources

education is worth four Camrys or that a Camry is worth one-fourth of a college education, we could say that the opportunity cost of a car is $25,000 and that of a college education is $100,000.

Useful as it is to have a common unit of measurement, great care must be taken when opportunity costs are expressed in terms of money because not all out-of-pocket money expenditures represent the sacrifice of opportunities to do something else. At the same time, not all sacrificed opportunities take the form of money spent. *Applying Economic Ideas 1.1*, which analyzes both the out-of-pocket expenditures and the opportunity costs of a college education, shows why.

The importance of opportunity cost will be stressed again and again in this book. The habit of looking for opportunity costs is one of the distinguishing features of the economic way of thinking.

Deciding How to Produce: Efficiency and Entrepreneurship

A second basic economic choice is that of how to produce. There is more than one way to produce almost any good or service. Cars, for example, can be made in highly automated factories, using a lot of capital equipment and relatively little labor; or they can be built one by one in smaller shops, using a lot of labor and only a few general-purpose machines. Toyota Camrys are built the first way, Tesla Roadsters the second way. The same kind of thing could be said about education. Economics can be taught in a small classroom with one teacher and a blackboard serving twenty students; or it can be taught in a large lecture hall in which the teacher uses video technology to address hundreds of students.

Economic efficiency

A state of affairs in which it is impossible to make any change that satisfies one person's wants more fully without causing some other person's wants to be satisfied less fully

EFFICIENCY   Efficiency is a key consideration in deciding how to produce. In everyday usage, efficiency means producing with a minimum of expense, effort, and waste. Economists use a more precise definition. **Economic efficiency**, they say, refers to a state of affairs in which it is impossible to make any change that satisfies one person's wants more fully without causing some other person's wants to be satisfied less fully.[2]

Although this formal definition of economic efficiency may be unfamiliar, it is actually closely related to the everyday notion of efficiency. If there is some way to make you better off without making me worse off, it is wasteful (inefficient) to pass up the opportunity. If I have a red pen that I am not using, and you need one just for a minute, it would be wasteful for you to buy a red pen of your own. It is more efficient for me to lend you my pen;

Automation in the car industry can produce many cars with little labor

Applying Economic Ideas 1.1
THE OPPORTUNITY COST OF A COLLEGE EDUCATION

How much does it cost you to go to college? If you are a resident student at a typical four-year private college in the United States, you can answer this question by making up a budget like the one shown in Figure A. This can be called a budget of out-of-pocket costs because it includes all the items—and only those items—that you or your parents must actually pay for in a year.

Your own out-of-pocket costs may be much higher or lower than those listed. Chances are, though, that these are the main categories that first come to mind when you think about the costs of college. As you begin to think more like an economist, you may find it useful to restate your college budget in terms of opportunity costs. Which of the items in Figure A represent opportunities that you have forgone in order to go to college? Are any forgone opportunities missing? To answer these questions, compare Figure A with Figure B, which shows a budget of opportunity costs.

Some items are both opportunity costs and out-of-pocket costs. The first three items in Figure A show up again in Figure B. To spend $14,000 on tuition and fees and $1,200 on books and supplies, you must give up the opportunity to buy other goods and services—to buy a car or rent a ski condo, for instance. To spend $1,100 getting to and from school, you must pass up the opportunity to travel somewhere else or to spend the money on something other than travel. Not all out-of-pocket costs are also opportunity costs, however. Consider the last two items in the out-

What are opportunity costs of your education?

of-pocket budget. By spending $7,000 on room, board, and personal expenses during the year, you are not really giving up the opportunity to do something else. Whether or not you were going to college, you would have to eat, live somewhere, and buy clothes. Because these are expenses that you would have in any case, they do not count as opportunity costs of going to college.

Finally, some items are opportunity costs without being out-of-pocket costs. Think about what you would be doing if you were not going to college. If you were not going to college, you probably would have taken a job and started earning money soon after leaving high school. As a high-school graduate, your earnings would be about $16,000 during the nine months of the school year. (You can work during the summer even if you are attending college.) Because this potential income is something that you must forgo for the sake of college, it is an opportunity cost even though it does not involve an outlay of money.

Which budget you use depends on the kind of decision you are making. If you have already decided to go to college and are doing your financial planning, the out-of-pocket budget will tell you how much you will have to raise from savings, money earned, parents' contributions, loans, and scholarships to make ends meet. But if you are making the more basic choice between going to college and pursuing a career that does not require a college degree, the opportunity cost of college is what counts.

Figure A	Budget of Out-of-Pocket Costs	Figure B	Budget of Opportunity Costs
Tuition and fees	$14,000	Tuition and fees	$14,000
Books and supplies	1,200	Books and supplies	1,200
Transportation to and from home	1,100	Transportation to and from home	1,100
Room and board	7,000	Forgone income	16,000
Personal expenses	1,400		
Total out-of-pocket costs	**$24,700**	**Total opportunity costs**	**$32,300**

it makes you better off and me no worse off. If there is a way to make us both better off, it would be all the more wasteful not to take advantage of the opportunity. You lend me your bicycle for the afternoon, and I will lend you my volleyball. If I do not ride a bicycle very often and you do not play volleyball very often, it would be inefficient for us both to own one of each item.

The concept of economic efficiency has a variety of applications. One such application centers on the question of *how* to produce. **Efficiency in production** refers to a situation in which it is not possible, given available productive resources and existing knowledge, to produce more of one good without forgoing the opportunity to produce some of another good. The concept of efficiency in production, like the broader concept of economic efficiency, includes the everyday notion of avoiding waste. For example, a grower of apples finds that beyond some certain quantity, using more water per tree does not increase the yield of apples; so using more than that amount would be wasteful. Better to transfer the extra water to the production of, say, peaches. That way, more peaches can be grown without any reduction in the apple crop.

The economist's definition also includes more subtle possibilities for improving the efficiency of production in cases where the waste of resources is less obvious. For example, it is possible to grow apples in Georgia. It is also possible, by selecting the right tree varieties and using winter protection, to grow peaches in Vermont. Some hobbyists do grow both fruits in both states. However, doing so on a commercial scale would be inefficient even if growers in both states followed the most careful cultivation practices and avoided any obvious waste, like using too much water. To see why, suppose that initially apple and peach trees were planted in equal numbers in the two states. Then compare this with a situation in which 500 fewer struggling peach trees had been planted in Vermont, and 500 thriving apple trees had been planted instead. At the same time, suppose 500 fewer heat-stressed apple trees had been planted in Georgia, and peaches had taken their place. The second alternative would increase the output of both fruits without increasing the total land, labor, and capital used in fruit production. This shows that the original distribution of trees was inefficient.

HOW TO INCREASE PRODUCTION POTENTIAL   Once efficiency has been achieved, more of one good can be produced only by forgoing the opportunity to produce something else, assuming that productive resources and knowledge are held constant. Over time, accumulating more resources and finding new ways of putting them to work can expand production potential.

In the past, discovery of new supplies of natural resources has been an important way of increasing production potential. Population growth has always been, and still is, another way. However, as the most easily tapped supplies of natural resources are depleted and as population growth slows in most parts of the world, capital will increasingly be the factor of production that contributes most to the expansion of production potential.

The act of increasing the economy's stock of capital—that is, its supply of productive inputs made by people—is known as **investment**. Investment involves a trade-off of present consumption for future consumption. To build more factories, roads, and computers, we have to divert resources from the production of bread, movies, hair-

Efficiency in production

A situation in which it is not possible, given available knowledge and productive resources, to produce more of one good without forgoing the opportunity to produce some of another good

Investment

The act of increasing the economy's stock of capital—that is, its supply of means of production made by people

cuts, and other things that satisfy immediate wants. In return, we put ourselves in a better position to satisfy our future wants.

Increased availability of productive resources is not the only source of economic growth, however. Even more important are improvements in human knowledge—the invention of new technology, new forms of organization, and new ways of satisfying wants. The process of looking for new possibilities—making use of new ways of doing things, being alert to new opportunities, and overcoming old limits—is called **entrepreneurship**. It is a dynamic process that breaks down the constraints imposed by existing knowledge and limited supplies of factors of production.

Entrepreneurship

The process of looking for new possibilities—making use of new ways of doing things, being alert to new opportunities, and overcoming old limits

Entrepreneurship does not have to mean inventing something or starting a new business, although it sometimes does. It may mean finding a new market for an existing product—for example, convincing people in Germany that Japanese sushi makes a quick and tasty lunch. It may mean taking advantage of price differences between one market and another—for example, buying hay at a low price in Pennsylvania, where growing conditions have been good in the past year, and reselling it in Virginia, where the weather has been too dry.

Households can be entrepreneurs, too. They do not simply repeat the same patterns of work and leisure every day. They seek variety—new jobs, new foods, and new places to visit. Each time you try something new, you are taking a step into the unknown. In this sense, you are an entrepreneur.

Entrepreneurship is sometimes called the fourth factor of production. However, entrepreneurship differs from the three classical factors of production in important ways. Unlike labor, capital, and natural resources, entrepreneurship is intangible and difficult to measure. Although entrepreneurs earn incomes reflecting the value that the market places on their accomplishments, we cannot speak of a price per unit of entrepreneurship; there are no such units. Also, unlike human resources (which grow old), machines (which wear out), and natural resources (which can be used up), the inventions and discoveries of entrepreneurs are not depleted as they are used. Once a new product or concept has been invented—such as gasoline-electric hybrid power for cars, text messaging on cell phones, or life insurance as a form of financial investment, the required knowledge does not have to be created again (although, of course, it may be supplanted by even better ideas). All in all, it is more helpful to think of entrepreneurship as a process of learning better ways of using the three basic factors of production than as a separate factor of production.

Deciding Who Will Do Which Work: the Division of Labor

The questions of what will be produced and how to produce it would exist even for a person living in isolation. Even the fictional castaway Robinson Crusoe had to decide whether to fish or hunt birds; and if he decided to fish, he had to decide whether to do so with a net or with a hook and line. In contrast, the economic questions of who will do which work and for whom output will be produced exist only for people living in society—another reason economics is considered one of the social sciences.

The question of who will do which work is a matter of organizing the social division of labor. Will everyone do everything independently—be a farmer in the morning, a tailor in the afternoon, and a poet in the evening? Or will people cooperate—work together, trade goods and services, and specialize in one particular job? Economists answer these questions by pointing out that it is more efficient to cooperate. Doing so allows a given number of people to produce more than they could if each of them worked alone. Three things make cooperation worthwhile: teamwork, learning by doing, and comparative advantage.

First, consider *teamwork*. In a classic paper on this subject, Armen Alchian and Harold Demsetz used the example of workers unloading bulky crates from a truck.[3] The crates are so large that one worker alone cannot move them at all without unpacking them. Two people, each working independently, would take hours to unload the truck. If they work as a team, however, they can easily pick up the crates and stack them on the loading dock. This example shows that even when everyone is doing the same work, and even when little skill is involved, teamwork pays.

A second reason for cooperation applies when there are different jobs to be done and different skills to be learned. In a furniture plant, for example, some workers operate production equipment, others use office equipment, and still others buy materials. Even if all the workers start out with equal abilities, each gets better at a particular job by doing it repeatedly. *Learning by doing* thus turns workers of average productivity into specialists, thereby creating a more productive team.

A third reason for cooperation comes into play after the process of learning by doing has developed different skills, and it also applies when workers start out with different talents and abilities—the principle of division of labor according to *comparative advantage*. **Comparative advantage** is the ability to do a job or produce a good at a relatively lower opportunity cost than someone else.

The following example will illustrate the principle of comparative advantage. Suppose two clerical workers, Bill and Jim, are assigned the job of getting out a batch of personalized letters to clients. Jim is a whiz. He can prepare a letter in five minutes and stuff it into an envelope in one minute. Working alone, he can finish ten letters in an hour. Bill is slow and clumsy. It takes him ten minutes to prepare a letter and five minutes to stuff it into the envelope. Alone, he can do only four letters an hour. In summary form:

Jim:	Prepare one letter in five min.	Stuff one envelope one in min.
Bill:	Prepare one letter in ten min.	Stuff one envelope five in min.

Without cooperation, the two workers' limit is fourteen letters per hour between them. Could they do better by cooperating? It depends on who does which job. One idea might be for Jim to prepare all the letters while Bill does all the stuffing because that way they can just keep up with each other; but at five minutes per letter, that kind of cooperation cuts their combined output to twelve letters per hour. It is worse than not cooperating at all.

Instead, they should divide the work according to the principle of comparative advantage. Even though Bill is slower at preparing the letters, he has a *comparative advantage* in preparation because the opportunity cost of that part of the work is lower for him: The ten minutes he takes to prepare a letter is equal to the time he needs to stuff two envelopes. For Jim, the five minutes he takes to prepare a letter could be used to stuff five envelopes. For Bill, then, the opportunity cost of preparing one letter is to

Comparative advantage

The ability to produce a good or service at a relatively lower opportunity cost than someone else

forgo stuffing *two* envelopes, whereas for Jim the opportunity cost of preparing one letter is to forgo stuffing *five* envelopes.

Because Bill gives up fewer stuffed envelopes per letter than Jim, the principle of comparative advantage says that Bill should spend all his time preparing letters. If he does, he can produce six letters per hour. Meanwhile Jim can spend forty-five minutes of each hour preparing nine letters, and the last fifteen minutes of each hour stuffing all fifteen envelopes. By specializing according to comparative advantage, the two workers can increase their total output to fifteen letters per hour, the best they can possible do.

In this example, the principle of comparative advantage points the way toward an efficient division of labor between two people working side by side. However, the principle also has broader implications. It can apply to a division of labor between individuals or business firms working far apart—even in different countries. In fact, the earliest application of the principle was to international trade (see *Who Said It? Who Did It? 1.1*). Today comparative advantage remains one of the primary motiva-

Who Said It? Who Did It? 1.1
DAVID RICARDO AND THE THEORY OF COMPARATIVE ADVANTAGE

David Ricardo was born in London in 1772, the son of an immigrant who was a member of the London stock exchange. Ricardo's education was rather haphazard, and he entered his father's business at the age of fourteen. In 1793, he married and went into business on his own. These were years of war and financial turmoil. The young Ricardo developed a reputation for remarkable astuteness and quickly made a large fortune.

In 1799, Ricardo read Adam Smith's *The Wealth of Nations* and developed an interest in political economy (as economics was then called). In 1809, his first writings on economics appeared. These were a series of newspaper articles on "The High Price of Bullion," which appeared during the following year as a pamphlet. Several other short works added to his reputation in this area. In 1814, he retired from business to devote all his time to political economy.

Ricardo's major work was *Principles of Political Economy and Taxation*, first published in 1817. This work contains, among other things, a pioneering statement of the principle of comparative advantage as applied to international trade. Using a lucid numerical example, Ricardo showed why, as long as wool can be produced comparatively less expensively in England, it was to the advantage

Ricardo's comparative advantage describes exporting wool and importing wine between England and Portugal

of both countries for England to export wool to Portugal and to import wine in return, even though both products could be produced with fewer labor hours in Portugal.

International trade is only one topic in Ricardo's *Principles*. The book covers the whole field of economics, as it then existed, beginning with value theory and progressing to a theory of economic growth and evolution. Ricardo held that the economy was growing toward a future "steady state." At that point, economic growth would come to a halt, and the wage rate would be reduced to the subsistence level. This gloomy view and the equally pessimistic views of Ricardo's contemporary, Thomas Malthus, gave political economy a reputation as "the dismal science."

Ricardo's book was extremely influential. For more than half a century thereafter, much of the writing on economic theory published in England consisted of expansions and commentaries on Ricardo's work. Economists as different as Karl Marx, the revolutionary socialist, and John Stuart Mill, a defender of liberal capitalism, took Ricardo's theories as their starting point. Even today, there are "neo-Ricardian" and "new classical" economists who look to Ricardo's works for inspiration.

tions for mutually beneficial cooperation, whether on the scale of the workplace or on that of the world as a whole.

Whatever the context, the principle of comparative advantage is easy to apply provided one remembers that it is rooted in the concept of opportunity cost. Suppose there are two tasks, A and B, and two parties, X and Y (individuals, firms, or countries), each capable of doing both tasks, but not equally well. First ask what is the opportunity cost for X of doing a unit of task A, measured in terms of how many units of task B could be done with the same time or resources. Then ask the same question for Y. The party with the lower opportunity cost for doing a unit of task A has the comparative advantage in doing that task. To check, ask what is the opportunity cost for each party of doing a unit of task B, measured in terms how many units of task A could be done with the same time or resources. The party with the lower opportunity cost for doing a unit of task B has the comparative advantage in doing that task. Both A and B will be better off if each specializes according to comparative advantage.

Deciding for Whom Goods Will Be Produced: Positive and Normative Economics

Together, the advantages of team production, learning by doing, and comparative advantage mean that people can produce more efficiently by cooperating than they could if each worked in isolation. Cooperation raises yet another issue, however: For whom will goods be produced? The question of the distribution of output among members of society has implications in terms of both efficiency and fairness.

EFFICIENCY IN DISTRIBUTION   Consider first a situation in which production has already taken place and the supply of goods is fixed. Suppose, for example, that 30 students get on a bus to go to a football game. Bag lunches are handed out. Half the bags contain a ham sandwich and a root beer; the other half contain a tuna sandwich and a cola. What happens when the students open their bags? They do not just eat whatever they find—they start trading. Some swap sandwiches; others swap drinks. Maybe there is not enough of everything to give each person his or her first choice. Nevertheless, the trading makes at least some people better off than they were when they started. Moreover, no one ends up worse off. If some of the students do not want to trade, they can always eat what was given to them in the first place.

This example shows one sense in which the "for whom" question is partly about efficiency: Starting from any given quantity of goods, their distribution can be improved through trades that result in better satisfaction of some people's preferences. As long as it is possible to trade existing supplies of goods in a way that permits some people to satisfy their wants more fully without making others worse off, **efficiency in distribution** can be improved even while the total quantity of goods remains fixed.

Efficiency in distribution and efficiency in production are two aspects of the general concept of economic efficiency. When both aspects are taken into account, the relationship between distribution and efficiency is not restricted to situations in which the total amount of goods is fixed in advance. That is so because the rules for distribu-

Efficiency in distribution

A situation in which it is not possible, by redistributing existing supplies of goods, to satisfy one person's wants more fully without causing some other person's wants to be satisfied less fully

tion affect the patterns of production. For example, suppose rewards for providing nursing care are increased relative to the rewards for producing clothing. As a result, some people will switch jobs, so that more nursing care and less clothing is produced. Another reason is that rules for distribution affect incentives for entrepreneurship. If there are great rewards for discovering new ways of doing things, people will make greater efforts to improve products, methods of production, and means of distribution.

FAIRNESS IN DISTRIBUTION   Efficiency is not the whole story when it comes to the question of for whom goods will be produced. One can also ask whether a given distribution is fair. Questions of fairness often dominate discussions of distribution.

One widely held view judges fairness in distribution in terms of equality. This concept of fairness is based on the idea that all people, by virtue of their shared humanity, deserve a portion of the goods and services turned out by the economy. There are many versions of this concept. Some people think that all income and wealth should be distributed equally. Others think that people have an equal right to a "safety net" level of income but that inequality in distributing any surplus beyond that level is not necessarily unfair. Still others think that certain goods, such as health care and education, should be distributed equally but that it is fair for other goods to be distributed less equally.

An alternative view, which also has many adherents, judges fairness not in terms of how much each person receives but instead, in terms of the process through which goods are distributed. In this view, fairness requires that certain rules and procedures be observed, such as respect for property or nondiscrimination on grounds of race and gender. As long as those rules are followed, any resulting distribution of income is viewed as acceptable. In this view, equality of opportunity is emphasized more than equality of outcome.

POSITIVE AND NORMATIVE ECONOMICS   Some economists make a sharp distinction between questions of efficiency and fairness. Discussions of efficiency are seen as part of **positive economics**, the area of economics that is concerned with facts and the relationships among them. Discussions of fairness, in contrast, are seen as part of **normative economics**, the area of economics that is devoted to judgments about whether particular economic policies and conditions are good or bad.

Normative economics extends beyond the question of fairness in the distribution of output. Value judgments also arise about the fairness of the other three basic choices faced by every economy. In choosing what will be produced, is it fair to permit production of alcohol and tobacco but to outlaw production of marijuana? In choosing how to produce, is it fair to allow people to work under dangerous or unhealthy conditions, or should work under such conditions be prohibited? In choosing who does which work, is it fair to limit access to specific jobs according to age, gender, race, or union membership? As you can see, normative issues extend to every corner of economics.

Positive economics, rather than offering value judgments about outcomes, focuses on understanding the processes by which the four basic economic questions are or could be answered. It analyzes the way economies operate, or would operate, if certain institutions or policies were changed. It traces relationships between facts, often looking for regularities and patterns that can be measured statistically.

Positive economics

The area of economics that is concerned with facts and the relationships among them

Normative economics

The area of economics that is devoted to judgments about whether economic policies or conditions are good or bad

Most economists consider positive economics their primary area of expertise, but normative considerations influence the conduct of positive economics in several ways. The most significant of those influences is the selection of topics to investigate. An economist who sees excessive unemployment as a glaring injustice may study that problem; one who sympathizes with victims of job discrimination may take up a different line of research. Also, normative views are likely to affect the ways in which data are collected, ideas about which facts can be considered true, and so on.

At one time it was thought that a purely positive economics could be developed, untouched by normative considerations of values and fairness. Within its framework, all disputes could be resolved by reference to objective facts. Today that notion is less widely held. Nevertheless, it remains important to be aware that most major economic controversies, especially those that have to do with government policy, have normative as well as positive components and to be aware of the way each component shapes the way we think about those controversies.

Coordinating Economic Choices

To function effectively, an economy must have some way of coordinating the choices of millions of individuals regarding what to produce, how to produce it, who will do each job, and for whom the output will be produced. This section discusses how households, businesses, and the government interact in the coordination of economic choices.

A Non-Economic Example

You, like almost everyone, have probably had the experience of shopping at a supermarket where there are several long checkout lines. In such a situation, you and other shoppers want to get through the checkout process as fast as possible. The store, too, would like to avoid a situation in which customers in some lines have a long wait for service while the cashiers in other lines stand idle for lack of customers. How can this be done?

Hierarchy

A way of achieving coordination in which individual actions are guided by instructions from a central authority

Spontaneous order

A way of achieving coordination in which individuals adjust their actions in response to cues from their immediate environment

One way would be for the store to follow the example of the U.S. Customs service at New York's busy Kennedy International Airport where an employee is on duty to direct arriving passengers to the agent with the shortest wait. Supermarkets, however, do not usually work that way. Instead, supermarkets leave shoppers to decide for themselves which line to join based on information from their own observations. As you approach the checkout area, you first look to see which lines are the shortest. You then make allowance for the possibility that some shoppers have carts that are heaped full, while others have only a few items. Using your own judgment based on your own observations, you head for the line you think will be fastest.

The coordination system used by the Customs Service at JFK airport is an example of coordination by **hierarchy**. Hierarchy is a way of achieving coordination in which individual actions are guided by instructions from a central authority. The approach used in supermarkets is an example of coordination by **spontaneous order**. Under this system, coordination is achieved when individuals adjust their own actions as they see best in response to cues received from their immediate environment. This method is *orderly* because it achieves an approximately equal waiting time in each checkout line. It is *spontaneous* in that coordination is achieved without central direction. Even though no shopper has the specific goal of equalizing the lines, approximate equalization is the end result.

Spontaneous Order in Markets

Market

Any arrangement people have for trading with one another

In economics, markets are the most important example of the coordination of decisions through spontaneous order. A **market** is any arrangement people have for trading with one another. Some markets have formal rules and carry out exchanges at a single location, such as the New York Stock Exchange. Other markets are more informal, such as the word-of-mouth networks through which domestic workers get in touch with people who need their services. Despite the wide variety of forms that markets take, they all have one thing in common: They provide the information and incentives people need to coordinate their decisions.

Just as shoppers need information about the length of checkout lines, participants in markets need information about the scarcity and opportunity costs of various goods and factors of production. Markets rely primarily on prices to transmit this information. If a good or factor of production becomes scarcer, its price is bid up. The increase in the price tells people it is worth more and signals producers to make greater efforts to increase supplies. For example, when platinum first began to be used in catalytic converters to reduce pollution from automobile exhaust, new buyers entered the market. As automakers began to compete with makers of jewelry and other traditional users, platinum became more difficult to acquire. Competition for available supplies bids up the price of platinum. This provided buyers with a cue that the value of platinum had increased and provided an incentive to be careful with its use. At the same time, producers learned that, where possible, they should increase the quantity of platinum mined.

Instead, suppose a new technology were to reduce the cost of producing platinum, for example, by allowing extraction of platinum from mine wastes that were discarded in earlier periods when platinum was less valuable. Markets would transmit information about the reduced cost in the form of a lower price. People could then consider increasing the quantity of platinum they use.

In addition to knowing the best use for resources, people must also have incentives to act on that information. Markets provide incentives to sell goods and productive resources where they will bring the highest prices and to buy them where they can be obtained at the lowest prices. Profits motivate business managers to improve production methods and to design goods that match consumer needs. Workers who stay alert to opportunities and work where they are most productive receive the highest wages. Consumers are motivated to use less expensive substitutes where feasible.

Adam Smith, often considered the father of economics, saw coordination through markets as the foundation of prosperity and progress. In a famous passage in *The Wealth of Nations*, he called markets an "invisible hand" that nudges people into the economic roles they can play best (see *Who Said It? Who Did It? 1.2*). To this day, an appreciation of markets as a means of coordinating choices remains a central feature of the economic way of thinking.

Who Said It? Who Did It? 1.2
ADAM SMITH ON THE INVISIBLE HAND

Adam Smith is considered the founder of economics as a distinct field of study, even though he wrote only one book on the subject: *The Wealth of Nations*, published in 1776. Smith was fifty-three years old at the time. His friend David Hume found the book such hard going that he doubted that many people would read it. Hume was wrong—people have been reading it for more than two hundred years.

The wealth of a nation, in Smith's view, is not a result of the accumulation of gold or silver in its treasury, as many of his contemporaries believed. Rather, it is the outcome of the activities of ordinary people working and trading in free markets. To Smith, the remarkable thing about the wealth produced by a market economy is that it is not a result of any organized plan but that it is rather the unintended outcome of the actions of many people, each of whom is pursuing the incentives the market offers with his or her own interests in mind. As he put it:

It is not from the benevolence of the butcher, the brewer, or the baker that we expect our dinner, but from their regard to their own interest ... Every individual is continually exerting himself to find out the most advantageous employment for whatever capital he can command ... By directing that industry in such a manner as its produce may be of the greatest value, he intends only his own gain; and he is in this, as in many other cases, led by an invisible hand to promote an end which was no part of his intention. *

Much of the discipline of economics as it has developed over the past two centuries consists of elaborations on ideas found in Smith's work. The idea of the "invisible hand" of market incentives that channels people's efforts in directions that are beneficial to their neighbors remains the most durable of Smith's contributions to economics.

_____

* Adam Smith, *The Wealth of Nations* (1776), Book 1, Chapter 2.

The Role of Hierarchy

Important as markets are, they are not the only means of achieving economic coordination. Some decisions are guided by direct authority within organizations, that is, by the mechanism of hierarchy. Decisions made by government agencies are one important example. Government decisions are often implemented, not through the spontaneous choices of individuals, but via directives issued by a central authority: pay your taxes, do not dump toxic wastes in the river, and so on. Business firms, especially large corporations, are another important example of the hierarchical form of organization. The Toyota Motor Corporation uses directives from a central authority to make many important decisions—for example, the decision to build a new hybrid version of its popular Camry in Kentucky rather than in Japan.

Although governments and corporations use hierarchical methods to make choices within their organizations, they deal with one another and with individual consumers through markets. Markets and hierarchies thus play complementary roles in achieving economic coordination. Some economies rely more on markets, others on government or corporate planning. At one extreme, the centrally planned economy of North Korea places heavy emphasis on government authority. Economies like that of the United States make greater use of markets, but no economy uses one means of coordination to the exclusion of the other. Government regulatory agencies in the United States establish laws to control pollution or protect worker safety; on the other hand, North Korea uses small-scale markets to distribute some goods. Large corporations use commands from higher authority to make many decisions, but they also often subcontract with outsiders through the market; and they sometimes encourage their own divisions to deal with one another on a market basis.

In short, wherever one turns in economics, the question of coordination arises. Understanding economic coordination means understanding the complementary roles of markets, on the one hand, and of government and corporate hierarchies, on the other.

Economic Method

We have seen that economists have a distinctive way of thinking about the world based on the concepts of scarcity, choice, and exchange. They also have some distinctive methods of approaching problems and expressing the conclusions that they reach. We will conclude the chapter with a few comments about method.

Theories and Models

Economists try to understand the choices people make in terms of the context in which the choices are made. The relationships they propose between choices and context are called **theories** or **models**. The terms mean almost the same, although economists tend to use the term theory to refer to more general statements about economic relationships and the term model to refer to more particular statements, especially those that take the form of graphs or mathematical equations.

Theory

A representation of the way in which facts are related to one another

Model

A synonym for theory; in economics, often applied to theories that are stated in graphical or mathematical form

Economics needs theories and models because facts do not speak for themselves. Take, for example, the fact that in the spring of 2008 U.S. farmers planted more acres in corn than ever before. Economists have a theory as to why this happened. They relate the change in crop patterns to a record-high price for corn at the time of planting. The relationship between the price of corn and the choice of what crop to grow is seen as a particular instance of a broader theory according to which an increase in the price of any good, other things being equal, leads producers to increase their output of the good.

The theory, as stated, is a simple one. It relates crop choices to just one other fact, the price of corn. A more complete theory would bring in other factors that influence choice, such as the prices of gasoline, for which corn-based ethanol is a substitute; the price of soybeans, which can be grown on the same land

Choosing to plant corn is generally based on the price of corn compared to other crops.

as corn; tax advantages provided by Congress to producers of biofuels; and so on. Where does one draw the line? How much detail does it take to make a good theory?

There is no simple answer to this question because adding detail to a theory involves a trade-off. On the one hand, if essential details are left out, the theory may fail altogether to fit the facts. On the other hand, adding too much detail defeats the purpose of understanding because key relationships may become lost in a cloud of complexity. The only real guideline is that a theory should be just detailed enough to suit the purpose for which it is intended, and no more.

By analogy, consider the models that aircraft designers use. A scaled-down wind-tunnel model made to test the aerodynamics of a new design would need to represent the shapes of the wings, fuselage, and control surfaces accurately, but it would not need to include tiny seats with tiny tables and magazine pockets. On the other hand, a full-scale model built for the purpose of training flight crews to work on the new plane would need seats and magazine pockets, but it would not need wings.

In much the same way, the theories and models presented in this book are designed to highlight a few key economic relationships. They are helpful in understanding economics in the same way that playing a flight simulation game on a laptop computer is helpful in understanding the basics of flying. Professional economists use more detailed models, just as professional pilots train with complex flight simulators rather than with simple computer games. Nevertheless, the basic principles learned from the simple models should not contradict those that apply to the more complex ones. In the simple games, just as in the complex simulators, adjusting the rudder makes the plane turn and adjusting the elevators makes it climb or dive.

The Use of Graphs

The theories introduced so far have been stated in words. Words are a powerful tool for developing understanding, but they are even more powerful when pictures supplement them. Economists support their words with pictures called graphs. An example will illustrate how economists use graphs to represent theories.[4]

THE PRODUCTION POSSIBILITY FRONTIER   Recall our earlier discussion of the trade-off between education and cars. Figure 1.1 shows the trade-off in graphical form for an economy in which only those two goods are produced. The horizontal axis measures the quantity of education in terms of the number of college graduates produced per year; the vertical axis measures the production of cars. Any combination of education and cars can be shown as a point in the space between the two axes. For example, production of 10 million graduates and 5 million cars in a given year would be represented by point E.

In drawing this graph, supplies of productive resources and the state of knowledge are assumed to remain constant. Even if all available resources are devoted to education, there is a limit to the number of graduates that can be produced in a year: twenty million. The extreme possibility of producing twenty million graduates and no cars is shown by point A. Likewise, the maximum number of cars that would be produced if no resources were put into education is eighteen million cars, shown by point B. Between those two extremes is a whole range of possible combinations of education

Figure 1.1	Production Possibility Frontier

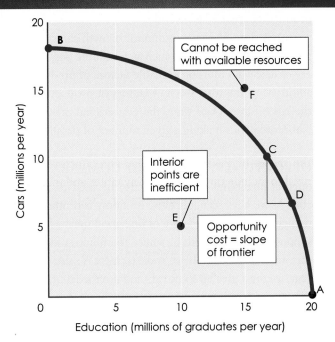

This figure shows combinations of cars and education that can be produced in a simple economy in which they are the only two products. Quantities of available factors of production and the state of existing knowledge are assumed to be fixed. If all factors are devoted to education, 20 million college graduates can be produced each year (point A). If all factors are devoted to making cars, 18 million cars can be produced each year (point B). Other combinations of the two goods that can be produced using available factors efficiently, such as those represented by points C and D, lie along a curve called a production possibility frontier. The slope of the frontier indicates the opportunity cost of education in terms of cars. Interior points, such as E, represent inefficient use of resources. Beginning from such a point, more of one good can be produced without producing less of the other. Points outside the frontier, such as F, cannot be reached using available factors of production and knowledge.

Production possibility frontier

A graph that shows possible combinations of goods that can be produced by an economy given available knowledge and factors of production

and cars. Those intermediate possibilities are shown by points such as C and D, which fall along a smooth curve. The curve is known as a **production possibility frontier**.

EFFICIENCY AND ECONOMIC GROWTH   The production possibility frontier is a boundary between the combinations of education and cars that can be produced and those that cannot, using given knowledge and productive resources. As such, it serves nicely to illustrate the concept of efficiency in production. Points inside the frontier, such as point E, represent inefficient production. Beginning from such a point, more cars can be made without cutting the output of education (shown by a vertical move toward the frontier); more education can be produced without cutting the output of cars (a horizontal move toward the frontier); or the output of both goods can be increased (a move up and to the right toward the frontier).

Points such as A, B, C, and D that are on the frontier represent efficient production. Starting from any of those points, it is not possible to produce more of one good without producing less of the other. For example, in moving from C to D, output of education is increased but output of cars falls. Points such as F that lie outside the frontier cannot be reached even when the currently available knowledge and factors of production are used efficiently.

Over time, however, economic growth can stretch the production possibility frontier outward so that points such as F become possible. As mentioned earlier, the discovery of new ways of using available factors of production is one source of growth. So are additions to the total stock of factors of production—for example, through growth of the labor force. Over time, the educational process itself improves the quality of the labor force, thus making a given number of people capable of producing more.

OPPORTUNITY COST AND COMPARATIVE ADVANTAGE   The production possibility frontier can also be used to represent the concept of opportunity cost. As we have seen, once the economy is producing efficiently at a point on the frontier, choosing to make more of one good means making less of the other. For example, suppose we start at point C, where 16 million students graduate each year and 10 million cars are being made. If we want to increase the output of graduates to 18 million per year, we must give up some cars and use the labor, capital, and natural resources freed in this way to build and staff classrooms. In moving from point C to point D, we trade off production of 4 million cars for the extra 2 million graduates. Over that range of the frontier, the opportunity cost of each extra graduate is about two cars. The slope of the frontier shows the opportunity cost of graduates, measured in terms of cars.

As more graduates are produced and the economy moves down and to the right along the frontier, the frontier becomes steeper and the opportunity cost of producing graduates increases. A major reason is that not all factors of production—especially not all workers—are alike. Suppose we start all the way up at point B, where no education is produced, and transfer enough resources to education to open one small college. The first people we would pull off the assembly line to staff the classrooms would be those who have a comparative advantage in teaching. By the time enough resources have been transferred to education from the auto industry to reach point D, the most suitable recruits for academic life have already been used. Increasingly, to produce still more education we have to take some of the best production workers with no assurance that they will be good teachers. The opportunity cost of increasing the output of education (shown by the slope of the frontier) is correspondingly greater.

Theory and Evidence

Theories are of no use in explaining relationships among facts unless they fit those facts. Theory building is a matter of constantly comparing proposed explanations with evidence gleaned from observations of the actual choices people make—that is, with empirical evidence. When **empirical** evidence is consistent with the relationships proposed in a theory, confidence in the validity of the theory is increased. When evidence is not consistent with the theory, the theory needs to be reexamined. The relationships proposed in it may be invalid, or they may be valid only under circumstances different from those that prevailed when the observations were made. The theory then needs to be modified by changing the proposed relationships or adding detail.

Empirical

Based on experience or observation

Government agencies and private firms generate mountains of empirical data on economic activity. Economists constantly examine those data in an effort to confirm theories or find inconsistencies that point the way to better theories. Statistical analysis of empirical economic data is known as **econometrics**—the science of economic measurement.

Econometrics

The statistical analysis of empirical economic data

Theories and Forecasts

Economic theories can help us understand things that happened in the past—trends in crop patterns over the past decade, the effects of new, twenty-first century communication technologies, and so on; but understanding the past is not always enough. People also want forecasts of future economic events.

Within limits, economic theory can be useful here, too. Any theory that purports to explain a relationship between past events provides a basis for predicting what will happen under similar circumstances in the future. To put it more precisely, economic theory can be used to make **conditional forecasts** of the form "If A, then B, other things being equal." Thus, an economist might say, "If gasoline prices rise, and if at the same time consumer incomes and the prices of other goods do not change, purchases of low-mileage vehicles will fall."

Conditional forecast

A prediction of future economic events in the form "If A, then B, other things being equal"

Thousands of economists make a living from forecasting. Decision-makers in business and government use economic forecasts extensively. Forecasts are not perfect, however; and forecasters sometimes make conspicuous mistakes. There are at least three reasons for the mistakes.

First, insufficient attention is sometimes paid to the conditional nature of forecasts. The news might report, for example, that "economists predict a drop in SUV sales," yet people keep right on buying big vehicles. In such a case, the news report may have failed to note the forecasters' precautionary comments. The forecasters may have said that SUV sales would drop in response to a gas price increase if consumer incomes and technology remained the same; but consumers got richer and new technology made SUVs less gas-hungry, so SUV sales did not fall after all.

Second, a forecast may be invalid because the theory on which it is based is incorrect or incomplete. Economists do not always agree on what theory best fits the facts. Some theories give more weight to one fact, others to different facts. The competing theories may imply conflicting forecasts under some conditions. At least one of the forecasts will then turn out to be wrong. Finding out which theories yield better forecasts than others is an important part of the process through which valid theories are distinguished from inadequate ones.

Third, economic forecasts can go wrong because some of the things that business managers and government officials most want to know are among the hardest to predict. For example, a competent economist could produce a fairly accurate forecast of vehicle sales based on certain assumptions about incomes and the prices of gasoline and other goods. However, what the marketing people at General Motors would like to know is what will happen to the social image of SUVs: Will they continue to be a symbol of high status, or will they become an embarrassment in a more environmentally conscious society? Social attitudes are not among the variables that economists can forecast accurately.

Despite these limitations, most economists take the view that well-founded conditional forecasts, for all their limitations, are a better basis for business and public policy decisions than whims and guesswork. Still, they caution against relying too heavily on forecasts.

Theory and Policy

Economists are often asked to use their theories to analyze the effects of public policies and forecast the effects of policy changes. The government may, for example, be considering new measures to aid unemployed workers, new responses to global warming, or new measures to regulate international trade. How will the effects of such policies be spread through the economy? How will they affect people's lives?

Economists have their own characteristic way of thinking about public policy, just as they have their own way of thinking about other topics. In particular, economists are concerned with identifying both the direct and indirect effects of policy, as well as any indirect or unintended consequences. They are also constantly alert to both the long-term and short-term effects of policy. For example:

- Unemployment compensation has the intended effect of aiding unemployed workers; but it also has the unintended effect of increasing the number of workers who are unemployed because workers receiving compensation can afford to take their time finding just the right new job. Many observers see generous unemployment compensation in some parts of Europe as one reason unemployment rates there are higher than in the United States.

- Regulations intended to improve the fuel efficiency of automobiles encourage production of cars that weigh less, but the lighter cars are somewhat less safe. Increased highway deaths among drivers of the lighter cars may thus be an unintended consequence of efforts to save fuel.

- After widespread banking failures in the 1980s, U.S. regulators made rule changes intended to stabilize the banking system by strengthening the balance sheets of commercial banks. Those regulations also raised the cost of bank loans relative to loans from other sources outside the banking system. As an unintended consequence, much lending activity, including home mortgage lending, moved to an emerging "shadow banking system" consisting of mortgage brokers, securitized loans, and special purpose financial vehicles. When a crisis came, the new financial system turned out, in some ways, to be not more but less stable than the old one.

While policies may have unintended consequences, it would be wrong to conclude that the government should never act simply because its actions may do some harm as well as some good. Sometimes the harm may outweigh the good, and sometimes not. What is important, economists say, is that policy-makers look at the whole picture, not just part of it, before they make a decision. As Henry Hazlitt once put it, the whole of economics can be reduced to a single lesson:

The art of economics consists in looking not merely at the immediate but at the longer effects of any act or policy; it consists in tracing the consequences of that policy not merely for one group but for all groups.[5]

As you progress through your study of economics—both the macro and micro branches—you will repeatedly encounter examples of the way economic theory can help understand the choices people make and the complex effects of policies intended to regulate those choices.

Summary

1. **What is the subject matter of economics?** Economics is a social science that seeks to understand the choices people make in using scarce resources to meet their wants. Scarcity is a situation in which there is not enough of something to meet everyone's wants. *Microeconomics* is the branch of economics that studies choices that involve individual households, firms, and markets. *Macroeconomics* is the branch of economics that deals with large-scale economic phenomena, such as inflation, unemployment, and economic growth.

2. **What considerations underlie the choice of what an economy will produce?** Producing more of one good requires producing less of something else because productive resources that are used to produce one good cannot be used to produce another at the same time. Productive resources are traditionally classified into three groups, called *factors of production*. *Labor* consists of the productive contributions made by people working with their hands and minds. *Capital* consists of all the productive inputs created by people. *Natural resources* include anything that can be used as a productive input in its natural state. The *opportunity cost* of a good or service is its cost in terms of the forgone opportunity to pursue the best possible alternative activity with the same time or resources.

3. **What considerations underlie the choice of how to produce?** Goods and services can be produced in many different ways, some of which are more efficient than others. *Economic efficiency* refers to a state of affairs in which it is impossible to make any change that satisfies one person's wants more fully without causing some other person's wants to be satisfied less fully. *Efficiency in production* refers to a situation in which it is not possible, given the available productive resources and existing knowledge, to produce more of one good or service without forgoing the opportunity to produce some of another good or service. Once efficiency has been achieved, production potential can be expanded by increasing the availability of resources or by improving knowledge. The process of increasing the economy's stock of capital is known as *investment*. The process of looking for new possibilities—making use of new ways of doing things, being alert to new opportunities, and overcoming old limits—is known as *entrepreneurship*.

4. **What considerations underlie the choice of who will do which work?** Economic efficiency is greatly enhanced by cooperation with others. Three things make cooperation worthwhile: teamwork, learning by doing, and comparative advantage. Teamwork can enhance productivity even when there is no specialization. Learning by doing improves productivity even when all workers start with equal talents and abilities. Comparative

advantage comes into play when people have different innate abilities or, after learning by doing, have developed specialized skills. Having a *comparative advantage* in producing a particular good or service means being able to produce it at a relatively lower opportunity cost than someone else.

5. **What considerations underlie the choice of for whom goods will be produced?** In part, deciding for whom goods will be produced revolves around issues of efficiency. *Efficiency in distribution* refers to a state of affairs in which, with a given quantity of goods and services, it is impossible to satisfy one person's wants more fully without satisfying someone else's less fully. Efficiency is part of *positive economics*, the area of economics that is concerned with facts and the relationships among them. *Normative economics* is the area of economics that is devoted to judgments about which economic conditions and policies are good or bad.

6. **What mechanisms are used to coordinate economic choices?** The two principle methods of coordinating choices are *hierarchy* and *spontaneous order*. Markets are the most important example of spontaneous order. The internal decisions made by large corporations and units of government are the most important examples of hierarchy.

7. **How do economists use theory, graphs, and evidence in their work?** A *theory* or *model* is a representation of the ways in which facts are related to one another. Economists use graphs to display data and make visual representations of theories and models. For example, a *production possibility frontier* is a graph that shows the boundary between combinations of goods that can be produced and those that cannot, using available factors of production and knowledge. Economists refine theories in the light of *empirical* evidence, that is, evidence gleaned from observation of actual economic decisions. The economic analysis of empirical evidence is known as *econometrics*. Economic models are often used to make *conditional forecasts* of the form "If A, then B, other things being equal."

Key Terms

Problems and Topics for Discussion

1. **Opportunity cost** Gasoline, insurance, depreciation, and repairs are all costs of owning a car. Which of these can be considered opportunity costs in the context of each of the following decisions?

a. You own a car and are deciding whether to drive 100 miles for a weekend visit to a friend at another university.

b. You do not own a car but are considering buying one so that you can get a part-time job located 5 miles from where you live.

In general, why does the context in which you decide to do something affect the opportunity cost of doing it?

2. **Comparative advantage in international trade** Suppose that in the United States a car can be produced with 200 labor hours while a ton of rice requires 20 labor hours. In China, it takes 250 labor hours to make a car and 50 labor hours to grow a ton of rice. What is the opportunity cost of producing rice in each country, stated in terms of cars? What is the opportunity cost of cars, stated in terms of rice? Which country has a comparative advantage in cars? Which in rice?

3. **Efficiency in distribution and the food stamp program** The federal food stamp program could have been designed so that every low-income family would receive a book of coupons containing so many bread coupons, so many milk coupons, and so on. Instead, it gives the family an allowance that can be spent on any kind of food the family prefers. For a given cost to the federal government, which plan do you think would better serve the goal of efficiency in distribution? Why?

Now consider a program that would allow families to trade their food stamps for cash (some such trading does occur, but it is restricted by law) or one in which poor families are given cash, with which they can buy whatever they want. Compare these alternatives with the existing food stamp program in terms of both positive and normative economics.

4. **Spontaneous order in the cafeteria** Suppose that your college cafeteria does not have enough room for all the students to sit down to eat at once, so it stays open for lunch from 11:30 a.m. to 1:30 p.m. Consider the following three methods of distributing diners over the two-hour lunch period in such a way that everyone can have a seat.

a. The administration sets a rule: First-year students must eat between 11:30 and 12:00, sophomores between 12:00 and 12:30, and so on for juniors and seniors.

b. The lunch period is broken up into half-hour segments with green tickets for the first shift, blue tickets for the second, and so on. An equal number of tickets of each color is printed. At the beginning of each semester an auction is held in which students bid for the ticket color of their choice.

c. Students can come to the cafeteria whenever they want. If there are no empty seats, they have to stand in line.

Compare the three schemes in terms of the concepts of (1) spontaneous order and hierarchy, (2) information and incentives, and (3) efficiency.

5. **A production possibility frontier** Bill Schwartz has four fields spread out over a hillside. He can grow either wheat or potatoes in any of the fields, but the low fields are better for potatoes and the high ones are better for wheat. Here are some combinations of wheat and potatoes that he could produce:

Number of Fields Used for Potatoes	Total Tons of Potatoes	Total Tons of Wheat
All 4	1,000	0
Lowest 3	900	400
Lowest 2	600	700
Lowest 1	300	900
None	0	1,000

Use these data to draw a production possibility frontier for wheat and potatoes. What is the opportunity cost of wheat, stated in terms of potatoes, when the farmer converts the highest field to wheat production? What happens to the opportunity cost of wheat as more and more fields are switched to wheat?

Case for Discussion

Cow Power

As natural resources go, it doesn't have much glamour; but unlike oil, the United States has plenty of it. We're talking about cow manure. The average cow puts out about 30 gallons a day. Multiply that by something like 8 million cows on the nation's 65,000 dairy farms, and you have—well, what do you have—a big problem or a big opportunity?

In the past, manure would, on balance, have been considered a problem. True, it makes good fertilizer, but with big drawbacks. Most dairy farms stored it in open lagoons before spreading it on fields. The smelly lagoons created a nuisance to neighbors. What is more, they were a big source of methane, a greenhouse gas that, pound for pound, contributes 10 times more to global warming than carbon dioxide.

Methane burns, however; and that's where cow manure becomes an opportunity. If farmers pump it into an anaerobic digester instead of into an open lagoon, it produces a purified gas that can either be burned on the farm to produce electricity or transported by pipeline to be burned elsewhere.

Marie and Earl Audet's dairy farm in Bridport, Vermont, expects to sell $200,000 worth of cow power a year to Central Vermont Public Service, the local electric utility. There are other benefits as well. The process also produces a clear liquid that can be used as fertilizer; and the farm will save another $50,000 by using the dry, odorless, fluff that is left over from the digester as bedding for the cows, in place of expensive sawdust.[6]

Cow power is not a free lunch, however. To make the economics favorable to farmers, Central Vermont Public Service pays them 12 cents per kilowatt-hour, a 4-cent premium over the normal rate. The utility makes up the difference by selling premium-priced "green electricity" to customers who want to feel they are doing something for the planet. Other state and federal agencies subsidize an estimated 100 cow power digesters elsewhere in the country.

Boosters of cow power hope the need for subsidies will disappear as costs of manufacturing the digesters fall and as gas and electric prices continue to rise. "The business model of producing energy along with food will transform the economics of rural America," said Michael T. Eckhart, president of the American Council on Renewable Energy, based in Washington.[7]

QUESTIONS

1. Based on the information given in the case, do you think the out-of-pocket costs of producing electricity from cow manure are greater, less, or about the same as the cost of conventional power sources? On what information in the case do you base your answer?

2. Anaerobic digestion of cow manure reduces harm to neighbors (less smell) and harm to the environment (less greenhouse gas). How do these benefits enter into the calculation of the opportunity cost of producing cow power? Do these benefits tend to make the opportunity cost greater than, or less than, the out-of-pocket costs?

3. Based on information in the case, do you think the growth of the cow power industry is based on the principle of spontaneous order or that of hierarchy? Or, is it a little bit of both? Explain your reasoning.

End Notes

1. The Austrian economist Ludwig von Mises suggested that *catallactics*, meaning the science of exchange, would be a better term than *economics*, which has the original meaning of household management. For better or worse, the term catallactics has never come into wide use.

2. Efficiency, defined this way, is sometimes called Pareto efficiency after the Italian economist Vilfredo Pareto.

3. Armen A. Alchian and Harold Demsetz, "Production, Information Cost, and Economic Organization," *American Economic Review* (December 1972): 777–795.

4. A review of basic graphical concepts, including axes, points and number pairs, slopes, and tangencies, is provided in the appendix to this chapter.

5. Henry Hazlitt, *Economics in One Lesson* (New York: Arlington House, 1979), 17.

6. Martha T. Moore, "Cows Power Plan for Alternative Fuel," *USA Today,* Dec. 6, 2006, http://www.usatoday.com/news/nation/2006-12-03-cow-power_x.htm.

7. Claudia H. Deutsch, "Tapping Latent Power in What's Left Around the Barnyard," *New York Times,* July 4, 2006.   http://select.nytimes.com/search/restricted/article?res=F20B13FD39540C778CDDAE0894DE404482

Appendix to Chapter 1:
WORKING WITH GRAPHS

Which is smarter—a computer or the human brain? The computer certainly does some things faster and more accurately, say, dividing one twenty-digit number by another. The human brain, however, is programmed to solve other kinds of problems with speed and accuracy beyond the ability of most computers. Working with pictures is one of the areas in which the human brain excels. Three key abilities give the brain a comparative advantage where pictures are involved.

1. An ability to store and retrieve a vast number of images quickly and accurately (Think of how many people's faces you can recognize.)

2. An ability to discard irrelevant detail while highlighting essentials (Think of how easily you can recognize a politician's face in a political cartoon drawn with just a few lines.)

3. An ability to see key similarities between patterns that are not exactly the same (That is why you can usually match two pictures of a person taken 20 years apart.)

Graphs are an invaluable aid in learning economics precisely because they make use of these three special abilities of the human brain. Graphs are not used to make economics harder but to make it easier. All it takes to use graphs effectively as a learning tool is the inborn human skill in working with pictures plus knowledge of a few simple rules for extracting the information that graphs contain. This appendix outlines those rules in brief. Additional details and exercises can be found in the *Study Guide* that accompanies this textbook.

Pairs of Numbers and Points

The first thing to master is how to use points on a graph to represent pairs of numbers. The table in Figure 1A.1 presents five pairs of numbers. The two columns are labeled "*x*" and "*y*." The first number in each pair is called the *x value* and the second the *y value*. Each pair of numbers is labeled with a capital letter. Pair A has an *x* value of 2 and a *y* value of 3, pair B has an *x* value of 4 and a *y* value of 4, and so on.

The diagram in Figure 1A.1 contains two lines that meet at the lower left-hand corner; they are called *coordinate axes*. The horizontal axis is marked off into units representing the *x* value and the vertical axis into unit representing the *y* value. In the space between the axes, each pair of numbers from the table can be shown as a point. For example, point A is found by going two units to the right along the horizontal axis and then three units straight up, parallel to the vertical axis. That point represents the *x* value of 2 and the *y* value of 3. The other points are located in the same way.

The visual effect of a graph usually can be improved by connecting the points with a line or a curve. By doing so, the relationship between *x* values and *y* values can be seen at a glance: As the *x* value increases, the *y* value also increases.

FIGURE 1A.1 NUMBER PAIRS AND POINTS

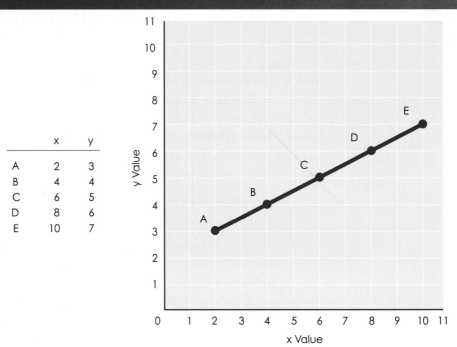

	x	y
A	2	3
B	4	4
C	6	5
D	8	6
E	10	7

Each lettered pair of numbers in the table corresponds to a lettered point on the graph. The x value of each point corresponds to the horizontal distance of the point from the vertical axis; the y value corresponds to its vertical distance from the horizontal axis.

Slope

For a straight line, the ratio of the change in the *y* value to the change in the *x* value between any two points on the line

Positive slope

A slope having a value greater than zero

Direct relationship

A relationship between two variables in which an increase in the value of one variable is associated with an increase in the value of the other

Slopes and Tangencies

The lines or curves used in graphs are described in terms of their slopes. The **slope** of a straight line between two points is defined as the ratio of the change in the *y* value to the change in the *x* value between the two points. In Figure 1A.2, for example, the slope of the line between points A and B is 2. The *y* value changes by six units between these two points, whereas the *x* value changes by only three units. The slope is the ratio 6/3 = 2.

The slope of a line between the points (*x*1, *y*1) and (*x*2, *y*2) can be expressed in terms of a simple formula that is derived from the definition just given:

$$\text{Slope} = (y_2 - y_1)/(x_2 - x_1)$$

Applied to the line between points A and B in Figure 1A.2, the formula gives the following result:

$$\text{Slope} = (7 - 1)/(4 - 1) = 6/3 = 2$$

A line such as that between A and B in Figure 1A.2, which slopes upward from left to right, is said to have a **positive slope** because the value of its slope is a positive number. A positively sloped line represents a **direct relationship** between the variable represented on the *x* axis and that represented on the *y* axis—that is, a relationship in which an increase in one variable is associated with an increase in the other. The relationship

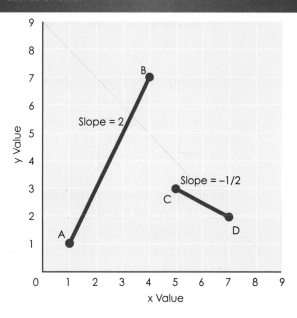

FIGURE 1A.2   SLOPES OF LINES

The slope of a straight line drawn between two points is defined as the ratio of the change in the *y* value to the change in the *x* value as one moves from one point to the other. For example, the line between points A and B in this figure has a slope of +2, whereas the line between points C and D has a slope of –1/2.

of the age of a tree to its height is an example of a direct relationship. An example from economics is the relationship between family income and expenditures on housing.

When a line slants downward from left to right, like the one between points C and D in Figure 1A.2, the *x* and *y* values change in opposite directions. Going from point C to point D, the *y* value changes by –1 (that is, decreases by one unit) and the *x* value changes by +2 (that is, increases by two units). The slope of this line is the ratio –1/2.

When a negative number gives the slope of a line, the line is said to have a **negative slope**. Such a line represents an **inverse relationship** between the *x* variable and the *y* variable—that is, a relationship in which an increase in the value of one variable is associated with a decrease in the value of the other variable. The relationship between the temperature in the room and the time it takes the ice in your lemonade to melt is an example of an inverse relationship. To give an economic example, the relationship between the price of gasoline and the quantity that consumers purchase, other things being equal, is an inverse relationship.

The concepts of positive and negative slopes, and of direct and inverse relationships, apply to curves as well as to straight lines. However, the slope of a curve, unlike that of a straight line, varies from one point to the next.[1] We cannot speak of the slope

Negative slope

A slope having a value less than zero

Inverse relationship

A relationship between two variables in which an increase in the value of one variable is associated with a decrease in the value of the other

---
[1] Economists try to be consistent, but in talking about lines and curves, they fail. They have no qualms about calling something a "curve" that is a straight line. For example, later we will encounter "demand curves" that are as straight as a stretched string. Less frequently, they may call something a line that is curved.

of a curve in general, but only of its slope at a given point. The slope of a curve at any given point is defined as the slope of a straight line drawn tangent to the curve at that point. (A **tangent** line is one that just touches the curve without crossing it.) In Figure 1A.3, the slope of the curve at point A is 1 and the slope at point B is –2.

Using Graphs to Display Data

Graphs are used in economics for two primary purposes: for visual display of quantitative data and for visual representation of economic relationships. Some graphs are primarily designed to serve one purpose, some the other, and some a little of both. We begin with some common kinds of graphs whose primary purpose is to display data.

Figure 1A.4 shows three kinds of graphs often used to display data. Part (a) is *pie chart*. Pie charts are used to show the relative size of various quantities that add up to a total of 100 percent. In this case, the quantities displayed are the percentages of U.S. foreign trade accounted for by various trading partners. In the original source, the graph was drawn as part of a discussion of U.S. trade with Canada, Japan, and Western Europe. The author wanted to make the point that trade with these countries is very important. Note how the graph highlights Canadian, Japanese, and Western European trade with the U.S. and, at the same time, omits details not relevant to the discussion by lumping together the rest of Europe, Africa, the rest of Asia, and many other countries under the heading "rest of the world." In reading graphs, do not just look at the numbers; ask yourself, "What point is the graph trying to make?"

Part (b) of Figure 1A.4 is a *bar chart*. Bar charts, like pie charts, are used to display numerical data (in this case, unemployment rates) in relationship to some non-numerical

Tangent

A straight line that touches a curve at a given point without intersecting it

---

FIGURE 1A.3 SLOPES OF CURVES

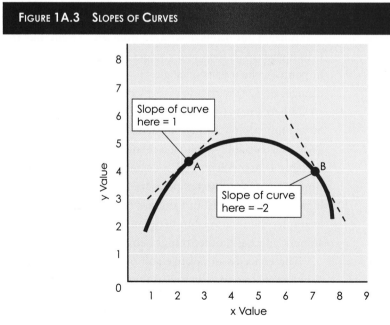

The slope of a curve at any point is defined as the slope of a straight line drawn tangent to the curve at that point. A tangent line is one that just touches the curve without crossing it. In this figure, the slope of the curve at point A is 1, and the slope at point B is –2.

FIGURE 1A.4 USING GRAPHS TO DISPLAY DATA

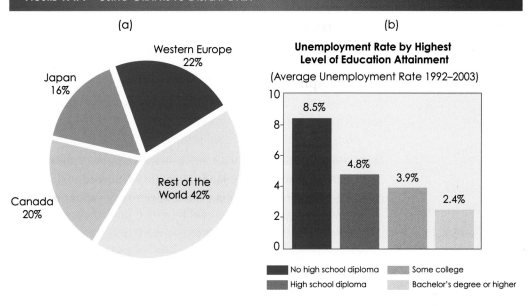

(a)

Western Europe
22%

Japan
16%

Canada
20%

Rest of the
World 42%

(b)

**Unemployment Rate by Highest
Level of Education Attainment**

(Average Unemployment Rate 1992–2003)

8.5%

4.8%

3.9%

2.4%

■ No high school diploma   ■ Some college
■ High school diploma   ■ Bachelor's degree or higher

(c)

Civilian Unemployment Rate
(1980–2003)

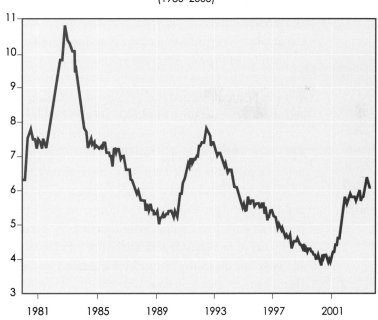

This figure shows three common kinds of data display graphs. The *pie chart* in part (a) is used when the data items sum to 100 percent. The *bar chart* in part (b), like the pie chart, is used when reporting numerical data that are associated with nonnumerical categories (in this case educational attainment). The bar chart does not require data items to sum to 100%. The *time-series graph* in part (c) shows the values of one or more economic quantities on the vertical axis and time on the horizontal axis.

SOURCE: Part (a), U.S. Council of Economic Advisers, *Economic Report of the President* (Washington, D.C.: Government Printing Office, 2002), Table B-105, 397; part (b), Bureau of Labor Statistics, *Current Population Survey*; and part (c), Bureau of Labor Statistics, *The Employment Situation*.

classification of cases (in this case, educational attainment). Bar charts are not subject to the restriction that data displayed must total 100 percent. What point do you think the author of this graph was trying to make?

Part (c) of Figure 1A.4 is an example of a data display graph very common in economics—the *time-series graph*. A time-series graph shows the values of one or more economic quantities on the vertical axis and time (years, months, or whatever) on the horizontal axis. This graph shows the ups and downs of the U.S. unemployment rate by month over the period 1980 through 2003.

Note one feature of this time-series graph: the scale on the vertical axis begins from 3 percent rather than from 0. By spreading out the data points in the range 3 to 11 percent, one can show the trend of unemployment in greater detail. The advantage of greater detail has an offsetting danger, however. Careless reading of the graph could cause one to exaggerate the amount by which unemployment rises during a recession. For example, the unemployment line is more than three times higher above the horizontal axis in 2003 than in 2000. However, careful reading of the graph shows that the unemployment rate was actually only about half again as high (6 percent versus 4 percent) in 2003 as in 2000. The moral of the story: Always examine the vertical and horizontal axes of a graph carefully.

Using Graphs to Display Relationships

Some graphs, rather than simply recording observed facts, attempt to represent theories and models—that is, to show the relationships among facts. Figure 1A.5 shows two typical graphs whose primary purpose is to display relationships.

Part (a) of Figure 1A.5 is the production possibility frontier that we encountered in Chapter 1. The graph represents the inverse relationship between the quantity of cars that can be produced and the quantity of education that can be produced, given available knowledge and productive resources.

Part (b) of Figure 1A.5 represents a relationship between the quantity of labor that a person is willing to supply (measured in worker-hours per year) and the wage rate per hour the person is paid. According to the theory portrayed by the graph, raising the wage rate will, up to a point, induce a person to work more hours; but beyond a certain point (according to the theory), a further increase in the wage will actually cause the person to work fewer hours. Why? Because the person is so well off, he or she prefers the luxury of more leisure time to the reward of more material goods.

Note one distinctive feature of this graph: There are no numbers on the axes. It is an abstract graph that represents only the qualitative relationships between the hours of labor supplied per year and the wage rate. It makes no quantitative statements regarding how much the number of hours worked will change as a result of any given change in wage rate. Abstract graphs are often used when the point to be made is a general one that applies to many cases, regardless of quantitative differences from one case to another.

Packing Three Variables into Two Dimensions

Anything drawn on a flat piece of paper is limited to two dimensions. The relationships discussed so far fit a two-dimensional framework easily because they involve just two variables. In the case of the production possibility frontier, the two are the quantity of

FIGURE 1A.5   USING GRAPHS TO SHOW RELATIONSHIPS

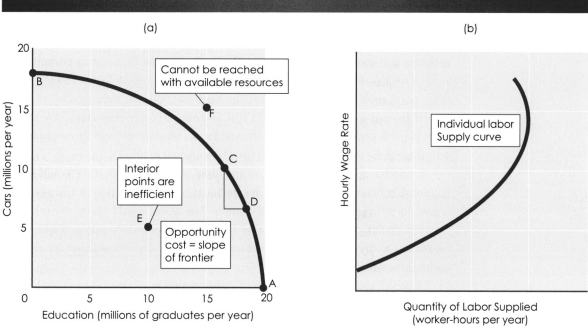

Relational graphs are visual representations of theories, that is, of relationships among facts. Two typical relational graphs are shown here. Part (a) is the production possibility frontier discussed in Chapter 1. It relates quantities of cars to quantities of education that can be produced with given factors of production and knowledge. Part (b) represents a theory of individual labor supply, according to which an increase in the hourly wage rate, after a point, will cause a person to reduce the quantity of labor supplied. Part (b) is an abstract graph in that it shows only the general nature of the relationship, with no numbers on either axis.

education (horizontal axis) and the quantity of cars (vertical axis). In the case of the labor supply, they are hours worked per year (horizontal axis) and wage rate per hour (vertical axis), but reality does not always cooperate with geometry. Often one must take three or more variables into account in order to understand relationships among facts.

A number of methods have been devised to represent relationships involving three or more variables. For example, a map of the United States might use coordinates of latitude and longitude to indicate position, contour lines to indicate altitude and shadings of various colors to indicate vegetation. An architect might use a perspective drawing to give the illusion of three dimensions—height, width, and depth—on a flat piece of paper. This section deals with one simple method of packing three variables into two dimensions. Although the method is a favorite of economists—it will be used in dozens of graphs in this book—we will show its generality by beginning with a non-economic example.

A Non-Economic Example   The example concerns heart disease, the leading cause of death in the United States. The risk of heart disease is closely linked to the quantity of cholesterol in a person's blood. Studies have indicated, for example, that a 25 percent reduction in cholesterol can cut the risk of death from heart attack by nearly 50 percent. Knowing this, millions of people have had their cholesterol levels tested and, if results were found to be high, have undertaken programs of diet, exercise, or drug therapy to reduce their risk of heart disease.

Important though cholesterol is, however, just knowing your cholesterol level is not enough to tell you your risk of dying of a heart attack in the coming year. Other variables also enter into the risk of heart disease. One of the most important of these variables is age. For example, for men aged 20 with average cholesterol levels, the mortality rate from heart disease is only about 3 per 100,000. For men aged 60, the mortality rate rises to over 500 per 100,000, still assuming average cholesterol. We thus have three variables with which to deal—mortality, cholesterol, and age. How can we represent these three variables using only two-dimensional graphs?

A possible approach would be to draw two separate graphs. One would show the relationship between age and heart disease for the male population as a whole, without regard to differences in cholesterol counts. The other would show the relationship between cholesterol and heart disease for the male population as a whole, without regard to age. By looking from one diagram to the other, we could get an idea of the entire three-variable relationship.

However, such a side-by-side pair of graphs would be clumsy. There must be a better way to represent the three variables in two dimensions. The better way, shown in Figure 1A.6, is to use cholesterol and mortality as the *x* and *y* axes, and to take age into account by plotting separate lines for men of various ages. That chart is far easier to interpret than the side-by-side pair would be. If you are a man and know your age and cholesterol count, you just pick out the appropriate line and read off your risk of mortality. If you do not like what you see, you go on a diet.[2]

The multi-curve graph is a lovely invention. One of the great things about it is that it works for more than three variables. For example, we could add a fourth variable, gender, to the graph by drawing a new set of lines in a different color to show mortality rates for women of various ages. Each line for women would have a positive slope similar to the men's lines; however, it would lie somewhat below the corresponding line for men of the same age because women, other things being equal, experience lower mortality from heart disease.

Shifts in Curves and Movements Along Curves Economists use three-variable, multi-curve graphs often enough that it is worth giving some attention to the terminology used in discussing them. How can we best describe what happens to a man as he ages, given the relationship shown in Figure 1A.6?

One way to describe the effects of aging would be to say, "As a man ages, he moves from one curve to the next higher one on the chart." There is nothing at all wrong with saying that; but an economist would tend to phrase it a bit differently saying, "As a man ages, his cholesterol-mortality curve shifts upward." The two ways of expressing the effects of aging have exactly the same meaning. Preferring one or the other is just a matter of habit.

---

[2] We could instead have started with the age-mortality chart and drawn separate lines for men with different cholesterol levels. Such a chart would show exactly the same information. We could even draw a chart with cholesterol and age on the axes, and separate contour lines to represent various levels of mortality. The choice often depends on what one wants to emphasize. Here, we emphasize the cholesterol-mortality relationship because cholesterol is something you can do something about. You cannot do anything about your age, so we give age slightly less emphasis by not placing it on one of the two axes.

FIGURE 1A.6   THREE VARIABLES IN TWO DIMENSIONS

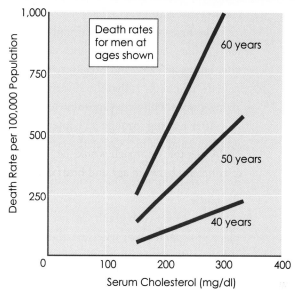

This graph shows a common way of representing a three-variable relationship on a two-dimensional graph. The three variables in this case are serum cholesterol (a measure of the amount of cholesterol in the blood), age, and death rate from heart disease for the U.S. male population. The relationship among the three variables is most easily interpreted, if all three variables are included in one graph, by drawing separate cholesterol-death rate lines for each age group. As a man ages, his cholesterol-death rate line shifts upward.

If we express the effects of aging in terms of a shift of the cholesterol-mortality curve, how should we express the effects of a reduction in cholesterol for a man of a given age? An economist would say it this way: "Cutting a man's cholesterol count through diet or exercise will move him down along his cholesterol-mortality curve."

Before you finish this book, you will see the phrases "shift in a curve" and "movement along a curve" a great many times. How can you keep them straight? Nothing could be easier.

- If you are talking about the effect of a change in a variable that is shown on one of the coordinate axes of the diagram, the effect will be shown as a movement along one of the curves. For example, the effect of a change in cholesterol (horizontal axis) on mortality (vertical axis) is shown by a movement along the line for a given age.

- If you are talking about the effect of a change in a variable that is not shown on one of the coordinate axes of the diagram, the effect will be shown by a shift in one of the curves. For example, the effect of a change in age (not the unit for either axis) on mortality (vertical axis) is shown by a shift in the curve relating cholesterol to mortality.

Study Hints

So much for the basic rules of graphics. Once you master them, how should you study a chapter that is full of graphs?

The first—and most important—rule is to *avoid trying to memorize graphs as patterns of lines*. In every economics course, at least one student comes to the instructor after failing an exam and exclaims, "But I learned every one of those graphs! What happened?" The reply is that the student should have learned economics instead of memorizing graphs. Following are some hints for working with graphs.

After reading through a chapter that contains several graphs, go back through the graphs one at a time. Cover the caption accompanying each graph, and try to express the graph's "picture" in words. If you cannot say as much about the graph as the caption does, reread the text. Once you can translate the graph into words, you have won half the battle.

Next, cover each graph and use the caption as a guide. Try to sketch the graph on a piece of scratch paper. How are the graph's axes labeled? How are the curves labeled? What are the slopes of various curves? Are there important points of intersection or tangencies? If you can go back and forth between the caption and the graph, you will find that the two together are much easier to remember than either one separately.

Finally, try going beyond the graph that is shown in the book. If the graph illustrates the effect of an increase in the price of butter, try sketching a similar diagram that shows the effect of a decrease in the price of butter. If the graph shows what happens to the economy during a period of rising unemployment, try drawing a similar graph that shows what happens during a period of falling unemployment. This is a good practice that may give you an edge on your next exam.

Making Your Own Graphs   For some students, the hardest test questions to answer are ones that require original graphs as part of an essay. Suppose the question is, "How does a change in the number of students attending a university affect the cost per student of providing an education?" Here are some hints for making your own graph.

1. Write down the answer to the question in words. If you cannot, you might as well skip to the next question. Underline the most important quantities in your answer, such as "The larger the *number of students* who attend a college, the lower the *cost per student* of providing them with an education because fixed facilities, such as libraries, do not have to be duplicated."

2. Decide how you want to label the axes. In our example, the vertical axis could be labeled "cost per student" and the horizontal axis "number of students."

3. Do you have specific numbers to work with? If so, the next step is to construct a table showing what you know and use it to sketch your graph. If you have no numbers, you must draw an abstract graph. In this case, all you know is that the cost per student goes down when the number of students goes up. Your graph would thus be a negatively sloped line.

4. If your graph involves more than one relationship between quantities, repeat steps 1 through 3 for each relationship you wish to show. When constructing a graph with more than one curve, pay special attention to points at which you think the curves should intersect. (Intersections occur whenever both the x and y values of the two relationships are equal.) Also, note the points at which you think two curves ought to be tangent (which requires that their slopes be equal), the points of maximum or minimum value, if any, and so on.

5. When your graph is finished, try to translate it back into words. Does it really say what you want it to?

A Reminder   As you read this book and encounter various kinds of graphs, turn back to this appendix now and then. Do not memorize graphs as patterns of lines; if you do, you will get lost. If you can alternate between graphs and words, the underlying point will be clearer than if you rely on either one alone. Keep in mind that the primary focus of economics is not graphs; it is people and the ways in which they deal with the challenge of scarcity.

CHAPTER *2*

Supply and Demand: the Basics

WE BEGAN THE preceding chapter with a discussion of recent record-breaking ups and downs in the prices of commodities, ranging from corn and wheat to crude oil and gold. These are just a few among millions of goods and services for which prices, quantities sold, and other market conditions vary from day to day and from year to year. Whether they are goods that we ourselves buy and sell, or goods that our employers, neighbors, or family members buy and sell, the changing market conditions affect our lives in many ways. The factors determining market prices and quantities are thus central to any discussion of economics.

Supply

The willingness and ability of sellers to provide goods for sale in a market

Demand

The willingness and ability of buyers to purchase goods

Law of demand

The principle that an inverse relationship exists between the price of a good and the quantity of that good that buyers demand, other things being equal

Economists use the term **supply** to refer to sellers' willingness and ability to provide goods for sale in a market. **Demand** refers to buyers' willingness and ability to purchase goods. This chapter will show how supply and demand work together to determine the prices of goods and services.

Demand

According to the **law of demand**, the quantity of a demanded good tends to rise as the price falls and to fall as the price rises. We expect this to happen for two reasons. First, if the price of one good falls while the prices of other goods stay the same, people are likely to substitute the cheaper good. Second, when the price of one good falls while incomes and other prices stay the same, people feel a little richer. They use their added buying power to buy a bit more of many things, including, in most cases, a little more of the good whose price went down.

The terms *demand* and *quantity demanded*, as used in economics, are not the same as *want* or *need*. For example, I think a Porsche is a beautiful car. Sometimes when I see one on the street, I think, "Hey, I want one of those!" Alas, my income is limited. Although in the abstract I might want a Porsche, there are other things I want more. Thus, the quantity of Porsches I demand at the going price is zero.

On the other hand, I might *need* dental surgery to avoid losing my teeth. However, suppose I am poor. If I cannot pay for the surgery or find someone to pay for it on my behalf, I am out of luck. The quantity of dental surgery I demand, therefore, would be zero, however great my need for that service. Demand, then, combines both willingness and ability to buy. It is not desire in the abstract, but desire backed by the means and the intent to buy.

The Demand Curve

The law of demand states a relationship between the quantity of a good that people are willing and able to buy, other things being equal, and the price of that good. Figure 2.1 represents this relationship for a familiar consumer good, chicken. It would be possible to discuss the demand for chicken of a single consumer; but more frequently, as in the following discussion, we focus on the total demand for the good by all buyers in the market.

The figure shows the demand relationship in two different ways. First look at part (a). The first row of the

The demand curve is based upon quantity and price.

FIGURE 2.1   A DEMAND CURVE FOR CHICKEN

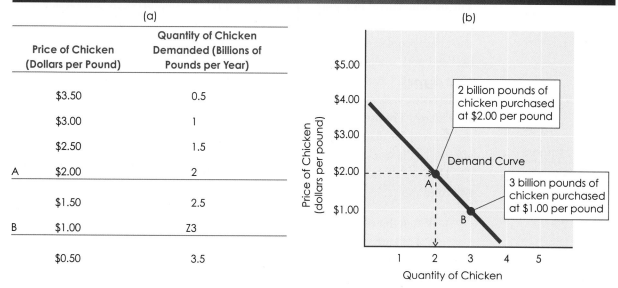

	Price of Chicken (Dollars per Pound)	Quantity of Chicken Demanded (Billions of Pounds per Year)
	$3.50	0.5
	$3.00	1
	$2.50	1.5
A	$2.00	2
	$1.50	2.5
B	$1.00	Z3
	$0.50	3.5

Both the table and the chart show the quantity of chicken demanded at various prices. For example, at a price of $2.00 per pound, buyers are willing and able to purchase 2 billion pounds of chicken per year. This price-quantity combination is shown by row A in part (a) and point A in part (b).

Demand curve

A graphical representation of the relationship between the price of a good and the quantity of that good that buyers demand

Change in quantity demanded

A change in the quantity of a good that buyers are willing and able to purchase that results from a change in the good's price, other things being equal, shown by a movement from one point to another along a demand curve

table shows that when the price of chicken is $3.00 a pound, the quantity demanded per year is 1 billion pounds. Reading down the table, we see that as the price falls, the quantity demanded rises. At $2.50 per pound, buyers are willing and able to purchase 1.5 billion pounds per year; at $1.50, 2.5 billion pounds; and so on.

Part (b) of Figure 2.1 presents the same information in graphical form. The graph is called a **demand curve** for chicken. Suppose we want to use the demand curve to find out what quantity of chicken will be demanded at a price of $2.00 per pound. Starting at $2.00 on the vertical axis, we move across, as shown by the arrow, until we reach the demand curve at point A. Continuing to follow the arrow, we drop down to the horizontal axis. Reading from the scale on that axis, we see that the quantity demanded at a price of $2.00 per pound is 2 billion pounds per year. That is the quantity demanded in row A of the table in part (a).

The effect of a change in the price of chicken, other things being equal, can be shown as a movement from one point to another along the demand curve for chicken. Suppose that the price drops from $2.00 to $1.00 per pound. In the process, the quantity that buyers plan to buy rises. The point corresponding to the quantity demanded at the new, lower price is point B (which corresponds to row B of the table). Because of the inverse relationship between price and quantity demanded, the demand curve has a negative slope.

Economists speak of a movement along a demand curve as a **change in quantity demanded**. Such a movement represents buyers' reactions to a change in the price of the good in question, other things being equal.

Shifts in the Demand Curve

The demand curve[1] in Figure 2.1 represents a relationship between two variables: the price of chicken and the quantity of chicken demanded. Changes in other variables can also affect people's purchases of chicken, however. In the case of chicken, the prices of beef and pork would affect demand. Consumer incomes are a second variable that can affect demand. Changes in expectations about the future are a third; and changes in consumer tastes, such as an increasing preference for foods with low carbohydrate content, are a fourth. The list could go on and on—the demand for ice is affected by the weather; the demand for diapers is affected by the birthrate; the demand for baseball tickets is affected by the won-lost record of the home team; and so on.

How are all these other variables handled when drawing a demand curve? In brief, two rules apply.

1. When drawing a single demand curve for a good, such as the one in Figure 2.1, all other conditions that affect demand are considered to be fixed or constant under the "other things being equal" clause of the law of demand. As long as that clause is in force, the only two variables at work are quantity demanded (on the horizontal axis) and price (on the vertical axis). Thus, a movement along the demand curve shows the effect of a change in price on quantity demanded.

2. When we look beyond the "other things being equal" clause and find that there is a change in a variable that is not represented on one of the axes, such as the price of another good or the level of consumer income, the effect is shown as a shift in the demand curve. In its new position, the demand curve still represents a two-variable price-quantity relationship, but it is a slightly different relationship than before because one of the "other things" has changed.

These two rules for graphical representation of demand relationships are crucial to understanding the theory of supply and demand as a whole. It will be worthwhile to expand on them through a series of examples.

CHANGES IN THE PRICE OF ANOTHER GOOD   We have already noted that the demand for chicken depends on what happens to the price of beef, as well as what happens to the price of chicken. Figure 2.2, which shows demand curves for both goods, provides a closer look at this relationship.

Suppose that the price of beef is initially $3.00 per pound and then increases to $4.50 per pound. The effect of this change on the quantity of beef demanded is shown in part (a) of Figure 2.2 as a movement along the beef demand curve from point A to point B. Part (b) of the figure shows the effect on the demand for chicken. With the price of beef higher than before, consumers will tend to buy more chicken *even if the price of chicken does not change*. Suppose the price of chicken is $2.00 per pound. When beef was selling at $3.00 a pound, consumers bought 2 billion pounds of chicken a year (point A′ on demand curve D_1). After the price of beef goes up to $4.50 a pound, they will buy 3.5 billion pounds of chicken a year, assuming that the price of chicken does not change (point B′ on demand curve D_2).

FIGURE 2.2   EFFECTS OF AN INCREASE IN THE PRICE OF BEEF ON THE DEMAND FOR CHICKEN

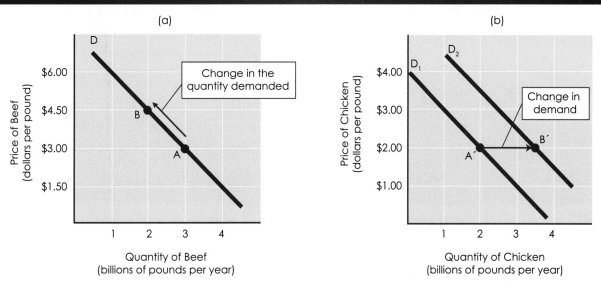

An increase in the price of beef from $3.00 to $4.50 per pound, other things being equal, causes a movement from point A to point B on the beef demand curve—a decrease in the quantity of beef demanded. With the price of chicken unchanged at $2.00 per pound, consumers will substitute chicken for beef. That will cause an increase in the demand for chicken, which is shown as a shift in the chicken demand curve from D_1 to D_2.

Change in demand

A change in the quantity of a good that buyers are willing and able to purchase that results from a change in some condition other than the price of that good, shown by a shift in the demand curve

Substitute goods

A pair of goods for which an increase in the price of one causes an increase in demand for the other

A rise in the price of beef would cause consumers to buy more chicken regardless of the initial price of chicken. If the price of chicken had started out at $3.00 a pound and remained there while the price of beef went up, consumers would have increased their chicken consumption from 1 billion pounds a year to 2.5 billion pounds a year. At a price of $1.00 a pound for chicken, the quantity would have risen from 3 billion pounds to 4.5 billion pounds, and so on. We see, then, that a change in the price of beef causes the entire demand curve for chicken to shift. The "other things being equal" clause of the new demand curve, D_2, incorporates a price of $4.50 a pound for beef, rather than the price of $3.00 a pound assumed in demand curve D_1.

Earlier we explained that economists refer to a movement along a demand curve as a "change in quantity demanded." The corresponding term for a shift in a demand curve is a **change in demand**. A change in quantity demanded (a movement along the curve) is caused by a change in the price of the good in question (the variable on the vertical axis). In contrast, a change in demand (a shift in the demand curve) is caused by a change in some variable other than the price of the good in question (one that does not appear on either axis).

In the example in Figure 2.2, people bought more chicken when the price of beef went up, replacing one meat with the other in their dinners. Economists call such pairs of goods **substitutes** because an increase in the price of one causes an increase in the demand for the other—a rightward shift in the demand curve.

Consumers react differently to price changes when two goods tend to be used together. One example is cars and gasoline. When the price of gasoline goes up, people's selection of cars will be affected. In particular, they will buy fewer low-mileage, large SUVs even if there is no change in the price of those vehicles. An increase in the price of gasoline thus causes a movement upward along the gasoline demand curve and a *leftward* shift in the demand curve for SUVs. Pairs of goods that are related in this way are known as **complements**.

Complementary goods

A pair of goods for which an increase in the price of one results in a decrease in demand for the other

Whether a given pair of goods is a substitute or complement good depends on buyers' attitudes toward those goods; these terms do not refer to properties of the goods themselves. Some people might regard cheese and beef as substitute sources of protein in their diets; others, who like cheeseburgers, might regard them as complements.

One more point regarding the effects of changes in the prices of other goods is also worth noting: In stating the law of demand, it is the price of a good *relative to those of other goods* that counts. During periods of inflation, when the average level of all prices rises, distinguishing between changes in *relative prices* and changes in *nominal prices*— the number of dollars actually paid per unit of a good—is especially important. When the economy experiences inflation, a good can become relatively less expensive even though its nominal price rises, provided that the prices of other goods rise even faster.

Consider chicken, for example. Between 1950 and 2005 the average retail price of a broiler rose by almost 40 percent, from $.59 per pound to $1.05 per pound. Over the same period, however, the average price of all goods and services purchased by consumers rose by about 600 percent. The relative price of chicken thus fell during the period even though its nominal price rose. The drop in the relative price of chicken had a lot to do with its growing popularity on the dinner table.

CHANGES IN CONSUMER INCOMES The demand for a good can also be affected by changes in consumer incomes. When their incomes rise, people tend to buy larger quantities of many goods, assuming that the prices of those goods do not change.

Figure 2.3 shows the effect of an increase in consumer income on the demand for chicken. Demand curve D_1 is the same as the curve shown in Figure 2.1. Suppose now that consumer income rises. With higher incomes, people become choosier about what they eat. They do not just want calories; they want high-quality calories from foods that are tasty, fashionable, and healthful. These considerations have made chicken increasingly popular as consumer incomes have risen.

More specifically, suppose that after their incomes rise, consumers are willing to buy 2.5 billion pounds of chicken instead of 1 billion pounds at a price of $3.00 per pound. The change is shown as an arrow drawn from point A to point B in Figure 2.3. If the initial price of chicken had been $2.00 per pound, even more chicken would be bought at the new, higher level of income. At the original income level and a price of $2.00, the amount purchased would be 2 billion pounds, as shown by point C. After the increase in incomes, buyers would plan to purchase 3.5 billion pounds, shown by the arrow from point C to point D.

Whatever the initial price of chicken, the effect of an increase in consumer income is shown by a shift to a point on the new demand curve, D_2. The increase in demand for chicken that results from the rise in consumer income thus is shown as a shift in the

FIGURE 2.3 EFFECTS OF AN INCREASE IN CONSUMER INCOME ON THE DEMAND FOR CHICKEN

Demand curve D_1 assumes a given level of consumer income. If their incomes increase, consumers will want to buy more chicken at any given price, other things being equal. That will shift the demand curve rightward to, say, D_2. If the prevailing market price at the time of the demand shift is $3.00 per pound, the quantity demanded increases to 2.5 billion pounds (B) from 1 billion (A); if the prevailing price is $2.00 per pound, the quantity demanded will increase to 3.5 billion pounds (D) from 2 billion (C); and so on.

entire demand curve. If consumer income remains at the new, higher level, the effects of any changes in the price of chicken will be shown as movements along the new demand curve. There is, in other words, a chicken demand curve for every possible income level. Each represents a one-to-one relationship between price and quantity demanded, given the assumed income level.

In the example just given, we assumed that an increase in income would cause an increase in the demand for chicken. Experience shows that this is what normally happens. Economists, therefore, call chicken a **normal good**, meaning that when consumer income rises, other things being equal, people will buy more of it.

There are some goods, however, that people will buy less of when their income rises, other things being equal. For example, as the economy slipped into a deep recession in 2008, sales of new shoes fell, but demand for shoe repair services increased sharply. Hormel Foods Corp. reported a surge in sales of staple products like Spam and Dinty Moore beef stew, even while demand for its upscale single-serving microwaveable foods fell. Goods like shoe repair services and Spam, for which demand increases as consumer income falls, are called **inferior goods**. When consumer income rises, the demand curve for an inferior good shifts to the left instead of to the right. As in the case of substitutes and complements, the notions of

Normal good

A good for which an increase in consumer income results in an increase in demand

Inferior good

A good for which an increase in consumer incomes results in a decrease in demand

inferiority and normality arise from consumer choices; they are not inherent properties of the goods themselves.

CHANGES IN EXPECTATIONS   Changes in buyers' expectations are a third factor that can shift demand curves. If people expect the price of a particular good to rise, relative to the prices of other goods, or expect something other than a price increase to raise the opportunity cost of acquiring the good, they will step up their rate of purchase before the change takes place.

For example, suppose that in May, consumers rush to buy airline tickets in response to a series of news reports indicating that prices will be raised for tickets ordered after June 1. The people who buy their tickets in May would probably include many who were planning to travel late in the summer and ordinarily would have waited several more weeks before making their purchase. Thus, many more tickets will be sold in May than would have been sold at the same price if consumers had not anticipated the June price rise. We can interpret the surge in ticket sales in May as a temporary rightward shift in the demand curve.

CHANGES IN TASTES   Changes in tastes are a fourth source of changes in demand. Sometimes these changes occur rapidly, as can be seen, for example, in such areas as popular music, clothing styles, and fast foods. The demand curves for these goods and services shift often. In other cases, changes in tastes take longer to occur but are more permanent. For example, in recent years consumers have been more health conscious than they were in the past. The result has been reduced demand for cigarettes and foods with high content of trans fats, along with increased demand for fish, organic vegetables, and exercise equipment.

Supply

The Supply Curve

We now turn from the demand side of the market to the supply side. As in the case of demand, we begin by constructing a one-to-one relationship between the price of a good and the quantity that sellers intend to offer for sale. Figure 2.4 shows such a relationship for chicken.

Supply curve

A graphical representation of the relationship between the price of a good and the quantity of that good that sellers are willing to supply

The positively sloped curve in Figure 2.4 is called a **supply curve** for chicken. Like demand curves, supply curves are based on an "other things being equal" condition. The supply curve for chicken shows how sellers change their plans in response to a change in the price of chicken, assuming that there are no changes in other conditions—the prices of other goods, production techniques, input prices, expectations, or any other relevant condition.

Why does the supply curve have a positive slope? Why do sellers, other things being equal, plan to supply more chicken when the prevailing market price is higher than they plan to supply when the price is lower? Without going too deeply into a discussion of microeconomic theory, we can consider some common-sense explanations here.

FIGURE 2.4   A SUPPLY CURVE FOR CHICKEN

(a)

	Price of Chicken (Dollars per Pound)	Quantity of Chicken Supplied (Billions of Pounds per Year)
	$4.00	4
	$3.50	3.5
A	$3.00	3
	$2.50	2.5
B	$2.00	2
	$1.50	1.5
	$1.00	1

(b)

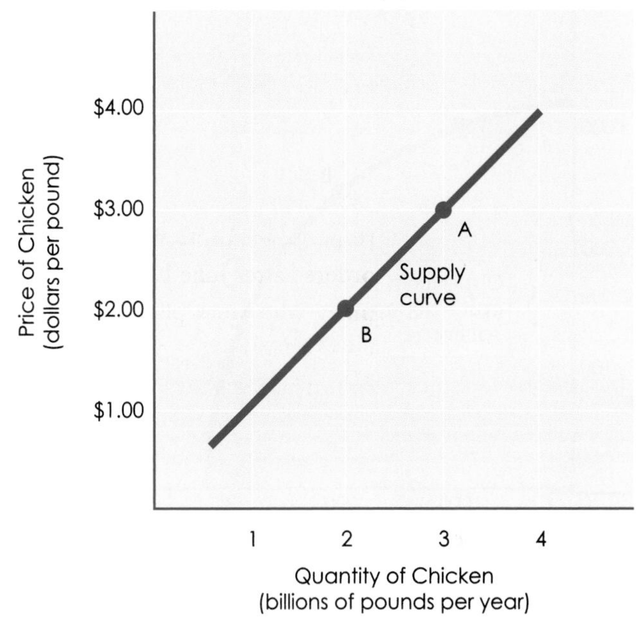

Parts (a) and (b) of this figure show the quantity of chicken supplied at various prices. As the price rises, the quantity supplied increases, other things being equal. The higher price gives farmers an incentive to raise more chickens, but the rising opportunity cost of doing so limits the supply produced in response to any given price increase.

One explanation is that the positive slope of the supply curve represents *producers' response to market incentives*. When the price of chicken goes up, farmers have an incentive to devote more time and resources to raising chickens. Farmers who raise chickens as a sideline may decide to make chickens their main business. Some people may enter the market for the first time. The same reasoning applies in every market. If parents are finding it hard to get babysitters, what do they do? They offer to pay more. If a sawmill cannot buy enough timber, it raises the price it offers to loggers, and so on. Exceptions to this general rule are rare.

Another explanation is that the positive slope of the supply curve reflects *the rising cost of producing additional output in facilities of a fixed size*. A furniture factory with a fixed amount of machinery might be able to produce more chairs only by paying workers at overtime rates to run the machinery for more hours. A farmer who is trying to grow more wheat on a fixed amount of land could do so by increasing the input of fertilizer and pesticides per acre, but beyond a certain point each unit of added chemicals yields less additional output.

Finally, the positive slope of the supply curve can be explained in terms of *comparative advantage and opportunity cost*. Figure 2.5a shows a production possibility frontier for an economy in which there are only two goods, tomatoes and chicken. Farmers can choose which product they will specialize in, but some farmers have a comparative

FIGURE 2.5   THE PRODUCTION POSSIBILITY CURVE AND THE SUPPLY CURVE

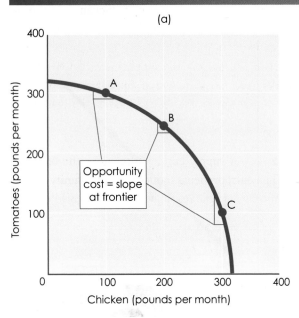

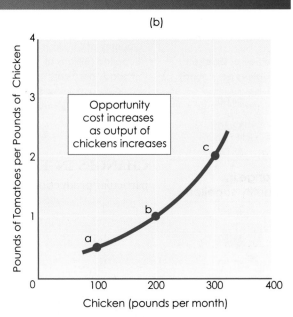

This figure offers an interpretation of the supply curve in terms of the production possibility frontier for an economy in which two goods are produced, tomatoes and chicken. Part (a) shows a production possibility frontier. The slope of the frontier, at any point, shows the opportunity cost of producing an additional pound of chicken measured in terms of the quantity of tomatoes that could have been produced using the same factors of production. The frontier curves because some farmers have a comparative advantage in producing tomatoes and others have a comparative advantage in producing chicken. As more chicken is produced, those with the greatest comparative advantage in producing chicken are the first to stop producing tomatoes. Because the frontier gets steeper as more chicken is produced, the opportunity cost rises, as shown in part (b). The curve in part (b) can be interpreted as a supply curve, in the sense that an incentive, in the form of a higher price, will cause factors of production to be shifted from tomatoes to chicken despite the rising opportunity cost of producing chicken.

advantage in growing tomatoes, others in raising chickens. Beginning from a situation in which only tomatoes are produced, farmers with the strongest comparative advantage in raising chickens—that is, those who are able to produce chicken at relatively the lowest opportunity cost—will switch from tomatoes to chicken even if the price of chicken is low. As the point of production moves along the frontier, the price of chicken must rise to induce farmers with relatively higher opportunity costs to make the switch. The slope of the frontier, at any point, represents the opportunity cost of producing more chicken for a farmer who finds it worthwhile to switch from tomatoes to chicken just at that point.

In Figure 2.5, the slopes at points A, B, and C in part (a) are graphed on a new set of axes in part (b). The graph can be interpreted as a supply curve if it is noted that the price of chicken must rise relative to the price of tomatoes to induce more farmers to switch to chicken as the opportunity cost rises.

Each of these common-sense explanations fits certain circumstances. Together, they provide an intuitive basis for the positive slope of the supply curve.

Change in supply

A change in the quantity of a good that suppliers are willing and able to sell that results from a change in some condition other than the good's price; shown by a shift in the supply curve

Change in quantity supplied

A change in the quantity of a good that suppliers are willing and able to sell that results from a change in the good's price, other things being equal; shown by a movement along a supply curve

Shifts in the Supply Curve

As in the case of demand, the effects of a change in the price of chicken, other things being equal, can be shown as a movement along the supply curve for chicken. Such a movement is called a **change in quantity supplied**. A change in a condition other than the price of chicken can be shown as a shift in the supply curve. Such a shift is referred to as a **change in supply**. Four sources of change in supply are worth noting. Each is related to the notion that the supply curve reflects the opportunity cost of producing the good or service in question.

CHANGES IN TECHNOLOGY   A supply curve is drawn on the basis of a particular production technique. When entrepreneurs reduce the opportunity costs of production by introducing more efficient techniques, it becomes worthwhile to sell more of the good than before at any given price. Figure 2.6 shows how an improvement in production technology affects the supply curve for chicken.

FIGURE 2.6   SHIFTS IN THE SUPPLY CURVE FOR CHICKEN

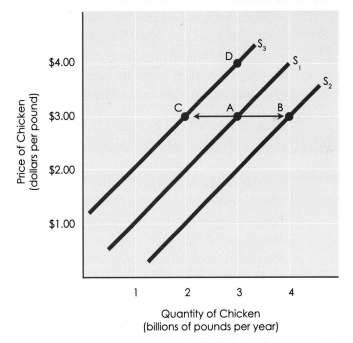

Several kinds of changes can cause the supply of chicken to increase or decrease. For example, a new production method that lowers costs will shift the curve to the right, from S_1 to S_2. The shift is to the right because, taking into account the new, lower cost of production per unit, producers will be willing to supply more chicken at any given price. An increase in the price of inputs, other things being equal, will shift the curve to the left, from S_1 to S_3. The shift is to the left because, taking into account the new, higher price of inputs, producers will be willing to supply less chicken at any given price. Changes in sellers' expectations or in the prices of competing goods can also cause the supply curve to shift.

Supply curve S_1 is the same as the one shown in Figure 2.4. It indicates that farmers will plan to supply 3 billion pounds of chicken per year at a price of $3.00 per pound (point A). Now suppose that the development of a faster-growing bird reduces the amount of feed used in raising chickens. With lower costs per unit, farmers will be willing to supply more chicken than before at any given price. They may, for example, be willing to supply 4 billion pounds of chicken at $3.00 per pound (point B). The move from A to B is part of a shift in the entire supply curve from S_1 to S_2. Once the new techniques are established, an increase or decrease in the price of chicken, other things being equal, will result in a movement along the new supply curve.

CHANGES IN INPUT PRICES   Changes in input prices are a second item that can cause supply curves to shift. An increase in input prices, other things being equal, increases the opportunity cost of producing the good in question; hence, it tends to reduce the quantity of a good that producers plan to supply at a given price. Refer again to Figure 2.6. Suppose that starting from point A on supply curve S_1, the price of chicken feed increases and no offsetting changes occur. Now, instead of supplying 3 billion pounds of chicken at $3.00 per pound, farmers will supply, say, just 2 billion pounds at that price (point C). The move from A to C is part of a leftward shift in the supply curve, from S_1 to S_3.

If the price of feed remains at the new level, changes in the price of chicken will cause movements along the new supply curve. For example, farmers could be induced to supply the original quantity of chicken—3 billion pounds—if the price of chicken was raised enough to cover the increased cost of feed. As you can see in Figure 2.6, that would require a price of $4.00 per pound for chicken (point D).

CHANGES IN THE PRICES OF OTHER GOODS   Changes in the prices of other goods that could be produced using the same factors of production can also produce a shift in the chicken supply curve. In our earlier example, farmers could use available resources to produce either chickens or tomatoes. Suppose that the price of tomatoes rises while the price of chicken stays at $3.00. The rise in the price of tomatoes gives some farmers who would otherwise have produced chickens an incentive to shift the use of their labor, land, and capital to the production of tomatoes. Thus, the effect of an increase in the price of tomatoes can be shown as a leftward shift in the chicken supply curve.

CHANGES IN EXPECTATIONS   Changes in expectations can cause supply curves to shift in much the same way that they cause demand curves to shift. Again, we can use farming as an example. At planting time, a farmer's selection of crops is influenced not so much by current prices as by the prices expected at harvest time. Expectations over a time horizon longer than one growing season also affect supply. Each crop requires special equipment and know-how. We have just seen that an increase in the price of tomatoes gives farmers an incentive to shift from chicken to tomatoes. The incentive will be stronger if the price of tomatoes is expected to remain at the higher level. If it is, farmers are more likely to buy the special equipment needed for that crop and to learn the necessary production techniques.

The Interaction of Supply and Demand

Markets transmit information, in the form of prices, to people who buy and sell goods and services. Taking these prices into account, along with other knowledge they may have, buyers and sellers make their plans.[2] As shown by the demand and supply curves, buyers and sellers plan to buy or sell certain quantities of a good at any given price.

Each market has many buyers and sellers, each making plans independently. When they meet to trade, some of them may be unable to carry out their plans on the terms they expected. Perhaps the total quantity of a good that buyers plan to purchase is greater than the total quantity that suppliers are willing to sell at the given price. In that case, some of the would-be buyers must change their plans. Perhaps planned sales exceed planned purchases at the given price. In that case, some would-be sellers will be unable to carry out their plans.

Market Equilibrium

Equilibrium

A condition in which buyers' and sellers' plans exactly mesh in the marketplace, so that the quantity supplied exactly equals the quantity demanded at a given price

Sometimes no one is surprised. The total quantity of a good that buyers plan to purchase exactly matches the total quantity that producers plan to sell. When buyers' and sellers' plans mesh when they meet in the marketplace, no buyers or sellers need to change their plans. Under these conditions, the market is said to be in **equilibrium**.

Supply and demand curves, which reflect the plans of sellers and buyers, can be used to give a graphical demonstration of market equilibrium. Figure 2.7 uses the same supply and demand curves as before, but this time both curves are drawn on the same diagram. If the quantity of planned sales at each price is compared with the quantity of planned purchases at that price (either the table or the graph can be used to make this comparison), it can be seen that there is only one price at which the two sets of plans mesh. That price—$2.00 per pound—is the equilibrium price. If all buyers and sellers make their plans with the expectation of a price of $2.00, no one will be surprised and no plans will have to be changed.

Shortages

Excess quantity demanded (shortage)

A condition in which the quantity of a good demanded at a given price exceeds the quantity supplied

Inventory

A stock of a finished good awaiting sale or use

What will happen if for some reason people base their plans for buying or selling chicken on a price other than $2.00 a pound?[3] Suppose, for example, that they base their plans on a price of $1.00. As Figure 2.7 shows, at that price buyers will plan to purchase chicken at a rate of 3 billion pounds per year, but farmers will plan to supply only 1 billion pounds. When the quantity demanded exceeds the quantity supplied, as in this example, the difference is an **excess quantity demanded** or, more simply, a **shortage**. In Figure 2.7 the shortage is 2 billion pounds of chicken per year when the price is $1.00 per pound.

In most markets the first sign of a shortage is a drop in the **inventory**, that is, in the stock of the good in question that has been produced and is waiting to be sold or used. Sellers plan to hold a certain quantity of goods in inventory to allow for minor changes in demand. When they see inventories dropping below the planned level, they change

FIGURE 2.7   EQUILIBRIUM IN THE CHICKEN MARKET

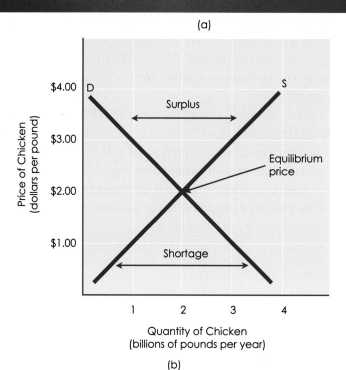

(a)

(b)

Price (per Pound)	Quantity Demanded (Billions of Pounds)	Quantity Supplied (Billions of Pounds)	Shortage (Billions of Pounds)	Surplus (Billions of Pounds)	Direction of Pressure on Price
$3.50	0.5	3.5	—	3	Downward
$3.00	1	3	—	2	Downward
$2.50	1.5	2.5	—	1	Downward
$2.00	2	2	—	—	Equilibrium
$1.50	2.5	1.5	1	—	Upward
$1.00	3	1	2	—	Upward
$0.50	3.5	0.5	3	—	Upward

This figure shows the supply and demand curves for chicken presented earlier in graphical and numerical form. The demand curve shows how much buyers plan to purchase at a given price. The supply curve shows how much producers plan to sell at a given price. At only one price—$2.00 per pound—do buyers' and sellers' plans exactly match. That is the equilibrium price. A higher price causes a surplus of chicken and puts downward pressure on price. A lower price causes a shortage and puts upward pressure on price.

their plans. Some may try to rebuild their inventories by increasing their output if they produce the good themselves; or, if they do not make it themselves, they may order more from the producer. Some sellers may take advantage of the strong demand for their product to raise the price, knowing that buyers will be willing to pay more. Many sellers will do a little of both. If sellers do not take the initiative, buyers will—they will offer to pay more if sellers will supply more. Whatever the details, the result will be an upward movement along the supply curve as both price and quantity increase.

As the shortage puts upward pressure on price, buyers will change their plans, too. Moving up and to the left along their demand curve, they will cut back on their planned purchases. As both buyers and sellers change their plans, the market will move toward equilibrium. When the price reaches $2.00 per pound, both the shortage and the pressure to change buying and selling plans will disappear.

In the markets for most goods, sellers have inventories of goods ready to be sold. There are exceptions, however. Inventories are not possible in markets for services—haircuts, tax preparation, lawn care, and the like. Also, some goods, such as custom-built houses and machine tools that are designed for a specialized need, are not held in inventories. Sellers in these markets do not begin production until they have a contract with a buyer.

In markets in which there are no inventories, the sign of a shortage is a queue of buyers. The queue may take the form of a line of people waiting to be served or a list of names in an order book. The queue is a sign that, given the prevailing price, buyers would like to purchase the good at a faster rate than that at which producers have planned to supply it. However, some plans cannot be carried out—at least not right away. Buyers are served on a first-come, first-served basis.

The formation of a queue of buyers has much the same effect on the market as a decrease in inventories. Sellers react by increasing their rate of output, raising their prices, or both. Buyers react by reducing the quantity they plan to purchase or by offering a higher price. The result is a movement up and to the right along the supply curve and, at the same time, up and to the left along the demand curve until equilibrium is reached.

Surpluses

Having considered what happens when buyers and sellers initially expect a price below the equilibrium price, we now turn to the opposite case. Suppose that for some reason buyers and sellers of chicken expect a price that is higher than the equilibrium price—say, $2.50 per pound—and make their plans accordingly. Figure 2.7 shows that farmers will plan to supply 2.5 billion pounds of chicken per year at $2.50, but their customers will plan to buy only 1.5 billion pounds. When the quantity supplied exceeds the quantity demanded, there is an **excess quantity supplied** or a **surplus**. As Figure 2.7 shows, the surplus of chicken at a price of $2.50 per pound is 1 billion pounds per year.

Excess quantity supplied (surplus)

A condition in which the quantity of a good supplied at a given price exceeds the quantity demanded

When there is a surplus of a product, sellers will be unable to sell all that they had hoped to sell at the planned price. As a result, their inventories will begin to grow beyond the level they had planned to hold in preparation for normal changes in demand.

Sellers will react to the inventory buildup by changing their plans. Some will cut back their output. Others will lower their prices to induce consumers to buy more and thus reduce their extra stock. Still others will do a little of both. The result of these changes in plans will be a movement down and to the left along the supply curve.

As unplanned inventory buildup puts downward pressure on the price of chicken, buyers change their plans too. Finding that chicken costs less than they had expected, they buy more of it. In graphical terms, they move down and to the right along the demand curve. As that happens, the market is restored to equilibrium.

In markets in which there are no inventories, surpluses lead to the formation of queues of sellers looking for customers. Taxi queues at airports are a case in point. At some times of the day, the fare for taxi service from the airport to downtown is more than high enough to attract a number of taxis that is equal to the demand. A queue of cabs waiting for passengers then forms. In some cities drivers who are far back in the queue try to attract riders by offering cut-rate fares. Often, though, there are rules against fare cutting. The queue then grows until the next peak period when a surge in demand shortens it.

Changes in Market Conditions

On a graph, finding the equilibrium point looks easy. In real life, though, it is a moving target. Market conditions, by which we mean all the items that lie behind the "other things being equal" clause, change frequently. When they do, both buyers and sellers revise their plans; and market prices and quantities adjust.

RESPONSE TO A SHIFT IN DEMAND   We will first consider a market's response to a shift in demand. Suppose, for example, that television news broadcasts a warning that eating chicken meat might transmit a new virus. The result would be an immediate decrease in demand for chicken. Part (a) of Figure 2.8 interprets this case in terms of the supply-and-demand model.

As the figure is drawn, the chicken market is initially in equilibrium at E_1. There, the price is $3.00 per pound, and the quantity produced is 2 billion pounds per year. Now the temporary change in tastes caused by the health warning shifts the demand curve to the left, from D_1 to D_2. (There is a shift in the demand curve rather than a movement along it because a change in tastes is not one of the items represented by the axes of the diagram.) What will happen next?

At the original price of $3.00 per pound, there will be a surplus of chicken. The supply curve shows that at that price chicken farmers will plan to produce 2 billion pounds per year. However, according to the new demand curve, D_2, consumers will no longer buy that much chicken at $3.00 per pound. Instead, given their new tastes, they will buy only 1 billion pounds at that price.

The price does not stay at $3.00 for long, however. As soon as the demand curve begins to shift and the surplus begins to develop, chicken inventories rise above their planned levels, putting downward pressure on the price. As the price falls, producers revise their plans. They move down and to the left along their supply curve, reducing the quantity supplied. (There is a movement along the supply curve, not a shift in the curve, because the producers are responding to a change in the price of chicken, the variable shown on the vertical axis. Nothing has happened to change the "other things being equal" conditions, such as technology, input prices, and so on, which could cause the supply curve to shift.)

As farmers move downward along their supply curve in the direction shown by the arrow in part (a) of Figure 2.8, they eventually reach point E_2, where their plans again mesh with those of consumers. At that point the price has fallen to $2.25 per pound and production to 1.5 billion pounds. Although health-conscious consumers would not have bought that much chicken at the old price, they will do so at the

FIGURE 2.8   EFFECTS OF CHANGING CONDITIONS IN THE CHICKEN MARKET

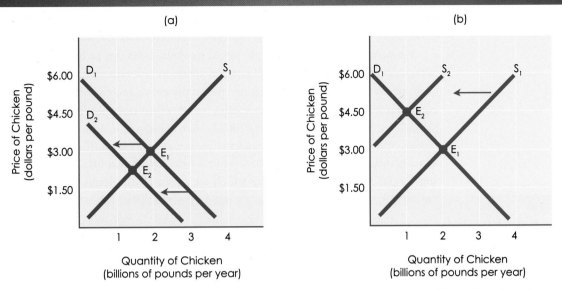

Part (a) of this figure shows the effects of a decrease in demand for chicken caused by a health warning about the safety of eating chicken. Initially the market is in equilibrium at E_1. The change in tastes causes a shift in the demand curve. At the original equilibrium price of $3.00 per pound, there is a temporary surplus of chicken. This causes inventories to start to rise and puts downward pressure on the price. As the price falls, producers move down along their supply curve to a new equilibrium at E_2. There both the price and quantity of chicken are lower than before the shift in demand. Part (b) shows the effects of a decrease in supply caused by an increase in the price of chicken feed. The shift in the supply curve causes a shortage at the initial price of $3.00 per pound. The shortage puts upward pressure on price. As the price rises, buyers move up and to the left along the demand curve until a new equilibrium is reached at E_2. In each case, note that only one curve needs to shift to bring about the new equilibrium.

new, lower price. E_2 thus is the new equilibrium point. Later, if the health scare proves to be baseless, the demand curve will shift back D_1, and the market price and quantity will return to their original values.

RESPONSE TO A SHIFT IN SUPPLY   The original equilibrium might be disrupted by a change in supply rather than by a change in demand. For example, beginning from a condition of equilibrium, increased demand for corn used to make ethanol fuel could cause the price of chicken feed, also made with corn, to increase. That would shift the supply curve to the left while the demand curve remained unchanged, as shown in part (b) of Figure 2.8.

Given the new supply curve, there will be a shortage of chicken at the original price. Inventories will decline, and the prices will rise in response. As the price increases, producers will move upward and to the right along their new supply curve, S_2; and consumers will move upward and to the left along their demand curve, D_1, which remains in its original position. A new equilibrium is established when the price reaches $4.50 per pound.

One of the most frequent mistakes people make in learning the supply-and-demand model is to think that *both* curves always must shift in order to restore equilibrium. The examples given in Figure 2.8 show clearly that this is not the case. In part (a), after the demand curve shifts, a movement along the supply curve is enough to establish the new equilibrium. No shift in the supply curve is needed. Similarly, in part (b), after the supply curve shifts, the demand curve does not need to shift to reach the new equilibrium.

However, in the turmoil of real-world markets, cases can be found in which both curves do shift at once. This will happen when two separate changes in conditions occur at the same time, one acting on the supply curve and the other on the demand curve. *Economics in the News 2.1* provides a real-world example. It shows how wheat prices were pushed upward in early 2008 by two simultaneous changes in market conditions. One was increasing demand for grain as food and animal feed in India and

Economics in the News 2.1
WHEAT PRICES SOAR ON RISING DEMAND, DROUGHT

The United Nations World Food Program is a lifeline for 73 million people in more than 80 countries around the world. WFP assistance does a lot of good; but, not surprisingly, its help does not come cheap. The agency began 2008 with a budget of $2.9 billion, enough to do the job, it was thought. The year was less than a quarter gone, however, before a new disaster struck that led to an appeal for $500 million in extra funds.

This time it was neither natural disaster nor war that led to the emergency appeal. Instead, it was high prices for grain, especially wheat, which hit an all-time high of over $12 a bushel in March, and also for corn, rice, and other staple foods. What was behind the run-up in prices?

A dwindling supply of wheat eventually led to higher prices.

Supply was one problem. In 2007, a serious drought affected Western Australia, one of the world's great wheat producing regions. This caused inventories around the world to fall to dangerously low levels. Then, in the spring of 2008, the bad weather news continued, this time with more dry weather in the wheat producing states of Kansas, Oklahoma, and Texas in the United States. A threat of strikes in wheat-producing regions of Argentina made matters even worse.

Weather was not the only factor affecting supply. Worried about energy dependence and global warming, the U.S. Congress, late in 2007, passed an energy bill that contained generous subsidies for corn-based ethanol. Corn competes with wheat for cropland, so a record acreage planted in corn meant reduction in the planting of wheat.

Demand-side events were also at work to push up wheat prices in 2008. India, the world's biggest wheat importer, and China, also a major importer, were among the fastest growing economies. Increased urbanization and millions of consumers emerging from poverty were not only eating more wheat in the form of bread but also eating more grain-fed meat, as well.

Some countries in East Africa, Southeast Asia, and South America began to see food riots. Josette Sheeran, head of the WFP, warned that the rise in world food prices was creating a "new face of hunger."[a] She said, "There is food on shelves, but people are priced out of the market. There is vulnerability in urban areas we have not seen before. There are food riots in countries where we have not seen them before."

Toward the end of 2008, the food crisis began to ease. This time, the dominant factor was a slowdown in demand as a result of the spreading global economic crisis. Long-term planners in agencies like the UN World Food Program worried that the relief from high prices was only temporary, however. Sooner or later, growth would resume in the giant economies of South and East Asia. When it did, the world's poorest consumers, like those in Sub-Saharan Africa, would once again feel the pinch of supply and demand.

_____

[a] Cited by Amando Doronilla, "Analysis: New Face of Hunger," *The Phillippine Enquirer,* March 26, 2008,

China. That shifted the demand curve to the right. At the same time, bad weather in major wheat-producing regions of the United States and Australia shifted the supply curve to the left. Either change acting alone would have been enough to raise the price. Both changes acting together had an especially sharp impact. Later in the year, the price fell again. This time the dominant factor was a drop in demand as a result of the growing global economic crisis.

Equilibrium as Spontaneous Order

The way that markets move toward a new equilibrium following a disturbance is an example of economic coordination through spontaneous order. In the case we have been following, the disturbance began either with a change in health consciousness among consumers or with a change in the weather. To make the adjustment to new conditions, the decisions of thousands of farmers, wholesalers, retailers, as well as that of millions of consumers, must somehow be coordinated. How can that be done?

In a market economy, no central planning agency or regulatory bureaucracy is needed. The required shift in the use of scarce resources is brought about through information and incentives transmitted in the form of changing market prices. The trend toward low-carbohydrate, high-protein diets in the early 2000s is a typical example. As demand for beef, chicken, and other high-protein foods rose, farmers responded to higher prices by raising more chickens and cattle. Labor, capital, natural resources, and entrepreneurial energy flowed into chicken and beef production without any central authority giving an order. At the same time, investments in donuts, a high-carb food that had boomed in the 1990s, slowed substantially.

The process was remarkably smooth for so vast a shift in resource use. Behind the scenes, surpluses and shortages nudged choices in the needed directions, but at no time did shortages occur in the acute form of empty meat coolers at the supermarket or lines of chicken-hungry consumers stretching down city streets. Similarly, slack demand for donuts signaled entrepreneurs to turn away from building new outlets, but it did not give rise to mountains of rotting donuts that had to be dumped into landfills.

No one *intended* this process of adjustment. Equilibrium is not a compromise that must be negotiated by a committee of consumers and producers. Just as shoppers manage to equalize the length of supermarket checkout lines without the guidance of a central authority, markets move toward equilibrium spontaneously, through the small, local adjustments that people make in their efforts to serve their own interests. As Adam Smith might have put it, we have not the benevolence of Tyson Foods or the Beef Industry Council to thank for our dinner; instead it is their self-interest that puts the right food on our table.

Price Floors and Ceilings: An Application

Economics—both macro and micro—encompasses a great many applications of the concepts of supply and demand. Although each situation is unique, each to some extent draws on ideas developed in this chapter. This section, which uses the model to analyze the effects of government-imposed price floors and ceilings, provides some examples. Many more will be added in later chapters.

Price Supports: the Market for Milk

In our earlier example of the market for beef, a decrease in demand caused a surplus, which in turn caused the price to decrease until the surplus was eliminated. Markets are not always free to respond by adjusting prices, however. The market for milk is a case in point.

The market for milk is supported by a floor price subsidy.

Figure 2.9 shows the market for milk in terms of supply and demand curves. The quantity of milk is measured in hundredweight, the unit used for bulk milk sales, equal to roughly 12 gallons. Suppose that initially the market is in equilibrium at point E_1. The wholesale price of milk is $13 per hundredweight, and 110 million hundredweight is produced per year. Then suppose that a trend in taste away from high-cholesterol foods shifts the demand curve for milk to the left. The result would be a surplus of milk at the $13 price, as shown by the arrow in Figure 2.9.

At this point a new factor comes into operation that was not present in our earlier discussion of the chicken market. In that case, chicken prices were free to fall in response to a surplus, but in the milk market they are not. Instead, an elaborate set of government-imposed controls and subsidies puts a floor under the price of milk. As part of the controls, the government agrees to pay a minimum price for all milk that cannot be sold at that price on the open market. In our example, the support price is assumed to be $13.

With the demand curve in its original position D_1, there was no surplus and the government did not need to buy any milk. However, with the demand curve in position D_2, there is a surplus of 40 million hundredweight per year. Under the price support law the government must buy this surplus and store it in the form of powdered milk, cheese, butter, and other products with long shelf lives. Without price supports, the shift in demand would cause the price of milk to fall to the new equilibrium price of $10 per hundredweight. When price supports are applied to a product at a level higher than the equilibrium price, however, the result is a persistent surplus. The effects of the price support can be understood in terms of conflicting signals sent to producers and consumers. To consumers, the price of $13 says, "Milk is scarce. Its opportunity cost is high. Hold your consumption down." To producers, it says, "All is well. Incentives are unchanged. Feel free to continue

FIGURE 2.9 PRICE SUPPORTS FOR MILK

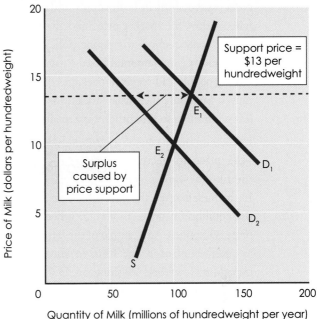

Quantity of Milk (millions of hundredweight per year)

Suppose that initially the market for milk is in equilibrium at E_1. A shift in tastes away from high-cholesterol foods then shifts the demand curve to D_2. If the price were free to fall, there would be a temporary surplus that would push the price down to a new equilibrium at $10 per hundredweight. Instead, suppose that the government maintains a support price for milk at a level higher than the equilibrium price, as it did for many years ($13 per hundredweight in this example). The government would then need to buy the surplus milk and stores it in the form of powdered milk, butter and cheese to keep the price from falling.

using scarce resources to produce milk." Without price supports, a drop in the price to $10 would send a different set of messages. Consumers would hear, "Milk is cheaper and more abundant. Although it is not cholesterol free, give in to temptation! Drink more of it!" Producers would hear, "The milk market is not what it once was. Look at your opportunity costs. Is there perhaps some better use for your labor, capital, and natural resources?"

During the 1980s and 1990s, the government's price support was consistently higher than the equilibrium price. The program became very expensive, more than $1,000 per U.S. family by some estimates, enough to buy each family its own cow. From time to time the government has tried to eliminate the milk surplus by shifting the supply curve to the left so that it would intersect the demand curve near the support price. Under one program, for example, farmers were encouraged to sell their cows to be slaughtered for their meat, thereby reducing the size of dairy herds; but such programs have failed to eliminate the milk surplus. The chief reason is the dairy farmers' entrepreneurial response to the high price of milk. The government's efforts to cut the size of herds were largely offset by increased output per cow as a result of genetic improvements and better farm management practices. The government accumulated mountains of surplus dairy products.

Then, during the early years of the twenty-first century, conditions in the milk market changed. Increasing demand from emerging-market countries and rising feed costs caused shifts in both supply and demand curves. By 2005, the support price had fallen below the market price and the surplus had disappeared. This, too, had unintended consequences for public policy. Under the U.S. Department of Agriculture's Commodity Supplemental Food Program, as many as 100,000 mothers, children, and elderly people had received packages of free milk powder drawn from government surpluses. Suddenly these vast stocks were threatened with exhaustion, and officials were left scrambling to find other ways to aid needy citizens.

Price Ceilings: the Case of Rent Control

In the milk market, the government maintains a support price that has often been above the equilibrium price. In certain other markets, a price ceiling below the equilibrium price is imposed. An example of the latter situation is rent control in housing markets.

Rent control in one form or another has been used in several major U.S. cities, including New York, Washington, D.C., San Francisco, and Los Angeles. The controls vary from one city to another; however, in all cases law, at least for some categories of apartments, establishes maximum rents. The purpose of rent control is to aid tenants by preventing landlords from charging "unreasonably high" rents. What is unreasonably high is determined by the relative political strength of landlords and tenants rather than by the forces of supply and demand.

INTENDED EFFECTS   Figure 2.10 interprets the effects of rent control in terms of supply and demand. For the sake of simplicity, it is assumed that the supply of rental housing consists of units of equal size and rental value. Part (a) of the figure shows the effects of rent control in the short run. Here the short run means a period that is too short to permit significant increases or decreases in the supply of rental housing. (The short-run supply curve, which is drawn as a vertical line, indicates that a change in price will not result in any change in the quantity of apartments.[4])

Under the conditions shown, the equilibrium rent per standard housing unit is $1,250 per month for each of the 200,000 units in the city. Now suppose that a rent ceiling of $500 is imposed. The result is a gain to tenants of $750 per unit per month. The total sum transferred to tenants (that is, the benefit to them from below-market rents) is $750 per unit multiplied by 200,000 units, or $150 million, in all. In graphical terms, that sum is equal to the area of the shaded rectangle in Figure 2.10. The benefit to tenants at the expense of landlords is the principal intended effect of rent control.

UNINTENDED EFFECTS The policy of rent control, which aims to benefit tenants at the expense of landlords, provides a classic illustration of the law of unintended consequences. In the short run, when the stock of apartments is fixed, the unintended consequences stem from the apartment shortage created by the controls. The shortage occurs because the quantity demanded is greater at the lower ceiling price than at the higher equilibrium price.

Figure 2.10   Effects of Rent Control

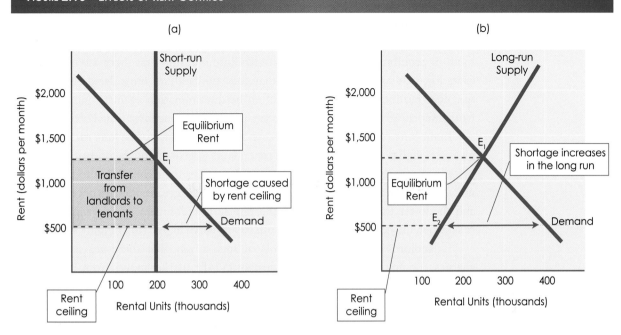

Part (a) shows the short-run effects of rent control. In the short run, the supply of rental apartments is considered to be fixed. The equilibrium rent is $1,250 per month. A rent ceiling of $500 per month is then put into effect. One possible outcome is that landlords will charge disguised rent increases, which will bring the true price back to $1,250 per month. If such disguised increases are prohibited, there will be a shortage of 350,000 units at the ceiling price. Part (b) shows the long-run effects when there is time to adjust the number of units in response to the price. If the ceiling price is enforced, landlords move down their supply curve to E_2. The shortage then becomes even more severe than in the short run.

The greater quantity demanded has several sources. First, people who would otherwise own a house or condominium may now want to rent. Second, people who would otherwise live in non–rent-controlled suburbs may now seek rent-controlled units in the city. Third, each tenant may want more space, which results in a demand for more of the standardized units shown in Figure 2.10.

The shortage creates a problem for both landlords and tenants: How will the limited supply of apartments be rationed among those who want them? Both landlords and tenants devise a number of creative responses—*entrepreneurial* responses, as an economist would say.

One response on the part of landlords is to seek disguised rent increases. These may take the form of large, nonrefundable "key deposits" or security deposits. As an alternative, they may sell old, used furniture or drapes at inflated prices as a condition for renting the apartment. Finally, the costs of certain maintenance or security services for which the landlord might otherwise have paid may be transferred to tenants.

Tenants, too, may get into the act. When they decide to move, they may sublet their apartments to other tenants rather than give up their leases. Now it is the tenant who collects the key money or sells the old drapes to the subtenant. The original tenant may have moved to a distant city but maintains a bank account and a post office box for use in paying the rent. The subtenant is instructed to play the role of a "guest" if the landlord telephones.

Advocates of rent control view these responses as cheating and often try to outlaw them. If prohibitions are enforced, the landlord will find that there are many applicants for each vacant apartment. In that case, the landlord must decide to whom to rent the apartment. The result will often be discrimination against renters who are from minority groups, who have children, or who have unconventional lifestyles.

In the long run, rent control has other unintended effects. The long run in this case means enough time for the number of rental units to grow through construction of new units or shrink through abandonment of old ones (or their conversion to condominiums). Other things being equal, the higher the rent, the greater the rate of construction; and the lower the rent, the greater the rate of abandonment or conversion. This is reflected in the positively sloped long-run supply curve in part (b) of Figure 2.10.

If landlords enforce rent controls in such a way that there are no disguised charges, the number of rental units shrinks and the market moves from E_1 to E_2. At E_2, the unintended effects that appeared in the short run become more pronounced. The intensity of housing discrimination increases relative to the short-run case because the difference between the number of units available and the number sought by renters increases. Graphically, that difference is shown by the horizontal gap between the supply and demand curves at the ceiling price. In the short run, there is a shortage of 50,000 units; in the long run, the shortage increases to 75,000 units.

Rent controls are often defended as being beneficial to the poor; but when all of the unintended effects of rent control are taken into account, one may question whether poor families really benefit. In cases in which disguised rent increases are possible, the true cost of rental housing is not really decreased. Further, it is hard to believe that the tendency of landlords to discriminate against minority group members, single-parent families, and tenants with irregular work histories will benefit the poor. The most likely beneficiaries of rent control are stable, middle-class families who work at the same jobs and live in the same apartments for long periods.

Why does rent control persist as a policy, given its many seemingly perverse unintended consequences? Some economists explain the popularity of rent control in terms of the political power of the middle-class tenants who are most likely to benefit from rent controls and who see "helping the poor" as nothing more than a convenient cover for their own self-interest. Some explain their popularity in terms of the short time horizon of government officials: The adverse effect on tenants of ending rent control would appear very quickly, whereas such benefits as increased construction of new apartments would materialize only long after the next election. Others attribute the popularity of rent control to the simple fact that many voters do not give much thought to the policy's unintended consequences. Whatever the reason, it appears that very gradually rent control is weakening its hold, even in New York, long home of the strongest controls. In the past decade, some 10 percent of the 1 million or so apartments once covered by New York's rent controls have left the system; and the trend is expected to continue.

THIS CHAPTER HAS covered the basics of the supply-and-demand model and described a few applications of that model. There are many more applications in both macro- and microeconomics. In macroeconomics, the supply-and-demand model can be applied to financial markets, labor markets, and the problem of determining the rate of inflation and real output for the economy as a whole. In microeconomics, the model can be applied to product markets, markets for productive resources, and policy issues ranging from pollution to farm policy to international trade, to name just a few. As the great economist Alfred Marshall once put it, nearly all of the major problems of economics have a "kernel" that reflects the workings of supply and demand (see *Who Said It? Who Did It? 2.1*).

When one takes a detailed look at the underpinnings of the model, it appears to fit some kinds of markets more closely than others. The fit is best for markets in which there are many producers and many customers, the goods sold by one producer are much like those sold by others, and all sellers and buyers have good information on market conditions. Markets for farm commodities, such as wheat and corn, and financial markets, such as the New York Stock Exchange, meet these standards reasonably well.

Who Said It? Who Did It? 2.1
ALFRED MARSHALL ON SUPPLY AND DEMAND

Alfred Marshall, often considered to have been the greatest economist of his day, was born in London in 1842. His father was a Bank of England cashier who hoped the boy would enter the ministry. Young Marshall had other ideas, however. He turned down a theological scholarship at Oxford to study mathematics, receiving his M.A. from Cambridge in 1865.

While at Cambridge, Marshall joined a philosophical discussion group. There he became interested in promoting the broad development of the human mind. He was soon told, however, that the harsh realities of economics would prevent his ideas from being carried out. Britain's economic potential as a country, it was said, could never allow the masses sufficient leisure for education. This disillusioning episode appears to have triggered Marshall's fascination with economics.

At the time, the classical school founded by Adam Smith and David Ricardo dominated British economics. Marshall had great respect for the classical writers. Initially, he saw his own work as simply applying his mathematical training to strengthen and systematize the classical system. Before long, however, he was breaking new ground and developing a system of his own. By 1890, when he brought out his famous *Principles of Economics*, he had laid the foundation of what we now call the neoclassical school.

In an attempt to explain the essence of his approach, Marshall included the following passage in the second edition of his *Principles*:

In spite of a great variety in detail, nearly all the chief problems of economics agree in that they have a kernel of the same kind. This kernel is an inquiry as to the balancing of two opposed classes of motives, the one consisting of desires to acquire certain new goods, and thus satisfy wants; while the other consists of desires to avoid certain efforts or retain certain immediate enjoyment ... in other words, it is an inquiry into the balancing of the forces of demand and supply.

Marshall's influence on economics—at least in the English-speaking world—was enormous. His *Principles* was the leading economics text for several decades, and modern students can still learn much from it. As a professor at Cambridge, Marshall taught a great many of the next generation's leading economists. Today his neoclassical school continues to dominate the profession. It has received many challenges, but so far it has weathered them all.

However, even in markets that do not display all of these features, the fit is often close enough so that the supply-and-demand model provides useful insights into what is going on. The rental housing market is an example. Not all rental units are, in fact, alike, even when measurement is standardized for objective characteristics such as floor space. Nevertheless, most economists would agree that applying the supply-and-demand model to that market could lead to valid conclusions about the effects of rent control. Thus, the supply-and-demand model serves a precise analytical function in some markets and a broader, more metaphorical function in others. That flexibility makes the model one of the most useful items in the economist's tool kit.

☙

Summary

1. **How does the price of a good or service affect the quantity of it that buyers demand?** Economists use the term *demand* to refer to the willingness and ability of buyers to purchase goods and services. According to the *law of demand*, there is an inverse relationship between the price of a good and the quantity of it that buyers demand. The *quantity demanded* is the quantity that buyers are willing and able to pay for. The law of demand can be represented graphically by a negatively sloped *demand curve*. A movement along the demand curve shows a change in the quantity demanded.

2. **How do other market conditions affect demand?** A change in any of the variables covered by the "other things being equal" clause of the law of demand causes a shift in the demand curve; this is known as a *change in demand*. Examples include changes in the prices of goods that are *substitutes* or *complements* of the good in question as well as changes in consumer incomes, expectations, and tastes.

3. **How does the price of a good affect the quantity supplied by sellers?** *Supply* refers to sellers' willingness and ability to offer products for sale in a market. In most markets an increase in the price of a good will increase the quantity of the good that sellers are willing to supply.

This relationship can be shown as a positively sloped *supply curve*. The higher price gives producers an incentive to supply more, but rising opportunity costs set a limit on the amount they will supply at any given price.

4. **How do changes in other market conditions affect supply?** A change in any of the items covered by the "other things being equal" clause of the supply curve will shift the curve. Examples include changes in technology, changes in the prices of inputs, changes in the prices of other goods that could be produced with the same resources, and changes in expectations.

5. **How do supply and demand interact to determine the market price of a good or service?** In a market with a positively-sloped supply curve and a negatively-sloped demand curve, there is only one price at which the quantity of a good that sellers plan to supply will exactly match the quantity that buyers plan to purchase. That is known as the *equilibrium* price. At any higher price there will be a *surplus*, and at any lower price there will be a *shortage*.

6. **Why do market prices and quantities change in response to changes in market conditions?** A change in any market condition that shifts the supply or demand curve will change the equilibrium price and quantity in a market. For example, the demand curve may shift to the right as a

result of a change in consumer incomes. This causes a shortage at the old price, and the price begins to rise. As the price rises, suppliers move up along the supply curve to a new equilibrium. No shift in the supply curve is required. On the other hand, better technology may shift the supply curve to the right. In that case, there is a surplus at the old price, and the price will fall. As the price decreases, buyers will move down along their demand curve to a new equilibrium. No shift in the demand curve is required.

7. **How do price supports and price ceilings affect the operation of markets?** A price support prevents the market price from falling when the demand curve shifts to the left or the supply curve shifts to the right. The result may be a lasting surplus. A price ceiling prevents the price from rising to its equilibrium level. The result may be a permanent shortage. The total quantity supplied may then be less than the quantity that buyers would like to purchase at the ceiling price or even at the equilibrium price.

Key Terms

Problems and Topics for Discussion

1. **A shifting demand curve** A vending machine company has studied the demand for soft drinks sold in cans from machines. On a 70-degree day consumers in the firm's territory will buy about 2,000 cans at a price of $0.75. For each $.05 rise in price, the quantity sold falls by 200 cans per day; for each 5-degree rise in the temperature, the quantity sold rises by 150 cans per day. The same relationships hold for decreases in price or temperature. Using this information, draw a set of curves showing the demand for soft drinks on days when the temperature is 60, 70, and 85 degrees. Then draw a separate diagram with temperature on the vertical axis and quantity on the horizontal axis. Draw a line representing the relationship between temperature and quantity when the price is $0.75. Next, draw additional temperature-quantity lines for prices of $0.50 and $1.00. Do the two diagrams give the same information? Discuss. (Note: If you have any trouble with this exercise, review the appendix to Chapter 1, "Working with Graphs," especially the section entitled "Packing Three Variables into Two Dimensions.")

2. **Demand and the relative price of motor fuel in the 1980s** In 1979 and 1980, the nominal price of motor fuel rose much more rapidly than the general price level, pushing up the relative price of motor fuel. As we would expect, the quantity sold decreased. In 1981 and 1982, the relative price leveled off and then began to fall; but the quantity sold continued to fall. Which one or more of the following hypotheses do you think best explains the behavior of motor fuel sales in 1981 and 1982? Illustrate each hypothesis with supply and demand curves.

   a. In the 1970s the demand curve had the usual negative slope. However, in 1981 and 1982, the demand curve shifted to an unusual positively sloped position.

b. The demand curve had a negative slope throughout the period. However, the recession of 1981 and 1982 reduced consumers' real incomes and thus shifted the demand curve.

c. The demand curve has a negative slope at all times, but the shape depends partly on how much time consumers have to adjust to a change in prices. Over a short period, the demand curve is fairly steep because few adjustments can be made. Over the long term, it has a somewhat flatter slope because further adjustments, such as buying more fuel-efficient cars or moving closer to the job, can be made. Thus, the decreases in fuel sales in 1981 and 1982 were delayed reactions to the price increases that occurred in 1979 and 1980.

3. **Shortages, price controls, and queues**   During the late 1980s and early 1990s, economic reforms initiated by Soviet President Mikhail Gorbachev began to raise consumer incomes; but the Soviet government continued to impose price ceilings on basic goods like food, clothing, and household goods. As a result, there were severe shortages of many goods and long lines at all kinds of stores became common. Then, in January 1992, the new Russian government, under President Boris Yeltsin, removed retail price controls on most goods. Within a month, prices more than doubled on average and lines disappeared. Analyze these events using the supply and demand model. First draw a supply and demand diagram for some common good, i.e., butter, showing the market in equilibrium before the beginning of the Gorbachev reforms. Next, use shifts of the appropriate curves to show why the combination of rising incomes plus price ceilings produced shortages and lines. Finally, show what happened when price controls were removed in 1992.

4. **Eliminating queues through flexible pricing**   You are a member of the Metropolitan Taxi Commission, which sets taxi fares for your city. You have been told that long lines of taxis form at the airport during off-peak hours. At peak hours, on the other hand, few taxis are available and there are long lines of passengers waiting for cabs. It is proposed that taxi fares from the airport to downtown be cut by 10 percent during off-peak hours and increased by 10 percent during peak hours. How do you think these changes would affect the queuing patterns of taxis and passengers? Do you think the proposal is a good one from the passengers' point of view? From the cabbies' point of view? From the standpoint of economic efficiency? What do you think would happen if the Taxi Commission stopped setting fares altogether and allowed passengers and drivers to negotiate any price they wanted? Discuss.

5. **Rent control**   Turn to part (b) of Figure 2.10, which shows the long-run effects of rent control. If the controls are enforced and there are no disguised rent charges, landlords move down the supply curve to E_2. Buildings are abandoned or converted because of the low rent they bring in. Now consider some alternative possibilities.

a. Suppose that the controls are poorly enforced so that landlords—through key deposits, furniture sales, or some other means—are able to charge as much as the market will bear. What will the resulting equilibrium price and quantity be, taking both open and disguised rental charges into account?

b. Now suppose that the controls are enforced so that landlords really cannot collect more than $500 per month. However, the controls are not enforced against tenants who sublet. What will the equilibrium quantity and price be, including both the rent paid to landlords and the disguised rental payments made by subtenants to their sublessors?

Case for Discussion

The hottest topic at a recent exposition for suppliers and users of off-road heavy equipment was tire shortages. Booming Chinese demand for raw materials meant that mining companies in China, Russia, and Indonesia were stocking up on new earth moving equipment and wearing tires out faster on equipment they already owned.

While demand soared, supply had a hard time keeping up. Building a new production line for large tires can take more than two years. The *Financial Times* reported that some tire makers were reactivating mothballed production lines for old-fashioned bias-ply tires. While not as good as modern radial tires, they were good enough to satisfy demand from customers who just wanted something "black and round," according to Prashant Prabhu, president of the earth-mover and industrial tire business of Michelin, the French tire maker. Prabhu also said his company was revising its pricing for large tires to take the shortage into account. Other suppliers have been buying tires of unknown, possibly inferior, quality from Russia and China.

According to *Light and Medium Truck Magazine*, the shortages of huge off-road tires were spilling over into the market for heavy-duty truck tires. In addition to sharply increased demand, it blamed rising prices for materials, including both natural and synthetic rubber. The magazine predicted that the shortage would last two years or more.

Expectations, based on past experience, were a significant factor slowing the adjustment of supply to the shortage. In 2000–2003, demand for heavy-duty tires from equipment makers had dropped by more than 50 percent, leaving some tire makers with serious overcapacity. The fear that recent high demand might not last led some manufacturers to take a "wait-and-see" attitude, but world demand for tires did hold up. In 2008, Canadian miners, trying to meet orders for strip-mined coal and oil shale, were still struggling to keep their giant vehicles rolling—using every little trick from keeping their roads free of sharp rocks to even digging up tires discarded years ago, but now, perhaps, capable of being reconditioned and used again.

SOURCES: *Financial Times*, Materials squeeze leads to tyre shortage, By James Mackintosh Published: April 28 2005 03:00; *Light and Medium Truck Magazine*, May 2005,

http://www.ttnews.com/lmt /May05/tire.asp (May 22, 2005); *Rental Management Online*, http://www.rentalmanagement-mag.com/newsart.asp?ARTID=1776, May 22, 2005; *Business Edge*, "Tire Shortage Poses Challenges to Miners," March 7, 2008, http://www.businessedge.ca/article.cfm/ newsID/ 17370.cfm.

QUESTIONS

1. Beginning from a position of equilibrium, use supply and demand curves to show how the tire market is affected by an increase in demand for earth-moving equipment. Does the supply curve shift? The demand curve? Both? Explain.

2. Now draw a diagram that has two supply curves, one that applies to the short run and the other to the long run. How does the long-run impact of an increase in demand differ from the short-run impact?

3. As the world fell into recession in 2008 and 2009, demand for earthmoving equipment decreased sharply. How would this affect the market for tires?

End Notes

1. Before continuing, the reader may want to review the Chapter 1 appendix, "Working with Graphs," especially the section entitled "Packing Three Variables into Two Dimensions."

2. The "plans" referred to need not be formal or thought out in detail, and are subject to change. A consumer might, for example, make out a shopping list for the supermarket based on the usual prices for various foods, but then revise it to take into account unexpected price increases or sales on certain items. On specific occasions, consumer decisions may even be completely impulsive, with little basis in rational calculation. The model of supply and demand does not require that every decision be based on precise analysis, but only that consumer intentions, on the average, are influenced by prices and other economic considerations.

3. Why might buyers and sellers enter the market expecting a price other than the one that permits equilibrium? It may be, for example, that market conditions have caused the supply or demand curve to shift unexpectedly, so that

a price that formerly permitted equilibrium no longer does so. It may be that buyers or sellers expect conditions to change, but they do not change after all; or, it may be that government policy has established a legal maximum or minimum price that differs from the equilibrium price. Later sections of the chapter will explore some of these possibilities.

4. This is a fairly restrictive assumption. In practice, a small number of housing units can move into or out of the rental market quickly in response to changing conditions. "Mother-in-law apartments" in private homes are an example. If conditions in the rental market are unfavorable, the owners of such units may simply leave them vacant. Allowing for such fast-reaction units means that the short-run supply curve, while still quite steep, would not be vertical. However, a vertical short-run curve simplifies the geometry while capturing the essential features of the situation.

CHAPTER *3*

Supply, Demand, and Elasticity

After reading this chapter, you will understand the following:

1. How the responsiveness of quantity demanded to a price change can be expressed in terms of elasticity
2. How elasticity of demand is related to revenue
3. How elasticity applies to changes in market conditions other than price
4. How elasticity is useful in interpreting issues of taxation and other public policies

Before reading this chapter, make sure you know the meaning of the concepts:

1. Supply and demand
2. Demand, quantity demanded
3. Supply, quantity supplied
4. Substitutes and complements
5. Normal and inferior goods

HOW MUCH DID you pay for this textbook? Was it more expensive or less expensive than the books you buy for other courses? As a student, you probably have a strong desire to pay less for your books if you can. Have you ever wondered why your professors sometimes choose books that are so expensive?

This chapter will help you understand the effect of price on choices that people make among alternative goods—like different textbooks, different foods, or different modes of transportation. It will focus on the concept of *elasticity*, a word economists use to say how sensitive such choices are to price. As a student, your choice of textbook is probably very sensitive to price—your demand is *elastic*, to use the economist's term. However, your professor, who does not pay for the books, cares less about how much they cost. Your professor's demand may be *inelastic*. In the following pages you will learn how to define, measure, and apply the important concept of elasticity.

Elasticity

The responsiveness of quantity demanded to a change in price can be expressed in many ways, depending on the units of measurement that are chosen. Consider the demand for chicken, an example used in the preceding chapter. A study of the budget of a single American household might find that an increase of ten cents per pound would decrease consumption by 1 pound per week. A study done in France might find that a price increase of 1 euro per kilogram would decrease consumption of all consumers in the city of Lille by 25,000 kilos per month. Are the findings of these studies similar? It is hard to tell because the units used are different. It would require more information, and some calculations, to know whether the sensitivity of demand to price as measured in different countries using different currencies are the same. A further problem with the examples given is that they do not tell us where prices or quantities started. Ten cents a pound is not a very large increase—if it refers to premium free-range, boneless, chicken breasts that began at $3.49 a pound. One euro per kilogram might represent a doubling of the price, however, for a low-quality, commercial grade of chicken.

To avoid confusion arising from the choice of different units of measurement and differing starting points for price changes, it is useful to standardize. One common way of doing so is to express all changes as percentages. Suppose, for example, that the studies of both American and French consumers found that a 20 percent increase in price was associated with a 10 percent decrease in quantity demanded. Stating changes in percentages would take into account the size of a price change relative to the starting or ending price and quantity. The percentages would also stay the same regardless of whether the original data were stated in dollars per pound, euros per kilo, or any other measurement.

The use of percentages to express the response of one variable to a change in another is widespread in economics. The term **elasticity** is used to refer to relationships expressed in percentages. Like equilibrium, elasticity is a metaphor borrowed from physics. Much as equilibrium calls to mind a pendulum that has come to rest hanging straight down, elasticity conjures up the image of a rubber band that stretches by a certain percentage of its length when the force applied to it is increased by a given percentage. This chapter introduces several applications of elasticity in economics.

Price Elasticity of Demand

The **price elasticity of demand** is the ratio of the percentage change in the quantity of a good demanded to a given percentage change in its price. Figure 3.1 presents five demand curves showing different degrees of price elasticity of demand. In part (a), the quantity demanded is strongly responsive to a change in price. In this case, a decrease in price from $5 to $3 causes the quantity demanded to increase from three units to six.

Changes in price and quantity are reflected in the **revenue** earned from sale of the product. Revenue means the price times the quantity sold. In part (a) of Figure 3.1, the percentage change in quantity demanded is greater than the percentage change in price, so the drop in price causes total revenue from sales of the good to increase. On a supply-and-demand diagram, revenue can be shown as the area of a rectangle drawn under the demand curve, with a height equal to price and a width equal to quantity

---

Elasticity

A measure of the response of one variable to a change in another, stated as a ratio of the percentage change in one variable to the associated percentage change in another variable

Price elasticity of demand

The ratio of the percentage change in the quantity of a good demanded to a given percentage change in its price, other things being equal

Revenue

Price multiplied by quantity sold

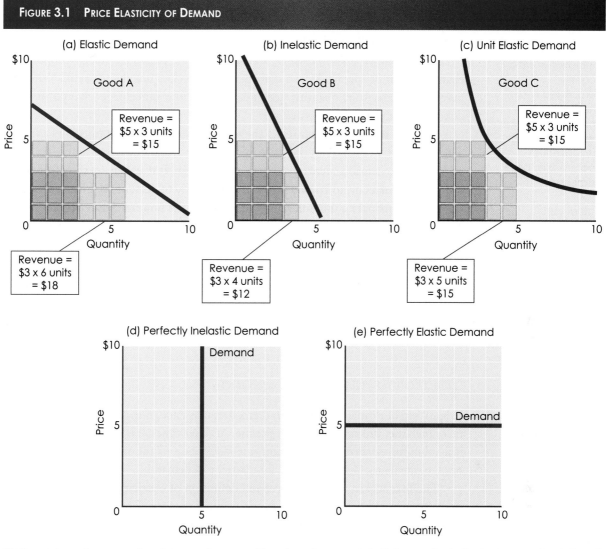

FIGURE 3.1   PRICE ELASTICITY OF DEMAND

This figure shows five examples of demand curves with various degrees of elasticity over the indicated range of variation of price and quantity. The examples illustrate elastic, inelastic, unit elastic, perfectly inelastic, and perfectly elastic demand. For the first three cases, the revenue change associated with a change in price is shown. When demand is elastic, a price decrease causes revenue to increase. When demand is inelastic, a price decrease causes revenue to decrease. When demand is unit elastic, revenue does not change when price changes.

Elastic demand

A situation in which quantity demanded changes by a larger percentage than price, so that total revenue increases as price decreases

demanded. In this case, comparison of the shaded rectangles representing revenue before the price reduction ($5 per unit × 3 units = $15) and afterward ($3 per unit × 6 units = $18) shows that revenue is greater after the price has been reduced. When the quantity demanded changes by a greater percentage than price, so that a price decrease causes total revenue to increase, demand is said to be **elastic**.

Part (b) of Figure 3.1 shows a case in which the quantity demanded is only weakly responsive to a change in price. Here, a $2 decrease in price, from $5 to $3 per unit, causes the quantity demanded to increase by just one unit—from three to four. This

Inelastic demand

A situation in which quantity demanded changes by a smaller percentage than price, so that total revenue decreases as price decreases

Unit elastic demand

A situation in which price and quantity demanded change by the same percentage, so that total revenue remains unchanged as price changes

Perfectly inelastic demand

A situation in which the demand curve is a vertical line

Perfectly elastic demand

A situation in which the demand curve is a horizontal line

time the percentage change in quantity demanded is less than that in price. As a result, the decrease in price causes total revenue to fall (again note the shaded rectangles). In such a case, demand is said to be **inelastic**.

Part (c) shows a case in which a change in price causes an exactly proportional change in quantity demanded, so that total revenue does not change at all. When the percentage change in quantity demanded equals the percentage change in price, demand is said to be **unit elastic**.

The final two parts of Figure 3.1 show two extreme cases. Part (d) shows a vertical demand curve. Regardless of the price, the quantity demanded is five units—no more, no less. Such a demand curve is said to be **perfectly inelastic**. Part (e) shows a demand curve that is perfectly horizontal. Above a price of $5, no units of the good can be sold; but as soon as the price drops to $5, there is no limit on how much can be sold. A horizontal demand curve like this one is described as **perfectly elastic**. The law of demand, which describes an inverse relationship between price and quantity, does not encompass the cases of perfectly elastic and inelastic demand; and we do not expect market demand curves for ordinary goods and services to fit these extremes. Nevertheless, we will see that perfectly elastic and inelastic curves sometimes provide useful reference points for theory building, even though they do not resemble real-world market demand curves.

Calculating Elasticity of Demand

In speaking of elasticity of demand, it is sometimes enough to say that demand is elastic or inelastic, without being more precise. At other times, it is useful to give a numerical value for elasticity. This section introduces one of the most common methods used to calculate a numerical value for elasticity of demand.

The first step in turning the general definition of elasticity into a numerical formula is to develop a way to measure percentage changes. The everyday method for calculating a percentage change is to use the initial value of the variable as the denominator and the change in the value as the numerator. For example, suppose the quantity of California lettuce demanded in the national market is initially 12,000 tons per week and then demand decreases by 4,000 tons per week; we say that there has been a 33 percent decrease (4,000/12,000 = .33). The trouble with this convention is that the same change in the opposite direction gives a different percentage. By everyday reasoning, an increase in the quantity of lettuce demanded from 8,000 tons per week to 12,000 tons per week is a 50 percent increase (4,000/8,000 = .5).

Decades ago the mathematical economist R. G. D. Allen proposed an unambiguous measure of percentage changes that uses the midpoint of the range over which change takes place as the denominator. To find the midpoint of the range over which a change takes place, we take the sum of the initial value and the final value and divide by 2. In our example, the midpoint of the quantity range is (8,000 + 12,000)/2 = 10,000). When this value is used as the denominator, a change of 4,000 units becomes a 40 percent change (4,000/10,000 = .4). Using Q_1 to represent the quantity before the change and Q_2 to represent the quantity after the change, the midpoint formula for the percentage change in quantity is

$$\text{Percentage change in quantity} = \frac{Q_2 - Q_1}{(Q_1 + Q_2)/2}$$

The same approach can be used to define the percentage change in price. Suppose that in our case, the price of lettuce increased from about $700 per ton to about $900 per ton. Using the midpoint of the range, or $800, as the denominator [(700 + 900)/2 = 800], we conclude that the $200 increase in price is a 25 percent increase (200/800 = .25). The midpoint formula for the percentage change in price is

$$\text{Percentage change in price} = \frac{P_2 - P_1}{(P_1 + P_2)/2}$$

THE MIDPOINT FORMULA FOR ELASTICITY   Defining percentage changes in this way allows us to write a useful formula for calculating elasticities. We can simplify the formula by omitting the terms "/2", which cancel out. With P_1 and Q_1 representing price and quantity before a change, and P_2 and Q_2 representing price and quantity after the change, the midpoint formula for elasticity is

$$\text{Price elasticity of demand} = \frac{(Q_2 - Q_1)/(Q_1 + Q_2)}{(P_2 - P_1)/(P_1 + P_2)} = \frac{\text{Percentage change in quantity}}{\text{Percentage change in price}}$$

Following is the complete calculation for the elasticity of demand for lettuce when an increase in price from $700 per ton to $900 per ton causes the quantity demanded to fall from 12,000 tons per day to 8,000 tons per day:

P_1 = price before change = $700

P_2 = price after change = $900

Q_1 = quantity before change = 12,000

Q_2 = quantity after change = 8,000

$$\text{Elasticity} = \frac{(8,000 - 12,000)/(8,000 + 12,000)}{(\$900 - \$700)/(\$700 + \$900)}$$

$$= \frac{-4,000/20,000}{200/1,600}$$

$$= \frac{-.2}{.125}$$

$$= -1.6$$

Because demand curves have negative slopes, price and quantity change in opposite directions. As a result, this formula yields a negative value for elasticity. When the price decreases, the term $(P_2 - P_1)$, which appears in the denominator of the formula, is negative, whereas the term $(Q_2 - Q_1)$, which appears in the numerator, is positive. When the price increases, the numerator is negative and the denominator is positive. However, in this book we follow the widely used (but not universal) practice of dropping the minus sign when discussing price elasticity of demand. For example, we will refer to the elasticity of demand for lettuce in our example as approximately 1.6 over the range studied.

A numerical elasticity value such as 1.6 can be related to the basic definition of elasticity in a simple way. That definition stated that price elasticity of demand is the ratio of the percentage change in quantity demanded to a given percentage change in price. Thus, an elasticity of 1.6 means that the quantity demanded will increase by 1.6 percent for each 1 percent change in price. An elasticity of 3 would mean that quantity demanded would change by 3 percent for each 1 percent change in price, and so on.[1]

ELASTICITY VALUES AND TERMINOLOGY   Earlier in the chapter we defined *elastic, inelastic, unit elastic, perfectly elastic,* and *perfectly inelastic* demand. Each of these terms corresponds to a numerical value or range of values of elasticity. A perfectly inelastic demand curve has a numerical value of 0 since any change in price produces no change in quantity demanded. The term *inelastic* (but not perfectly inelastic) *demand* applies to numerical values from 0 up to, but not including, 1. *Unit elasticity,* as the name implies, means a numerical value of exactly 1. *Elastic demand* means any value for elasticity that is greater than 1. *Perfectly elastic* demand, represented by a horizontal demand curve, is not defined numerically; as the demand curve becomes horizontal, the denominator of the elasticity formula approaches 0 and the numerical value of elasticity increases without limit.

Varying- and Constant-Elasticity Demand Curves

The midpoint formula shows elasticity of demand over a certain range of prices and quantities. Measured over some other range, the elasticity of demand for the same good may be the same or different, depending on the shape of the demand curve, as shown in Figure 3.2.

Part (a) of Figure 3.2 shows a demand curve that, like most of those in this book, is a straight line. The elasticity of demand is not constant for all ranges of price and quantity along this curve. For example, when measured over the price range $8 to $9, the elasticity of demand is 5.66; when measured over the range $2 to $3, it is .33. (The calculations are shown in the figure.)

The calculations illustrate the general rule that elasticity declines as one moves down and to the right along a straight-line demand curve. It is easy to see why. With such a demand curve, a $1 reduction in price always causes the same absolute increase in quantity demanded. At the upper end of the demand curve, a $1 change is a small percentage of the relatively high price, while the change in quantity is a large percentage of the relatively low quantity demanded. At the lower end of the curve, however,

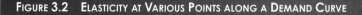

FIGURE 3.2   ELASTICITY AT VARIOUS POINTS ALONG A DEMAND CURVE

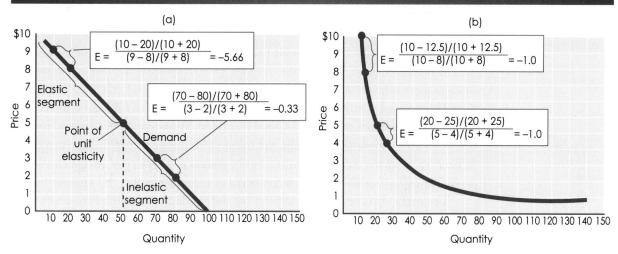

Elasticity varies along a straight-line demand curve, as part (a) of this figure illustrates. At the upper end of the curve, where the price is relatively high, a $1 change in price is a relatively small percentage change; and because the quantity demanded is low, the corresponding change in quantity is relatively large in percentage terms. Demand is thus elastic near the top of the demand curve. At the lower end of the curve, the situation is reversed: a $1 change in price is now a relatively large change in percentage terms, whereas the corresponding change in quantity is smaller in percentage terms. Thus demand is inelastic. As part (b) shows, a curved demand curve can be drawn such that elasticity is constant for all ranges of price and quantity change.

the situation is reversed: A $1 change is now a large percentage of the relatively low price, while the increase in quantity is smaller in relation to the relatively larger quantity demanded. Because it is percentages, not absolute amounts that matter in elasticity calculations, a linear demand curve is less elastic near the bottom than near the top.

If the demand curve is not a straight line, other results are possible. There is an important special case in which the demand curve has just the curvature needed to keep elasticity constant over its entire length. Such a curve is shown in part (b) of Figure 3.2. As can be seen from the calculations in the figure, elasticity is 1.0 at every point on that curve. It is possible to construct demand curves with constant elasticities of any value. Econometric studies of demand elasticity often look for the constant-elasticity demand curve that most closely approximates buyers' average sensitivity to price changes as revealed by market data over time.

Determinants of Elasticity of Demand

The fact that elasticity often varies along the demand curve means that care must be taken in making statements about the elasticity of demand for a good. In practice, what such statements usually refer to is the elasticity, measured by the midpoint formula or some alternative method, over the range of price variation that is commonly observed in the market for that good. With this understanding, we can make some generalizations about what makes the demand for some goods elastic and the demand for others inelastic.

SUBSTITUTES, COMPLEMENTS, AND ELASTICITY   One important determinant of elasticity of demand is the availability of substitutes. When a good has close substitutes, the demand for that good tends to be elastic because people willingly switch to the substitutes when the price of the good goes up. Thus, for example, the demand for corn oil is elastic because other cooking oils can usually be substituted for it. On the other hand, the demand for cigarettes is inelastic because for a habitual smoker there is no good substitute.

This principle has two corollaries. One is that the demand for a good tends to be more elastic the more narrowly the good is defined. For example, the demand for coffee as a whole is inelastic. However, the demand for medium-roast Colombian coffee is likely to be elastic because if the price of that particular type rises, people can switch to similar coffee from Nicaragua or Sumatra.

The other corollary is that demand for the product of a single firm tends to be more elastic than the demand for the output of all producers operating in the market. As one example, the demand for cigarettes as a whole will be less elastic than the demand for any particular brand. The reason is that one brand can be substituted for another when the price of a brand changes.

The complements of a good can also play a role in determining its elasticity. If something is a minor complement to an important good (that is, one that accounts for a large share of consumers' budgets), demand for it tends to be inelastic. For example, the demand for motor oil tends to be inelastic because it is a complement to a more important good, gasoline. The price of gasoline has a greater effect on the amount of driving a person does than the price of motor oil.

PRICE VERSUS OPPORTUNITY COST   Elasticity measures the responsiveness of quantity demanded to the monetary price of a good. In most cases, the price, in money, is an accurate approximation of the opportunity cost of choosing a good; but that is not always the case. We mentioned one example at the beginning of the chapter: The price of a textbook is an opportunity cost to the student who buys it; but it is not an opportunity cost to the professor who assigns it because the students pay for the book, not the professor. As a result, publishers have traditionally assumed that professors will pay little attention to the price of the text, and demand will be

Textbook prices are opportunity costs for students.

highly inelastic. However, in recent years students have increasingly been making their influence felt, so that price-elasticity of demand for textbooks may be increasing.

The textbook market is a relatively small one, but there are other much more important markets where the responsibility for choice does not lie with the party who bears the opportunity cost. Medical care provides many examples. Doctors choose what drug to offer to patients, but either the patient or the patient's insurance company pays for the drug. As a result, demand for drugs is very inelastic; and doctors sometimes prescribe expensive brand-name drugs when cheaper generic drugs are available to do the same job.

Business travel is still another example of the separation of price and opportunity cost. Business travelers do not pay for their own airline tickets, hotels, and meals, so their demand for these services tends to be inelastic. When vacationers purchase the same services, they bear the full opportunity cost. Not surprisingly, business travelers often choose more expensive options. In many cases airlines and hotels take advantage of the separation of price and opportunity cost by charging different rates to business and vacation travelers.

TIME HORIZON AND ELASTICITY   One of the most important considerations determining the price elasticity of demand is the time horizon within which the decision to buy is made. For several reasons, demand is often less elastic in the short run than in the long run.

One reason is that full adjustment to a change in the price of a good may require changes in the kind or quantity of many other goods that a consumer buys. Gasoline provides a classic example. When the price of gasoline rises, people can cut out some nonessential driving; but the total quantity of gasoline demanded is not much affected. Short-run demand elasticity for gasoline has been estimated as about .25, that is, just one quarter of one percent reduction in quantity demanded for each 1 percent increase in price. As time goes by, though, consumers can make many kinds of adjustment to the higher price. They can buy fewer fuel-hungry SUVs and more higher-mileage hybrid cars. They can change their jobs or move in order to shorten their daily commute. They can switch to public transportation, if it is available; or if it is not, they can demand that local governments expand public transportation options. The long-run demand for gasoline is estimated to be about .6 to .8, considerably higher than the short-run elasticity.

Another reason elasticity tends to be greater in the long run than in the short run is that an increase in the price of one good encourages entrepreneurs to develop substitutes, which, as we have seen, can be an important determinant of elasticity. To take an example from history, consider the response to what has been called America's first energy crisis: a sharp increase in the price of whale oil, which was widely used as lamp fuel in the early nineteenth century. At first candles were the only substitute for whale-oil lamps, and not a very satisfactory one. People, therefore, cut their use of whale oil only a little when the price began to rise. The high price of whale oil, however, spurred entrepreneurs to develop a better substitute, kerosene. Once kerosene came onto the market, the quantity of whale oil demanded for use as lamp fuel dropped to zero. Today market forces are spurring the development of many alternative forms of energy, ranging from ethanol as a motor fuel to wind, wave, and solar energy for generating electricity.

A final reason for greater elasticity of demand in the long run than in the short run is the slow adjustment of consumer tastes. The case of beef and chicken, featured in the preceding chapter, provides an example. Chicken, originally the more expensive meat, achieved a price advantage over beef many years ago; but eating lots of beef was a habit. Gradually, though, chicken developed an image as a healthy, stylish, versatile food; and finally it overtook beef as the number-one meat in the United States.

Income Elasticity of Demand

Determining the response of quantity demanded to a change in price is the most common application of the concept of elasticity, but it is by no means the only one. Elasticity can also be used to express the response of demand to any of the conditions covered by the "other things being equal" assumption on which a given demand curve is based. As we saw in the preceding chapter, consumer income is one of those conditions.

Income elasticity of demand

The ratio of the percentage change in the quantity of a good demanded to a given percentage change in consumer incomes, other things being equal

The **income elasticity of demand** for a good is defined as the ratio of the percentage change in the quantity of that good demanded to a percentage change in income. In measuring income elasticity, it is assumed that the good's price does not change. Using Q_1 and Q_2 to represent quantities before and after the change in income, and y_1 and y_2 to represent income before and after the change, the midpoint formula for income elasticity of demand can be written as follows:

$$\text{Income elasticity of demand} = \frac{(Q_2 - Q_1)/(Q_1 + Q_2)}{(y_2 - y_1)/(y_1 + y_2)} = \frac{\text{Percentage change in quantity}}{\text{Percentage change in income}}$$

For a normal good, an increase in income causes demand to rise. Because income and demand change in the same direction, the income elasticity of demand for a normal good is positive. For an inferior good, an increase in income causes demand to decrease. Because income and demand change in opposite directions, the income elasticity of demand for an inferior good is negative.

Some of the considerations that determine price elasticity also affect income elasticity. In particular, whether a good is considered to be normal or inferior depends on how narrowly it is defined and on the availability of substitutes. For example, a study by Jonq-Ying Lee, Mark G. Brown, and Brooke Schwartz of the University of Florida looked at the demand for frozen orange juice.[2] Orange juice considered as a broad category is a normal good; people tend to consume more of it as their income rises. However, when the definition is narrowed so that house brand and national brand frozen orange juice are treated as separate products, the house brand product turns out to be an inferior good. As their incomes rise, consumers substitute the higher-quality national brands, which have a positive income elasticity of demand.

Cross-Elasticity of Demand

Another condition that can cause a change in the demand for a good is a change in the price of some other good. The demand for chicken is affected by changes in the price of beef, the demand for SUVs by changes in the price of gasoline, and so on. The

Cross-elasticity of demand

The ratio of the percentage change in the quantity of a good demanded to a given percentage change in the price of some other good, other things being equal

cross-elasticity of demand for a good is defined as the ratio of the percentage change in the quantity of that good demanded to a given percentage change in the price of another good. The midpoint formula for cross-elasticity of demand looks just like the one for price elasticity of demand, except that the numerator shows the percentage change in the quantity of one good while the denominator shows the percentage change in the price of some other good.

Cross-elasticity of demand is related to the concepts of substitutes and complements. Because lettuce and cabbage are substitutes, an increase in the price of cabbage causes an increase in the quantity of lettuce demanded; the cross-elasticity of demand is positive. Because SUVs and gasoline are complements, an increase in the price of gasoline causes a decrease in the quantity of SUVs demanded; the cross-elasticity of demand is negative. The previously mentioned study of frozen orange juice found a positive cross-elasticity of demand between house brand and national brand juices, indicating that the two are substitutes.

Price Elasticity of Supply

Price elasticity of supply

The ratio of the percentage change in the quantity of a good supplied to a given percentage change in its price, other things being equal

Elasticity is not confined to demand; it can also be used to indicate the response of quantity supplied to a change in price. Formally, the **price elasticity of supply** of a good is defined as the percentage change in the quantity of the good supplied divided by the percentage change in its price. The midpoint formula for calculating price elasticity of supply looks like the one for determining price elasticity of demand, but the Qs in the numerator of the formula now refer to quantity *supplied* rather than quantity *demanded*. Because price and quantity change in the same direction along a positively sloped supply curve, the formula gives a positive value for the elasticity of supply. Figure 3.3 applies the elasticity formula to two supply curves, one with constant elasticity and the other with variable elasticity.

In later chapters we will look in detail at the considerations that determine the elasticity of supply for various products. Two of those considered are especially important, however, and deserve some discussion here.

One determinant of the elasticity of supply of a good is the mobility of the factors of production used to produce it. As used here, *mobility* means the ease with which factors can be attracted away from some other use, as well as the ease with which they can be reconverted to their original use. The trucking industry provides a classic example of mobile resources. As a crop such as lettuce or watermelons comes to harvest in a particular region of a country, hundreds of trucks are needed to haul it to market. Shippers compete for available trucks, driving up the price paid to truckers in the local market. Independent truckers throughout the country learn—from their own experience, from trucking brokers, and from Internet sites— where they can earn the best rates for hauling produce. It takes only a modest rise in the price for hauling a load of Georgia watermelons to attract enough truckers to Georgia to haul the crop to market. When the harvest is over, the truckers will move elsewhere to haul peaches, tomatoes, or whatever.

In contrast, other products are produced with resources that are not so mobile. Petroleum provides a good example. When oil prices rise, producers have an incentive

FIGURE 3.3   CALCULATING PRICE ELASTICITY OF SUPPLY

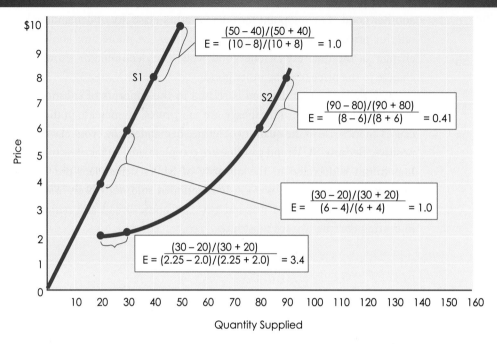

$$E = \frac{(50 - 40)/(50 + 40)}{(10 - 8)/(10 + 8)} = 1.0$$

$$E = \frac{(90 - 80)/(90 + 80)}{(8 - 6)/(8 + 6)} = 0.41$$

$$E = \frac{(30 - 20)/(30 + 20)}{(6 - 4)/(6 + 4)} = 1.0$$

$$E = \frac{(30 - 20)/(30 + 20)}{(2.25 - 2.0)/(2.25 + 2.0)} = 3.4$$

This figure gives four examples of the way price elasticity of supply is calculated. Price elasticity of supply is shown for two ranges on each of the two supply curves. Supply curve S_1, which is a straight line passing through the origin, has a constant elasticity of 1.0. Supply curve S_2, which is curved, is elastic for small quantities and inelastic for larger ones.

to drill more wells. However, given limited numbers of drilling rigs and other highly specialized equipment, not to mention limited numbers of sites worth exploring, even a doubling of oil prices has only a small effect on oil output. Factor mobility in this industry is limited in the other direction, too. Once a well has been drilled, the investment cannot be converted to a different use. Thus, when world demand falls, as it did in the late 1990s, and again beginning in late 2008, prices fall sharply but the quantity of oil produced falls by much less than price.

A second determinant of elasticity of supply is time. As in the case of demand, price elasticity of supply tends to be greater in the long run than in the short run. In part, the reason for this is connected with mobility of resources. In the short run, the output of many products can be increased by using more of the most flexible inputs—for example, by adding workers at a plant or extending the hours of work. Such short-run measures often mean higher costs per unit for the added output, however, because workers added without comparable additions in other inputs (such as equipment) tend to be less productive. If a firm expects market conditions to warrant an increase of supply in the long run, it will be worthwhile to invest in additional quantities of less mobile inputs such as specialized plants and equipment. Once those investments have been made, the firm will find it worthwhile to supply the greater quantity of output at a lower price than in the short-run case because its costs per unit supplied will be lower. The Case for Discussion at the end of Chapter 2, which discussed the market for heavy-duty tires, provides an example of the difference between short-run and long-run elasticity of supply.

Applications of Elasticity

Elasticity has many applications in both macro- and microeconomics. In macroeconomics, it can be applied to financial markets, to the aggregate supply and demand for all goods and services, and to foreign exchange markets, to name just a few. In microeconomics, elasticity plays a role in discussions of consumer behavior, the profit-maximizing behavior of business firms, governments' regulatory and labor policies, and many other areas. To further illustrate elasticity, we conclude this chapter with applications featuring the problems of tax incidence and drug policy.

Elasticity and Tax Incidence

Who pays taxes? One way to answer this question is in terms of *assessments*—the issue of who bears the legal responsibility to make tax payments to the government. A study of assessments would show that property owners pay property taxes, gasoline retailers pay gasoline taxes, and so on. However, looking at assessments does not always settle the issue of who bears the economic burden of a tax—or, to use the economist's term, the issue of **tax incidence**.

Tax incidence

The distribution of the economic burden of a tax

The incidence of a tax does not always coincide with the way the tax is assessed because the economic burden of the tax, in whole or in part, often can be passed along to someone else. The degree to which the burden of a tax may be passed along depends on the elasticities of supply and demand. Let's consider some examples.

INCIDENCE OF A GASOLINE TAX   First consider the familiar example of a gasoline tax. Specifically, suppose that the state of Virginia decides to impose a tax of $1 per gallon on gasoline beginning from a situation in which there is no tax. The tax is assessed against sellers of gasoline, who add the tax into the price paid by consumers at the pump.

How do supply and demand affect gasoline prices?

Figure 3.4 uses the supply-and-demand model to show the effects of the tax. Initially, the demand curve intersects supply curve S_1 at E_1, resulting in a price of $2 per gallon. The supply curve is elastic in the region of the initial equilibrium. The elasticity of supply reflects the fact that we are dealing with the gasoline market in just one state; only a slight rise in the price in Virginia is needed to divert additional quantities of gasoline from elsewhere in the nation because of the wide geographic reach of the wholesale gasoline market. The

FIGURE 3.4   INCIDENCE OF A TAX ON GASOLINE

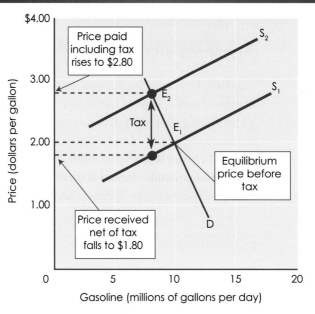

S$_1$ and D are the supply and demand curves before imposition of the tax. The initial equilibrium price is $2 per gallon. A tax of $1 per gallon shifts the supply curve to S$_2$. To induce sellers to supply the same quantity as before, the price would have to rise to $3. However, as the price rises, buyers reduce the quantity demanded, moving up and to the left along the demand curve. In the new equilibrium at E$_2$, the price rises only to $2.80. After the tax is paid, sellers receive only $1,80 per gallon. Thus, buyers bear $.80 of the tax on each gallon and sellers the remaining $.20. Buyers bear the larger share of the tax because demand, in this case, is less elastic than supply.

retail gasoline market is more local. If the price in Virginia rises, some consumers living near the border may cross a state line to fill up in Maryland or North Carolina; but most people will continue to fill up in Virginia. In the short run, they have only limited ways to save gas, such as cutting back on non-essential trips. As a result, demand for gasoline is less elastic than the supply in the region of the initial equilibrium.

The effect of the tax is to shift the supply curve to the left until each point on the new supply curve is exactly $1 higher than the point for the corresponding quantity on the old supply curve. (We could instead say that the supply curve shifts *upward* by $1.) Because sellers must now turn over $1 to the state government for each gallon of gas sold, they would have to get $3 per gallon to be willing to sell the same quantity (10 million gallons per day) as initially. However, when sellers attempt to pass the tax on to motorists, motorists respond by reducing the amount of gas they buy. As the quantity sold falls, sellers move down and to the left along supply curve S$_2$ to a new equilibrium at E$_2$.

In the new equilibrium, the price is $2.80 per gallon—just $.80 higher than the original price. The new price includes the $1 tax, which sellers add to their net price of $1.80 per gallon—a net price that is $.20 less than before. The amount of the tax—$1 per gallon—is shown by the vertical gap between the supply and demand curves. The economic burden of the tax is divided between buyers and sellers, but in this case it falls more heavily on the buyers.

INCIDENCE OF A TAX ON APARTMENT RENTS   In the preceding example, the incidence of the gasoline tax falls more heavily on buyers than on sellers because demand is less elastic than supply. If the elasticities are reversed, the results will also be reversed, as can be seen in the case of a tax on apartment rents.

In Figure 3.5, the market for rental apartments in Ogden, Utah (a small city) is initially in equilibrium at $500 per month. The supply of rental apartments is inelastic. An increase in rents will cause a few new apartments to be built, whereas a reduction will cause a few to be torn down; but in either case, the response will be moderate. On the other hand, demand is fairly elastic because potential renters consider houses or condominiums a fairly close substitute for rental apartments.

Given this situation, suppose that the local government decides to impose a tax of $250 per month on all apartments rented in Ogden. This tax, like the gasoline tax, is assessed against landlords, who include the tax payment in the monthly rental they charge to tenants. As in the previous example, the tax shifts the supply curve to the left until each point on the new supply curve lies above the corresponding point on the old supply curve by the amount of the tax. (Again, we could instead say the supply curve

---

FIGURE 3.5   INCIDENCE OF A TAX ON APARTMENT RENTS

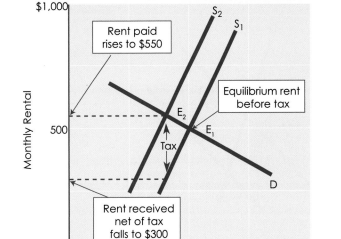

This figure shows the incidence of a tax imposed in a market in which supply is less elastic than demand. Initially, the equilibrium rent is $500 per month. A $250-per-month tax on apartment rents shifts the supply curve to S_2. The new equilibrium is at E_2. Landlords end up absorbing all but $50 of the tax. If they tried to pass more of the tax on to renters, more renters would switch to owner-occupied housing, and the vacancy rate on rental apartments would rise.

shifts upward by the amount of the tax.) After the shift, the market reaches a new equilibrium at E_2. There the rental price paid by tenants rises to only $550 per month, as indicated by the intersection of the new supply and demand curves. Landlords succeed in passing only $50 of the $250 monthly tax along to tenants. Their net rental income, after turning over the tax receipts to the town government, is now just $300, down from $500 before imposition of the tax. In this case, because supply is inelastic and demand is elastic, suppliers bear most of the incidence of the tax and buyers only a little.

INCIDENCE AND TAX REVENUE   When the government considers imposing a tax on gasoline, cigarettes, apartments, or any other item, the price elasticity of demand and supply is important, not only for how the burden is shared between buyers and sellers, but also for how much tax revenue the government collects. When buyers or sellers are more responsive to changes in price (when demand or supply is more elastic), a tax will generate less revenue for the government.

Figure 3.6 compares the markets for two items: milk and pork. The elasticities of supply are similar, but the price elasticities of demand differ. Pork has many obvious substitutes—beef, chicken, turkey, and other meats. Milk has few substitutes, so its demand is more inelastic. The markets for milk and pork are shown in Figure 3.6. The equilibrium price of milk is $0.50 per gallon and 12 million gallons are sold each year at this price. The milk market equilibrium is point E_1 on the left panel of Figure 3.6.

FIGURE 3.6   COMPARISON OF THE MARKETS FOR MILK AND PORK

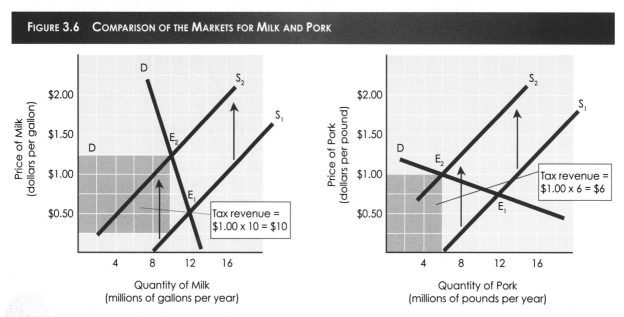

A tax imposed on a good that has an inelastic demand will generate more tax revenue than a tax on a good with elastic demand, assuming similar supply conditions. The diagrams above compare the effects of a $1.00 tax on the markets for milk (inelastic demand) and pork (elastic demand). In the market for milk, the tax reduces the equilibrium quantity by 2 million gallons, from point E_1 (12 million gallons) to E_2 (10 million gallons). Therefore, the government collects a total of $10 million from the milk tax. The same $1.00 tax on pork causes a large reduction in the quantity sold, from 12 million pounds (point E_1) to 6 million pounds (point E_2). This means the government will only collect $6 million, as only 6 million pounds of pork are sold at the new equilibrium.

The equilibrium (shown by the point E_1 on the right panel of Figure 3.6) is $0.75 per pound, and 12 million pounds are sold each year.

Suppose now that the government imposes a $1.00 tax on each product. In the milk market, where demand is inelastic, the tax leads to a small decrease in the quantity, from 12 to 10 million gallons. The government collects $1.00 on each gallon of milk sold, for tax revenue of $10 million on the 10 million gallons sold after the tax. In the market for pork, the tax leads to a larger reduction in the quantity people buy, from 12 to 6 million pounds. The government will collect a total of $6 million from the tax on pork, collecting $1.00 on each of the 6 million pounds sold. When comparing the two taxes, the government collects more revenue from the tax on milk. Today, governments rely for most of their revenue on broad-based taxes like income taxes, sales taxes, and value-added taxes. In past centuries, however, taxes on individual goods were more important than they are now. In those days, taxes on goods with highly inelastic demand, like salt, tobacco, and matches, were especially popular.

Elasticity and Prohibition

In the case of gasoline and apartment rents, a tax led to a reduction in the quantity consumed, which we characterized as an unintended consequence of the tax. In a few cases, the reduction in quantity consumed may be an *intended* consequence of the tax. Modern taxes on tobacco products are one example: because tobacco is regarded as harmful, a reduction in quantity consumed is seen as desirable. Taxes on environmentally harmful products, such as the chemicals responsible for ozone depletion, are another example.

Prohibition is a more extreme policy aimed at reducing the quantity of a product consumed. Alcoholic beverages were subject to prohibition in the United States during the 1920s; and drugs like marijuana, heroin, and cocaine are subject to prohibition today. Prohibition is a common method of environmental regulation as well. For example, use of the pesticide DDT and lead additives for gasoline are not just taxed but also completely prohibited in the United States.

On the surface, a policy of prohibition may seem very different from a tax; since unlike a tax, prohibition raises no tax revenue for the government. However, if we use economic analysis to look below the surface, we see some similarities as well as differences between taxation and prohibition.

First, passage of a law prohibiting production and sale of a good does not make it impossible to supply the good; it simply makes it more expensive to do so. After the prohibition is in effect, the supplier must consider not only the direct costs of production but also the extra costs of covert

Drugs like heroin and cocaine are subject to prohibition in the United States.

transportation and distribution systems, the risk of fines or jail terms, the costs of hiring armed gangsters to protect illegal laboratories, and so on. From the law-breaking supplier's point of view, these costs can be seen as an implicit tax. If the price rises by enough to cover them, the good is still supplied. Thus, the effect of prohibition of a good is to shift its supply curve to the left until each point on the new supply curve lies above the corresponding point on the old curve by a distance equal to the extra costs associated with evading the prohibition.

Second, the effects of the prohibition, like those of a tax, depend on the elasticities of demand and supply. This is illustrated in Figure 3.7, which compares the effects of prohibition on the U.S. markets for DDT and cocaine. The demand for DDT is shown as elastic because effective substitutes are available at a price only a little higher than the banned pesticide. The demand for cocaine is shown as inelastic, in part because once people become addicted, they will find it hard to cut back on their use of the drug even if its price rises sharply.

In the case of elastic demand for DDT (Figure 3.7a), even a weakly enforced prohibition, which raises costs of illegal supply only a little, will sharply reduce the

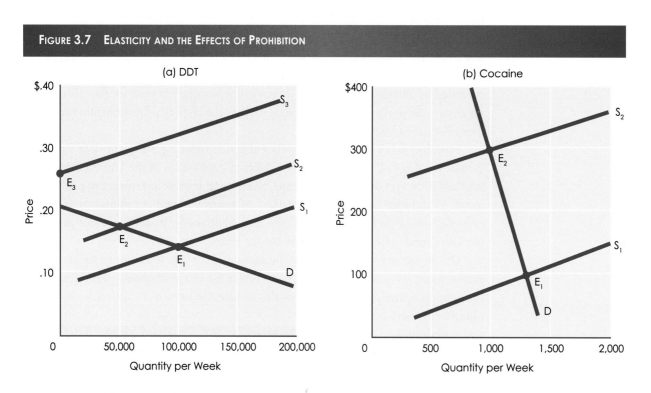

FIGURE 3.7   ELASTICITY AND THE EFFECTS OF PROHIBITION

(a) DDT

(b) Cocaine

A law prohibiting production and sale of a good, like a tax on the good, shifts its supply curve to the left. The new supply curve will lie above the old supply curve at any given quantity by a distance equal to the cost of evading the prohibition. The effects on price, quantity, and revenue depend on the elasticity of demand. Part (a) uses DDT to illustrate prohibition of a good with elastic demand. A weakly enforced prohibition (S_2) raises the price, reduces the quantity, and reduces total revenue earned by producers from sale of the product. A strongly enforced prohibition reduces quantity and revenue to zero (S_3). Part (b) uses cocaine to illustrate prohibition of a good with inelastic demand. In this case, even strong efforts to enforce prohibition do not reduce quantity sold to zero. Because quantity sold increases by a smaller percentage than price increases, there is an increased total revenue and expenditure on the good.

quantity sold. Such a weak prohibition, represented by a shift in the supply curve from S_1 to S_2, is already enough to reduce the total revenue earned by producers (price times quantity sold) from $14,000 per week to $8,500 per week. A more vigorously enforced prohibition, as represented by supply curve S_3, raises the cost of supply by enough to eliminate use of the product altogether.

In the case of cocaine, with its inelastic demand, even a strongly enforced prohibition has a small effect on quantity sold. This case is represented in Figure 3.7b by a shift in the supply curve to S_2. Because quantity demanded is not much affected by the price increase, total revenue from the sale of cocaine rises sharply, from $130,000 per week at equilibrium E_1 to $300,000 per week at equilibrium E_2. As long as demand is inelastic, increasing strictness of enforcement, which drives the supply curve still higher, will make the sales revenue of drug suppliers increase still further.

Elasticity of demand is important in understanding the intended and unintended consequences of prohibition. The intended consequence, of course, is to reduce or eliminate use of the product. As we see, the more elastic the demand for the product, the more successful is the policy of prohibition in achieving its intended effects. The unintended effects of prohibition are those associated with the change in revenue that the policy produces. These are very different in the case of elastic and inelastic demand.

Where demand is elastic, there is a moderate loss of revenue to DDT producers and a small rise in the cost of growing crops as farmers switch to more expensive pesticides. Neither has major social consequences. Chemical companies will offset the loss of revenue from producing DDT by increased revenue from production of substitutes. The increased cost of growing crops is offset by the benefits of a cleaner environment.

On the other hand, where demand is inelastic, the intended consequences are smaller and the unintended consequences greater. With inelastic demand, prohibition increases total expenditure on the banned product. The social consequences may be severe. First, users of cocaine must spend more to sustain their habit. At best this means impoverishing themselves and their families; at worst it means an increase in muggings and armed robberies by users desperate for cash. Second, the impact of the prohibition on suppliers must be considered as well. For suppliers, the increase in revenue does not just mean an increase in profit (although profits may increase) but also an increase in expenditures devoted to evading prohibition. In part, the result is simply wasteful, as when drug suppliers build special submersible boats that are discarded after a single one-way smuggling voyage rather than shipping their product cheaply by normal transportation methods. Worse, another part of suppliers' increased expenditures takes the form of hiring armies of thugs to battle the police and other suppliers, further raising the level of violence on city streets, or bribing government officials, thereby corrupting the quality of government.

The issue of drug prohibition, of course, involves many normative issues that reach far beyond the concept of elasticity. One such issue is whether people have a right to harm themselves through consumption of substances like tobacco, alcohol, or cocaine; or whether, instead, the government has a duty to act paternalistically to prevent such harm. Another concerns the relative emphasis that should be placed on prohibition versus treatment in allocating resources to reduce drug use. The analysis given here cannot answer such questions. However, it does suggest that the law of unintended consequences applies in the area of drug policy as elsewhere, and that elasticity of demand is important in determining the nature and severity of those consequences.

Summary

1. **How can the responsiveness of quantity demanded to a price change be expressed in terms of elasticity?** *Elasticity* is the responsiveness of quantity demanded or supplied to changes in the price of a good (or changes in other factors), measured as a ratio of the percentage change in quantity to the percentage change in price (or other factor causing the change in quantity). The *price elasticity of demand* between two points on a demand curve is the percentage change in quantity demanded divided by the percentage change in the good's price.

2. **How is the elasticity of demand for a good related to the revenue earned by its seller?** If the demand for a good is elastic, a decrease in its price will increase total revenue. If it is inelastic, an increase in its price will increase total revenue. When the demand for a good is unit elastic, revenue will remain constant as the price varies.

3. **How can elasticity be applied to changes in market conditions other than price?** The concept of elasticity can be applied to many situations besides movements along demand curves. The *income elasticity of demand* for a good is the ratio of the percentage change in quantity demanded to a given percentage change in income. The *cross-elasticity of demand* between goods A and B is the ratio of the percentage change in the quantity of good A demanded to a given percentage change in the price of good B. The *price elasticity of supply* is the ratio of the percentage change in the quantity of a good supplied to a given change in its price.

4. **What determines the distribution of the economic burden of a tax?** The way in which the economic burden of a tax is distributed is known as the *incidence* of the tax. The incidence depends on the relative elasticities of supply and demand. If supply is relatively more elastic than demand, buyers will bear the larger share of the tax burden. If demand is relatively more elastic than supply, the larger share of the burden will fall on sellers. If the good is subject to prohibition rather than to a tax, elasticity of demand will determine how many resources are likely to be devoted to enforcement and evasion of the prohibition.

Key Terms

Problems and Topics for Discussion

1. **Time horizon and elasticity**   Suppose a virus infects the California lettuce crop, cutting production by half. Consider three time horizons: (a) The

"very short" run means a period that is too short to allow farmers to change the amount of lettuce that has been planted. No matter what happens to the price, the quantity supplied will be the amount already planted, less the amount destroyed by the virus. (b) The "intermediate" run means a period that is long enough to allow farmers to plant more fields in lettuce, but not long enough to permit them to develop new varieties of lettuce, introduce new methods of cultivation, or acquire new specialized equipment. (c) The "long" run means a period that is long enough to allow farmers to develop new varieties of virus-resistant lettuce and improve cultivation techniques. Discuss these three time horizons in terms of the price elasticity of supply. Sketch a figure showing supply curves for each of the time horizons.

2. **Calculating elasticity**   Draw a set of coordinate axes on a piece of graph paper. Label the horizontal axis from 0 to 50 units and the vertical axis from $0 to $20 per unit. Draw a demand curve that intersects the vertical axis at $10 and the horizontal axis at 40 units. Draw a supply curve that intersects the vertical axis at $4 and has a slope of 1. Make the following calculations for these curves, using the midpoint formula:

    a. What is the price elasticity of demand over the price range $5 to $7?

    b. What is the price elasticity of demand over the price range $1 to $3?

    c. What is the price elasticity of supply over the price range $10 to $15?

    d. What is the price elasticity of supply over the price range $15 to $17?

3. **Elasticity and revenue**   Look at the demand curve given in Figure 2.1 of the preceding chapter. Make a third column in the table that gives revenue for each price-quantity combination shown. Draw a set of axes on a piece of graph paper. Label the horizontal axis as in Figure 2.1, and label the vertical axis from 0 to $5 billion of revenue in increments of $1 billion. Graph the relationship between quantity and revenue using the column you added to the table. Discuss the relationship of your revenue graph to the demand curve, keeping in mind what you know about elasticity and revenue and about variation in elasticity along the demand curve.

4. **Elasticity of demand and revenue**   Assume that you are an officer of your campus theater club. You are at a meeting at which ticket prices are being discussed. One member says, "What I hate to see most of all is empty seats in the theater. We sell out every weekend performance, but there are always empty seats on Wednesdays. If we cut our Wednesday night prices by enough to fill up the theater, we'd bring in more money." Would this tactic really bring in more revenue? What would you need to know in order to be sure? Draw diagrams to illustrate some of the possibilities.

5. **Cross-elasticity of demand**   Between 1979 and 1981, the price of heating oil rose by 104 percent. Over the same period, use of fuel oil fell slightly while use of LP gas, another heating fuel, rose. Assuming that there was no change in the price of LP gas, what does this suggest about the cross-elasticity of demand for LP gas with respect to the price of fuel oil? Draw a pair of diagrams to illustrate these events. (Suggestion: Draw upward-sloping supply curves for both fuels. Then assume that the supply curve for heating oil shifts upward while the supply curve for LP gas stays the same.)

Case for Discussion

VP Asks Cigarette Firms for Sacrifice

Rendi A. Witular, *The Jakarta Post,* Jakarta, Indonesia, June 1, 2005

The lower profits cigarette-makers are likely to experience when the government raises the retail price on cigarettes should be viewed as a sacrifice to the state, [Indonesian] Vice President Jusuf Kalla said on Tuesday.

"The tobacco industry is one of the most profitable sectors in [Indonesian] business. Raising the (retail) rate won't affect tobacco firms much since they will still be able to make a profit. Remember that cigarette prices here are still the lowest in the world," Kalla said.

By increasing the retail price of cigarettes, the government planned to make more money on the excise duty it charged manufacturers, which was calculated on the final retail price.

The amount of the increase has not been finalized, but last week the Minister of Finance Jusuf Anwar suggested it would be in the range of 15 to 20 percent. This extra revenue would help plug the state budget deficit that has increased in line with the rising costs of the government's fuel subsidy.

PT H. M. Sampoerna, the country's second-largest cigarette maker by sales, said that more than a 10 percent increase in the cigarette prices could hurt producers as it would affect sales.

Sampoerna is 98 percent owned by U.S. cigarette giant Philip Morris International.

"Less than a 10 percent increase in the price is likely to be OK, but more (than that) could disturb sales," Sampoerna director Angky Camaro said after meeting Kalla earlier in the day.

Angky said the industry had not yet fully recovered from the aggressive excise rate hikes in 2002 and 2003, which had resulted in declines in the volumes of cigarette produced and lower profits across the board.

Last year, local cigarette company profits rose on increased consumption spurred on by higher general economic growth and the absence of any increases in excise duty.

The Indonesian Cigarette Producer Union (Gappri) estimates that some 141 million of the country's 220 million people are smokers.

SOURCE: Rendi A. Witular, *The Jakarta Post*, Jakarta, Indonesia, June 1, 2005 (Downloaded June 5, 2005 from http://www.thejakartapost.com/yesterdaydetail.asp?field=20050601.L04).

QUESTIONS

1. On the basis of this article, do you think that price elasticity of demand for cigarettes in Indonesia is elastic, inelastic, unit elastic, perfectly elastic, or perfectly inelastic? Cite the specific passages supporting your conclusion, and note any apparent contradictions in the article.

2. According to the article, 64 percent of the people of Indonesia, where cigarette prices are among the lowest in the world, are smokers, compared to less than 25 percent in the United States, where prices are higher. What does this suggest about the price elasticity of demand for tobacco in the long run? Why might the long-run elasticity of demand for cigarettes be greater than the short-run elasticity?

3. According to Angky Camaro of Sampoerna, a tax increase that reduced quantity sold would hurt producers. Using a diagram similar to Figure 3.4, explain why this would be true even if the percentage decrease in quantity were less than the percentage increase in price.

4. According to the article, in 2004, cigarette sales increased as income increased, while taxes were unchanged. What does this tell you about the income elasticity of demand?

End Notes

1. As we have said, the midpoint formula (also sometimes called *arc-elasticity*) is not the only one for calculating elasticity. A drawback of this formula is that it can give misleading elasticity values if applied over too wide a variation in price or quantity. Because of this limitation, the midpoint formula works best over fairly small ranges of variation in price or quantity. An even more

precise approach is to use an alternative formula that gives a value for elasticity for a single point on the demand curve. For a linear demand curve having the formula $q = a - bp$ (with q representing quantity demanded, p the price, and a and b being constants), the *point formula* for elasticity of demand (stated, as elsewhere, as a positive number) is

$$Elasticity = bp/(a - bp).$$

2. Jonq-Ying Lee, Mark G. Brown, and Brooke Schwartz, "The Demand for National Brand and Private Label Frozen Concentrated Orange Juice: A Switching Regression Analysis," *Western Journal of Agricultural Economics* (July 1986): 1–7.

PART 2

Markets and Government

CHAPTER 4

Choice, Markets, and Government

After reading this chapter, you will understand the following:

1. The basic structure of economic theory
2. Why rationality is of central importance in economics
3. The meaning of market performance and market failure
4. Some alternative theories of the economic role of government

Before reading this chapter, make sure you know the meaning of the concepts:

1. Positive and normative economics
2. Entrepreneurship
3. Law of unintended consequences
4. Supply and demand

THE THEORY OF supply and demand introduced in the preceding two chapters shows how choices made by consumers and producers interact to determine market prices and quantities. In this chapter and the next, we will take a closer look at those choices. In doing so, we will ask some general questions about the structure of economic theory, the reliability with which markets work, and the nature of the individuals and organizations, including government organizations, that populate the economist's world. Then, in Chapters 6 and 7, we will apply what we have learned to important policy issues, environmental policy and global trade.

The Structure of Economic Theory

To *analyze* something means to break it down into its component parts. A literary critic might analyze a novel in terms of such basic components as plot, character, and dialog. A detective might analyze a murder in terms of motive, means, and opportunity. Similarly, economic decisions can be analyzed in terms of the concepts of objectives, constraints, and choices.

Objectives, Constraints, and Choices

The elements of which every economic theory is composed are three types of statements: statements about objectives, statements about constraints on opportunities, and statements about choices.

STATEMENTS ABOUT OBJECTIVES   An *objective* is anything people want to achieve. A business owner may have the objective of earning the greatest possible profit. A consumer may strive for the greatest possible material satisfaction with a given income. People in any situation may blend their pursuit of material or monetary objectives with considerations like family values and social responsibilities. The terms *aims, goals,* and *preferences* are interchangeable with *objectives.*

STATEMENTS ABOUT CONSTRAINTS ON OPPORTUNITIES   A key part of every economic theory is a statement of the constraints on the set of opportunities from among which a person may choose in a given situation. In a world of scarcity, alternatives are never unlimited, so constraints are universal.

Some constraints relate to what is physically possible, given available resources and knowledge. Only so many bales of hay can be loaded into a truck that can hold 1,000 cubic feet of cargo. Only so many pounds of iron can be smelted from a ton of ore of a given quality.

Other constraints take the form not of physical limits but of opportunity costs, often defined in terms of prices. For example, there is no physical limit to the number of pairs of shoes a person can own; but if shoes cost $60 a pair and sweaters cost $30 apiece, each pair of shoes purchased means forgoing the opportunity to buy two sweaters (or something else of equal value).

Still other constraints take the form of legal rules. Particularly important sets of legal constraints are those that define *property rights*. **Property rights** are legal

Property rights

Legal rules that establish what things a person may use or control, and the conditions under which such use or control may be exercised

rules that establish what things a person may use or control and the conditions under which that use or control may be exercised. In short, they establish what a person *owns*.

As an everyday example, consider the property rights associated with a person's ownership of a house. Those rights include the

Legal constraints define property rights.

right to live in the house, to modify its structure, and to control the arrangement of furniture in its rooms. In some communities, ownership may include the right to park a boat trailer in the driveway and to have a swing set on the front lawn. In others, those particular rights may be limited by zoning laws or restrictive covenants. As this example shows, the broad concept of "ownership" may be associated with different bundles of specific property rights depending on the circumstances.

Property rights extend to more abstract relationships as well. For example, ownership of a share of common stock in ConocoPhillips Corporation gives the stockholder a complex package of rights, including the rights to vote on issues affecting the firm and to share in the firm's profits. As another example, a software firm's copyright on a program it has produced gives it control over the conditions under which others may license the program for use.

STATEMENTS ABOUT CHOICES   The final component of an economic theory is a statement of the choice that is most likely to be made, given particular objectives and constraints on opportunities. For example, the next chapter will look at the choices that underlie the law of demand. There, consumers will be seen as having the objective of obtaining the greatest possible satisfaction—given the constraints placed on their opportunities by their budgets, the range of goods available, and the prices of those goods. Given those objectives and constraints, the law of demand states that people can be expected to choose to increase their purchases of a good when its price is reduced, other things being equal.

Economic Theory and Rationality

Although all economic theories contain the three types of statements just listed, a successful theory is more than just a list; its elements need to form a coherent whole. Our understanding of the structure of economic theory would be incomplete without a discussion of a key assumption that serves to hold the three elements of a theory together: the assumption that people choose the *best* way of accomplishing their objectives, given the constraints they face—that is, the assumption that people are *rational*.

Rationality

Acting purposefully to achieve an objective, given constraints on the opportunities that are available

Rationality, as the term is used in economics, means acting purposefully to achieve an objective, given the constraints on available opportunities. The concept of rationality is built into the definition of economics given at the beginning of this book, which speaks of choosing the best way to use scarce resources to meet human wants. To say that some ways of using scarce resources are better than others, and that those are the ones people tend to choose, is to express the essence of rationality.

The assumption of rationality, so central to economics, is sometimes misunderstood as a psychological or philosophical assertion about human nature—an assertion that people are always coolly calculating, not emotional or impulsive. A critic once ridiculed economists for seeing the human individual as a "lightning calculator of pleasures and pains, who oscillates like a homogeneous globule of desire under the impulse of stimuli … [who] spins symmetrically about his own spiritual axis until the parallelogram of forces bears down upon him, whereupon he follows the line of the resultant. "[1] However, used properly, the rationality assumption does not imply that sort of caricature of "economic man."

The rationality assumption, properly understood, is simply a tool for giving structure to theories about the choices people make. Economists then fill in the specifics of the structure by observing what people do in various situations—that is, what choices they make when faced with certain opportunities.

Consider a very simple example. Suppose Bundy Hall, a dormitory, and Carpenter Hall, where economics classes are held, are located at opposite corners of a grassy quadrangle in the middle of a college campus. Across the diagonal of the quad between Bundy and Carpenter, a well-worn path has been beaten into the grass. Why is the path there, even though there are perfectly good sidewalks around all four sides of the quad?

If you ask an economist that question, the answer you get will probably be something like this: "The students' objective is to minimize the time it takes to get to class so that they can sleep as late as possible. Of the limited numbers of routes to class, the diagonal path is the shortest one; so that's the path they choose to take."

Most people would probably accept that theory as a reasonable explanation of the path across the quad. Why? First and most important, it is consistent with the observation that the path is there and students use it. Second, adding to its appeal, the theory corresponds with our intuition about what we would do in the given situation. Although economists are wary of relying too heavily on their own experience to verify their theories, in practice introspection plays a significant role. Finally, our theory about the path across the quad is likely to be accepted partly because it is simple. Economists, like their colleagues in other social and natural sciences, tend to prefer simple theories to complex ones when both are consistent with given observations. (The preference for simple theories over complex ones is known as **Ockham's razor**, after a fourteenth-century philosopher who urged its use to "shave away" unnecessary theoretical complexities.)

So far, so good. Suppose now that a transfer student arrives from another campus and says, "At Treelined University there is a big quad just like this one, and there is no diagonal path across it. Here's a picture to prove it. What do you say to that, O Wise Economist?"

This is not a far-fetched possibility. Observations that are inconsistent with previously accepted theories cross economists' desks frequently. When that happens, they look for a way to modify the theory so that it provides a rational basis for the new observation. Given the structure of economic theory, we can expect the search to take one of two directions.

First, closer investigation will often show that the original theory failed to allow for some *constraint* on the opportunities available to people in the situation under study. For example, it might be that the campus police at Treelined University have a nasty practice of slapping a $20 fine on any student caught walking on the grass. A modified theory is then formulated that takes this constraint into account: "Even when the shortest distance to class is a diagonal across the quad, a fine that raises the opportunity cost of walking on the grass will induce a certain percentage of students to take the sidewalk. The percentage taking the sidewalk will increase as the fine increases, so that with a sufficiently large fine, not enough students will take the shortcut to wear a path in the grass." This more general theory is consistent with observations made on both campuses.

Second, if closer investigation fails to turn up some previously unnoticed constraint on opportunities, it may turn out that the original theory was based on a mis-

---

Ockham's razor

The principle that simpler theories are to be preferred to more complex ones when both are consistent with given observations

taken understanding of the *objectives* of the people involved. In the case under discussion, it was assumed that students on both campuses placed a high priority on getting to class on time. However, perhaps the students of Treelined University take great pride in the appearance of their campus. They would rather be late to class than trample on the grass. Thus, there is a path on one campus and not on the other because students at the two schools rank their objectives differently.

Clearly differing choices can sometimes properly be attributed to differing objectives. For example, if Marcia buys pistachio ice cream while Mark buys chocolate ice cream, and the two flavors cost the same, we are comfortable concluding that their choices differ because their preferences do. However, as a rule, economists like first to see whether an explanation of different choices can be framed in terms of differing constraints on opportunities—prices, regulations, climate, and so on. If constraints are not checked first, explaining things in terms of differing preferences is simply too easy. Take, for example, the fact that people in the United States drive larger cars, on average, than people in Italy. Who would be satisfied just to say that Italians prefer little cars, without noting that drivers in Italy face different constraints, in particular, narrower streets and more expensive gasoline?

Something similar can be said about the rationality assumption. Just as economists are wary of relying too much on differences in preferences to explain choices, they are also wary of explaining choices in nonrational terms. Suppose, for example, that an economist sees a student, obviously late for class, who, instead of cutting across the quad or even hurrying around by the sidewalk, is walking slowly in circles in the middle of the grass. The economist, seeking a rational explanation, questions the student. "Have you lost a contact lens? Are you exercising?" If an explanation cannot be found in terms of constraints and the rational pursuit of objectives, the economist is faced with a dilemma. One alternative would be to give up on studying this particular aspect of human behavior and call in some other specialist, perhaps a psychotherapist. The other could be to consider whether the concept of rationality itself needs to be rethought in order to understand what is going on. Increasingly, economists are choosing to rethink the concept of rationality.

Full and Bounded Rationality

One way in which the rationality assumption can be modified is to distinguish between full and bounded rationality.

Theories based on **full rationality** assume that people make optimal use of all available information in calculating how best to meet their objectives. In some versions of full rationality, the cost of making decisions, the possibility of error, and often, the cost of acquiring information are assumed to be zero. Other versions assume that these aspects of the decision-making process are themselves handled with optimal efficiency.

On the other hand, theories based on **bounded rationality** assume that people *intend* to make choices that best serve their objectives, but that they have limited ability to acquire and process information. Rather than optimally weighing all available information and efficiently adjusting efforts to acquire and process new information, they are viewed as relying on incomplete information and rules of thumb that do not necessarily make full use of the information they do have.

Full rationality

The assumption that people make full use of all available information in calculating how best to meet their objectives

Bounded rationality

The assumption that people intend to make choices that best serve their objectives, but have limited ability to acquire and process information

For example, consider the task of choosing which university to attend. If college applicants strictly followed the assumption of full rationality, they would make full use of all sources of information available. They would carefully study the information on the Web site of every college of possible interest, allocating their research efforts according to the opportunity cost of the time needed to make their search. On the basis of that information, they would outline preferred four-year programs of study at each school. Based on their preliminary Web search, they would systematically interview people who had attended the schools that rated near the top of their list and would perhaps visit those schools. Only when all information that could be gathered in a cost-effective manner was in hand would they make a choice; in doing so, they might weigh such factors as the probable grades they would earn at each school, the influence of grades and choice of school on their lifetime incomes, and so on.

On the other hand, if applicants followed the assumptions of bounded rationality, they would conduct a more limited search. Perhaps they would arbitrarily limit their search in advance to schools from a certain region. They might listen to what friends and relatives said about schools they had attended and consult only the web sites of schools recommended by people they know. Their final choice might be based more on advice from people they trusted and less on systematic balancing of objective information.

In the chapters that follow, we will encounter examples of theories based both on full and on bounded rationality.

Self-Regarding Versus Other-Regarding Preferences

Another way to modify the assumption of rationality is to expand the definition of objectives to include human feelings like fairness, altruism, trust, spite, and envy. Distinguishing between **self-regarding** and **other-regarding preferences** can capture these feelings. People who are concerned only with their own material welfare are said to have self-regarding preferences. People who balance considerations of their own material welfare with the welfare of others and also take into account what others think about them are said to have other-regarding preferences.

One simple example of other-regarding preferences is revealed in the "ultimatum game" described in *Applying Economic Ideas 4.1*. Results from repeated experiments around the world suggest that people often behave in ways that are better explained on the basis of other-regarding rather than strictly self-regarding preferences. Somewhat more controversial is the issue of whether to describe choices based on altruism, envy, and similar feelings as rational. The tendency in economics today seems to be toward expanding the concept of rationality in a way that allows for other-regarding preferences.

Richard H. Thaler of the University of Chicago suggests that including ideas like bounded rationality and other-regarding preferences will once again make economics more of a social science, as it was in the past. In the 19th and early 20th centuries, economists seemed comfortable with discussing emotional and psychological elements of economic behavior. As rigorous mathematical modeling came to dominate economics in the second half of the twentieth century, these elements were elimi-

Self-regarding preferences

A set of objectives that depend only on the material welfare of the decision maker

Other-regarding preferences

A set of objectives that includes not only the material welfare of the decision maker, but also the material welfare of others and their attitudes toward the decision maker

Applying Economic Ideas 4.1
ULTIMATUMS, DICTATORS, AND OTHER GAMES

In recent years, games have become increasingly popular as a tool of economic research. One game that consistently produces results that contradict narrow definitions of economic rationality is the so-called *ultimatum game*.

The game works like this—Player A is given a sum of money, say $10. She is then asked to offer some share of the money to Player B. Next Player B has the option of accepting the offer or rejecting it. If B rejects A's offer, neither player gets to keep anything. If player B accepts, they divide the money according to the terms that A proposed. The name of the game comes from the fact that there is only one offer and only one chance to refuse—no extended bargaining is allowed, no repeated play during which considerations like developing a reputation or building trust might come into play.

Exchanging of money to multiple parties is part of the ultimatum game.

Under the assumptions of full rationality and self-regarding preferences, the outcome of the game is easy to predict. First, we conclude that Player B will never rationally reject any nonzero offer. To do so would give up a certain (although perhaps small) reward in favor of getting nothing at all. Second, we conclude that Player A, knowing that B will never reject any nonzero offer, no matter how small, will rationally make the smallest offer allowed. (Sometimes the rules set by the experimenter might say this is one cent, sometimes one dollar, or whatever.)

That is not at all what happens when the game is actually played, however. In practice, Player A—not always, but more often than not—offers a substantial amount, say 30 to 50 percent of the total. Furthermore, B typically rejects offers that are perceived as too low, with the frequency of rejection rising sharply for offers below 20 percent or so of the total. The experiment has been repeated thousands of times, not only with American college students, but also with African hunter-gatherers, Wall Street brokers, residents of Mongolia, and many other groups. The average amount offered and the threshold for rejection differ somewhat from one society to another, but it seems that the narrowly rational result is never observed.

What is going on? One hypothesis is that, when placed in the Player A position, people behave altruistically. They take pleasure from pleasing Player B. Another hypothesis is that Player A is not altruistic but, rather, is strategically motivated by the fear that a too-low offer will be rejected. But if so, what motivates Player B? Why are low offers rejected when there is nothing material to gain by doing so? Is B motivated by some innate aversion to inequality? By a spiteful desire to draw pleasure from punishing an insufficiently generous Player A?

One way to try to sort out the motives is to play the related *dictator game* with a similar group of subjects. In the dictator game, Player A gets to keep her share regardless of whether B accepts or rejects the offer. Since there is no fear of rejection, any nonzero offer must be motivated purely by altruism. Interestingly, although the dictator game typically produces smaller offers than the ultimatum game, the offers are still substantially above zero. Seemingly, both altruism and fear of rejection play a role.

There are many, many variants of the games. Sometimes the players are known to each other, sometimes anonymous. Sometimes the game is played in a "double-blind" form where neither the players nor the experimenter knows the individual identities of the players or amount specific individuals offer or reject. (The double-blind variant is supposed to eliminate the possibility that Player A might be ashamed of appearing "too selfish" in the eyes of the experimenter.) No matter what, the offers never fall to zero. Human behavior is stubbornly more complex than narrowly rational, self-regarding preferences can account for!

nated. Almost all models of the period were based on full rationality and self-regarding preferences. While admitting that it is harder to construct models that incorporate the full range of human behavior, Thaler is hopeful that today's generation of economists are up to the task.[2]

Market Performance and Market Failure

Economic choices are not made in a vacuum. They are made within the context of a set of institutions, of which markets and government are two of the most important. This section offers a preview of what coming chapters will have to say about markets, especially the key concepts of *market performance* and *market failure*. The next section will preview the role of government in the economy.

Market Performance

Market performance

The degree to which markets work efficiently in providing arrangements for mutually beneficial trade

Earlier, we defined a *market* as any arrangement that people have for trading with one another. When economists speak of **market performance**, then, they are referring to how efficiently markets do their job of providing arrangements for mutually beneficial trade.

Ideally, markets would make it possible to carry out every exchange that is to the mutual benefit of the parties involved. Suppose we are talking about the market for peaches. The parties to peach trading are farmers and consumers. An exchange will benefit consumers if the satisfaction they get from a peach is at least as great as the satisfaction they would get from spending the same amount on the next most attractive good (say, an apple). The exchange will benefit producers if the price paid for a peach is at least high enough to cover the opportunity cost of producing it. If there is a price that makes the trade beneficial both to consumers and to producers, then carrying out the trade will be *efficient* inasmuch as it will leave at least one party better off and neither worse off.

Although the details will require several chapters to work out, a simple diagram can give an intuitive idea of efficient market performance. Figure 4.1 shows two curves that represent the market for peaches. The demand curve represents the benefit of peaches to consumers as reflected by their willingness to buy peaches, given the price of peaches, the prices of alternative goods, and so on. The supply curve represents the opportunity costs of producing an additional peach as reflected by the willingness of farmers to produce and sell the product under given conditions.

At any point to the left of the intersection of the two curves, the price consumers would willingly pay for a peach (as indicated by the height of the demand curve) is greater than the minimum needed to cover farmers' opportunity costs (as indicated by the height of the supply curve). To the left of the intersection, trades carried out at any price between the two curves are mutually beneficial to consumers and producers. However, to the right of the intersection, the maximum consumers would find it worthwhile to pay for still more peaches is less than what is needed to cover farmers' costs. There is no price at which further trades would benefit both parties; therefore, production beyond the intersection point would not be efficient.

It follows, then, that a market in which production is carried out just up to, but not beyond, the intersection point performs efficiently. At a lower quantity, some mutually beneficial exchanges would not occur. At a higher quantity, no price could be found that would benefit both parties. Not only is the quantity indicated by the intersection of the two curves just right, but the price is, too. Any higher price would lead to a wasteful sur-

FIGURE 4.1   PERFORMANCE OF THE MARKET FOR PEACHES

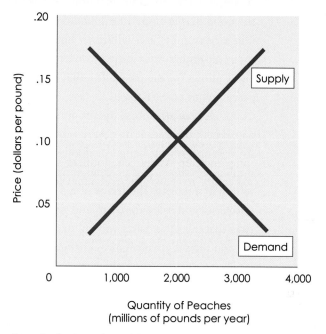

Quantity of Peaches
(millions of pounds per year)

This exhibit shows hypothetical supply and demand curves for peaches. The demand curve reflects the willingness of consumers to buy peaches, given the price of peaches and the prices of alternative goods. The supply curve represents the willingness of farmers to sell peaches, given the price of peaches and the opportunity costs of production. At any point to the left of the intersection of the curves, the price that consumers would willingly pay for a peach (as indicated by the height of the demand curve) is greater than the minimum needed to cover farmers' costs (as indicated by the height of the supply curve). Thus, up to that point, exchanges carried out at a price between the two curves are mutually beneficial to consumers and producers. At any point to the right of the intersection, the maximum amount that consumers would be willing to pay for still more peaches is less than the amount needed to cover farmers' costs. Thus, production beyond the intersection point would not be efficient. It follows, then, that a market in which production is carried out just up to but not beyond the intersection point performs efficiently.

plus of peaches, whereas any lower price would lead to a shortage in which some consumers' wants would not be satisfied.

It is hard to exaggerate the enthusiasm that economists have for markets that generate such efficient outcomes. From those pursuing economic reform in the nations of the former Soviet Union to candidates touting new solutions to problems of American capitalism, there is widespread agreement that within large areas of economic life, markets can be an efficient means of solving basic economic problems. Yet even the most enthusiastic fans of markets recognize that they do not always function perfectly. Several conditions must be met before markets reach a stable equilibrium exactly at the intersection of the supply and demand curves. Let's look briefly at some of the situations in which market performance falls short of the ideal, again leaving details to later chapters.

Transaction Costs and Market Performance

A supply curve like that in Figure 4.1 reflects the opportunity costs of producing the good in question. The demand curve in the figure, and others like it, show how much consumers are willing to buy, assuming that the price paid is the only cost that consumers must bear in order to buy it. Neither the supply nor the demand curve allows for the possibility that buyers or sellers may incur other costs as part of carrying out an exchange.

Among other things, the simple supply and demand model implicitly assumes that consumers are able, at no cost in terms of time, money, or mental effort, to obtain full information on the range of goods available, their quality, and their prices. It also implicitly assumes that no time, money, or mental effort is needed by either buyers or sellers to negotiate the terms of a sale. Finally, the model implicitly assumes that all purchases and sales are clean and final. Once an agreement is reached, there are no risks that the other party will fail to do what was promised and no costs of renegotiating contracts if circumstances change.

Transaction costs

The costs, other than production costs, of carrying out a transaction

In practice, costs of gathering information, finding a potential partner, negotiating and enforcing agreements, and renegotiating when conditions change can be considerable. Economists use the term **transaction costs** to refer to all such costs. For a simple transaction, like buying a single peach, transaction costs are likely to be small. For a larger consumer purchase, like buying a house or condominium, transaction costs, in the form of brokers' commissions, bank closing costs, and fees paid to insurers and surveyors can add significantly to the quoted price. In the case of complex business transactions, say the merger of two corporations, transaction costs can be enormous.

When transaction costs are taken into account, it is more difficult to specify whether a market is operating efficiently. It is no longer valid to say that efficiency requires operating exactly at the point where the supply and demand curves intersect. Instead, before the market approaches the intersection, it may reach a point where the gap between the opportunity cost of production (as shown by the supply curve) and consumers' willingness to pay (as shown by the demand curve) is smaller than the transaction costs needed to carry out additional exchanges. To take a trivial example, you might be driving down the street when you are struck by hunger for a luscious, ripe peach. You see a supermarket; but you start thinking about the time it will take to park and stand in line for checkout, the chance that the store may not have any peaches for sale today, and the possibility that a peach that looks attractive on the shelf won't taste as good as you would like. The gap between your hunger for the peach and the price isn't great enough to make it worth the effort and uncertainty involved in stopping.

It would be going too far, however, to say that markets are necessarily operating efficiently when they reach the point where the gap between supply and demand curves is just equal to transaction costs. Sometimes transaction costs themselves may be inefficiently large. For example, the Japanese economy, which has a world-class reputation for efficiency in manufacturing, also has a retail trade system that is outdated and hampered by cumbersome regulations. As a result, transaction costs facing Japanese consumers are sometimes much greater than those for Americans that are able to buy their peaches super-fresh from a farm stand, super-cheap in a big-box discounter, or super-fast in at

24-hour convenience store. In this sense, it would be reasonable to say that high Japanese transaction costs are a sign of inefficiency.

As we add detail to our discussion of markets in coming chapters, we will return to the subject of transaction costs at many points.

Market Failure

A **market failure** is a situation in which a market fails to coordinate choices in a way that achieves efficient use of resources. Not every situation in which the market does not reach the exact intersection of supply and demand should be considered a market failure. Transaction costs, as well as costs of production, need to be taken into account. When economists talk of market failure, they have in mind situations where conditions other than transaction costs alone prevent buyers and sellers from carrying out all potentially beneficial exchanges. Of the many possible sources of market failure, three deserve special attention. We will discuss them under the headings of *externalities*, *public goods*, and *insufficient competition*. Other sources of market failure will be mentioned more briefly.

EXTERNALITIES   One type of market failure is failure to transmit information about scarcity in the form of prices. For markets to perform their job efficiently, prices should reflect the opportunity costs of producing the goods or services in question. Ordinarily, market prices do reflect at least a reasonable approximation of opportunity costs. However, situations arise in which producers' (and consumers') actions have effects on third parties, that is, people other than the buyer and seller who carry out a transaction. These third-party effects, which are not reflected in prices, are known as **externalities**. When externalities are present, the price system does not transmit accurate information about opportunity costs.

The classic example of an externality is pollution. Suppose a utility burns coal in its boilers to generate electricity. The costs of fuel, capital, and labor come to $.10 per kilowatt hour of electricity produced. They are called *internal costs* because they are borne by the utility itself. Those costs are reflected in market transactions—payments to coal producers, workers, stockholders and bondholders, and so on. Internal costs are part of the opportunity cost of making electricity because they represent the forgone opportunities of using the same natural resources, capital, and labor in some other industry. To stay in business, the utility must receive a price of at least $.10 per kilowatt hour, that is, a price at least equal to the internal opportunity costs.

The internal costs, however, are not the only costs of making electricity. In the process of burning coal, a utility spews out clouds of carbon dioxide, sulfur dioxide, soot, and other pollutants. The pollution damages health, kills trees, and corrodes buildings in areas downwind from the plant and contributes to global warming. Those effects are referred to as *external costs* of generating electricity because they are borne by third parties—people who are neither buyers nor sellers of electricity or any of the inputs used in making it. From the viewpoint of the economy as a whole, external costs are also part of the opportunity cost of generating power. They represent the value of the factors of production that are destroyed by the pollution (such as dead trees or workers in other firms taking extended sick leave) or required in order to repair its effects (repainting houses, treating pollution-related diseases).

Suppose that pollution damage of all kinds comes to $.02 per kilowatt hour of power produced. Added to the $.10 in internal costs, the $.02 of external costs brings the overall opportunity cost of electricity to $.12 per kilowatt hour. This figure reflects the value of the factors of production used directly by the utility plus those that are destroyed or diverted from other uses by the pollution.

If the price of electric power is set by supply and demand, its equilibrium value will tend toward the level of $.10 per kilowatt hour that just covers internal costs. This, however, sends a false signal to users of electricity: It tells them that producing a kilowatt hour puts a smaller drain on the world's scarce factors of production than is really the case. As a result, electricity users will use more power than they should. They will be less inclined to buy new, more efficient machinery, to design products so as to use less electricity, to shift to cleaner natural gas, and so on. In short, the market will fail to achieve efficient resource allocation because prices will have sent users the wrong information.

We will return to the economics of pollution in Chapter 6. There, we will examine several possible solutions to market failures resulting from externalities.

PUBLIC GOODS   The goods and services discussed in all the examples used to this point—chicken, peaches, apartments, and so on—have two properties in common: (1) The supplier can decide to supply the good to some people and to exclude others; this is termed the *property of exclusion.* (For example, if I run a multiplex movie theater, I can exclude people who do not buy tickets.) (2) Use of a unit of the good by one person limits the possibility of use of that unit by other people; this is termed the *property of rivalry.* (For example, if I sell you a peach, I cannot sell that same peach to someone else.) Some goods do not possess the properties of exclusion and rivalry, however. These are known as **public goods**. Lacking the property of exclusion, they cannot be provided for one person without also being provided for others. Lacking the property of rivalry, once they are provided for one person, they can be provided for others at no extra cost. Public goods, like externalities, are a potential source of market failure.

Perhaps the closest thing to a pure public good is national defense. One person cannot be protected against nuclear attack or invasion without the protection being extended to everyone. Also, it costs no more to protect a single resident of an area than to safeguard an entire city or region. Although pure public goods are rare, other goods may lack the properties of exclusion or rivalry to some extent. These can be called impure public goods. Police protection provides one example. In their functions of promoting public safety in general and deterring street crime, the police are providing a public good; but in their function of solving an individual crime, such as a burglary, they are providing a private good to the person who hopes to recover the stolen property. Maintenance of urban streets, the provision of parks, and even the space program have been cited as examples of goods that are neither purely public nor purely private.

Public goods

Goods that (1) cannot be provided for one person without also being provided for others and (2) when provided for one person can be provided for others at zero additional sum

Private firms have difficulty making a profit selling products that, once they are provided to one customer, become available to others at no additional cost. To see why the market may fail in such cases, imagine that someone tries to set up a private missile defense system—call it Star Wars, Inc.—to be funded by selling subscriptions to people who want protection from a nuclear attack. Even if I think the system will work and that there is a real threat, there are two reasons I might choose not to subscribe. First, I know that if my neighbors subscribe and get their homes protected, my home will be protected too, even if I do not pay. I could take a *free ride* on a public good paid for by others. Second, I might be willing to contribute if I had *assurance* that at least, say, 1,000 of my neighbors did so. That would raise enough money to buy at least one missile. However, I would not contribute without the assurance that this minimum would be met. Contributing along with just 500 neighbors would buy only half a missile, which would be useless; and my contribution would be completely wasted.

Economists have long argued that the *free-rider problem* and the *assurance problem*, which make people reluctant to contribute voluntarily to the support of public goods, mean that government may have to provide those goods if they are to be provided at all. (We say *may* because, as *Applying Economic Ideas 4.2* illustrates, private firms provide some things that have the characteristics of public goods.) However, many goods and services that are provided at public expense are public goods only to a small extent, if at all. Take education, for example. The principal beneficiaries of public education are students. It is not impossible to exclude students from the schools. Only a few schools, public or private, operate on an "open admission" basis. Others select their students according to neighborhood, ability to pay, or scholastic achievement. Moreover, education clearly has the property of rivalry in consumption. Students cannot be added to a school without some additional expense. The more students a school admits, the more teachers, classrooms, laboratories, and other facilities it must provide. Thus, education fits the definition of a public good, if at all, only to the extent that it has some benefit beyond that received by individual students—for example, promoting good citizenship in a way that makes life better for everyone in the community.

INSUFFICIENT COMPETITION A third source of market failure is insufficient competition. As we have seen, market prices should reflect opportunity costs if they are to guide resource allocation efficiently. In the case of harmful externalities, market failure occurs because prices fall below opportunity costs. Where competition is insufficient, however, market failure can occur because prices are too high.

Utility companies have been considered examples of a monopoly.

Applying Economic Ideas 4.2
PRIVATE PROVISION OF PUBLIC GOODS

Many economists argue that private firms cannot supply public goods because of the assurance and free rider problems that arise whenever goods have the properties of non-exclusion and nonrivalry. In practice, however, many private firms and voluntary organizations do find methods of providing goods that have these properties. Examples include broadcast radio and television, computer software, and amenities like streets and parks in residential neighborhoods.

In some cases, private firms simply alter the product in a way that makes it possible to exclude free riders. Thus, satellite television signals can be scrambled so only subscribers who rent a decoder can receive them; computer software can be copy protected so that the original purchasers cannot easily make free copies for their friends; and roads can be equipped with tollbooths. In this case, the good ceases to be a public good, even though it continues to have the property of nonrivalry.

Exclusion has its disadvantages, however. The necessary technology may be expensive and less than fully reliable, and the attempt to exclude may be offensive to customers the firm would like to attract. To avoid these disadvantages, private firms and voluntary organizations often use other techniques to provide public goods.

A public road ceases to be a public good when a tollbooth is installed.

- One approach is to link the public good to an ordinary good, offering the two as a package deal. Thus, some public radio stations send their contributors magazines with movie reviews and program guides, computer software companies provide advice via telephone to legitimate registered purchasers, and real estate developers find it worthwhile to build residential streets as part of a package included with the sale of private homes.

- Another approach is to tap the power of other-regarding preferences. Voluntary organizations build on the psychological satisfaction of contributing to a good cause or the psychological discomfort of being recognized as a free rider. This works best in small communities where everyone knows everyone else; but organizations, like public radio stations, can achieve something of the same effect by publicly thanking contributors over the air.

- Still another device is the "assurance contract." Sometimes people hesitate to contribute to a good cause because they fear their contribution will be in vain unless others join them. In such a case, the provider can accept pledges of support that will be activated only if an agreed minimum of support is received. Thus, families might be asked to contribute checks to a fund to build a neighborhood playground on the understanding that the checks will be returned if a necessary minimum is not raised.

As these examples show, the economic category of "public good" does not always mean a good that must be provided by the government.

Monopoly

A situation in which there is only a single seller of a good or service

As an extreme case, consider a market in which there is only a single seller of a good or service; such a market is termed a **monopoly**. Residential electric service is a frequently cited example. Suppose that Metropolitan Electric can generate power at an opportunity cost of $.10 per kilowatt hour. Selling electric power at that price would guide customers in choosing between electricity and other energy sources, such as oil or gas, and in undertaking energy-saving investments, such as home insulation and high-efficiency lighting.

If homeowners could buy electricity from anyone they chose the way they buy eggs or gasoline, the forces of competition, acting through supply and demand, would push the market price toward the level of opportunity costs. In a competitive market, any seller that tried to raise prices much above opportunity costs would be undercut by others; and the utility would not sell power at a price below opportunity costs because doing so would put it out of business.

However, utilities do not compete in selling to residential customers. Every home is normally connected to only one set of power lines. In this case, if not restrained by government regulation, a utility could substantially increase its profits by charging a price higher than opportunity costs. Of course, raising the price would mean that less power would be sold as customers moved up and to the left along their demand curves. Up to a point, however, the greater profit per kilowatt hour sold would more than outweigh the effects of the reduction in quantity demanded.

If too high a price is charged, homeowners will get a false message regarding the opportunity cost of electricity. They may make substitutions that are not economically justified. For example, they may switch from electricity to oil for heat, even in regions where cheap hydroelectric power is available, or from electric air conditioning to gas air conditioning, even in areas where the opportunity cost of electricity is below that of gas.

Market failures due to insufficient competition are not necessarily limited to the extreme case of monopoly. Under some circumstances, competition among a small number of firms may also lead to prices that are above opportunity costs, especially if the firms engage in collusion. The circumstances under which competition is or is not sufficient to ensure the efficient operation of markets is the subject of a large body of economic research and of more than a few controversies, as we will see in coming chapters.

OTHER MARKET FAILURES   Some economists would list other sources of market failure in addition to the three just discussed. For example, the macroeconomic phenomena of inflation and cyclical unemployment are sometimes considered to be market failures. Certainly, an economy that is subject to excessive inflation and unemployment provides a poor environment in which to coordinate the actions of buyers and sellers of individual goods and factor services. However, the effects of inflation and unemployment, together with policies intended to keep them under control, lie outside the scope of the microeconomics course.

As we have defined it, market failure means failure to achieve an *efficient* allocation of scarce resources. In addition, the market may or may not achieve an *equitable* allocation of resources. Whether unfairness, inequality, and economic injustice in a market economy should be given the label *market failure* is more a matter of terminology than of substance. In this book, market failure is defined in a way that makes it an issue of efficiency alone, but this definition is not meant to deny the importance of issues of economic justice. Such issues will be discussed extensively at several points in the following chapters, although not under the heading of market failure.

The Economic Role of Government

Although markets play a big role in answering the key questions of who, what, how, and for whom, not all economic decisions are made in markets. Some important economic decisions are made in hierarchies. Allocation of resources within a business firm is one example of hierarchical decision making; we will focus on that later. Here we are concerned with the role of government, the other major example of hierarchy in economics.

If we want to understand the microeconomic role of government, a good place to begin is by asking: Why does government play any role in the economy at all? Why cannot all decisions be made by households and private firms coordinating their actions through markets? Economists offer two answers, one based on the notion of market failure, the other on that of *rent seeking*. The answers are partly contradictory and partly complementary. Each will figure prominently in coming chapters, and each deserves a brief preview here.

The Market Failure Theory of Government

According to the market failure theory of government, the principal economic role of government is to step in where markets fail to allocate resources efficiently and fairly. Each type of market failure calls for a particular type of governmental intervention.

Take the case of pollution. Earlier we gave the example of a utility whose contribution to air pollution caused $.02 worth of damage for every kilowatt hour of electricity. Government can do a number of things to correct the resulting market failure. For example, it can require the utility to install pollution control equipment that will prevent poisonous gas from escaping into the atmosphere or impose a tax equal to the external costs of pollution.

When markets fail to supply public goods, government also is called in. Often, as in the case of national defense, the government simply becomes the producer of the public good. In other cases, such as education, which some economists consider to be in part a public good, the government need not be the sole producer. Private schools and colleges are encouraged with subsidies and tax benefits to add to the supply of education produced by public institutions.

Government has attempted to remedy market failures arising from insufficient competition in a variety of ways. In some cases, government uses *antitrust laws* to preserve competition by preventing mergers of competing firms, or even by breaking large firms up into a number of smaller ones. In other cases, such as the electric power industry, *regulation* is used to control prices charged by a monopoly firm. In a few cases, such as the Tennessee Valley Authority's electric power facilities, the government itself may become a monopoly producer of a good or service. These activities of government will be discussed in Chapter 12.

The Public Choice Theory of Government

The market failure theory of government is sometimes criticized for being normative rather than positive—more of a theory about what the government ought to do than about

The government can require a utility to install pollution control equipment or impose taxes.

what it actually does. In practice, many government programs, rather than correcting market failures, seem to promote inefficiency or inequality in markets that would function well without government intervention. Price supports for milk, discussed in Chapter 2, are an example. That program long held the price of milk above its equilibrium level, causing persistent surpluses. That is hardly efficient. Further, although some benefits of farm programs go to farmers who are in financial difficulty, thus arguably serving the goal of fairness, many of the subsidies go to farmers who are financially well off.

Critics of the market failure theory maintain that government policies should be understood not in terms of broad social goals like efficiency and fairness but in terms of how people use the institutions of government to pursue their own self-interest. This approach to policy analysis is known as **public choice theory**.

RENTS AND RENT SEEKING   One of the key concepts of public choice theory is *economic rent*. In everyday language, a *rent* is simply a payment made for the use of something, say, an apartment or a car. Public choice theorists use the term in a more specialized sense, however. An **economic rent** is any payment to a factor of production in excess of its opportunity cost. An example is the huge income a popular author like J. K. Rowling or Dan Brown earns from a new novel—an income much higher than the author could earn working the same amount time in the next-best paying line of work.

When rents are earned through innovation in competitive markets, they are called *economic profits*. Entrepreneurs are always on the lookout for ways to earn such profits—for example, by introducing a new product superior to that of rival firms or by being the first to implement a cost-saving production method. When they are successful, the income they earn may be substantially higher than what others are able to earn by employing similar factors of production in less imaginative ways.

Profit that entrepreneurs earn through private market activity is not the only category of economic rent, however. Firms, workers, and resource owners often turn to government in search of rents, rather than trying to outwit their rivals in the marketplace. A dollar earned because of a regulation that raises the price at which a firm sells its output or lowers the prices at which it buys its inputs is worth just as much as a dollar of profit earned through purely private efforts at innovation. In some cases it may even be better. Profits earned from innovation in a competitive market may be short lived because rivals will soon come out with an even better product or introduce an even cheaper production method. However, government regulations can, not only create opportunities to earn rents, but also shield those opportunities from competitors. Obtaining and defending rents through government action is known as **political rent seeking**, or often simply as **rent seeking**, with the political aspect implied.[3]

Consider the case of subsidies for corn-based ethanol used as a gasoline substitute. Politicians attempt to justify those subsidies as a way to offset externalities—in this case, the carbon dioxide produced from burning gasoline. However, many economists argue that the process of producing ethanol releases nearly as much carbon dioxide into the atmosphere as burning gasoline does, or even more. Public choice theorists see ethanol subsidies as a classic case of *political rent seeking*. The benefits of ethanol subsidies go not just to small family farms but also to large agribusinesses, owners of ethanol refineries, even growers of competing crops like wheat and soybeans whose prices are pushed up

Public choice theory

The branch of economics that studies how people use the institutions of government in pursuit of their own interests

Economic rent

Any payment to a factor of production in excess of its opportunity cost

Political rent seeking (rent seeking)

The process of seeking and defending economic rents through the political process

when corn acreage expands. The result is a program that draws wide political support even though its environmental benefits are far less than is sometimes claimed.

Government restrictions on competition are another way of generating rents. For example, tariffs and import quotas on clothing, cars, sugar, steel, and other products shield domestic firms and their employees from foreign competition. Thus, the firms are able to earn rents by raising prices above the competitive market level, and the employees are able to earn rents in the form of higher wages. Examples of government restrictions on competition can be found within the domestic economy as well. For example, licensing fees and examinations restrict the number of competitors who can enter such professions as law and medicine and, often, even such occupations as manicuring and hair styling.

FROM THE LAW OF UNINTENDED CONSEQUENCES TO GOVERN-MENT FAILURE   The notion that government policies do not always promote efficiency and equity is not new. Economists have long been aware of the law of unintended consequences—the tendency of government policies to have effects other than those desired by their proponents; but public choice theory goes beyond the notion of unintended consequences, which could be traced simply to incomplete analysis on the part of policy makers. Rather, the element of rent seeking in the formulation of government policy suggests that the inefficient results of many government programs are not unintended at all. In this view, there is a systematic tendency for government programs to cause rather than to cure economic inefficiencies—a tendency, that is, toward **government failure**.

Government failure

A situation in which a government policy causes inefficient use of resources

In introducing the notion of government failure, public choice theorists do not intend to imply that government always makes a mess of things or that the market always functions perfectly. Rather, they want to level the playing field by showing that both markets and government are imperfect institutions. In deciding whether government or the market better performs a given function, the possibilities of government failure must be weighed against those of market failure.

Neoclassical and Other Approaches to Microeconomics

This chapter began by introducing the idea of economics as the study of rational choice when objectives and constraints are given. Rational choice lies at the core of neoclassical economics, which can be traced to the work of Alfred Marshall at the end of the 19th century (see *Who Said It? Who Did It? 2.1*) and has long been the dominant school of economics in the United States. Much of the material in the following chapters, including the theory of consumer choice, the theory of profit maximization by firms, and the theory of factor markets, is based on the neoclassical tradition. In addition to the general principles of rational choice that have been discussed already in this chapter, neoclassical economics often incorporates additional simplifying assumptions:

1. An assumption of full rationality where decision makers are seen as having well-defined objectives (for example, profit maximization) and as being competent to make use of all available information in choosing how best to pursue those objectives

2. An assumption of self-regarding preferences, models in which decision makers are understood as being motivated by material gain for themselves

3. An emphasis on the price system as the economy's key mechanism for transmitting information, where the prices of all goods and services are typically assumed to be public information available free to all households and firms and, for the most part, costs of acquiring information and other transaction costs are ignored

4. An emphasis on formal models of economic behavior that can be stated in graphical or mathematical terms, and a focus on conditions of equilibrium

5. Treatment of households, firms, and where considered, government agencies as "black boxes" with the main focus on the interactions of these units in the marketplace and relatively little attention paid to the workings of their internal hierarchies

The very restrictiveness of these assumptions is the source of much of the success of neoclassical theory. Neoclassical economics is like a spotlight that is able to illuminate objects brightly precisely because it is focused narrowly. In the following chapters, we will encounter one situation after another, ranging from highway safety to negotiations among OPEC oil ministers, where neoclassical economics provides insights of striking clarity and predictions that stand up remarkably well to the test of experience.

Despite the successes of neoclassical microeconomics, economists have long been aware that there are some problems that its narrowly focused spotlight cannot adequately illuminate. We have already mentioned difficulties posed by bounded rationality, other-regarding preferences, and transactions costs—all of which require modifications or extensions of neoclassical models. Also, neoclassical economics tends to take market and government institutions as given, without asking why they exist and how they evolve. Finally, the focus on equilibrium in neoclassical economics has limited its ability to address issues of innovation, change, and entrepreneurship. In coming chapters, we will discuss extensions and alternatives to neoclassical economics whenever they are helpful in understanding the important economic issues of our day.

Summary

1. **What is the basic structure of economic theory?** Economic theories are constructed from statements about people's objectives, aims, and preferences; statements about the constraints on available opportunities; and statements about how people choose among the available opportunities so as to best meet their objectives.

2. **Why is rationality of central importance to economics?** To be rational means to act purposefully to achieve one's objectives, given the available opportunities. In some cases, economists assume *full rationality*, which means that they assume that people make full use of all available information in calculating how best to meet their objectives. In other cases, they assume *bounded rationality*, which means that they assume that people intend to make the choices that best serve their objectives, but have limited ability to acquire and process information. The assumption of rationality is sometimes further modified to allow for other-regarding as well as self-regarding preferences.

3. **What is the meaning of market performance and market failure?** *Market performance* refers to how efficiently markets do their job of providing

arrangements for mutually beneficial trade. Ideally, markets would make it possible to carry out every possible mutually beneficial trade, in which case they would operate perfectly efficiently. Sometimes, however, *market failure* occurs, in which case markets fail to carry out their job efficiently. *Externalities*, *public goods*, and insufficient competition (leading to *monopoly*) are among the most widely discussed sources of market failure.

4. **What are some alternative theories of the economic role of government?** According to the market failure theory of government, everything that markets can do efficiently should be left to them. Government should intervene only to correct market failures, whether narrowly or broadly defined. *Public choice theory* maintains that many government policies are not efforts to correct market failure but, instead, result from *political rent seeking*. Rent seeking refers to the process of seeking payments in excess of opportunity costs.

Key Terms

Problems and Topics for Discussion

1. **Alternative path theories**   The chapter proposes a simple theory to explain the existence of a path across a grassy area on a certain college campus. Here is another theory that might also explain the path: "Economics lectures are so boring that students prefer to be late to them. However, near the sidewalk on one side of the quad there is a beehive, and many students have suffered stings; and on the other side of the quad is the chemistry building, which smells bad when the wind blows a certain way. Sometimes if you cut across the middle of the quad, you find four-leaf clovers that give you good luck on your exams. Those are the reasons that there is a path across the quad." Applying the principle of Ockham's razor, which theory do you think is better? Why? Would you reject the more complex theory out of hand, or would you first want to make some observations? What observations would you make?

2. **Italians in America**   According to a theory suggested in the chapter, people drive smaller cars in Italy than in the United States not because of different preferences but because they face different constraints on their opportunities—higher gasoline prices, narrower streets, and so on. On the basis of that theory, what prediction would you make about the cars driven by Italians who move to the United States? What kind of observations would you suggest to test whether preferences or constraints are the key factor in the choice of car size?

3. **What makes a fair offer?**   J. B. is a woman of limited income and almost no savings who faces a sudden financial emergency. The only way she can think of to raise the money she urgently needs is to sell her car. She has little experience in the used car market, so she offers her car to a nearby dealer, the first one she can think of. The dealer, R. S., thinks he can resell the car for about $3,000. Normally he would offer about $2,000,

which would leave him enough margin to cover the costs and risks of his business plus some profit. He might even raise his offer a bit if the seller were a hard bargainer. However, R. S. quickly sees that J. B. is desperate for cash and that she does not know of any other way to find a buyer quickly. He sees that he is in a position to offer an ultimatum, so he offers $600 in cash for the car, immediate sale, take it or leave it. Answer the following questions:

a. Put yourself in J. B.'s position. Even though you are an unsophisticated seller, you realize that $600 is a low offer. Would you be tempted to reject the offer even if you know of no other immediate buyer and even if the $600 is enough to solve your immediate financial emergency? Discuss your reasoning.

b. Put yourself in R. S.'s position. Would you offer more than $600 for the car? Why or why not? Discuss your reasoning.

c. Put yourself in the position of J. B.'s neighbor. She accepts the offer and later, when it is too late for you to advise her or offer her financial help (if you are able to do so), she tells you the story. You go to R. S. and demand an explanation of why he made such a low offer. He candidly tells you that he would have offered more if he thought she had any alternative and if she were not so desperate for cash. He points out that J. B. must have believed that she was better off with the $600 than without it; otherwise she could have refused the offer. Accepting that J. B.'s conduct was entirely legal, do you think it was ethical? Discuss.

4. **The economics of voting**   Did you vote in the most recent state or national election? If so, how was your choice of a candidate influenced by your objectives and constraints? If you did not vote, was your decision not to vote influenced by objectives and constraints? Do you think your choice of a candidate (or your choice not to vote) was a rational one? Discuss.

5. **Government failure versus market failure**   When the possibilities of both government failure and market failure are taken into account, does the fact that a government policy causes inefficiency necessarily mean that abolishing the policy would result in greater efficiency? Does the fact that a certain market fails to work efficiently necessarily mean that intervention by government would improve the situation? Discuss.

Case for Discussion

A Price That's Too Good to Be Bad

Almost any aisle of any supermarket is a battleground in the never-ending war between house brands and national brands. The weapons of the national brands are advertising, reputation, and brand recognition. The big gun on the side of the house brands is price. One day recently, for example, shoppers at a Virginia Safeway store could take their choice of Johnson & Johnson baby powder for $3.29 or a can of the Safeway brand at $2.59, of Kellogg's cornflakes at $1.97 per box or the house brand at $1.59, of Wesson vegetable oil at $4.59 per bottle or Safeway's product at $3.39 per bottle, or of Heinz distilled vinegar at $1.93 per quart with Safeway's Townhouse brand at $1.23.

What logic lies behind this competition? One's first thought might be that it all depends on the law of demand. If so, one would think, the lower the price of the house brand, the higher its sales relative to the national brand. Marketers of consumer products have found that the law of demand applies only up to a point in the competition between house brands and national brands. Paradoxically, a price that is *too* low can actually hurt the sales of the house brand.

Consider the case of Pathmark supermarkets' Premium All Purpose cleaner. This house brand product was designed to compete head-to-head with Fantastik, the leading national brand. The two products were chemically identical. The house brand's packaging mimicked that of the national brand; and Pathmark's product was priced at just $.89, versus $1.79 for Fantastik.

Yet, from its first introduction, Premium All Purpose cleaner was a slow seller. Frustrated Pathmark marketers even added a sticker to the label that said, "If you like Fantastik, try me!" The sticker did not help. Finally, Pathmark decided to drop the product.

What went wrong? Interviewed by *The Wall Street Journal*, Robert Wunderle, a spokesman for Supermarket General Corporation, Pathmark's corporate parent, blamed the failure on a price "so low that it discredited the intrinsic value of the product."

Many retailers consider it risky to price their house brands more than 20 to 25 percent below the national brand. There are exceptions, however. If the product is so simple and familiar that consumers believe there can be no quality difference, it is safe to establish a bigger discount. Thus, for example, Safeway puts a bigger discount on its house brand vinegar and vegetable oil than on its house brand baby powder or cornflakes.

Peter Schwartz, president of Daymon Associates, Inc., a private-label research and marketing firm, explains the problem this way: "The further the distance from the national brand, the higher the credibility problem for consumers. Once you get outside the customer's comfort zone, the consumer psychology becomes, 'Gee, they must have taken it out in quality.' "

SOURCE: Based in part on Alix M. Freedman, "A Price That's Too Good May Be Bad," *The Wall Street Journal*, November 15, 1988, B1.

QUESTIONS

1. Would you characterize the behavior of consumers who buy Fantastik brand cleaner instead of Pathmark's Premium All-Purpose cleaner as full rationality, irrationality, or bounded rationality? Explain.

2. The case suggests that in choosing among alternative brands of goods, consumers sometimes rely on the rule of thumb that higher prices tend to be associated with higher quality. From your own experience as a shopper, how valid do you think that this rule of thumb is on the average— valid always or, rarely valid? Give examples.

3. A consumer who followed the assumptions of bounded rationality would be most likely to apply the preceding rule of thumb, rather than seeking independent information on product quality, in purchasing which kinds of goods?

    a. Major purchases such as automobiles

    b. Goods that are purchased frequently and can easily be inspected, such as clothing

    c. Goods like household cleaners that are purchased infrequently constitute a small part of the consumer's budget and cannot easily be inspected or tested before purchase. Discuss why the rule of thumb is more reasonable in some cases than others, and give additional examples of each case.

End Notes

1. Thorstein Veblen, "In Dispraise of Economists," in *The Portable Veblen*, ed. Max Lerner (New York: Viking Press, 1958), 232–233.

2. See Richard H. Thaler, "From Homo Economicus to Homo Sapiens," *Journal of Economic Perspectives*, Volume 14, No. 1 (Winter 2000): 133–141.

3. For a representative collection of papers on the theory of rent seeking, see James M. Buchanan, Robert D. Tollison, and Gordon Tullock, eds., *Toward a Theory of the Rent-Seeking Society* (College Station: Texas A&M Press, 1980).

CHAPTER *5*

Choices by Consumers

After reading this chapter, you will understand the following:

1. The elements involved in consumers' rational choices
2. How consumers balance their choices of goods and services to achieve equilibrium
3. What lies behind the effect of a price change on the quantity of a good demanded
4. Why demand curves have negative slopes
5. Why both consumers and producers gain from exchanges
6. Why the burden of a tax exceeds the revenue raised by government

Before reading this chapter, make sure you know the meaning of the concepts:

1. Substitutes and complements
2. Normal and inferior goods
3. Incidence of a tax

THIS CHAPTER EXPLORES the theory of rational choice as applied to choices made by consumers. Perhaps the first image that comes to mind when you read the words "consumer choice" is one of people filling their shopping carts in a supermarket. The theory of consumer choice does apply in a supermarket, but it is broader than that. It extends to choices involving health and safety, like whether to smoke or whether to wear a seatbelt when driving. It extends to life choices like whether to marry and have children. As we will see in this chapter, it applies to any scenario in which people make choices in order to satisfy their objectives as best they can, given the constraints that they face. This chapter begins by outlining a theory of rational choice by consumers. Later, it will explore a number of applications of the theory, some of them quite ordinary, others more surprising.

Utility and the Rational Consumer

Economic theories have a typical structure that can be described in terms of statements about objectives, constraints, and choices. Theories of consumer choice fit this pattern. The study of consumer choice thus gives us a chance to fill in the general structure of economic theory with some specific content.

Utility

We begin with the question of consumer *objectives*—why is it that people consume goods and services at all? The answer that people usually give when they think about their own motivations is that consumption of goods and services is a source of pleasure and satisfaction. A loaf of bread to eat, a warm bed to sleep in, a book to read—each serves a particular consumer want or need.

Utility

The pleasure, satisfaction, or need fulfillment that people obtain from the consumption of goods and services

Economists use the term **utility** to refer to the pleasure or satisfaction people get from the consumption of goods and services. The term goes back some 200 years to the work of the eccentric English social philosopher Jeremy Bentham (1748–1832). Bentham, who studied English law and came to hate it, was obsessed with reforming the law in a way consistent with the principle of the "greatest good for the greatest number." He thought ordinary words such as *pleasure, satisfaction,* or *happiness* were too weak to convey the power of his vision of maximum bliss; so he coined the new word *utility* and established a movement called utilitarianism to promote the idea. Over the centuries, the term *utility* has lost the mystical overtones that it had for Bentham and his followers; but economists still use it in preference to its more ordinary synonyms when they refer to the objective that consumers pursue when choosing among goods and services.

Constraints on Opportunities

Having established utility as the objective, the next step in constructing the theory of consumer choice is to find a way of describing the constraints that shape the set of opportunities available to consumers. Those constraints encompass all the circumstances that, in a world of scarcity, prevent people from consuming all they want of everything they want.

The most important constraints are limits on the types of goods available, the prices of those goods, and the size of the consumer's budget. A restaurant menu provides a simple example of a constrained opportunity set. You may want tofu salad for lunch, but it is not on the menu. Among the dishes that are on the menu, your favorite might be the filet mignon, but the filet is $24 a serving, and your budget constrains you to spend no more than $5 on lunch. In the end, you settle for a cheeseburger.

To be sure, there are situations in which constraints other than budgets and market prices may be the most important ones. In choosing how fast to drive your car, the "price" (opportunity cost) of greater safety may be taking more time to get where you are going. In choosing a spouse, one constraint is a law that says you can be married to only one person at a time. *Economics in the News 5.1* gives further examples of the many considerations, in addition to prices and budgets, which shape our choices as consumers.

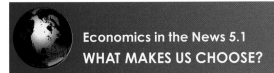

Economics in the News 5.1
WHAT MAKES US CHOOSE?

Economic theory has long focused on prices and consumer budgets as the two biggest factors that shape consumer choices among alternative goods. Certainly no one thinks that these traditional constraints are unimportant. However, the rapidly expanding theory of behavioral economics has shed new light on the many other considerations that affect the way we choose.

Consider the matter of eating popcorn at a movie theater. How much you eat is entirely a rational choice, depending on the price, your budget, and maybe on how hungry you are, right? Wrong! According to Brian Wansink, Cornell Professor and author of the book *Mindless Eating*, rationality has little to do with it. To make his point, Wansink gave away free popcorn to patrons of a suburban Chicago movie theater. The popcorn wasn't even very fresh, but that didn't seem to matter much. What did matter was the size of the container. Some moviegoers got huge buckets of popcorn, while others got truly colossal buckets. Although both sizes held more than a normal person could eat, those with the colossal buckets ate more than those with the merely huge ones. After the experiment was over, the subjects of the experiment had a hard time believing the results. "Things like that don't fool me," one said.

In other experiments, Wansink showed that big dinner plates make

The size of the popcorn container affected how much popcorn was eaten.

people eat more, short, fat glasses that hold exactly the same amount of liquid as tall, skinny ones make portions look smaller and encourage people to drink more; and kitchen cabinets with glass doors, or no doors, cause people to eat more than cabinets that keep the food out of sight. Even the choice of how to arrange items inside our refrigerators can influence how much we eat.

John A. Barg, a professor of psychology at Yale, explains some of the choices we make in terms of the role of the unconscious mind. He sees the unconscious mind as constantly at work making suggestions about choices before our conscious mind takes up the job of making the choice. As an example, he cited one experiment in which a stranger, whose hands were full with a clipboard, books, and other items, asks a student to help out by holding a cup of coffee for a moment. Sometimes it was hot coffee, sometimes iced coffee. When the students were asked to rate a hypothetical individual's personality a few minutes later, those who had recently handled hot coffee described a warm, friendly personality while those who had handled the iced coffee saw the individual as colder and more selfish.

Makers of luxury goods take practical advantage of the power of context to influence our decisions. Have you ever entered a store and wondered who on earth would buy the $14,000 Ralph Lauren handbag or the $6,900 Beefeater barbeque grill? According to Swarthmore College professor Barry Schwarz, luxury goods makers can profit from displaying those items even if no one buys them. Their real purpose is to set a context in which other items that cost a lot, but not quite as much, fall into the category of "affordable luxury." Swartz himself admits to having once bought an $800 suit he didn't need just because it looked reasonable next to others that cost $3,000. "I got sucked in. And I knew what was happening," he says.

SOURCES: For Wansink's work, David Leonhardt, "Your Plate is Bigger than your Stomach," *The New York Times*, May 2, 2007; for Bargh's, Benedict Carey, "Who's Minding the Mind," *The New York Times*, July 31, 2007; for Schwarz's, Christina Binkley, "The Psychology of the $14,000 Handbag," *The Wall Street Journal*, August 9, 2007.

In constructing a theory of the choices consumers make to maximize utility within their budget constraints, we will proceed in two steps. First, we look at a traditional version of the theory based directly on the notion of utility; then we look at a more modern version in which utility plays a less explicit role.

Diminishing Marginal Utility and Consumer Choice

Jeremy Bentham's notion of "the greatest good for the greatest number" was anything but scientific. In the late nineteenth century, economists took a major step forward in their understanding of rational choice by consumers when they developed the principle of diminishing marginal utility The British economist William Stanley Jevons was the first economist to put the new theory into print, but he shares credit for the "marginal revolution" with at least three others who were working along the same lines simultaneously. The Austrian economist Carl Menger also published his version of marginal utility theory in 1871. Three years later, the Swiss economist Leon Walras, who was not aware of the work of Jevons or Menger, came out with still another version. Finally, Alfred Marshall worked out the basics of marginal utility theory at about the same time in his lectures at Cambridge although he did not publish his version until 1890.

The theory of marginal utility was based on the insight that most of the choices consumers make are not all-or-nothing matters (such as whether to take up smoking or to swear off smoking forever); instead, they are incremental decisions (such as whether to order a 12-oz. or a 16-oz. coffee). Whenever economists refer to the effects of doing a little more or a little less of something, they apply the adjective *marginal*. Thus, the **marginal utility** of a good is the amount of added utility that a consumer gains from consuming one more unit of that good, other things being equal.

The most important principle arrived at by Jevons and others is that of **diminishing marginal utility**. According to this principle, the greater the quantity of any good consumed, the less the marginal utility derived from consuming one more unit of that good.

Let's look at how the principle of diminishing marginal utility can be applied to an everyday situation. Assume that you are seated at a lunch counter where pizza is being sold at a price of $2 for a rather skimpy slice and lemonade is being sold at a price of $1 for a small glass. You have $10 to spend on lunch. What will you order?

Your objective is to choose a lunch that will give you the greatest possible utility. Will you spend all your money to buy five pieces of pizza? Probably not. However much you like pizza, you will not get as much satisfaction out of the fifth piece as the first—at least not according to the principle of diminishing marginal utility. Probably you will be willing to pass up the fifth piece of pizza to have a couple of glasses of lemonade with which to wash the first four down. Doing so will increase your total utility because the first two lemonades will give you a lot of satisfaction and the last piece of pizza only a little. How about the fourth piece of pizza? Maybe you will be willing to give up half of it for one more glass of lemonade. As you cut back on pizza and increase your consumption of lemonade, the marginal utility of pizza rises and that of lemonade falls. Finally, you get to the point at which you cannot increase your utility by spending less on one good and more on the other within a given budget. You have reached a point of **consumer equilibrium**.

You reach consumer equilibrium when the marginal utility you get from a dollar's worth of one good equals the marginal utility you get from a dollar's worth of the other. Another way to state this is that the ratio of the marginal utility of a good to its price must be the same for all goods. Thus:

Marginal utility

The amount of added utility gained from a one-unit increase in consumption of a good, other things being equal

Principle of diminishing marginal utility

The principle that the greater the consumption of some good, the smaller the increase in utility from a one-unit increase in consumption of that good

Consumer equilibrium

A state of affairs in which a consumer cannot increase the total utility gained from a given budget by spending less on one good and more on another

$$\frac{\text{Marginal utility of good A}}{\text{Price of good A}} = \frac{\text{Marginal utility of good B}}{\text{Price of good B}}$$

This formula can be applied using an imaginary unit of utility, the "util." Suppose, for example, you have adjusted the quantities of pizza and lemonade you buy so that you get 10 utils from another slice of pizza at a price of $2 per slice and 5 utils from another glass of lemonade at a price of $1 per glass. At these ratios, you get no more added satisfaction from an extra dollar's worth (one half-slice) of pizza than from an extra dollar's worth (one glass) of lemonade. It is not worthwhile to trade off some of either good for some of the other. You are in consumer equilibrium.

On the other hand, suppose you get 18 utils from another slice of pizza (9 utils per half-slice) and 4 from another glass of lemonade, still given the same prices. Now you are not in consumer equilibrium. Cutting back by one lemonade would lose you just 4 utils. You could then use the dollar you saved to buy another half-slice of pizza, thereby gaining 9 utils. By making this adjustment in your consumption pattern, you would not only gain total utility but also move closer to consumer equilibrium because the marginal utility you would get from pizza would fall slightly as you consumed more and the marginal utility you would get from lemonade would rise a little as you consumed less.

Attaching numbers to things in this way helps explain the principle involved. Remember, though, that in practice consumer choice is a much more subjective process. Some people count calories when they sit down to lunch; some count the pennies in their pockets; but no one counts "utils"—they cannot really be counted. Utility is something we feel, not something we think about. Because some people feel differently about what they eat than others do, they make different choices. Perhaps you would rather have a calamari salad and a glass of San Pelegrino than either pizza or lemonade. Although your choice might differ from someone else's, the logic of the decision—the calculation of utility, the concept of equilibrium—is the same.

From Consumer Equilibrium to the Law of Demand

The concepts of consumer equilibrium and diminishing marginal utility can be combined to give an explanation of the law of demand. Suppose you have adjusted your pattern of consumption until you have reached equilibrium in which, among other things,

$$\frac{\text{MU of pizza}}{\$2} = \frac{\text{MU of lemonade}}{\$1}$$

As long as this equality holds, you will not benefit from increasing your consumption of pizza; doing so would soon push down the marginal utility of pizza. The marginal utility per dollar's worth of pizza would drop below the marginal utility per dollar's worth of lemonade, making you better off if you switched back to more lemonade.

What if the price of pizza were to drop to, say, $1.50 per slice, upsetting the equality just given? To make the two ratios equal again, given the new price of pizza, either the marginal utility of lemonade would have to rise or that of pizza would have to fall. According to the principle of diminishing marginal utility, one way to get the marginal utility of pizza to fall is to consume more pizza; and one way to get the marginal utility of lemonade to rise is to consume less lemonade. Perhaps you would do a little of both—that is, cut back a little on lemonade and consume a little more pizza. In so doing, you would be acting just as the law of demand would predict: A decrease in the price of pizza would have caused you to buy more pizza.

This line of reasoning connects the law of demand with the principle of diminishing marginal utility in a way that appeals to common sense. However, that is not good enough for all economists. In the next section, we will look at an alternative line of reasoning.

Substitution and Income Effects

In the view of many economists, the whole concept of utility is suspect because of its subjective, immeasurable nature. Instead, they favor an explanation of the law of demand based on the concepts of substitution and income effects of a change in price. The two approaches to demand are, in a broad sense, consistent; but the explanation based on income and substitution effects avoids the need to measure utility.

The Substitution Effect

One reason people buy more of a good whose price falls is that they tend to substitute a good with a lower price for other goods that are relatively expensive. In our earlier example, we looked at the effects of a drop in the price of pizza. The change in price will cause people to substitute pizza for other foods that they might otherwise have eaten—hamburgers, nachos, whatever. Broader substitutions are also possible. With the price of pizza lower than before, people may substitute eating out for eating at home or a pizza party for an evening at the movies. The portion of the increase in the quantity demanded of a good whose price has fallen, which is caused by the substitution of that good for other goods that are now relatively more costly, is known as the **substitution effect** of a change in price.

Substitution effect

The part of the increase in quantity demanded of a good whose price has fallen that is caused by substitution of that good for others that are now relatively more costly.

The Income Effect

A second reason that the change in a good's price will cause a change in the quantity demanded has to do with the effect of price changes on real income.

In economics, the term *nominal* is used to refer to quantities measured in the ordinary way, in terms of the dollar prices at which transactions actually take place. The term *real* is used to indicate quantities that have been adjusted to take into account the effects of price changes. The distinction between real and nominal income is a typical application of these terms. If your monthly paycheck is $1,000, that is your nominal income—the number of dollars you earn. If your nominal income stays at $1,000 while inflation doubles the average prices of all goods and services, your *real* income—your ability to buy things taking price changes into account—will fall by half. If your nominal income stays at $1,000 while the average prices of goods and services drop by half, your real income will double.

In macroeconomics the distinction between real and nominal income is widely used in connection with inflation, which involves changes in the prices of many goods at once. The distinction, however, can also be applied in microeconomics, which tends to emphasize the effects of price changes for one good at a time. The reason is that if the price of even one good changes, while the prices of other goods remain constant, there will be some effect on the average price level and, hence, on real income.

With this in mind, let's return to our example. Again suppose that the price of pizza falls while your nominal income and the prices of all other goods and services remain the same. Although pizza occupies only a small place in your budget, a fall in its price means a slight fall in the average level of all prices and, hence, a slight increase in your real income. If you continued to buy the same quantity of pizza and other goods and services as before, you would have a little money left over. For example, if the price of pizza goes down by $.50 a slice and you usually buy ten slices a month, you would have $5 left over after making your usual purchases. That is as much of an increase in your real income as you would get if your paycheck were increased by $5 and all prices remained constant.

The question now is: What will you spend the $5 on? The answer: You will use it to buy more of things that are normal goods. If pizza is a normal good, one of the things you will buy with your increased real income is more pizza. The portion of the change in quantity demanded of a good whose price has fallen that is caused by the increase in real income resulting from the drop in price is known as the **income effect** of the price change.

Income effect

The part of the change in quantity demanded of a good whose price has fallen that is caused by the increase in real income resulting from the price change

Income and Substitution Effects and the Demand Curve

In the case of a normal good, the income effect is an additional reason for buying more of a good when its price falls. With both the income and substitution effects causing the quantity demanded to increase when the price falls, the demand curve for a normal good is certain to have a negative slope. We can reach this conclusion with no reference to the awkward concept of utility. So far, so good.

If we are dealing with an inferior good, the situation is a little different. Let's say that hot dogs are an inferior good for you. You eat them if you are hungry and they are all you can afford; but if your income goes up enough to buy pizza, you phase out hot dogs. What will happen if the price of hot dogs goes down while the prices of all other goods and services remain constant?

First, there will be a substitution effect. Hot dogs, now, are relatively cheaper compared with lemonade, pizza, pretzels, haircuts, or whatever. Taken by itself, the substitution effect will cause you to buy more hot dogs. Other things (including real income) being equal, the rational consumer will always buy more rather than less of something when its opportunity cost (in this case, its price relative to other goods) goes down; but here other things are not equal. At the same time that the fall in the price of hot dogs tempts you to substitute hot dogs for other things, it also raises your real income slightly. Taken by itself, the increase in your real income would cause you to buy fewer hot dogs because hot dogs are an inferior good for you. Thus, in the case of an inferior good, the substitution and income effects work at cross-purposes when the price changes.

What, then, is the net effect of a decrease in the price of hot dogs? Will you buy more or fewer of them than before? In the case of a good that makes up only a small part of your budget, such as hot dogs, it is safe to assume that a fall in price will cause you to buy more and a rise in price to buy less. The reason is that a change in the price of something of which you buy only a little anyway will have only a small income effect, which will be outweighed by the substitution effect. Thus, when the substitution effect is larger than the income effect, the demand curve for an inferior good will still have a negative slope.

However, there is a theoretical possibility that the demand curve for an inferior good might have a positive slope. For this to be the case, the good would have to make up a large part of a person's budget so that the income effect would be large. Imagine, for example, a family that is so poor that they spend almost all of their income on food, and almost the only foods they can afford to buy are bread and oatmeal. They eat bread as a special treat on Sunday, but the rest of the week they must make do with inferior-tasting, but cheaper, oatmeal. One day the price of oatmeal goes up, but not by enough to make it more expensive than bread. The rise in the price of oatmeal is devastating to the family's budget. They are forced to cut out their one remaining luxury: The Sunday loaf of bread disappears and is replaced by oatmeal. The paradoxical conclusion, then, is that a rise in the price of oatmeal causes this family to buy more, not less, oatmeal. The family's demand curve for oatmeal has a positive slope. An inferior good that has a positively sloped demand curve because the income effect outweighs the substitution effect is called a **Giffen good** after a nineteenth-century English writer, Robert Giffen, who supposedly mentioned the possibility.[1]

The conditions required for a positively sloped demand curve—an inferior good that makes up a large portion of the consumer's budget—are very special. Such conditions are unlikely to be encountered in the markets in which people usually conduct transactions. If you are in the pizza business—or even in the oatmeal business—you can be virtually certain that, taking the world as it really is, raising the price of any good or service will cause people to buy less of it and cutting the price will cause them to buy more of it. The Giffen-good phenomenon has been demonstrated under carefully controlled experimental circumstances, however, as reported in *Applying Economic Ideas 5.1*. Nothing in the pure logic of rational choice disproves the possibility of such a situation occurring in an actual market situation.

Giffen good

An inferior good accounting for a large share of a consumer's budget that has a positively sloped demand curve because the income effect of a price change outweighs the substitution effect

Applications of Income and Substitution Effects

The law of demand and the concepts of income and substitution effects can be applied to any situation in which a consumer seeks to maximize utility in the face of established alternatives and constraints, even when the "goods" in question are not "for sale," and even when constraints and the opportunity costs of the available alternatives are not stated in money. This section will look at some of the wider applications of the theory of consumer choice.

The Demand for Safety

Let's begin with an example from the field of automobile safety. When you get into a car to go somewhere, you face a trade-off between travel time and safety. A quick trip is good, but so is a safe one. Making the trip safer by driving more

Applying Economic Ideas 5.1
TESTING CONSUMER DEMAND THEORY WITH WHITE RATS

Traditionally, most empirical work in economics uses observation of actual market behavior as its data source. In recent years, however, a growing number of economists have engaged in laboratory experimentation. Many of the experiments involve students as their subjects. For example, a group of students might simulate the operation of a stock exchange, with shares of stocks exchanged for tokens or pennies.

The use of human subjects in economic experiments has its limitations, however. For one thing, it is hard to get subjects to agree to participate in long-term experiments that might change their whole way of life. Moreover, human subjects inevitably are aware that they are participating in an experiment. This awareness might affect their behavior. To get around these drawbacks, economists John Kagel of the University of Houston and Ray Battalio of Texas A&M seized on the idea of using animal subjects in economic experiments. Their pioneering experiments have borne out many of the predictions of consumer choice theory in the laboratory.

For example, in one experiment, two white male rats were placed in standard laboratory cages with food and water freely available. At one end of each cage were two levers that activated dipper cups. One dipper cup provided a measured quantity of root beer when its lever was depressed; the other provided a measured quantity of a different non-alcoholic soft drink, Collins mix. Previous experimentation had shown that rats prefer these beverages to water.

John Kagel and Ray Battalio used rats to test theories on consumer choices.

Within this setup, each rat could be given a fixed "income" of so many pushes on the levers per day. The pushes could be distributed in any way between the two levers. Experimenters could also control the "price" of root beet and Collins mix by determining the number of pushes the rat had to "spend" to obtain one milliliter of liquid.

In an initial experimental run lasting two weeks, the rats were given an income of 300 pushes per day, and both beverages were priced at 20 pushes per milliliter. Under those conditions, rat 1 settled down to a pattern of drinking about 11 milliliters of root beer per day and about 4 milliliters of Collins mix. Rat 2 preferred a diet of almost all root beer, averaging less than one milliliter of Collins mix per day.

Once the initial conditions were established, the experimenters were ready to see how the rats would respond to changes in prices and incomes. First, the price (in pushes per milliliter) of root beer was doubled and the price of Collins mix was cut in half. At the same time, each subject's total income of pushes was adjusted to make it possible for each to afford to continue the previous consumption pattern if it were chosen. (That adjustment in total income was made in order to eliminate any possible income effect of the price change and to concentrate solely on the substitution effect.) Economic theory predicts that under the new conditions the rats would choose to consume more Collins mix and less root beer than before, even though their income would be sufficient to maintain the original pattern of consumption if they chose to do so.

The rats' behavior exactly fitted these predictions. In two weeks of living under the new conditions, rat 1 settled down to a new consumption pattern of about 8 milliliters of root beet and 17 milliliters of Collins mix per day. Rat 2, which had chosen root beer almost exclusively before, switched over to about 9 milliliters of root beer and 25 milliliters of Collins mix.

Another experiment focused on income effects. In this case, the two liquids chosen were root beer, which rats love, and quinine water, which they are more reluctant to drink. At the beginning of the experiment, the price of root beer was set at twice the price of quinine water. If the rats' income of pushes per day was kept low, they would drink some of the relatively cheap quinine water along with some of the more expensive root beer. As their income was raised, they would switch away from quinine water toward more root beer. The conclusion: For rats, root beer is a normal good and quinine water an inferior good.

Having established that quinine water was an inferior good, Kagel and Battalio set out to see if they could demonstrate the Giffen-good effect. That effect requires an inferior good that also accounts for a large part of the subject's total expenditures. To produce these conditions, the rats were kept in "poverty." Their budget was kept so low that without drinking a fair amount of quinine they would become dehydrated.

Without changing the total budget of pushes, the price of quinine water was then reduced. If they maintained their previous consumption pattern, the rats would

continues

have pushes left over. What would they spend the extra pushes on? Root beer, of course. Being able to afford more root beer, the rats could now cut back on their consumption of quinine without risking dehydration. The net result: Cutting the price of quinine with no change in nominal income (pushes per day) caused the rats to drink less quinine. For impoverished rats, quinine water is a true Giffen good.

SOURCES: The root beer-Collins mix experiment is reported in John H. Kagel and Raymond C. Battalio, "Experimental Studies of Consumer Demand Behavior," *Economic Inquiry* 8 (March 1975): 22–38, *Journal of the Western Economic Association.* Reprinted with permission. Kagel and Battalio's root beer–quinine experiment is summarized in Timothy Tregarthen, "Found! A Giffen Good," *The Margin* (October 1987): 8–10.

slowly, stopping for yellow lights, and so on has an opportunity cost in terms of time. Cutting travel time by driving faster and going through yellow lights has an opportunity cost in terms of safety.

If the opportunity costs change, the choices drivers make also tend to change. For example, suppose there is snow on the road; that makes the road less safe and raises the opportunity cost of speed. When it snows, then, drivers slow down and shift their choices away from speed in the interest of safety, just as the substitution effect would predict.

A change in the design of cars to make them safer, for example by adding seat belts as was done starting in the 1960s and air bags as in the 1990s, also changes the opportunity cost of speed relative to that of safety. Cutting travel time by speeding up and running yellow lights entails giving up less safety in a car with seat belts or air bags than in one without those devices. Because the opportunity cost of speed is lower in a safer car, logically the substitution effect would cause people to drive faster and less carefully. Does this really happen? In a classic 1975 study, economist Sam Peltzman reported evidence that it does. In a stunning example of the law of unintended consequences, he reported that while drivers who wore seat belts increased their own safety, they drove faster and less carefully, with the result being that they killed more pedestrians and bicyclists.[2] Since the time of Peltzman's initial work, numerous other studies have confirmed that "offsetting behavior," as it is called, in response to improved risk-avoidance technology is widespread, although it is not always so strong that new safety devices or regulations are completely ineffective.

Some studies have found an income effect as well as a substitution effect on driving behavior. Robert W. Crandall and John D. Graham suggest that safety is an inferior good. It seems that as people's incomes go up, they begin to feel that their time is too valuable to spend in a

Adding seat belts to cars may change the behavior of drivers.

car. Perhaps they speed up so they can get to their high-paying jobs or fashionable parties more quickly. If they decide to run a greater risk of killing themselves and others along the way—well, that is part of the logic of consumer choice. Maybe people with less exciting destinations have less reason to be in a hurry.

Children as Durable Consumer Goods

University of Chicago economist Gary Becker, winner of the 1992 Nobel Memorial Prize for economics, has made his reputation by applying economic reasoning to areas of choice that many people think of as noneconomic. Some of his best-known research concerns choices made within the family. As an example, consider Becker's analysis of the number of children a family chooses to have.

Children, in Becker's view, are durable consumer goods. They return benefits to parents over many years in such forms as love, family pride, and mowing the lawn; but there are opportunity costs associated with having children. Those costs include the goods and services forgone to pay the extra grocery bills, clothing bills, and doctors' bills for the children. In Becker's view, the biggest opportunity cost of having children is the time parents spend caring for them. Time not spent caring for children could be spent working to earn income. Thus the higher the parents' earning power, the greater the opportunity cost of having children.

What does this imply about the number of children a family chooses to have? It has been widely observed in many societies that as family income rises, the number of children per family tends to fall. Does this mean that children are inferior goods? Not at all, says Becker. Children are normal goods; other things being equal, the income

Gary S. Becker, left, from the University of Chicago, receives the 1992 Nobel Economics Prize from Sweden's King Carl Gustav in Stockholm, Sweden.

effect would cause a family to want more children as its income increases. But other things are not equal. As Becker notes, there is also a substitution effect because if the higher income reflects a higher hourly wage, it increases the opportunity cost of each hour spent caring for children. On the average, the substitution effect outweighs the income effect, so higher-income families end up having fewer children.

As confirmation of his analysis, Becker notes that the income and substitution effects can be partially distinguished by looking separately at the effects of changes in men's and women's incomes. Traditionally, women perform a greater proportion of childcare than men. In a family where this is the case, an increase in a woman's income would have a stronger substitution effect than an increase in a man's income. The reason is that, in such a family, a woman with a high income would encounter a high opportunity cost for each hour taken off from work to devote to childcare, whereas, by assumption, the man would take few hours off for childcare regardless of his income. Empirical data, in fact, reveal such a pattern to be prevalent: Birth rates tend to vary directly with incomes earned by men because the income effect outweighs the relatively weak substitution effect. Birth rates vary inversely, however, with incomes earned by women, who experience a relatively stronger substitution effect.

What is it that parents substitute for a greater quantity of children when their incomes rise? Some, no doubt, substitute ski vacations in Austria, BMWs, and other luxuries. Becker notes, however, they have another reaction as well, one that is consistent with the theory of consumer choice. In place of a greater number of children, he says, upper-income families substitute investment in higher-quality children: piano lessons from the age of five, tutors to help cram for SAT exams, tuition payments to Yale Law School. It's all so *rational*, says Becker.

Consumer Surplus

This chapter has related consumer choice to the demand curve from two perspectives—that of utility theory and that of income and substitution effects. In both cases, the demand curve was viewed as answering the question, How much of a good will consumers wish to purchase at any given price? In this section, we turn to a different question to which the demand curve also can provide an answer: How much will consumers be willing to pay for an additional unit of a good, given the quantity they already have?

The Demand Curve as Willingness to Pay

Figure 5.1 shows a demand curve for apples for a college student, Hannah Lee. Lee stocks up on snack foods at a local supermarket and often includes apples in her purchases. The demand curve given in the figure shows that the number of apples she eats each month depends on their price. Currently the price of an apple is $.40. At this price, she buys ten per month. On other days, she substitutes an orange or a banana.

The demand curve indicates that $.40 is the maximum that Lee would be willing to pay for the tenth apple. If the price rose to $.45, she would substitute some other fruit for the tenth apple. However, she would not cut out apples altogether. Although

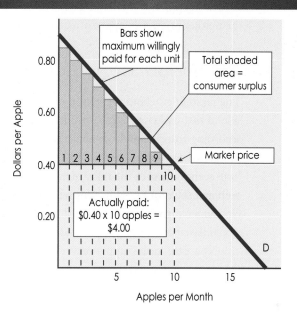

FIGURE 5.1   CONSUMER SURPLUS

The height of a demand curve shows the maximum that this consumer would be willing to pay for an additional unit of a good. For example, she would be willing to pay up to $.85 for the first apple bought each month but only $.55 for the seventh. A vertical bar shows the maximum she would willingly pay for each unit. In this case, the market price is $.40; thus, she buys 10 apples a month, paying a total of $4.00. The difference between what she actually pays at the market price and the maximum she would have been willing to pay, shown by the shaded area, is called consumer surplus.

$.40 is the maximum she is willing to pay for the tenth apple, she would not give up the ninth apple unless the price rose above $.45. Similarly, she would be willing to pay up to $.50 before giving up the eighth apple, up to $.55 before giving up the seventh, and so on. The height of the demand curve at each point (emphasized here by a vertical bar) shows the maximum that she would willingly pay for each unit consumed. That maximum decreases as the quantity consumed increases, in accordance with the principle of diminishing marginal utility.

Measuring the Surplus

Figure 5.1 shows the maximum that Lee is willing to pay for various quantities of apples, but it also shows that she need not actually pay this amount. At the going price of $.40, she pays only a total of $4 for the ten apples she buys each month. Except in the case of the last unit purchased, she gets each unit for less than what she would willingly have paid for it. The difference between what she would willingly have paid for each unit and the amount actually paid at the market price is called the **consumer surplus** for that unit. The shaded portion of the corresponding vertical bar shows the consumer surplus on each unit. For example, the surplus on the first apple, for which Lee would have willingly paid $.85 if necessary, is $.45, because she actually paid only

Consumer surplus

The difference between the maximum that a consumer would be willing to pay for a unit of a good and the amount that he or she actually pays

$.40. The total consumer surplus on all units purchased is shown by the sum of the shaded portions of the bars. The area of the triangle between the demand curve and the market price is an approximate measure of consumer surplus.[3]

Consumer Surplus, Producer Surplus, and Gains from Exchange

The reasoning behind the notion of consumer surplus can be extended to the producers' side of the market as well. Consider Figure 5.2, which shows a typical market operating according to principles of supply and demand. The equilibrium market price is established at the point where the supply and demand curves cross. The demand curve, as we have seen, measures the maximum amount that consumers would be willing to pay for each unit sold; for example, they will pay no more than $1.50 for the one thousandth unit. Consumer surplus is a measure of the difference between the maximum that consumers would have been willing to pay and what they actually pay at the market price.

Now turn to the supply curve. The height of the supply curve at any point represents the minimum that producers would willingly accept for the unit. For example, producers

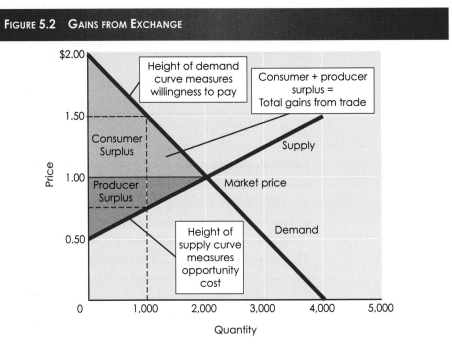

FIGURE 5.2   GAINS FROM EXCHANGE

This figure shows that both consumers and producers gain from exchange. Here the equilibrium market price is $1 per unit. The demand curve shows the maximum that consumers would willingly pay for each unit. Consumers' gain from exchange takes the form of consumer surplus, shown by the area between the demand curve and the market price. The supply curve shows the minimum that producers would willingly accept rather than put their resources to work elsewhere. Producers earn a surplus equal to the difference between what they actually receive at the market price and the minimum they would have been willing to accept. The area between the supply curve and the market price shows the producer surplus. Assuming equilibrium is reached at the point of intersection of the two curves, total gains from exchange are thus the entire area between them up to the intersection.

would be unwilling to accept less than $.75 for the one thousandth unit sold. If they could not get at least that much, the producers would divert their resources to an alternative use rather than produce the one thousandth unit of this product.

However, as the figure is drawn, producers receive the market price of $1 per unit for all units sold, including the one thousandth. On that unit, they earn a producer surplus of $.25. The **producer surplus** earned on each unit is the difference between the market price and the minimum that the producers would have been willing to accept in exchange for that unit—the difference between $1 and $.75 for the one thousandth unit in our example. The area between the supply curve and the market price shows the total producer surplus earned on all units.

We see, then, that the concept of surplus in the market is symmetrical. Consumers buy the goods, except for the very last unit, for less than the maximum amount they would have been willing to pay, and producers sell the goods, except for the very last unit, for more than the minimum amount they would have been willing to accept. Thus, *both buyers and sellers gain from exchange.* That is why markets exist. As long as participation is voluntary, markets make everyone who buys and sells in them better off than they would be if they did not participate. Assuming an equilibrium at the intersection of the supply and demand curves, as in Figure 5.2, the total of the mutual gains from exchange—consumer surplus plus producer surplus—is equal to the entire shaded triangle between the supply and demand curves to the left of their intersection point.

Application: the Excess Burden of a Tax

Figure 5.3 provides an application of the concepts of consumer and producer surplus to the effects of a price of a tax on gasoline. Imposing a $1.00-per-gallon tax on gasoline shifts the supply curve upward by that amount and raises the equilibrium price, including tax, from $2.00 to $2.80 per gallon. The price received by sellers, after tax, falls from $2.00 to $1.80 per gallon.

The concepts of consumer and producer surplus offer additional insight into the issue of tax incidence beyond those we gain by looking at price changes alone. Figure 5.3 shows that the tax brings in $8 million per day in revenue to the government. This equals the after-tax quantity Q_2, which is 8 million gallons, times the amount of the tax, which is $1.00 per gallon. Part of that revenue is paid by consumers at the expense of the consumer surplus they otherwise would have earned by being able to buy 8 million gallons at $2.00 rather than at $2.80. Part is paid by suppliers at the expense of the producer surplus they would have earned by being able to sell 8 million gallons at $2.00 rather than at $1.80. The sum of that part of the consumers' burden and that part of the producers' burden is equal to the tax revenue collected by the government.

However, there is an additional burden on consumers and producers that is not reflected in the government's revenue from the tax. That burden is associated with the reduction in quantity purchased from 10 million to 8 million gallons per day because of the tax. Consumers would have enjoyed a surplus on the extra 2 million gallons equal to the triangle above the pretax price of $2.00 between Q_1 and Q_2; producers would have enjoyed a surplus equal to the triangle below the pretax price between Q_1 and Q_2. The lost consumer-plus-producer surplus is called the **excess burden of the tax**.

Producer surplus

The difference between what producers receive for a unit of a good and the minimum they would be willing to accept

Excess burden of the tax

The part of the economic burden of a tax that takes the form of consumer and producer surplus that is lost because the tax reduces the equilibrium quantity sold

FIGURE 5.3   EXCESS BURDEN OF A TAX

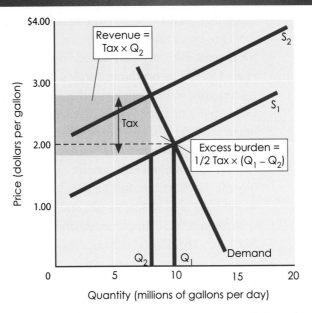

Imposition of a tax of $1.00 per gallon on gasoline raises the equilibrium price from $2.00 to $2.80 per gallon. The price that sellers receive after the tax is paid falls to $1.80. Revenue collected by the government equals the tax times Q_2, the equilibrium quantity after tax. The economic burden of the revenue is divided between consumers and sellers. There is also an excess burden, which takes the form of the consumer and producer surpluses that would be realized from the sale of the additional quantity that would have been sold without the tax. This is shown by the area of the triangle between the supply and demand curves and between the pretax quantity, Q_1, and the after-tax quantity, Q_2.

The common sense behind this is that the tax imposes a burden on consumers and producers that is larger than the amount the government takes in as revenue. It does so because the tax discourages buyers and sellers from doing as much business as they would have done without the tax. The potential mutual gain from pushing exchange in the gasoline market all the way out to 10 million gallons per day is lost. In geometric terms, the size of the excess burden can be calculated by applying the rule that the area of a triangle equals one-half of its height times its base. The height is the tax ($1.00), and the base is $Q_1 - Q_2$ (2 million gallons). Thus, the excess burden is $1 million per day. The total burden on consumers plus producers equals the $8 million collected by the government plus this $1 million excess burden, or $9 million.

The example can be generalized to all taxes because virtually any tax causes firms or individuals to change their behavior by engaging in less of the taxed activity. For instance, income taxes have an excess burden related to their reduction of incentives to work and save. Similarly, tariffs (taxes on imports) have an excess burden related to the fact that they discourage international trade. The excess burden of taxes is just as much a part of the opportunity cost of the services that the government supplies as are the taxes actually collected by the government.

Summary

1. **What elements are involved in consumers' rational choices?** Objectives and constraints on opportunities provide the setting for rational choice by consumers. Consumers are said to choose rationally when they set goals and make systematic efforts to achieve them. The objective of consumer choice is *utility*—the pleasure and satisfaction that people get from goods and services. The added utility obtained from a one-unit increase in consumption of a good or service is its *marginal utility*. The greater the rate of consumption of a good, the smaller the increase in utility from an additional unit consumed.

2. **How do consumers balance their choices of goods and services to achieve equilibrium?** *Consumer equilibrium* is said to occur when shifting spending from one good to another cannot increase the total utility obtained from a given budget. In equilibrium, the marginal utility of a dollar's worth of one good must equal the marginal utility of a dollar's worth of any other good.

3. **What lies behind the effect of a price change on the quantity of a good demanded?** The change in quantity demanded that results from a change in a good's price, other things being equal, could be separated into two parts. The part that comes from the tendency to substitute cheaper goods for more costly ones is the *substitution effect*. The part that comes from the increase in real income that results from a decrease in the price of the good, other things being equal, is the *income effect*.

4. **Why do demand curves have negative slopes?** For a normal good, the substitution and income effects work in the same direction. The demand curves for normal goods, therefore, have negative slopes. For inferior goods, the income effect and the substitution effect work in opposite directions. For inferior goods, therefore, the demand curve will have a negative slope only if the substitution effect outweighs the income effect. In

practice, this is virtually always the case although *Giffen goods* with positively sloped demand curves are a theoretical possibility.

5. **Why do both consumers and producers gain from exchange?** When consumers buy a product at a given market price, they pay the same amount for each unit purchased. However, because of the *principle of diminishing marginal utility*, the first units purchased are worth more to them than the last ones purchased. The difference between what consumers actually pay for a unit of a good and the maximum they would be willing to pay is the *consumer surplus* gained on that unit of the good. Similarly, the difference between what sellers actually receive for a good and the minimum they would have accepted is known as *producer surplus*.

6. **Why does the burden of a tax exceed the revenue raised by government?** When a tax is imposed on a good or service, the equilibrium price, including the tax, rises while the equilibrium price net of the tax falls. As a result, the equilibrium quantity falls, making both consumers and producers forgo some surplus. The forgone surplus is not captured in the form of tax revenue and is called the *excess burden of the tax*. It is a burden on consumers and producers over and above the sum that the government collects as tax revenue.

Key Terms

Problems and Topics for Discussion

1. **Externalities of automobile safety** The increase in deaths of pedestrians and bicyclists resulting from drivers' use of seat belts or air bags is an example of an *externality*, a concept introduced in Chapter 4. What could the government do to prevent this externality while still achieving the goal of increased driver safety? Bonus question: If you complete the appendix to this chapter, analyze the trade-off between speed and safety using an indifference curve diagram. How does the installation of seat belts in a car change the budget line?

2. **Can there be increasing marginal utility?** Can there be increasing marginal utility in some cases? For example, suppose it would take eight rolls of wallpaper to decorate your kitchen. If someone gave you seven rolls of wallpaper, you would get only limited utility from them. An eighth roll, however, would give you great utility. Do you think this is a valid exception to the principle of diminishing marginal utility?

3. **Consumer equilibrium, marginal utility, and prices** Martha Smith consumes two pounds of pork and five pounds of beef per month. She pays $1.50 a pound for the pork and $2 per pound for the beef. What can you say about the ratio of the marginal utility of pork to the marginal utility of beef, assuming that this pattern represents a state of consumer equilibrium for Smith? Is the ratio 3/4, 4/3, 5/2, 2/5, or none of these?

4. **Excess burden of a tax** Figure 3.5 in Chapter 3 demonstrates the incidence of a tax on apartment rents. Using the approach outlined in this chapter, calculate the revenue raised by this tax and the excess burden of the tax. How much of the excess burden is borne by landlords? How much by tenants?

Case for Discussion

Fears Grow as Rice Prices Hit Record High

Rice prices rose more than 10 percent yesterday to a record high as African countries joined southeast Asian importers in the race to head off social unrest by securing supplies from the handful of exporters still selling the grain in the international market.

The rise in prices—50 per cent in two weeks—threatens upheaval and has resulted in riots and soldiers overseeing supplies in some emerging countries in which the grain is a staple food for about 3 billion people.

The increase also risks stoking further inflation in emerging countries, which have been suffering the impact of record oil prices and the rise in price of other agricultural commodities—including wheat, maize [corn] and vegetable oil—in the past year.

Kamal Nath, India's trade minister, said the government would crack down on hoarding of essential commodities to keep a lid on food prices. "We will not hesitate to take the strongest possible measures, including using some of the legal provisions that we have against hoarding," he said yesterday.

Food aid officials said consumption could rise further because record food prices are forcing families to move from a diversified diet to just one staple.

Farmers delaying their harvest and middleman hoarding stocks were also contributing to the crisis, said governments and traders.

SOURCE: Javier Blas and Roel Landingin, "Fears Grow over Rice Supplies as Prices Hit Record," *Financial Times*, April 5, 2008, p. 1.

QUESTIONS

1. Why have the prices of all grains tended to rise together? Does this give you any clue as to whether consumers treat the goods as complements or as substitutes?

2. Why would an increase in the price of a good like rice lead to hoarding and delayed harvest? Do you think laws preventing hoarding will make things better for consumers in the short run? In the long run?

3. Why are food officials worried that an increase in the price of rice could cause an increase in rice consumption? Explain in terms of the income and substitution effects. What does this possibility suggest about the slope of the demand curve for rice? *Bonus question: Using tools introduced in the appendix, sketch a set of indifference curves and budget lines to illustrate the case in which an increase in the price of rice leads to an increase in the quantity demanded.*

End Notes

1. The positive slope of the demand curve for a Giffen good assumes a fully rational consumer. The Case for Discussion in Chapter 4 introduced the possibility that goods, like house-brand supermarket goods, may also have positively-sloped demand curves, but for a different reason. In the case of house brand goods, consumers buy less of a product that is "too cheap" because bounded rationality causes them to rely on a rule of thumb that associates higher price with higher quality.

2. Sam Peltzman, "The Effects of Automobile Safety Regulation," *Journal of Political Economy* 83 (August 1975): 677–725. In a follow-up study, Robert W. Crandall and John D. Graham ("Automobile Safety Regulation and Offsetting Behavior: Some New Empirical Estimates," *American Economic Review* 74 (May 1984): 328–331) also found that safety regulation had unintended consequences on driving behavior.

3. An advanced microeconomics course would explain that for reasons associated with the income effect, the triangle does not provide a precise measure of consumer surplus. However, the approximation is close for goods that make up only a small part of consumers' total expenditures.

Appendix to Chapter 5:
INDIFFERENCE CURVES

This chapter described two versions of the theory of consumer choice—one based on marginal utility and the other on income and substitution effects. This appendix gives a third version that can be related to the other two, using what are known as *indifference curves*. Indifference curves are not featured in this book, but they are often used in intermediate- and advanced-level economic writings. Many students and instructors find it worthwhile to study them, even if briefly, as part of an introductory course. This appendix will serve their needs.

Constructing an Indifference Curve

Begin by supposing that I am an experimenter and you are my subject. I want to find out how you feel about consuming various quantities of meat and cheese. It would be convenient if I had a utility meter, but I do not. Therefore, to find out your attitudes toward the consumption of these goods, I offer you a number of baskets (two at a time) containing varying amounts of meat and cheese.

As I offer each pair of baskets, I ask: "Would you prefer the one on the left to the one on the right? Would you prefer the one on the right to the one on the left? Or are you indifferent between the two?" In this way, I hope to get a meaningful answer from you. I know I have a better chance of getting such an answer this way than I would if I asked you how many utils you would get from each basket.

At some point in the experiment, I offer you basket A, which contains eight pounds of meat and three pounds of cheese, and basket B, which contains six pounds of meat and four pounds of cheese. I ask you the usual questions, and you answer that you are indifferent between the two baskets. You feel that the extra pound of cheese in basket B just makes up for the fact that it has two pounds less meat than basket A. This gives me a useful bit of information: It tells me that for you baskets A and B belong to an **indifference set**—a set of consumption choices each of which yields the same amount of satisfaction such that no member of the set is preferred to any other. Exploring the matter further, I find that two other baskets, C and D, also belong to the same indifference set, which now has the following four members:

Indifference set

A set of consumption choices, each of which yields the same utility so that no member of the set is preferred to any other

Basket	Meat (Pounds)	Cheese (Pounds)
A	8	3
B	6	4
C	5	5
D	4	7

Having thanked you for taking part in my experiment, I get out a piece of graph paper. First I draw a pair of axes, as in Figure 5A.1. Pounds of meat are measured on the horizontal axis and pounds of cheese on the vertical axis. Each basket of goods can be

FIGURE 5A.1   AN INDIFFERENCE CURVE

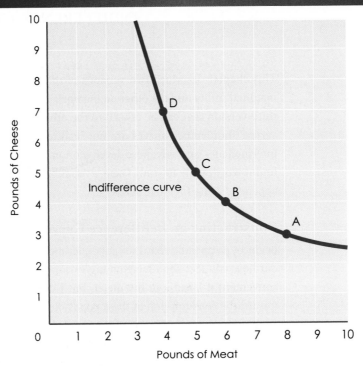

Each point in this diagram stands for a basket of meat and cheese. A, B, C, and D are baskets among which a certain consumer is indifferent. All give equal utility. Those points and all the others on a smooth curve connecting them form an indifference set. An indifference curve is a graphical representation of an indifference set.

shown as a point in the area between the two axes. The points representing baskets A B, C, and D are shown in their proper places on the graph. These points and all those between them that lie on the smooth curve joining them are members of the same indifference set. The curve itself is an **indifference curve**—a curve composed of points that are all members of the same indifference set.

Indifference curve

A graphical representation of an indifference set

Some Characteristics of Indifference Curves

Indifference curves have characteristics that reflect certain regularities in patterns of consumer preferences. Five of these are of interest to us:

1. *Indifference curves normally have negative slopes.* For example, the curve in Figure 5A.2 is not possible if both meat and cheese are desired goods—that is, if the consumer prefers more to less, other things being equal. The basket shown by point A contains more of both goods than that shown by point B. This implies that if greater amounts of meat and cheese give greater satisfaction, A must be preferred to B; it cannot be a member of the same indifference set as B.

2. *The absolute value of the slope of an indifference curve at any point is the ratio of the marginal utility of the good on the horizontal axis to the marginal utility of the good on the*

FIGURE 5A.2 INDIFFERENCE CURVES HAVE NEGATIVE SLOPES

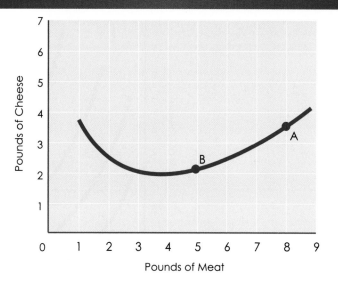

Indifference curves normally have negative slopes. The positively sloped portion of the indifference curve shown here is impossible if both goods give increased satisfaction with increased quantity. A has more of both goods than B. Therefore, point A should be preferred to point B and, hence, could not lie on the same indifference curve.

vertical axis. For example, look at Figure 5A.1. Between D and C, the slope of the curve is approximately −2 (or simply 2 when the minus sign is removed to give the absolute value). This shows that the marginal utility of meat is approximately twice that of cheese when the amounts consumed are in the region of baskets C and D. Because the marginal utility of meat is twice that of cheese in this region, the consumer will feel neither a gain nor a loss in total utility in trading basket D for basket C—that is, in giving up two pounds of cheese for one extra pound of meat. Because it shows the rate at which meat can be substituted for cheese without a gain or loss in satisfaction, the slope of the indifference curve is called the **marginal rate of substitution** of meat for cheese.

Marginal rate of substitution

The rate at which one good can be substituted for another with no gain or loss in satisfaction

3. *Indifference curves are convex; their slopes decrease as one moves downward and to the right along them.* This implies that the ratio of the marginal utility of meat to the marginal utility of cheese (or the marginal rate of substitution of meat for cheese) decreases as one moves downward and to the right along the curve. Look once more at Figure 5A.1. In the region between D and C the slope of the curve is approximately −2, indicating that the ratio of the marginal utility of meat to that of cheese is approximately 2:1. By comparison, in the region between B and A the slope is only about −1/2. The substitution of meat for cheese has caused the ratio of the marginal utility of meat to the marginal utility of cheese to fall to approximately 1:2.

4. *An indifference curve can be drawn through the point that represents any basket of goods.* Figure 5A.3 shows the same indifference curve as in Figure 5A.1, but here the curve is labeled I_1. Point E, which represents a basket containing seven pounds of meat and five

FIGURE 5A.3   MULTIPLE INDIFFERENCE CURVES

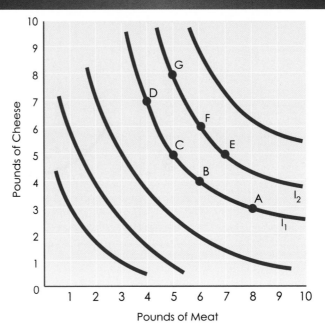

An indifference curve can be drawn through any point. Here curve I$_1$ represents an indifference set containing points A, B, C, and D, and I$_2$ represents a set including points E, F, and G. All points on I2 are preferred to all points on I$_1$. A representative set of indifference curves like the one shown here can be called an *indifference map*.

pounds of cheese, is not a member of the indifference set represented by this curve. Because it lies above and to the right of point B and has more of both products than B, it must be preferred to B. Other points, such as F and G, have more cheese and less meat than E and, on balance, give the same satisfaction as E. The consumer is indifferent among E, F, G, and all other points on curve I$_2$ and prefers all of these points to any of those on I$_1$.

Any point taken at random, along with the other points that happen to give the same amount of satisfaction, can form an indifference curve. Several other (unlabeled) curves are sketched in Figure 5A.3. Were all possible curves drawn in, they would be so close together that the lines would run into a solid sheet, completely filling the space between the axes. A selection of indifference curves showing their general pattern but leaving enough space to make the graph easy to read is called an **indifference map**.

Indifference curves do not cross. Consumer preferences have **transitivity**, meaning that if you prefer A to B and B to C, you will prefer A to C. Looking at Figure 5A.4, you can see that crossed indifference curves are not possible. Consider points A, B, and C. A and B lie on the same indifference curve, I$_1$; hence, the consumer is indifferent between them. A and C both lie on I$_2$; thus, the consumer is indifferent between them, too. Because consumer preferences are transitive, if B is as good as A and A is as good as C, C is as good as B. However, C lies above and to the right of B. It represents a mix of goods that contains more of both meat and cheese. If more is better, the consumer must prefer C to B. Because crossed indifference curves imply a contradictory set of preferences, we must conclude that they cannot cross.

Indifference map

A selection of indifference curves for a single consumer and pair of goods

Transitivity

The principle that if A is preferred to B and B is preferred to C, A must be preferred to C.

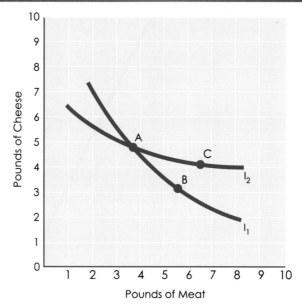

FIGURE 5A.4 INDIFFERENCE CURVES CANNOT CROSS

Because consumer preferences are transitive, indifference curves cannot cross. The impossible curves shown here represent contradictory preferences. A and B are both on I_1; therefore, the consumer must be indifferent between them. A and C are both on I_2; hence, the consumer must be indifferent between them as well. Transitivity implies that the consumer is indifferent between B and C, but this is impossible because C contains more of both goods than B does.

The Budget Line

The range of choices open to a consumer with a given budget and with given prices can be shown on the same kind of graph we have used for indifference curves. Figure 5A.5 shows how this can be done. Suppose you have a food budget of $10 per week; the price of meat is $2 a pound, and the price of cheese is $1 a pound. If you spend all your money on meat, you can have up to five pounds of meat; if you spend all your money on cheese, you can have up to ten pounds of cheese. Combinations such as two pounds of meat and six of cheese or four pounds of meat and two of cheese are also possible. Taking into account the possibility of buying a fraction of a pound of meat or cheese, these choices can be shown on the graph as a diagonal line running from 10 on the cheese axis to 5 on the meat axis. Such a line is called a budget line.

Using m to stand for amount of meat and c for amount of cheese, the equation for the budget line can be written as

$$2m + 1c = 10.$$

This equation simply says that the number of pounds of meat bought times the price of meat plus the number of pounds of cheese bought times the price of cheese must add up to the total budget if all the money is spent. In more general terms, the

Budget line

A line showing the various combinations of goods and services that can be purchased at given prices with a given budget

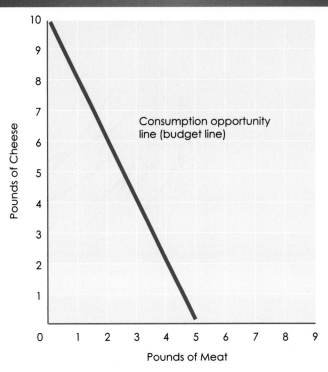

FIGURE 5A.5   THE BUDGET LINE

Consumption opportunity
line (budget line)

Pounds of Cheese

Pounds of Meat

Suppose you have a food budget of $10 per week. You can spend your money on meat at $2 a pound, on cheese at $1 a pound, or on some mix of the two. The consumption opportunity line (budget line) shows all the possible combinations given these prices and your budget.

equation for a budget line for goods x and y—with P_x the price of x, P_y the price of y, and B the consumer's total budget is

$$P_xX + P_yY = B.$$

The slope of such a budget line is $-P_x/P_y$. In the case shown in Figure 5A.5, where the price of meat is $2 a pound and the price of cheese is $1 a pound, the slope of the budget line is –2.

A Graphic Representation of Consumer Equilibrium

Indifference curves and the budget line can be used to give a graphic representation of consumer equilibrium. Figure 5A.6 shows the budget line from Figure 5A.5 superimposed on an indifference map like the one shown in Figure 5A.3. In this way, we can easily compare consumer preferences and consumption choices. For example, point B is preferred to point A because it lies on a "higher" indifference curve (one that at some point, such as C, passes above and to the right of A). By similar reasoning, point B is preferred to point D. Of all the points on or below the budget line, it is clear that point E, which represents two and a half pounds of meat and five pounds of cheese, is the most preferred, because all the other points on it lie on lower indifference curves. Every point that is better (like F) lies outside the range of consumption choices.

FIGURE 5A.6　CONSUMER EQUILIBRIUM

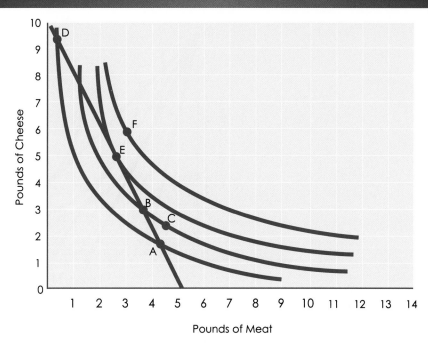

E is the point of consumer equilibrium given the indifference curves and budget line shown. All points that are better than E (such as F) lie outside the budget line. All other points for goods that the consumer can afford to buy (such as A and D) lie on lower indifference curves than E and hence are less preferred.

Because E is the point that gives the greatest possible satisfaction, it is the point of consumer equilibrium. At E, the relevant indifference curve is just tangent to the budget line; this means that the slopes of the curve and the budget line are the same at that point. The slope of the indifference curve, as shown earlier, equals the ratio of the marginal utility of meat to the marginal utility of cheese. The slope of the budget line equals the ratio of the price of meat to the price of cheese. Thus, it follows that in consumer equilibrium,

$$\frac{\text{Marginal utility of meat}}{\text{Marginal utility of cheese}} = \frac{\text{Price of meat}}{\text{Price of cheese}}$$

This is a restatement of the condition for consumer equilibrium given in this chapter.

Derivation of the Demand Curve

This appendix concludes with Figure 5A.7, which shows how a demand curve for meat can be derived from a set of indifference curves. Along with the curves, Figure 5A.7 shows a set of budget lines. Each line is based on the assumption that the price of cheese is $1 a pound and the consumer's budget is $10, as before. Now, however, each budget line assumes a different price, P_m, of meat. The budget line running from 10 on the vertical axis to 2.5 on the horizontal axis assumes that $P_m = \$4$. The budget line running from 10 on the vertical axis to 5 on the horizontal axis assumes that $P_m = \$2$. (This is the same budget line as the one in Figures 5A.5 and 5A.6.) The other two budget lines assume that $P_m = \$1.50$ and $P_m = \$1$, respectively.

FIGURE 5A.7   DERIVATION OF A DEMAND CURVE

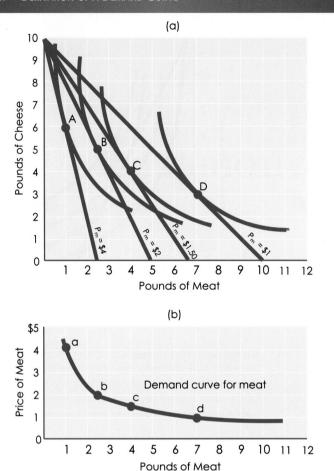

Part (a) of this figure shows a consumer's indifference map for meat and cheese and a set of budget lines. Each budget line corresponds to a different price, P_m, of meat. All four budget lines assume the price of cheese to be $1 and the total budget to be $10. Points A, B, C, and D in part (a) show the choices the consumer makes at meat prices of $4, $2, $1.50, and $1. In part (b), the data on meat consumption at the various prices is plotted on a new set of axes. The smooth line connecting points a, b, c, and d is the consumer's demand curve for meat.

The equilibrium pattern of consumption differs for each price of meat, other things being equal. When P_m = $4, point A, which represents six pounds of cheese and one pound of meat, is the best the consumer can do; when P_m = $2, B is the most preferred point. Given this information, it is a simple matter to draw the consumer's demand curve for meat. Part (b) of Figure 5A.7 shows a new set of axes, with the quantity of meat on the horizontal axis as before but the price of meat on the vertical axis. From part (a) of Figure 5A.7 when P_m = $4, the consumer chooses combination A, which includes one pound of meat. In part (b), therefore, point a is marked as the quantity of meat demanded at a price of $4; then point b, which corresponds to point B in part (a), is added; and so on. Drawing a smooth line through points a, b, c, and d gives the consumer's demand curve for meat. As expected, it has the downward slope predicted by the law of demand.

CHAPTER *6*

The Economics of Climate Change and Environmental Policy

After reading this chapter, you will understand the following:

1. How the price of a good or service affects the quantity demanded by buyers
2. How other market conditions affect demand
3. How the price of a good affects the quantity supplied by sellers
4. How other market conditions affect supply
5. How supply and demand interact to determine the market price of a good or service
6. Why market prices and quantities change in response to changes in market conditions
7. How price supports and price ceilings affect the operations of markets

Before reading this chapter, make sure you know the meaning of the concepts:

1. Spontaneous order
2. Markets
3. Opportunity cost
4. Law of unintended consequences

I N CHAPTER 4 we introduced the term externality to refer to effects of production or consumption that have an impact on third parties. Problems of pollution, ranging from local smog to global climate change, are examples of externalities. They hinder the efficient operation of the price system because harm to pollution victims is not reflected in market prices. As a result, users of the product that causes the pollution receive a false signal that tells them "use more," when the true opportunity cost would tell them "use less."

For example, when you fill the gas tank on your car, the price at the pump reflects costs of extracting the crude oil, transporting it, refining it, and distributing it through the retail network. However, the price does not reflect the damage done locally, and to the whole planet, as a result of carbon dioxide and other greenhouse gasses emitted through your tailpipe. According to widely used scientific models, these greenhouse gasses contribute to global warming. The gradual average warming of the planet, in turn, has the potential to trigger many types of climate change, including not just changes in temperature, but also in rainfall patterns, storm tracks, ocean currents, and so on. On balance, the changes in climate appear more likely to be harmful than helpful. This chapter takes a closer look at the problem of climate change and other pollution issues, and at potential solutions that attempt to restore the efficient working of price systems.

Pollution Abatement as a Problem of Scarcity

Pollution, says the *American Heritage Dictionary*, is "the contamination of soil, water, or the atmosphere by noxious substances." That is a fine definition—from the victim's point of view. An understanding of pollution as an economic problem, however, must take into account the polluter's point of view as well. People do not—at least we hope they do not—pollute the environment just for the fun of it. Instead, they pollute because it is an inexpensive way of getting rid of wastes from production or consumption. Seen from this perspective, it is clear that pollution is a problem of scarcity. The earth's scarce air, water, and other resources cannot absorb unlimited waste disposal without serious damage.

The Costs of Pollution Abatement

Most of the types of pollution that dominate the news involve noxious gases, toxic chemicals, and bulky solids that are byproducts of commercial activities. Left to their own devices, polluters have an incentive to choose the lowest-cost method of getting rid of these byproducts, which often means discharging them directly into the environment. *Pollution abatement* means taking measure to reduce discharge of harmful byproducts into the environment through changes in production methods, recycling, capture and storage, or other methods. Pollution abatement reduces the impact on the environment; but, at the same time, it increases the cost to the polluter of waste disposal.

Figure 6.1 illustrates the cost of pollution abatement with the example of carbon dioxide (CO_2) emissions from a coal-burning power plant. If no abatement measures are undertaken, the amount of CO_2 emitted by the plant is marked "business as usual." Beginning from that point, the plant could reduce emissions using several strategies, some more effective, but also more expensive, than others. The least expensive

Toxic chemicals are a major concern in dealing with the pollution of the environment.

FIGURE 6.1   COST OF POLLUTION ABATEMENT

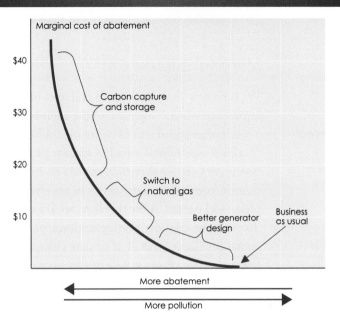

This graph shows the marginal cost of abatement for the case of carbon dioxide emitted by a coal-fired electric power plant. With no pollution control, the plant would emit an amount of CO_2 shown as "business as usual." The cheapest method of pollution abatement, improving the efficiency of the generating equipment, could eliminate about a third of the pollution at a cost of less that $10 per ton. Switching to natural gas would eliminate more pollution, and using still-experimental carbon capture and storage technology could eliminate almost all of it. As pollution is progressively reduced, more and more expensive abatement technologies must be introduced. For that reason, as the amount of pollution decreases, the marginal cost of abatement Increase.

Marginal cost of abatement

The cost of reducing waste discharged into the environment by one unit

approach would be to improve the efficiency of the generating equipment. All of the CO_2 from burning the coal would still be released into the atmosphere, but less coal would have to be burned per kilowatt-hour of electricity. Perhaps a third of the CO_2 could be eliminated in this way, at a cost of less than $10 per ton. If the plant wanted to reduce CO_2 pollution still more, it could switch its fuel from coal to natural gas. The figure suggests that doing so could eliminate about half of the remaining pollution, but at a higher marginal cost of abatement—up to $15 per ton of CO_2 avoided. Finally, using still-experimental technology to capture and store the CO_2 instead of releasing it into the atmosphere could theoretically eliminate nearly all of the CO_2. The figure shows that doing so might cost up to $40 per ton of avoided CO_2, or even more.

The numbers in the figure are only illustrative. The costs would vary from one source to another and would change as technology and costs of alternative fuels changed. However, they suggest a general principle that applies to nearly every source of pollution: The cost of reducing pollution by one more unit, known as the **marginal cost of abatement**, increases as the degree of abatement decreases. Since the diagram shows increasing pollution from left to right and increasing abatement from right to left, the principle of increasing marginal cost of abatement is shown by a negatively-sloped curve, one that becomes higher from right to left as it approaches the vertical axis.

Marginal External Cost

We turn now from the cost to polluters of reducing waste to the costs that pollution imposes on others. The total of the additional costs borne by all members of society as a result of an added unit of pollution can be termed the **marginal external cost**.

Marginal external cost

The total of the additional costs borne by all members of society as the result of an added unit of pollution

Each type of pollution has its own particular characteristics. In some cases pollution up to a certain threshold may do no harm. For example, a small amount of carbon dioxide from human activity can be absorbed harmlessly in the natural carbon cycle of plants and oceans. After this threshold is reached, further increases become harmful. To illustrate, consider a rising sea level, only one of the many harmful effects that scientists predict as a result of climate change caused by CO_2 emissions. Rises of even a few inches can damage beachfront property. Further rises would cause flooding of low-lying farmland in countries like Bangladesh and could threaten to flood some small island countries completely. In principle, investment in dikes and barriers could offset some or even most of that damage; but as the ocean level rises further, the costs of barriers would increase greatly. Some models predict catastrophic sea level rises of up to 20 feet, although a majority of scientists think the probability of such a catastrophe in this century is small. A 20-foot sea-level rise would cause enormous damage and would overwhelm any human efforts to build barriers.

The same pattern is seen when other types of harm from climate change are considered—damage from changes in rainfall, from extreme weather events, from reduction in biodiversity, and so on. In short, studies of many different effects of climate change suggest that as the earth's temperature rises, the harm done by an additional degree of warming—the marginal external cost—increases.

The Optimal Quantity of Pollution

Figure 6.2 combines a marginal cost of abatement curve similar to that in Figure 6.1 with a positively sloped curve representing marginal external cost. This time, the figure represents not the CO_2 emissions from a single plant but emissions for the world as a whole. The horizontal axis is labeled in gigatons (billions of tons) of carbon dioxide equivalent (CO_2E). CO_2E is a measure of greenhouse gasses that includes the effect not only of CO_2 but also of other gasses like methane and nitrous oxide.

The point of intersection of the two curves represents the economically optimal quantity of pollution. To the right of the intersection in Figure 6.2, then, it would be worthwhile to undertake additional abatement efforts because the external costs saved in the form of crop damage, sea level rise, and so on would be less than the cost of reducing greenhouse gas emissions.

To the left of the intersection, however, the marginal cost of abatement exceeds the marginal external cost. In that region, further pollution abatement is not economi-

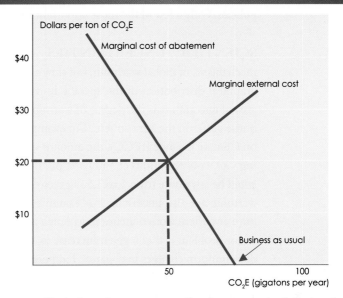

FIGURE 6.2   THE OPTIMAL QUANTITY OF POLLUTION

This figure shows a positively sloped curve representing the marginal external cost of greenhouse gas emissions together with a negatively sloped curve representing the marginal cost of abatement. (To simplify the diagram, both curves are drawn as straight lines.) The point where the two curves intersect is the economically optimal quantity of pollution. To the right of that point, the harm done by pollution exceeds the cost of eliminating it. To the left of that point, the cost of abatement is greater than the harm done by pollution.

cally justified. The relatively small avoided harm done is not enough to offset the scarce resources used to further reduce pollution.

To economists, the logic of the optimal quantity of pollution is no different from that underlying the choice of the least-cost method of producing running shoes or the choice of the optimal balance of oil and vinegar in making a salad dressing. Clearly cleaning up the environment entails costs and trade-offs. Few people would advocate choosing either of the extremes—the whole world as an uninhabitable sewer or a pristine wilderness from which all humans have been eliminated. If we reject both extremes, says the economist, there must be an optimal point between them.

However, it should be pointed out that some people reject the optimal-pollution concept as a guide to public policy. The criticisms are of two types, some focusing on problems of measurement and some on problems of rights.

Problems of Measurement

Economists and climate scientists working together have made many attempts to estimate both the costs of climate change (the marginal external costs in our terminology) and the costs of mitigation (marginal costs of abatement). A consensus has been reached on some aspects of the problem, but the range of estimates remains very wide.[1] Some critics say that the range of estimates is so wide as to offer no useful guidance at all. Others say the estimates are not only imprecise but are also biased toward business-as-usual policies. Only a few of the most important issues can be discussed here.

SCIENTIFIC UNCERTAINTIES   Climate scientists understand the basic mechanisms of global warming, but they are not always able to agree on the size or geographical distribution of the specific impacts of the resulting changes in climate. One area of uncertainty is the degree of warming associated with any given increase in greenhouse gasses in the atmosphere. For example, according to the Intergovernmental Panel on Climate Change (IPCC), the amount of additional warming associated with stabilizing CO_2 concentrations at 550 parts per million (well below the business-as-usual level) could be anywhere from 1 to 3.5 degrees centigrade. The effects of any given amount of warming are also uncertain. For example, 2 degrees of additional warming could produce anywhere from 6 inches to as much as a meter of additional sea level rise. Another major problem is that a given increase in the average global temperature does not produce uniform changes in climate. Temperatures tend to change more near the poles and less near the equator. Storm tracks, rainfall patterns, and other details of climate change are still harder to predict, even though exactly those details may be critical to calculating damages. Complex climate feedback loops cause especially great difficulties in forecasting climate change. For example, warming increases the release of methane from permafrost, which in turn causes additional warming; but warming also may increase cloud cover, which would reflect some solar energy back into space and slow warming.

MARKET AND NONMARKET DAMAGES   Once climate scientists have done their best to forecast the degree of future warming and the details of its effects on the climate, economists have to convert the costs and benefits into dollar terms. Costs that can, in principle, be assigned a monetary value are called market damages. For example, economists try to estimate the value of damage to crops. Many regions, especially near the tropics, will suffer a loss in farm productivity; but farm output in some northern regions will probably increase, at least with moderate degrees of warming. Monetary values can also be assigned to damage from sea level rise, increased storm intensity, and changes in energy used for heating and cooling. Nonmarket damages are harder to convert to monetary terms. For example, health effects from the spread of malaria or changes in death from heat and cold can only be partly converted to monetary terms. Damages to biodiversity and the recreational value of natural areas are even harder to estimate.

THE INTERACTION OF ECONOMIC GROWTH AND CLIMATE CHANGE   Special problems are raised by the complex interaction between economic growth and climate change. On the one hand, economic growth is the root cause of increased greenhouse gas emissions. The global warming forecasts of the IPCC, the IMF, and others all assume continued economic growth in both developed and undeveloped countries. For example, the IMF estimates that by the middle of the twenty-first century, the level of real income (that is, income expressed in today's dollars to eliminate the effect of inflation) will be about three times what it is now in the United States and about six times what it is now in developing countries (excluding

Economics in the News 6.1
USING PROPERTY RIGHTS TO PROTECT THE LAND

The Brazilian Amazon, and the vast adjacent forest known as the *Mato Grosso*, is one of the world's environmental battlegrounds. Every year, deforestation adds millions of tons of carbon dioxide to the earth's atmosphere and further reduces habitat for endangered species.

The Brazilian government is well aware of the threat. It has passed laws that restrict deforestation and require ranchers to keep up to 80 percent of their land in forest. If they have previously cleared too much, they must replant. The laws, unfortunately, are not always enforced. Corrupt local officials sometimes turn a blind eye to violations. Land speculators team up with gangs of illegal land invaders who burn first and then stake claims to the devastated land. Police are sometimes afraid to go into the forest to confront the heavily armed gangs.

Fire in the Amazon rainforest in northern Brazil. Ranchers, farmers, and loggers burned and cut down a near-record area of the Amazon rainforest.

John Cain Carter is one rancher who has had enough of the lawlessness and destruction. A transplanted Texan with a Brazilian wife, he founded the *Aliança da Terra* (Land Alliance), an organization that aims to use market forces to protect the environment. In comments published on the web site *Amazônia*, Carter says, "People think farmers in the Amazon are bandits, so we're trying to show there are good people who are trying to make a difference and reduce their impact …. We're turning the system on its head, adding transparency and credibility to turn it into a worldwide example of good land stewardship."

Carter's organization sends environmental engineers and agronomists to help ranchers improve land management practices by replanting forests, protecting fragile waterways from damage done by cattle, and limiting ero-

sion and pollution. Their reward comes not just in terms of increased self-respect but in increased profits, too. Some of the profits come from payments earned for carbon reduction credits when land is reforested. Another source of profit is the sale of beef and soy that is certified as environmentally friendly. McDonald's, Burger King, and other big buyers are willing to pay premium prices for these products to show that they are environmentally friendly.

Not-for-profit groups like the World Wildlife Fund have supported the efforts of the Land Alliance and other local groups, like the Roundtable on Responsible Soy Association. Not all environmentalists are enthusiastic. Some shun alliances with farmers and ranchers in favor of activities like eco-tourism and gathering forest products for sale. However, speaking to the *Washington Post*, Christopher Wells, head of the soy producers' group, sees cooperation of business and environmentalists as essential. Unless everyone works together, he says, "We'd go back to a world of bitter debate between NGOs (nongovernmental organizations) and big industry. That's where we were five years ago. I don't see any other way other than this."

SOURCES: Jonathan Wheatley, "Edge of Destruction," Financial Times, April 26, 2008, Life and Arts p. 1; Monte Reel, "Applying Capitalism to Protect Dwindling Brazilian Forestland," Washington Post, April 25, 2008 (http://www.washingtonpost.com/wp-dyn/content/article/2008/04/24/AR2008042403392_pf.html); "Land Invasions Undermine Amazon Forest Law," Amazonia, April 3, 2008 (http://www.amazonia.org.br/english/noticias/noticia.cfm?id=265626).

they agree to a list of restrictions on loud parties, lights, boats, garbage, and so on. In most cases, neighbors comply with the covenants voluntarily because they find it mutually beneficial to do so; but the covenants can be enforced in court if necessary.

Another example of the use of markets to handle externalities concerns the pollination of crops by honeybees. Although most of the examples discussed in this chapter concern harmful externalities, this one concerns a beneficial externality. In this case, farmers pay fees to beekeepers to bring their hives by truck to locations near their apple orchards, blueberry farms, or whatever. Such fees total tens of millions of dollars a year in the United States. The fees the farmers pay are more than compensated by the increase in crop yield. Beekeepers, in turn, gain a second source of revenue, in addition to sales of honey.

Without such a market, beekeepers would limit the number of hives to the quantity justified by sales of honey alone. The external benefit to fruit growers would not enter into their calculations. When they can earn extra revenue by selling pollination services, they expand the number of hives. Doing so benefits not only beekeepers and fruit growers but also consumers, who get more of both honey and fruit.

Transaction Costs as Barriers to Voluntary Resolution of Externalities

In practice, private negotiations are not always able to resolve problems of externalities because, in the real world, transaction costs are far from zero. To see why, we will move away from small-scale local externalities, like those of land use and beekeeping, and resume our earlier discussion of climate change.

SCIENTIFIC UNCERTAINTIES   To resolve a pollution dispute through private negotiations, one must know the source of the pollution and the nature of the damage. Acquiring such knowledge is often expensive and sometimes impossible. As we saw earlier, it is known that emissions of CO_2 and other greenhouse gasses contribute to global warming; but beyond that, there are many scientific uncertainties. We do not know exactly where the greatest damages will occur. We do not know how to trace the damage in a certain place (for example, coastal flooding damage to the land of a farmer in Bangladesh) back to a certain source of pollution (for example, an electric power plant in Illinois). Because of this, victims of climate change do not know with whom they should negotiate. Also, because we do not know the exact magnitude of the relationship between a given amount of CO_2 emissions and a given rise in the sea level (or other form of damage), we cannot know how much damage will be avoided by any given reduction in emissions. Because of this, victims would not know how much compensation for which to ask—even if they knew from whom to ask it.

EFFECTIVENESS OF THE LEGAL SYSTEM   Resolution of disagreements over environmental property rights depend, in part, on the effectiveness of *tort law*— the area of civil law concerned with harms (torts) done by one person to another. Lawsuits involving accidental personal injury, product defects, and damage to property through negligence are familiar examples of tort litigation.

The areas of tort law that touch most directly on pollution are *nuisance and trespass*. The law of nuisance can be used for protection against externalities such as a neighbor's noisy parties or a firm's malodorous manufacturing processes. Trespass traditionally covers one person's entry onto another person's land; but it has been extended to include harmful invasions by smoke, chemical leakage, and so on. Pollution often raises issues of both nuisance and trespass.

However, the successful use of tort law to enforce property rights and provide a clear framework for private negotiation requires agreement about the initial distribution of property rights and a court willing to rule on disputes. In practice, environmental property rights are often unclear, and there are often no courts with the needed authority. In the case of climate change, industries in developed countries may claim a right to continue emitting greenhouse gasses on the grounds that their factories complied with all pollution regulations that existed at the time those factories were built. The government of a low-income country like China may counter that industry in developed countries has already used more than its fair share of the limited capacity of the earth's atmosphere to absorb pollution. The advanced countries should start cleaning up their act now, while low-income countries get their chance to catch up. There are no global legal codes or courts to resolve disputes of this kind. Without the backup of appeal to effective courts, private negotiations among citizens living in different countries have small chance of succeeding.

COSTS OF NEGOTIATION AMONG MANY PARTIES   Still another factor increasing transaction costs is the large number of parties involved in many environmental disputes. When there are many parties, the process of negotiating and enforcing an agreement to resolve an externality might be prohibitively expensive even if there were no legal or scientific uncertainties. In the case of climate change, the parties include millions of businesses and billions of individuals throughout the world. It is hard to imagine successful private negotiations on such a scale.

In sum, private negotiations supported by tort law cannot be relied on to resolve all large-scale environmental problems, however useful they may be on a local scale. We turn next to the possibility of controlling pollution through regulation.

Controlling Externalities Through Regulation

As awareness of environmental problems has increased, the pressure has grown for governments in the United States and around the world to do something. The response has included a wide variety of environmental laws and regulation. This section provides an overview of the three most common types of environmental policies: command and control, emission charges, and cap-and-trade systems that use marketable permits.

Command and Control

Many of the U.S. government's earliest efforts to control pollution took a command-and-control approach. This strategy was embodied in the Clean Air Act, the Clean Water Act, the National Environmental Policy Act, the Noise Control Act, and several other laws enacted during the 1970s. Command-and-control laws often state that a specific pollution control technology must be used, without considering its cost compared with alternative methods. In other cases a quantitative goal, such as 90 percent cleanup, is applied to all pollution sources without consideration of differences in cost of abatement among sources. Sometimes, in areas in which pollution is especially bad, new pollution sources are banned entirely.

The early command-and-control regulations had some success in reducing air and water pollution. Over time, though, they have come under increasing criticism because requirements to use specific cleanup technologies reduce the incentive to discover new, lower-cost methods. If no attempt is made to balance marginal abatement costs among various cleanup technologies, various sources, and various categories of pollution, the total costs of achieving any given environmental goal is increased. High costs can lead to political pressure to cut back on pollution-control efforts. For that reason, excessive reliance on command-and-control can be self-defeating.

Today economists see command-and-control as the wrong response to most environmental problems. At best, command-and-control may make sense for a narrow range of pollutants where a zero emission level is both desirable and technologically feasible—for example, banning lead additives for gasoline. For broader categories of pollution, where 100 percent cleanup is not a possible or appropriate goal, other approaches are likely to be both more cost effective and more politically feasible.

Emission Charges (Pollution Taxes)

Economic approaches to pollution control operate by bringing external costs to bear on the pollution source. When this happens, polluters are given an incentive to balance marginal abatement costs with the marginal external costs and move toward an optimal level of pollution. The most direct way to do this is for the government to impose an *emission charge*, sometimes also called a *pollution tax*, of a fixed amount per unit of waste. For example, all sources of sewage might be required to pay a charge of $40 per ton of sewage discharged into lakes and rivers. In the case of climate change, a *carbon tax* has been proposed, which would be a charge per ton of carbon dioxide (or CO_2 equivalent) that is released into the atmosphere.

Figure 6.4 shows how a carbon tax would work. As discussed earlier, the optimal quantity of pollution is determined by the intersection of the curves for marginal cost of abatement and marginal external cost of pollution. With a carbon tax in force, pollution sources will prefer to reduce emissions rather than pay the charge whenever the marginal cost of abatement is less than the charge. In Figure 6.4, that would be the case for levels of pollution greater than 50 gigatons per year. For levels of pollution less than 50 gigatons per year, polluters would prefer to pay the tax. If, as in the figure, the tax is set exactly at the level where the marginal abatement cost and marginal external cost curves intersect, the result will be the optimal level of pollution.

Of course, it is possible that the charge would be set too low or too high. Measurement problems may make it hard to tell just where the curves intersect and how high the tax should be. Even if the tax is initially set at the optimal level, changes in economic conditions may shift one or both of the curves, in which case the old tax will be too high or too low. However, advocates point out that a carbon tax would encourage the use of efficient techniques to achieve a given level of emissions even if the chosen tax rate is not the optimal one. That is so because a charge applied

FIGURE 6.4   EFFECT OF A CARBON TAX

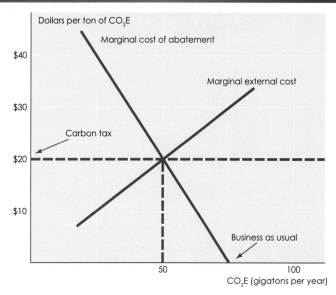

This figure shows the effect of a carbon tax. For levels of pollution above 50 gigatons per year, marginal abatement cost is less than the tax, so it would be more profitable for pollution sources to reduce CO_2 output than to pay the tax. For pollution levels less than 50 gigatons per year, it would cost less to pay the tax than to make further reductions in emissions. If the carbon tax is set at a level equal to the intersection of the marginal abatement cost and marginal external cost curves, the result will be an optimal level of emissions. A tax that was too high, too low, or that did not apply equally to all pollution sources would still result in a reduction of pollution relative to the business-as-usual level, but it would not be fully efficient.

uniformly to all pollution sources would exert equal pressure on all polluters to cut back at least a few units on their output of wastes. It would encourage them to eliminate pollution first from the sources that can be controlled most cheaply, using the least-cost available technology. Thus, it would avoid the problem that occurs under command-and-control, in which all sources are subject to the same regulations even though some sources cause less harm than others. For example, a command-and-control approach to CO_2 emissions might impose strict mileage standards on cars regardless of the number of miles per year the car is driven or the purpose for which it is used. If the marginal cost of abatement is not equalized for all sources of pollution, the cost of a given degree of pollution reduction will be higher than it needs to be.

One example of the successful use of emission charges was the control of chlorofluorocarbons under the 1987 Montreal Protocol. These chemicals, once used for items ranging from spray cans to refrigerators, are damaging to the earth's protective ozone layer. To meet its initial commitment to reduce emissions of chlorofluorocarbons under the Montreal Protocol, the U.S. government imposed a heavy tax. Later, after less environmentally damaging substitutes had been developed and brought into production, the most damaging chemicals were banned altogether.

Cap and Trade

Emission charges are one way of using market incentives to encourage efficiency in attaining environmental goals. Another approach to the same goal is the use of marketable waste-discharge permits, a technique commonly known as "cap-and-trade."

Figure 6.5 shows how a cap-and-trade system works. The vertical line in the diagram corresponds to the "cap," that is, the overall limit on the amount of pollution allowed from all sources in the affected area. As applied to greenhouse gasses and climate change, the area would be the entire country; but for some other types of pollutants, it might be a region or a single city. Ideally, as shown in the figure, the limit corresponds to the optimal quantity of pollution.

Once the overall limit has been determined, it is divided into a fixed number of permits that are distributed among pollution sources. The permits can then be freely bought and sold. Polluters whose marginal cost of abatement is relatively high become buyers of permits, and those with relatively low marginal abatement costs become sellers. As the market for permits approaches equilibrium, the marginal cost of abatement will be equalized for all firms. Thus, as in the case of emission charges, there is an incentive to use efficient means to achieve the target level of pollution abatement.

FIGURE 6.5   EFFECT OF EMISSIONS TRADING

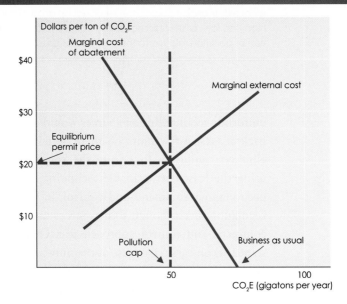

This figure shows the effect of a policy of a cap and trade regulation strategy applied to greenhouse gas emissions. The total amount of CO_2 equivalent that may be discharged is limited by the number of permits issued, in this case, 50 gigatons. Permits will be traded among pollution sources. Those with higher marginal abatement costs will buy permits from those with lower marginal abatement costs. An equilibrium will be established when the marginal cost of abatement is equalized among all pollution sources. The equilibrium price of a permit will be determined by the intersection of the marginal cost of abatement curve with the line representing the number of permits. If the correct number of permits is issued, the optimum quantity of pollution will be achieved.

The cap-and-trade approach has been used to control pollution both in the United States and abroad. It has been used to control air pollution from electric power plants under 1990 amendments to the *Clean Air Act*. It is also used in several cities to control local air pollution. More recently, it has been used in the European Union to control carbon emissions.

Environmental Policy and Public Choice

Chapter 1 introduced a distinction between positive and normative economics. Our discussion of environmental policy to this point has taken a normative perspective. It has focused on how policy ought to be designed in order to avoid market failure and achieve the goal of efficiency. This section offers a positive perspective on environmental policy. It uses concepts of public choice theory to explain why real-world environmental policies are not always crafted to achieve the goal of efficiency, and why the political process sometimes leads to government failure rather than the correction of market failure.

Environmental Policy in a Democracy

Public choice theory looks at environmental policy in terms of the way people pursue their economic interests through the political process. In a democracy, the focus is on political choices made by voters and by their elected representatives.

Median voter model

A model showing that there is a tendency for decisions in a democracy to reflect the interests of voters whose preferences lie near the middle of the scale

One of the simplest models in public choice theory is the **median voter model**. This model suggests that political choices in a democracy reflect the interests of voters whose preferences lie near the middle of the range represented in the community. To use a simple example, consider a community where all citizens gather once a year to vote on important issues. This year the big issue is whether the town should use some tax money to improve its schools or, instead, give a tax break to an organization that wants to construct an assisted living facility. Young parents are more likely to vote in favor of schools, while older voters are more likely to favor tax breaks for assisted living. According to the model, the outcome of the vote will depend on the age of the *median* voter—that is, the voter whose age is such that exactly half the citizens are older and half are younger. In a community where the median age is young, families that favor schools are likely to be in the majority. In a community where the median age is older, assisted living is more likely to win.

It is not hard to find examples in which environmental policy appears to be consistent with the median voter model. For example, in 2007, California's Republican governor proposed the nation's strongest policies for reducing carbon dioxide emissions. Could it be that the median California voter is more concerned about the environment than in other parts of the country? Very likely so, but environmentalism is not confined to California. Economists consider environmental quality to have a relatively high income elasticity of demand. Over time, as economic growth raises the income of the median voter, we would expect stronger political support for policies that promote clean air, improved opportunities for outdoor recreation, and increased concern for the future of the planet. That is just what democratic political systems have produced in most high-income countries.

Vote Trading and Special Interests

Despite the ability of the median voter model to explain some trends in environmental policy, it is by no means a complete theory. Public choice economists are quick to point out that the median voter model, which emphasizes the political choices of individual citizens, must be modified to take into account the frequently disproportionate influence of small groups that share intensely felt interests.

Just what features of the political system tend to amplify the voice of special interests—even when they represent a small minority of voters? Public choice theory identifies two that are especially important.

COSTS OF LOBBYING AND POLITICAL EXPRESSION   Like everything we do, participation in democratic politics has an opportunity cost. The opportunity cost is not limited to making the effort to roll out of bed early once a year in order to vote in an election. Other forms of political action, like writing to elected representatives, calling in to local talk shows, attending meetings, or marching in demonstrations also take time and effort from other activities. Actions like making campaign contributions or employing professional lobbyists cost not just time but also money. Finally, there is a large opportunity cost just to keeping informed about how you yourself are affected by what goes on in the political world.

When you are a member of an organized group, all members of which are affected similarly by some policy, you can often share the opportunity cost of political action. You can keep informed through a web site or newsletter supported by your organization. Your job or your leisure interests naturally keep you in touch with like-minded people. Your organization may use dues or a special fund-raising drive to sponsor lobbyists or political ads. As a result of lower opportunity costs, members of groups speak with a louder voice, relative to their numbers, than do unorganized individuals.

Small, well-organized groups also have another source of strength. Political action by a group has the property of a public good—all members benefit whether they contribute or not. As explained in Chapter 4, production of public goods is hampered by the *free rider problem*. Group members would like to gain from the group's political activities without bearing their fair share of the costs. Small, well-organized groups have ways of overcoming the free-rider problem. Some, like labor unions and professional associations, may have compulsory dues. Others, like churches or parent-teacher groups, may bring social pressures to bear on group members that don't seem willing to do their fair share. In contrast, the free rider problem makes it nearly impossible to mobilize large groups in pursuit of shared interests that are not central to the life of each member.

LOGROLLING   Representative democracy is a second factor that increases the political impact of small groups that share intense interests. In the modern world, relatively few issues are decided by direct democracy, in which individual citizens vote on specific issues. Local town meetings and referendums in some states are the exception, not the rule. Instead, citizens usually express themselves in a two-stage process: First they vote for representatives—senators, members of congress, state legislators—and then the representatives vote on each issue.

Logrolling

The practice of trading votes among members of a legislative body

Representative democracy adds an important element to the political process—vote trading, or **logrolling** as it is popularly known. Logrolling is possible because voting in legislatures differs in two important ways from voting in general elections. First, legislative voting is almost never by secret ballot. Second, legislators vote frequently on very specific issues, rather than only now and then on more general issues. As a result, it is possible for one representative to promise her vote on issue A in exchange for a promise that her colleague will provide his vote on issue B.

Logrolling often allows minority interests to prevail, provided they are strongly felt. Senators from dairy states can gather votes for higher milk prices by trading away votes on issues like flood control or highway funds that are important to voters in other states, but not theirs. Although logrolling is sometimes used to pursue the narrowly economic interests of groups like dairy farmers, it can also be used to promote non-economic interests of any minority group. For example, logrolling has helped pass civil rights laws and protections for disabled persons, causes that might have been slow to win majority support if every issue were decided according to the preferences of the median voter.

SPECIAL INTERESTS AND ENVIRONMENTAL POLICY   When it comes to specific issues of environmental policy, majority interests, as expressed through the influence of the median voter, and special interests, expressed through small-group action and logrolling, can interact in complex ways. The case of regulations controlling sulfur dioxide emissions from coal-fired electric power plants provides a case in point.

There are a variety of technologies for reducing sulfur dioxide emissions. Typically, switching to a low-sulfur coal is the cheapest alternative, and scrubbing the sulfur from combustion gases is the most expensive. Nonetheless, in its 1977 amendments to Section 111 of the *Clean Air Act*, Congress required that any newly constructed electric power plant meet the emissions limit by scrubbing. That requirement applied, regardless of how clean or dirty the plant's fuel or combustion technology was. Many old plants, including some of the dirtiest ones that burned the most sulfurous midwestern coal, were not forced to scrub. Instead, they were allowed to meet standards for local pollution by building tall smokestacks—up to 1,000 feet high—that keep the air in surrounding communities fairly clean. However, pollution injected into the upper atmosphere by the tall stacks contributes to the problem of acid rain hundreds of miles downwind.

Why did Congress choose this approach to controlling sulfur dioxide emissions? The

To meet local pollution standards some smoke stacks were built up to 1,000 feet high rather than installing scrubbers.

answer appears to lie in the coalition that passed the *Clean Air Act*, which included the following:

- Coal-mining interests in the high-sulfur areas of Ohio, Illinois, and elsewhere wanted to strengthen demand for their product. These factions, including both unions and mine owners, were afraid that changing fuels would result in the loss of coal production jobs to western states where low-sulfur coal is found.

- Industrial and political interests from eastern and midwestern states wanted to protect profits by stopping the flight of industry to western and southern states. By focusing control efforts on newly built plants, the *Clean Air Act* gave old, dirty plants a few more years of life. Moreover, by focusing on scrubbing rather than changing fuels, the act ensured that coal-burning plants in the South and West are unable to exploit the cost advantage of a location close to sources of low-sulfur coal.

- Environmentalists, who were unable to obtain a majority in Congress by themselves, were willing to enter an "unholy alliance" on the theory that any pollution control measure was better than none.

After the passage of the 1977 Clean Air amendments, environmentalists became dissatisfied with the deal that had been made. The degree of pollution reduction was less than had been hoped, partly because scrubbers are not always reliable and partly because the regulations slowed the replacement of old, dirty facilities with new, cleaner ones. Thus, important elements of the coalition changed by the time the 1990 amendments were under consideration. This time, environmentalists broke with the midwestern coal and industrial interests, supporting the use of a cap-and-trade strategy. As discussed in *Applying Economic Ideas 6.1*, the new approach turned out to be much more effective.

Alternative energy resources are another area in which economics, science, and politics clash. Many analysts see alternative energy from windmills, solar arrays, or biomass fuels as the best approach to reducing carbon dioxide emissions. Each alternative technology has its supporters and critics. Given a level playing field, we might hope over time that the forms of alternative energy that produce the greatest environmental benefits at the lowest costs would be developed most rapidly. However, that has not happened. As the Case for Discussion at the end of this chapter shows, political considerations have led to a disproportionately rapid development of one technology, namely, corn-based ethanol, despite its questionable environmental effects and serious, unintended consequences.

The examples given help explain why government policies do not always resolve environmental issues in an efficient manner and, sometimes, even make environmental problems worse rather than better. The insights of public choice theory suggest the evaluation of policy alternatives comes down to a matter of balancing market failures, on the one hand, against government failures, on the other.

ᕳ

Applying Economic Ideas 6.1
CAP AND TRADE FOR ACID RAIN

In the 1980s, before climate change began to make the headlines, acid rain was the most widely discussed environmental problem in the United States. Acid rain occurs when sulfur dioxide (SO_2) and other pollutants, mainly from coal-fired power plants, rise into the atmosphere and undergo chemical reactions that increase the acidity of rain that falls on areas downwind. Steadily increasing acidity of rain was destroying forests, damaging crops, and creating a constant haze throughout the Eastern United States. Early environmental legislation took a command-and-control approach by mandating stack scrubbers and other technology for midwestern power plants. However, those controls turned out to be insufficient, and damage from acid rain continued to increase.

By 1990, it was time to try a new approach. A set of amendments to the *Clean Air Act* permitted the Environmental Protection Agency (EPA) to try a cap-and-trade approach to control of SO_2 emissions. There were many skeptics. Some environmentalists feared that the incentives of cap-and-trade would be too weak to persuade industry to cut back on pollution. Representatives of industry feared that the controls would be too tight and

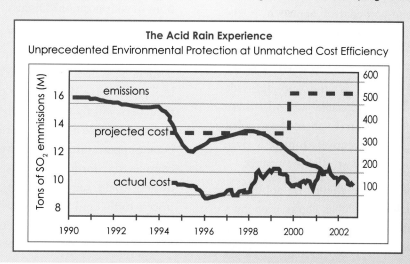

Bavarian Forest around the Lusen mountain—the old forest died as a result of acid rain and the bark beetle in 1996, but now a new forest is growing.

that the market price of permits would soar to unaffordable levels. However, despite the many doubts, the EPA went ahead with its program.

The result surprised almost everyone. Cap-and-trade for acid rain control became one of the greatest environmental success stories of recent time. As the chart shows, SO_2 emissions fell by more than half over the next decade; and the cost of the program was far below projections. Rather than rising to a range of $500 to $2,000 per ton, as had been projected by some critics, the equilibrium price of permits fell steadily. By 2003, it was only $150 per ton. The acidity of rain in the Adirondacks and New England fell by 25 to 50 percent. Forests and streams began to recover their ecological health. The success of the acid rain program has become one of the strongest arguments in favor of using a similar approach to the problem of climate change.

SOURCES: Environmental Defense Fund, "The Cap-and-Trade Success Story," www.edf.org/page.cfm?tagID=1085; Environmental Protection Agency, "Cap and Trade: Acid Rain Program Results", www.epa.gov/airmarkets.

The Acid Rain Experience
Unprecedented Environmental Protection at Unmatched Cost Efficiency

Summary

1. **How can the problem of pollution be understood in terms externalities?** Pollution occurs when firms (or sometimes consumers) discharge wastes into soil, water, or the atmosphere. The optimal quantity of pollution is the quantity beyond which the marginal external cost of pollution exceeds the marginal cost of abatement.

2. **How can property rights and private negotiation help control externalities?** In a world without transaction costs, problems of externalities would be resolved through voluntary negotiation. According to the *Coase theorem*, voluntary exchange would result in efficient resource allocation regardless of the initial assignment of property rights, provided that there were no transaction costs. In practice, high transaction costs limit the power of negotiations to resolve environmental problems.

3. **What government policies are available to control pollution?** Early pollution control policies in the United States followed a command-and-control approach. Economists have criticized the command-and-control approach for poor performance in terms of efficiency because they often do not take marginal abatement costs into account and do not provide incentives to employ the least-cost control technology. One alternative to the command-and-control approach is the imposition of emission charges (pollution taxes), which would require pollution sources to pay a per-unit fee for the discharge of wastes into the environment. Another is the cap-and-trade approach based on marketable waste-discharge permits. Economists favor these approaches because they include incentives to meet a given pollution control target in an efficient manner.

4. **How can public choice theory be applied to environmental issues?** Public choice economics can help explain what environmental policies are politically successful. The median voter model suggests that the relatively high income elasticity of demand for environmental quality helps explain the strengthening of environmental policy over time in high-income countries. Public choice theory can, also, help explain why the pollution control policies adopted by government are not always the most efficient ones. Often those policies reflect the influence of regional interests and logrolling. Environmental policy thus provides many examples of government failure as well as market failure.

Key Terms

Problems and Topics for Discussion

1. **Environmental rights** "Pollution is garbage. Just as no one has a right to dump garbage on his/her neighbor's property, no one has a right to pollute the planet. A pollution-free environment is a basic human right." Do you agree, disagree, or agree in part? What are the economic implications of your position? Discuss.

2. **Beneficial externalities and property rights** Beekeepers need flowers to produce honey, and farmers need bees to pollinate crops. At present, beekeepers have the right to place hives where their bees will fly onto neighbors' property, and the neighbors do not have the right to exclude the bees. Suppose instead that invasion by bees was considered a form of trespass, so that property owners could sue beekeepers who allowed the insects to fly onto their land without permission. How would this alter the economic relations between farmers and beekeepers? Do you think

that it might lead to a situation in which beekeepers have to pay farmers for access to the blossoms of their crops? Discuss in terms of the Coase theorem and the Miller-Forester example.

3. **Smoking in restaurants** Smoking results in externalities that are unpleasant for nonsmokers. Given this fact, why would a restaurant find it profitable to establish smoking and nonsmoking areas? Do you think that the problem of smoking in restaurants is adequately resolved by voluntary market incentives, or should there be a government policy mandating (or preventing) designated smoking areas in restaurants? Do you think that the same conclusions apply to smoking on airplanes? In a government office? Discuss.

4. **Automobile pollution** One way to control automobile pollution is by the use of catalytic converters and other devices that limit pollution to a certain quantity per mile driven. For comparison, imagine a system in which drivers had to pay an annual tax based on the total pollution emitted by their cars. The tax would be calculated by measuring the quantity of pollution per mile, using a testing device such as those now used for vehicle inspections, and multiplying that figure by the number of miles per year shown on the car's odometer. People could choose to buy catalytic converters, more expensive and more effective devices, or no control devices at all. What considerations would determine the type of pollution control device purchased? Do you think that the tax system would be more efficient than the current command-and-control system? Would it be as effective in reducing pollution? Would it be as fair? Discuss.

Case for Discussion

Fill It Up with Ethanol?

Stand on any street corner in Rio de Janeiro, and you will notice a faint aroma reminiscent of a camping trip or a fondue feast—the aroma of burning alcohol. Nearly all cars in Brazil run on alcohol, more exactly, ethanol produced from sugar cane. Brazilians can buy gasoline at their local filling station if they must, but the price is higher, even taking into account the fact that gasoline has higher energy content than ethanol and, accordingly, produces better mileage.

Ethanol-based motor fuel is growing in popularity in the United States, as well. Unlike the case in Brazil, few U.S. cars can run on pure ethanol, but blends containing anywhere from 10 percent to 85 percent ethanol are being promoted as a solution to the national "addiction" to imported oil. Since little sugar cane is grown in the United States, most ethanol produced there is made from corn. In late 2007, Congress passed new energy legislation that further increased already generous subsidies for ethanol production. Does it make economic or environmental sense?

Among the first scientists to cast suspicion on the case for corn-based ethanol were Cornell University's David Pimentel and Tad Patzek of the University of California, Berkeley. Their research showed that corn-based ethanol consumes about 30 percent more energy than the fuel yields. Furthermore, much of the energy used to drive tractors and fuel ethanol plants is petroleum based. Far from being a solution to the energy crisis, corn-based ethanol makes it worse. The corn lobby soon struck back with new research sponsored by the U.S. Department of Agriculture. Those studies said that Pimentel and Patzek based production costs on average technology, which included some now-obsolete plants, not the most efficient technology embodied in the newest plants. They also failed to include the energy-saving value of ethanol byproducts like high-protein cattle feed. When these and other considerations are added, corn-based ethanol appeared to produce a small but positive net gain to the nation's energy balance. Still more recent research, published in *Science* in early 2008, argues that all of the earlier studies failed to include the effects of land use. As farmers in the U.S. and around the world plow up previously unfarmed land for crops, massive amounts of CO_2 and other greenhouse gasses are released into the air. When land use effects are taken into account, corn-based ethanol and most other biofuels unambiguously do more harm than good to the environment.

If food-based biofuels are such a bad idea, why are they so heavily subsidized? The answer is to be found not in economics but in politics. Midwestern corn farmers are delighted to see the demand for their product grow as more and more subsidized ethanol plants are built. Use of corn to make ethanol drives up world food prices, but hungry people in Africa and Asia do not vote in U.S. elections. U.S. consumers (at least this is what members of Congress seem to hope) can be easily fooled into believing that, when they fill up their tank with ethanol, they are helping make the world a better place to live in.

QUESTIONS

1. Suppose each gallon of gasoline consumed results in $.50 of harmful externalities while each gallon of ethanol results in just $.15 of harmful externalities. If ethanol costs $.35 cents more per gallon to produce, would it be efficient to encourage ethanol-based fuels? Why or why not? What if, when land-use effects are taken into account, the externalities from corn-based ethanol are the same as those from gasoline? Discuss in terms of concepts from this chapter.

2. In order to persuade motorists to use ethanol as fuel, the price of ethanol (adjusted for its lower energy content) must be the same as or lower than gasoline. Do you think it would be better to encourage use of ethanol by putting a tax on gasoline or by subsidizing production of ethanol? Which would result in the greater total saving in gasoline use? Why? What political considerations might affect the choice between tax and subsidy?

3. If there are fewer corn farmers than motorists, why has Congress blocked imports of Brazilian

ethanol, which is much cheaper than that produced in the United States, rather than encouraging such imports? Discuss in terms of concepts from public choice theory.

End Notes

1. For an overview of the issues involved in measuring the impacts of climate change and the costs of mitigation, consult one or both of the following studies: Intergovernmental Panel on Climate change, *Climate Change 2007 Synthesis Report, Summary for Policymakers,* http://www.ipcc.ch/, or International Monetary Fund, *World Economic Outlook,* April 2008, Chapter 4: Climate Change and the Global Economy, http:// www.imf.org/ external/pubs/ ft/weo/2008/01/index.htm.

2. Although IPCC and IMF forecasts show world income increasing steadily for the indefinite future, there is one grim scenario that could produce an absolute decrease in world income, not just a decrease relative to a growing baseline. That scenario is one in which rising greenhouse gas concentrations reached a "tipping point" that triggered strong feedback effects, like melting permafrost or collapsing polar icecap. Once the feedback effects materialized, no possible reduction in the human component of global warming would be enough to stop further catastrophic climate change. At present, this is considered a low-probability scenario, but not one that can be excluded altogether.

3. For a more extended discussion of the issues raised in this section, see Edwin G. Dolan, "Science, Public Policy, and Global Warming: Rethinking the Market Liberal Position," *Cato Journal,* Fall 2006, http://www.cato.org/ pubs/journal/ cj26n3/cj26n3-3.pdf.

4. The theorem is implicit in Ronald Coase, "The Problem of Social Cost," *Journal of Law and Economics* (October 1960): 1–44. Coase's colleague, George Stigler, first used the term "Coase theorem" for this proposition. Since then, there has been a long controversy regarding how the theorem should be interpreted. For a thorough review, see Glenn Fox, "The Real Coase Theorems," *Cato Journal,* Fall, 2007.

Appendix to Chapter 6:
VALUING COSTS AND BENEFITS OVER TIME

In the world of business, managers frequently encounter situations that require the comparison of the value of costs and benefits that occur at different points in time. Should a trucking company build a new warehouse in Tulsa? Doing so will require an investment now and will produce cost savings and service improvements over many years in the future. If the warehouse is built, how much insulation should be put in the roof? More insulation increases the immediate construction cost but saves future heating costs.

Discounting   The method used to make comparisons between costs and benefits that occur at different points in time is known as *discounting*. To understand discounting, begin by imagining a firm that has surplus funds available for investment. If it puts funds to work earning interest by placing them in a bank account, making a loan, or buying a security, the original sum it invests will grow year by year. At 10 percent interest per year, $100 invested today will be worth $110 a year from now. After two years, it will be worth $121—the $11 gain in the second year reflects interest of $10 on the original principal and $1 interest on the $10 interest earned in the first year. Because interest is paid on previously earned interest, this process is termed *compound interest*. Mathematically, we can say that the value V of $1 invested for t years at a rate of interest of r percent per year is given by the formula $Vt = (1 + r)^t$.

In a world in which funds can be loaned out at compound interest, it is always advantageous to receive a payment earlier rather than later. The opportunity cost of receiving a sum later rather than sooner is the interest that could have been earned otherwise. Consider, for example, the cost of receiving $100 a year from now rather than today, assuming an interest rate of 10 percent per year. Delaying receipt of the sum would mean forgoing a year's interest. Rather than give up that interest, a firm would be just as well off to receive a smaller sum now as to receive the $100 a year from now. To be precise, it would be just as good to get $91 now as $100 a year from now because the $91 placed for a year at 10 percent would grow to $100 (give or take a few cents). Similarly, $100 payable two years from now is equivalent to about $83 today, assuming 10 percent interest; $100 three years from now is worth about $75 today; and so on.

This kind of example can be generalized to any time period and any interest rate. Let V_p be the sum of money that, if it is invested today at r percent interest, will grow to the sum V_t after t years. V_p is known as the **present value** of the sum V_t, payable t years from now, discounted at r percent per year. The formula for calculating the present value of any future sum is

$$V_p = \frac{V_t}{(1 + r)^t}$$

Present value

The value today of a sum payable in the future (In mathematical terms, the present value of a sum V_p, payable t years in the future, discounted at r percent interest, would grow to the value Vt in t years; the present value formula is $V_p = V_t / (1 + r)^t$.)

An Example   Suppose you own a chain of stores selling hiking shoes. You think your customers will react favorably if you "go green" by converting your stores to a carbon-neutral source of electric power. A supplier of electrical equipment gives you a choice of two methods for doing this: a solar-electric panel or a bio-diesel generator. For the sake of discussion, we will consider the environmental benefits of the two methods to be equal.

The economic costs and benefits are not the same, however. The solar panel will cost $25,000 to install, but it has very low operating cost. It requires no fuel and just $100 per year for routine maintenance. The bio-diesel generator is much less expensive to install— just $10,000. However, it will require annual costs of $2,000 per year for fuel and maintenance. Both installations have an expected lifetime of 10 years. Which should be chosen?

If we just add up total expenses over the 10-year period, the solar solution wins hands down. It has a total cost of just $26,000, compared to $30,000 for the bio-diesel alternative. However, that comparison is misleading. The major cost of the solar electric panel occurs immediately, while the high fuel costs of the bio-diesel generator occur later. If future dollars are worth less than present dollars, as the discounting approach suggests, a more detailed analysis is required.

The complete analysis of the problem is given in Table 6A.1. There, in addition to the undiscounted information of costs and benefits, additional columns give the discounted value of future costs and benefits at two possible discount rates, 4 percent per year and 6 percent per year. For example, we can use the table to determine that the present value of the $2,000 that will be spent on diesel fuel in year 5 is $1,494.52 if a 6 percent discount rate is used $(2000 \times (1.06)^5)$ and $1,643.85 if a 4 percent discount rate is used $(2000 \times (1.04)^5)$.

Looking across the bottom row, we see that the total present value of installation costs plus future operating costs, discounted at 6 percent, is $25,736.01 for the solar

TABLE 6A.1   COST COMPARISON

Year	Solar-Electric Panel			Bio-Diesel Generator		
	Undiscounted Expense	Discounted at 6%	Discounted at 4%	Undiscounted Expense	Discounted at 6%	Discounted at 4%
0	25,000	25,000	25,000	10,000	10,000	10,000
1	100	94	96	2,000	1,887	1,920
2	100	89	92	2,000	1,780	1,849
3	100	84	89	2,000	1,679	1,778
4	100	79	85	2,000	1,584	1,710
5	100	75	82	2,000	1,495	1,644
6	100	70	79	2,000	1,410	1,581
7	100	67	76	2,000	1,330	1,520
8	100	63	73	2,000	1,255	1,461
9	100	59	70	2,000	1,184	1,405
10	100	56	68	2,000	1,117	1,351
TOTAL	25,000	25,736	25,811	30,000	24,720	26,219

installation compared to just $24,720.17 for the bio-diesel option. At that interest rate, the benefit of postponing some expenses to a future date outweighs the fact that total undiscounted expenses are greater. However, discounted at a 4 percent discount rate, the solar electric option is less expensive by a small margin.

It turns out, then, that the choice between solar electric and bio-diesel depends not just on the pattern of costs over time but also on the discount rate used. For the case under discussion, it is not hard to determine the proper discount rate. The discount rate used should be the opportunity cost of funds for the firm. If the firm must borrow money to install the equipment, the opportunity cost is the interest rate charged on the loan. If it has spare cash that can be used for the project, the opportunity cost is the next-best alternative investment, for example, using the funds to buy government bonds.

Applying Discounting to Climate Change   The problem of deciding how much to spend now to mitigate future climate change is similar in some ways to the problem of deciding between alternative methods of generating electricity. In both cases, costs and benefits are spread over time. In both cases, costs are concentrated more heavily in the near future while benefits accrue over the more distant future. In both cases, the method of discounting can be applied to compare the present value of costs and benefits that occur at different times.

The main difference is that the costs and benefits of climate change policy are spread over a vastly longer time horizon. Decisions made now to slow emissions of greenhouse gasses will affect atmospheric concentrations of gasses, global temperatures, and sea levels for centuries to come. When the discount formula is applied over such very long periods, it tells us that costs and benefits in the far distant future have very little value today. For example, the present value of $1,000, discounted at 4 percent for 100 years, is less than $20. Discounted for 300 years at 4 percent, the present value of $1,000 is only about one cent. Translated into everyday language, the discount formula seems to tell us that we should hardly care at all about something that will not happen for 100 years and that we should be almost completely indifferent even to huge catastrophes if we think they will not happen for 300 years.

Many people, confronted with the mathematics of discounting over long periods, reject the results out of hand. Forget the math, they say—we do care! We like our little planet; it's the only one we have! We do not want to destroy it—not tomorrow and, just as certainly, not 100, 300, or even 1,000 years from now!

Economists who study climate change policy react to these protests in different ways. Some brush them aside, saying, in effect, that it is not rational to care much about the distant future. Others attempt to reconcile the protests with the discounting method by reconsidering the proper interest rate that should be applied. Perhaps the market-based interest rates in the range of 3 to 5 percent that are appropriate for ordinary commercial decisions and short-term policy making should not be applied when thinking about the distant future. Perhaps instead we should use a much smaller interest rate or one that starts at a market-based rate for the near future and falls over time.

It turns out that for the question of how much to do now to mitigate climate change, the choice of a discount rate makes more difference than any other consideration. One way to compare policy recommendations is to frame them in terms of a carbon tax. A strong policy recommendation is equivalent to a high tax (or a strict cap-and-trade policy that would produce a high price for carbon permits). A weak policy recommendation is equivalent to a low tax, or even none. Often the carbon tax is expressed in dollars per ton. In more familiar terms, a carbon tax of $1 per ton is equivalent to a tax of about one cent per gallon of gasoline.

William Nordhaus of Yale University is one of the best known among economists who applies the standard discounting approach to climate change. His work uses a discount rate that starts with a market-based rate of about 4 percent, gradually decreasing to about 2 percent for the distant future. Based on these discount rates, Nordhaus calculates that an optimal carbon tax (or equivalent cap-and-trade permit price) would be about $35 per ton, as of 2008. That is close to the market price for carbon permits being traded in the European Union as of mid-2008. In consumer terms, such a tax would add about $.35 per gallon to the cost of gasoline. Some economists who use market-based discount rates come up with even lower recommendations for the optimal carbon tax.

On the other hand, economists like Nicholas Stern, author of a widely-cited climate change study sponsored by the British Treasury, advocates using a much lower discount rate based on the ethical principle that human life has equal value regardless of the century in which people are born. As a result of applying a low discount rate, Stern estimates the optimal carbon tax to be more than $300 per ton, almost 10 times as high as Nordhaus's recommendation. A carbon tax of that level would impose much higher costs on consumers and businesses, and would be equivalent to a much stricter cap-and-trade program than that implemented by the European Union, currently the world's strictest policy.

Who is right? Economics, in this case, simply cannot supply the answer. Either we care about the distant future, or we do not. Either we believe that human life has equal value regardless of a person's century of birth, or we believe current life has greater value than future life. The most economics can do is to help us understand the consequences of whatever policy choices we make.

CHAPTER *7*

Global Trade and Trade Policy

After reading this chapter, you will understand the following:

1. How the principle of comparative advantage can be applied to international trade
2. How the notion of competitiveness is related to that of comparative advantage
3. The trend of international trade policy in recent years
4. How international trade affects income distribution within each country
5. How protectionist policies can be understood in terms of public choice theory and rent seeking

Before reading this chapter, make sure you know the meaning of the concepts:

1. Opportunity cost
2. Comparative advantage
3. Political rent seeking
4. Public choice theory

MARKETS ARE NOT confined to national borders. They are world wide, and global trade is changing the world economy. During the second half of the twentieth century, the volume of world trade increased by a factor of seventeen, compared with a six-fold growth of output; and the growth of trade continues. Figure 7.1 shows shares of the biggest players in terms of imports and exports. Not surprisingly, the United States is the world's largest importer both of goods and services. More surprisingly, in light of the constant hand-wringing about its international competitiveness, the United States also exports more goods and services than any other country, although the combined merchandise exports of the twenty-seven European Union countries are greater than those of the United States.

Figure 7.1 shows only the raw data of trade. The most interesting questions will require digging beneath the surface. How do choices made by consumers and firms interact to determine

FIGURE 7.1 **WORLD EXPORT AND IMPORT LEADERS**

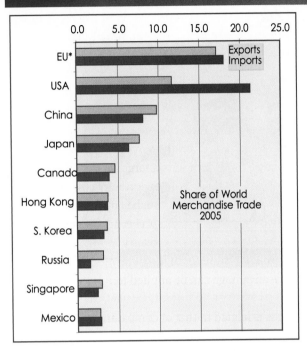 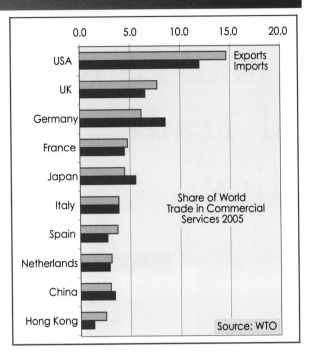

The United States is the world's largest importer of both goods and services. It also exports more goods and services than any other single country although the combined merchandise exports of the European Union are larger.

SOURCE: World Trade Organization *Excludes intra-EU merchandise trade

who exports to whom and who imports from whom? Does the growth of imports and exports make markets more efficient? Does it make people better off or worse off? How are trade patterns affected by national and international trade policy; and what forces, in turn, determine trade policy? The rest of the chapter will explore these issues.

The Theory of Comparative Advantage: Review and Extensions

The answer to the first question—who trades with whom?—begins with the concept of *comparative advantage*, first introduced in Chapter 1. Although it can be applied to the division of labor within an economy of a single country, David Ricardo originally developed the concept as an explanation of trade between countries. We will begin our discussion of international trade by reviewing this theory, first using a numerical example and then applying a graphical approach.

Numerical Approach

For illustrative purposes, imagine a world with just two countries—Norway and Spain. Both have farms and offshore fishing grounds, but Spain's moderate climate makes both the farms and the fishing grounds there more productive. A ton of fish can be produced in Spain with four hours of labor and a ton of grain with two hours of labor. In Norway, five labor hours are required to produce a ton of fish and five labor hours to produce a ton of grain. We will consider only labor costs in this example; other costs can be assumed to be proportional to labor costs. Also, we will assume constant per-unit labor costs for all output levels.

Absolute advantage

The ability of a country to produce a good at a lower cost, in terms of quantity of factor inputs, than the cost at which trading partners can produce the good

Because it takes fewer labor hours to produce both fish and grain in Spain, Spain can be said to have an **absolute advantage** in the production of both goods. However, absolute cost differences do not matter for international trade; it is the difference in opportunity costs between the two countries that matters. For opportunity costs, the situation is different. In Norway, producing a ton of fish means forgoing the opportunity to use five labor hours in the fields. A ton of fish thus has an opportunity cost of one ton of grain there. In Spain, producing a ton of fish means giving up the opportunity to produce two tons of grain. In terms of opportunity costs, then, fish is cheaper in Norway than in Spain and grain is cheaper in Spain than in Norway. The country in which the opportunity cost of a good is lower is said to have a *comparative advantage* in producing that good.

Considering only labor costs, mutually beneficial trade between Spain and Norway might not seem possible. Norwegians might like to get their hands on some of those cheap Spanish goods, but why would the Spanish be interested? After all, couldn't they produce everything at home more cheaply than it could be produced abroad? If that is the case, how could they gain from trade? A closer analysis shows that this view is incorrect and that absolute advantage is unimportant in determining patterns of trade; only comparative advantage matters.

To see the possibilities for trade between the two countries, imagine that a Norwegian fishing boat decides to sail into a Spanish port with a ton of fish. Before the Norwegians' arrival, Spanish merchants in the port will be used to exchanging two tons of locally produced grain for a ton of fish, while the Norwegians will be accustomed to getting only one ton of Norwegian grain for each ton of Norwegian fish. Thus, any exchange ratio between one and two tons of grain per ton of fish will seem attractive to

An example of absolute advantage is when a country can produce a product cheaper than a competing country.

both parties. For instance, a trade of one and a half tons of grain for a ton of fish will make both the Spanish merchants and the Norwegian fishers better off than they would be if they traded only with others from their own country.

The profit made by the first boatload of traders is only the beginning of the story. Additional benefits come as each country begins to specialize in producing the good in which it has a comparative advantage. Norwegians will discover that instead of working five hours to raise a ton of grain from their own rocky soil, they can fish for five hours and trade their catch to the Spaniards for one and a half tons of grain. In Spain, people will find that it is no longer worth their while to spend four hours catching a ton of fish. Instead, if they can work just three hours in the fields, the one and a half tons of grain that they grow will get them a ton of fish from the Norwegians. In short, the Norwegians will find it worthwhile to specialize in fish, and the Spaniards will find it advantageous to specialize in grain.

Now suppose that trade continues at the rate of one and a half tons of grain per ton of fish until both countries have become completely specialized. Spain no longer produces any fish, and Norway no longer produces any grain. Norwegians catch 200 tons of fish, half of which is exported to Spain. The Spanish grow 500 tons of grain, 150 tons of which is exported to Norway. Table 7.1 compares this situation with a nonspecialized, pre-trade situation in which each country produces some of both products. The comparison reveals

TABLE 7.1   EFFECTS OF TRADE ON PRODUCTION

	Spain	Norway	World Total
Before Trade			
Fish			
Production	75	100	175
Consumption	75	100	175
Grain			
Production	350	100	450
Consumption	350	100	450
After Trade			
Fish			
Production	0	200	200
Consumption	100	100	200
Grain			
Production	500	0	500
Consumption	350	150	500

All figures represent tons produced or consumed

This table shows production and consumption of fish and grain in Spain, Norway, and the world as a whole before and after trade. The example assumes that each country specializes in the product in which it has a comparative advantage and that fish are traded for grain at the rate of 1.5 tons of grain per ton of fish.

three things. First, the Norwegians are better off than before; they have just as much fish to eat and fifty tons more grain than in the pre-trade equilibrium. Second, the Spaniards are also better off; they have just as much grain to consume as ever—and more fish. Looking at both countries together, we see that total world output of both grain and fish has risen as a result of trade. Everyone is better off, and no one is worse off.

Graphical Presentation

Comparative advantage can be illustrated graphically using a set of production possibility frontiers based on the example just given. This is done in Figure 7.2, which shows three production possibility frontiers.

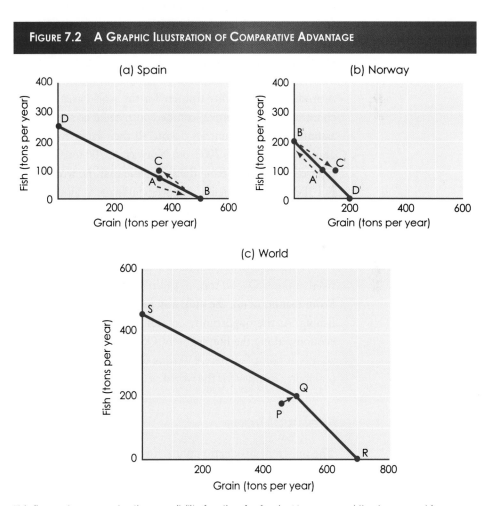

FIGURE 7.2   A GRAPHIC ILLUSTRATION OF COMPARATIVE ADVANTAGE

This figure shows production possibility frontiers for Spain, Norway, and the two countries combined. Before trade, Spain produces and consumes at point A and Norway at point A'. Together these correspond to world consumption point P, which is inside the world production possibility frontier. After trade begins, Spain specializes in producing grain (point B) and trades part of the grain for fish, moving to consumption point C. Norway specializes in producing fish (point B') and reaches consumption point B' through trade. As a result, world efficiency is improved and point Q on the world production possibility frontier is reached.

Part (a) is the production possibility frontier for Spain. Given 1,000 available labor hours and a cost of two labor hours per ton of grain, Spain can produce up to 500 tons of grain per year if it produces no fish (point B′). If it produces no grain, up to 250 tons of fish per year can be caught at a cost of four hours per ton of fish (point D′). The line running from B to D represents the combinations of grain and fish that Spain can produce.

Part (b) shows the production possibility frontier for Norway. In Norway, fish and grain both take five labor hours per ton to produce. If Norwegians devote all their time to fishing, they can catch up to 200 tons of fish per year (point B′). If they devote all their time to farming, they can grow up to 200 tons of grain (point D′). The line between B_1 and D_1 represents Norway's production possibility frontier.

According to the example summarized in Figure 7.2, before trade begins, Spain produces and consumes 350 tons of grain and seventy-five tons of fish. This is shown as point A on Spain's production possibility frontier. Norway is assumed to produce and consume 100 tons each of fish and grain. This is shown by point D′ on Norway's frontier.

The World Production Possibility Frontier

A production possibility frontier for the world as a whole (consisting of just these two countries in our example) can be constructed as shown in part (c) of Figure 7.2. First, assume that both countries devote all their labor to grain. That results in 500 tons of grain from Spain plus 200 from Norway, or 700 tons of grain in all (point R in part (c) of Figure 7.2). Starting from there, assume that the world output of fish is to be increased. For the sake of efficiency, Norwegian farmers should be the first to switch to fishing because the opportunity cost of fish is lower in Norway (one ton of grain per ton of fish) than in Spain (two tons of grain per ton of fish). As Norwegians switch to fishing, then, world production moves upward and to the left along the line segment RQ.

When all Norwegians have abandoned farming for fishing, the world will have arrived at point Q—500 tons of grain (all Spanish) and 200 tons of fish (all Norwegian). From that point on, the only way to get more fish is to have Spanish farmers switch to fishing. At the opportunity cost of two tons of grain per ton of fish, this moves the economy along the line segment QS. When all Spanish farmers are fishing, the world arrives at point S, where 450 tons of fish and no grain are produced. The production possibility frontier for the world as a whole, then, is the kinked line RQS.

Effects of Trade

The pre-trade production point for the world as a whole lies inside the world production possibility frontier. Adding together the quantities of fish and grain from A and A′, we arrive at point P in part (c) of Figure 7.2—450 tons of grain and 175 tons of fish. This is inefficient; the world economy as a whole could produce more of both goods. To increase efficiency, both countries must specialize.

Suppose that Spain shifts its production from 350 tons of grain and seventy-five tons of fish (point A) to 500 tons of grain and no fish (point B). It then trades the extra 150 tons of grain for 100 tons of Norwegian fish. Spain's consumption thus ends up at point C, while its production remains at B. At the same time, Norway shifts its production from A' to B', that is, it specializes entirely in fish. The extra 100 tons of fish are traded for the 150 tons of Spanish grain, moving Norwegian consumption to point C'.

As a result of specialization plus trade, then, both Spain and Norway have moved to points that lie outside their own production possibility frontiers. As they do so, the world as a whole moves from point P inside its production possibility frontier to point Q on the frontier. Thus, specialization improves the efficiency of the world economy as a whole, increases production of both goods, and leaves both countries better off than they would be if they did not trade.

Empirical Evidence on Comparative Advantage

Ricardo's theory of comparative advantage suggests that each country will export goods for which its labor is relatively productive compared with that of its trading partners. A number of economists have put this simple version of the theory to empirical tests.

One of the first to do so was G. D. A. MacDougal. In 1951 MacDougal published a study of U.S.-British trade, using data from 1937.[1] He compared a number of industries in terms of relative labor productivity in the two countries with the ratio of their exports of the products of those industries. The results strongly supported the Ricardian theory. Labor productivity was higher in the United States than in the United Kingdom for all of the industries studied, indicating that the United States had a Ricardian absolute advantage in all of the products. As predicted by the theory, however, the United Kingdom was relatively successful in exporting the goods in which its labor productivity disadvantage was lowest. British exports were greater than U.S. exports for all the industries studied in which British labor was more than half as productive as U.S. labor (for example, woolen cloth, footwear, hosiery). U.S. exports exceeded British exports for all the industries in which U.S. labor was more than twice as productive as British labor. Later studies using different sets of data have tended to confirm this result.

Comparative Advantage with Multiple Factors of Production

The Ricardian model of comparative advantage focused on a single factor of production: labor. Studies such as MacDougal's indicate that the single-factor version of the theory has considerable explanatory power. However, it can also be extended to take multiple factors of production into account.

Heckscher-Ohlin theorem

The proposition that countries tend to export goods that make intensive use of the factors of production that the country possesses in relative abundance

THE HECKSCHER-OHLIN THEOREM   Early in the twentieth century two Swedish economists, Eli Heckscher and Bertil Ohlin, developed a model that took into account two factors of production: capital and labor. They reasoned that countries with abundant supplies of labor and little capital would have a comparative advantage in labor-intensive goods, whereas countries with abundant capital and relatively less labor would have a comparative advantage in capital-intensive goods. The proposition that countries would tend to export products that use their relatively more abundant factor more intensively has come to be known as the **Heckscher-Ohlin theorem.** An illustration of this theorem is the pattern in which the United States exports capital-intensive aircraft to China in exchange for labor-intensive clothing.

The Importance of Demand

Both single-factor and multiple-factor versions of the theory of comparative advantage focus on supply conditions as the explanation of trade patterns. They implicitly assume that the consumer tastes that underlie the demand for goods and services are identical in all countries. In practice, however, patterns of trade contain some features that can be explained only by taking demand into account.

One such feature is the tendency of countries to trade most heavily with others at a similar level of economic development. This is not predicted by the simple Ricardian theory, which suggests that trade would be most profitable between countries that differ from each other as much as possible. For example, simple comparative advantage would suggest that the United States would have more trade with Mexico, structurally a very different economy, than with Canada, which not only has a much smaller population than Mexico, but also is more similar in many ways to the United States. However, Canada turns out to be the largest U.S. trading partner; and several distant countries, including Germany and Japan, rank close to nearby Mexico.

A closely related puzzle is the fact that countries both import and export the products of many industries. The United States is both a major importer and exporter of motor vehicles, textiles, computers, foodstuffs, and footwear, to name just a few examples.

Comparative advantage can explain these trade patterns only at the expense of trivializing the concept—by saying, for example, that Germany has a comparative advantage in producing Audis and the United States has a comparative advantage in producing Cadillacs. A better explanation is that such trade patterns reflect the influence of demand and tastes. Firms in developed countries sell where the demand for their products is greatest—in other developed countries. Cross-trade within product categories reflects patterns of tastes: Although U.S. automakers pattern their cars to fit the tastes of a majority of domestic consumers, some domestic buyers share European tastes for Audis and BMWs. These demand-side influences are not taken into account by the Ricardian theory and its modern variants, which look only at production costs.

Comparative Advantage and "Competitiveness"

As noted at the beginning of the chapter, U.S. involvement in world trade has grown greatly in recent decades. However, as U.S. exports have set records, imports have grown even more rapidly. In the first decade of the twenty-first century, the *trade deficit*—the amount by which imports exceed exports—reached an all-time high. This became a major cause of national concern. News reporters, editorialists, and politicians feared that the United States was no longer "competitive" in the world economy. Competitiveness means different things to different people, but at the heart of it is a concern that foreign workers work harder and foreign business managers have become smarter than their U.S. counterparts. "Soon the Japanese, the Koreans, and the Europeans will be better at everything than we are," people have said. "Eventually we won't be able to export anything at all!"

Some aspects of U.S. trade trends are a legitimate cause for concern. However, the theory of comparative advantage casts doubt on the notion that a country can reach a point at which it imports everything and exports nothing. In fact, classical trade theory, as embodied in the Spain-Norway example presented earlier, maintains that a country always has a comparative advantage in producing something even when it has an absolute disadvantage (in terms of labor hours or other factor inputs) for all goods. In terms of comparative advantage, then, a country must always be "competitive" in producing something.

Nevertheless, comparative advantage does not guarantee an exact match between the value of a country's exports and the value of its imports. The numerical examples given earlier, which suggest that this must be the case, omit two important details. First, they leave out international financial transactions, including purchases and sales of corporate stocks, government bonds, and other securities, as well as several kinds of international banking transactions. Second, they assume that trade takes the form of barter, whereas in practice most international trade uses money as a means of payment. Let us look briefly at the implications of each of these considerations for comparative advantage and competitiveness.

FINANCIAL TRANSACTIONS AND THE BALANCE OF TRADE   International financial transactions are important because they allow a country to import more goods and services than it exports, or to export more than it imports, in a given year. To take a very simple case, suppose that U.S. consumers decide to buy $100 million worth of television sets from Korean firms. What will the Korean firms do with the $100 million they receive? They can use it to buy airliners built in the United States, in which case trade in goods between the United States and Korea will balance. However, they can instead use it to buy U.S. government bonds or make deposits in U.S. banks. In that case, no U.S. goods will be exported in the current year to balance the imports. The Korean owners of the bonds or bank deposits have a claim on future exports from the United States; they can cash in their financial assets and spend them any time they like. Meanwhile, despite the U.S. comparative advantage in producing airliners, the U.S. trade accounts will not be balanced.

Could we say, then, that recent U.S. balance-of-trade deficits reflect a comparative advantage for the United States in the production of financial assets? That would certainly be one way to look at it. We could also say that Korean buyers simply prefer future U.S. airliners to current ones. That would be closer to the truth. A large part of the current U.S. trade deficit can be explained by the fact that many other countries, especially in Asia, have much higher savings rates than the United States, which does indicate a preference for future consumption over current consumption. Looked at in this light, we should be cautious about assuming that the imbalance in merchandise trade reflects a loss of "competitiveness" in the sense of lost comparative advantage.

EXCHANGE RATES AND COMPETITIVENESS   To understand international trade fully, we must also take into account the fact that it is conducted in terms of money. However, there is no world money; each country has its own currency. Thus, before one can buy goods, services, or financial instruments from abroad, one must first visit the *foreign-exchange markets,* in which one currency can be traded for another. The windows at international airports where tourists can use dollars to buy European euros or British pounds are a tiny part of these markets. Larger exchanges of currency are carried out through major banks in New York, London, Tokyo, and other world financial centers.

The forces of supply and demand determine the rates at which two currencies are exchanged. These vary greatly from day to day and from year to year. For example, in early 2000, a U.S. dollar was worth 1.10 euros; by early 2008, it was worth just over .60 euros. As exchange rates vary, so do the prices of countries' imports and exports. At 1.10 euros to a dollar, an American firm need spend only $50 to import a 55-euro bottle of French wine. At 0.60 euros to the dollar, it takes $92 to buy the same 55-euro bottle. Similarly, at 1.10 euros to the dollar, a French buyer would have to lay out 2,200 euros to buy a $2,000 software package produced in the United States. At 0.60 euros to the dollar, the price to the French buyer would be much less—only 1,200 euros.

We see, then, that the ability of U.S. exporters to compete in world markets—and the ability of U.S. firms to compete against imports in their home markets—depends not only on Ricardian considerations of factor productivity but also on exchange rates.

That is one reason why countries that do not allow their exchange rates to fluctuate freely in response to market forces are often subject to criticism. For example, for many years China held its exchange rate fixed at about 8 yuan per U.S. dollar, despite strong indications that supply and demand conditions would dictate a stronger yuan. U.S. politicians saw this as giving China an "unfair" advantage by making its exports cheaper for U.S. buyers, and making U.S. goods more expensive in China. When China, in mid-2005, began to move toward a more flexible exchange rate policy, U.S. exporters and firms that competed with imports from China breathed a sigh of relief. However, it often takes several years for changes in exchange rates to affect trade patterns, so the long-run effects of the change in Chinese policy were just beginning to be seen by 2008. Furthermore, as the Chinese yuan began to strengthen relative to the U.S. dollar, the change affected not just the volume of trade between the two countries but also the composition of trade. With a stronger exchange rate, China began to find it less attractive to export low-value-added products like clothing and, instead, began moving into higher-value-added sectors like electronics and automotive equipment.

Trade Policy and Protectionism

Up to this point we have not mentioned governmental policy regarding international trade. We have pictured a world in which Norwegian fishers and Spanish farmers are free to trade as dictated by comparative advantage. In practice, however, governments are deeply involved in the regulation and promotion of trade. In this section we examine government's role in international trade.

Moves Toward Freer Trade since World War II

The post–World War II period saw a broad movement toward freer trade aided by several new international organizations. The International Monetary Fund was

Protectionism

Any policy that is intended to shield domestic industries from import competition

Tariff

A tax on imported goods

Import quotas

A limit on the quantity of a good that can be imported over a given period

created in 1944 to maintain a stable financial climate for trade. The General Agreement on Tariffs and Trade (GATT) was founded in an attempt to combat **protectionism**—policies designed to shield domestic industries from competition by imports. In 1995, the World Trade Organization (WTO), which is now the world's principal authority overseeing international trade, replaced GATT.

WTO rules permit taxes on imports, known as **tariffs**, but restrict their use. Under the so-called most-favored-nation principle, WTO member nations are supposed to charge the same tariff rates for imports from all WTO countries. A series of multinational negotiations sponsored by the WTO succeeded in lowering the average level of tariffs from 40 percent at the end of World War II to less than 10 percent today. Throughout this period, as noted earlier, the volume of world trade grew consistently faster than the volume of world output. Also, the WTO has tried, with far from complete success, to discourage the use of **import quotas**—restrictions on the quantity of a good that can be imported during a given period.

REGIONAL TRADING BLOCS   In addition to the activities of the WTO, there have been efforts to set up regional trading blocs in several parts of the world. The best known of these is the European Union (EU). A key aim of the EU has been to eliminate all barriers to trade among the major European countries, eventually leading to a situation in which trade among these countries is nearly as free as trade among the states of the United States.

Not all goals of the EU have been achieved in full. Differences in levels of economic development among the countries of the EU, which are greater than those among the states of the United States, have been a recurring source of problems. Also, the goal of a single currency for Europe has proved more difficult to achieve than many had hoped. Nonetheless, after its expansion to 27 countries in 2007, the EU, with a population of nearly 500 million, can fairly be considered the world's largest unified economic zone in most respects.

On the other side of the Atlantic, progress was under way toward the formation of an even larger trading bloc. Its foundations were laid when the United States reached an agreement with Canada, its largest trading partner, to eliminate almost all trade barriers over a ten-year period beginning in 1989. (The U.S.-Canada treaty does allow for continued use of quotas on some farm, forest, and fishery products, and in some other respects falls short of the free-trade ideal.) The North American Free Trade Agreement (NAFTA), discussed in *Applying Economic Ideas 7.1*, soon followed.

Still another regional trading bloc, formed in late 1992, unites six countries of the Association of Southeast Asian Nations in the ASEAN Free Trade Area (AFTA). The member countries—Thailand, Philippines, Malaysia, Brunei, Singapore, and Indonesia—have a total population of 320 million people. A similar regional trading block, MECOSUR, links several of the most important economies of Latin America.

There is a downside to regional free trade blocs, however. That is the tendency of such blocs to raise protectionist barriers against outsiders. Thus, NAFTA contains provisions protecting North American (mainly U.S.) firms against competition

Applying Economic Ideas 7.1
NAFTA—AT FIFTEEN YEARS

In 1994, Mexico, Canada, and the United States entered into the North American Free Trade Agreement (NAFTA). Over the past fifteen years, many of the agreement's promised benefits have materialized, but there have been some disappointments, too.

NAFTA did bring some obvious positive results. Trade within NAFTA countries more than doubled. Mexico replaced Japan as America's second largest trading partner behind Canada. Early winners included U.S. export powerhouses like Caterpillar, Inc. The construction equipment giant saw its exports to Mexico triple in the five years after NAFTA was initiated and captured the lion's share of future growth in this market. A key reason: NAFTA resulted in elimination of Mexico's 20 percent import tariff on U.S. construction equipment while leaving the tariff in place on equipment made by Japanese rivals.

U.S. firms responded to the opening of the Mexican market not only with exports but also with construction of new plants south of the border. Hoover Company, for example, started building handheld vacuum cleaners in Ciudad Juarez, just across the border from El Paso, Texas. Hoover previously manufactured these machines in Asia, but believed it would be more economical to move the work to Mexico.

Caterpillar, Inc. was an early winner of NAFTA tripling exports to Mexico.

The free trade agreement was not limited to manufacturing. It created significant opportunities for U.S. service industries, as well. Southwestern Bell Corporation helped to rebuild Mexico's creaky telephone system. Bank of America, which already had branches in every U.S. state along the Mexican border, expanded into Mexico itself as barriers to international banking were relaxed. Some promises, however, were not kept. Fifteen years after NAFTA, the United States, citing safety concerns, had still not met its pledge to open its highways to Mexi-

can trucks, leading to retaliation by Mexico against imports from the north.

Not all results of NAFTA's first 10 years were as positive as had been hoped by those who conceived and negotiated the pact in the 1990s. In particular, effects on Mexican labor markets were mixed. More than half a million new manufacturing jobs were created, but gains in productivity growth due to foreign investment did not always feed through to the labor force in the form of higher real wages. NAFTA also opened Mexico's farm sector to competition from efficient, and often subsidized, U.S. producers. This put pressure on Mexican farmers to improve productivity, and they did so; but still, more farm jobs were lost than were gained in the factory sector. "It's a race against time," said Antonio Hernández, an agronomist who advises farmers for a coalition of farming associations in Jalisco state, in an interview with the *New York Times*. "We have to demonstrate [the benefits to farmers] before people abandon the land."

"NAFTA has had positive effects in Mexico, but they could have been better," said David de Ferranti, World Bank Vice President for Latin America and the Caribbean, summarizing his organization's report on NAFTA. "Free trade definitely brings new economic opportunities, but the lessons from NAFTA for other countries negotiating with the United States are that free trade alone is not enough without significant policy and institutional reforms."

SOURCE: Daniel Lederman, Louis Maloney, and Louis Serven, *Lessons from NAFTA*, World Bank, 2003; John J. Audley and Demetrios Papademetriou, Sandra Polaski, and Scott Vaugh, *NAFTA's Promise and Reality*, Carnegie Endowment for World Peace, 2003; and Elizabeth Malkin, "NAFTA's Promise Unfulfilled," *New York Times*, March 23, 2009.

from Asian and European rivals. The EU is notorious for shielding its farmers from outside competition. Serious worries remain about the possibility of open trade war between the blocs. AFTA, on the other hand, is composed of relatively poor nations that cannot afford to cut themselves off from world trade. Their bloc is based on the principle of "open regionalism" that will lower barriers within the group without raising them against outsiders.

Countertrends: the New Protectionism

Spurred by the strengthening of free-trade institutions, the volume of world trade has increased greatly in recent decades. However, protectionism is far from dead. In addition to the continued use of traditional tariffs and quotas, especially in agriculture, new types of protectionism have sprung up, resulting in the imposition of additional restrictions on international trade. The new protectionism consists in part of devices such as "orderly marketing agreements" and "voluntary export restraints." These involve the use of political pressure—usually backed by the threat of a tariff or quota—to restrain trade in a particular good.

A leading example of the new protectionism was the so-called Multifiber Agreement (MFA), formally adopted in 1974.[2] This agreement, which began as a temporary restriction on imports of Japanese cotton textiles into the United States, grew into a vast web of quotas that all major trading countries used to manage trade in all types of textiles and apparel. The agreement was a major violation of WTO principles, not only in its emphasis on quotas, but also in its open discrimination among exporting nations. By imposing much more stringent limits on imports from developing countries than from industrialized exporters in the EU and elsewhere, the MFA undermined not only the principles of the WTO but also the stated U.S. policy of promoting economic development in low-income countries. Several developing countries complained about unfair treatment because of the MFA restrictions, which cost them as much as 20 million jobs each year. These complaints led to the termination of the MFA at the end of 2004. Termination of the MFA will potentially rationalize patterns of international textile trade; however, it has had some painful effects in the short run. Under the MFA, some countries were subject to tighter restrictions than others, with the result of a shift in textile production patterns among developing countries. Since the end of the MFA, countries like Bangladesh, which had large quotas under the MFA, have lost market share to more efficient producers in China.

The new protectionism not only applies to preventing the import of foreign goods but also to preventing the export of jobs. Many companies in the United States and other countries have shifted their operations away from the high-wage environment at home to one with cheaper labor to lower their costs of production. This practice of shifting jobs from one country to another is known as outsourcing. India has become a popular locale for outsourcing everything from customer service centers to city government administrative services. In the early 2000s, the backlash against the foreign outsourcing of U.S. jobs grew in state legislatures around the country. Bills aimed at curbing the outflow of jobs were introduced in several states. Most required that state contracts go only to companies that certify the work will be done inside the United States.

Many forms of the new protectionist agreements are referred to as voluntary, but their effects on consumers scarcely differ from those of a compulsory tariff or quota. Prices go up and reductions in efficiency occur as production moves against the direction of comparative advantage. For example, the cost of the Multifiber Agreement to U.S. consumers was estimated at more than $20 billion per year, or about $238 per U.S. household as of 1986.

Antidumping rules are another aspect of the new protectionism. A country is said to be "dumping" its goods when it sells them in a foreign market for less than the price at which it sells them at home or for less than the cost of producing them. Under certain provisions of U.S. law, domestic producers facing competition from imports that have been "dumped" on the U.S. market can seek tariffs. Steel is one of the industries that have sought this type of protection.

Application of anti-dumping rules has been a constant source of friction between the United States and the EU. The WTO has ruled against the United States in several recent antidumping cases, including an attempt by President George W. Bush to impose antidumping tariffs on steel imports.

The steel industry has sought protection from having imports "dumped" on the U.S. market.

Understanding Protectionism: Impacts of Trade on Income Distribution

Why is it that protectionist measures are so widely used, despite the potential economic efficiency to be gained from free trade? To understand the sources of protectionism, we can begin by considering the effects of trade on the distribution of income within each country. A modification of the Spain-Norway example to take into account more than one factor of production will illustrate some basic principles.

Suppose that fishing requires a relatively large capital investment per worker, in the form of expensive boats, nets, and navigation equipment, while farming requires a relatively small investment in tractors and plows. Fishing can then be said to be capital intensive and farming to be labor intensive. Also assume, as before, that in the absence of trade, the opportunity cost of fish will be higher in Spain than in Norway, so that Spain has a comparative advantage in grain and Norway has a comparative advantage in fish. As in the single-factor example, international trade will still make it possible for total world production of both fish and grain to increase. It will still enable the quantities of both goods available in both countries to rise. Now, however, a new question arises:

How will the gains from trade be distributed within each country?

To answer this question, we must look at what happens in factor markets as trade brings about increasing specialization in each country. In Norway, production shifts from farming to fishing. As grain production is phased out, large quantities of labor and relatively small quantities of capital are released. The shift in production thus creates a surplus of labor and a shortage of capital. Factor markets can return to equilibrium only when wages fall relative to the rate of return on capital. Only then will fisheries adopt more labor-intensive production methods. Meanwhile the opposite process occurs in Spain where the shift from fishing to farming depresses the rate of return on capital and increases the wage rate.

These changes in relative factor prices determine how the gains from trade are distributed among the people of each country. Spanish workers and Norwegian boat owners will gain doubly from trade—first because trade increases the size of the pie (the total

Economics in the News 7.1
OUTSOURCING

Shifting U.S. jobs overseas has become a hot-button political issue, but the bottom line for companies is that outsourcing saves them a lot of money.

Early in 2004, Gregory Mankiw, chairman of President Bush's Council of Economic Advisers, took a lot of heat from both sides of the political aisle for suggesting that outsourcing to India and other countries is a win-win for both sides. Democratic presidential candidate John Kerry and Republican House Speaker Dennis Hastert sharply criticized the senior Bush aide, saying jobs should stay in the United States. Kerry said offshoring is done by "Benedict Arnold CEOs."

Just as China is the top low-cost manufacturer, India is the equivalent in business services. India exported nearly $10 billion in tech services in 2003, mostly to the United States. The volume is said to be growing more than 30 percent a year. Some big changes in the past decade are driving this growth. India has opened itself to trade and eased business restrictions. Plus, communications advances have made it far easier to have operations around the world. That $10 billion makes up less than 3 percent of global spending on IT services, says Ashish Thadhani, senior vice president of Brean Murray & Co. "So there's lots of room to grow," he said.

Putting a stop to such growth now won't be easy. Savings are a big draw, with quality of work a close second. "The rule of thumb is that each employee in India translates into annual savings of $20,000 to $30,000," said Thadhani. "General Electric is saving well over $300

Outsourcing saves money.

million doing captive in-house business process outsourcing in India. Recently IBM indicated its savings (in information technology services) could be more than $150 million a year," he said.

GE spokesman Peter Stack, echoing Mankiw's win-win sentiment, says savings are only part of the allure. "The abilities of (developing) countries to rapidly grow middle classes and well-compensated work forces benefits us tremendously. They create markets for us to sell into," he said. "It's about global competitiveness."

Since entering India in 1997, GE's work force there has swelled to over 20,000. Stack says jobs done in India are increasingly sophisticated and include pure science research and development.

China and India have a seemingly endless supply of lower cost workers. India's 1.1 billion population is second only to China's 1.3 billion, but India has a steady stream of high-caliber professionals. They are English-speaking engineers, software technicians, and other high-tech specialists. They're also call-center personnel trained to modify their Raj-rooted Anglo-Indian accents and speak like Americans. "The Indian education system places strong emphasis on technical and quantitative skills, English proficiency and a diligent work ethic," Thadhani said.

SOURCE: Marilyn Alva, "U.S. Firms' Outsourcing To India Reaps Big Savings, Political Heat," *Investor's Business Daily*, February 20, 2004. Portions reprinted with permission.

quantity of goods) and second because the shifts in factor prices give them a larger slice of that pie. For Norwegian workers and Spanish owners of agricultural capital, in contrast, one of these effects works against the other. These groups still benefit from the growth of the pie, but they get a smaller piece of it than before. They may or may not end up better off as a result of the trade.

Suppose that the comparative advantage in the pre-trade situation is large and the difference in factor intensity between the two countries is small. Norwegian workers and owners of Spanish farms will still gain from trade in an absolute sense, even though they will lose ground relative to others in their own country. If conditions are less favorable, however, they can end up worse off than they were before trade began. Who gains and who loses depends partly on the degree of specialization of factors of production.

So far we have looked at matters only in terms of broadly defined labor, as if workers could move from job to job without cost. However, suppose instead that we think not in terms of labor in general but in terms of people with farming skills and people with fishing skills, or auto workers and textile workers. When specialized skills and locational factors are taken into account, the effects of trade include not only changes in relative wages but also periods of unemployment, costs of retraining, and moving expenses. The uneven impact of changes in trade patterns on the lives and jobs of specific categories of workers turns out to be one of the main sources of political support for protectionism, as we will see in the next section.

Protectionism and Public Choice

International competition, like other forms of competition, tends to drive wages and returns to other factors of production toward the level of opportunity costs. Protection against foreign competition relieves the pressure and permits the protected firms and workers to earn rents—that is, profits and wages in excess of opportunity costs. Thus, the political process that results in trade restrictions can be analyzed in terms of public choice theory and rent seeking.

As a specific example, consider the costs and benefits of U.S. trade restrictions on sugar imports. Historically, the United States produced about half of the sugar it consumed and imported the rest.[3] By the early 2000s, as a result of trade restrictions, it was importing only about 12 percent of its sugar. As a result, sugar prices in the United States have ranged from two to three times the world price, at a cost to U.S. consumers of some $1.9 billion per year. The United States not only maintains barriers to direct imports of sugar but also has a high tariff on the indirect import of sugar in the form of ethanol distilled from sugar cane in Brazil and other countries. That not only helps keep the U.S. price of sugar high but also raises the price of corn, as well, since in the United States, ethanol is primarily made from corn rather than sugar cane.

What explains the willingness of U.S. consumers to pay high prices for sugar? It is, apparently, a classic case of the disproportionate political influence of small, well-organized interest groups. The benefits of restrictions on sugar imports are concentrated on producers, who are few in number. Large companies like Flo-Sun and U.S. Sugar contribute hundreds of thousands of dollars to candidates of both major parties during each election cycle. On the other hand, the $1.9 billion cost of sugar quotas to consumers comes to just $6 per individual. For them, sugar policy is an insignificant consideration in making political choices.

Sugar policy can also be viewed in terms of its impact on jobs. Only about 16,000 U.S. workers are employed in sugar production and refining in the United States, and an end to quotas would threaten the jobs of only about 3,000 of those. Production of corn sweetener, which benefits indirectly from high sugar production, employs more workers, perhaps as many as 250,000; but the threat to those jobs is also less direct. If sugar quotas were removed, the chief employment bene-fit would be creation of new jobs in the food processing industry, which already employs far more workers, more than 500,000. The political impact of changes in the job market, however, is not proportional to the number of jobs affected. The key consideration is that workers in sugar production know who they are and understand that their jobs might be threatened by a policy change. Potential new workers in food processing, currently employed elsewhere or unemployed, do not specifically identify sugar policy as a factor affecting their welfare. As a result, sugar workers are politically active on the issue and potential new food processing workers are not.

This analysis could be repeated for any protected market. For example, the cost to consumers of each job saved in the apparel industry by the MFA was estimated at $46,000 per year, compared with average earnings of just $11,000 per year for textile workers.[4] Studies of tariffs and quotas on peanuts, books, ceramic tile, and other prod-ucts give similar results. In each case economic investigators have found that total gains to producers fall short of total costs to consumers; however, the benefits are con-centrated on compact, politically active groups while the costs are spread among mil-lions of households.

A Race to the Bottom?

Often opponents of free trade speak a simple language of self-interest, using money and political power to advance their position regardless of effects on others. However, some opponents of globalization in high-income countries have a genuine concern for possible adverse effects of trade on people in their low-income trade partners.

One such concern is that free trade leads to a "race to the bottom" in global labor standards. Trade based on comparative advantage is all well and good, they would say, if a country does have a genuine advantage in producing something at a low cost. They would hardly want Iceland to be self-sufficient in coffee or the city-state of Sin-gapore to have to produce all its own rice. Still, they say, some kinds of cost advantage should not be recognized as a legitimate basis for trade. For example, critics argue that countries should not be encouraged to lower health and safety protections for workers in an attempt to gain a comparative advantage based on lower labor costs.

In evaluating such concerns about labor standards, some observers distinguish between "cash standards" and "core standards." Cash standards mean wages and non-wage labor benefits like employer-paid health care or paid vacation. To insist that workers in poor countries be paid the same as those in rich ones could be to deprive them entirely of the benefits of trade-based growth. Refusing to buy products from people who are poor seems like a strange way to help them become rich. Experience shows, instead, that countries like Korea or Taiwan, where living standards grew rap-idly in the late twentieth century, were relatively open to trade during their early years as low-wage countries. Similarly, in China, relatively primitive textile and footwear factories, where wages can be as low as $2 per day, are increasingly being forced out of business by changing patterns of trade. Workers are, instead, moving to more modern factories producing photovoltaic panels or computer chips, where wages are $10 per day or more. These wages are still very low by U.S. or European standards; but for the workers involved, they represent the next step from poverty to economic security.

Core labor standards, on the other hand, are seen more as a matter of universal human rights than simply of labor costs. They include such things as abolition of forced labor and abusive child labor, the right for workers to associate freely and bargain collectively, and the absence of discrimination in employment. A true "race to the bottom" would occur if policies encouraged production to move to the countries that most flagrantly ignored core labor standards.

A similar concern is that trade policy could promote a "race to the bottom" in terms of environmental standards. As we saw in Chapter 6, sustainable waste disposal practices are typically more costly for producers than dumping untreated wastes into the environment. Again, a distinction could be made between environmental standards that reflect economic choices and those that could be regarded as core standards. With regard to economic choice, it can be argued that people in low-income countries might not be willing to sacrifice as much material consumption for a given improvement in local air or water quality as those in high-income countries. Environmental quality is a "normal good" as we defined it in Chapter 5. As incomes rise, people are willing to "buy" more environmental quality, and trends over time show that they do so. (Compare urban air quality in London today with that in Charles Dickens' time, for example.)

On the other hand, companies and sometimes countries may be tempted to cut costs by ignoring more fundamental environmental standards. Suppose, for example, that two countries both have well-designed environmental laws; but in one, the laws are enforced, whereas in the other, corrupt inspectors take bribes and turn their backs on violations. Would it be right to say that the latter country had a comparative advantage based on lower costs? Economic analysis says that it would not. Total costs of production, including both internal and external costs, are likely to be higher, not lower, in the country where externalities go uncontrolled. Costs only appear lower because lax enforcement allows producers to impose the costs on their neighbors. If the pollution in question has a cross-border nature, like emissions of greenhouse gasses or the chemicals that destroy the earth's protective ozone layer, it is even harder to argue that world efficiency gains when trade moves production to high-pollution countries.

There is no reason to expect the war of words over globalization and trade policy to end soon. The presidential election of 2008 featured many sharp exchanges on trade policy. During the presidential debates, winning candidate Barak Obama pledged to review past trade agreements, including NAFTA, and renegotiate any provisions that were found not to be in the interests of U.S. workers, consumers, and businesses. We can only hope that an understanding of the economics of international trade can help in evaluating the claims made by the various participants in this ongoing debate.

Summary

1. **How can the principle of comparative advantage be applied to international trade?** A country is said to have a comparative advantage in the production of a good if it can produce it at a lower opportunity cost than its trading partner can. When each country exports goods in which it has a comparative advantage, total world production of all goods and services, as well as total consumption in each trading country, can increase. The *Heckscher-Ohlin theorem* proposes that countries will tend to have a comparative advantage in goods that make intensive use of the factors of production that are relatively abundant in that country.

2. **How is the notion of competitiveness related to that of comparative advantage?** In recent years, U.S. imports have expanded more rapidly than exports, leaving the country with a record trade deficit. Some observers interpreted this situation as indicating a loss of competitiveness, implying that U.S. firms were no longer capable of producing goods that other countries wanted. However, trends in imports and exports cannot be evaluated without consideration of international financial transactions and exchange rates. When these are taken into account, a country that is "competitive" in the sense that it produces high quality goods using state-of-the-art management and technology can still import more than it exports.

3. **What has been the trend of international trade policy in recent years?** The general trend in international trade policy has been toward a reduction of traditional *tariff* and QUOTA barriers to trade. Another important trend has been the formation of regional trade groups like the European Union and NAFTA. However, recent years have also seen increased use of protectionist devices such as orderly marketing agreements, voluntary quotas, antidumping laws, and restrictive product standards.

4. **How does international trade affect income distribution within each country?** In a world with two or more factors of production, trade tends to increase the demand for factors that are used relatively intensively in producing goods for export and to decrease the demand for factors that are used relatively intensively in producing goods that compete with imported goods. Thus, although trade benefits a country as a whole, it may not benefit owners of factors that are specialized for producing goods that compete with imports.

5. **How can protectionist policies be understood in terms of public choice theory and rent seeking?** Because protectionist policies shield firms and factor owners from international competition, they allow rents—that is, payments in excess of opportunity costs—to be earned. Often those who benefit from these rents are small, well-organized groups that have political influence out of proportion to their numbers. Although the overall costs of protectionism tend to outweigh the benefits, the costs are spread widely among consumers, each of whom is affected less than producers by any given trade barrier.

Key Terms

Problems and Topics for Discussion

1. **NAFTA and comparative advantage** What does the example of NAFTA (*Applying Economic Ideas 7.1*) suggest about U.S. versus Mexican comparative advantage in the production of construction equipment? Of vacuum cleaners?

Do these examples suggest a pattern of trade that would be consistent with the Heckscher-Ohlin theorem? What are the potential benefits and costs of NAFTA for U.S. and Mexican workers? Consumers? Owners of productive resources other than labor?

2. **A change in costs and comparative advantage** Suppose that new, high-yield grains are introduced in Norway and that the number of labor hours needed to grow a ton of grain there is cut from 5 hours to 2.5 hours. What will happen to trade between Norway and Spain? If the number of labor hours needed to grow a ton of grain in Norway falls all the way to 2, what will happen to the pattern of trade?

3. **Competitiveness** Consider the following statement: "The United States may still be number one, but I don't think we will be much longer. The European Union, Japan—all areas of the world are catching up. Soon it will no longer be economical for us to produce anything." On the basis of what you have learned about the principle of comparative advantage, do you think it is possible to reach a point at which it is no longer worthwhile to produce anything—that is, a point at which it becomes economical to import all goods? Discuss.

4. **Trade bargaining** If you were a strong supporter of free trade and in charge of U.S. international trade policy, would you cut tariffs and quotas, or would you negotiate with the nation's trading partners, maintaining trade barriers unless they lowered theirs too? Discuss.

5. **The globalization debate** Do a Web search for "globalization + environment standards" or "globalization + labor standards." Reading pro- and anti-globalization sources, can you identify "economic" issues and "core" issues? Can you identify any cases in which it appears that parties to the debate are using altruistic rhetoric to defend simple self-interest?

Case for Discussion

WTO Ruling in Cotton Subsidy Case Makes U.S. Farmers Nervous

A ruling by the World Trade Organization condemning U.S. subsidies to cotton producers could open the door to similar cases, perhaps forcing advanced countries to agree to deeper cuts in their subsidies, say trade officials and agricultural experts.

The WTO ruled in a confidential decision that the U.S. had fallen foul of its WTO obligations by providing subsidies of $12.5 billion to U.S. cotton growers between 1999 and 2002, boosting U.S. exports and depressing prices at the expense of Brazilian cotton growers and other producers.

Under its left-leaning president, Luis Inacio Lula da Silva, Brazil has taken a lead among emerging countries in pushing for reductions of agricultural subsidies in the developed world.

The threat of further cases should help strengthen the bargaining position of agricultural exporting countries. Farm exporters are pressing for big cuts in domestic supports for rich-country producers, but the U.S. and European Union say developing countries must also make concessions, for instance, by cutting tariffs on agricultural and industrial goods.

U.S. farmers are nervous that the ruling could set a broad precedent. Payments similar to the cotton subsidies are made for other U.S. commodities such as soybeans, rice, and wheat.

SOURCE: Jonathan Wheatley, Edward Alden, and Frances Williams, "Brazil Victory Could Prompt Subsidies Cases," Financial Times, April 28, 2004, p. 8.

QUESTIONS

1. A subsidy on exports is, in a sense, the opposite of a tariff on imports. If a tariff lowers efficiency, would you expect a subsidy to increase efficiency or, also, lower it? How do tariffs and subsidies compare in the way they distort trade according to comparative advantage?

2. Who gains and who loses from U.S. cotton subsidies? Consider each of the following groups: U.S. producers, U.S. taxpayers, Brazilian producers, and consumers in both countries? Do you think total gains exceed or fall short of total losses?

3. How could you explain the expenditure of billions of taxpayer dollars to subsidize a relatively few, highly prosperous U.S. cotton producers? Do the categories of public choice theory help here?

End Notes

1. G. D. A. MacDougal, "British and American Exports: A Study Suggested by the Theory of Comparative Costs," *Economic Journal* (December 1951).

2. For a thorough discussion of the MFA, see Thomas Grennes, "The Multifiber Arrangement and the Management of International Textile Trade," *Cato Journal* (Spring/Summer 1989): 107–131.

3. Information on sugar policy and its effects based on Mark A. Groombridge, "American's Bittersweet Sugar Policy," Cato Institute Center for Trade Policy Studies, December 4, 2001.

4. See Grennes. The comparison of consumers' costs to workers' wages actually understates the true cost-benefit ratio because the MFA's cost to consumers continued year after year, whereas displaced apparel workers are out of work less than six months, on the average. Taking this fact into account, it has been estimated that consumers bear $31 in costs through higher apparel prices for each $1 benefit to apparel workers.

PART 3

Economics of
the Firm

CHAPTER *8*

Production and Cost

After reading this chapter, you will understand the following:

1. How economists view the concepts of cost and profit
2. The distinction between short-run and long-run time horizons
3. How costs vary in response to changes in the quantity of a variable input
4. How a firm's cost structure can be represented in geometric terms
5. The choices a firm faces in the course of long-run expansion

Before reading this chapter, make sure you know the meaning of the concepts:

1. Opportunity cost
2. Entrepreneurship
3. Economic rent
4. Rational choice

B USINESS FIRMS, WHETHER giants like Microsoft or midgets like a local lawn service, are one of the basic units of microeconomic analysis. The chapters in this section look at firms from several perspectives. This chapter looks at firms as mechanisms for transforming inputs of labor, capital, and natural resources into outputs. Chapters 9, 10, and 11 look at firms as profit maximizers in markets with a variety of competitive structures. Chapter 12 looks at issues in public policy that are raised by the behavior of firms in various market structures.

Costs and Profits

As in our discussion of consumer choice, we can begin our study of the firm by looking at the objectives and constraints that shape its choices. Our theory will assume that the principal objective of any private firm is to maximize its profit. The principal constraints on its opportunities are, first, its costs of production, and second, the demand for its output. We will bring demand into the picture beginning in the next chapter. In this chapter, we will explore costs and their relationship to profit.

The Profit Motive

The assumption that profit is the principal objective of the business firm often meets an objection similar to that raised against the assumption of rationality. It implies too narrow a view of human nature. To be sure, critics say, profit is important, but it is hardly the only thing businesses are interested in. Managers of some firms seem to display other-regarding preferences. They spend large amounts on supporting the arts or aiding the homeless and exhibit concern for their workers, their customers, and the environment beyond any level that might increase profits by enhancing the firm's public image. Other firms are led by egotists who will risk all, including profit itself, in pursuit of building a personal empire. Still others are run by people who prefer to take Wednesday afternoons off for golf as long as their firms earn a minimum level of profit needed to survive.

After our discussion of rational choice in Chapter 4, it should not be hard to guess how economists answer this objection.

One answer, true to the spirit of neoclassical economics, is that the assumption of profit maximization is not intended to serve as a comprehensive description of the motives behind business decisions. Rather, it is a simplification, the purpose of which gives a sharper structure to theories about the way changes in costs or demands affect decisions. A simple theory should be discarded for a more complex one only if it fails to explain behavior observed in the real world. In practice, theories based on the assumption of profit maximization are able to explain a great deal of what firms are observed to do. In some special situations, theories can be improved by taking into account objectives other than profit. Such situations are few, however.

The *survivorship principle* is a second defense of the assumption of profit maximization. Imagine that ownership of firms is at first distributed randomly among people who are inclined to pursue the objective of profit and others who favor the objectives of benevolence, ego satisfaction, or the easy life. Over time, the firms that maximized profit would increase their capital and grow steadily through investment or acquisition. Those that pursued other objectives would at best have fewer profits to invest in expansion and at worst might be forced out of business by losses. As time went on, then, the survivors of the competitive process would tend to be the profit maximizers.

The Nature of Costs

Profit is the difference between revenue and costs, so we cannot get far in discussing profits without looking at costs. As we learned in Chapter 1, economists think first and foremost in terms of opportunity cost. Because of scarcity, no production can take place without an *opportunity cost*. There are never enough resources to satisfy all wants; and, therefore, the decision to produce any one thing implies the need to forgo using the same resources to produce something else. The opportunity costs of production are a fundamental constraint on a firm's ability to maximize its profits. In this section, we will explore several aspects of production costs and explain their relationship to one another.

IMPLICIT AND EXPLICIT COSTS   The opportunity costs that a firm faces include the compensation it must pay to workers, investors, and owners of natural resources in order to attract factors of production away from alternative uses, as well as the payments it must make to other firms that supply it with intermediate goods, such as parts, semi-finished materials, and business services. Those costs can be classified in several ways. We begin with the distinction between explicit and implicit costs.

Explicit costs

Opportunity costs that take the form of explicit payments to suppliers of factors of production and intermediate goods

Implicit costs

Opportunity costs of using resources contributed by the firm's owners (or owned by the firm itself as a legal entity) that are not obtained in exchange for explicit payments

Explicit costs are opportunity costs that take the form of explicit payments to suppliers of factors of production and intermediate goods. They include workers' wages, managers' salaries, salespeople's commissions, payments to banks and other suppliers of financial services, fees for legal advice, transportation charges, and many other things.

Long as this list is, explicit costs do not include all of the opportunity costs that a firm bears when it engages in production. There are also **implicit costs**—opportunity costs of using resources contributed by the firm's owners (or owned by the firm itself as a legal entity) that are not obtained under contracts calling for explicit payments.

The owners of many small businesses contribute resources to their firms without the guarantee of an explicit payment. For example, if the proprietor of a small firm works along with the firm's hired employees without receiving a salary, he or she gives up the opportunity to work for someone else. The correct measure of the opportunity cost of the owner's labor would be the wage or salary that could be earned in the next-best employment opportunity. Also, small-business owners often invest their own savings in the firm without receiving an explicit interest payment. The correct measure of the opportunity cost of capital for such a firm would be the interest or dividend that could be earned by using the same amount of capital to make a similarly risky investment elsewhere. Firms normally do not record implicit costs in their accounts, but this does not make those costs any less real.

For a publicly traded corporation, the most important implicit cost is the opportunity cost of capital contributed by shareholders. Shareholders will not buy a corporation's stock unless they expect to be compensated through dividends or through increases in the market price of their shares. There is some minimum rate of return (which will vary from one company to another, depending on risks, taxes, and other considerations) needed to persuade people to buy the stock. This minimum depends on what potential shareholders think they could earn by investing their money in the stock of some other corporation subject to similar risks and tax treatments.

Pure economic profit

The sum that remains when both explicit and implicit costs are subtracted from total revenue

Accounting profit

Total revenue minus explicit costs

COSTS AND PROFITS   The distinction between explicit and implicit costs is important in understanding what economists mean by profit—the firm's chief objective. Economists use the term profit to mean the difference between a firm's total revenues and all of its opportunity costs, including both explicit and implicit costs. To distinguish this meaning from other possible meanings, we will call it **pure economic profit**. Special care must be taken to distinguish economic profit from two other uses of the term profit.

First, in the business world, *profit* is often used to mean revenue minus explicit costs only, without giving consideration to implicit costs. Economists call this concept **accounting profit** because it considers only the explicit payments that appear in the firm's written accounts.[1] The relationship between accounting profit and pure economic profit is as follows:

$$\text{Pure economic profit} = \text{Accounting profit} - \text{Implicit costs}$$

or alternatively

$$\text{Accounting profit} = \text{Pure economic profit} + \text{Implicit costs}$$

Second, pure economic profit needs to be distinguished from so-called normal profit, a term that is sometimes used to refer to the opportunity cost of capital contributed by the firm's owners (*equity capital*, in financial terminology). **Normal return on capital** is an equivalent term. Suppose that you use $200,000 of your own savings as capital for a new business. You could, instead, have invested in securities that paid a 10 percent rate of return, or $20,000 per year. That $20,000 would be your opportunity cost of capital. It represents the return your funds would have earned in the best alternative use. The same reasoning would be applied if the capital were contributed by outside shareholders rather than by an entrepreneur who actively participated in managing the business.

Normal profit (normal return on capital)

The implicit opportunity cost of capital contributed by the firm's owners (equity capital)

To understand how the opportunity cost of owners' capital comes to be called *normal profit*, consider a firm that has no other implicit costs. In order for such a firm to earn zero economic profit, its accounting profit would have to be equal to its implicit opportunity cost of capital. Such a rate of accounting profit could be called "normal" in the sense that it is just enough to make it worthwhile for owners to invest their capital in this firm, rather than in the best alternative line of business available. Lines of business that earned more than this (that is, a positive pure economic profit), would be perceived as "abnormally" profitable and would swiftly attract new investors and competitors. Those that earned less would be perceived as less than "normally" profitable and would tend to shrink as investors channeled their capital elsewhere.

If a firm has other implicit costs in addition to those of owners' capital, its accounting profit must be sufficient to cover them, too, in order to earn zero economic profit. This idea can be expressed in terms of any of the following equations, all of which are equivalent:

Accounting profit = Pure economic profit + Implicit costs

= Pure economic profit + Implicit cost of capital + Other implicit costs

= Pure economic profit + Normal profit + Other implicit costs

AN EXAMPLE   At several points in this chapter and the next, it will be convenient to use an imaginary business as a basis for numerical examples of concepts that we introduce. Our imaginary business will be called Fieldcom, Inc. It is a small business started by a couple named Ralph and Andrea Martin. The Martins buy commonly available computer parts and assemble them into special-purpose Personal Digital Assistants (PDAs) that are "ruggedized" so that they can be used, not only in an office or on a commuter train, but also in stressful environments like a desert oil field, a tropical mining site, or aboard an ocean racing yacht.

Figure 8.1 uses Fieldcom, Inc., to illustrate the concepts of pure economic profit, accounting profit, and normal profit. The figure shows Fieldcom as having earned total revenues of $600,000 in the past year. Explicit costs—salaries paid to employees and materials purchased—came to $400,000. That left an accounting profit of $200,000. The explicit costs do not include all of the firm's opportunity costs, however. Both Andrea and Ralph Martin gave up high-paying jobs to start the firm. Their combined former income of $160,000 is listed in Figure 8.1 as an implicit cost of production. Also listed as an implicit cost is $20,000 of forgone income that the Martins could have earned on $200,000 of personal savings if they had invested it elsewhere instead of in their business. This is the firm's opportunity cost of capital—the normal profit or normal return on capital required to attract capital to this use rather than to the best alternative use. When both explicit and implicit costs (including normal profit) are subtracted from revenue, the firm is left with a pure economic profit of $20,000.

COSTS ARE SUBJECTIVE   A final word is in order regarding the nature of costs. In turning from the theory of consumption set forth in Chapter 5 to the theory of production costs, it may at first appear that we are moving from an area of economics governed by *subjective* valuations to one of *objective* valuations. This is true only in part, if at all.

It is true that business managers and their accountants do make serious efforts to record costs in numerical form and, in doing so, to apply consistent, rational methods that are as free as possible from wishful thinking and intentional bias. In this sense, the process of cost accounting is objective.

FIGURE 8.1   ACCOUNTS OF FIELDCOM, INC.

Total Revenue	$600,000
Less explicit costs:	
Wages and salaries	300,000
Materials and other	100,000
Equals accounting profit	$200,000
Less implicit costs:	
Forgone salary, Andrea Martin	80,000
Forgone salary, Ralph Martin	80,000
Opportunity cost of capital	20,000
Equals pure economic profit	$20,000

This figure shows the implicit and explicit costs of the imaginary firm Fieldcom, Inc., owned by entrepreneurs Ralph and Andrea Martin. Total revenue minus explicit costs equals accounting profit. Subtracting implicit costs from this quantity yields pure economic profit. The opportunity cost of capital contributed by the Martins is sometimes referred to as normal profit.

In a deeper sense, however, the theory of cost is just as much rooted in subjective judgment as is the theory of consumer choice. That is because all costs, as explained above, are *opportunity costs*. Opportunity costs reflect the value that would have been produced by resources in the best alternative use, but the value of other products that might be produced with the same resources depends on the demand for those products. For that reason, there can be no clear line between "objective" determinants of cost and "subjective" determinants of demand.

Furthermore, opinions can differ as to what the best alternative is and what its value is. For example, what really is the opportunity cost to the Martins of investing their $200,000 savings in their computer firm? Ralph might think that the best alternative use would have been to purchase a portfolio of blue-chip stocks paying a 10 percent rate of return. Andrea might think the best alternative use would have been to buy shares in an aggressive hedge fund, a riskier use of their savings, but one yielding an expected return of 15 percent. Who is to say which one is right? Which alternative use of the $200,000 is best depends not only on subjective estimates of the likely return from alternative investments but also on the subjective attitude toward risk of the person making the investment.

The same is true of the opportunity costs of resources other than capital. For example, an assessment of the opportunity cost of assigning a talented worker to one task must take into account not just what the worker is paid but also what he or she could have contributed elsewhere in the firm. It will rarely be possible to measure the worker's productivity objectively in both tasks, so the decision will usually be made on the basis of a manager's subjective judgment. In short, because choices are subjective, costs are subjective, too.

Profit, Rents, and Entrepreneurship

Pure economic profit, as we have defined it, is the difference between what a firm receives for the products it sells and the opportunity cost of producing those products. We first introduced the notion of payments in excess of opportunity costs in Chapter 4, where we called them *economic rents*. Pure economic profit, then, is a type of economic rent. Nevertheless, the two terms are not fully interchangeable.

For one thing, economic rent is a broader notion than profit. *Profit* is usually used in connection with the activities of a business firm, whereas *rents* can be said to be earned by any factor of production. Consider, for example, the income of rock stars, sports professionals, and other people with exceptional talents in a certain line of work. Their opportunity cost of pursuing their chosen line of work may be low, in the sense that their income from their best-paying alternative occupation (say, selling insurance or working as a lifeguard) may be far lower than what they now earn. The amount by which their extraordinary income as a rock star, sports professional, or whatever exceeds their income from their best alternative occupation can properly be called economic rent; however, that income would not usually be called profit.

A distinction is also sometimes made between *profit seeking* and *rent seeking*. Profit seeking is commonly associated with the activity of entrepreneurship. Entrepreneurs seek profits by finding ways to use factors of production, which they purchase at market prices, to create goods and services of greater value or lower cost than those of their competitors. Our imaginary Martins are an example of entrepreneurs who seek profits by finding new ways of satisfying customer needs. Thus, *profit seeking* means finding ways to create new value.

The incomes of professional athletes often include a large share of economic rent.

However, some firms seek to increase their revenues not through innovation and cost reduction but by seeking restrictions on competition. For example, the Martins might try to boost their firm's earnings by persuading Congress to ban imports of similar PDAs made in China and Korea. That would be an example not of entrepreneurship but of political rent seeking.[2]

The distinction between profits earned by entrepreneurs and rents earned by rent seekers is certainly not watertight. In both cases, we are dealing with revenues that exceed opportunity costs. Data like those presented in Figure 8.1 do not tell us all we might want to know about the origin of the $20,000 of pure economic profit. Was that $20,000 earned by entrepreneurial creation of a new product superior to the products of competitors, or was it earned by rent seeking activity that persuaded the government to implement restrictions that drove the superior products of competitors out of the market? The issues raised by this kind of question go beyond the cost and revenue data that we deal with in this chapter and the next one, but we will return to them in later chapters.

Fixed Costs, Variable Costs, and Sunk Costs

The implicit-explicit distinction provides one way to classify costs, but it is not the only one. Another important classification of costs is based on the time horizon within which production decisions are made.

The amounts of the inputs a firm uses vary as the amounts of output change. The amount of some inputs used can be adjusted quickly; for example, the amount of electricity used can be increased or decreased just by flipping a switch. Quantities of other inputs take longer to adjust. For example, constructing a new office building takes many months, even years. In general, inputs that take longer to adjust are those that define the size of the firm's plant, including structures and production equipment. They are known as **fixed inputs**. The cost of providing fixed inputs are called **fixed costs**.

In addition to fixed inputs, the firm uses **variable inputs** that can be adjusted quickly and easily within a plant of a given size as output changes. The costs of providing variable

Fixed inputs

Inputs that cannot be increased or decreased in a short time in order to increase or decrease output

Fixed costs

The explicit and implicit opportunity costs associated with providing fixed inputs

Variable inputs

Inputs that can be varied within a short time in order to increase or decrease output

Variable costs

The explicit and implicit costs of providing variable inputs

inputs are called **variable costs**. Raw materials, energy, and hourly labor are variable inputs for most firms. However, which inputs are fixed and which are variable depends on the situation. For example, a firm that hires workers on an hourly basis may treat wages as a variable cost. Another firm that hires workers on a yearly contract, subject to a "no lay-off" agreement, would treat wages as a fixed cost, at least within the time limits of the contract. Public policies may also affect the distinction between fixed and variable costs. For example, in the United States, most firms operate under the principle of *employment at will*, meaning that they can lay off workers whenever they think doing so would improve their profits. Under *employment at will*, wages are a variable cost. In contrast, Germany, France, and many other European countries have strong labor protection laws that require advance notice, complex paperwork, and large severance payments when workers are laid off. For firms in those countries, wages are more of a fixed cost.

The difference between fixed and variable inputs is the basis for the distinction between two time horizons: the short run and the long run. These time horizons are operational concepts, not periods of calendar time. The **short run** is a length of time in which changing the quantity of variable inputs used can change output, but that is too short to permit changes in the size of a firm's plant (that is, its fixed inputs). For example, an automaker can vary output from month to month by adding extra shifts of workers without installing additional equipment or building new factories. The **long run** is a length of time that is long enough to permit changes in the amounts of fixed inputs. For example, an automaker can increase capacity to meet expected growth of demand over a period of a few years by building new plants, as well as by adding extra shifts of workers within its old plants.

Short run

A time horizon within which output can be adjusted only by changing the amounts of variable inputs used while fixed inputs remain unchanged

Long run

A time horizon that is long enough to permit changes in both fixed and variable inputs

IMPLICIT AND EXPLICIT COSTS   In all cases, cost means opportunity cost and, therefore, includes both implicit and explicit costs. Particular attention must be paid to this fact in dealing with fixed costs.

Fixed costs are "fixed" in the sense that they do not vary with the firm's rate of output. However, they are ongoing costs that must be borne by the firm each day it continues to lease or own the facilities it needs in order to stay in business. If those ongoing costs take the form of periodic payments, they are explicit fixed costs. If they reflect the opportunity cost of ownership of facilities that have been purchased by the firm, they are implicit fixed costs.

As an example, consider a trucking firm. One of the facilities it needs is a warehouse. The warehouse is a fixed cost that the firm incurs regardless of how much freight is hauled in a given month, but it might take either an explicit or an implicit form. The firm might, for example, lease the warehouse for an annual payment of $12,000 in installments of $1,000 per month. That would make the warehouse an explicit cost. The firm might, instead, choose to set aside some of its profits to buy the warehouse for a price of $120,000. The $120,000 in cash used to buy the warehouse could have been used for some other purpose—say, to buy securities yielding 10 percent interest. The income ($12,000 a year or $1,000 a month) that could have been earned with these funds if they had not been used to buy the warehouse is an opportunity cost of owning the warehouse—an implicit fixed cost. The cost continues as long as the firm keeps the warehouse, even if it goes a month without carrying any freight at all; but if the firm decides to quit the trucking business, it can sell the warehouse and recover the $120,000 for use elsewhere. In that case it would cease to bear the $1,000-a-month fixed cost of the facility.

Sunk costs
_____

Once-and-for-all costs that, once incurred, cannot be recovered

SUNK COSTS   Fixed costs, especially implicit fixed costs, should not be confused with **sunk costs**. Sunk costs reflect once-and-for-all expenditures that, once made, cannot be recovered even if the firm leaves its line of business. For example, the trucking firm just mentioned might have paid $1,000 to have "Taylor Trucking" painted on the wall of its warehouse. That is a sunk cost. If the firm sells the warehouse (or terminates its lease), the sign becomes worthless. There is no way to recover the $1,000 that was paid for it because the next owner or tenant will want a different sign.

If a firm is planning to enter a new line of business or to expand its operations, the sunk costs of doing so are an opportunity cost associated with entry into the new venture. Thus, in considering serving a new city, the trucking firm must think, "$120,000 to buy the warehouse plus $1,000 to paint the sign." Because they cannot be recovered, sunk costs, unlike fixed and variable costs, are *not* counted as part of the firm's ongoing costs of doing business. Once the commitment has been made, the sunk cost is no longer an opportunity cost to the firm because the firm has, once and for all, lost the opportunity to do anything else with the funds in question. In deciding whether to remain in business, the firm should think only, "We could get $120,000 by selling the warehouse." The $1,000 paid for the sign would not enter into the decision at all. In business, the irrelevance of sunk costs to ongoing operations is often expressed in the phrase "bygones are bygones."

The remainder of this chapter will be concerned only with firms' ongoing fixed and variable costs of doing business. Sunk costs will not enter into the picture. In later chapters we will return to the subject of sunk costs when discussing the processes through which firms enter and leave particular markets.

Production and Costs in the Short Run

Now that we have pinned down the meaning of cost, our next task is to build a theory to explain how a firm's costs vary with its level of output. The cost that a firm must bear to produce a given level of output is, as we have said, one of the basic constraints that shape a firm's decisions. Our discussion of cost theory will be divided into two parts, corresponding to the time horizons that we have called the short run and the long run.

Production with One Variable Input in the Short Run

Although most firms have several inputs that can be varied even in the short run, it will simplify matters to begin with a case in which only one input—the quantity of labor employed—can be varied. Let us turn once again to Fieldcom for an example.

Total physical product
_____

The total output of a firm, measured in physical units

Figure 8.2 shows what happens to the daily production rate measured in physical terms, or **total physical product**, as the number of workers is varied from zero to eight. If no workers are employed, no production can take place. In this firm, one worker alone cannot produce anything either since some parts of the job require a minimum of two people working together. Two workers can get production moving; but because they use a lot of time setting up jobs and changing from one job to

FIGURE 8.2   RESPONSE OF OUTPUT TO CHANGES IN ONE VARIABLE INPUT

(a)

(1) Input (Workers per Day)	(2) Total Physical Product (Units per Day)	(3) Marginal Physical Product (Units per Worker)
0	0	0
1	0	1
2	1	2
3	3	4
4	7	3
5	10	2
6	12	1
7	13	0
8	13	

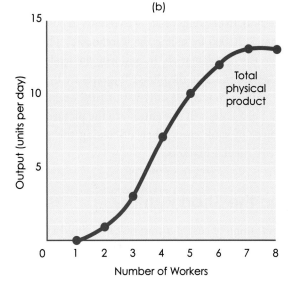

(b)

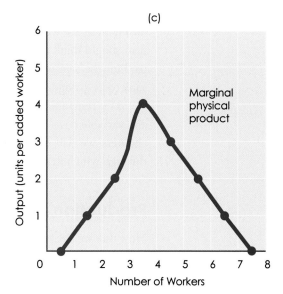

(c)

This figure shows how the output of PDAs at Fieldcom, Inc., responds to changes in one variable input—labor. All other inputs remain constant while the number of workers is varied. One worker can produce nothing since some equipment takes a minimum of two employees to operate. Output increases—at first rapidly, then more slowly, as more workers are used. After seven workers are on the job, all equipment is in use; thus additional workers add nothing more to output. Column 3 of part (a) and the chart in part (c) show the amount of added output that results from each added worker. This is known as the *marginal physical product* of the variable input.

another, they are able to produce at a rate of only one PDA per day. When a third worker is added, some degree of specialization becomes possible, and production increases to three units per day. A fourth worker gets things moving really smoothly, and production rises to seven units per day. Adding workers five, six, and seven boosts the plant's output to its maximum of thirteen PDAs per day. At that point it does no good to add more workers; all the tools and equipment are in use, and any extra workers would have to stand around waiting for a turn to use them.

Of course, output could be increased by adding *other* inputs in addition to workers—more assembly tables, more testing equipment, and so on. For the moment, however, we are looking at the effects of increasing just one variable input, other things being equal.

MARGINAL PHYSICAL PRODUCT   The chart in part (b) and columns 1 and 2 in part (a) of Figure 8.2 show the relationship between labor inputs and daily output. In the range of one to seven workers, output rises as labor input increases, but not at a constant rate. Column 3 of the table and the chart in part (c) of the figure show how much output changes for each successive worker. The amount by which output changes in each instance is called the **marginal physical product** of the variable input. (As elsewhere, the adjective *marginal* refers to the effect of a small change in a quantity—here, the quantity of a variable input.) Adding one full-time worker at a time, as in the table, gives the progression of marginal physical products shown in part (c).

At Fieldcom, as the input of labor is increased from one worker to two, the marginal physical product is one unit of output; as it is stepped up from two to three workers, marginal physical product rises to two units; and so on. The step from three workers to four gives the greatest boost to output. After that, output increases at a diminishing rate with each added worker. Once the staff reaches seven workers, the marginal physical product drops to zero.

THE LAW OF DIMINISHING RETURNS   The example just given shows a pattern that economists consider typical for the marginal product of a single variable input such as labor. At first, as workers are added, marginal product increases. Increasing marginal product reflects the advantages of cooperation: the superiority of team production and the benefits of specialization by comparative advantage. After a point, however, as more workers are added, marginal product stops rising and begins to fall. In the case of a single variable input, the principal reason for the eventual decline in marginal physical product is the overcrowding of complementary fixed inputs—in our example, such things as work space, tools, and testing equipment.

Part (c) of Figure 8.2 shows the relationship of marginal physical product to the number of workers in the form of a graph called the *marginal physical product curve*. The part of the curve with a negative slope illustrates a principle known as the **law of diminishing returns**. According to this principle, as the amount of one variable input is increased while the amounts of all other inputs remain fixed, a point will be reached beyond which the marginal physical product of the input will decrease.

The law of diminishing returns applies to all production processes and to all variable inputs. The example just given is drawn from manufacturing, but the law could be demonstrated just as well with an example from, say, farming, with fertilizer as the variable input. As more fertilizer is added to a field, output increases; but beyond some point the gain in output brought about by an additional ton of fertilizer tapers off. (In fact, too much fertilizer could poison the plants, in which case marginal physical product would become negative.) Oil refineries, power plants,

Marginal physical product

The increase in output, expressed in physical units, produced by each added unit of one variable input, other things being equal

Law of diminishing returns

The principle that as one variable input is increased while all others remain fixed, a point will be reached beyond which the marginal physical product of the variable input will begin to decrease

barber shops, government bureaus—indeed, *any* production process—could be used to illustrate the law of diminishing returns. There can be no exceptions.

From Marginal Physical Product to Marginal Costs

The relationship between inputs and output in terms of physical units is an important constraint on a firm's profit-maximizing activities. However, most business decisions are not made in terms of physical units but in terms of money. Our next step, then, is to restate the constraint implied by the marginal physical product curve in money terms, that is, to ask how much each added unit of output *costs*.

Marginal cost

The increase in cost required to raise the output of some good or service by one unit

The change in cost associated with a one-unit change in output is called **marginal cost**. To make the conversion from marginal physical product to marginal cost, we proceed as follows, again using Fieldcom as an example. The first step is to rearrange the data given in Figure 8.2 in terms of input per unit of output. This is done in Figure 8.3. The table in part (a) of the figure reverses the order of the first two columns. Also, the charts in parts (b) and (c) are flipped so that units of output, rather than units of labor input, occupy the horizontal axis.

The next step is to convert physical units of input into costs stated in dollars. To do so, we need to know the cost per unit of input. To keep things simple, this example assumes that the variable input, labor, carries an explicit price of $100 per day. Multiplying the labor inputs in column 2 of the figure by the $100-per-day wage yields total labor costs, which are shown in column 3. Those data are used to plot a total labor cost curve in part (b) of the figure. Taking the rearrangement of the axes and the change in units into account, that curve can be recognized as the mirror image of the total physical product curve shown in Figure 8.2.

Finally, column 4 of the table in Figure 8.3 is filled in to show marginal cost, that is, the change in cost, stated in dollars per unit change in output. Increasing output from zero to one requires adding two workers, so the added cost per unit in that range is $200; increasing output by two more units (from one to three) requires one more worker at $100 per day, so the cost per added unit of output in that range is $50; and so on. The marginal cost curve shown in part (c) of the figure is plotted from columns 1 and 4 of the table. As in the case of marginal product, the effect of adding one full-time worker at a time becomes a smooth curve if smaller increments are considered. Again, considering the change in units and rearrangement of the axes, part (c) of Figure 8.3 looks much like a mirror image of the marginal physical product curve shown in part (c) of Figure 8.2.

More than One Variable Input

The Fieldcom example assumes that only one input is varied. In practice, short-run increases or decreases in Fieldcom's output would require changes in many—though not all—of its inputs. For example, if the firm wanted to raise its output, it might not only have to hire more workers but also burn more fuel to keep the shop heated longer each day and double the rate at which it orders parts.

The appendix to this chapter outlines a way of analyzing changes in two or more variable inputs. Without going into detail, it can be stated that as long as at least some inputs remain fixed, the law of diminishing returns continues to apply. Also, a

FIGURE 8.3 COST AND OUTPUT WITH ONE VARIABLE INPUT

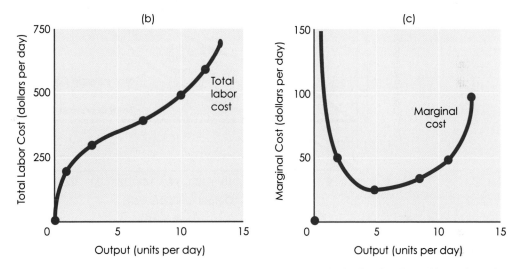

(a)

(1) Output (Units per Day)	(2) Labor Input	(3) Total Labor Cost (Dollars per Day)	(4) Marginal Cost (Dollars per Unit)
0	0	0	
1	2	200	200
3	3	300	50
7	4	400	25
10	5	500	33
12	6	600	50
13	7	700	100

This figure shows how the cost of production at Fieldcom, Inc., changes as output varies. The table and graphs are based on the data used in Figure 8.2, but here they are recast to stress cost assuming a daily wage of $100 per worker. Column 3 of the table and the chart in part (b) show total labor cost for various output levels. Column 4 of the table and the chart in part (c) show marginal cost—the amount by which cost increases per added unit of output. For example, increasing the number of workers from three to four raises output by four units, from three to seven PDAs per day. Over this range, then, the cost of each added PDA is one-quarter of a day's wage, or $25.

region of increasing marginal physical product will often exist at low levels of output. When such a relationship between variable inputs and physical product is combined with a constant price for each input, the result is a total cost curve with a reverse-S shape and a U-shaped marginal cost curve, as in the case of a single variable input.

A Set of Short-Run Cost Curves

Variable cost and marginal cost curves with the shapes just described are shown in Figure 8.4. Those curves are the basis of a whole set of short-run cost curves that can be constructed for an enterprise such as Fieldcom. The figure gives the full set of curves in both graphical and tabular form and also contains some often-used formulas and abbreviations that pertain to cost curves.

FIGURE 8.4   A SET OF SHORT-RUN COST CURVES

(a)

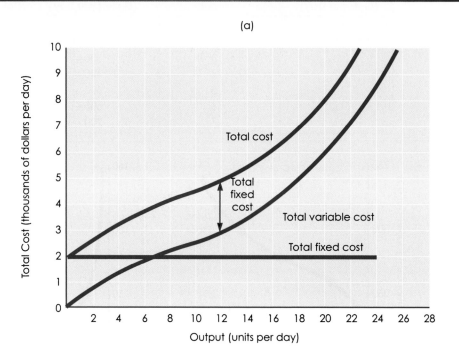

(b)

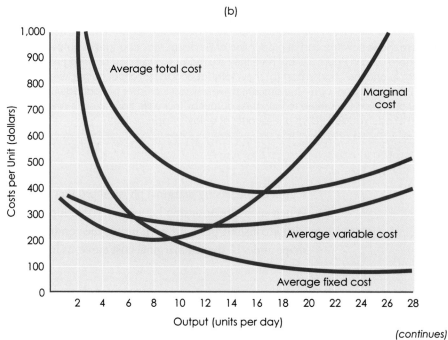

(continues)

FIGURE 8.4   A SET OF SHORT-RUN COST CURVES, CONTINUED

(c)

Quantity of Output (Units per Day) (1)	Total Variable Cost (Dollars per Day) (2)	Total Fixed Cost (Dollars per Day) (3)	Total Cost (Dollars per Day) (4)	Marginal Cost (Dollars per Unit) (5)	Average Variable Cost (Dollars per Unit) (6)	Average Fixed Cost (Dollars per Unit) (7)	Average Total Cost (Dollars per Unit) (8)
0	$ 0	$2,000	$ 2,000		—	—	—
1	380	2,000	2,380	$380	$380	$2,000	$2,380
2	720	2,000	2,720	340	360	1,000	1,360
3	1,025	2,000	3,025	305	342	667	1,009
4	1,300	2,000	3,300	275	325	500	825
5	1,550	2,000	3,550	250	310	400	710
6	1,780	2,000	3,780	230	296	333	629
7	1,995	2,000	3,995	215	285	286	571
8	2,200	2,000	4,200	205	275	250	525
9	2,400	2,000	4,400	200	266	222	488
10	2,605	2,000	4,605	205	260	200	460
11	2,820	2,000	4,820	215	256	181	437
12	3,050	2,000	5,050	230	254	169	421
13	3,300	2,000	5,300	250	254	154	408
14	3,575	2,000	5,575	275	255	143	398
15	3,880	2,000	5,880	305	259	133	392
16	4,220	2,000	6,220	340	264	125	389
17	4,600	2,000	6,600	380	271	118	389
18	5,025	2,000	7,025	425	279	111	390
19	5,500	2,000	7,500	475	289	105	394
20	6,030	2,000	8,030	530	302	100	402
21	6,620	2,000	8,620	590	315	95	410
22	7,275	2,000	9,275	655	331	91	422
23	8,000	2,000	10,000	725	348	87	435
24	8,800	2,000	10,800	800	367	83	450

(d)

Common abbreviations

Q   Quantity of output

TC   Total cost

TFC   Total fixed cost

TVC   Total variable cost

MC   Marginal cost

AVC   Average variable cost

AFC   Average fixed cost

ATC   Average total cost

Useful formulas:

$$TC = TFC + TVC$$

$$MC = \frac{\text{Change in TC}}{\text{Change in Q}} = \frac{\text{Change in TVC}}{\text{Change in Q}}$$

$$AVC = \frac{TVC}{Q}$$

$$AFC = \frac{TFC}{Q}$$

$$ATC = \frac{TC}{Q}$$

A whole set of short-run cost curves can be derived from data on fixed and variable costs, as this figure shows. The data are presented in the form of a table and a pair of graphs. The figure also lists a number of useful abbreviations and formulas.

Total variable cost is shown graphically in part (a) of Figure 8.4 and numerically in column 2 of part (c). The total variable costs in this example are analogous to the costs shown in the preceding example, except that these allow for more than one variable input. In addition to variable costs, *total fixed costs* (office staff, testing equipment, rent, and so on), which are assumed to be $2,000 per day, are shown in column 3 of part (c). Adding columns 2 and 3 gives short-run *total cost* (variable plus fixed costs), which is shown in column 4. The total fixed cost and total cost curves are plotted together with the total variable cost curve in part (a). Because by definition total fixed cost does not vary as output changes, the total fixed cost curve is a horizontal line $2,000 above the horizontal axis. Total fixed cost is the amount by which total cost exceeds total variable cost, so the total cost curve parallels the total variable cost curve at a higher level. The vertical distance between the total cost and total variable cost curves equals total fixed cost.

The next column in part (c) of Figure 8.4 is marginal cost. Marginal cost data appear on lines between the total cost entries in order to stress that marginal cost shows how total cost changes as the level of output varies. The marginal cost curve is plotted in part (b) of the figure.

All of the cost concepts shown in total terms in part (a) of the figure can also be expressed on a per-unit basis. This is done in the last three columns in the table and the chart in part (b) of Figure 8.4. *Average variable cost* equals total variable cost divided by quantity of output, *average fixed cost* equals total fixed cost divided by output, and *average total cost* equals total cost divided by output. The three average cost curves are drawn together with the marginal cost curve in part (b) of the figure.

Some Geometric Relationships

Parts (a) and (b) of Figure 8.4 demonstrate some important geometric relationships among the cost curves. First, compare the marginal cost curve with the total variable cost curve. The bottom of the U-shaped marginal cost curve lies at exactly the level of output at which the slope of the reverse-S-shaped total variable cost curve stops flattening out and starts getting steeper. (In the language of geometry, this is the *inflection point* of the total variable cost curve.) This relationship holds because the slope of the total variable cost curve shows the rate at which total variable cost changes as output changes, and that is the definition of marginal cost. In graphical terms, then, the *height* of the marginal cost curve always equals the slope of the total variable cost curve.

A second feature of the cost curves in Figure 8.4 also deserves comment. The marginal cost curve intersects both the average variable cost and the average total cost curves at their lowest points. This is not a coincidence; it is a result of a relationship that can be called the **marginal-average rule**, which can be explained as follows. Beginning at any given point, ask what the cost of making one more unit of output will be. The answer is given by marginal cost. Then ask whether that cost is more or less than the average cost of all units produced up to that point. If the added cost of the next unit made is less than the average cost of all the previous units, making that unit will have the effect of pulling down the average. If the next unit costs more, making that unit will pull the average up. It follows that whenever marginal cost is below average variable cost, the average variable cost curve must be falling (negatively sloped);

Marginal-average rule

The rule that marginal cost must equal average cost when average cost is at its minimum and whenever marginal cost is above average variable cost, the average variable cost curve must be rising (positively sloped). This, in turn, implies that the marginal cost curve cuts the average variable cost curve at its lowest point. The same is true of the relationship between marginal cost and average total cost.

The marginal-average rule is not unique to economics; it can be seen in many everyday situations. Consider, for example, the effect of your grade in this course on your grade point average. You could call this grade your "marginal grade" because it represents the grade points earned by taking one more course. If your grade in this course (that is, your marginal grade) is higher than your average grade in other courses, the effect of taking this course will be to pull up your average. Your grade point average thus must be rising if your marginal grade exceeds your average grade. If you do worse than average in this course, your grade point average will fall. When your marginal grade falls short of your average grade, your grade point average must be falling. This relationship is the same as the one between marginal cost and average cost. If the cost of making one more unit is less than the average cost of making previous units, the average will be pulled down; if it is more, the average will be pulled up.

Some people find it easier to remember the relationships among the various cost concepts if they are presented as formulas. If you are one of those people, you may find the formulas in part (d) of Figure 8.4 useful. The figure also presents some common abbreviations. They are not used in this text, but you may want to use them in your note taking, and your instructor will probably use them on the blackboard.

Long-Run Costs and Economies of Scale

In the first part of the chapter, we pointed out that different kinds of costs are relevant to different kinds of decisions. The costs that we call variable are relevant to decisions regarding short-run changes in output using a given quantity of fixed inputs. For example, how much corn should a farmer grow, given a certain available acreage and stock of farm equipment? Any change in prices or quantities supplied that does not involve a change in the quantity of fixed inputs used will be made with reference to the position of the firm's short-run cost curves.

In other cases, however, attention centers on plans for lasting expansion or contraction of the firm's stock of fixed inputs. For example, corn growers might adjust to legislation that provides long-term subsidies for corn-based ethanol by buying additional land or farm equipment. Such decisions must be made with reference to long-run costs, to which we turn in this section. For the time being, we consider only fixed costs that are recoverable in the event that the firm leaves its line of business or permanently scales back its operations. Sunk costs are assumed to be zero.

Planning for Expansion

Put yourself in the position of an entrepreneur about to set up a small firm. You think it would be wise to start with a small plant, but you want to do some long-range planning, too. In consultation with specialists, you put together information on plants of five possible sizes, each of which could represent a stage in the future growth of your firm.

Short-run average total cost curves for each of the plants are drawn in Figure 8.5. The first one shows short-run average total costs for the range of output that is possible given the firm's first small plant, the one in the converted gas station; the second curve corresponds to a slightly larger plant; and so on.

The size of plant you actually choose will depend on the level of output you plan to produce over a time horizon long enough to change from one size of plant to the next. Choosing a plant of a certain size does not commit a firm forever, but the choice is not a trivial one. As *Applying Economic Ideas 8.1* shows, a small firm cannot afford to take on the costs of a permanently larger plant just to fill a single order. It may not make sense to expand the size of your plant unless these fixed costs can be spread out over a long enough period at the output level for which a plant is designed. Only when the firm expects a long-term increase in its output should it move from one of the short-run curves shown in Figure 8.5 to the next.

The five short-run cost curves in the figure represent only a sampling of possible plant sizes. Taking into account the short-run curves that correspond to intermediate-sized plants as well as those shown, we can draw a *long-run average cost curve* such as the one in the figure. Such a curve is the "envelope" of all the possible short-run average

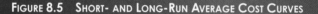

FIGURE 8.5   SHORT- AND LONG-RUN AVERAGE COST CURVES

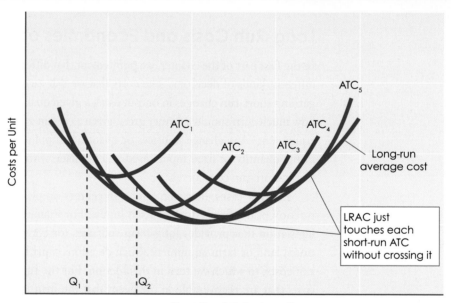

The position of the short-run average total cost curve for a firm depends on the size of the plant. In the long run, the firm has a choice of operating with any size of plant it chooses. Each plant size can be represented by a U-shaped, short-run average total cost curve. Five such curves are shown in this graph. A new firm might begin with a plant that can be represented by a short-run average total cost curve such as ATC₁. Then, as demand for its product expands, it might move to one of those farther to the right. The firm's long-run average cost curve is the "envelope" of these and other possible short-run average total cost curves; that is, it is a smooth curve drawn so that it just touches the short-run curves without intersecting any of them.

Applying Economic Ideas 8.1
SONY CORPORATION FACES COSTS AND OPPORTUNITIES

Several years ago Akio Morita, chairman of the Japanese electronics giant, Sony Corporation, was asked to talk about the early days of his firm. Here he describes what it was like to be just a small company.

Akio Morita, co-founder of Sony Corporation, presents a seven-inch portable color television July 1967.

Our first transistor radio of 1955 was small and practical—not as small as some of our later efforts, but we were very proud of it. I saw the United States as a natural market. I took my little $29.95 radio to New York and made the rounds of possible retailers.

While making the rounds, I came across an American buyer who looked at the radio and said he liked it very much. He said his chain, which had about 150 stores, would need large quantities. He asked me to give him a price quotation only on quantities of 5,000, 10,000; 30,000, 50,000 and 100,000 radios. What an invitation!

But back in my hotel room, I began pondering the possible impact of such grand orders on our small facilities in Tokyo. We had expanded our plant a lot since we outgrew the unpainted, leaky shack on Gotenyama [a hill on the southern edge of Tokyo]. We had moved into bigger, sturdier buildings adjacent to the original site and had our eye on some more property, but we did not have the capacity to produce 100,000 transistor radios a year and also make the other things in our small product line. Our capacity was less than 10,000 radios a month. If we got an order for 100,000, we would have to hire and train new employees and expand our facilities even more. This would mean a major investment, a major expansion and a gamble.

I was inexperienced and still a little naive, but I had my wits about me. I considered all the consequences I could think of, and then I sat down and drew a curve that looked something like a lopsided letter U. The price for 5,000 would be our regular price. That would be the beginning of the curve. For 10,000 there would be a dis-

count, and that was at the bottom of the curve. For 30,000 the price would begin to climb. For 50,000 the price per unit would be higher than for 5,000, and for 100,000 units the price would have to be much more per unit than for the first 5,000.

My reasoning was this: If we had to double our production capacity to complete an order for 100,000 and if we could not get a repeat order the following year we would be in big trouble, perhaps bankrupt, because how in that case could we employ all the added staff and pay for the new and unused facilities? ... In Japan, we cannot just hire people and fire them whenever our orders go up or down. We have a long-term commitment to our employees and they have a commitment to us.

I returned the next day with my quotation. The buyer looked at it and blinked as though he couldn't believe his eyes. He put down the paper and said, patiently, "Mr. Morita, I have been working as a purchasing agent for nearly thirty years and you are the first person who has ever come in here and told me that the more I buy the higher the unit price will be. It's illogical!" I explained my reasoning to him, and he listened carefully to what I had to say. When he got over his shock, he paused for a moment, smiled, and then placed an order for 10,000 radios—at the 10,000 unit price—which was just right for him and for us.

SOURCE: Akio Morita, "When Sony Was an Up and Comer," *Forbes*, October 6, 1986, 98–102. Adapted from *Made in Japan: Akio Morita and Sony* by Akio Morita with Edwin M. Reingold and Mitsuko Shimomura. Copyright 1986 by E. P. Dutton, a division of NAL Penguin, Inc. Reprinted by permission of the publisher, E. P. Dutton.

Sony Corporation in Tokyo, Japan

cost curves, meaning that it just touches each of the possible short-run curves without crossing them. The size of plant chosen for each output in the long run will be the one that corresponds to a short-run average total cost curve that is just tangent to the long-run average total cost curve at that point.

Figure 8.5 shows that there is one best plant size for any given level of output that the firm plans to produce in the long run. It may be physically possible to produce a given level of output in a larger or smaller plant, but that would involve a penalty in terms of cost per unit. For example, in Figure 8.5 the output level Q_1 is produced at least cost in a plant of the size corresponding to the short-run curve ATC_1. The same level of output could also be produced in the larger plant corresponding to ATC_2, but only at a higher cost per unit because the larger plant would not be used to its designed capacity. On the other hand, the larger plant represented by ATC_2 is the best plant size for output Q_2. That larger output could be produced in the smaller plant, but only by running it at a rate higher than the one for which it is designed. The penalty, in terms of unit cost, is shown by the fact that ATC_1 lies above ATC_2 at the output level Q_2.

If a firm wants to produce at an unusually high or low rate for a short time, it may make sense to do so by moving along the short-run average total cost curve corresponding to its present plant size. An example would be a firm that decides to run overtime to fill an exceptionally large order, or one that cuts back to half-shifts to weather a temporary business downturn. When sustained increases in output level are under consideration, costs are minimized by building a larger plant, such as a young firm like Sony will build when it has enough confidence in long-term demand for its product to expand. Likewise, a firm that is planning to reduce its output permanently will eliminate some plant rather than keep production facilities operating at lower levels of output than those for which they were designed. Decisions of that kind represent movements out or back along the firm's long-run average cost curve.

Economies of Scale

Movements along a firm's long-run average cost curve, during which the firm is free to adjust quantities of all the inputs it uses, are referred to as changes in the *scale* of production. Some special terminology is used to describe the way long-run average cost changes as the scale of production changes. In any output range in which long-run average cost *decreases* as output increases, the firm is said to experience **economies of scale**. In any output range in which long-run average cost *increases*, the firm is said to experience **diseconomies of scale**. Finally, if there is any range of output for which long-run average cost does not change as output varies, the firm is said to experience **constant returns** to scale in that range.

The long-run average cost curve in Figure 8.5 is smoothly U-shaped, so there is no range of constant returns to scale. However, empirical studies suggest that the long-run cost curves of actual firms may have long flat sections in the middle over which average cost changes relatively little as output changes. Economies of scale for such a firm appear only over a range of rather low output levels, and diseconomies appear only over a range of very high output levels. For a firm with such a long-run average cost curve, the level of output at which economies of scale end and constant returns to scale begin can be called the firm's **minimum efficient scale**.

Economies of scale

A situation in which long-run average cost decreases as output increases

Diseconomies of scale

A situation in which long-run average cost increases as output increases

Constant returns to scale

A situation in which there are neither economies nor diseconomies of scale

Minimum efficient scale

The output level at which economies of scale cease

SOURCES OF ECONOMIES OF SCALE   Where do economies of scale come from? If firms grew simply by increasing fixed and variable inputs in exact proportion, so that a large plant amounted to nothing more than a lot of small plants built side by side, one might expect changes in scale to have no effect at all on average cost. That is not the way firms expand, however. As they grow, they tend to change the technologies they use and their methods of internal organization to take advantage of new opportunities offered by the higher output level. Those changes give rise to economies of scale.

In part, economies of scale stem from human factors like the advantages of team production and specialization according to comparative advantage. A firm can get very large before it completely exhausts the possibilities for cooperation and specialization. In a small firm, for example, the marketing function may be something the owner does from 3:00 P.M. to 4:00 P.M., after touring the plant floor and perhaps taking a turn running a machine. A somewhat larger firm can afford to hire a marketing manager who devotes full time to the job. In a still larger firm, subspecialties develop—a sales manager, a director of product development, an advertising specialist, all under the direction of the marketing manager.

Other economies of scale have origins in technology. In many lines of production, for example, a machine that is capable of doing twice the work of a smaller one costs less than twice as much to build and operate. A pizza oven that is big enough to bake 60 pizzas an hour costs less than twice as much as a 30-pizza-per-hour model and takes less than twice the energy to operate. A tractor that can plow 50 acres a day costs less than twice as much as one that can plow only 25 acres, and the large model still requires only one driver. For a firm that is too small to make full use of a large piece of equipment, the smaller model can be the appropriate choice. As the firm grows, however, technological economies lower its average costs.

What is more, growth of a firm does not just mean constant expansion of a single plant. Operation of multiple plants can yield further economies of scale even after each plant reaches the minimum efficient scale at which technical economies are exhausted. The McDonald's hamburger chain provides a good example. The minimum efficient scale for a single plant (restaurant) is very small in the fast-food industry. Yet McDonald's gains some important economies by running a large number of restaurants as a system. Some of these are production economies. Individual food items and ingredients can be made in central kitchens, managers can be trained at "Hamburger University", and so on. A multi-plant firm such as McDonald's also realizes economies of scale in such areas as finance and marketing.

SOURCES OF DISECONOMIES OF SCALE   Although there are many sources of economies of scale, they are not limitless. As a firm expands, it encounters diseconomies of scale as well as economies. Technological sources of diseconomies can often be avoided. For example, as an airline grows, at first it may buy larger and larger planes; but beyond a point, it starts buying more and more planes of optimal size. In other lines of business, firms can avoid potential technical diseconomies by building multiple plants of optimal size.

The most important diseconomies are organizational. As a firm grows, it finds itself depending more and more on hierarchical means of coordinating its employees' activities. As a hierarchy grows, the cost of channeling information to key decision makers tends to rise. Moreover, individual incentives tend to get diluted in a large hierarchical organization. More and more managerial skill has to be devoted to maintaining employee loyalty and motivation. There is an increasing risk that departments and divisions will pursue parochial interests that diverge from those of the firm as a whole.

In some lines of business, firms can grow to a very large size before the diseconomies start to outweigh the economies. Huge firms, such as General Motors, AT&T, Microsoft, and IBM, successfully manage hierarchies that are bigger than the governments of many countries; but the very mention of such corporate giants calls to mind their vulnerability to smaller, more aggressive rivals. All three of the companies just listed have lost sales in recent years to smaller competitors in important product lines.

In other lines of business, comparatively small firms seem to have the edge. In farming, services, and many sectors of retail trade, small units predominate. In still other industries, franchising is used to combine economies of scale in a few functions such as marketing and product development with the production advantages of small-unit operation.

Much more could be written about costs and production functions, but we have now covered the most important points. Coming chapters will repeatedly make use of the concepts of marginal and average costs, economies of scale, and profit maximization to show how firms make decisions in a variety of market contexts.

In many sectors of the retail trade, small shops predominate.

Summary

1. **How do economists view the concepts of cost and profit?** *Explicit costs* are opportunity costs that take the form of explicit payments to suppliers of factors of production and intermediate goods. *Implicit costs* are the opportunity costs associated with using resources contributed by the firm's owners (or owned by the firm itself as a legal entity) that are not obtained under contracts calling for explicit payments. Implicit costs include the opportunity cost of capital needed to attract owners' capital to the firm. If only explicit costs are subtracted from revenue, the result is *accounting profit*. Revenue minus all costs, both implicit and explicit, is *pure economic profit*.

2. **What is the distinction between short-run and long-run time horizons?** *Fixed inputs* cannot be increased or decreased in a short time; they are linked with the size of the firm's plant. The costs of such inputs are termed *fixed costs*. *Variable inputs* can be varied quickly in order to increase or decrease output; they include hourly labor, energy, and raw materials. The costs of those inputs are termed *variable costs*. *Sunk costs* are once-and-for-all expenditures that cannot be recovered once they have been made. The *short run* is a period within which only variable inputs can be adjusted. In the *long run* changes can be made in fixed inputs, including plant size.

3. **How do costs vary in response to changes in the quantity of a variable input?** As the amount of one input to a production process increases while the amounts of all other inputs remain fixed, output will increase, at least over some range. The amount of output added by each one-unit increase in the variable input is known as the *marginal physical product* of that input. According to the *law of diminishing returns*, as the amount of one variable input used in a production process increases (with the amounts of all other inputs remaining fixed), a point will be reached beyond which the amount of output added per unit of added variable input (that is, the marginal physical product of the variable input) will begin to decrease. The principle applies to all production processes.

4. **How can a firm's cost structure be represented in geometric terms?** A whole set of cost curves can be constructed for a firm, given data on its fixed and variable costs. The most commonly used cost curves are total cost, total fixed cost, total variable cost, average fixed cost, average variable cost, average total cost, and marginal cost. According to the *marginal-average rule*, the marginal cost curve intersects the average variable cost and average total cost curves at their lowest points.

5. **What choices does a firm face in the course of long-run expansion?** In the long run, a firm can adjust the amounts of fixed inputs that it uses by expanding or reducing its plant. Each possible plant size has a U-shaped short-run average total cost curve. The firm's long-run average cost curve is a shallower U-shaped curve based on a set of short-run curves. When long-run average cost decreases as output increases, the firm is said to experience *economies of scale*. When long-run average cost increases as output increases, the firm is said to experience *diseconomies of scale*. If there are neither economies nor diseconomies of scale, the firm is said to experience *constant returns to scale*.

Key Terms

Problems and Topics for Discussion

1. **Entrepreneurship and risk** One of the opportunity costs borne by anyone who starts a

new business, whether it is Akio Morita of Sony or our imaginary Ralph and Andrea Martin, is that of exchanging the secure life of employees of large firms for the risky life of entrepreneurs. Do you think they would be willing to do this if they expected to earn no more than their previous salaries plus a "normal profit" on the capital they invested in the firm? Do you think that pure economic profit can be viewed as compensation to entrepreneurs for the risk they bear? Discuss.

2. **Implicit and explicit costs**   List the basic costs of owning and operating an automobile. Which are explicit costs? Which are implicit costs? Does driving an automobile impose any external opportunity costs on the economy as a whole that do not show up on your list as either implicit or explicit costs? If so, what are they?

3. **Fixed and variable costs**   Divide the costs of owning and operating an automobile into fixed and variable costs. Suppose that you were deciding whether to drive to a football game at a nearby college or to take the bus instead. Would you take both fixed and variable costs into account? Suppose that you were deciding whether to buy a house in a neighborhood where you could walk to work or a house in a neighborhood where you would have to buy a second car to drive to work every day. Would you take both fixed and variable costs into account? Explain the difference between the two situations.

4. **Economies and diseconomies of scale**   Do you think the business of running a college is subject to economies or diseconomies of scale? Which parts of the college's operation (such as library, dormitories, faculty salaries, moving students between classes, and so on) are subject to economies of scale, diseconomies of scale, or constant returns to scale?

5. **Total cost curves**   Draw a set of coordinate axes on a piece of graph paper. Label the x axis "Output" (0 to 20 units) and the y axis "Cost" (0 to 20 units). Plot the following (x, y) points on your graph: (0, 4); (2, 6); (4, 7); (7, 8); (9, 9); (11, 11); (13, 14). Connect these points with a smooth

curve and label it "total cost." Working from this curve, construct a total fixed cost curve and a total variable cost curve for the same firm.

6. **Marginal and average cost curves**   Draw a second set of coordinate axes on another piece of graph paper. Label the horizontal axis "Output" (0 to 20 units) and the vertical axis "Cost per Unit" (0 to 2 units, in tenths of a unit). Using as a basis the total cost, total variable cost, and total fixed cost curves you drew for problem 5, construct the following curves on your new graph: marginal cost, average total cost, average variable cost, and average fixed cost.

7. **Relating the long- and short-run cost curves**   Turn to Figure 8.5 and copy the diagram onto a sheet of graph paper, drawing the long-run average total cost curve and one of the short-run average total cost curves. Use these curves to construct the corresponding long- and short-run total cost curves. Both total cost curves should be reverse-S shaped and tangent to each other at the same output level for which the average total cost curves are tangent.

8. **Diminishing returns**   Suppose that you examine the relationship between the amount of coal burned per week in a certain power plant and the amount of electricity generated per week. You find that for small amounts of coal—too small even to bring the boiler up to the temperature needed to make steam—no electricity can be produced. After a certain minimum amount of coal is burned, the plant begins to operate. From that point on, the added amount of electricity generated per added ton of coal burned is constant over a wide range. Then a point is reached beyond which burning more coal produces no more electricity. Sketch the total physical product curve for this plant, and draw a graph showing how marginal physical product varies as output changes. Does this production process obey the law of diminishing returns?

9. **More on diminishing returns**   It has been said that were it not for the law of diminishing returns, all the food that the world needs could

be grown in a flowerpot. Discuss this statement. (Suggestion: Think of land as the only fixed factor and fertilizer as the only variable factor. How much food could be grown in the flowerpot if the marginal physical product of fertilizer were constant regardless of the amount used per unit of land?)

Case for Discussion

Tennis at the Grand Slam

The Grand Slam Sport and Health Club is a large, modern facility in the suburbs of a medium-sized American city. The club offers many activities, including swimming, weight training, and aerobics; but its leading attractions are its excellent indoor tennis courts. Members may play on clay or two types of hard-surface courts. To add to members' enjoyment of the sport, the club offers private and group lessons; tournament, ladder, and team competitions; and numerous social events.

To join the club, a single individual pays a $1,000 nonrefundable initiation fee. In addition, there is an $88 monthly membership charge, which must be paid whether or not the member uses the facilities. Those two fees cover most of the club's costs, so it is able to keep the charge for actual playing time quite low. The fee for an hour's use of a court is only $2.

At first the low hourly court fee created a problem for the club. The fee was so low that members would not bother to call to cancel a court reservation if they changed their minds about playing. Other members would then be told that no reservations were available, when in fact the courts stood empty.

To overcome this problem, the club introduced a new rule: Members who make reservations and use the court pay the usual $2 per hour; but a member who makes a reservation and does *not* show up, pays a penalty rate of $10 per hour for the unused time. A reservation can be canceled nine hours or more in advance with no charge at all. This rule has proved successful in reducing abuses of the reservation sys-

tem and making court time more readily available to all members.

QUESTIONS

1. Classify the costs of membership in the Grand Slam as fixed, variable, and sunk.
2. Suppose that you are thinking about joining the Grand Slam to play indoor tennis. Which of the costs of membership are opportunity costs that would be relevant to your decision?
3. Suppose you are a member of the Grand Slam but are considering dropping your membership so that you can afford to do other things, such as traveling. Which of the costs of membership in the club are opportunity costs that would be relevant to your decision?
4. Suppose that you are a member of the club and are deciding whether to spend next Saturday afternoon playing tennis there. Which of the costs of membership are opportunity costs that would be relevant to your decision?
5. Suppose that it is noon on Saturday. You have made a reservation for an hour of court time at 5:00 p.m. A friend asks you to join a pickup basketball game at that time instead. What is the opportunity cost associated with abandoning the tennis reservation to join the basketball game?

End Notes

1. If you have studied accounting, you will recognize that this description of "accounting profit" is somewhat oversimplified. Accountants and economists have different objectives in analyzing the operations of a business firm. As a result, their concepts of costs and profits do not always allow precise comparison. Although the comparison is not exact, what economists call "accounting profit" most closely corresponds to what corporate accountants would call "net operating profit after taxes" (NOPAT) plus interest expense.
2. See James M. Buchanan, "Rent Seeking and Profit Seeking," in *Toward a Theory of the Rent-Seeking Society,* eds. James M. Buchanan, Robert D. Tollison, and Gordon Tullock (College Station: Texas A&M University Press, 1980), 3–15.

Appendix to Chapter 8:
COST AND OUTPUT WITH TWO VARIABLE INPUTS

In this chapter we looked at the relationship between cost and output when just one input is varied and all other inputs are kept constant. Now, we extend the theory of cost to the case in which more than one input is varied.

Substitution of Inputs

The main new feature of situations in which more than one input is varied is the possibility of substituting one input for another. Consider the case of Henry Hathaway, a farmer who grows corn. Hathaway spends all his time working on his farm and does not hire anyone to help him. For him, the amount of labor used in growing corn is a fixed input. In addition to fixed amounts of labor and machinery, he uses two variable inputs: land and fertilizer.

Hathaway can grow a given quantity of corn—say, 200 bushels—in many different ways. Some of the possibilities are shown in Figure 8A.1. One way to grow 200 bushels of corn is to use 2.5 tons of fertilizer and 10 acres of land. This is represented by point P on the graph. If Hathaway wants to grow the same amount of corn on less land, he can

FIGURE 8A.1   AN ISOQUANTITY LINE

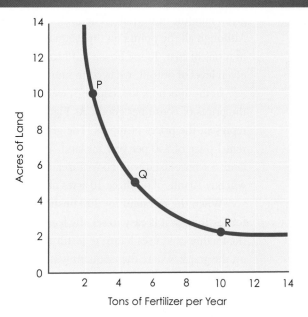

This graph shows an isoquantity line, or isoquant, for the production of 200 bushels of corn. The variable inputs are land and fertilizer; the other inputs, labor and machinery, are assumed to be fixed. Points P, Q, and R represent various ways of growing the given quantity of corn. A movement downward along the isoquant represents the substitution of fertilizer for land while output is maintained at 200 bushels per year. As more and more fertilizer is substituted for land, the isoquant becomes flatter because of diminishing returns.

substitute fertilizer for land. For example, at point Q he can grow 200 bushels of corn on 5 acres by using 5 tons of fertilizer. By substituting still more fertilizer for land, he can move to point R, where the 200 bushels are grown on just 2.5 acres using 10 tons of fertilizer.

Diminishing Returns in Substitutions

In this chapter, we defined the law of diminishing returns as it applies to a situation in which one input is varied while all others remain constant. In that situation, after a certain point the amount of the variable input needed to make an extra unit of output increases. (This is another way of saying that the marginal physical product of the variable input decreases.) A similar principle applies when one input is substituted for another in such a way as to keep output at a constant level: As the amount of input x is increased, the amount of x needed to replace one unit of y increases.

The example in Figure 8A.1 illustrates this principle. In moving from point P to point Q, 2.5 tons of fertilizer replace 5 acres of land while output stays constant at 200 bushels. But in moving from point Q to point R, 5 more tons of fertilizer are needed to replace just 2.5 acres of land.

As a result of the law of diminishing returns in substituting one input for another, a curve connecting points P, Q, and R becomes flatter as one moves downward and to the right along it. This reflects the decreasing ratio of the marginal physical product of fertilizer to the marginal physical product of land as more fertilizer is substituted for land.

Choosing the Least-Cost Production Method

Isoquantity line (isoquant)

A line showing the various combinations of inputs with which a given quantity of output can be produced

The line connecting points P, Q, and R in Figure 8A.1 is called an **isoquantity line** or **isoquant** because it shows the combinations of inputs that can be used to produce a given amount of output. (The prefix *iso* comes from a Greek word meaning "equal.") Although all the points on the isoquant are equal in terms of output, they are not equal in terms of cost. To see how a producer can choose the least-cost method of producing a given level of output, we need to know the prices of the inputs.

In the appendix to Chapter 5, we used budget lines as a graphical device to represent the prices of consumer goods. As Figure 8A.2 shows, the same technique can be used to represent the prices of inputs. The graph assumes a cost of $50 a ton for fertilizer and a rental price of $50 per year for land. The sum of $400 can buy 8 tons of fertilizer and no land, 8 acres of land with no fertilizer, or any of the other points on line A; the sum of $500 will buy 10 tons of fertilizer, 10 acres of land, or any of the other points on line B; and so on.

When the isoquant for 200 bushels of corn is drawn on top of a set of budget lines for the inputs, it is easy to see the least-cost method of producing that output level: It is the method that uses 5 tons of fertilizer and 5 acres of land. This corresponds to point Q on the graph, where the isoquant just touches budget line B. Points P and R are possible ways of growing 200 bushels of corn, but they lie on budget line C, which corresponds to a cost of $625. Note also that a budget of less than $500 (say, $400, as shown by budget line A) is not enough to reach the 200-bushel isoquant no matter how it is split between fertilizer and land.

Responses to Changes in Input Prices

If input prices change, the least-cost combination of inputs is likely to change as well. Suppose that the suburbs begin to expand in the direction of Hathaway's farm, driving

FIGURE 8A.2   FINDING THE LEAST-COST PRODUCTION METHOD

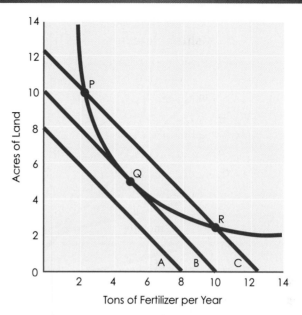

This graph shows how the least-cost method of production can be found from among the points on an isoquant given the prices of the variable inputs. Here, the price of fertilizer is assumed to be $50 a ton and the rental price of land $50 per year. A set of budget lines is drawn to represent various levels of spending on inputs. Line A, which corresponds to a total variable cost of $400, does not provide enough inputs to produce 200 bushels of corn. Line C, which corresponds to a total variable cost of $625, provides enough inputs to grow 200 bushels of corn using methods P or R. Line B, which corresponds to a total variable cost of $500, permits the 200 bushels to be grown using method Q, which is the least-cost method given these input prices.

up the price of land. Land that used to rent for $50 per acre per year now rents for $200 per acre. The price of fertilizer remains unchanged at $50 a ton.

The results of the increase in the price of land are shown in Figure 8A.3. Now $500 will not be enough to buy the combinations of inputs that fall along budget line B. Even if all the money were spent on land, only 2.5 acres could be rented. The new $500 budget line is C, which does not reach the 200-bushel isoquant at any point.

To grow 200 bushels, Hathaway must now spend more than $500. As he increases his budget for land and fertilizer, the budget line shifts upward but stays parallel to C. When the budget line reaches D, which corresponds to spending $1,000 on inputs, it just touches the isoquant at R. We see that now $1,000 is the lowest cost at which 200 bushels of corn can be grown, given a price of $50 a ton for fertilizer and $200 an acre for land. With those prices, R is the least-cost combination of inputs.

In this case, the effect of an increase in the price of an input is typical. Less of the input whose price has gone up is used; and the other input, which has become relatively less costly, is substituted for it. We will return to this topic in later chapters where we discuss the markets for productive resources.

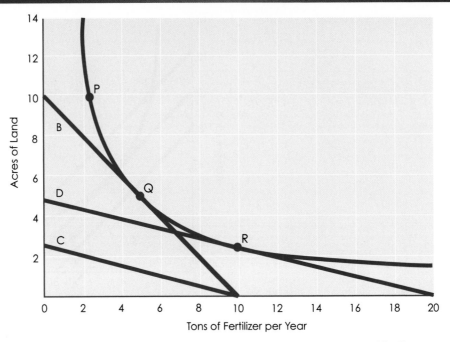

FIGURE 8A.3   EFFECTS OF A CHANGE IN INPUT PRICES

If the rental price of land increases from $50 to $200 per year while the price of fertilizer remains fixed at $50 a ton, 200 bushels of corn can no longer be produced for $500. The $500 budget line shifts from position B to position C and now falls short of the 200-bushel isoquant. Increasing the amount spent on variable inputs to $1,000 shifts the budget line up to position D, where it just touches the isoquant at point R. The increase in the price of land thus not only raises the total variable cost of growing 200 bushels of corn but also causes fertilizer to be substituted for land, which is now relatively more costly.

Varying Output

The isoquant technique can also be used to analyze variations in output with two variable inputs. Part (a) of Figure 8A.4 shows an isoquant "map" with three sets of points that correspond to three output levels. As before, P, Q, and R represent three ways of growing 200 bushels of corn. Points S, T, and U represent three ways of growing 100 bushels, and points V, W, and X are three ways of growing 300 bushels. An isoquant has been drawn through each set of points.

In this figure, we return to the assumption that land costs $50 an acre and fertilizer $50 a ton. Using these prices, a set of budget lines has been drawn, each corresponding to a different total variable cost, $300, $500, and $1,000.

As the graph clearly shows, there is a least-cost method for producing each output level given these prices. Point T is the best way to produce 100 bushels, Q is best for 200 bushels, and W is best for 300 bushels. Other output levels would be possible as well; these would lie along the line drawn from the origin through points T, Q, and W. This line is called the firm's **expansion path**. As the firm moves along its expansion path, more of both the variable inputs, land and fertilizer, is used. Meanwhile, the fixed inputs—labor and machinery, in Hathaway's case—remain constant.

Expansion path

A line on an isoquant diagram showing the least-cost combinations of inputs used to produce various levels of output, for given input prices

sFigure 8A.4   Expansion of Output and Total Variable Costs

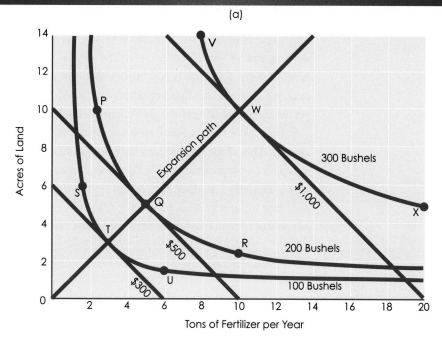

(a)

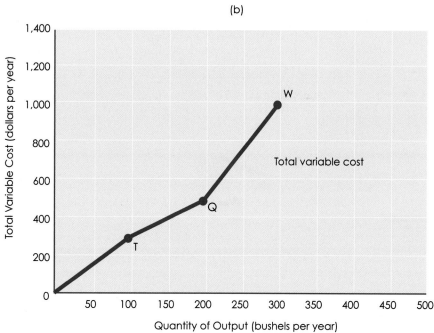

(b)

Part (a) of this figure shows three isoquants for the production of corn corresponding to outputs of 100, 200, and 300 bushels per year. Assuming input prices of $50 an acre for land and $50 a ton for fertilizer, budget lines can be drawn to show the minimum total variable cost for each output level. As output expands, the firm will move from T to Q and then to W along the expansion path. Part (b) of the figure plots the amount of output and the total variable cost for each of these points. The result is a reverse-S-shaped total variable cost curve that shows the effects of diminishing returns for output levels above 200 bushels per year.

Deriving a Cost Curve from the Isoquant Map

Once the expansion path has been identified, we can easily construct a total variable cost curve. All we need do is construct a graph that links each output point on the expansion path with the variable cost level of the corresponding budget line. This is done in part (b) of Figure 8A.4. At the origin, both output and total variable cost are zero. At point T, output is 100 bushels per year and total variable cost is $300 per year; at Q, we have 200 bushels and $500; and at W, 300 bushels and $1,000. Plotting these points and connecting them give the firm's total variable cost curve.

This curve has the same reverse-S shape as the cost curve discussed earlier in this chapter. This shape results from the law of diminishing returns, here applied to the case in which two inputs vary while all others remain fixed. Beyond point Q, the amounts of inputs needed to produce each added unit of output begin to rise, just as they did when only one input was allowed to vary. Only if all inputs are allowed to vary and none is allowed to remain fixed can a firm escape the effects of the law of diminishing returns.

CHAPTER *9*

Supply Under Perfect Competition

After reading this chapter, you will understand the following:

1. What characteristics define the structure of a market
2. What determines the profit-maximizing output level in the short run for a perfectly competitive firm
3. Under what conditions a firm will continue to operate even if it sustains a loss
4. How a firm's short-run supply curve is related to its cost curves
5. The conditions for long-run equilibrium in a perfectly competitive industry
6. What determines the shape of the long-run supply curve for a perfectly competitive industry
7. How efficiently markets perform under perfect competition

Before reading this chapter, make sure you know the meaning of the concepts:

1. Entrepreneurship
2. Efficiency
3. Theories and models
4. Perfectly elastic demand
5. Objectives, constraints, and choices
6. Market performance
7. Monopoly
8. Short- and long-run costs

IN A MARKET economy, competition is everywhere. Competition may take the form of giants such as Ford and Toyota struggling to dominate a market through advertising or introduction of new brands and styles. Sometimes it takes the form of intense rivalry between small firms for purely local markets—for example, two fast-food restaurants on opposite sides of a busy road. Sometimes competition takes the less visible form of small producers selling products like wheat or sugar that are nearly identical for

all firms in the market. In this chapter and the two that follow, we will examine all of these varieties of competition.

Economists refer to the conditions under which competition occurs in a market as **market structure**. Market structure is defined in terms of the number and size of firms, the nature of the product, ease of entry and exit, and availability of information.

In this book we will look at four market structures that have traditionally been emphasized in neoclassical economics. The first, to which this chapter is devoted, is **perfect competition**. The defining characteristics of perfect competition are the presence of many firms, none with a significant share of the market; a product that is homogeneous; easy entry into the industry and exit from it; and equal access to information by buyers and sellers. In saying that no firm has a "significant" share of the market, we mean that each firm is so small that its actions, alone, have no noticeable effect on the market price. By a "homogeneous product," we mean that the various firms' products are so nearly alike that they are perfect substitutes in the eyes of buyer. By "ease of entry," we mean that firms that are just starting to produce the product can do so on an equal footing with existing firms in terms of the prices paid for inputs, availability of technology, access to government permits or licenses, and so on. By "ease of exit," we mean that firms face no legal barriers to leaving the market and are able to find buyers or other uses for their fixed inputs. Finally, by "equal access to information," we mean that all buyers and sellers have complete information about the price of the product and of the inputs used to produce it, that buyers know all they need to know about product characteristics, and that all producers have equal knowledge of production techniques.

A second market structure, *monopoly*, is at the opposite extreme from perfect competition. A monopoly is a market in which a single firm accounts for 100 percent of sales of a product that has no close substitutes. Monopoly will be examined in detail in the next chapter.

Perfect competition and monopoly are "ideal type" market structures. Few if any markets exactly fit the definitions, although many approximate them. The next two market structures are more descriptive. **Oligopoly** means a market with only a few firms, at least some of which have a significant share of the market. The product may be either homogeneous or differentiated; there may or may not be significant barriers to entry; and buyers and sellers need not have equal access to all kinds of information. Most familiar markets for branded products, from automobiles to toothpaste, fit in this category. **Monopolistic competition** resembles perfect competition in that there are many small firms and easy entry and exit, but under monopolistic competition the various firms' products are differentiated from one another. Many sectors of retail trade and small service firms fit this category.

The characteristics of the four market structures are summarized in Table 9.1.

Perfect Competition and Supply in the Short Run

In building a model to fit the market structure of perfect competition, our objectives are first, to show how the profit-maximizing decisions of individual firms determine the quantity they will supply at various prices and, second, to show how individual

---

Market structure

The key traits of a market, including the number and size of firms, the extent to which the products of various firms are different or similar, ease of entry and exit, and availability of information

Perfect competition

A market structure that is characterized by a large number of small firms, a homogeneous product, freedom of entry and exit, and equal access to information

Oligopoly

A market structure in which there are only a few firms, at least some of which are large in relation to the size of the market

Monopolistic competition

A market structure in which there are many small firms, a differentiated product, and easy entry and exit

	TABLE 9.1 MARKET STRUCTURES			
	Number and Size of Firms	**Nature of Product**	**Entry and Exit Conditions**	**Information Availability**
Perfect Competition	Many firms, all small	Homogenous	Easy	Equal access to all information
Monopolistic Competition	Many firms, all small	Differentiated	Easy	Some restrictions
Oligopoly	Few firms, at least some of them large	Differentiated or homogeneous	May be some barriers to entry	Some restrictions
Monopoly	One firm	Unique product	Barriers to entry are common	Some restrictions

The structure of a market refers to the conditions under which firms compete in it—the number and size of firms, the nature of the product, the ease of entry and exit, and the availability of information. Perfect competition and monopoly are "ideal" types of structures. Few—if any—markers fit their definitions perfectly. Monopolistic competition and oligopoly are descriptive of most markets in the real wold.

firms' decisions generate market supply curves. We will look first at the short run and then at the long run.

The Constraints

The models used in neoclassical economics assume that, regardless of market structure, the firm's objective is to maximize profit. That means that differences in the choices that firms make under various market structures must be traced to differences in the constraints they face rather than to differences in objectives.

COST CONSTRAINTS One set of constraints, those imposed by costs, was discussed in the preceding chapter. In the case of perfect competition, we make three special assumptions regarding costs:

1. All firms in the market have access to the same technology and know where to buy inputs at the same prices. These conditions are implied by the assumptions of a homogeneous product and equal access to information by all firms. As a result, all firms have identical long- and short-run cost curves.

2. Economies of scale are exhausted at a small level of output relative to the quantity demanded at the prevailing price. As a result, there is room in the market for many firms producing at the minimum long-run average cost. Without this assumption, it would not be possible to maintain many firms, each small relative to the market.

3. There are no sunk costs. Firms that leave the market are able to recover implicit fixed costs by selling their plant and equipment to other firms. This is part of the requirement of free entry and exit.

DEMAND CONSTRAINTS: THE FIRM AS PRICE TAKER   Demand is the other principal constraint on the choices made by a profit-maximizing firm. Under perfect competition, the demand constraint has a special form. Because all firms in such an industry are small and have homogeneous products, each firm is a **price taker**. This means that the price at which each firm sells its output is determined by forces beyond the firm's control, namely, supply and demand conditions in the market as a whole. If an individual firm were to raise its price even a fraction above the prevailing market price, it would lose all of its customers. Equally, there would be no point in lowering its price even a fraction below the prevailing market price. If it did so, it would be overwhelmed by more orders than it could possibly fill. In graphical terms, we can say that each firm in a perfectly competitive market faces a horizontal demand curve, as shown in Figure 9.1.

Part (a) of Figure 9.1 shows the supply and demand curves for the market for chicken as given in earlier chapters. The equilibrium price is $2.00 per pound, and the

Price taker

A firm that sells its output at prices that are determined by forces beyond its control

---

FIGURE 9.1   MARKET DEMAND AND DEMAND FOR THE PERFECTLY COMPETITIVE FIRM

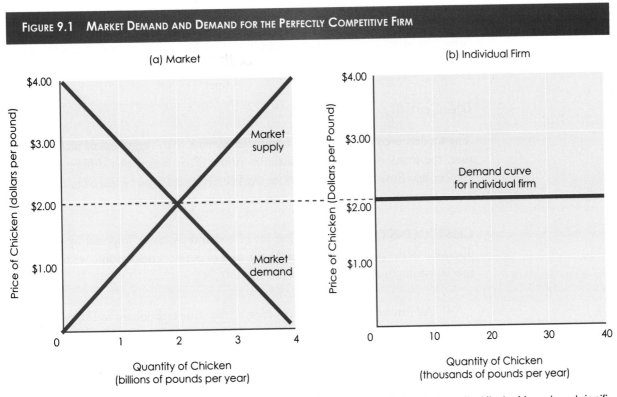

The perfectly competitive firm is a price taker. It is so small relative to the market as a whole that its decisions do not significantly affect the market price. In this example, the market equilibrium price is $2.00 per pound. The price will not be much affected if the individual firm shown in part (b) produces 20,000 rather than 40,000 pounds out of the billions of pounds produced in the market as a whole. Because the individual competitive firm is a price taker, the demand curve it faces is perfectly elastic. As a result, revenue equals price for a perfectly competitive firm.

equilibrium quantity is 2 billion pounds per year. Part (b) shows how the market looks from the viewpoint of an individual producer. The range of possible outputs is measured in terms of thousands rather than billions of pounds. The range of choice over which any one firm can vary its output is so small relative to the total quantity demanded that the market price will not be perceptibly affected whether the firm produces 10,000, 20,000, or 40,000 pounds of chicken a year. A 10,000-pound movement is too small even to see on the scale of the market supply and demand curves. As far as the individual firm is concerned, then, the demand curve it faces appears to be horizontal (perfectly elastic) at the market price, even though, when viewed from the perspective of the market as a whole, the demand curve has the usual negative slope.

Marginal revenue

The amount by which total revenue changes as a result of a one-unit increase in quantity sold

Previously we introduced the term *marginal cost* to refer to the amount by which total cost changes when output changes by one unit. Now we can introduce a similar term, **marginal revenue**, to refer to the amount by which total revenue changes as a result of a one-unit change in output. Recall that *revenue* means price times quantity sold. For a firm with a perfectly elastic demand curve, marginal revenue simply equals price. For example, if the price of chicken is $2 per pound, the firm will receive revenue of $200 from the sale of 100 pounds of chicken and revenue of $202 from the sale of 101 pounds. A 1-pound increase in output yields a $2 increase in revenue, that is, an increase in revenue equal to the product's price. Although marginal revenue and price are equal for a perfectly competitive firm, we will see in the next chapter that this is not the case for market structures in which the firm's demand curve is not perfectly elastic.

Short-Run Profit Maximization for the Firm

How does an individual firm in a perfectly competitive market maximize profits, given the constraints imposed by its cost and demand curves? A simple numerical example will help us answer this question. Our example will be based on the imaginary firm Fieldcom, which was introduced in the last chapter.[1]

Part (a) of Figure 9.2 shows short-run cost data for Fieldcom as given in the last chapter. It also shows the revenue Fieldcom earns from the sale of each quantity of output, assuming a market price of $500 per unit.

Subtracting total cost in column 3 from total revenue in column 2 yields the total profit the firm earns at each output level. The maximum is reached at 19 units per day, where a profit of $2,000 per day is earned. The profit-maximizing output level is shown graphically in part (b) of Figure 9.2. There the firm's total profit is indicated by the distance between the total revenue and total cost curves. That distance is greatest at 19 units of output.

Instead of comparing total cost and total revenue, we can find the profit-maximizing output level by comparing marginal cost and marginal revenue. Look first at columns 5 and 6 of part (a) of Figure 9.2. Column 5 gives data on marginal cost. (Marginal cost data are printed on lines between the entries in the first four columns to show that marginal cost is the change in cost as output moves from one level to another.) Column 6 shows marginal revenue, which, as explained, is equal to the product's price. Each PDA that Fieldcom sells adds $500 to its total revenue.

As the table shows, both total cost and total revenue rise as output increases. If the increase in revenue exceeds the increase in cost (that is, if marginal revenue is greater than marginal cost), boosting output by one unit increases total profit. If the increase in cost exceeds the increase in revenue (that is, if marginal cost is greater than marginal revenue), raising output by one unit reduces total profit. Therefore, to maximize profit a firm should expand its output as long as marginal revenue exceeds marginal cost and should stop as soon as rising marginal cost begins to exceed marginal revenue. A comparison of columns 5 and 6 of Figure 9.2 shows that for Fieldcom this means producing 19 units of output per day—the same number we arrive at when we compare total cost and total revenue.

FIGURE 9.2   SHORT-RUN PROFIT MAXIMIZATION UNDER PERFECT COMPETITION

(a)

Quantity of Output (1)	Total Revenue (2)	Total Cost (3)	Total Profit (2) – (3) (4)	Marginal Cost (5)	Marginal Revenue (6)
0	$ 0	$2,000	–$2,000	$380	$500
1	500	2,380	–1,880	340	500
2	1,000	2,720	–1,720	305	500
3	1,500	3,025	–1,525	275	500
4	2,000	3,300	–1,300	250	500
5	2,500	3,550	–1,000	230	500
6	3,000	3,780	–780	215	500
7	3,500	3,955	–495	205	500
8	4,000	4,200	–200	200	500
9	4,500	4,400	100	205	500
10	5,000	4,605	395	215	500
11	5,500	4,820	680	230	500
12	6,000	5,050	950	250	500
13	6,500	5,300	1,200	275	500
14	7,000	5,575	1,425	305	500
15	7,500	5,880	1,620	340	500
16	8,000	6,220	1,780	380	500
17	8,500	6,600	1,900	425	500
18	9,000	7,025	1,975	475	500
19	9,500	7,500	2,000	530	500
20	10,000	8,030	1,970	590	500
21	10,500	8,620	1,880	655	500
22	11,000	9,275	1,725	725	500
23	11,500	10,000	1,500	800	500
24	12,000	10,800	1,200		

(continues)

This figure shows the profit-maximizing level of output chosen by a perfectly competitive firm, Fieldcom, Inc., given a market price of $500 per unit. That level of output can be found by comparing total cost and total revenue, as shown in parts (a) and (b). It can also be found by comparing marginal cost and marginal revenue. (Because the firm is a price taker, marginal revenue is equal to price.) Profit increases up to the point at which rising marginal cost begins to exceed marginal revenue; after that point, it declines. Regardless of the approach used, the profit-maximizing output is 19 units per day and the maximum profit per day is $2,000.

The marginal approach to short-run profit maximization is shown graphically in part (c) of Figure 9.2. Up to about 19 units of output, the marginal cost curve lies below the marginal revenue curve, so each added unit of output increases profit. (The graph, unlike the table, pictures output as a continuous quantity so that profit maximization need not occur exactly at an even number of units.) Beyond that point, the marginal cost

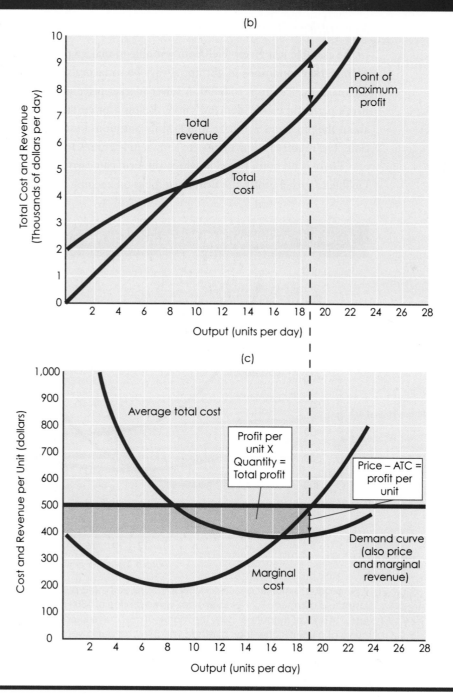

FIGURE 9.2   SHORT-RUN PROFIT MAXIMIZATION UNDER PERFECT COMPETITION, CONTINUED

curve rises above the marginal revenue curve so each added unit of output reduces profit. The point of profit maximization—the point at which the rising section of the marginal cost curve intersects the marginal revenue curve—matches the point in part (b) at which the spread between total revenue and total cost is greatest.

In part (c), the vertical distance between the demand curve, which shows price, and the average total cost curve represents the profit per unit. Profit per unit multiplied by the number of units gives total profit. Thus, from the standpoint of part (c), total profit equals the area of the shaded rectangle.

Minimizing Short-Run Losses

In the example just given, Fieldcom was able to make a profit at a price of $500. However, market conditions might not always be so favorable. Suppose, for example, that the market price drops to $300. A lower market price means a downward shift in the firm's perfectly elastic demand curve. Being a price taker, the firm can do nothing about the price and will have to adjust its output as best it can to meet the new situation. The required adjustments are shown in Figure 9.3.

There is no output level at which the firm can earn a profit given a price of $300. Unable to earn a profit, the firm must focus on keeping its losses to a minimum. With

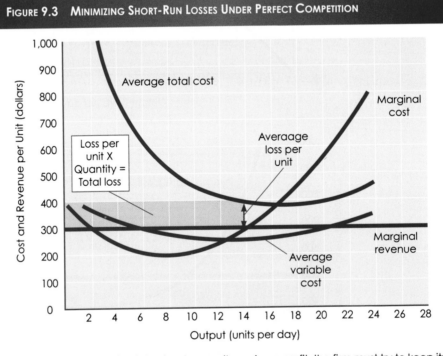

FIGURE 9.3   MINIMIZING SHORT-RUN LOSSES UNDER PERFECT COMPETITION

If the product's market price is too low to permit earning a profit, the firm must try to keep its losses to a minimum. For Fieldcom, Inc., given a price of $300 per unit, the point of minimum loss is 14 units of output per day. The marginal cost curve intersects the marginal revenue curve at a point higher than average variable cost but lower than average total cost. Each unit of output sold earns more than its share of variable cost but not enough to pay for its share of total cost when its share of fixed cost is included.

a price of $300 per unit, the minimum loss occurs at 14 units of output. As in the previous case, that is the output level beyond which marginal cost begins to exceed the product's price.

In graphical terms, we note that the point at which the rising section of the marginal cost curve intersects the marginal revenue curve lies between the average total cost and average variable cost curves.[2] Because the demand curve is below the average total cost curve, there is a loss on each unit sold. The total loss is equal to the shaded rectangle (loss per unit times quantity of output). However, the demand curve lies above the average variable cost curve. This means that revenue per unit is more than enough to cover variable cost and, hence, that each unit sold makes at least some contribution to covering fixed cost. Thus, losses are smaller than they would be if no output were produced, assuming that fixed costs must be paid even when output drops to zero.

As an aid to understanding the logic of the loss-minimizing decision, suppose for a moment that wages are the firm's only variable cost and that rent on its building is its only fixed cost. At the point shown, the firm is bringing in more than enough revenue to pay its wage bill (variable costs); the remainder will help pay the rent. If the firm shuts down temporarily, it will have to pay the rent with no help at all from current revenue. That would mean a loss equal to fixed cost—even more of a loss than at 14 units of output per day.

The logic of continuing operations in order to minimize losses applies only in the short run, when the costs of fixed inputs must be borne regardless of how much output is produced. A firm would not continue to operate indefinitely with the price below average total cost as shown in Figure 9.3. In the long run, a firm can free itself of fixed costs by selling its equipment, allowing long-term leases to expire, and so on. We will return to the conditions under which firms will leave the industry later in the chapter.

Shutting Down to Cut Short-Run Losses

What would happen if the price of PDAs dropped even lower than $300? Would it then still be worthwhile for the firm to keep making them even though it was losing money? The answer, as shown in Figure 9.4, is no.

The figure assumes a price of $225 per unit. With such a low price the firm cannot make a profit at any output level. But this time the best thing for the firm to do in the short run is to shut down. As illustrated by *Economics in the News 9.1*, temporary shutdowns are a normal way of adapting to changing supply and demand conditions. The example illustrates the point that shutting down is not at all the same as going out of business. Provided that the outlook for the future is good, it makes sense for a firm to keep its plant intact, pay its rent, and even continue some benefits for employees to ensure that they will be ready to come back when called. The firm therefore does not escape its fixed costs. When market conditions improve, inventories are brought into line with demand, and as the market price rises again, the firm can resume operations. Only if market conditions are never expected to improve will the firm consider winding up its affairs and going out of business.

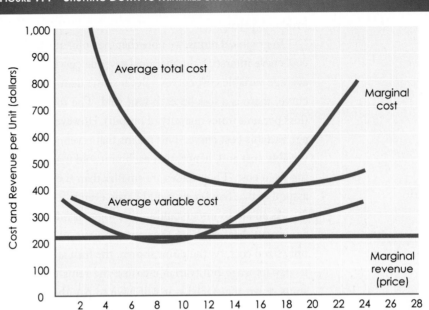

FIGURE 9.4   SHUTTING DOWN TO MINIMIZE SHORT-RUN LOSS

The price of a firm's output may drop so low that the firm must shut down in order to keep short-run losses to a minimum. As illustrated here, such a situation occurs for Fieldcom at a price of $225 per unit. Marginal cost rises above marginal revenue at about 11 units of output. That output yields a smaller loss ($2,345) than those slightly greater or lower. However, the loss can be reduced to just $2,000 a day if the firm shuts down. The marginal cost curve in this case intersects the marginal revenue curve at a point below average variable cost. That is the signal to shut down.

In the case of a temporary shutdown, it can be misleading to follow the rule of expanding output until marginal cost begins to exceed marginal revenue. With the price at $225, such a point is reached at about 11 units of output per day. That output level does give the firm a lower loss than a level slightly higher or slightly lower; but in this case the firm incurs an even smaller loss by not producing at all.

The reason 11 units of output does not minimize loss is that the demand curve lies below the average variable cost curve at that point. Suppose again that wages are the firm's only variable cost and rent is its only fixed cost. At 11 units of output, revenue is not enough even to meet the firm's payroll. The firm will do better to send its workers home and save the cost of wages, even though when it does this the owners will have to pay the entire rent from reserves, without any help from current sales revenue.

The Firm's Short-Run Supply Curve

The examples just given provide the information needed to draw a short-run supply curve for a perfectly competitive firm. Let's work through an example like the one

Economics in the News 9.1
CHANGING WITH THE SEASONS

Croatia is a small country that must make the most of its resources as it hurries to catch up to the living standards of the rest of Europe. One asset that will help it do so is a stunning Adriatic coastline with brilliant sun, sparkling clear water, and hundreds of islands, perfect for get-away weekends by Parisians or Berliners.

In the opinion of many, the crown jewel among the Croatian islands is Hvar. The tiny port of Hvar Town is a tourist paradise of ancient red-roofed houses cascading down a steep hill from an old fort at the top to a quaint fishing harbor below. Taking advantage of some fine, clear weather in mid-March, a recent visitor found the streets of Hvar Town lined with hotels, restaurants, and souvenir shops—all of them closed! Although it has facilities to serve thousands of tourists in the summer, all but one hotel and all but three or four restaurants close for the season each winter, to open again in the late spring.

At first it seems like such a waste. All that natural beauty is still there, and the water is just as clear even if the air is a few degrees cooler. Why don't the hotels and restaurants just offer low, off-season rates in order to stay busy all winter? With a little thought, though, the economic logic of the decision to shut down becomes clear. Hotel and restaurant owners have to take a close look at their costs when deciding whether to operate on a year-round or seasonal basis. Some costs, like property taxes and interest on bank loans can't be avoided by shutting down, but others, especially labor costs for clerks and kitchen staff, can be eliminated when the establishment is closed. To a certain point, it pays to stay open by offering lower, off-season rates, but when those rates fall so low that they don't even cover the wages of the cooks and cleaners, it is time to put up the shutters and wait for spring.

And what about the one hotel that stays open in the winter? Is the owner just ignorant of economics? No, there's an economic logic behind this hold-out strategy, too. If just one hotel stays open while all others shut, the few visitors to the town are enough to push its revenues above the break-even point. It's all an example of competition in action.

Ancient street on the island of Hvar, Croatia

shown in Figure 9.5 starting with a price of $500. As we saw earlier, Fieldcom will turn out 19 devices a day at that price. Point E_1 of the firm's short-run marginal cost curve thus is a point on its supply curve.

Now suppose that the demand for PDAs slackens and the market price begins to fall. As it does so, the point at which marginal revenue equals marginal cost moves downward along the firm's marginal cost curve. Soon point E_2 is reached—the point at which marginal cost and average total cost are equal. This occurs at an output of about 17 units and a price of about $385. At that price, the best the firm can do is break even; either a greater or a smaller output will result in a loss.

If the price falls still lower, the firm's objective becomes one of keeping its loss to a minimum. At a price of $300, for example, the firm minimizes its loss by making 14 units (point E_3). In the range of prices between minimum average total cost and minimum average variable cost, the supply curve continues to follow the marginal cost curve.

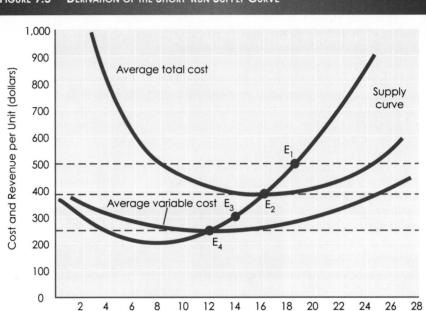

FIGURE 9.5   DERIVATION OF THE SHORT-RUN SUPPLY CURVE

This graph shows how a short-run supply curve for Fieldcom, Inc. can be derived from its cost curves. When the price and marginal revenue is $500, the firm will produce at point E_1. As the price falls the firm will move downward along its short run marginal cost curve as shown by points E_2 and E_3. The firm will continue to produce at the point at which price equals marginal cost until marginal cost falls below average variable cost. E_4 thus is the lowest point on the firm's supply curve. Below that price the firm will shut down.

At about $250 the price reaches the lowest point on the average variable cost curve. There the firm is just on the edge of shutting down—it is covering its variable costs with nothing to spare. Its loss is equal to its fixed costs. At any lower price the firm will minimize its losses by shutting down. Thus, point E_4 is the lowest point on the marginal cost curve that can be considered part of the firm's supply curve.

The preceding discussion of the firm's short-run supply decision can be summed up as follows: *The short-run supply curve of a profit-maximizing firm operating in a perfectly competitive market coincides with the upward sloping part of the marginal cost curve lying above its intersection with the average variable cost curve.*

The Industry's Short-Run Supply Curve

Once we have a supply curve for each firm in an industry, we can add them together to construct a supply curve for the industry as a whole. Figure 9.6 shows how this can be done, beginning with the supply curves for three firms. To get the total supply of the three firms at each price, the quantities supplied by each firm are added together. In graphical terms this means adding the supply curves horizontally. To generalize the process to an industry with many firms, the individual supply curves of the remaining firms in the industry would be added to the three shown.

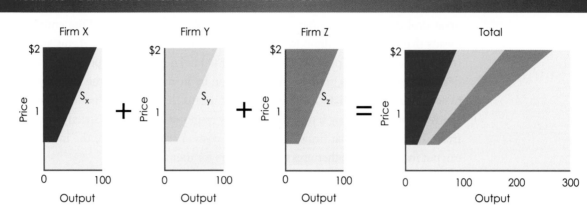

FIGURE 9.6 DERIVATION OF A SHORT-RUN INDUSTRY SUPPLY CURVE

A short-run industry supply curve can be obtained by summing the supply curves of individual firms. Here this method is shown for the first three firms in an industry. The supply curves of additional firms would be added in the same way. If the prices of inputs change as industry output varies, the industry supply curve will need to be adjusted.

In adding the firms' supply curves together, we assumed that input prices did not change as output expanded. For a small firm in a perfectly competitive industry, this is a realistic assumption. However, if all firms in an industry try to grow at the same time, the assumption may not hold. In fact, input prices will rise unless a greater quantity of inputs can be purchased without paying higher prices, that is, unless the short-run supply curves for inputs to the industry are perfectly elastic. If input prices rise as the industry's total output grows, each firm's cost curves will shift upward as the output of all firms increases. That will make the short-run industry supply curve somewhat steeper than the sum of the individual supply curves.

Long-Run Equilibrium Under Perfect Competition

Up to this point we have considered changes in industry output that result from firms' decisions to produce more or less as the market price changes. In doing so, however, we have neglected an important part of a competitive industry's response to changes in demand: the processes of entry and exit.

Consideration of entry and exit moves us from the short run to the long run. In the last chapter we distinguished between the long run, when all inputs can be varied, and the short run, when some inputs are fixed. The ability to vary all inputs in the long run—even durable ones such as land, structures, and major pieces of equipment—allows firms to enter a market for the first time, starting with a new plant and work force. It also means that they can leave a market for good, releasing all their employees and selling their plant and equipment. (Sometimes firms leave voluntarily, with the owners selling the firm's assets and dividing up the proceeds. Other times they leave the market only when forced to do so, such as when creditors resort to a bankruptcy court to force a sale of the firm's assets in order to pay its debts.) Typically, as an industry expands and contracts, many firms enter and leave it.

Free entry and exit of firms is one of the basic traits of a perfectly competitive market. Free entry does not mean that firms can enter at no cost. They may have to pay a great deal to purchase equipment, hire key employees, and so on. Free entry simply means that if they are willing to make the necessary investment, new firms are free to compete with existing ones on a level playing field. They are not kept out by patents or licensing requirements, trade secrets, collusion by firms already in the industry, or lack of access to raw materials. Likewise, free exit means that firms face no legal barriers to shutting down or moving if they find that they cannot make a profit. Strictly interpreted, free exit also means that firms have no sunk costs. When they leave the industry, they can put fixed assets to other uses or find buyers for them.

Free entry and exit did not play a direct role in our discussion of a firm's short-run supply decision. However, as we will now see, it is crucial to understanding how a competitive market works in the long run.

Long-Run Equilibrium for a Competitive Firm

At numerous points we have used the term *equilibrium* to refer to a state of affairs in which economic decision makers have no incentive to change their plans. Three conditions are required for a perfectly competitive firm to be in equilibrium in the long run:

1. The firm must have no incentive to produce a larger or smaller output given the size of its plant (that is, the amount of fixed inputs it uses). That requires that short-run marginal cost be equal to short-run marginal revenue, which in turn means that the short-run equilibrium condition is also a condition for long-run equilibrium.

2. Each firm must have no incentive to change the size of its current plant (that is, the amount of fixed inputs it uses).

3. There must be no incentive for new firms to enter the industry or for existing firms to leave it.

Figure 9.7 shows a perfectly competitive firm for which these three requirements are met. First, short-run marginal cost equals price at 25 units of output per day, which is the level of output the firm will choose in order to make the maximum profit. Second, the firm has a plant that is just the right size to make short-run average total cost equal to the lowest possible long-run average cost at the chosen output level. The short-run average total cost curve for a plant of any other size would give a higher average total cost for the chosen output. Third, both long-run average cost and short-run average total cost are equal to price at the equilibrium level of output. This guarantees that there is no incentive for entry or exit. As always, average total cost comprises both explicit and implicit costs, including the opportunity cost of capital, or "normal profit." When price equals average total cost, then, firms are earning zero economic profit. Any positive economic profit would attract new firms into the industry, whereas negative economic profits (economic losses) would cause firms to leave the industry.

FIGURE 9.7   A PERFECTLY COMPETITIVE FIRM IN LONG-RUN EQUILIBRIUM

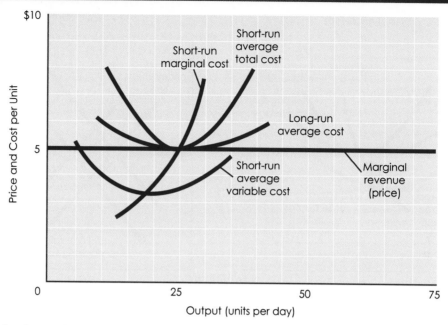

Long-run equilibrium in a perfectly competitive industry requires that the typical firm (1) have no short-run incentive to change the level of its output; (2) have no long-run incentive to change the size of the plant used to produce its output; and (3) have no long-run incentive to enter or leave the industry. This requires that price, short-run marginal cost, short-run average total cost, and long-run average cost all have the same value in equilibrium as shown here.

The three conditions for long-run equilibrium are summarized in the following equation.

Price = Marginal cost = Short-run average total cost = Long-run average cost

If any part of this equation does not hold, firms will have a reason to change their plans. If price does not equal short-run marginal cost, they will have an incentive to change their output levels by changing the quantity of variable inputs used, even if they cannot, in the short run, change the size of their plants. If short-run average total cost does not equal long-run average cost, their current plant is too large or too small to produce their current level of output at the least possible cost. They will want to change the size of the plants they are using, so their plant will be the ideal size to produce their current output. If price is lower than long-run average cost, firms in the industry will want to leave it; if price is above long-run average total cost, firms outside the industry will want to enter it.

Industry Adjustment to Falling Demand

A state of long-run equilibrium, such as that shown in Figure 9.7, exists only as long as outside conditions do not change. Suppose, though, that those conditions do change—for example, there is a long-run decrease in the market demand for the firm's product. Figure 9.8 shows what will happen.

FIGURE 9.8   LONG-RUN ADJUSTMENT TO DECLINING DEMAND

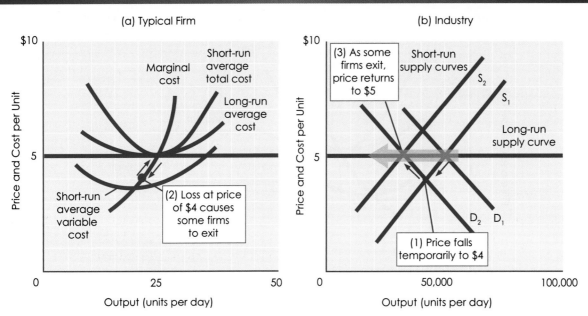

Part (a) represents a typical firm in a perfectly competitive industry; part (b) represents the industry as a whole. At first, both the firm and the industry are in long-run equilibrium at a price of $5. Then something happens to shift the market demand curve leftward from D_1 to D_2. In the short run, the price falls to $4 at the intersection of D_2 and S_1. The firm's short-run response is to move downward along its marginal cost curve. Because the price is still above average variable cost, the firm does not shut down. After a while, some firms (not the one shown) get tired of taking losses and leave the industry. This causes the market supply curve to shift toward S_2 and the market price to recover. The typical firm returns to the break-even point. The market has traced out part of its long-run supply curve as shown by the large arrow.

Part (a) of Figure 9.8 shows a set of cost curves for a typical firm. Part (b) is a supply-and-demand diagram for the market as a whole. The short-run industry supply curves shown are built up from those of the individual firms in the market (see Figure 9.6). The demand curves in part (b) are market demand curves.

Suppose that initially the short-run market supply and demand curves are in the positions S_1 and D_1. The equilibrium price is $5. Each firm takes this price as given and adjusts its output on that basis, producing 25 units. At that price and output, a typical firm would just break even. (Remember, though, that "breaking even" in the economic sense means earning enough to cover all costs, including the opportunity cost of capital.)

Now something happens—say, a change in consumer tastes or incomes—that shifts the demand curve to a new position, D_2. The short-run result is a drop in the market price, to $4. Each firm, being a price taker, will view the decline in price as beyond its control and will adjust to it as best it can. As shown in part (a) of Figure 9.8, this means cutting back output slightly in order to keep losses to a minimum, but not shutting down completely. Each firm's movement downward along its short-run marginal cost curve is what causes the movement of the market as a whole downward and to the left along the short-run supply curve.

However, the new situation cannot be a long-run equilibrium because each firm is operating at a loss. The firms' owners are not earning a normal rate of return, that is, they are not earning enough to cover the opportunity costs of keeping their capital invested in the industry. If the market demand curve shows no hope of shifting back to the right, some owners will pull their capital out of the industry. They may go bankrupt, abandoning their fixed assets to their creditors. They may sell their plant and equipment and get out while they can, or they may keep their firms running but convert their plants to make goods for other, more profitable markets.[3]

For the sake of the example, suppose that the typical firm shown in Figure 9.8 is not one of the first to leave. As some other firms withdraw, industry output falls by the amount of their output. The short-run market supply curve, which now comprises fewer individual supply curves, shifts to the left toward S_2. As it does so, the market price begins to move upward along demand curve D_2. When the price gets all the way back to $5, the firms remaining in the industry will no longer be losing money. Firms will stop leaving the industry, and the market will have reached a new long-run equilibrium. At the new equilibrium price, short-run marginal cost, short-run average total cost, and long-run average cost will once again be equal.

This sequence of events has traced out a portion of the industry's *long-run supply curve*, as shown by the large horizontal arrow. A long-run supply curve for an industry shows the path along which equilibrium price and quantity move when there is a lasting change in demand. Movement along this curve requires enough time for firms to adjust the sizes of their plants or enter or leave the market.

Industry Adjustment to Rising Demand

When there is a long-run increase in demand, freedom of entry plays the same role that freedom of exit plays when demand falls. Such a case is shown in Figure 9.9. The starting position in this figure is the same as that in Figure 9.8. Short-run supply curve S_1 and demand curve D_1 result in an equilibrium price of $5. The individual firm breaks even at an output of 25 units. Now watch what happens as the demand curve shifts to the right, to D_2. The short-run result is an increase in the market price, to $6. The typical firm adjusts to the new price by moving up along its short-run marginal cost curve. As all firms do this, the market moves up and to the right along short-run supply curve S_1.

Again, however, the short-run position is not the new long-run equilibrium, because now all firms are making an economic profit. Entrepreneurs will soon spot this healthy, growing market as a good one in which to invest. Some of them may start new firms in this market; others may shift plant and equipment from making something else to making goods for this industry. Whether the entry is by new firms or by existing ones that are producing for this market for the first time, new entries will cause the supply curve to shift to the right, toward S_2.

As the short-run market supply curve shifts to the right, the price falls. It does not fall far enough to drive the new entrants out of the market, but it does fall far enough to drive pure economic profits back to zero. Entry of firms into the market will stop, and the market will reach a new long-run equilibrium at the intersection of S_2 and D_2.

Once again a portion of the long-run supply curve for the industry has been traced out, as shown by the large horizontal arrow in Figure 9.9. This long-run supply

FIGURE 9.9   LONG-RUN ADJUSTMENT TO AN INCREASE IN DEMAND

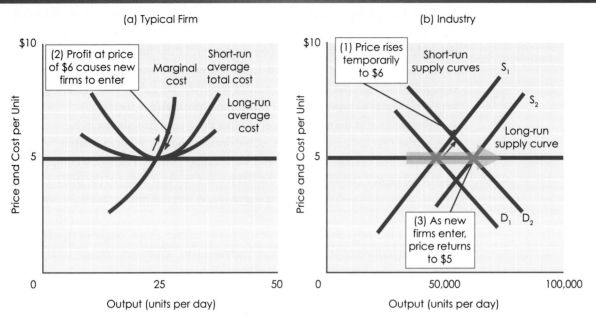

In this figure, both the firm and the industry start out in equilibrium at a price of $5. Then something happens to shift the market demand curve rightward to D_2. In the short run, the price rises to $6 at the intersection of D_2 and S_1. The firm's short-run response is to move upward along its marginal cost curve, earning better-than-normal profits. After a while, the high profits attract new firms into the industry. As those firms enter, the market supply curve shifts toward S_2. Profits for the typical firm return to zero, and new firms stop entering the industry. Again the market has traced out part of its long-run supply curve as shown by the large arrow.

curve again is perfectly elastic. A rightward shift in the demand curve has, in the long run, produced an increase in quantity supplied but no rise in price.

As a final detail, note the importance of the assumption that there are no sunk costs in the industry. If entering the industry required specialized investments that could not be recovered later, firms would view them as opportunity costs when deciding whether to enter the market. They would not enter unless the price was high enough (and was expected to stay high enough) to give them a normal rate of return on the nonrecoverable investments. Once in the industry, however, those sunk costs would no longer affect decisions, according to the "bygones are bygones" principle. They would not count as part of the fixed (but not sunk) costs that must be covered by revenue for continued operation to be worthwhile. Thus, existing firms may stay in business indefinitely even if the price falls somewhat below what would be needed to attract new firms. When sunk costs are present, then, the industry supply curve is no longer a two-way street. Such an industry would, in effect, follow one supply curve when expanding and a different, lower one when contracting.

Although the theoretical model of perfect competition does not allow for sunk costs, such costs are common in the real world. Consider the history of that uniquely American entertainment establishment, the drive-in theater. In the early years after World War II, drive-in theaters were a growing business. With demand high, many entrepreneurs entered the industry. Later, demand for this form of entertainment decreased. Even when market demand dropped well below the level needed to make it worthwhile to construct new drive-ins, existing operators stayed in business. They did so even though they were no longer earning enough to cover the original sunk cost of their screens and projection houses because those facilities could neither be moved nor converted to any other use. Only when demand fell still lower, so that revenues no longer covered recoverable fixed costs (such as the cost of land) and variable costs (such as wages, electricity, and film rentals) did drive-in theater operators finally leave the market.

The Elasticity of Long-Run Supply

The long-run industry supply curve in Figures 9.8 and 9.9 is perfectly elastic. Given such a curve, a change in demand affects only the equilibrium quantity, not the price, in the long run. However, that is not the only possible case. Supply curves that are positively sloped, negatively sloped, and U-shaped are also possible.

The shape of the long-run industry supply curve depends mainly on what happens to the industry's input prices in the long run as output expands. If the long-run supply curves for all inputs to the industry are perfectly elastic, the prices of those inputs will not change as the quantities of them demanded by the industry increase. It may also be that the industry uses such a small part of the total supply of each input that any change in input prices that does occur will be slight. For example, cookie stores use such a small part of the total supply of flour and eggs that expansion or contraction of such stores will have no perceptible effect on the market prices of those inputs. Industry output can therefore expand without affecting the costs of the individual firms, and the supply curve will be perfectly elastic.

Suppose, however, that the industry is a heavy user of relatively specialized inputs whose outputs can be boosted only at an increasing cost. An example is the home construction business, which uses a substantial portion of all lumber produced. An expansion of the construction industry will cause lumber suppliers to exhaust the lowest-cost stands of trees and begin harvesting higher-cost timber. The home construction industry also employs a significant proportion of all carpenters in the country. If the industry expands, carpenters' wages may have to rise relative to those of, say, auto mechanics in order to attract additional workers into the occupation.

Figure 9.10 shows what happens in such an industry as a permanent increase in demand causes output to expand. As in the preceding case, the shift in demand first pushes up price along the short-run supply curve. New firms enter the market. However, the expansion of the industry raises input prices. Each firm's short-run marginal cost and average total cost curves are shifted upward from MC_1 to MC_2 and from ATC_1 to ATC_2 as shown. As a result, the new long-run equilibrium is at a higher price than the initial equilibrium. The long-run industry supply curve, drawn through the two points of short-run equilibrium, therefore has a positive slope.

It is also possible for the price of an input to decrease as the industry's total output increases. For example, as sales of electronic equipment expand, the firms that make components for such equipment may be able to use cheaper production methods. If

---

FIGURE 9.10   A POSITIVELY SLOPED LONG-RUN INDUSTRY SUPPLY CURVE

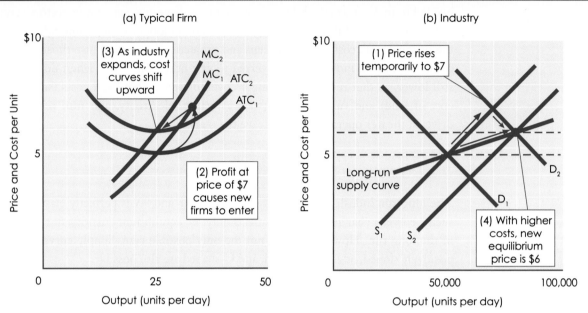

(a) Typical Firm

(3) As industry expands, cost curves shift upward

(2) Profit at price of $7 causes new firms to enter

MC₂   MC₁   ATC₂   ATC₁

(b) Industry

(1) Price rises temporarily to $7

Long-run supply curve

(4) With higher costs, new equilibrium price is $6

S₁   S₂   D₁   D₂

In Figures 9.8 and 9.9, it was assumed that input prices do not change as industry output expands. This pair of diagrams shows what happens if industry expansion causes input prices to rise. As output expands, rising input prices push up the firm's marginal cost curve from MC₁ to MC₂ and its average total cost from ATC₁ to ATC₂. The result is a new long-run equilibrium price that is higher than the initial price. The long-run industry supply curve thus has a positive slope.

---

that occurs, the short-run cost curves for all firms will drift downward as new firms enter the industry. The long-run supply curve then will be negatively sloped.

Finally, it is possible for these various forces to operate together. At first long-run supply is influenced by the falling price of one special input, but beyond a certain point some other special input becomes a limiting factor that causes the long-run supply curve to bend upward. The long-run industry supply curve then becomes U-shaped.

As we have seen, many variations are possible. Only through direct observation of the industry in question can we tell which possibility applies.

Market Performance Under Perfect Competition

In Chapter 4 we introduced the notion of *market performance* to indicate how efficiently markets do their job of allowing buyers and sellers to capture mutual gains from trade. Perfectly competitive markets have long earned high marks for several aspects of performance. In this section we look at market performance under perfect competition as it relates to the questions of *what* should be produced and *how* it should be produced.

What Should Be Produced

When the concept of market performance was introduced, we used a diagram similar to Figure 9.11 to show the quantity of a good (peaches, in this case) that must be pro-

FIGURE 9.11 EFFICIENT OUTPUT UNDER PERFECT COMPETITION

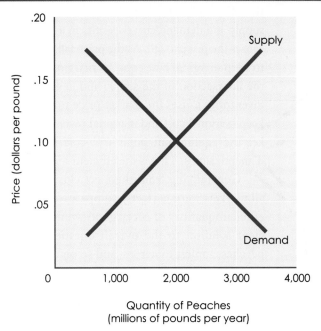

Quantity of Peaches
(millions of pounds per year)

This figure shows supply and demand curves for a perfectly competitive market for peaches. Under perfect competition, each firm's efforts to keep marginal cost equal to marginal revenue ensure that the industry will produce at some point on the supply curve. Equilibrium for the market as a whole can occur only at the point where the supply and demand curves intersect. That represents an efficient resolution to the question, What should be produced?

duced for a market to perform efficiently. The demand curve, we said, represents the amount consumers are willing to pay for an additional pound of peaches, given any level of output. That amount reflects the benefit of the marginal pound as perceived by consumers. The supply curve represents the amount suppliers require if they are to produce an additional pound of peaches. That amount corresponds to the opportunity cost to producers of supplying the marginal pound. As long as the demand curve is higher than the supply curve, trade at a price between the two curves can potentially benefit both parties. Accordingly, opportunities for mutually beneficial trades are exhausted (and efficiency is achieved) only if production is carried out to the point of intersection between the supply and demand curves, but not beyond that point.

In this chapter we have shown that the supply curve in a perfectly competitive market is the summation of the marginal cost curves of the individual firms. At any given market price, producers will supply the quantity that makes marginal cost equal to marginal revenue, which in turn is equal to the market price. Thus, the price-quantity combination at which transactions take place in a competitive market will be some point on the supply curve.

For the market to end up at the right point on the supply curve, the market price must correspond to the intersection of the supply curve with the demand curve. To see why this will happen in a competitive market, we can put Chapter 2's analysis of market equilibrium together with this chapter's conclusions regarding perfect competition. From Chapter 2, we know that a price that is higher than the intersection of the supply and demand curves results in a surplus. Unplanned accumulation of inventory causes the price to fall. As the price falls, firms move down along the supply curve so as to keep marginal cost equal to marginal revenue. Similarly, a price that is lower than the intersection of the supply and demand curves results in a shortage. Depletion of inventories causes the market price to rise. Firms move up along the supply curve to keep marginal cost and marginal revenue equal. Thus, in a perfectly competitive market the equilibrium point will correspond to the intersection of the supply and demand curves. That is the efficient outcome.

Generalizing from these conclusions, we can see that in an economy in which all markets were perfectly competitive and in which there were no externalities the efficient quantity of every good would be produced. That would represent an efficient solution to the overall question of what should be produced—how many peaches, apples, tomatoes, and so on. Beginning from a situation in which the competitive markets for all products were in equilibrium, it would not be possible to substitute any one good for another (say, by producing more peaches at the expense of using fewer resources to produce apples) in a way that would make any person better off without making at least one other person worse off.

How to Produce

The preceding conclusion about what should be produced holds in both short- and long-run equilibrium. In addition, in the long run only, perfectly competitive markets ensure that each good is produced at the lowest possible cost—a key aspect of how goods should be produced.

To understand why goods are produced at the lowest cost in a situation of long-run competitive equilibrium, review Figures 9.8 and 9.9. In those figures the point of long-run equilibrium is shown to occur at the point where the typical firm operates at the minimum point of both the short-run average total cost curve and the long-run average cost curve.

Starting from such a point, a decrease in demand causes the market price to fall. In response, each firm reduces its output to the point where short-run marginal cost equals the new price. Although short-run marginal cost is lower at that output, short-run average total cost is higher because the firm moves up and to the left along the average total cost curve as output falls. Thus, at this point in the adjustment to falling demand, the given level of output is not being produced at the lowest possible cost. That is inefficient.

However, the inefficient situation does not last. Because short-run average total cost exceeds the market price, the firms suffer an economic loss, and some of them will leave the industry. Assuming no further change in demand, as the number of firms in the industry decreases, each firm is able to increase its output and move back toward its point of least-cost production. Similar reasoning applies to the expansion of industry output in response to an increase in demand.

Under perfect competition, firms are led not only to produce at the lowest possible short-run average total cost, given the size of their plants, but also to select the correct plant size to minimize average cost in the long run. To see why, suppose that one firm had a plant that was not the optimal size. As we saw in the last chapter, the short-run average total cost curve for such a firm would be tangent to its long-run average cost curve at a point above and to the right of the point of long-run minimum cost (if the plant were too large) or above it and to the left (if the plant were too small). The firm with the wrong size plant would thus be at a cost disadvantage relative to its competitors. As competition drove the market price toward a level equal to minimum long-run average cost, the firm would either adjust the size of its plant to the cost-minimizing level or leave the industry because of economic losses.

Other Aspects of Market Performance

The tendency of perfectly competitive markets to produce the efficient quantity of each good and to produce those quantities at the lowest cost are important strengths of this market structure. In Chapter 13 we will extend the analysis of perfect competition to factor markets. In doing so, we will see that perfectly competitive markets perform efficiently with regard to the questions of *who* and *for whom* as well as those of *what* and *how*. In these respects, long-run equilibrium in perfectly competitive markets sets a standard against which the performance of other market structures can be judged.

Nevertheless, it would be claiming far too much to say that perfect competition has the best possible market performance under all conditions, and it would be premature to condemn every feature of real-world markets that differs from the structural characteristics of perfect competition. Before we write off all markets that are not made up exclusively of small firms, all markets in which products are not homogeneous, all markets in which newly entering firms encounter entry barriers or incur sunk costs, or all markets in which some participants know things that others do not, many questions must be asked. Among them are the following:

- Is it possible that other market structures equal or at least approximate the efficiency of perfect competition?

- How do alternative market structures perform when attention is focused on innovation and entrepreneurship rather than on equilibrium under conditions where technology and product characteristics are assumed to be unchanging?

- When markets fail to perform efficiently, what public-policy options are available? How should the dangers of government failure be weighed against the dangers of market failure?

Only when these additional aspects of the problem have been explored will we be in a position to make a balanced judgment of market performance under various market structures.

Summary

1. **What characteristics define the structure of a market?** A *market structure* is defined in terms of the number and size of firms in the market, the nature of the product, ease of entry and exit, and availability of information. A *perfectly competitive market* has the following traits: (1) There are many buyers and sellers, each of which is small compared with the market as a whole; (2) the product is homogeneous; (3) it is easy to enter or leave the market; and (4) all buyers and sellers have equal access to information. Other market structures to be studied in this course include *monopoly, oligopoly, and monopolistic competition.*

2. **What determines the profit-maximizing output level in the short run for a perfectly competitive firm?** In the short run the relationship between marginal cost and *marginal revenue* (price) determines the profit-maximizing output level for a perfectly competitive firm. The firm should expand output up to, but not beyond, the point at which marginal cost rises to the level of marginal revenue, provided that marginal revenue is at least equal to average variable cost at that point.

3. **Under what conditions will a firm continue to operate even if it sustains a loss?** If marginal revenue is below average total cost at the point at which marginal cost and marginal revenue are equal, the firm cannot earn a profit. It will minimize loss in the short run by staying open if marginal revenue is above average variable cost. If marginal revenue is below average variable cost at the same point, the firm will minimize loss by shutting down.

4. **How is a firm's short-run supply curve related to its cost curves?** The short-run supply curve for a perfectly competitive firm is the upward-sloping part of the marginal cost curve lying above its intersection with the average variable cost curve.

5. **What are the conditions for long-run equilibrium in a perfectly competitive industry?** Long-run equilibrium in a perfectly competitive industry requires (1) that price be equal to short-run marginal cost so that each firm is content with the level of output it is producing; (2) that short-run average total cost be equal to long-run average cost so that firms are satisfied with the size of their plants, given their output rate; and (3) that price be equal to long-run average cost so that there is no incentive for new firms to enter the industry or for existing firms to leave it.

6. **What determines the shape of the long-run supply curve for a perfectly competitive industry?** A perfectly competitive industry adjusts to long-run changes in demand through exit of firms (in the case of a drop in market demand) or entry of new firms (in the case of a rise in market demand). If input prices do not change as the industry's output changes, the industry's long-run supply curve will be perfectly elastic. If input prices rise, the long-run supply curve will have a positive slope; if they fall, it will have a negative slope.

7. **How efficiently do markets perform under perfect competition?** Under conditions of equilibrium, a perfectly competitive market produces a quantity of output that corresponds to the intersection of the market's supply and demand curves. In an economy in which all markets are in perfectly competitive equilibrium and there are no externalities, the question of what to produce is thus resolved efficiently. Also, in a situation of long-run equilibrium the output of a perfectly competitive market is produced at the lowest possible cost. This means that the question of how to produce is also resolved efficiently.

Key Terms   Page

Problems and Topics for Discussion

1. **Market structures**   Give examples (other than those presented in the text) of industries that fit, or approximate, the market structures of perfect competition, monopoly, oligopoly, and monopolistic competition.

2. **Buyers as price takers**   The concept of price taking can apply to buyers as well as to sellers. A price-taking buyer cannot influence prices by changing the amount purchased. Are you a price taker for the goods you buy? Can you give an example of a firm that might not be a price taker in the market in which it buys one or more of its inputs?

3. **Changes in fixed cost and the supply curve** Fieldcom buys some automated equipment to speed up production of its PDAs. The equipment adds $500 per day to the firm's fixed costs, but it saves $50 per unit in variable costs. Rework the graph in Figure 9.5 to show how the new equipment affects Fieldcom's supply curve. (You may want to rework part (a) of Figure 9.2 as a basis for the new supply curve.) What is the minimum price the firm must now charge to continue operating in the short run? What is the lowest price at which it can break even?

4. **Long- and short-run elasticity of supply**   In Chapter 3 it was asserted that, other things being equal, the elasticity of supply of a good tends to be greater the more time firms have to adjust to new market conditions. Using the theory of perfect competition as presented in this chapter, explain the basis for that assertion.

5. **Long-run supply with falling input prices** Figure 9.10 shows the long-run adjustment of a competitive industry to an increase in demand in the case in which input prices rise as industry output increases. Assume instead that input prices fall as output rises. Draw a new set of diagrams to show how a typical firm and the industry as a whole would respond to an increase in demand.

Case for Discussion

Independent Truckers as a Perfectly Competitive Industry

The next time you are out on the highway, take a look at the trucks that are passing you. You will see many that belong to large firms, such as UPS, that haul large numbers of small shipments all over the country on regular schedules. You will also see trucks that bear the names of companies such as Sears or Sun Oil, for which transportation of their own products is a small part of their total operations.

If you look closely, though, you will see that about one truck in four looks a little different. The tractors, many of which are brightly painted and highly chromed, often have sleepers attached to them. The trailers, often refrigerated, are likely to be filled with farm produce moving to market. These are the trucks of independent owner-operators, who move much of the nation's output of farm goods and some manufactured goods.

Each firm in this market consists of a person who owns and drives just one truck. There are tens of thousands of owner operators—just how many is hard to count.

From the shipper's point of view, one refrigerated truck is about as good as another as long as it is headed in the right direction. And most independent truckers will go wherever their loads take them.

Entry into the market is easy. Some people go into business with a used truck and as little as $5,000. Most operators buy their trucks on credit. Exit is also easy—too easy, some say. Many independent truckers go broke every year, and the number of firms rises and falls with the state of the economy.

Information is the lifeblood of the owner-operator. Truckers cannot make money unless they can find loads. Empty return runs after making a delivery are deadly to profitability. In the past, truck stop payphones and gossip over a cup of coffee were the main information channels, but the Internet has revolutionized the flow of information among shippers and truckers. Several competing web sites, some of which are free, others of which charge brokerage fees, match truckers to loads.

People who run the giant trucking companies that haul manufactured goods often look down their noses at the independent truckers with their loads of apples and potatoes. They call them gypsies or worse. But this system succeeds in putting fresh produce on dinner tables in every town every day.

QUESTIONS

1. In what ways does the independent trucking industry approximate the requirements of perfect competition? Are there any ways in which it does not meet those requirements?

2. On the average, the firms in a perfectly competitive industry earn no pure economic profits. However, average conditions do not always apply. What would you expect to happen to the profits of independent truckers when the economy enters a recession? When it enters a period of prosperity? What do you think would happen to the number of firms in the industry at such times?

3. Diesel fuel is a major input for independent truckers. What would you expect to happen to the profits of independent truckers and the num-

ber of firms in the industry as the price of fuel rises and falls? Outline the sequence of events in each case. (Drawing a graph may help.)

End Notes

1. Bear in mind that in the real world, it is hard to find firms that exactly fit the ideal type of perfect competition. For example, the description of Fieldcom in Chapter 8 implied that the firm's PDAs had special qualities of "ruggedization" that set them apart from other computers. This would violate the assumption of product homogeneity. For the purposes of this chapter, we will imagine that the idea of "ruggedized" PDAs did not work out, but that the Martins instead have discovered that they can survive by making "generic" PDAs that function just like others on the market.

2. This graph shows why we emphasize that profit maximization occurs where the *rising* section of the marginal cost curve intersects the marginal revenue curve. There is sometimes also an intersection of the *falling* section of the marginal cost curve with the $300-per-unit marginal revenue curve, as is the case at about 2 units of output in Figure 9.3. That intersection is *not* a point of profit maximization, but rather, one of loss maximization.

3. The discussion of exit from a perfectly competitive market seems to pose a paradox: If all firms are *exactly* alike, why don't they all stay in the market as long as conditions are favorable, and then all leave the market at the same instant when conditions become unfavorable? However, real-world markets only approximate the conditions of perfect competition. In such markets, small differences in firms' circumstances of cost or demand, or in the temperaments of their owners, will cause some to leave the market before others do.

CHAPTER *10*

The Theory of Monopoly

After reading this chapter, you will understand the following:

1. The circumstances in which monopoly can exist
2. How the profit-maximizing price and output for a monopoly are determined
3. How long-run equilibrium is achieved under monopoly
4. Kinds of pricing strategies used by monopolies
5. How monopoly affects market performance

Before reading this chapter, make sure you know the meaning of the concepts:

1. Market performance and market failure
2. Rent seeking
3. Consumer and producer surplus
4. Market structure

A MONOPOLY IS defined in neoclassical economics as a market in which a single firm is the sole supplier of a product that has no close substitute. There are few firms that meet this requirement, if it is taken literally. Is Microsoft a monopolist in the market for operating systems? No, it has a large market share, but Linux users would deny a lack of substitutes. Does the U.S. Postal Service have a monopoly on delivery of mail? Yes, if narrowly defined as first-class postal mail, but Federal Express, e-mail, and fax are close substitutes. Does your local electric company have a monopoly? Probably yes, if you mean delivery of electric power by wire, but industrial users of co-generation equipment and green consumers with off-the-grid systems provide examples of substitutes. Still, we can learn much from studying the market structure that we call monopoly, even if we have a hard time finding perfect real-world examples. One reason is that many features of the monopoly model introduced in this chapter apply to all firms that are not price takers, even if they are not pure monopolists. Also, we will learn much about real world markets by asking why monopoly in its pure form is rare and, where it exists, why it does not last forever.

Varieties of Monopoly

We can begin by distinguishing among three types of circumstances in which a single firm could occupy the position of sole supplier to a market.

Closed monopoly

A monopoly that is protected by legal restrictions on competition

1. A **closed monopoly** is protected by legal restrictions on competition. For example, state law in Washington prevents anyone from offering competing car ferry service to islands served by the Washington State Ferry System. Patents and copyrights can also be viewed as closed monopolies—competing authors are not allowed to write novels based on J. K. Rowling's character Harry Potter. Note, however, that these closed monopolies do not prevent sale of substitutes, for example, air service to Washington islands or books featuring other child heroes.

Natural monopoly

An industry in which long-run average cost is minimized when only one firm serves the market

2. A **natural monopoly** is an industry in which long-run average cost is minimized when just one firm serves the entire market. Distribution of natural gas to residential customers is an example. In such an industry the minimum efficient scale of production for a good is close to (or even larger than) the quantity that is demanded at any price high enough to cover per-unit production costs. Thus, dividing production between two or more firms (for example, running two sets of gas pipes down every street) would result in an inefficiently high cost per unit for each. Closely related to natural monopolies based on economies of scale are monopolies based on ownership of a unique natural resource. For example, for many years ownership of a uniquely productive mine in Utah gave the Brush Wellman Company a near monopoly over production of beryllium, an ultra-light metal used in aerospace applications.

Open monopoly

A monopoly in which one firm is, at least for a time, the sole supplier of a product but has no special protection from competition

3. An **open monopoly** is a case in which a firm becomes, at least for a time, the sole supplier of a product without having the special protection against competition that is enjoyed by a closed or natural monopoly. The first firm to venture into the market for a new product often finds itself in such a position, although other competitors may enter later. An example is Apple's iPhone, which had a monopoly in the market for touch-screen cell phones until competitor Blackberry introduced a similar product.

The classification of monopolies into these three categories is a loose one. Some firms may belong to more than one category. For example, local utilities like electric and gas companies may be both natural monopolies (because of economies of scale) and closed monopolies (because of regulatory barriers to competition). Also, the classification may depend on the time horizon in question. For example, patent protection may give a firm a closed monopoly in the short run; but the monopoly may be open in the long run, not only because patents eventually expire, but also because competitors are able to invent new products or processes that circumvent them. Patented pharmaceuticals illustrate this phenomenon.

Ultimately, all monopolies can probably be considered open. The legal restrictions that protect closed monopolies from competition are subject to challenge in legislatures and courtrooms. Long-distance telephone service, on which AT&T once held a monopoly, is a case in point. Technological change may doom other monopolies. For example, Polaroid's once lucrative monopoly on instant-film cameras became nothing but a technological curiosity with the rise of digital photography. All monopolists face competition by substitutes for the products they produce. Later in the chapter we will return to the tendency of monopolies to attract competitors. First we will develop a formal model of this market structure.

Simple Monopoly

Like the model of perfect competition presented in the preceding chapter, the model of monopoly aims to explain the operation of markets in terms of the firm's objectives and constraints. For monopoly, as for perfect competition, standard neoclassical models assume that the firm's objective is profit maximization. The differences in market outcomes between the two cases, then, stem from differences in the constraints that are assumed to define the set of opportunities open to the firm.

Constraints Faced by Monopoly

The monopolist's ability to earn a profit, like that of other firms, is constrained in part by its production costs. The model presented here is based on the theory of cost presented in Chapter 8. The special restrictions imposed in perfect competition (a minimum efficient scale that is small relative to the size of the market and no sunk costs) do not apply to monopoly.

The other principal constraint on the monopolist's profit-making opportunities is the demand for its product. Because a monopolist is by definition the only firm in its market, the demand curve faced by the firm is the same as the market demand curve for the product. The monopolist's demand curve, then, is negatively sloped—the quantity of output that can be sold decreases as the price increases.

The monopolist is assumed to know the characteristics of the demand curve for its product, whether from econometric studies, trial and error, or simple intuition. Because both price and quantity vary along the negatively sloped demand curve, the monopolist, unlike a perfectly competitive firm, is not a price taker. Instead, its demand curve represents a menu of possible price-quantity combinations from which it selects the combination that will yield the maximum profit. Because it searches for the most profitable price in a range of possible prices, a monopolist can be called a **price searcher**.

The model of monopoly presented in this section incorporates one additional constraint: The monopolist is assumed to offer its output at a single price that is uniform for all customers and to allow all buyers to purchase as much or as little as they want at that price. A monopoly that follows this pricing policy is called a **simple monopoly**. Other pricing strategies will be discussed later in the chapter.

Output, Price, and Marginal Revenue Under Simple Monopoly

We first noted the relationship between price and total revenue along the demand curve in Chapter 3, in connection with the concept of elasticity. There we saw that when demand is *elastic* a drop in price causes total revenue to rise. (The reason is that

Price searcher

Any firm that faces a negatively sloped demand curve for its product

Simple monopoly

A monopoly that offers its output at a single price that is uniform for all customers and allows all buyers to purchase as much or as little as they want at that price

in percentage terms the quantity sold rises by more than the price falls; thus, the product of price times quantity, which equals revenue, increases.) In contrast, when demand is *inelastic* revenue falls when the price drops. (This occurs because with inelastic demand the percentage increase in quantity is less than the percentage decrease in price.) With a straight-line demand curve, such as the one in part (b) of Figure 10.1, the upper half is elastic and the lower half inelastic. That accounts for the shape of the "revenue hill" in part (c).

Earlier we defined *marginal revenue* as the change in total revenue that results from a one-unit increase in a firm's output. Column 4 in part (a) of Figure 10.1 presents data on marginal revenue for the firm in this example. The figures in the column are the differences between the entries in column 3. Part (b) of the exhibit shows the firm's marginal

FIGURE 10.1 DEMAND, TOTAL REVENUE, AND MARGINAL REVENUE UNDER SIMPLE MONOPOLY

(a)

Quantity of Output (1)	Price (2)	Total Revenue (3)	Marginal Revenue (4)
1	$9.75	$9.75	
2	9.50	19.00	9.25
3	9.25	27.75	8.75
4	9.00	36.00	8.25
5	8.75	43.75	7.75
19	5.25	99.75	
20	5.00	100.00	0.25
21	4.75	99.75	-0.25
22	4.50	99.00	-0.75
36	1.00	36.00	
37	0.75	27.75	-8.25
38	0.50	19.00	-8.75
39	0.25	9.75	-9.25
40	0.00	0.00	-9.75

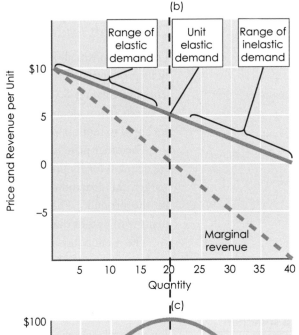

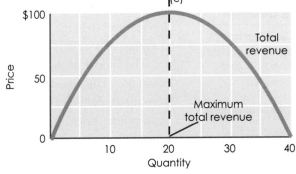

This figure shows how demand, total revenue, and marginal revenue are related under simple monopoly. Total revenue is found by multiplying price by output at each point on the demand curve. Marginal revenue is the increase in total revenue that results from a one-unit increase in output. When demand is elastic, marginal revenue is more than zero and total revenue is increasing. When demand is inelastic, marginal revenue is less than zero and total revenue is decreasing. Marginal revenue is less than price at all levels of output.

revenue curve. The marginal revenue curve is above the horizontal axis when total revenue is increasing (elastic demand) and below it when total revenue is decreasing (inelastic demand). It intersects the horizontal axis at the point of maximum total revenue.

An easy rule can be used to sketch the marginal revenue curve corresponding to any straight-line demand curve: *The marginal revenue curve for a straight-line demand curve always cuts the horizontal distance from the demand curve to the vertical axis exactly in half.* Following this rule, the point where the marginal revenue curve intersects the horizontal axis can be placed halfway between the origin and the horizontal intercept of the demand curve (that is, the point where the demand curve intersects the horizontal axis). In Figure 10.1 the marginal revenue curve cuts the horizontal axis at 20, half of 40. The vertical intercept of the marginal revenue curve is the same as that of the straight-line demand curve. (The vertical intercept is at $10 in Figure 10.1.) This rule does not apply to curved demand curves, but to keep things simple, we will look only at linear demand curves here.

The marginal revenue curve is always below the demand curve. For a simple monopolist, the marginal revenue that the firm gets from the sale of one additional unit is less than the price at which the unit is sold, not equal to the price as in a perfectly competitive firm. The gap between price and marginal revenue stems from the fact that the firm sells all units supplied in a given period at the same price. This means that it must cut the price on all units sold per period, not just on the last one, in order to increase the quantity sold. For example, if our monopolist wants to increase sales from 19 units per period to 20 units per period, it must cut the price on all 20 units from $5.25 to $5. Although the firm gains $5 in revenue from the sale of the twentieth unit, its total revenue increases by only $4.25, from $99.75 to $100. The added revenue from the twentieth unit is mostly offset by a revenue reduction of $.25 per unit on the first 19 units sold.

The fact that the marginal revenue curve for a monopolist lies below its demand curve illustrates the marginal-average rule discussed in the preceding chapter. The average revenue realized by the simple monopolist, as represented by the height of the demand curve for any given level of output, must be falling if marginal revenue is less than average revenue.

Finding the Point of Maximum Profit

Figure 10.2 adds the monopolist's cost curves to its demand and marginal revenue curves. The data presented there can be used to identify the price-quantity combination that will yield the maximum profit. As in the preceding chapter, this can be done either by comparing total cost with total revenue or by taking a marginal approach.

A monopolist maximizes profits by producing the quantity of output for which marginal cost equals marginal revenue. The price it charges for the product is determined by the height of the demand curve (rather than the height of the marginal revenue curve) at the profit-maximizing output. Note that maximizing profit is not the same as maximizing revenue. Beyond 13 units of output (the profit-maximizing level in this case), total revenue continues to rise for a while; however, profit falls because total cost rises even more rapidly.

FIGURE 10.2 PROFIT MAXIMIZATION FOR A MONOPOLIST

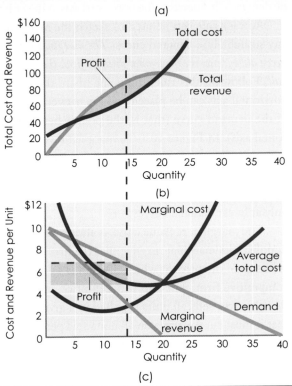

(a)

(b)

(c)

Quantity of Output (1)	Price (2)	Total Revenue (3)	Marginal Revenue (4)	Marginal Cost (5)	Total Cost (6)	Total Profit (7)
0	$10.00	$0.00		$5.05	$25.00	$-25.00
1	9.75	9.75	$9.75	4.60	29.60	-19.85
2	9.50	19.00	9.25	4.20	33.80	-14.80
3	9.25	27.75	8.75	3.85	37.65	-9.90
4	9.00	36.00	8.25	3.55	41.20	-5.20
5	8.75	43.75	7.75	3.30	44.50	-0.75
6	8.50	51.00	7.25	3.10	47.60	3.40
7	8.25	57.75	6.75	2.95	50.55	7.20
8	8.00	64.00	6.25	2.85	53.40	10.60
9	7.75	69.75	5.75	2.80	56.20	13.55
10	7.50	75.00	5.25	2.80	59.00	16.00
11	7.25	79.75	4.75	2.85	61.85	17.90
12	7.00	84.00	4.25	2.95	64.80	19.20
13	**6.75**	**87.75**	**3.75**	**3.10**	**67.90**	**19.85**
14	6.50	91.00	3.25	3.30	71.20	19.80
15	6.25	93.75	2.75	3.55	74.75	19.00
16	6.00	96.00	2.25	3.85	78.60	17.40
17	5.75	97.75	1.75	4.20	82.80	14.95

A monopolist maximizes profits by producing the quantity of output for which marginal cost equals marginal revenue. The price it charges for the product is determined by the height of the demand curve (rather than the height of the marginal revenue curve) at the profit-maximizing output. Beyond 13 units of output (the profit-maximizing level in this case), total revenue continues to rise for a while, but profit falls because total cost rises even more rapidly.

Total cost for the firm at various output levels is given in column 6 of part (c) of Figure 10.2. Subtracting total cost from total revenue (column 3) gives total profit (column 7). A glance at column 7 shows that the profit-maximizing output level is 13 units. The total revenue–total cost approach to profit maximization is shown graphically in part (a) of the exhibit. Total profit equals the vertical gap between the total cost and total revenue curves. It reaches a maximum at about 13 units of output, where the two curves are farthest apart. Note that maximizing profit is not the same as maximizing revenue. Between 13 and 20 units of output, total revenue continues to rise; but because total cost rises even more rapidly, profit falls.

The marginal approach to profit maximization is illustrated by the data in columns 4 and 5 in part (c) of Figure 10.2. Marginal revenue is the amount by which total revenue increases when output is increased by one unit; marginal cost is the amount by which total cost increases. It follows that as long as marginal revenue exceeds marginal cost, adding one more unit of output adds more to total revenue than to total cost and hence adds to total profit. Beyond 13 units of output, marginal revenue falls below marginal cost; therefore, any further expansion of output reduces total profit. The logic here is exactly the same as for a perfectly competitive firm, except that now marginal revenue is variable rather than constant.

Part (b) of Figure 10.2 compares marginal revenue and marginal cost in graphical terms. The profit-maximizing output is found at the point where the positively sloped section of the marginal cost curve intersects the marginal revenue curve—that is, at about 13 units of output. Profit per unit at that output is equal to the vertical gap between the demand curve (which shows the price at which the product is sold) and the average total cost curve. Profit per unit times quantity of output equals total profit, as shown by the shaded rectangle.

The intersection of the marginal cost and marginal revenue curves in Figure 10.2 gives the profit-maximizing *output* for the firm, but the profit-maximizing *price* is given by the height of the demand curve for that level of output. For a monopolist, that price is always above marginal cost when profit is being maximized. For the firm in our example, marginal cost at 13 units of output is $3.10 per unit; but according to the demand curve, consumers are willing to buy 13 units at a price of $6.75 per unit. Therefore, $6.75, not $3.10, is what the monopolist will charge for the 13 units of output in order to earn the maximum profit.

Profit Maximization or Loss Minimization?

If market conditions are unfavorable, a monopolist, like a perfectly competitive firm, may be unable to earn a profit in the short run. In such a case, it will aim to minimize losses. Whether a profit is possible depends on the position of the demand curve relative to the firm's average total cost curve.

The possibility of a loss is shown in Figure 10.3. In this diagram, fixed costs are assumed to be higher than in our earlier example, so that the demand curve lies below the average total cost curve at all points. The monopolist might find itself in such a position as the result in the increase of the price of some fixed input. Following the usual rule, the profit-maximizing (or loss-minimizing) level of output is found at the point where the marginal cost and marginal revenue curves intersect, which is still at

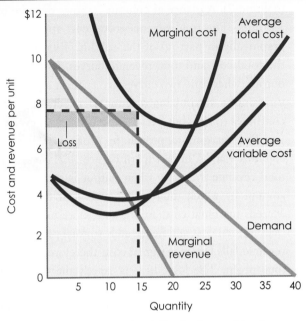

FIGURE 10.3   A MONOPOLIST SUFFERING A SHORT-RUN LOSS

Sometimes costs may be too high in relation to demand to allow a monopolist to earn a profit. In this graph, for example, the demand curve lies below the average total cost curve at all points. The best the monopolist can do in the short run is cut losses by producing at the point at which marginal cost equals marginal revenue. If the demand curve were to shift downward even further, preventing the firm from obtaining a price that would cover average variable cost, the short-run loss-minimizing strategy would be to shut down.

about 13 units of output. According to the demand curve, that much output cannot be sold for more than $6.75 per unit, even though average total cost at 10 units of output is $8.30. At a price of $6.75 per unit, then, the firm will lose $1.55 on each unit sold. The total loss is shown by the shaded rectangle.

Although the firm suffers a loss at 3 units of output, no other output level will yield a smaller loss. In Figure 10.3, the price of $6.75 per unit is more than enough to cover average variable costs. A monopolist, like a perfect competitor, is better off staying in business in the short run, even at a loss, as long as the price at which it can sell its output is greater than the average variable cost. If poor market conditions caused the demand curve to shift so far to the left that it fell below the average variable cost curve at all points, the firm would minimize its short-run losses by shutting down.

We see, then, that being a monopolist does not guarantee that a firm will be able to earn a profit. It can do so only if cost and demand conditions allow the product to be sold at a price that exceeds the cost of producing it. If the situation shown in Figure 10.3 were only temporary, the firm would ride it out, waiting for better times to return. Sometimes, however, a monopolist faces a permanent increase in cost or decline in demand. A privately owned, profit-maximizing monopolist will then leave the industry, freeing itself of its fixed costs by selling its assets, terminating its long-term leases, and so on. *Applying Economic Ideas 10.1* illustrates this possibility with the case of urban mass transit systems, which, in many cities, formerly operated as privately owned closed monopolies. When the demand for mass transit services fell, the systems could no longer operate at a profit and might have disappeared entirely but for public subsidies.

Applying Economic Ideas 10.1
SUBSIDIZED MONOPOLY: THE CASE OF MASS TRANSIT

To many people, monopoly is synonymous with vast profits. Not all monopolies are profitable, however. A case in point is the mass transit systems of most large U.S. cities.

Until the 1960s, the majority of urban bus lines in the United States were privately owned. Often there was more than one transit firm in a city—Chicago had more than thirty at one point. However, city governments granted each firm a closed monopoly over the routes it operated, so that people were often unable to choose among transit systems to get to any given destination.

In 1950 this largely private transit system carried some 17 billion passengers. Gradually, however, more and more commuters and shoppers began to travel by car. By 1970 ridership on urban mass transit systems had fallen to just 7 billion. Along the way, the business became unprofitable for most private firms, despite their monopoly status. In 1963, for the first time, urban mass transit as a whole experienced an operating loss. Since that date it has never regained profitability.

At one point mass transit systems were privately owned and routes were monopolized.

City governments could simply have let the private transit systems go out of business. In some cases, especially trolley systems, they did so. However, all subway and most urban bus systems were gradually transferred to city ownership where they remain to this day.

These government-owned monopoly transit systems, like their private predecessors, must decide how to price their product. One possible rule would be to equate marginal cost and marginal revenue in order to minimize losses and keep subsidies for the system to a minimum. However, because of several considerations, many cities offer fares lower than what would be dictated by the rule of equating marginal cost and marginal revenue. Consequently, they must offer larger subsidies than would result from a simple loss-minimization strategy.

One such consideration is efficiency. It could be argued that for commuters to choose efficiently between mass transit and driving their own cars, the transit fare should be equal to the marginal cost of providing an additional ride on the public transit system A subsidy-minimizing price would be higher than marginal cost and, thus, higher than the efficient level.

Second, it can be argued that a further adjustment of the fare should be made to allow for traffic congestion, a form of negative externality that in itself results in inefficient use of transportation resources. A low fare that causes people to choose mass transit rather than travel by car can be defended as a means of offsetting the adverse effects of traffic congestion.

Finally, low transit fares are often defended as a means of benefiting low-income households, which tend to be heavy users of public transportation. Without affordable public transportation as a means of getting to work, it is argued, some lower-income people would not be able to keep their jobs and, instead, would have to depend on the assistance of public welfare payments.

In practice, then, most mass transit systems do not set fares to minimize subsidies. To do so would require operating at a point at which marginal revenue is positive, indicating that the system is operating on the elastic part of its demand circle. However, fare increases on most systems result in higher revenues, showing that they are on the inelastic portion of the demand curve. As a rule, city governments leave transit fares low until taxpayers start complaining about the size of the necessary subsidies. Then they raise fares to the point at which the strength of the marginal complaint from transit riders balances that of the marginal complaint from taxpayers.

Profit Maximization in the Long Run

In presenting the model of perfect competition, we distinguished between two time horizons. In the short run, each firm had a plant of fixed size, and the number of firms in the industry was also fixed. In the long run, each firm was free to adjust the size of its plant, and firms were free to enter or leave the industry. Each case gave rise to a clearly defined equilibrium. The simple model of monopoly presented in the preceding section is oriented toward the short run. The issues raised by consideration of the long run under monopoly conditions are more complex. Not all of them can be resolved in terms of simple equilibrium solutions. Nevertheless, some of the issues are worth considering.

Long-Run Equilibrium Without Threat of Entry

The simplest situation is that of a monopolist that faces no threat of entry into its market by competitors. For such a firm, a graph such as Figure 10.2 can represent long-run as well as short-run profit maximization—only the interpretation of the curves changes. The curve that is labeled average total cost in Figure 10.2 would now be interpreted as the firm's long-run average cost curve, allowing for free adjustment of fixed inputs as in the long-run competitive case. The marginal cost curve would be the corresponding long-run marginal cost curve, and the demand curve would be the long-run demand curve. The long-run equilibrium would occur at the output where long-run marginal cost equals long-run marginal revenue, and the long-run equilibrium price would be given by the height of the long-run demand curve at that point. Beyond what has already been said about the short run, three things are worth noting about such a long-run equilibrium.

1. The firm must at least break even in the long-run equilibrium. The loss-minimizing situation shown in Figure 10.3 cannot be a long-run equilibrium because the firm would leave the market if it could not at least recover its long-run average cost.

2. Unlike the case of perfect competition, long-run equilibrium under monopoly need not occur at the minimum point on the firm's long-run total cost curve. It could occur at an output below minimum long-run average cost (as shown in Figure 10.2) or at an output greater than minimum long-run average cost (as would be the case if the demand curve in Figure 10.2 were to shift strongly to the right). Whatever its long-run equilibrium output, the monopolist will select the size of plant that is best suited to that level of output. In graphical terms, this would mean a short-run aver-age total cost curve tangent to the long-run average cost curve at the equilibrium output.

3. The price that will maximize long-run profit for the firm will be lower than the price that will maximize short-run profit if, as is usually the case, demand is more elastic in the long run than in the short run. Beginning from a point of long-run equilibrium, a monopolist could temporarily increase its profit by raising its price and cutting output to move up along its less elastic short-run

demand curve. Given that higher price, customers would make long-run adjustments in their consumption patterns, reducing the quantity demanded until they were back on the long-run demand curve at a correspondingly lower level of output. The monopolist's profit at the higher price would then be less than at the original long-run equilibrium price.

Open Monopoly, Entrepreneurship, and Limit Pricing

In the cases we have examined up to this point, it is easy to identify a specific equilibrium point. The situation becomes more complex if we introduce the possibility of entrepreneurship. If we do so, demand and cost curves can no longer be treated as given because any firm that earns a pure economic profit for any length of time is sure to attract the attention of entrepreneurs eager to get a piece of the action. They will have their own ideas about what is given and what is subject to change.

Consider long-run equilibrium for an open monopolist. Such a firm is currently the sole supplier of its product but is not protected by the decisive cost advantages of a natural monopoly or the legal barriers to entry of a closed monopoly. With little or no built-in protection from would-be rivals, what options does it have?

One option is to push the price all the way up to the short-run profit-maximizing level, enjoy pure economic profits while they last, and accept the fact that sooner or later other firms will enter the market and take away part or all of those profits. In many cases that is just what firms do. The consumer electronics industry provides some familiar examples. The first firm to reach the market with a DVD player, a flat-screen TV, or a touch-screen cell phone typically sets a high initial price. Soon other firms enter with products that closely imitate the original one. The market then becomes an oligopoly in which the first firm may still hold a significant market share, but with less pricing power. With luck, by the time pure economic profits disappear entirely, the firm's research department will come up with a new product from which the firm can again reap temporary monopoly profits. Often the hope of even short-lived monopoly profits is a strong spur to innovation.

Consumer electronics are typically set at a high price when they initially enter the market.

An alternative strategy, instead of setting the price at the short-run profit-maximizing level, is to set a somewhat lower price, one that gives it a moderate profit but at the same time makes the market a less attractive target for would-be competitors. Such a strategy is called limit pricing because it limits short-run profits in the hope of limiting entry.

Limit pricing

A strategy in which the dominant firm in a market charges less than the short-run profit maximizing price in order to limit the likelihood of entry by new competitors

Limit pricing tends to be more attractive if the monopolist enjoys any cost advantage, even a small one, over potential entrants. For example, a new entrant may need to incur sunk costs, say, to recruit a network of dealers or acquaint consumers with a new brand name. Or perhaps through "learning by doing" the first firm in the market has achieved lower production costs than another firm can achieve when it first enters the market. Given such a cost advantage, the first firm may be able to earn a pure economic profit at a price that is still low enough to deter other entrants.

There need not be an all-or-nothing choice between short-run profit maximization and limit pricing. A firm may set an intermediate price that merely slows entry without entirely preventing it. It may introduce its product at a high price and then "slide down the demand curve" as other firms enter. The variations are endless. As the firm's attention turns away from the marginal cost–marginal revenue calculus of the simple monopolist to strategic moves and countermoves against actual and potential rivals, the market structure that we have called open monopoly shades into oligopoly. That is a subject for another chapter.

Closed Monopoly and Rent Seeking

Let's turn now to the implications of entrepreneurship for a closed monopoly—one that is protected by a legal barrier, such as a government permit or a patent. If the market is truly closed to competition in any form, there is nothing to add beyond what was said earlier in the section on long-run equilibrium without threat of entry. However, few if any monopolies are closed that tightly. Instead, they face threats to their profits on two fronts: (1) the development of substitute products and (2) challenges to the legal barriers that seal the market off from competition.

First consider substitute products. Although the market structure of monopoly assumes that the product has no "close" substitutes, closeness is clearly a matter of degree. There is no such thing as a product without any substitutes whatsoever. Moreover, a monopolist must consider not only existing substitutes, but also the development of new ones. If one firm has a monopoly on a patented drug, rival researchers will strive to develop other therapies for the condition being treated. If a railroad charges a monopoly price on a route that has no competing rail service, it will encourage competition from pipelines, barges, and trucks.

Over time, then, the higher the price set by the monopolist and the longer that price is maintained, the more rival entrepreneurs will attempt to supply varied and attractive substitutes. As they do so, the monopolist's demand curve will gradually be pushed to the left.

Meanwhile, the same or other rivals will be at work on another front. Law may protect the closed monopolist's hold on the market; but lobbyists can persuade legislatures to change laws, and lawyers can find loopholes in them. If the closed monopoly is earning pure economic profits, lawyers and lobbyists are attractive investments for potential rivals. To combat them, the monopoly will have to invest in lawyers and lobbyists of its own.

The efforts of firms to break into or protect closed monopolies are examples of rent seeking. The "rents" being sought in this case are the pure economic profits that the monopolist earns over and above the opportunity costs of producing its product, but rent seeking and defenses against rent seeking are costly. They require a firm to hire lawyers, lobbyists, and researchers, and divert the time of its managers from other tasks. These costs must be added to production costs when computing profit. In terms of our model, expenditures that arise from rent seeking and defenses against it push a firm's cost curves upward.

Rent seeking need not be limited to rivals that seek to enter the firm's market. The firm's own employees may get in on the act. Monopoly profits earned by a protected employer—say, a municipal transit company or a firm with a monopoly contract to collect a city's garbage—are an attractive target for labor unions. Unions do not always depend only on their own bargaining power; sometimes they may seek legislative intervention in labor disputes. Rent seeking by a monopolist's suppliers and even by its customers may also occur.

The closed monopolist, thus, is caught in a vise. Entrepreneurs who develop substitute products push its demand curve to the left, and at the same time the need to defend itself against rent seekers pushes its costs upward. Even if no rivals enter the monopolist's market directly, it will gradually be forced toward the position shown in Figure 10.4, where it just breaks even. At that point, the price P that can be charged for

FIGURE 10.4   THE BREAK-EVEN POSITION FOR A MONOPOLIST

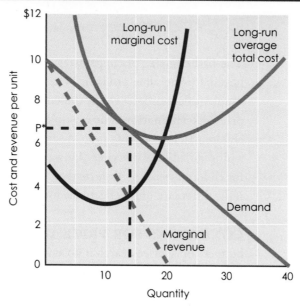

This exhibit shows a monopolist that is just breaking even. The firm earns enough revenue to cover all costs, including the opportunity cost of capital, but not enough to permit an economic profit. A closed monopoly could be driven to this position in the long run through erosion of demand as substitutes are developed or by the costs of defending its monopoly position against rent seekers.

the quantity of output where marginal cost equals marginal revenue is just enough to cover average total costs. When it reaches a situation of zero economic profit, an equilibrium will finally be established in which the introduction of substitutes and the level of rent-seeking expenditures stop increasing.

As an example of a monopolist caught in such a squeeze, consider the U.S. Postal Service. For two centuries it has fought for and held on to its closed monopoly on delivery of first-class mail. Yet the postal service, far from being richly profitable, is lucky if it breaks even. A large part of the explanation is found in the vigorous expansion of substitutes (UPS, Federal Express, electronic transmission of documents via fax or Internet) and the successful rent-seeking activities of postal employee unions.

To summarize, the life of a monopolist is not a bed of roses. True, extraordinary short-run profit opportunities may arise, but a monopolist must not be overly aggressive in exploiting them. New substitute products, newly entering firms, and rent-seeking all pose threats. In real life, being a monopolist requires a lot more work than just finding the point where a couple of lines cross on a graph.

Complex Pricing Strategies

The model of simple monopoly assumes that all units sold in a given period must be sold at the same price and that all customers are allowed to buy as much or as little as they want at that price. Not all monopolists use this simple pricing strategy; neither do all oligopolies or firms in monopolistically competitive markets. In this section, we look at two common pricing strategies that are more complex than that of simple monopoly.

Price Discrimination

Price discrimination

The practice of charging different prices for various units of a single product when the price differences are not justified by differences in cost

The first complex pricing strategy is that of charging different prices to different buyers for the same product. When the prices charged to different buyers do not simply reflect differences in the costs of serving them, the firm is said to practice **price discrimination**. For example, a theater that charges adults $8 for a seat and children $6 is practicing price discrimination; the cost of providing a seat to a child and to an adult is the same. However, a clothing maker that charges lower prices for children's sizes of T-shirts than adult sizes is not practicing price discrimination if the difference only reflects the lower cost of materials used in the smaller sizes.

CONDITIONS FOR PRICE DISCRIMINATION   Two conditions must be met for a price searcher to engage in price discrimination. First, it must be impossible or at least inconvenient for buyers to transfer or resell the product. For example, it is unlikely that your campus bookstore could get away with selling economics texts at list price to seniors and at a 25 percent discount to everyone else. If it tried to do so, seniors would just ask a friend in a lower class to do their book shopping for them. The bookstore's list-price sales would rapidly fall to zero. Second, the seller must be able to classify buyers into groups on the basis of the elasticity of their demand for the good. Those with highly inelastic demand can then be charged high prices, and those with more elastic demand can be charged lower prices. If the firm could not tell whose demand was more and whose was less elastic, it would not know who should be asked to pay the higher price.

Although it is convenient to discuss price discrimination in conjunction with monopoly, the practice may appear in other market structures, as well. Consider, for example, price discrimination by colleges and universities, which are certainly not monopolies. First, the school's business office sets tuition and fees at a level that it thinks is about as high as anyone would be willing to pay. Next, the admissions office gives its approval to a certain number of qualified applicants. Finally, the financial aid office gives selective price rebates, called scholarships, to students who would be unwilling or unable to attend if they were charged the full tuition.

A college or university is in an ideal position to practice price discrimination. For one thing, the product cannot be resold. If you are admitted to both Harvard and Dartmouth, and choose to attend Harvard, you cannot sell your Dartmouth admission to someone who did not get into either place. Also, the school insists that applicants supply a great deal of information on families' willingness and ability to pay. Because the demand for a good tends to be less elastic the smaller the share of income a family spends on it, rich families are likely to have less elastic demand for college education than poor families. Finally, an applicant's high-school grades and test scores also help in estimating his or her elasticity of demand. A student with relatively high grades probably has many alternatives and, hence, relatively elastic demand. A student with lower grades may be lucky to get into just one school. For this reason, it makes sense to charge lower prices (that is, give larger scholarships) to students with good grades.

In this case, as in others where markets can be divided into separate submarkets with distinct demand curves, the firm sets marginal cost equal to marginal revenue in each market. The result is a higher equilibrium price for customers whose demand is less elastic.

Fairness and Price Discrimination

Price discrimination is often viewed as unfair, especially by those who pay the higher prices. Many people, for example, are annoyed if they learn that the person sitting next to them on an airplane paid less than they did for a ticket on the same flight. In fact, many people think it is unfair for a firm to charge different prices to different customers even when the difference is justified by considerations of cost. An example is the practice of charging young men more than young women for automobile insurance. Insurance companies insist that different rates are justified by the fact that costs of insuring men are higher because they are involved in more accidents, but this does not end the perception that the difference in rates is unfair.

Economists tend to look more kindly on price discrimination. They not only see it as a practice that promotes efficiency but properly understood, as one that often promotes fairness as well. The example of college scholarships illustrates some of the reasons that price discrimination can be beneficial. This form of price discrimination makes it possible for some students to attend colleges that they otherwise could not afford while shifting part of the cost, in the form of high tuition, to the students who can most afford to pay. Similarly, price discrimination makes it easier for parents to take young children to the movies. It makes it possible for students who are willing to buy tickets in advance and stay at their destinations over a Saturday night to fill airline seats that business travelers would leave empty.

These examples emphasize that price discrimination may, in some circumstances, be beneficial in terms of fairness. Later in the chapter we will see that it can also allow markets to perform more efficiently. For these reasons, although price discrimination will always have its critics, economists often rise to its defense.

Two-Part Pricing

Two-part pricing

A pricing strategy in which people must pay for the right to become a buyer before choosing how much to buy at a given price

Access fee

The part of a two-part pricing strategy paid for the right to become a customer

User charge

The per-unit price offered in a two-part pricing strategy to qualified customers who have paid the access charge

Two-part pricing is another strategy that departs from the model of simple monopoly. Under two-part pricing, customers first pay for the right to become a buyer and only then have the right to buy as much as they want at a fixed per-unit price. To give them general names, the amount paid to become a buyer can be called the **access fee**; and the price per unit, once the access fee has been paid, can be called the **user charge**. The specific terms used vary from one application of this strategy to another.

Examples of two-part pricing are easy to find. Here are just a few with which everyone is familiar:

- Nightclubs often impose a cover charge (access fee) for admission and then sell food and drinks at prices (user charges) stated on a menu.

- Utilities—like electricity, telephone, and sometimes cell-phone service—charge a flat monthly connection charge (access fee), which sometimes includes a fixed minimum amount of use, plus a charge per kilowatt-hour or minute of phone service (user charge) beyond any amount covered by the access fee.

- Country clubs charge large membership fees (access fees), sometimes reaching tens of thousands of dollars, for the right to join. Members then pay small "greens fees" (user charges) each time they play golf.

- The popular discount chain Price Club charges an annual membership fee (access fee) for a card that gives admission to its stores. Members are then offered very low prices on merchandise (user fees).

A two-part pricing strategy helps a firm get around a dilemma that faces the simple monopolist. If a simple monopolist maximizes profit by setting a price corresponding to the quantity at which marginal revenue equals to marginal cost, it must turn away some potentially profitable business. The potentially profitable business represents extra units that could be sold by cutting the price below the simple monopoly price, but still leaving it above marginal cost. Price discriminators get around this dilemma by cutting the price for some, but not all, units sold. Two-part pricing gets around the dilemma in a different way. By offering a user charge on all units sold that is below the simple monopoly price, it "gives up" some revenue; but it recoups the "lost" revenue through the access fee. In some cases the best strategy may be to lower the user fee all the way to marginal cost.

Customers are often happy with two-part pricing because it gives them lower prices (at the margin), and sometimes higher quality as well, compared with simple monopoly. For example, Price Club, because of its membership fee, is able to offer merchandise at a lower mark-up over cost than rival Wal-Mart, which has no membership requirement; and country clubs that require membership fees provide higher-quality, less-crowded courses and clubhouses compared with public golf courses that rely on greens fees alone.

Two-part pricing is especially popular in markets where fixed costs are high and marginal costs are comparatively low. Electric power companies, telephone companies, and golf courses—all fit this model. Without access fees, per-unit prices would have to be very high relative to marginal costs in order for the firm to break even. Sometimes fixed costs constitute almost all the cost of a service, and marginal costs are nearly zero. In that case, the access fee may provide all of a firm's revenue, and the user fee may be set to equal zero (that is, equal to marginal cost). In the early days of the Internet, most Internet Service Providers charged a monthly connection charge plus a fee per hour of use. Later, as server and pipeline capacities grew, the marginal cost of an added hour of service fell close to zero. Today, most providers rely on the monthly access charge alone for revenue and set the user charge at zero. This model is rapidly spreading for cell phone service providers, too.

Market Performance Under Monopoly

In the last chapter we looked at market performance under perfect competition. That market structure received high marks in two respects. First, we noted that in competitive equilibrium marginal cost is equal to market price. Production thus proceeds to the point at which no further mutual gains for buyers and sellers are possible. In that sense, an economy of competitive markets provides an efficient solution to the question of what to produce. Second, we noted that in long-run equilibrium a perfectly competitive firm produces at the lowest point on its long-run average cost curve. This is a key aspect of efficiency in the choice of how to produce.

In this section we look at market performance under monopoly. First, we compare simple monopoly with perfect competition in terms of the questions of what and how to produce. We then look briefly at the question of for whom goods are produced. Finally, we explore some unresolved issues.

What to Produce: Consumer and Producer Surplus

The concepts of consumer and producer surplus, which were introduced in a previous chapter, provide a useful tool for analyzing market performance with regard to the quantity of each good that is produced. Figure 10.5 makes the comparison between perfect competition and simple monopoly.

FIGURE **10.5** MARKET PERFORMANCE UNDER MONOPOLY AND COMPETITION

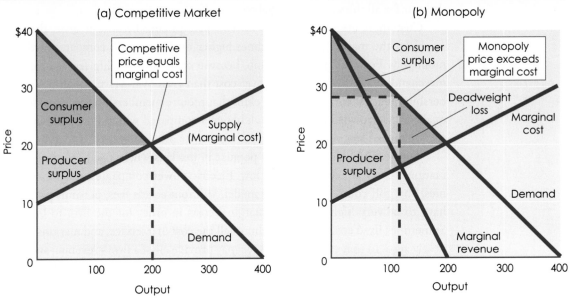

Under perfect competition, shown in part (a), production is carried out to the point at which the price consumers are willing to pay for the last unit produced just equals the opportunity cost of producing it. All possible gains from trade are realized in the form of producer and consumer surplus. Under monopoly, production stops short of that point. Consumer surplus is smaller and producer surplus larger than under competition, but the total of the two is smaller. Some potential gains from trade go unrealized. This deadweight loss is the reason monopoly is considered a form of market failure.

Part (a) of the exhibit shows a perfectly competitive market. As we saw in Chapter 5, the height of the demand curve measures the maximum amount that consumers would willingly pay for a given quantity of output. The height of the supply curve measures the minimum amount that suppliers would willingly accept for a given output. Because the supply curve is based on the marginal cost curves of individual firms, it reflects the opportunity cost of producing each additional unit. The equilibrium price is $20 and the equilibrium quantity 200 units. Consumers, who would be willing to pay more than $20 for all but the two hundredth unit, earn a consumer surplus equal to the area beneath the demand curve but above the market price. Producers, who produce all but the two hundredth unit at an opportunity cost of less than $20, earn a producer surplus equal to the area above the supply curve but beneath the market price. These surpluses represent consumers' and producers' mutual gains from exchange.

Under competitive conditions, production is carried to the point at which all potential gains from exchange are exhausted. Nothing would be gained from producing beyond the 200-unit mark. From the 201st unit on, the opportunity cost of the unit to producers as measured by the supply curve would exceed its value to consumers as measured by the demand curve.

Now consider the situation under simple monopoly, as shown in part (b) of the exhibit. To make the comparison easy, the demand and marginal cost curves for the monopolist in question are assumed to be the same as the market demand and supply curves for the competitive industry.

To maximize its profits, the simple monopolist limits production to 120 units and charges a price of $28 per unit. Even at that price, consumers are better off than they would be if the good were entirely unavailable. They realize a surplus equal to the area beneath the demand curve but above the $28 price. The monopolist, on the other hand, realizes a substantial producer surplus. The 120th unit, which is sold for $28, costs only $16 to produce, yielding a producer surplus of $12. Surpluses on earlier units, which are produced at a lower opportunity cost, are correspondingly greater. The total producer surplus equals the shaded area above the marginal cost curve but below the $28 price, bordered on the left by the vertical axis and on the right by the profit-maximizing quantity.

Comparison of the competitive case with the monopoly case reveals these three differences.

1. Consumer surplus is smaller under simple monopoly.

2. Producer surplus is larger under simple monopoly.

3. The total of producer and consumer surpluses is smaller under simple monopoly.

The third difference reveals the inefficiency of monopoly. It indicates that some potential gains from exchange are not realized. Other things being equal, production of units 121 through 200 would provide benefits to consumers that exceed their costs. This would make both producers and consumers better off. The potential gains from trade that are "wasted" are shown by the triangle lying between the supply and demand curves and bordered on the left by the monopolist's profit-maximizing quantity. That area represents a **deadweight loss**—a term that is often used to refer to any benefit that is lost by one party but not gained by another. The excess burden of a tax, illustrated in Chapter 5, is another example of a deadweight loss.

Deadweight loss

A loss of consumer or producer surplus that is not balanced by a gain to someone else

If producing another 80 units of output would make both producers and consumers better off, one might ask why this is not done. The answer lies in the assumption that a simple monopolist offers a single price per unit to all buyers. The complex pricing strategies examined above are designed to overcome this disadvantage of simple monopoly. Under price discrimination, the monopolist might be able to hold the price of the first 120 units at $28 while selling units 121 through 200 at a price of $20. If it did so, both the firm and its customers would benefit. A firm using two-part pricing could charge the marginal-cost price of $20 to its members and make up the lost revenue through an access fee. In either case, the deadweight loss would then be recaptured. In contrast, a simple monopolist must sell all units at a uniform price. Such a firm cannot cut the price on units 121 through 200 without also cutting the price on units 1 through 120. The intersection of the marginal cost and marginal revenue curves marks the limit of the simple monopolist's willingness to produce.

To summarize, the fact that a simple monopoly's price exceeds its marginal cost in a situation of equilibrium means that too little of the good is produced to realize all potential gains from trade. Simple monopoly, therefore, distorts the choice of what to produce. Compared with perfectly competitive industries, simple monopolies produce goods in inefficiently small quantities. However, in the real world monopolies, monopolistic competitors and oligopolists often use more complex pricing strategies that keep prices closer to marginal cost. The deadweight loss is thus less than implied by Figure 10.5.

How to Produce: Average Total Cost in Monopoly Equilibrium

A second favorable trait of perfect competition, as we saw in the preceding chapter, is the fact that its equilibrium output is produced at the least possible long-run average cost. This trait is not shared by monopoly. As we saw earlier in this chapter, equilibrium output for a monopoly can occur at any point along its long-run average cost curve. Thus, monopoly cannot lay claim to minimization of average total cost and, in this respect, can be said to be less efficient than perfect competition.

How serious the inefficiency is in practice depends on circumstances. Three cases need to be considered.

1. In the case of a natural monopoly, equilibrium will usually occur at an output at which the firm is still experiencing economies of scale. Dividing the industry's total output between two or more firms would mean that each of them would have to operate at an even lower, and hence less efficient, level of output. Thus, although the natural monopoly produces an inefficiently low level of output, it produces that output at the lowest possible cost given the demand and cost curves for the product.

2. Empirical cost studies indicate that many firms experience approximately constant returns to scale after a minimum efficient scale has been reached. If demand for the product is sufficient so that the profit-maximizing equilibrium output for such a firm is greater than that minimum efficient scale, that output will be produced at the minimum possible cost. This will be so even if the chosen output is smaller than the efficient level, that is, the level that would make price equal to marginal cost.

3. The equilibrium output may lie on the rising portion of the monopolist's average cost curve, where it encounters decreasing returns to scale. Dividing total output among two or more smaller firms would then decrease average total cost. In this case the monopolist not only produces an output that is too small to realize all potential consumer and producer surplus but also produces that output at an inefficiently high cost.

Failure to minimize average total cost appears to be a problem only when the monopolist experiences diseconomies of scale at the equilibrium output. This can happen only in a closed monopoly. A natural monopoly experiences economies of scale at its equilibrium output, and an open monopoly could not survive in the long run if it operated at a significant cost disadvantage relative to new firms entering the market. A limit pricing strategy would not work for such a firm, and a short-run profit-maximizing price would only speed the entry of rivals.

In addition to operating at an inefficient point on its long-run average cost curve, there is another reason that a closed monopolist's costs may be inefficiently high. Earlier we noted that closed monopolists might have to spend heavily on lobbying and legal battles to defend themselves against rent-seeking rivals that want to break down the legal protections the monopoly enjoys. Those costs add little or nothing to output or consumer satisfaction. Loss of the output that the lawyers or lobbyists could have produced if they had worked elsewhere, it can be argued, is another form of dead-weight loss from closed monopoly.

For Whom to Produce: Does Monopoly Promote Inequality?

Cartoonists draw monopolists as fat men with big cigars and long limousines. For good measure, they may show a child in rags watching the limousine drive by. Such cartoons reflect a common view that monopoly promotes inequality. To the extent that non-economists worry about monopolies at all, they are more likely to dislike monopolies because they are seen as rich and powerful than because they are seen as inefficient.

Sometimes monopoly does confer wealth and power. The "robber barons" that tried to monopolize the oil, steel, and tobacco industries at the turn of the century were a case in point. One of the richest people in the world today is Microsoft founder, Bill Gates. Although Microsoft's market is properly considered an oligopoly, its market share is so large that the term "monopoly" is often applied in popular discussion. Aside from such anecdotal evidence, does the theory of monopoly provide any reason to associate the market structure of monopoly with large private fortunes? Not necessarily.

For one thing, we must ask who owns the monopoly. If the monopoly is a giant corporation, such institutions as insurance companies and union pension funds may own much of its stock. If so, the monopoly's profits will benefit widows and orphans as well as fat cats with big cigars. Other monopolies are small operations such as, say, the only gas station or restaurant in an isolated small town. The owners may barely earn enough to cover costs. In still other cases, government owns monopolies—the U.S. Postal Service, the retail liquor monopolies of many states, and the Tennessee Valley Authority's monopoly of electric power in an area covering several states are examples. Any profits made by those monopolies become available to finance other areas of government activity rather than creating private fortunes. In other cases, such as public transit systems, monopoly profits are actually negative, and customers receive the benefit of subsidies.

Finally, as we have seen, there is no guarantee that monopolists will earn pure economic profits in the long run. Competition from substitute products erodes the profits of some monopolies. Closed monopolies may spend potential profits on measures to fend off rent seekers. Open monopolies may limit their profits in order to deter other firms from entering the market.

None of this is intended to deny that a market economy can produce large inequalities of wealth and income. Instead, the point is that monopoly, as a market structure, is neither a necessary nor a sufficient condition for inequality. There are poor monopolists, and there are people who grow rich under oligopoly, monopolistic competition, and even in markets that are close to perfect competition.

A Balance Sheet

Taking everything into account, where do we stand on the question of market performance under monopoly? What are its important failures, and what, if any, are its strengths? The material presented in this chapter supports the following conclusions:

1. Simple monopoly can result in market failure by leading to an equilibrium in which price exceeds marginal cost. However, the extent of the market failure is often reduced by strategies like limit pricing, price discrimination and two-part pricing.

2. No monopolist is entirely free of competition from substitute products and potential entrants. In some cases, such competition may be sufficient in the long run to eliminate pure economic profit and significantly narrow the gap between price and marginal cost.

3. Closed monopolies pose the most serious threat of market failure. Legal protections shield them, at least partially, from competition by entrants and substitutes; and costs associated with rent seeking may represent additional deadweight losses. However, there may be offsetting benefits. Closed monopolies based on patents and copyrights encourage innovation and creativity. Closed monopolies, like public transit systems, may operate in ways that reduce externalities like pollution and congestion.

4. Natural monopolies also pose a threat of market failure. Economies of scale protect them from the threat of entry by other firms unless new technology permits efficient small-scale production. Regulation designed to enhance the performance of natural monopolies will be discussed in Chapter 12.

5. Open monopolies pose the least serious threat of market failure. The threat of entry by potential competitors limits the ability of firms to earn pure economic profits in the long run. Limit pricing may keep prices close to the level of costs. A rapid pace of innovation may offset inefficiencies resulting from short-run monopoly pricing practices. We will return to the relationship between market structure and innovation in Chapter 12.

In short, considerably more remains to be said about the relationship between market structure and market performance. To take the next steps, we need to broaden the scope of our discussion to take into account the market structures that lie between perfect competition and monopoly—that is, oligopoly and monopolistic competition. That is the task of the next chapter.

Summary

1. **In what circumstances can monopoly exist?** A monopoly is a firm that is the sole supplier of a product that has no close substitutes. Three classes of monopoly can be distinguished: *closed monopolies*, which are protected by legal restrictions on competition; *natural monopolies*, which are protected by economies of scale; and *open monopolies*, which have no special protections against the entry of potential competitors.

2. **How are the profit-maximizing price and output for a monopoly determined?** A *simple monopoly* (one that does not practice price discrimination) earns a maximum profit by producing the quantity of output that makes marginal cost equal to marginal revenue. The price is determined by the height of the demand curve at the profit-maximizing level. If a monopoly cannot earn a profit in the short run, it will try to keep its loss to a minimum. If the loss-minimizing price is above average variable cost, the firm will continue to operate in the short run. If the loss-minimizing price is below average variable cost, it will shut down.

3. **How is long-run equilibrium achieved under monopoly?** In the long run, a monopoly that faces no threat of competition maximizes its profit at the level of output for which long-run marginal cost is equal to long-run marginal revenue. Because demand tends to be more elastic in the long run, the long-run profit-maximizing price may be lower than the price that would maximize short-run profit. An open monopoly may discourage other firms from entering the market by charging a price below that which would maximize short-run profit. Such a strategy is known as *limit pricing*.

4. **What pricing strategies are available to monopolies and other price-searching firms?** A monopolist or other firm that is not a price taker can practice *price discrimination* if buyers cannot resell its product and if it has some way of classifying buyers on the basis of elasticity of demand. Although price discrimination is resented by buyers who must pay higher prices, it may increase efficiency by allowing customers who value the product more than its marginal cost but less than the price that a simple monopolist would charge to buy the product. An alternative strategy is two-part pricing, which involves charging an access fee for the right to become a customer plus a per-unit user fee.

5. **How does monopoly affect market performance?** Monopoly can be a source of market failure in that the amount of output it produces is less than the amount that would make marginal cost equal to the price charged. As a result, some consumers who would be willing to pay a price that is higher than marginal cost are unable to buy from a monopolist. Because some gains from trade (consumer and producer surplus) are not realized under a simple monopoly, there is a *deadweight loss* to the economy. However, strategies like limit pricing, two-part pricing, and price discrimination may reduce the deadweight loss. Finally, under long-run equilibrium conditions a monopoly does not necessarily produce at the point of minimum long-run average cost.

Key Terms

Problems and Topics for Discussion

1. **Charging any price you like**   "A monopolist can always make a profit because with no competition it

can charge any price it likes." Do you think this statement is true? Suppose you own the only movie theater in a small town. Because your corrupt uncle is on the town's zoning board, you feel confident that no competitors will be allowed into the market. What factors might limit your ability to "charge any price you like"?

2. **Short-run shutdown for a monopolist** Redraw the graph in Figure 10.3, shifting the demand and marginal revenue curves to illustrate the case in which a monopolist will shut down in the short run rather than continue to produce at a loss.

3. **Price discrimination** Air travelers are sometimes surprised and annoyed to find that the price of a ticket for a short flight may exceed the price for a long flight. For example, on one recent day, a round-trip ticket from Washington, D.C., to Seattle on one airline cost $235, compared with the same airline's price of $278 from Washington, D.C., to Dayton, Ohio, less than a third of the distance. Travelers complain that such prices represent unfair discrimination against the residents of medium-sized cities such as Dayton. They say that airlines should be forced to charge prices that are scaled in proportion to the distance flown. The airlines answer that major city pairs, such as Washington, D.C.–Seattle, can be served at a lower cost (with larger planes and fewer empty seats) than less frequently traveled city pairs, such as Washington, D.C.–Dayton. Discuss the merits of the current price structure and the proposed alternative in terms of fairness and efficiency.

4. **Mass transit pricing and market failure** Reread the sections of Chapter 4 that deal with market failure and rent seeking. Can it be argued that the market failure theory of government justifies public ownership and subsidy of mass transit systems? What particular types of failure are involved here? What pricing policy would be called for under the market failure theory? Do

you think there are any elements of mass transit policy that can be explained under the theory of rent seeking?

Case for Discussion

The Postal Monopoly

The U.S. Post Office was organized in 1789 and immediately began losing money. One of the reasons that it lost money was competition. The post office charged the same price to deliver a letter anywhere in the country, but its costs were not the same in every case. For letters mailed between points in the East, the post office charged more than cost; for letters mailed to points in the West, it charged less than cost.

Competitors flocked to the routes on which costs were low. For example, in the 1840s Henry Wells, who later founded the famous Wells-Fargo Company, set up a mail service between Philadelphia and New York. He charged $.06 for a first-class letter, compared to the post office's rate of $.25. By the early 1840s private firms were carrying at least one-third of the mail in the United States.

To fight off the competition, the post office turned to Congress. In 1845 Congress strengthened the restrictions on private first-class mail service. This saved the post office from extinction and allowed it to continue its policy of uniform rates regardless of the cost of service. This policy remains in force for first-class mail: The price for mailing a letter to any address in the United States is the same, whatever the distance. However, the cost of delivering a letter clearly is not the same for all addresses. Deliveries to post office boxes are least expensive; deliveries to homes in suburban neighborhoods are a bit more costly; and rural free delivery service is more expensive still.

SOURCE: Based in part on *Economics of Public Policy*, 2nd ed. (Chapter 11), by John C. Goodman and Edwin G. Dolan (St. Paul, MN: West Publishing Company, 1982).

QUESTIONS

1. On the basis of information given in the case, should the postal monopoly on first-class mail be classified as closed, open, or natural? Why?

2. Do you think the practice of charging all customers the same price when costs differ from one customer to another should be viewed as price discrimination? Do you think it has any benefits? Discuss in terms of efficiency and fairness.

3. Although the U.S. Postal Service (USPS) has retained its monopoly on ordinary first-class mail, it allows competition from such firms as United Parcel Service (UPS) and Federal Express (FedEx) in carrying overnight and third-class mail (parcels). In these cases, both the USPS and its private competitors charge different prices according to weight and distance and according to whether pickup and delivery services are provided. Why does a policy of charging a single price regardless of cost not work in a market in which competition exists?

CHAPTER *11*

Industrial Organization, Monopolistic Competition, and Oligopoly

After reading this chapter, you will understand the following:

1. How the structure of markets in the U.S. economy has changed over time
2. How the interdependence of firms under oligopoly affects price and output decisions
3. Why oligopolistic firms sometimes collude to increase profits, and the problems they encounter when they do
4. The conditions that affect market performance under oligopoly
5. How equilibrium is achieved under monopolistic competition, and how well monopolistically competitive markets perform

Before reading this chapter, make sure you know the meaning of the concepts:

1. Consumer and producer surplus
2. Economies of scale
3. Market structure
4. Types of monopoly
5. Limit pricing

WHAT IS THE most competitive market in the world? Some people might choose the market for commercial aircraft. Every order placed for any but the smallest planes comes down to a hard-fisted slugfest between two heavyweights, U.S.-based Boeing and E.U.-based Airbus. In 2001 Airbus edged out Boeing in the race for new orders and held the lead for five straight years. Then Airbus stumbled. Wiring problems and other difficulties set back delivery of its flagship A380 Superjumbo, designed to carry more than 500 passengers. Meanwhile advance orders were brisk for Boeing's innovative 787 Dreamliner. In 2007 Boeing was back in the lead, but the American company again slipped to second place in 2008, based on a delayed schedule for its new 787.

The Boeing-Airbus example highlights the fact that the term *competition* has more than one meaning. In the phrase "perfect competition," it refers to *market structure*. A market is

The competition between Boeing and Airbus illustrates business rivalry.

perfectly competitive if it has large numbers of small firms, the product is homogeneous, all firms share information equally, and it is easy to enter or leave the market. In contrast, competition in the form of Boeing versus Airbus refers to business *rivalry*. In this sense, "rivalry" refers to the activities of entrepreneurs, not just those of business managers who are responding to conditions that they accept as given.

In the market structure of *oligopoly*, to which much of this chapter is devoted, rivalry becomes a central issue. Rivalry is also an important issue for the market structures that border on oligopoly. At one end of the spectrum, oligopoly shades into what we have called open monopoly, a market structure in which a single firm, although it is the sole supplier of a product at the moment, is threatened by the entry of potential rivals. At the other end, oligopoly shades into *monopolistic competition*. In monopolistically competitive markets, rivalry is likely to be strong among firms that are near neighbors. For example, rivalry among vendors on an urban street corner can be as sharp in its way as the rivalry between giant firms in the aircraft or breakfast cereal industry.

This chapter will take in the whole spectrum of market structures that fall somewhere between the ideal types of monopoly and perfect competition. It will begin with a look at some empirical data on the organization of industry. The next section will take up oligopoly, and the last section will discuss monopolistic competition.

Market Structure in the U.S. Economy

The structure of markets has long been of interest not only to economic theorists, but also to those who look at actual markets. A particular focus of this work has been the degree to which the largest firms dominate the economy as a whole, or particular markets within it. In this section, we will take a look at some data relating to the structure of markets in the United States, today and in the past.

Aggregate Concentration

Aggregate concentration

The degree to which the economy as a whole is dominated by the largest firms

One way to gauge the influence of the largest firms is to measure **aggregate concentration**, the degree to which the economy as a whole is dominated by the largest firms. There is a popular fear that large corporations have disproportionate power and influence. Social Critic Ralph Nader made a career by appealing to people who feel powerless against perceived corporate dominance of their lives. Statements such as, "Today, the increasing size and wealth of corporations point to more concentration of wealth and of political and economic power and influence than before," are commonplace on anti-capitalist and anti-globalization Web sites.[1] Frequent news of mergers of giant corporations with one another to form even larger entities fuel fears of corporate dominance. Do economic data on aggregate concentration back up these views?

Apparently, it does not. Lawrence J. White of New York University surveyed a wide range of available data on aggregate concentration in the U.S. economy. However measured, the data show little change over time in the relative economic influence of the largest firms.

The broadest measure of aggregate concentration is the share of total value added contributed by the largest firms. (Value added measures the value of output adjusted for the value of inputs bought from other firms.) Figure 11.1 shows trends in value added by

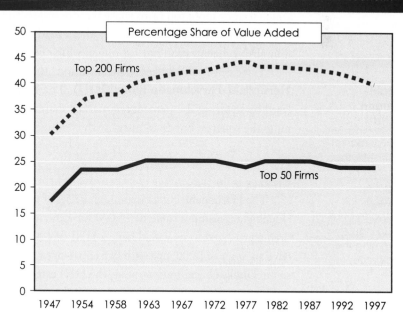

FIGURE 11.1   TRENDS IN AGGREGATE CONCENTRATION IN THE UNITED STATES ECONOMY

The relative size of the largest manufacturing corporations in the U.S. economy increased in the first two decades following World War II. Since that time, the relative size of the top 50 firms has changed little, and that of the top 200 firms, after peaking in the 1970s, has decreased.

SOURCE: Lawrence J. White, "Trends in Aggregate Concentration in the United States," *Journal of Economic Perspectives*, Volume 16, No. 4, Fall 2002, Table 1.

the top 50 and top 200 corporations in the United States. The share of the top 50 firms increased from the end of World War II until the early 1960s and has changed little since then. The share of the top 200 manufacturing firms reached a peak in the 1970s and has declined since then. Data on shares of total sales, total assets, and total employment also show no strong trend toward greater aggregate concentration in recent decades.[2] These data do not by themselves exclude the possibility that large corporations may have increased their political or social power without increasing their relative economic size, but neither do they support such a view.

Measures of Market Concentration

Market concentration

The degree to which a market is dominated by a few large firms

Concentration ratio

The percentage of all sales that is accounted for by the four or eight largest firms in a market

Herfindahl-Hirschmann Index (HHI)

An index of market concentration that is calculated by squaring the percentage market shares of all firms in an industry then summing the squared-values

If our interest is market structure rather than overall corporate power, we need to look not at aggregate concentration but **market concentration**, the degree to which a market is dominated by one or a few large firms. Market concentration gives us a clue as to whether a given sector of the economy more closely fits the structures of monopoly, oligopoly, monopolistic competition, or perfect competition.

A **concentration ratio** is the simplest measure of market concentration. A concentration ratio gives the percentage of all sales in a market that are accounted for by a specified number of firms in that market. The most commonly used such ratio is the four-firm concentration ratio, which shows the combined market share of the top four firms as a percent of sales in the market as a whole.

Concentration ratios have a number of limitations. Obviously, they do not distinguish between an industry in which a single firm dominates the market and one in which four or more top firms share it more or less equally. A market in which one firm held 77 percent and twenty-three others held 1 percent each would have the same four-firm concentration ratio as one in which five firms each held 20 percent.

A measure of market concentration that overcomes this drawback is the **Herfindahl-Hirschmann index (HHI)**. The HHI of market concentration is calculated by squaring the percentage market shares of each firm in the market and summing the squares. For an industry with n competing firms, the formula is

$$H = p_1^2 + p_2^2 + \dots + p_n^2,$$

where p_k is the percentage market share of firm k.

The Herfindahl-Hirschmann index rises as the market becomes more concentrated, reaching a maximum value of 10,000 for a monopoly. Thus, an industry with one hundred equal-sized firms would have a HHI of 100, one with ten equal-sized firms would have an index of 1,000, one with five equal-sized firms would have an index of 2,000, and so on. Unlike concentration ratios, the HHI can distinguish between degrees of concentration in markets with equal numbers of firms. For example, a market with eight firms of equal size has the same eight-firm concentration ratio as one in which one firm has 30 percent and seven others have 10 percent each; but the HHI for the latter market is 1,600 compared with 1,250 for the former. The difference in HHIs for the two markets reflects a widespread view that the presence of one dominant firm in a market makes that market less competitive in the sense that the dominant firm can exercise more influence over price and quantity than other firms in the market. Table 11.1 gives data on concentration ratios and HHIs for selected U.S. manufacturing industries.

| TABLE 11.1   MARKET CONCENTRATION FOR SELECTED U.S. MANUFACTURING INDUSTRIES |

Industry Description	Number of Companies	Share of Sales Accounted for by Largest Companies			HHI
		4 Largest	8 Largest	50 Largest	
Wood kitchen cabinets	4,303	19%	25%	46%	156
Book publishing	2,504	23%	38%	77%	251
Petroleum refining	131	30%	49%	97%	414
Meatpacking-plant products	1,296	50%	66%	88%	1,123
Household refrigerators and freezers	52	82%	98%	100%	1,891
Motor vehicles and car bodies	398	84%	91%	99%	2,676

The table above shows manufacturing industry concentration data, based on the 1992 U.S. Census. Note that the number of companies is not the only important determinant of the degree of competition in industries. Even though there are only 131 petroleum refiners in the United States, this is a relatively competitive industry. The largest four petroleum refiners account for only 30 percent of all sales in this industry. This is reflected in the low HHI value for petroleum refining. On the other hand, there were almost 400 motor vehicle and car-body manufacturers in the United States, but the four largest companies dominate more than three-fourths of this industry. The top 50 motor vehicle and car-body companies account for nearly all sales. The high concentration in the motor vehicle and car-bodies industry is shown by the relatively high HHI value of 2,676.

SOURCE: U.S. Census, *1992 Census—Concentration Ratios in Manufacturing.*

Blending Structural and Behavioral Evidence

Many economists think that structural evidence, such as concentration ratios or the Herfindahl-Hirschmann index, is not enough to judge the competitiveness of a market. In addition, they say, attention must be paid to the way firms actually behave. Can they block the entry of rivals into the market? Do domestic firms face competition from imports? Do they collude or compete in making pricing decisions? Do they compete vigorously in product innovation and other nonprice areas? Information about such issues should be considered along with structural data in determining competitiveness.

The results of one study that combined structural and behavioral evidence are given in *Applying Economic Ideas 11.1.* That study, conducted by William C. Shepherd, concluded that more than three-quarters of the U.S. economy was at the time "effectively competitive," a category that takes in perfect competition, monopolistic competition, and loose forms of oligopoly. Less than 3 percent of the economy was classified as pure monopoly, with most of that category consisting of public utilities.

Shepherd's results are interesting in that they indicate a strong trend toward increased competitiveness in the U.S. economy from 1958 to 1980. U.S. industries experienced an increase in business consolidation in the 1980s, but this lead to only modest increases in business concentration.[3] The trend toward greater competitiveness has continued, partially because of international pressure. From 1980 to 2008, total imports increased from 11 percent of total U.S. output of goods and services to almost 18 percent, totally transforming the competitive landscape in industries like automobiles, aircraft, electronics, and clothing. In addition, many foreign firms entered U.S. markets

Applying Economic Ideas 11.1
TRENDS IN COMPETITION IN THE U.S. ECONOMY

Economists have followed trends in competition and concentration in the U.S. economy for more than fifty years. In 1982, William C. Shepherd attempted to view all of these studies from a historical perspective. Relying on recent data, as well as on older published studies, he classified U.S. markets into four categories for the years 1939, 1958, and 1980. The categories, which combine measurements of market structure with information on the behavior of firms, are as follows:

1. *Pure monopoly*   Market share at or near 100 percent, plus effectively blocked entry, evidence of effective monopoly control over the level and structure of prices, and, in practice, includes mainly utilities and patented goods

2. *Dominant firms*   A market share of 50 percent to over 90 percent, no close rival, high barriers to entry, and ability to control pricing, set systematic discriminatory prices, influence innovation, and (usually) earn rates of return well above the competitive rate of return

3. *Tight oligopoly*   Four-firm concentration above 60 percent, with stable market shares,

Fisheries were one of the top competitive sectors from 1939 to 1980.

medium or high barriers to entry, a tendency toward cooperation (shown especially by rigid prices), and excess profits neither necessary nor sufficient to establish the existence of tight oligopoly

4. *Effective competition*   Four-firm concentration below 40 percent, with unstable market shares, flexible pricing, low barriers to entry, little collusion, and low profit rates

The data in the following table show that the competitiveness of U.S. markets increased slightly from 1939 to 1958 and dramatically from 1958 to 1980. Shepherd attributes the change to three factors: increased international competition, deregulation, and enforcement of antitrust laws. Increased international competition and further deregulation have probably resulted in a continuation of the trend toward competitiveness in the 1980s. Enforcement of antitrust law has played a reduced role in shaping market structure in the 1980s, but it has continued to play an active role in discouraging collusive behavior on the part of rival firms.

through purchases of U.S. companies or construction of manufacturing facilities in the United States. Also, 1980 marked the beginning of the trend toward deregulation in transportation, communications, and finance. In structural terms, regulatory reform has decreased concentration in some industries (such as telephone service) while increasing it in others (such as airlines). However, even when reform has been accompanied by numerous mergers of firms, thus increasing the concentration ratio, structural changes have been outweighed by greater freedom to compete with the result that regulated markets are, on the whole, more competitive than before.

Causes of Market Concentration

Given the evidence that some markets are more concentrated than others, it is natural to ask why. No single theory explains market concentration, but a variety of hypotheses have been proposed. We will discuss these under the headings of economies of scale, barriers to entry, and sunk costs.

Sectors of the Economy	National Income in Each Sector, 1978 ($ billions)[a]	The Share of Each Sector that Was Effectively Competitive		
		1939 (%)	1958 (%)	1980 (%)[a]
Agriculture, Forestry, and Fisheries	54.7	91.6	85.0	86.4
Mining	24.5	87.1	92.2	95.8
Construction	87.6	27.9	55.9	80.2
Manufacturing	459.5	51.5	55.9	69.0
Transportation and Public Utilities	162.3	8.7	26.1	39.1
Wholesale and Retail Trade	261.8	57.8	60.5	93.4
Finance, Insurance, and Real Estate	210.7	61.5	63.8	94.1
Services	245.3	53.9	54.3	77.9
TOTAL	1,506.5	55.0	61.7	79.5

The Share of Each Category in Total National Income	($ billions)	Percentage Shares		
		1939	1958	1980
1. Pure Monopoly	38.2	6.2	3.1	2.5
2. Dominant Firm	42.4	5.0	5.0	2.8
3. Tight Oligopoly	272.1	36.4	35.6	18.0
4. Effectively competitive	1,157.9	52.4	56.3	76.7
TOTAL	1,510.6	100.0	100.0	100.0

[a] 1980 figures reflect competitive conditions as of 1980. The industry weights are based on 1978 data for national income, the latest year available.

SOURCE: William G. Shepherd, "Causes of Increased Competition in the U.S. Economy, 1939–1980," *Review of Economics and Statistics* (November 1982), Table 2.

ECONOMIES OF SCALE   A firm is said to experience economies of scale if its long-run average cost declines as its output increases. At one extreme is the case of natural monopoly, in which economies of scale are so strong that minimum-cost production requires that the entire market supply be produced by a single firm. In less extreme cases, the *minimum efficient scale* for a firm—the point at which the average total cost curve stops falling and begins to flatten out—is so large that only a few firms can efficiently coexist in the market.

Suppose, for example, that the minimum efficient scale for a single plant producing refrigerators is 15 percent of U.S. consumption. The theoretical minimum four-firm concentration ratio implied by the minimum efficient plant size would then be 60 percent. The industry could not be any less concentrated than this without forcing some firms to use plants that are too small to produce at minimum long-run average cost. However, empirical studies suggest that economies of scale at *the plant level* clearly are not enough to explain the observed degree of market concentration.

Of course, as emphasized previously, there are many sources of economies of scale above the plant level. Operating more than one plant may result in savings in scheduling, transportation, research and development, finance, marketing, and administration costs. In addition to economies of scale in the ordinary sense, which pertain to a plant's rate of output per unit of time, a firm with a larger market share can also carry out longer production runs at an efficient rate of output. To the extent that cost savings can be achieved through "learning by doing," a plant with a large market share benefits from greater accumulated experience with each product than does one with a small market share. These kinds of economies may lie beyond the ability of economists and accountants to measure using the techniques commonly applied in studies of economies of scale.[4]

Even after all such qualifications are taken into account, however, it appears that economies of scale alone do not fully account for the degree of concentration found in U.S. industry. Let's turn, then, to the role of barriers to entry.

Barrier to entry

Any circumstance that prevents a new firm in a market from competing on an equal footing with existing ones

BARRIERS TO ENTRY   For our purposes, a **barrier to entry** may be defined as any circumstance that prevents a new firm from competing on an equal footing with existing firms in a particular market.[5] In a market with neither large economies of scale nor high barriers to entry, growth will tend to occur mainly through the entry of new firms, leading to a decrease in concentration over time. With the presence of barriers to entry, the first firms in the industry may be able to maintain their market shares as the industry grows, even without the help of economies of scale.

Sometimes federal, state, or local governments deliberately create barriers to entry. The markets that were referred to as closed monopolies in Chapter 10 are examples, but governments often let more than one firm into a market without opening it to all competitors. For example, to establish a new federally chartered bank, one must obtain permission from a federal agency, the Comptroller of the Currency. One factor that is considered in granting the permit is whether there are already enough banks in the area—in the judgment of the comptroller, not that of the market. The expense of obtaining the permit and the risk that the permit will be denied are significant barriers to competition in the banking industry.

A second kind of barrier to entry is control of a nonreproducible resource. The market for caviar, long controlled by the Soviet Ministry of Fishing, is an example. (Sadly, breakup of that monopoly after the fall of the Soviet Union led not to lower prices for consumers, but to near-extinction of the Caspian sturgeon.) Ownership of a nonreproducible resource gives existing firms an advantage over new ones and, in this way, acts as a barrier to entry.

Patents and copyrights, another class of barriers to entry, are important in both oligopoly and monopoly. A patent or copyright can be treated as a restrictive regulation. As an alternative, it can be treated like ownership of any other nonreproducible resource. In either case, patents and copyrights clearly can make entry difficult and contribute to market concentration. For example, patents held by Xerox Corporation slowed (but did not stop) entry of competing firms into the market for office copiers.

As the term is used here, a *barrier to entry* is something that keeps new firms from duplicating the performance of existing ones in terms of cost or product quality. It does not mean that every effort or expense that a firm must undertake to enter a market should be thought of as a barrier to entry. To start a new firm, an entrepreneur must take risks, find investors, recruit workers, attract customers, and so on. All of these activities are hard work—hard enough to discourage some people from making the effort; but the need for hard work is not a barrier to entry in the economic sense. When entrepreneurs are free to buy the building blocks for their new firms on the same terms as existing firms buy them, new entrants can penetrate even huge markets. Examples include Honda's entry into the automobile market, starting from the base of its motorcycle business or the entry of Russia's Lukoil brand into the U.S. retail gasoline market via its purchase of Getty Petroleum Marketing.

SUNK COSTS AND CONTESTABILITY OF MARKETS Sunk costs are another consideration that can play a role in determining market structure. Entry into many industries does require substantial sunk costs. The new firm may need to purchase custom-made equipment with little resale value, construct a plant in a place where it would have no other obvious use, or spend heavily on advertising and promotion to establish a new brand name in the minds of consumers.

As we have defined the term, sunk costs are not necessarily barriers to entry provided that firms that are already in the market had to undertake the same expenses when they entered. In a market in which the demand for a product is growing and is expected to remain high enough to enable a new firm with at least the minimum efficient scale to cover all of its opportunity costs, including sunk costs, entry can take place just as it would in an industry in which there are no sunk costs.

However, the situation may be different in markets in which there is a temporary increase in demand. In such a market, sunk costs affect the feasibility of what has been called hit-and-run entry—entry by firms that expect to leave the market again once demand conditions return to normal. A firm will not enter such a market on a temporary basis unless it is sure it can recover its fixed costs when it leaves.

In some cases, firms will not be sure whether changes in demand conditions justify entry. Under conditions of uncertainty, firms will be bolder about entering if sunk costs are low. Low sunk costs encourage firms to "test the waters" in a new market. For example, a greeting card retailer might rent a store in a new shopping center to test demand in that area, knowing that the lease can be terminated if the store turns out to be unprofitable. Another category of retailer might have to build a special building that could not be used for anything else, so it would be more cautious about entering a new market.

A market in which there are neither barriers to entry nor sunk costs and which, therefore, is open to hit-and-run entry is known as a contestable market. The airline industry is often cited as an example of a **contestable market**. In that industry, starting a whole new airline may entail sunk costs, but the relevant market is usually considered to be a city pair, such as Baltimore–Miami. Entry into an established city-pair market by a carrier not previously operating there may require little more than renting a few gates and reassigning some airplanes and crews.

Contestable market

A market in which barriers to entry and exit are low

Theory of Oligopoly: Interdependence and Collusion

Earlier chapters presented simple models of profit maximization for perfect competition and monopoly. Those models were based on the analysis of rational responses of managers to cost and demand constraints. In contrast, there is no single, general model of oligopoly. Instead, the theory of oligopoly consists of some broadly applied generalities plus a collection of more specific models that apply to special cases. This section looks at the general principles; the appendix to the chapter discusses some of the special-case models.

The Constraint of Oligopolistic Interdependence

The chief difficulty in analyzing oligopoly concerns the nature of the constraints the firm faces in a market in which there are just a few rival firms. Those firms, like firms in perfectly competitive and monopolistic markets, face constraints in the form of cost curves and market demand conditions. In addition, however, they face another constraint: the reactions of rival firms. The change in the profit that any one firm realizes as a result of a change in price, output quantity, or product characteristics depends not only on how customers respond (as is the case in the other market structures) but also on how other firms in the market respond. The linkage of each firm's choices to its rivals' reactions is called **oligopolistic interdependence**.

Oligopolistic interdependence

The need to pay close attention to the actions of rival firms in an oligopolistic market when making price or production decision

The problem of oligopolistic interdependence can be illustrated by how street vendors operate. Consider a hot-dog vendor named Suzy who sells hot dogs on the corner of 15th and L Streets. If she were the only hot-dog vendor in the market, her profit-maximizing strategy would be based on calculations of marginal cost and marginal revenues—or at least on Suzy's seat-of-the-pants estimates of those variables. If, on the other hand, there were enough firms in the market for perfect competition to exist, each firm would care only about an impersonal market price and would not care about individual rivals' reactions. The price would be treated as a given, and output would be adjusted by each firm until the price equaled marginal cost.

Now, consider what happens when Suzy faces competition from only three other vendors, one on each corner at 15th and L. Suppose that, initially, all four vendors charge $2 per hot dog. Can any one of them gain by changing the price? The decision depends not only on each vendor's estimates of marginal cost and marginal revenue but also on each one's estimates of its rivals' actions. Suzy may decide to raise her price, say to $2.50 instead of $2, banking on the loyalty of her customers to slow any shift to the cheaper vendors. Another vendor may try to undercut the market, charging $1.75 instead of $2. This vendor's strategy is based on the guess that the others' customers are not so loyal after all and that a higher sales volume will allow the low-price seller to earn a profit even at the low price. Thus, the price charged and quantity produced in an oligopoly can change, not only as a result of changes in "objective" conditions, such as cost and demand, but also as a result of purely subjective estimates of human traits, such as stubbornness, loyalty, patience, and anger.

An implication of oligopolistic interdependence is that any model of oligopoly must begin by specifying how each firm expects its rivals to react to changing conditions. We can begin with the special case in which the rival firms in a market agree to cooperate in the pursuit of profit.

Cartels

Oligopolistic interdependence may lead to intense rivalry, as in the case of the hot dog vendors, but it can also result in collusion. *Collusion* occurs when the firms in an oligopoly realize that they can jointly increase their profits by raising the product's price and working out an agreement for dividing the market among them. When collusion is open and formal and involves all or most of the producers in the market, the result is called a **cartel**.

A simple example will show how cartels work. Imagine an industry made up of one hundred small firms. Assume that the marginal cost of production for all firms in the industry is $1 per unit, regardless of the amount produced. Because marginal cost is the same for all units of output, the marginal cost curve also serves as the long-run average cost curve and the long-run supply curve for the industry. This perfectly elastic long-run supply curve is shown in Figure 11.2, along with a demand curve for the industry.

The industry's equilibrium price and level of output depend on how the market is organized. Initially, suppose that all firms act like perfect competitors. According to the theory set forth in Chapter 9, this will result in an equilibrium in which the market price is $1 per unit (equal to long-run average cost and long-run marginal cost) and 400,000 units of output are produced each month. In that equilibrium, firms earn no economic profit.

Now suppose that one day, the heads of the one hundred firms meet to form a cartel. They elect a cartel manager, who is asked to work out a production and marketing plan that will result in the maximum possible total profits for the industry, and to divide them fairly among the members.

Cartel

A group of producers that jointly maximize profits by fixing prices and limiting output

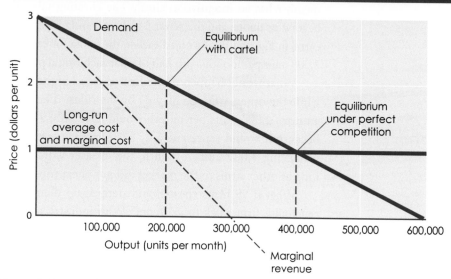

FIGURE 11.2　PROFIT MAXIMIZATION FOR A CARTEL

This graph shows an industry made up of one hundred firms, each producing at a constant long-run average and marginal cost. If the firms act like perfect competitors, the industry will be in equilibrium at the point at which the demand and marginal cost curves intersect. If the firms form a cartel, however, they can jointly earn profits by restricting output to the point at which marginal cost equals marginal revenue and raising the price from $1 to $2.

The profit-maximizing problem that the cartel manager faces is exactly the same as the one faced by a monopolist. Industry profits are highest at the output level at which marginal revenue equals marginal cost—200,000 units per month. If output is restricted to that quantity, the price can be raised to $2 per unit, which will yield $200,000 per month of pure economic profit.

To divide this profit among all the cartel members, the manager will give each firm an output quota of 2,000 units a month, half as much as each was producing before the cartel was formed. In that way, the member firms will reap the benefits of pure monopoly despite their small size and large number.

THE STABILITY PROBLEM   Although cartels are good for their members, they are not so good for consumers. For them, cartels mean a smaller supply of goods and higher prices. Fortunately for consumers, cartels have some built-in problems that make them hard to form and unstable over time.

The first problem faced by cartels is control over entry. As we have seen, any industry in which prices are higher than long-run average cost tends to attract new firms. Because the whole point of a cartel is to raise prices above the competitive level, a cartel acts as a magnet for entrepreneurs. The entry of new firms into the market, however, does not increase the total amount that the cartel can sell at the profit-maximizing price. More firms only mean that the profits must be divided into smaller shares. It is not enough simply to say that new producers cannot join the cartel. If they enter as independent producers, selling outside the framework of the cartel's market sharing agreement, they still depress the cartel's profits. Any cartel, then, needs to find a way to control entry into its market if it is to serve the interests of its founding members.

A second problem faced by cartels is that of enforcing output quotas. In a cartel each member has an incentive to cheat. The cheating takes the form of producing output beyond its quota; and the reward, if the cheating is successful, is greater profit. Take the cartel in Figure 11.2. As noted earlier, the quota for each of the one hundred members is 2,000 units per month—just half of what each would produce under perfect competition.

What would happen if one firm cheated on its quota by stepping up its output while the others went on playing by the rules? The answer is simple: Production of an extra 2,000 units per month would have only a small effect on the market price because it would represent only a 1 percent increase in total industry output. By producing 4,000 units a month, the cheater would double its monthly profit—as long as other firms in the market did not cheat too.

What if 99 firms cheated and stepped up their output to 4,000 units while the remaining firm stuck to its quota? With industry output at 398,000 units, the price would be forced down toward the competitive level of $1. The firm that played fair would gain nothing for having done so.

The conclusion to which this leads is that every member of a cartel will have an incentive to cheat if it expects other members to play fair—and it will also have an incentive to cheat if it expects others to cheat as well.

CARTELS IN PRACTICE   The problems of entry and cheating affect all cartels. The Organization of Petroleum Exporting Countries (OPEC) is a case in point.

In 1973, OPEC controlled about 60 percent of the oil imports of the industrialized countries. Taking advantage of its market power, in the next eight years it increased crude oil prices about tenfold, to a level approaching $40 per barrel (equivalent to over $100 a barrel in 2008 dollars). Output

OPEC is an example of a practicing cartel.

was divided among the cartel's members in proportion to formulas that were agreed upon at meetings of the oil ministers of the various OPEC countries. Saudi Arabia, the largest producer, had the greatest influence and the largest quota.

The price increase brought the OPEC countries fabulous wealth in the short run. However, it also spurred output in non-OPEC areas, such as Alaska, the North Sea, and Mexico. Moreover, the demand for oil proved more elastic in the long run than in the short run as factories installed energy conservation equipment and consumers bought more fuel-efficient cars. As a result of these changes, OPEC lost half of its former market share. Saudi Arabia cut back its own output to less than 25 percent of capacity and tried to persuade smaller member countries to accept lower quotas as well. Cheating in terms of both price and quantity became widespread. By 1986 the OPEC cartel was in disarray; at one point the market price of oil plunged below $10 a barrel.

In the early 2000s, oil prices recovered again, reaching a record high of more than $140 per barrel in mid-2008. One reason was a slowing pace of new discoveries. Another was booming oil demand in China and India. Most analysts agreed, however, that those peak prices have more to do with supply and demand conditions on the world market than with policy decisions by the OPEC cartel. This belief was confirmed when prices plunged after a spreading global recession undermined demand toward the end of 2008. OPEC's attempts to stop the decline of prices with output cuts had little effect.

Because cartels that depend on voluntary cooperation among members run into problems, some cartels have enlisted governments to enforce quotas and restrict entry. In the United States, agricultural cartels known as *marketing orders* are a case in point. However, as can be seen from *Economics in the News 11.1*, even government-assisted cartels may eventually collapse.

Coordination Without Collusion

Formal cartels are not unknown, but they are rare. They are uncommon partly because of their inherent instability, as explained in the preceding section. Also—at least in the United States—most cartels are illegal under the antitrust laws. (Those

Economics in the News 11.1
BIG TOBACCO, LAWSUITS, AND COMPETITION

The U.S. Department of Justice attempts to monitor industry competitiveness using industry concentration ratios and HHI values. This does not entirely prevent cartels among U.S. producers, especially those protected by regulations dating back to the early twentieth century. For instance, many people know that they are dealing with a cartel when they buy gasoline; but few people realize that for years they were doing the same whenever they bought a pack of cigarettes.

The U.S. tobacco industry is, to a large degree, controlled by the four largest cigarette companies: Altria, R. J. Reynolds, Brown & Williamson, and Lorillard. While not legally permitted to fix prices on tobacco products, these companies have implicitly colluded in the way they have dealt with their recent lawsuit settlements. For years, big tobacco fought off lawsuits that claimed the companies concealed the true health risks associated with smoking; however, a new wave of successful suits led to a large settlement between the big-four companies and state attorneys general in 1998. The settlement required that the companies pay about $200 billion over twenty-five years to cover the states' costs of health care for smokers. If the big four could not be sure of continued high revenues, they would have had a hard time paying these enormous sums; so the settlement enlisted states to support a big-brand cartel that keeps prices high by imposing fees on small rivals not covered by the settlement.

The agreement highlights an important relationship between regulation and competition: the big tobacco producers might not have settled unless the states tried to stop small rivals from undercutting its prices, and the states stood to reap higher payments if the major brands fared well. So, many states passed laws requiring

The settlement of a lawsuit against big tobacco firms put small rivals at a competitive disadvantage.

tobacco upstarts to pay the states fees equivalent to—or after taxes, even more than—what the big four companies pay in the settlement.

The settlement led to new anti-smoking ads, funded by the large tobacco producers themselves. While it appeared to the public a penalty on the big cigarette companies and a coup for state prosecutors, it actually benefits Altria, R. J. Reynolds, Brown & Williamson, and Lorillard. The increased fees paid by smaller tobacco companies make it harder for them to undercut the majors' prices.

Two small tobacco producers have filed a federal lawsuit challenging the settlement, claiming it violates federal antitrust laws. "This is not some bedroom conspiracy to fix prices that we have to prove. It's all there in the settlement," says lawyer David Dobbins, who represented the Las Vegas–based cigarette importer, Freedom Holdings. The big brands' "treble-damage liability is astronomical," he notes. "Eventually this cartel will be abolished and competition will return to the cigarette market."

The settlement may not be working out as well as the states and the big tobacco producers had hoped, however. States expect their settlement fees to fall 16 percent this year to a total $7.8 billion. The reason is entry of cheap, previously unknown brands, whose share has risen to nearly 10 percent of the market, up from 1 percent five years ago. This doesn't come as a surprise; the big brands raised their wholesale price $1.10, to over $3 a pack, several times the sum needed to fund their payments to the states.

SOURCE: Scott Woolley, "A Cozy Cancer Cartel," *Forbes,* January 29, 2004.

laws will be discussed in Chapter 12.) We are left with the question of whether the firms in an oligopoly can, even without open collusion, tacitly coordinate their price and output decisions in a way that will jointly maximize their profit. To put it another way, will an industry in which there are only a few firms, but no formal cartel, perform more nearly like the model of perfect competition or like that of monopoly?

There have been a number of attempts to answer this question with formal models similar to those of perfect competition and monopoly. Those attempts have not been particularly successful, however, because there is no simple way to handle the problem of oligopolistic interdependence—the dependence of each firm's behavior on its rivals' decisions.

To construct a formal model, one must make a specific assumption about how each firm reacts to what its rivals do and how it expects them to react to what it does. One model, for example, assumes that each firm reacts to its rivals' changes in prices or output but expects them not to respond to changes in its own prices and output. Another model assumes that rivals will always match price cuts but never match price increases. Still another assumes that each firm expects its rivals to do the worst thing possible and plans accordingly.

Several formal models are described in the appendix to this chapter. None of them, however, offers a general solution to the question of how price and output decisions are made under oligopoly. In the absence of a general, formal model, much of the writing on oligopoly deals with informal theories consisting of conjectures about the conditions that tend to make cooperation by oligopolists easier or more difficult. Under conditions that facilitate formal, tacit coordination, price and output may tend to more closely resemble the results of a cartel. Under conditions that make coordination more difficult, price and output may tend to more nearly approximate the result of perfect competition. Some of the most common themes of the informal theories are described next.

NUMBER AND SIZE OF FIRMS   There is little doubt that the number and size of the firms in a market make a big difference. Tacit coordination is easier in a market with only two or three large firms of roughly equal size than in a market in which a dozen equal-sized firms control half the market and the rest is controlled by smaller firms. If the number of firms is large enough and the size of the largest firms is sufficiently small, the market ceases to be an oligopoly. With a homogeneous product and easy entry and exit, it becomes perfectly competitive, as discussed in an earlier chapter. With a differentiated product and easy entry and exit, it becomes monopolistically competitive, a case that we will analyze later in this chapter.

The relative size and number of the various firms in the market are considered to be important on the grounds that cooperation is easier in an industry in which there is one dominant firm. That firm may be able to act as a price leader. Under the strongest form of **price leadership**, firms are no longer uncertain about how their rivals will react to price changes. The leader knows that the others will follow it, whether it raises or lowers the price. The others know that if they follow the leader, others will too, but not if they raise or lower prices on their own. When it works, this arrangement is tantamount to a cartel in that the dominant firm's efforts to maximize its own profit will also maximize the entire industry's profits. U.S. Steel and General Motors are examples of companies that were once thought to play the role

Price leadership

A situation in which price increases or decreases by a dominant firm in an oligopoly, known as the price leader, are matched by all or most of the other firms in the market

of price leaders in their markets although neither of these firms occupies the dominant position today that it once did.

THE NATURE OF THE PRODUCT   The nature of the product also affects the ease or difficulty of coordination. A homogeneous product for which there is a smooth flow of orders tends to make coordination easier; widely used steel products, such as railroad rails and wire, are examples. A variable product for which the flow of orders is irregular tends to make coordination more difficult; the ship building industry is a case in point. In such an industry, there are simply too many things to coordinate. It is not enough that all firms tacitly agree to sell at the same price; they must also agree on a set of price variations based on changes in quality, speed of delivery, size of order, and so on. Under these conditions an agreement to raise the price above the competitive level, even if it can be sustained, is unlikely to lead to higher profits. It is more likely to lead to an outbreak of competition by firms offering higher quality, more convenient scheduling, volume discounts, and so on. These factors will add to the cost of doing business or reduce revenue until excess profits disappear.

GROWTH AND INNOVATION   The rates of growth and innovation in a market are another factor that is likely to affect the ease or difficulty of coordination among rival oligopolists. In a market in which product features, production techniques, and buyers' and sellers' personalities do not change from year to year, an agreement among firms, whether it is tacit or overt, will never have to be revised. In a market with rapidly changing elements, any agreement will soon be made obsolete by changing conditions or be disrupted by the entry of new buyers or sellers. Given the uncertainties of tacit agreements and the fact that overt ones are illegal, one would expect that the faster the pace of growth and change, the less successful rival firms will be in coordinating their activities.

EASE OF ENTRY AND EXIT   Barriers to entry play an important role in the price and output decisions of an oligopoly. Even if there are only a few firms in the market, the threat of entry by new firms may force existing ones to practice limit pricing to avoid attracting new rivals. Under limit pricing, as explained in Chapter 10, the price is set below the profit-maximizing level implied by short-run demand, marginal revenue, and marginal cost.

Barriers to entry are also important in considering the effect of mergers on price and output decisions in an oligopoly. A merger within an oligopoly reduces the number of firms in the industry and, if the larger members are involved, increases the concentration ratio. Taken in isolation, a reduction in the number and an increase in the size of firms would tend to make coordination easier, perhaps leading to a more cartel-like result. Often, however, new firms quickly enter to fill any gaps left by mergers. The publishing industry is an example of one in which there have been several mergers of leading firms, but also many entries of new small firms, so that the degree of competition remains substantial. Also, as pointed out earlier in the chapter, sunk costs that cannot be recovered when the firm leaves the market can be as important as ease of entry in determining price and output decisions under oligopoly.

Market Performance Under Oligopoly

Neither the formal theories discussed in the appendix to this chapter nor the informal rules of thumb just presented give conclusive answers to the question of market performance under oligopoly. Depending on the situation, some oligopolies may behave much like perfectly competitive markets, with prices equal or close to marginal cost. Others, with or without open collusion, may behave more like a monopoly, with prices higher than marginal cost and a resulting deadweight loss.

When they cannot answer questions about market performance by means of pure theory, economists turn to statistical methods. Ideally, one would like to measure the gap between price and marginal cost at the point of market equilibrium, but it is rarely possible to do so. In the absence of reliable data on marginal cost, an indirect approach can be used. If firms in concentrated industries can be shown, on average, to earn returns that exceed the opportunity cost of capital, one can infer that they are behaving more like monopolists than like perfect competitors. If, on the other hand, firms in concentrated industries earn only "normal profits"—that is, rates of return on capital that are no higher, on average, than those earned by firms in less concentrated industries—one can conclude that oligopolies perform about as well as more competitive industries. Following this reasoning, much of the debate about market performance under oligopoly focuses on rates of return.

The first person to try this approach in a systematic way was University of California professor Joe Bain. In 1951 Bain published the results of a study of forty-two selected industries for the years 1936 to 1940. According to Bain's analysis of the data, industries with concentration ratios of over seventy earned higher profits than less concentrated ones. The link between profits and concentration was neither perfect nor strong, but it did exist.

During the 1950s and 1960s, many of Bain's students and followers repeated his studies for other industries and years. Most of them got the same results: a weak but persistent link between profits and concentration. Economists concluded that in general, the more highly concentrated an industry, the more it will tend to perform like a cartel or a monopoly. This would be true even if there were no agreement among rivals to raise prices and divide up markets.

As faith in this idea grew, economists tried as hard as they could to prove it, using the more advanced statistical techniques and better data that became available each year; but the harder they tried, the more elusive the connection became. Some studies showed that if the data are adjusted for the size of firms in different markets, the link between concentration and profits tends to disappear. Others indicated that if the data are adjusted for differences in advertising expenditures, the connection evaporates. Still others suggested that results like Bain's hold only in periods of recession and disappear with the return of prosperity.

Moreover, as the link between concentration and profits was becoming more ambiguous, economists were growing less certain about how such a link should be interpreted even if it could be confirmed. New reasons were found to explain why firms in more concentrated industries might appear to earn higher profits than firms in less concentrated ones. Those reasons had nothing to do with monopoly pricing or tacit coordination. For example, a concentrated industry that was growing rapidly might need to earn high profits to attract capital. Perhaps the high profits of the largest firms in each concentrated industry might simply reflect those firms' superior efficiency relative to smaller firms in the same industry. Finally, the higher profits that some concentrated industries appeared to earn might not be pure economic profits; they might merely reflect the fact that the categories used by accountants to record business transactions do not accurately reflect implicit costs.

The Theory of Monopolistic Competition

Up to this point we have looked at industries in which many small firms produce a homogeneous product and at others in which a few large firms make products that need not be alike. Those cases leave out a very large class of markets in which there are many small firms, each of which makes a product that differs somewhat from those of its competitors. This market structure is known as *monopolistic competition*. Examples include restaurants, service stations, bakeries, some types of publishing companies, and countless others.

Profit Maximization Under Monopolistic Competition

Although there is no general agreement on a formal model for oligopoly, there is a widely accepted model of monopolistic competition. As its name implies, this model, which dates from work done in the 1930s by Edward H. Chamberlin and independently by Joan Robinson, blends monopolistic and competitive aspects. Like a monopolist, the monopolistically competitive firm is a price searcher facing a negatively sloped demand curve. However, like the perfectly competitive firm, the monopolistic competitor is assumed to share the market with many other small firms. For this reason, the model of monopolistic competition ignores oligopolistic interdependence. It assumes that each firm in the market is so small that no one firm is significantly affected by what another one does.

The theory can be understood with the help of Figure 11.3, which shows short- and long-run equilibrium positions for a typical firm under monopolistic competition. The demand curve has a negative slope because each firm's product is a little different from its competitors' products. Each firm, therefore, can raise its price at least slightly without losing all its customers because some customers attach more importance than others to the special style, location, or other marketing advantage the firm offers. Given this negatively sloped demand curve, the short-run profit-maximizing position shown in part (a) of the figure is found in the same way as that for a simple monopolist: The output level is determined by the intersection of the marginal cost and marginal revenue curves, and the price charged is determined by the height of the demand curve at that point.

However, this particular short-run equilibrium cannot also be long-run equilibrium under monopolistic competition. The reason is that monopolistically competitive markets are highly contestable, with easy entry and exit. In the short-run position shown in part (a) of Figure 11.3, the firm is earning a pure economic profit; this is shown by the fact that price exceeds average total cost.

FIGURE 11.3   SHORT-RUN AND LONG-RUN EQUILIBRIUM UNDER MONOPOLISTIC COMPETITION

(a) The Short Run

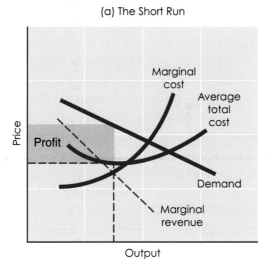

(b) The Long Run

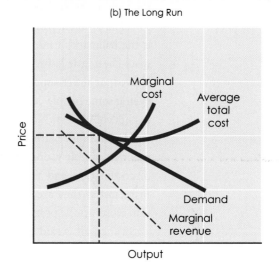

Under monopolistic competition, each firm is a price searcher with a negatively sloped demand curve; but there are no barriers to entry by new firms. In the short run, a firm that produces at the point at which marginal cost equals marginal revenue can earn pure economic profits, as shown in part (a). In the long run, however, new firms are attracted to the market. This diverts part of the demand from firms that are already in the market, thus lowering each one's demand curve. Also, those firms may fight to keep their share of the market, using means that will increase their costs. Entry by new firms will continue until a long-run equilibrium is reached in which profits are eliminated, as shown in part (b).

Profits attract new firms; and as new firms enter the market, two things happen. First, the demand curves of existing firms shift downward. This happens because the new firms' products, although they are not identical to those of the original firms, are substitutes for them. Second, in response to the new competition, firms that are already in the market may step up their advertising, improve their product in some way, or take other steps to win back customers. These efforts cause the firms' average total cost curves to shift upward. The downward shift in the original firms' demand curves or the upward shift in their cost curves, or both, continue until there are no more profits to attract new firms. The result is the long-run equilibrium position shown in part (b) of Figure 11.3.

The Performance of Monopolistically Competitive Industries

Some economists have argued that the long-run equilibrium position shown in Figure 11.3 indicates poor performance by monopolistically competitive industries. For one thing, as in the case of pure monopoly, each firm stops short of the output level that would maximize the sum of producer and consumer surplus. Likewise, the gap between price and marginal cost indicates potential added production that would benefit both the firm and its customers. In addition, under monopolistic competition a firm does not operate at the lowest point on its long-run average cost curve. If there were fewer firms, each producing a greater amount of output, the same quantity of goods could be provided at a lower total cost. Following this reasoning, it has been argued that monopolistic competition results in too many gas stations, supermarkets, and restaurants, each operating at less than full capacity and each charging inefficiently high prices. Yet despite the high prices, each earns only the minimum return it needs to stay in business.

The problem with this critique is that it ignores the value of the product variety that is the hallmark of monopolistic competition. It is beside the point to argue that prices would be a little lower if there were fewer barbershops, each somewhat less conveniently located; or fewer supermarkets, each a little more crowded; or fewer ice cream flavors, even if some people could not have their favorite flavor. Would a move in that direction benefit consumers? Not necessarily, if consumers are willing to pay something for variety.

Furthermore, the model of monopolistic competition assumes that each firm practices simple monopoly pricing. In practice, complex pricing strategies like price-discrimination and two-part pricing are available to monopolistically competitive firms just as they are to monopolies and oligopolies. These strategies bring production closer to the point where marginal cost and marginal revenue are equal.

When all is said and done, the prevailing view is that monopolistic competition and perfect competition are not all that different and that both serve customers reasonably well. Both fall into the category that Shepherd refers to as "effectively competitive." It is encouraging to consider, as reported earlier in *Applying Economic Ideas 11.1*, that more than three-quarters of the economy fits into this broad category.

Summary

1. **How has the structure of markets in the U.S. economy changed over time?** Aggregate concentration of U.S. industry has changed little in recent decades. *Concentration ratios* and the *Herfindahl-Hirschmann index* are two measures of the degree to which a market is dominated by a few firms. They can be used together with information about the behavior of firms to estimate the degree of competition in a market. More than three-quarters of U.S. output is produced in effectively competitive markets. The share of output produced by monopolies, oligopolies with dominant firms, and tight oligopolies appears to be declining.

2. **How does the interdependence of firms under oligopoly affect price and output decisions?** *Oligopolistic interdependence* refers to the need for each firm in an oligopoly to pay close attention to its rivals' actions when making decisions regarding price, output, or product characteristics. Oligopolistic interdependence makes it difficult to construct simple, generally applicable models of oligopoly.

3. **Why do oligopolistic firms sometimes collude to increase profits, and what problems do they encounter as a result?** A group of producers that jointly maximize profits by fixing prices and limiting output is known as a *cartel*. A cartel's profits are maximized by setting output at a level corresponding to the intersection of the marginal cost and marginal revenue curves for the industry as a whole. The chief problems encountered by cartels are controlling entry and preventing members from cheating on prices and output quotas.

4. **What conditions affect market performance under oligopoly?** Among the factors that are thought to affect market performance under oligopoly are the number and size of firms in the market, the presence or absence of *price leadership*, the

nature of the product (homogeneous or varied), the pace of growth and innovation, and the ease or difficulty of entry and exit. If barriers to entry and exit are low, a market is said to be *contestable*. Contestable markets are thought to perform well even if they are highly concentrated.

5. **How is equilibrium achieved under monopolistic competition, and how well do such markets perform?** A monopolistic competitor maximizes profit at the output level at which marginal cost equals marginal revenue. In the long run competition in such an industry results in an equilibrium in which price equals average total cost for each firm. In this equilibrium, price does not equal marginal cost and production does not take place at the point of minimum average total cost; nevertheless, consumers enjoy the benefit of product variety.

Key Terms

Problems and Topics for Discussion

1. **Oligopolistic interdependence in action** Look around your community for a case in which a firm is conducting a special sale or product promotion. To what extent, if at all, is the firm's action a response to something its rivals have done? To what extent, if at all, have its rivals reacted with their own sales or promotions?

2. **Barriers to entry** "Barriers to entry are lower in the restaurant industry than in the airline industry because a restaurant requires only a few workers and a few thousand dollars in capital, whereas even a small airline requires many workers and millions of dollars in capital." Do you agree? Why or why not?

3. **The market for college education** What market structure do you think best fits the market for college education? What factors do you believe affect the structure of the college education industry? How important are economies of scale? How important are barriers to entry and exit?

4. **Labor unions as cartels** In what ways do labor unions resemble cartels? In what ways do they differ from cartels? Do you think labor unions ever suffer from the problems of instability that plague cartels?

Case for Discussion

All Things Begin Small

In 1994, the German automobile maker BMW acquired Rover Group, adding the British Mini Cooper to its collection of cars. In 2001, the Mini Cooper premiered at the Detroit auto show and was available for sale in the U.S. the following year. Despite the phenomenal growth in sport-utility vehicles in the U.S., the compact Mini has been extremely popular.

The rest of the world seems to share this sentiment. In the fall of 2003, BMW was considering plans to increase production of its Mini plant at Oxford to about 200,000 a year to meet growing demand. BMW's chief executive Helmut Panke estimated Mini sales could top 165,000 this year after hitting a record of 144,000 in 2002. By 2003 annual output was about 160,000.

There have been fears that capacity constraints at the Oxford plant could force some Mini production abroad; but Panke said the car would be built only at Oxford, where BMW planned to streamline production to remove bottlenecks. One option being considered is to lengthen workers' shifts from the traditional eight to nine or ten hours.

Panke said that output at BMW car plants could grow by between 40,000 and 50,000 units a year—with minimum investment. Increased output and sales of the Mini are integral to BMW's plans to lift global sales from 1 to 1.4 million between 2003 and 2008.

Panke held up the Mini as "a UK manufacturing success story," destroying the myth that Britain's manufacturing sector would never make a comeback.

SOURCE: Based on David Gow, "BMW to boost production of 'UK success story,'" *Guardian Unlimited*, November 13, 2003.

QUESTIONS

1. How would you best characterize the market in which the Mini is sold: Perfectly competitive, oligopolistic, monopolistically competitive, or oligopoly? Why?
2. If the Mini enjoys strong demand, do you think that will allow BMW to charge a price higher than marginal cost? Why or why not?
3. How might BMW's rivals react to the introduction and success of the Mini? Do you think

BMW must take this into account when planning its marketing strategy?
4. What sunk costs does BMW encounter when bringing out a new car like the Mini? What does this say about the degree to which the automobile market is contestable?

End Notes

1. Anup Shah, "The Rise of Corporations," Globalissues.org, (http://www.globalissues.org/TradeRelated/Corporations/Rise.asp), July 16, 2005.
2. Lawrence J. White, "Trends in Aggregate Concentration in the United States," *Journal of Economic Perspectives*, Volume 16, No. 4 (Fall 2002): 137–160.
3. Julia Porter Liebeskind, Tim C. Opler, and Donald E. Hatfield, "Corporate Restructuring and the Consolidation of US Industry," *The Journal of Industrial Economics* 11(2) (March–April 1996).
4. See John S. McGee, "Efficiency and Economies of Size," in *Industrial Concentration: The New Learning*, eds. Harvey J. Goldschmid, Michael H. Mann, and Fred J. Weston (Boston: Little, Brown, 1974), 55–96.
5. Economists have struggled for decades to find consensus on the definition of "barrier to entry." For a survey of proposed definitions, see R. Preston MacAfee et. al., "What is a Barrier to Entry," *American Economic Review*, Papers and Proceedings (May 2004): 461–465.

Appendix to Chapter 11:
FORMAL THEORIES OF OLIGOPOLY

Over the years, many economists have proposed formal theories of oligopoly. The goal of such a theory is to determine the equilibrium price and output level for an oligopolistic firm and its industry given aspects of market structure such as number of firms, concentration ratio, cost and technology, and demand curve. No general theory has been developed, but some useful partial theories and interesting analyses of special cases exist. These provide some insight into the broader problem of oligopoly. The three theories discussed in this appendix are a sample from the literature on formal theories of oligopoly.

The Cournot Theory and Its Variations

The oldest attempt to develop a theory of oligopoly began with a work published by Augustin Cournot in 1838. Cournot recognized the problem of oligopolistic interdependence: the need for each firm to take its rivals' behavior into account when deciding on its own market strategy. The way to understand the behavior of rival firms, he thought, was to make a simple assumption about the way each firm would react to its rivals' moves.

In his initial statement of the problem, Cournot assumed that each firm would act as if it did not expect its rivals to change their output levels even if it changed its own. However, later theorists who expanded Cournot's theory usually made price rather than output the crucial variable. In the price-based version of the Cournot theory, each firm is assumed to set its price as though it expects other firms in the industry to leave their prices unchanged.

Figure 11A.1 shows how the price-based Cournot theory might work for an industry with just two firms. Corresponding to each price that its rival may charge, every firm has a price that will yield the maximum profit. These prices are shown in the form of *reaction curves*. For example, firm 1's reaction curve indicates that it will charge $60 if its rival charges $50 (point S). If firm 2 charges $150, firm 1 will charge $130 (point T). In the extreme case, firm 2 may charge so much that it will price itself out of the market, leaving firm 1 with a pure monopoly. In that event, firm 1 will maximize its profits by charging $150, as shown by the broken line labeled "Firm 1's monopoly price." Firm 2's monopoly price is shown in the same way. The two reaction curves can be derived from the two firms' cost and demand curves. The derivation is not given here, but it can be found in many advanced texts.

Given these reaction curves, the behavior of an oligopoly, according to Cournot, can be described somewhat as follows. Imagine that at first firm 1 is the only producer of the good in question. Because it has a pure monopoly, it maximizes profits by setting a price of $150. Then firm 2 enters the market. Under the Cournot theory, firm 2 will set its price as though it expected firm 1 to go on charging $150 indefinitely. Given this assumption, firm 2 sets its price at $125, as shown by point A on firm 2's reaction curve.

At this point, firm 1 begins to notice its rival. Seeing that firm 2 has taken away many of its customers with its much lower price, it moves to point B on its reaction curve, cutting its own price to $115.

FIGURE 11A.1 COURNOT THEORY WORKING IN AN INDUSTRY WITH TWO FIRMS

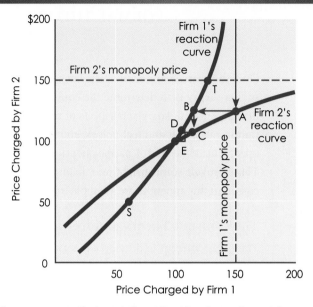

The Cournot theory assumes that each firm will set its price as though it expects its rivals' prices to remain fixed. The reaction curves show the best price for each of two firms given the other's price. For example, point S on firm 1's reaction curve indicates that firm 1 should charge $60 if firm 2 charges $50. If firm 1 has a monopoly, it will set a price of $150. If firm 2 then enters the market, it will touch off a price war, moving the industry step by step to points A, B, C, D, and finally E. Point E is a stable equilibrium.

Firm 2, which entered the market on the assumption that firm 1 would maintain its price at $150, must react next. Given firm 1's $115 price, firm 2 cuts its price to $108 (point C). That sparks a price cut by firm 1, which goes to $107 (point D). After a series of increasingly smaller moves and countermoves, the two firms' prices converge at an equilibrium of $100 at point E.

Two things are appealing about the Cournot theory. First, it gives a stable equilibrium. At prices above the intersection of the two reaction curves, each firm has an incentive to undercut its rival's price. At prices below the intersection, each firm has an incentive to charge more than its rival. Thus, given the assumptions, there is only one price that the market can reach. Second, as the theory is expanded beyond two firms to allow for multi-firm oligopolies, it can be shown that the equilibrium price moves steadily away from the monopoly price and toward a price equal to marginal cost. Thus, the Cournot equilibrium for an industry with one firm equals the monopoly price; that for an industry with an infinite number of firms equals the competitive price; and those for oligopolies of various sizes occur along a continuum between these extremes.

Still, there is one feature of the Cournot theory that has always troubled economists. The structure of the theory depends on each firm's assuming that its rivals will not react to its price changes, yet daily life in the Cournot world proves that assumption to be wrong. In the example in Figure 11A.1, firm 2 enters on the assumption that firm 1 will pay no attention to its entry and capture of a large chunk of firm 1's sales; but firm

1 does react, as does firm 2. Instead of this mindless price war, wouldn't each firm have second thoughts about its price-cutting, fearing its rival's reaction? The Cournot theory fails to acknowledge this possibility.

Recently, theorists have explored variations of the Cournot theory in which firms do not base their expectations regarding their rivals' behavior solely on what they did in the previous period. Instead, their expectations are gradually adapted to what the rivals have done over a sequence of previous periods. Under certain circumstances, such models produce outcomes similar to the simple Cournot model—outcomes in which equilibrium is stable and approaches the competitive case as the number of firms increase.

The Kinked Demand Curve Theory

In 1939, a century after Cournot, another major oligopoly theory was proposed. Known as the *kinked demand curve theory,* it was proposed at about the same time by the British economists R. L. Hall and C. J. Hitch and the American economist Paul M. Sweezy. Like the Cournot theory, the kinked demand curve theory begins from a simple assumption about oligopolists' reactions to price changes by rivals: Each firm expects that if it cuts its price, its rivals will match the cut; but that if it raises its price, no other firms will follow.

Figure 11A.2 shows how the market looks to an oligopolist who makes these two assumptions. Let P be the price ($1.70, in this case) that happens to prevail in the market. If the firm cuts its price below P, other firms will lower their prices in turn. Sales in the industry as a whole will expand. The firm in question will keep about the same share of the market and will move down the lower slope of the demand curve. In contrast, if the firm raises its price, the others will not follow suit. Instead of keeping its share of the market, our firm will lose customers to its rivals. As a result, the part of the firm's demand curve above price P is much more elastic than the part below it.

Now bring marginal cost and marginal revenue into the picture. Give the firm a short-run marginal cost curve with the usual positive slope. The marginal revenue curve contains a step that corresponds to the kink in the demand curve. To the left of the step, marginal revenue is very high, showing that revenue will be lost quickly if the firm moves up the very elastic part of the demand curve. To the right of the step, marginal revenue is much lower, indicating that little extra revenue can be obtained by moving down the less elastic part of the demand curve. As drawn, the marginal cost curve cuts the marginal revenue curve right at the step. The prevailing price is an equilibrium price for the firm because it will be unprofitable to move in either direction.

The kinked demand curve equilibrium for an oligopolist is a very stable kind of equilibrium. Unlike a pure monopolist, the oligopolist with a kinked demand curve will not change its price or output in response to small- or medium-sized changes in cost. The level of marginal cost shown in Figure 11A.2 can move by as much as $.30 in either direction, and the firm will not change its price or output. The marginal cost curve will still cross the marginal revenue curve at the step. Only if marginal cost changes by more than $.30 does the firm break with the prevailing price.

Like the Cournot theory, the kinked demand curve theory is simple and elegant. Its assumptions about the way each oligopolist views its rivals' actions are clearly more plausible than Cournot's. However, the kinked demand curve theory has a major limitation of its own. Although it explains why an oligopolist might be reluctant to change its

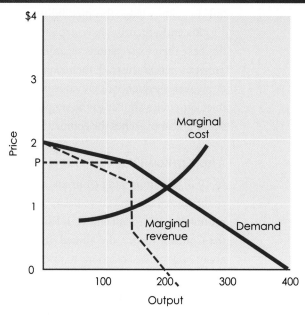

FIGURE 11A.2 THE KINKED DEMAND CURVE THEORY OF OLIGOPOLY

An oligopolist will have a kinked demand curve if its rivals will follow any price decrease it makes but will not follow price increases. There is a sharp step in the marginal revenue curve that corresponds to the kink in the demand curve. Here the marginal cost curve crosses the marginal revenue curve at the step. This makes the equilibrium very stable.

price once it has set that price, it fails to show how the price comes to be set at any particular level in the first place. The theory thus provides an answer to a question that is not central to the analysis of oligopoly. In addition, some empirical studies have failed to confirm the theory's prediction that prices will be changed less often under oligopoly than under monopoly.

Game Theory and Oligopoly Behavior

It has often been remarked that oligopoly is really a sort of a game—one in which, as in chess or poker, each player must try to guess the opponent's moves, bluffs, countermoves, and counterbluffs as many moves ahead as possible. Hence, economists who specialize in oligopoly theory were excited by the appearance in 1944 of a thick, highly mathematical book entitled *The Theory of Games and Economic Behavior*.[1] Could it be that the authors, John von Neumann and Oskar Morgenstern, had at last solved the oligopoly puzzle?

Clearly, Neumann and Morgenstern had taken a major step. Instead of starting from some arbitrary assumption about how one firm would react to others' moves, they decided to ask, in effect, what *optimal assumption* each firm should make about its rivals' behavior.

---

[1] John von Neumann and Oskar Morgenstern, *The Theory of Games and Economic Behavior* (Princeton, N.J.: Princeton University Press, 1944).

A simple example of an oligopoly game will convey the spirit of the Neumann-Morgenstern approach. Imagine a market in which there are only two firms—Alpha Company and Zed Enterprises. It costs $1 a unit to make their product. If each firm sets its price at $5 a unit, each will sell 100 units per month at a profit of $4 a unit, for a total monthly profit of $400. If each sets its price at $4 a unit, each will sell 120 units at a profit of $3 a unit, for a total profit of $360. Which price will the firms actually set? Clearly, $5 is the price that will maximize their joint profits, but under oligopoly this price may not be a stable equilibrium.

Figure 11A.3 shows why. It presents the pricing strategies available to Alpha Company. Besides the two already mentioned, Alpha must consider two more. One is to cut its price to $4 while Zed holds at $5. That will allow Alpha to take away a lot of Zed's customers and sell 150 units, for a profit of $450. The other is for Alpha to hold its price at $5 while Zed cuts its price to $4. Then Zed will take away many of Alpha's customers and leave Alpha selling only 60 units, for a total profit of $240.

What will happen? One way to seek an answer is to look at the effects of different assumptions that each firm might make about the other's behavior. If Alpha assumes that Zed will charge $5, Alpha will be best off charging $4. If Alpha assumes that Zed will charge $4, it will again be best off charging $4. It looks as though Alpha will be best off charging $4 regardless of what Zed does. Alpha will also be aware that Zed's view of the game is the mirror image of its own. After considering the likely effects of the different assumptions, each firm will see that it is rational to assume the worst. Unless the two firms can agree to keep the price at $5 (and such agreements are assumed to be against the rules of the game as it is played here), $4 is the equilibrium price.

The equilibrium reached in the situation described in Figure 11A.3 is called **Nash equilibrium** after the American mathematician and game theorist John Nash. In Nash

Nash equilibrium

An equilibrium solution to a game in which each player's strategy is optimal given the other players' choice of strategy

FIGURE 11A.3   A SIMPLE OLIGOPOLY GAME

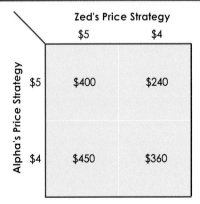

This figure shows the profits Alpha Company would earn under various pricing strategies for itself and its rival, Zed Enterprises. If both firms set their prices at $5, each will earn $400. If both lower their prices to $4, they will continue to split the market and each will earn $360. If Alpha lowers its price while Zed does not, Alpha will steal many of Zed's customers and earn $450. If Zed lowers its price while Alpha's remains at $5, Zed will steal many of Alpha's customers, leaving Alpha with only $240 in profits.

equilibrium, each player's strategy is optimal given the strategy chosen by its rivals. Thus, neither player has an incentive to change strategies after finding out what strategy the other player has chosen. The Cournot theory provides another example of Nash equilibrium. In the Cournot game, at first each firm changes its price as soon as it learns what its rival has done. Gradually, though, the prices converge toward Nash equilibrium.

As economists and mathematicians have developed more powerful analytical tools, they have explored increasingly complex oligopoly games. The games vary in terms of how much each player knows about what the other is doing, the number of times the game is expected to be repeated, the number of players, and the structure of the payoffs. Consideration has also been given to games in which players pursue "mixed strategies" under which they vary their response to rivals' moves on a random basis. (In sports, an example of a mixed strategy is a baseball pitcher's random use of fastballs, curves, and sinkers to keep the batter guessing.)

The research has led to many interesting results for plausible individual cases, but it has yielded no completely general conclusions. Some games have Nash equilibrium solutions, and some do not. Some converge toward the competitive outcome as the number of firms increase, and some do not. Some produce equilibrium solutions that are efficient (either from the point of view of the players or from that of the market), and some do not. Game theory continues to be an active area of oligopoly research.

CHAPTER *12*

Antitrust and Regulation

DEPARTMENT OF JUSTICE
WASHINGTON

After reading this chapter, you will understand the following:

1. Illegal business practices under the antitrust laws
2. How economists' views on antitrust policy have changed over time
3. How natural monopolies are regulated and what problems are posed by regulation
4. Why some industries are regulated despite their inherently competitive structure
5. Current trends in health and safety regulation

Before reading this chapter, make sure you know the meaning of the concepts:

1. Political rent seeking
2. Market failure
3. Public choice theory
4. Natural monopoly
5. Cartels

C HAPTER 4 INTRODUCED the market failure and public choice theories of the role of government in the economy. Chapters 6 and 7 illustrated both theories with examples from environmental policy and global trade policy. Now we turn our attention to another group of government policies that focus on the issues of market performance and competition.

Antitrust laws

A set of laws, including the Sherman Act and the Clayton Act, which regulate market structure and the competitive behavior of firms

Antitrust Laws and Policies

We begin with a discussion of **antitrust laws**—a set of laws, some of which date back more than 100 years, that regulate market structure and the competitive behavior of firms. *Applying Economic Ideas 12.1* summarizes the main U.S. antitrust laws. Today, most other countries also have antitrust laws that regulate market structure and competitive behavior.

Applying Economic Ideas 12.1
THE ANTITRUST LAWS

The antitrust laws of the United States derive their name from the nineteenth century giant "trusts," which were large industrial groupings that established dominant positions in railroads, oil, steel, and other industries. These trusts aroused public opposition because their wealth and power threatened the traditional livelihood of smaller-scale, traditional forms of business. As one judge of the period put it,

[Large firms] may even temporarily, or perhaps permanently, reduce the price of the article traded in or manufactured, by reducing the expense inseparable from the running of many different companies for the same purpose. Trade or commerce under those circumstances may nevertheless be badly and unfortunately restrained by driving out of business the small dealers and worthy men whose lives have been spent therein and who might be unable to readjust themselves to their altered surroundings. Mere reduction in the price of the commodity dealt in might be dearly paid for by the ruin of such a class.[1]

The first of the antitrust laws was the **Sherman Antitrust Act** of 1890, which outlawed contracts, combinations, trusts, and conspiracies in restraint of commerce. It also declared illegal conspiracies that monopolize or attempt to monopolize any area of commerce. The law allows both government actions to break up monopolies (as was done with Standard Oil and American Tobacco in 1911, and with AT&T in 1984) and private antitrust lawsuits.

In 1914, two more antitrust laws were enacted. The **Clayton Act** focused on mergers, "tying contracts" under which the seller of a good prohibits the buyer from doing business with competitors, and interlocking directorates that allow individuals to control boards of several competing firms. The **Federal Trade Commission Act** of the same year broadly outlawed "unfair methods of competition," without clearly defining the term, and established an independent agency, the Federal Trade Commission (FTC) to regulate business practices that are perceived as unfair.

In 1936, the **Clayton Act** was amended by the **Robinson-Patman Act,** which strengthened the law against price discrimination. It is often called the "Anti-Chain-Store Act" because its main purpose appears to have been to keep new, more efficient retailers like the A&P grocery chain from undercutting the prices of small local stores. In 1950, the **Clayton Act** was further amended by the **Celler-Kefauver Act,** which strengthened its provisions against mergers.

The wealth and power of trusts such as the railroads, oil, and steel threatened smaller scale businesses.

_____

[1] *United States vs. Trans-Missouri Freight Ass'n.,* 166 U.S. 323 (1897).

Antitrust Policy

The antitrust laws were not originally motivated by economic abstractions like market failure and deadweight loss. Those theoretical constructs had not yet been developed at the time they were passed. Later, however, economists attempted to reconcile the populist impulse behind the original antitrust laws with the considerations of efficiency and market performance that are focal points of neoclassical economics. This market-failure view of antitrust was expressed by the influential economist F. M. Scherer, who wrote that "the enforcement of antitrust laws is one of the more important weapons wielded by government in its effort to harmonize the profit-seeking behavior of private enterprises with the public interest."[2] Guided by this general concept, antitrust policy focused on several specific types of behavior.

Price fixing

Attempt by two or more firms to co-operate in setting prices

PRICE FIXING   Economists have often singled out **price fixing** as one of the practices that most clearly violates the Sherman Act's strictures against "substantial lessening of competition." Competing firms are not to form cartels. They must make their pricing decisions on their own. Following this view, the courts and antitrust officials have tended to treat price fixing as a per se violation of the law—which means that only the fact of a price-fixing agreement need be proven in order to win a conviction. It is not necessary to prove that the price-fixing attempt was successful or that the prices set were unreasonable. Also, accused price fixers cannot defend themselves on the ground that their action might have had beneficial effects.

Besides making price fixing illegal, the law has been interpreted as applying to other forms of cooperative conduct that might affect prices indirectly. For example, certain practices in which cartels engage, such as agreeing to restrict output or divide markets, have been treated just as severely as agreements on prices.

Horizontal mergers

Mergers of firms that compete in the same market

Vertical mergers

Mergers of firms with a supplier-purchaser relationship

Conglomerate mergers

Mergers of firms in unrelated markets

MERGERS   After the Clayton Act was amended by the Celler-Kefauver Act in 1950, regulation of mergers become a major part of antitrust policy. In addition to opposing **horizontal mergers** (mergers of firms that compete in the same market), the government often challenged **vertical mergers** (mergers of firms with a supplier-customer relationship, such as an automaker and a spark plug manufacturer). **Conglomerate mergers** (mergers of firms in unrelated markets, for example, an oil company and a retail chain) were also frequent targets of antitrust enforcement.

Mergers were never completely prohibited, however. Horizontal mergers, even between large firms, may be permitted if the merger would increase efficiency, perhaps because one of the firms would fail without the merger, or because international competition is strong enough to ensure good market performance. For example, the 1987 merger of Chrysler with failing American Motors reduced the number of U.S. auto makers by one but created a company that, it was hoped, would be more able to compete with Japanese rivals. A subsequent 1998 merger of Chrysler with Germany's Damlier Motors was approved based on similar hopes, but they proved unfounded. In 2007, Damlier sold Chrysler, leaving it once again independent but in a weaker competitive position than ever. Other large mergers that have been approved include the less than fully successful merger of AOL with Time-Warner and the more successful merger of Exxon with Mobil. Not all mergers are approved, however. For example, the government blocked the proposed merger of

One of the largest company mergers was between AOL and Time Warner

Coca-Cola with Dr Pepper, seeing no mitigating circumstances in that case. More recently, the government intervened to prevent a merger of defense giants Lockheed Martin and Northrop Grumman.

VERTICAL RESTRAINTS   Like vertical mergers, vertical restraints on trade involve agreements between a supplier and a customer. They are distinct from horizontal restraints, such as price-fixing, which involve agreements between direct competitors. Among the kinds of vertical restraints that have been challenged most often by antitrust authorities are resale price maintenance agreements, territorial restrictions, tying agreements, and exclusive dealing. Vertical restraints were at the heart of two of the antitrust suits filed against Microsoft Corporation in the 1990s by the U.S. Department of Justice and the European Commission. Those suits are described in *Economics in News 12.1.*

PRICE DISCRIMINATION   In the original Clayton Act, price discrimination was listed as an illegal practice, but that section was not widely enforced at first. Things changed in 1936. In that year the Clayton Act was amended by the Robinson-Patman Act, which greatly strengthened the law against price discrimination.

Economists have criticized the act for the ease with which it can be turned from a tool for promoting competition into a means by which a firm can shield itself from competition by its rivals. Largely for this reason, the government has sharply cut back its enforcement efforts against price discrimination in recent years.

Antitrust Reformers

In the mid-twentieth century, most economists accepted that antitrust policy was a logical corollary of the neoclassical view that any departure from perfect competition is a likely potential source of market failure. However, beginning in the 1980s, economists working from a number of perspectives became increasingly skeptical of antitrust policy, at least as then practiced.

Many antitrust reformers trace the flaws in past policy to its failure to take into account such considerations as transaction costs and the scarcity value of information. In the light of such considerations, many business practices that once seemed harmful now appear benign. According to reformers, the main enforcement targets should be conspiracies to fix prices or divide markets, horizontal mergers that would create very large market shares, and predatory actions aimed at harming competitors (with predation carefully distinguished from active competition). Enforcement actions should not overemphasize vertical restraints, nor should they be directed at small horizontal mergers or any vertical or conglomerate merger or at price discrimination.

In setting forth a program for the reform of antitrust policy, Robert Bork wrote, in 1978, that these are "not prescriptions for the nonenforcement of the antitrust laws, but rather for their enforcement in a way that advances, rather than retards, competition and consumer welfare."[3] Beginning about that time, a number of academic critics of traditional antitrust policy left their universities for influential government posts. Among them were William Baxter, who headed the antitrust

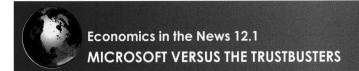

Economics in the News 12.1
MICROSOFT VERSUS THE TRUSTBUSTERS

Microsoft Corporation is one of the great entrepreneurial successes of our times. Founded in 1975 by Bill Gates and Paul Allen, it got its big break when it secured a license in 1981 to write an operating system for the new IBM PC. It used the success of the MS-DOS operating system it created for IBM to increase its market share among competing hardware makers until, by the end of the 1990s, it was selling more than 90% of all personal computer operating systems worldwide. In the process, Bill Gates became famous as the world's wealthiest individual.

Not surprisingly, a company with such a dominant position in the market became a target of antitrust investigations. In 1994, the U.S. Department of Justice brought a complaint against Microsoft based on the alleged illegal use of exclusionary contracts and predatory conduct to maintain its dominant market position. The heart of the case consisted of a series of allegations about the relationship between Microsoft's operating system and its Internet

Bill Gates, founder of Microsoft Corporation

Explorer browser. The government considered Microsoft's decision to "bundle" the browser together with the operating system to be an illegal exclusionary agreement. In addition, it considered the practice of giving away Internet Explorer without charge to be a form of predatory pricing. Both were seen as having the principal objective of placing the rival Netscape browser at a disadvantage.

Microsoft countered that the software market was more competitive than the Justice Department claimed. Its 90 percent market share could be attributed to "network effects" that are at work in any market where there is an advantage for two users to share a product or standard. However, it saw its dominant position as constantly under threat of "catastrophic entry" by some new technology. As a result, Microsoft was driven to keep its prices low (just one-sixteenth of the theoretical profit maximizing price, by one estimate) and constantly innovate. Although it was a large firm, it argued that it served its customers well.

After years of litigation, a final settlement with the Department of Justice was reached in 2004. The settlement did not prevent Microsoft from tying its browser to its operating system—the cornerstone of the government's original case. It did require Microsoft to be more generous in providing information on the details of its operating system to rival software developers. The final result has hardly had an earth-shattering impact on the software market.

The settlement with the DOJ did not end Microsoft's antitrust troubles, however. While the U.S. suit was in progress, the European Commission, which has antitrust authority for the European Union, brought its own case. Although it focused on Microsoft's media player and its rivals rather than Internet browsers, in many ways it was similar to that of the U.S. Department of Justice.

On balance, the European Commission has been tougher on Microsoft than the U.S. government. Its proposed settlement will—if fully implemented—prevent bundling of the media player, require strict sharing of information on software systems, and impose a large fine. At this writing, the parties are still litigating the final interpretation of the settlement.

division of the Department of Justice during the first term of the Reagan administration, and James C. Miller III, who headed the Federal Trade Commission. Other critics, including Bork, Richard Posner, and Ralph Winter, were appointed to federal judgeships.

Meanwhile, trends in legal education were also having an effect on the thinking of antitrust lawyers. Legal education has long stressed learning from past cases and judicial opinions. Today, however, this aspect of legal training is often supplemented with formal training in economics. As a result, students of antitrust law are encouraged to focus more closely on the questions of efficiency and consumer welfare raised by the cases with which they deal.

Entrepreneurship and Antitrust

Another group of critics, including representatives of the modern Austrian school, see a neglect of entrepreneurship as one of the fundamental problems of antitrust policy. Entrepreneurship, as defined in Chapter 1, is the activity of looking for new possibilities, making use of new ways of doing things, being alert to new opportunities, and overcoming old limits. In the world of business, the success or failure of a firm is critically dependent on its entrepreneurial abilities.[4]

Static efficiency

The ability of an economy to get the greatest degree of consumer satisfaction from given amounts of resources and technology

Dynamic efficiency

The ability of an economy to increase consumer satisfaction through innovation and technological change

The problem with traditional antitrust theory, say this group of critics, is that it focuses too much on **static efficiency**—the ability of an economy to get the greatest possible amount of consumer satisfaction with given amounts of resources and technology. Static efficiency measures how well the economy performs at a given time with given resources and technology; but the performance of an economy also depends on its **dynamic efficiency**—its success in increasing the rate of output per unit of resources. Dynamic efficiency is a measure of the rate at which the production possibility frontier shifts outward over time as a result of innovation and technological change. In the long run, dynamic—not static—efficiency is seen as the engine of growth and prosperity.

If every feature of the economy that promoted static efficiency also contributed to dynamic efficiency, the distinction between the two would hardly matter. However, there are reasons to think that this may not necessarily be the case. One key issue is the relationship between market structure and market performance. Much of traditional antitrust theory is built on the neoclassical view that perfectly competitive markets are the most efficient in the static sense, and monopoly is the least efficient. However, when efficiency is viewed in dynamic terms, the superiority of perfect competition is not so clear. It has been argued that the traditional categories of market structure are largely irrelevant to market performance measured in dynamic terms. This view is often referred to as the Schumpeter hypothesis, after the Austrian-born economist Joseph Schumpeter, who first brought it to widespread attention (see *Who Said It? Who Did It? 12.1*). Schumpeter and others suggested that in some cases large, oligopolistic firms might outperform small, perfectly competitive firms in dynamic terms.

According to Schumpeter, the source of innovation and technological change is competition—but competition among entrepreneurs, not the kind found in perfectly competitive markets. He saw two ways in which entrepreneurial competition promotes dynamic efficiency even when it leads, at least temporarily, to some degree of monopoly power.

First, Schumpeter points out, the hope of achieving monopoly power is often the entrepreneur's chief incentive for competition. The first firm to obtain new knowledge and put it to use is able to make pure economic profits because its new discovery gives it a temporary monopoly. If each new product had to be brought out at a price that just covered cost, or if each cost-reducing innovation had to be followed by a matching reduction in price, there would be little reason to innovate at all. If the first firm to adjust to changing conditions were unable to increase the gap between costs and revenues by doing so, there would be no incentive to be first. Competition among

Who Said It? Who Did It? 12.1
JOSEPH SCHUMPETER ON COMPETITION AND ENTREPRENEURSHIP

Joseph Schumpeter was born in 1883 in a small city in what is now the Czech Republic, then part of the Austro-Hungarian Empire. He studied law at the University of Vienna and attended lectures by the leading economists of the day, including some of the founders of the Austrian school. He served briefly as Austrian minister of finance after World War I. In 1932, he left Austria for Harvard University, where he wrote most of the works for which he is known today.

Schumpeter had little use for the kind of economics that reduces everything to graphs and equations. He thought economic theories paid too little attention to the role of the entrepreneur. He saw competition among entrepreneurs, rather than the abstract notion of perfect competition, as the source of economic progress. As he wrote in *Capitalism, Socialism, and Democracy:*

The competition that counts is competition from the new commodity, the new technology, the new source of supply, the new type of organization (the largest scale unit of control, for instance)—competition which commands a decisive cost or quality advantage and which strikes not at the margins of the profits and the outputs of the existing firms, but at their foundations and their very lives. This kind of competition is as much more effective than the other as a bombardment is in comparison with forcing a door, and so much more important that it becomes a matter of comparative indifference whether competition in the ordinary sense functions more or less promptly; the powerful lever that in the long run expands output and brings down prices is in any case made of other stuff.

"In this respect," Schumpeter added, "perfect competition is not only impossible but inferior and has not title to being set up as a model of ideal efficiency."

SOURCE: Joseph Schumpeter, *Capitalism, Socialism, and Democracy* (New York: Harper & Row, 1942, 1942k), 84–85, 105.

entrepreneurs is competition for monopoly power, at least in the short run. In this sense, monopoly is not the opposite of competition but, rather, a normal result of it.

Second, monopoly power acts to spur competition. This is true in the sense that an industry in which monopoly profits are being made tends to attract entrepreneurs from the outside. This applies both to the entry of new firms and to indirect competition by substitutes. For example, each attempt by OPEC to exploit its monopoly power over the price of oil has led to a speedup in the rate of oil exploration and also to innovations in alternative energy sources and conservation techniques. In this sense, monopoly is an impetus to competition.

The Future of Antitrust Policy

Over the years, reformers succeeded in making a number of important changes in antitrust policy. In many respects, their once-radical ideas have become the new conventional wisdom. Does this mean that antitrust policy will play a permanently reduced role in economic affairs, with possible repeal of some of the more restrictive statutes? Perhaps, but perhaps not.

For one thing, outside the economics profession the old populist view of antitrust action remains alive. As one critic of recent reforms has put it, "antitrust [law] was intended also to further a social and moral vision of America. At the core of that vision was a conviction that the past greatness, and future potential, of the country depended on the kind of character—resourceful, practical, and determined—that only competitive individualism would foster."[5] (Consumer activist and former FTC Chairman Michael Pertschuk put it more simply when he characterized the proper focus of antitrust policy as a "Jeffersonian preference for dispersed power" applied not only to the dispersion of power among various branches of government but also to the dispersion of economic power among a multitude of relatively small firms.)

Regulation of Natural Monopoly

The aim of antitrust policy is to prevent one firm, or a few firms acting in concert, from gaining control of a market. However, there are some cases, known as natural monopolies, in which there is no practical way to avoid the dominance of one firm. In this section we examine policies intended to improve the performance of these markets, and also the unintended consequences such policies sometimes bring about.

The Policy Problem

A *natural monopoly* is an industry in which total costs are kept to a minimum by having just one producer serve the whole market. Local gas, electric, cable TV, and water services are often cited as examples. It is easy for one such utility to hook up more customers once it has run its lines into their neighborhood, but it is wasteful and costly for a number of different companies to run lines down the same street.

The policy problem raised by a natural monopoly is how to keep the firm from taking advantage of its position to raise prices and restrict output. Consider the example shown in Figure 12.1. That firm, an electric utility, has constant marginal costs and a negatively sloped long-run average cost curve. The demand curve intersects the long-run average cost curve at quantity Q_1, not far from the minimum efficient scale of production. If this output were divided between two firms, each of which produced half of quantity Q_1, the cost per unit would be a lot higher—and still more so if there were more than two firms.

If one unregulated firm operates in a market, it can be expected to act like a pure monopolist. Instead of producing Q_1 it will produce Q_2, which corresponds to the intersection of the firm's marginal revenue and marginal cost curves. The price that corresponds to this output is P_2, which is far above marginal cost. This is too small an output and too high a price to permit efficient production.

The Regulatory Solution

It appears, then, that in a natural monopoly competition by two or more firms is inefficient, as is monopoly pricing by a single firm. The traditional solution is to allow just one firm to operate but to regulate the price at which it can sell its output. For example, the firm may be limited to a price of no more than P_1, the price at which the demand curve intersects the long-run average cost curve in Figure 12.1. With this price ceiling in force, the firm becomes a price taker for output levels up to Q_1, because even if it kept output below that level, it would be prevented from further raising the price. The

FIGURE 12.1   REGULATION OF A NATURAL MONOPOLY

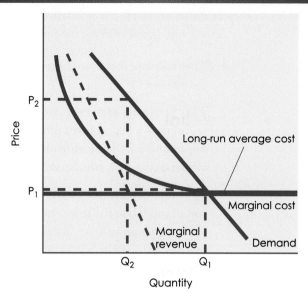

This graph shows the cost and demand curves for a natural monopoly such as an electric utility. As an unregulated monopolist, the firm would make the maximum profit by charging price P_2 and selling quantity Q_2. If regulators impose a maximum price of P_1, the firm will find it worthwhile to produce quantity Q_1.

maximum profit is earned under the regulated price by producing Q_1 units of output. This is a lower price and a greater quantity than would result either from an unregulated pure monopoly or from production by two or more competing firms.

For the market to be perfectly efficient, the price would have to be reduced to the level of marginal cost, which is slightly lower than P_1. At any price lower than P_1, however, the firm would suffer a loss. It could survive in the long run only if it were subsidized. By allowing the firm to charge price P_1, which is high enough to just cover all costs, the regulators would avoid the need for a subsidy while giving up only a small degree of efficiency.

RATE OF RETURN AS A FOCUS OF REGULATION   The correct regulated price in Figure 12.1 is easy to identify because the shapes and positions of the demand and cost curves are right there on the page. In the real world, however, regulators do not have complete information about demand and cost. Lacking this information, they set the regulated price indirectly by focusing on the **rate of return** earned by the firm. The rate of return is the firm's accounting profit expressed as a percentage of its net worth.

To see why the rate of return is a useful focus of regulatory policy, consider the implications of setting various prices. If the price is set equal to average total cost, the firm will earn a "normal profit," that is, a rate of return equal to the opportunity cost of capital. If the price is higher than average total cost, the firm will earn more than a normal profit, that is, enough to cover the opportunity cost of capital with some left

Rate of return

A firm's accounting profit expressed as a percentage of its net worth

320 over as economic profit. If the price is set below average total cost, the firm will earn

over as economic profit. If the price is set below average total cost, the firm will earn less than a normal profit. Because revenue is insufficient to meet all opportunity costs, including that of capital, the firm will suffer an economic loss.

Armed with this reasoning, the regulators proceed in five steps:

1. They measure the value of the firm's capital—say, $1.2 million. This is called the *rate base*.

2. They measure the average rate of return for the economy, that is, the normal rate of profit. Suppose this turns out to be 15 percent per year. (In practice, steps 1 and 2 are more difficult than they sound, but for our purposes the regulators can be given the benefit of the doubt.)

3. They multiply the rate base by the permitted rate of return to calculate a total cost of capital for the firm—in this case, $180,000 per year. This sum should be enough both to make interest payments on the portion of the firm's capital that was acquired by borrowing and to yield an accounting profit high enough to compensate the owners for their investment in the firm.

4. They ask the firm to propose a price or set of prices that it thinks will allow it to meet its capital costs.

5. As time goes by, they keep track of the firm's actual rate of return, cutting the price if it rises above the normal level and allowing it to rise if returns fall below the normal level.

LIMITATIONS OF RATE-OF-RETURN REGULATION   For a number of reasons, rate-of-return regulation may not always achieve its goals of lower prices and greater output. Economists of the public choice school point to possible influence over regulators by political rent seekers. This may occur, for example, if regulated firms "capture" the regulatory agency by gaining control over the appointment of regulators, or if regulators follow lax policies in the hope of finding well-paid jobs in the industry after their terms as regulators expire. On the other hand, in some areas groups that represent consumers have captured regulatory agencies. They seek the short-run gains that come from keeping rates low without regard for the regulated firms' long-run need to attract capital in order to maintain capacity and service quality.

Another possible problem is that regulators may not know enough about the industry to control its rate of return. It is by no means easy to measure such factors as the regulated firm's stock of capital, its actual rate of return, and the opportunity cost of capital. The more regulators must rely on guesswork, the less likely they are to be effective.

If regulators set rates of return that are either higher or lower than the opportunity cost of capital, serious problems may follow. For example, a study by Harvey Averch and Leland Johnson suggested that in the 1950s and 1960s regulated rates for electricity tended to be too high.[6] They allowed utilities to achieve a rate of return that was higher than the opportunity cost of capital. This gave the utilities' stockholders an indirect way of taking advantage of their monopoly position. They could raise capital to build new plants, whether they were needed or not, and then add the plants into their rate base. The regulators then would allow them to raise their rates enough not only to pass along the costs of the new plants but to earn a pure economic profit as well. The outcome—now known as the *A-J effect*—was that too high a rate of return led to wasteful overinvestment in the regulated industry.

By the 1980s the situation had changed. Some economists came to fear that rates of return had fallen too low. If this were so, it would cause the A-J effect to operate in reverse. Utilities would avoid investing in new plants even when the plants would be justified from the consumer's point of view. Such a policy of "rate suppression" might keep rates low for consumers for many years before problems become apparent; but as old plants wear out, the quality of service falls.

In short, either too high or too low an allowed rate of return is harmful. In their search for efficiency regulators must walk a narrow line between two kinds of errors.

Regulation of Competitive Industries

Natural monopolies are not the only industries to come under regulation. There are many others—transportation, banking, finance, and communications, to name just a few—that have long been regulated even though their market structures, in the absence of regulation, are oligopolistic, monopolistically competitive, and in some cases, close to perfectly competitive. In this section we look at the regulation of competitive behavior in such industries.

Historical Origins

Railroads first came under regulation in the late nineteenth century, but the big surge in regulation came in the 1930s. One tends to think of the Great Depression mainly in terms of high unemployment; however, another major feature of the Depression was low prices. Between 1929 and 1933 the consumer price index dropped about 25 percent. Today most economists would explain both the high unemployment and the falling prices in macroeconomic terms, blaming them on low aggregate demand, inappropriate monetary policy, and so on. At the time, however, people tended to blame the high unemployment levels on low prices. If only prices could be raised, business leaders said, it would be possible to put more workers on the payroll.

Many contemporary observers blamed excessive competition on low prices. Believing that too much competition was a barrier to economic recovery, Congress, in 1933, passed the National Recovery Act, which encouraged firms to use cartel-like methods to prop up prices. The Supreme Court declared that particular act unconstitutional, but similar legislation that applied only to specific industries survived. Two of the most important industries that were regulated in order to limit competition were trucking, which was brought under the control of the Interstate Commerce Commission (ICC) in 1935, and airlines, which came under the regulation of the Civil Aeronautics Board (CAB) in 1938.

Rate and Entry Regulations in Transportation

The case of transportation regulation reveals some key differences between the regulation of competitive industries and that of natural monopolies. Two of these differences were a focus on limiting entry by new firms and a tendency to set minimum rather than maximum prices. The traditional argument for regulation of natural monopolies was that without regulation prices would rise too high. In the case of airlines and trucking, the concern was that without regulation prices would fall too low.

It is generally agreed that regulation of trucking and airlines achieved the goal of raising prices and limiting the number of firms in those industries. As the years passed, however, many economists began to have second thoughts as to whether high prices and limited competition were the proper goals of government policy. With the advent of high inflation rates in the 1970s, the doubts about regulation grew stronger; economists turned almost unanimously against the regulation of entry and the setting of minimum rates in competitive industries.

Regulation and Political Rent Seeking

Critics of transportation regulation tended to view this area of policy as an example of political rent seeking. They saw regulation as a device that permits rival firms to form cartels, which enable them to raise prices above opportunity costs and earn profits in excess of those that would be possible in a more competitive environment.

It is easy to see why this theory developed. In an earlier chapter we saw that two major weaknesses of most cartels are inability to control competition by nonmembers and inability to keep members from cheating on price agreements. The laws that gave the ICC and the CAB authority over trucking and airlines were directed at these problems. Both agencies became highly restrictive in terms of entry by new firms. (The CAB did not let in a single new major airline for its first forty years, and the ICC was only slightly less restrictive.) Further, both agencies were granted, and used, the authority to prevent carriers from cutting prices below specified minimum levels, as well as the authority to regulate maximum rates.

A number of studies carried out in the 1960s and 1970s seemed to support the cartel theory of regulation. Many of them were based on comparisons of regulated and unregulated markets. One study, for example, showed that unregulated intrastate airline fares in California and Texas were only about half of the regulated interstate fares for similar distances. Other studies compared regulated freight rates for industrial goods with those for agricultural produce, which had been exempted from regulation. Again, the regulated rates seemed substantially higher.

Regulatory Reform

In the late 1970s long-standing criticisms of transportation regulation began to be translated into policy. Through legislation and the appointment of reform-minded regulators, restrictions on competition were eased for passenger airlines, air freight, trucking, and intercity bus service. There was also extensive deregulation of railroad rates and a relaxation of barriers to competition between railroads and motor freight. The CAB was abolished, and a few of its former powers were granted to the Federal Aviation Administration (FAA), whose main concern is air safety. The ICC stayed in business with a reduced staff and much more limited functions until 1995, when it, too, was terminated.

In addition to the reform of regulation in the transportation industries, there were significant regulatory reforms in other industries. In financial industries, banks were freed from regulations that had barred them from competing by offering higher interest rates and new services. In communications, the breakup of AT&T and the rise of cell phones brought competition to the telephone industry, and the Federal Communications Commission changed the regulatory atmosphere in radio and television broadcasting.

Despite generally positive outcomes, deregulation has not always been unqualified successes. Finding the right balance between overly restrictive and overly permissive regulation has been especially difficult in the financial industry. Many critics have placed at least part of the blame for the financial crisis that began in 2007 on inadequate regulation of banks and other financial institutions, which allowed them to take excessive risk while benefiting from an implicit promise of government bailouts in case of failure. It seems likely that in the aftermath of this crisis there will be a trend toward increased regulation of the financial industry.

Health and Safety Regulation

In the 1970s, as some forms of regulation dating from the Great Depression were being cut back, other areas of regulation were expanding. Among the agencies reflecting this trend were the Occupational Safety and Health Administration (OSHA), the Consumer Product Safety Commission (CPSC), the National Highway and Traffic Safety Administration (NHTSA), and the Environmental Protection Agency (EPA). In addition, some older agencies, such as the Food and Drug Administration (FDA), became more active than before. These agencies are not directly concerned with prices and competition; rather, their focus is on the kinds of goods that are produced and how they are produced. Let us take a look at what economists have to say about health and safety regulation, an issue that has provoked much debate.

Normative Issues

The goal of health and safety regulation is to make the world a safer, healthier, more pleasant place in which to live. Because this is a goal with which no one can argue, why are regulations designed to achieve it a matter of debate? Part of the answer is that even when goals are agreed upon, there can be disagreements about the best ways to pursue those goals. Such disagreements, which belong to the realm of positive economics, will be discussed shortly. Other major sources of controversy are normative. Although almost everyone believes that health and safety are good in themselves, there are disagreements about their relationship to other worthwhile goals. Two such normative disagreements often threaten to overshadow any consideration of the positive economics of health and safety regulation.

They are the question of valuing health and safety and that of deciding whose values should shape policy when values differ.

CAN HEALTH AND SAFETY BE ASSIGNED AN ECONOMIC VALUE?

The first issue is whether one should even consider trade-offs between human health and safety on the one hand and material well-being on the other. Many supporters of strong, strictly enforced health and safety regulations argue that there is no way to measure the value of human life. Regulations, therefore, should be set without regard to economic trade-offs or cost-benefit ratios of any kind.

Others, however, do not share this view. They do not belittle the value of human life; rather, they see no point in condemning something that people do every day—and people do sacrifice their own health and safety in favor of other goals daily. They choose the convenience of car travel over the discomforts of bus travel, even though buses are known to be many times safer than cars. They take high-paying jobs in cities rather than low-paying jobs in the country, even though city air is known to be much less healthful than country air. They have medical checkups once a year but not twice a year or once a month because the gain in terms of health is not worth the sacrifice in terms of time and money.

WHOSE VALUES?   The second normative question remains to be answered even if one concedes that cost-benefit analysis can be reasonably applied in the areas of health and safety. That is the question of whose values should govern any trade-offs made between health and safety on the one hand and economic costs on the other. Should policy be guided by the values of the people who receive the benefits and bear the costs, or should it be left to the judgment of experts? In practical terms, this comes down to the question of when people should simply be warned about health and safety hazards and when they should be forced to be safe and healthy whether they want to or not.

Strictly speaking, economics as a science has nothing to say about these normative issues. Nevertheless, economists often strongly believe that it is reasonable to consider economic costs and benefits in making health and safety decisions and to allow well-informed people to make those choices for themselves whenever possible. When such an economist discusses health and safety regulation with someone who believes in health and safety at any cost, what is likely to take place is a fight rather than a rational debate. This is unfortunate because there are some things that economics as a science—that is, positive economics—can contribute to the controversy over health and safety regulation.

Positive Issues

One area of positive economics on which economists and regulators should be able to agree is ensuring that regulatory goals, once chosen, are achieved at the lowest cost. Consider the matter of giving local decision makers the greatest possible leeway in choosing the lowest-cost means of complying with regulation. One way to do this is to issue regulations in the form of performance standards rather than engineering controls. Performance standards are rules that specify the results to be achieved, whereas engineering controls are rules that specify particular techniques to be used or equipment to be installed. Chapter 6 discussed the trend in environmental regulation toward performance-based regulations like cap-and-trade programs or emission charges and away from measures that mandate specific engineering controls. Although perhaps not to the same extent, health and safety regulation has moved in the same direction.

Another issue on which positive economics can focus is evaluating the benefits of a proposed regulation relative to its costs. For example, in 1984 the EPA issued a study that showed that banning lead in gasoline would have benefits totaling $1.8 billion. In the EPA's view, this would more than offset the cost, which it estimated at about $.02 per gallon of gasoline. Ethyl Corporation, which produced the lead additive that the EPA sought to ban, said that the agency had left out a major cost. According to Ethyl, banning lead would mean that older cars (which had been designed before lead-free gasoline was widely available) would need valve repairs much more often. In Ethyl's estimate, the cost of these repairs would be $18 billion per year, far more than the benefits. In this case, cost-benefit analysis narrowed the grounds of the dispute over elimination of lead in gasoline and allowed progress toward agreement on terms of the phase-out.

Still another area of regulation in which positive economics can be helpful is tracing the unintended consequences of regulation. For example, Chapter 5 discussed the unintended consequences of auto safety regulation, which were suspected of having the unintended effect of increasing hazards to pedestrians and bicyclists. Similarly, regulations requiring safety caps on aspirin bottles had the unintended effect of making it more likely that people would leave the caps off altogether, thus, in some cases, increasing hazards to children. A study by Richard L. Stroup and John C. Goodman detailed dozens of other cases in which well-intentioned health and safety regulations have had unintended effects that endanger health and safety.[7]

Summary

1. **Which business practices are illegal under the antitrust laws?** *Antitrust laws* seek to control market structure and the competitive behavior of firms. The oldest of the antitrust laws is the Sherman Act of 1890, which outlaws combinations and conspiracies in restraint of trade and makes any attempt to monopolize a market illegal. The Clayton and Federal Trade Commission Acts of 1914 seek to control unfair trade practices. The Clayton Act, together with the Celler-Kefauver Act of 1950, controls mergers. The Robinson-Patman Act of 1935 regulates price discrimination.

2. **How have economists' views on antitrust policy changed over time?** For many years vigorous enforcement of antitrust laws had widespread support among economists. Recently, however, economists' views have changed. Reformers, armed with new views about the efficiency effects of business practices, urge greater consideration for consumer welfare, fewer restrictions on all but the largest horizontal mergers, and less attention to vertical restraints and price discrimination. Public choice theorists see antitrust laws in terms of political rent seeking by small economic entities at the expense of large ones. Economists of the modern Austrian school see antitrust laws as damaging to entrepreneurship and innovations.

3. **How are natural monopolies regulated, and what problems are posed by regulation?** Natural monopolies, such as electric utilities, are

subject to regulation that aims to prevent excessive *rates of return*. Regulation does not always work smoothly, however. If too high or too low a rate of return is set, the regulated firm's investment incentives will be distorted.

4. **Why are some industries regulated despite their inherently competitive structure?** Many industries have been regulated even though they are not natural monopolies. Some economists have seen such regulation as a form of rent seeking. In effect, regulation amounts to government imposition of a cartel. The rents generated by regulatory "cartels" are shared among firms, their workers, and their customers.

5. **What are the current trends in health and safety regulation?** Regulation has been growing in the areas of health and safety at the same time that it has been decreasing in such industries as transportation, communication, and financial services. Disputes in these areas of regulation raise both normative and positive issues. The normative issues include the question of whether one can place an economic value on health and safety, as well as the issue of whose values should guide regulatory policy. The positive issues include finding ways to keep down the costs of regulation, compare its costs and benefits, and trace its unintended consequences.

Key Terms

Problems and Topics for Discussion

1. **Antitrust laws and economic rights** "Everyone should have the unrestricted right both to sell goods and services in any market and to withhold goods or services from sale." Are the antitrust laws consistent with this statement? Why or why not?

2. **Public ownership of utilities** In some cities, utilities such as electric companies and gas distribution companies are owned by the city government. What do you think are the advantages and disadvantages of public ownership of a natural monopoly compared with regulated private ownership? With unregulated private ownership?

3. **Value of trucking permits** Before 1980 the ICC limited the number of trucking firms that could serve any given route. Often the only way a new firm could get permission to serve a route was to buy the "certificate" (permit) of a firm that already served that route. Some of those permits were worth hundreds of thousands of dollars. Why were the permits worth so much? After deregulation the value of such permits fell to zero. Why do you think this happened?

4. **Regulation of taxis** How are taxis regulated in the area where you live? Is there free entry into the market? Are minimum or maximum fares set? How easy is it to get a cab if you need one? Would you suggest any changes in regulatory policy for your area?

5. **Highway speed limits** In 1987, states were given the option of raising the speed limit on rural interstate highways from 55 to 65 miles per hour. The move was controversial because it was feared that the rate of highway fatalities would increase as a result of higher speeds. How would you go about judging whether a change in the speed limit is a good idea? Discuss both positive and normative aspects of the question.

Case for Discussion

Tipping the Balance

The growing popularity of sport utility vehicles (SUVs) and the widely publicized rollover deaths in Ford Explorers using Firestone tires in the 1990s have drawn the critical eye of government regulators. After the Ford-Firestone incident, Congress required the National Highway Traffic Safety Administration (NHTSA) to test automobiles on a track. Prior to the increased fear of rollovers, the NHTSA used a mathematical formula to estimate a vehicle's star rating. For instance, a five-star rating meant that an automobile has a less than 10 percent chance of rollover in a single accident.

The NHTSA track tests were incorporated into safety ratings beginning with the 2004 models. Compared with prior years, the 2004 results showed improvement for a few SUVs. This added fuel to lobbyists' arguments against increased regulations targeting the SUV, such as gas mileage restrictions and subsidies for promoting the development of hybrids. "SUV Rollover Hysteria Appears Misplaced," said a news release from the lobbyist group Sport Utility Vehicle Owners of America.

Others remained unconvinced. "I think there are many SUVs, probably a majority of SUVs that have stability issues," said Brian O'Neill, president of the Insurance Institute for Highway Safety. "What consumers really need to know, if they're bound and determined to buy an SUV, is which ones are more stable than others." People often equate the size of SUVs with increased safety, but their high center of gravity makes them more prone to rollover compared with other automobiles.

"You don't have to get the C.G. [center of gravity] very high to get the vehicle to a point where it's unstable," said Paul Mercurio, an engineer for Bosch. Bosch makes stability control technology that helps reduce rollovers in cars and trucks.

Are rollovers common? The SUV industry lobbyists often cite that only 2.5 percent of accidents involve a rollover. However, among drivers and passengers involved in a rollover accident, one-third of them die as a result of the accident. So, while rollovers are rare, the chances of surviving are less than comforting. According to statistics from the Insurance Institute for Highway Safety, SUVs had higher fatality rates compared with cars. Between 2000 and 2001, 1997–1999 model year cars weighing between 3,500 and 3,999 pounds had a fatality rate of 87 per million registered vehicles. This compares with a fatality rate of 160 for SUVs in the same weight class and model years.

"Personally, I believe a minivan is as functional as an SUV without the handling questions," he said. "It's typically a less-expensive vehicle. It's just not trendy."

SOURCE: Information from Danny Hakim, "The Tipping Point for Safety," *The New York Times*, February 22, 2004.

QUESTIONS

1. Suppose that Ford and Firestone offered to pay $1 million per fatal accident in the Ford Explorer. Is this a reasonable figure? To put it in human terms, consider the following two ways of looking at the offer:

   a. Imagine yourself in a hospital following a fatal rollover accident. A representative of the Ford Motor Company enters the room and offers you a choice:
   You can either have $1 million or be restored to health. Which option would you take?

   b. Imagine that you are about to buy an SUV and that a stability control system is optional rather than required equipment. You expect to drive the car 100,000 miles before junking it. If the car has no stability control, your chances of being killed in a rollover accident over that period are about 16 in 10,000. If it has a stability control system and you use it regularly, your chances of being killed over the same period are about 2 in 10,000. If you value your life at $1 million, you should be willing to pay up to $1,000 for the stability control system.

What is the maximum you would actually be willing to pay?

2. Setting aside the issue of whether $1 million is the "right" value for a human life, do you agree in principle that a cost-benefit formula is the proper framework for making the decision about modifying the stability design of SUVs, or do you feel that cost doesn't really matter? If you were an SUV manufacturer, would you install stability-control safeguards at a cost of, say, $400 per vehicle? If you were a consumer rather than a manufacturer, how much would you pay for an optional, stability package that would prevent a rollover accident—more than $400, or less?

End Notes

1. *United States v. Trans-Missouri Freight Ass'n.*, 166 U.S. 323 (1897).

2. F. M. Scherer, *Industrial Market Structure and Economic Performance* (Chicago: Rand McNally, 1980), 491.

3. See Robert H. Bork, *The Antitrust Paradox* (New York: Basic Books, 1978), 405–406.

4. For a short exposition of Austrian antitrust views, see Armentano, "Efficiency, Liberty, and Antitrust Policy," *Cato Journal* (Winter 1985): 925–931. Those views are developed at greater length in *Antitrust and Monopoly: Anatomy of a Policy Failure* (New York: Wiley, 1982).

5. Robert A. Katzman, "The Attenuation of Antitrust," *Brookings Review* (Summer 1984): 24.

6. Harvey A. Averch and L. L. Johnson, "Behavior of the Firm under Regulatory Constraint," *American Economic Review* (December 1962): 1052–1069.

7. Richard L. Stroup and John C. Goodman, "Making the World Less Safe: The Unhealthy Trend in Health, Safety, and Environmental Regulation," National Center for Policy Analysis Policy Report no. 137, April 1989.

PART 4

Factor Markets and Income Distribution

CHAPTER 13

Pricing in Resource Markets

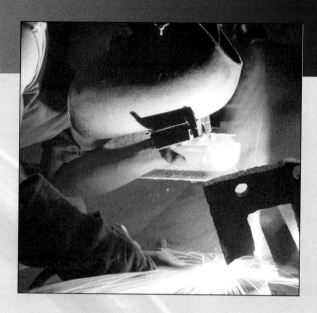

THIS CHAPTER TURNS to an important set of markets, called factor markets or resource markets, that we have referred to only indirectly up to this point. These are the markets in which firms obtain the inputs they need to carry on production. The first part of this chapter outlines a general theory of demand for inputs. In the second part, attention is focused on markets for labor, which is the most important category of input. In the final section we will apply the theory to markets for capital and natural resources.

Demand for Inputs

In many ways markets for inputs are similar to the product markets we have already studied. The theories of supply and demand and the tools of marginal analysis apply to resource markets just as they do to product markets. However, resource markets differ from product markets in one major respect. The buyers are firms, and the sellers, at least in some cases, are households. A theory of the demand for resources, therefore, must be based on an analysis of profit maximization by firms.

Objectives and Constraints

As in other branches of microeconomic theory, the first step toward a theory of demand for resources is to specify the objectives and constraints faced by firms. As in earlier chapters, we will assume that the objective is profit maximization. Three types of constraints will be considered.

1. *Production technology*   The firm is constrained in part by technology, which determines how inputs can be combined to produce outputs. When one variable input is considered, technological constraints can be represented as marginal physical product curves. Technology with more than one variable input can be represented using the graphical technique explained in the Chapter 8 Appendix, "Cost and Output with Two Variable Inputs."

2. *Demand for the product*   Firms buy resources not for their own sake but to use them as inputs in producing goods and services for sale. The demand for any input thus is said to be a **derived demand** because it ultimately reflects demand for the product that the input is used to produce.

3. *Resource cost*   The third constraint that a firm must consider in deciding how much of an input to purchase is the cost of obtaining that input. In competitive input markets that cost is simply the market price of the resource in question. Imperfectly competitive markets are considered later in the chapter.

Derived demand

Demand for a productive input that stems from the demand for the product the input is used to produce

Marginal Physical Product

In Chapter 8, we defined the *marginal physical product* of a resource as the increase in output that results from a one-unit increase in the input of that resource when the amounts of all other inputs used stay the same. For example, if using one additional worker-hour of labor to cultivate a turnip field yields an additional output of five turnips when no other input to the production process is changed, the marginal physical product of labor in that field is five turnips per labor hour.

As we saw earlier, the marginal physical product of a resource varies as the amount of it used changes, other things being equal. In particular, as the quantity of a single input increases while the quantities of all other inputs remain fixed, a point will be reached beyond which the marginal physical product of the variable input will decline. This principle is known as the *law of diminishing returns*.

Figure 13.1 shows total and marginal physical product curves for a firm that is subject to the law of diminishing returns over the range from 0 to 20 units of an input. As the

FIGURE 13.1   TOTAL AND MARGINAL PHYSICAL PRODUCT OF AN INPUT

(a)

Quantity of Input (1)	Total Physical Product (2)	Marginal Physical Product (3)
0	0	
1	20	20
2	39	19
3	57	18
4	74	17
5	90	16
6	105	15
7	119	14
8	132	13
9	144	12
10	155	11
11	165	10
12	174	9
13	182	8
14	189	7
15	195	6
16	200	5
17	204	4
18	207	3
19	209	2
20	210	1

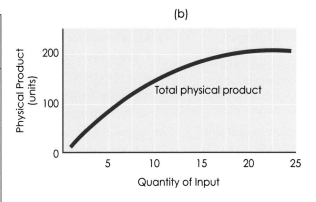

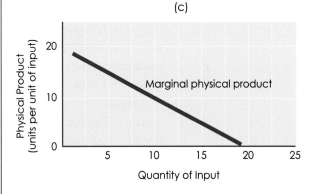

As the quantity of one resource input increases with the quantity of other inputs remaining unchanged, total physical product increases, but at a decreasing rate. As parts (a) and (c) of this figure show, marginal physical product decreases as the quantity of the employed input increases. This decrease is a direct result of the law of diminishing returns.

amount of this input is increased while the amounts of all other inputs used are held constant, output increases—but at a diminishing rate. The first unit of the input yields a marginal physical product of 20 units of output, the second a marginal physical product of 19 units of output, and so on. After the twentieth unit of input, marginal physical product drops to zero. A ceiling has been reached beyond which adding more of the variable input cannot produce more output unless the amounts of some of the fixed inputs are also increased. For example, if the variable input is labor, adding more than 20 workers may do nothing to increase output unless the amount of machinery available for the workers to use is increased as well. Beyond 20 units of input, where the marginal physical product of the variable input drops to zero, the total physical product curve becomes horizontal.

Marginal Revenue Product

Because the demand for a resource is a derived demand, the firm must consider the revenue it will earn from the sale of the output produced by an added unit of input as well

Marginal revenue product
_____

The change in revenue that results from the sale of the output produced by one additional unit of an input

Value of marginal product
_____

Marginal physical product times the product's per-unit price

as the input's marginal physical product. The change in revenue that results from the sale of the added output produced by a one-unit increase in the input of a resource is the **marginal revenue product** of that resource. The relationship of marginal revenue product to demand for the product must be considered separately for firms that are *price takers* and for those that are *price searchers* in their output markets.

For a firm that is a price taker in its output market, the price is constant regardless of the quantity sold. Marginal revenue for the competitive firm thus equals the price of the firm's output, which is constant for all quantities of output. For such a firm, then, marginal revenue product equals the **value of marginal product**, that is, marginal physical product times the output price.

If the firm is a price searcher in its output market, the price at which it sells its output will tend to vary as the amount of output changes. This will be the case in markets that are monopolies, oligopolies, or monopolistically competitive. As a price searcher, the firm must choose from among a menu of price-quantity combinations given by its negatively sloped demand curve. Because the price per unit decreases as output increases, marginal revenue per unit of output is always less than price per unit for a price searcher. (It is assumed that the firm uses simple monopoly pricing, not price discrimination or two-part pricing.) It follows, then, that the marginal revenue product for such a firm is less than the value of marginal product.

Figure 13.2 shows how marginal revenue product is calculated for a price searcher. The figure uses the same total physical product schedule that is used in Figure 13.1. Column 3 presents the firm's product demand curve, showing that the price at which output can be sold drops from $1.40 per unit at 20 units of output to $.45 at 210 units. Multiplying price by total physical product gives the total revenue that corresponds to each quantity of input, which is shown in column 4.

The differences between successive entries in the total revenue column give the marginal revenue product data, shown in column 5. For example, as input of the resource increases from 4 to 5 units, total output increases from 74 to 90 units while the price falls from $1.13 to $1.05 per unit. As column 4 shows, total revenue increases from $83.62 when 4 units of the input are used to $94.50 when 5 units of the input are used. This gives a marginal revenue product of $10.88 in the range from 4 to 5 units of input.

It can be verified that this marginal revenue product is less than the value of marginal product (not shown in the figure). The product price is $1.13 when 4 units of the input are used and $1.05 when 5 units of the input are used; thus, it averages $1.09 over the corresponding output range. Multiplying this by the marginal physical product of 16 (column 6 of the figure) gives a value of marginal product of $17.44 at the midpoint of the output range in question, compared with a marginal revenue product of $10.88.

As the price continues to fall, marginal revenue eventually becomes negative. Beyond that point, additional units of the input reduce total revenue even though they increase total physical product. The turning point comes at 10 units of input. Beyond that level, marginal revenue product is negative even though marginal physical product remains positive.

At every level of input, the marginal revenue product of the input equals the marginal physical product times the marginal revenue per unit of output. This relation-

FIGURE 13.2   MARGINAL REVENUE PRODUCT FOR A PRICE-SEARCHING FIRM

Quantity of Input (1)	Total Physical Product (2)	Price of Output (3)	Total Revenue (4)	Marginal Revenue Product (5)	Marginal Physical Product (6)	Marginal Revenue per Unit of Output (7)
0	0	—	0.00			
				$28.00	20	$1.40
1	20	$1.40	$28.00			
				22.90	19	1.21
2	39	1.31	50.90			
				18.36	18	1.02
3	57	1.22	69.26			
				14.36	17	.84
4	74	1.13	83.62			
				10.88	16	.68
5	90	1.05	94.50			
				7.88	15	.52
6	105	.98	102.38			
				5.32	14	.38
7	119	.91	107.70			
				3.18	13	.24
8	132	.84	110.88			
				1.44	12	.12
9	144	.78	112.32			
				.06	11	.01
10	155	.73	112.38			
				−1.00	10	−.10
11	165	.68	111.38			
				−1.76	9	−.20
12	174	.63	109.62			
				−2.24	8	−.28
13	182	.59	107.38			
				−2.48	7	−.35
14	189	.56	104.90			
				−2.52	6	−.42
15	195	.53	102.38			
				−2.38	5	−.47
16	200	.50	100.00			
				−2.08	4	−.52
17	204	.48	97.92			
				−1.66	3	−.55
18	207	.47	96.26			
				−1.16	2	−.58
19	209	.46	95.10			
				−.60	1	−.60
20	210	.45	94.50			

Note: Figures in columns 3, 4, 5, and 7 are rounded to the nearest cent.

This figure shows how marginal revenue product varies as the quantity of a resource input changes for a firm that faces a negatively sloped demand curve for its product. As column 3 shows, price falls as output increases in accordance with the demand for the firm's product. Total revenue begins to decrease after 10 units of output (the point at which marginal revenue per unit of output becomes negative) even though marginal physical product remains positive. Marginal revenue product can be calculated either as the difference between each entry in the total revenue column or as the product of marginal physical product and marginal revenue per unit of output.

Marginal resource cost

The amount by which a firm's total resource cost must increase for the firm to obtain an additional unit of that resource

ship is shown in columns 5 through 7 of Figure 13.2. The marginal revenue figures in column 7 are expressed in terms of dollars per unit of output, whereas those in column 5 are expressed in terms of dollars per unit of input.

Marginal Resource Cost

The third constraint that the firm must consider in determining how much of each resource to employ as a productive input is the cost of obtaining each additional unit of that resource, that is, its **marginal resource cost**.

We can begin by considering the case in which the markets where the firm buys its inputs are perfectly competitive, so that the firm is a price taker in those markets. This will be the case if the firm is only one of a large number of firms that are competing to buy a particular resource and if the amount of the resource it uses is only a small fraction of the total used by all firms. For a firm that buys as a price taker, the marginal resource cost equals the market price of that particular input. For example, if the market wage rate for clerical workers is $7 an hour, the marginal resource cost for clerical workers' labor is $7 an hour for any firm that is a price taker in the market for clerical workers.

Profit Maximization

To maximize profits, a firm must use just enough of each input to equalize marginal revenue product and marginal resource cost. If marginal revenue product exceeds marginal resource cost, hiring one more unit of the input will add more to revenue than to cost and, hence, will increase profit. If marginal resource cost exceeds marginal revenue product, *reducing* the amount of that input by one unit will reduce cost by more than revenue and thus increase profit. Only when marginal revenue product and marginal resource cost are equal will it be impossible for any change in the amount of the input to increase profit. In equation form, this rule can be stated as

$$MRC = MRP$$

where MRC stands for marginal resource cost and MRP for marginal revenue product. The rule applies both to firms that are price takers in their output markets and to those that are price searchers in their output markets.

Figure 13.3 illustrates the profit maximization rule. Both the table and the corresponding graph assume that the firm is a price taker in the output market and that the market price of the output is $1 per unit. The firm is also assumed to be a price taker in the *resource market*, buying inputs of that resource at $5 per unit. Note that profit rises as more of the resource is purchased, up to the 15th unit of input. The firm just breaks even on the purchase of the 16th unit of input, and thereafter profit declines. It is between the 15th and 16th units of input that marginal revenue product becomes exactly equal to marginal resource cost.

Resource Demand Curves

When a firm is a price taker in an input market, whether it is a price taker in the output market or not, its marginal revenue product curve for the input, like the one shown in Figure 13.3, is also its demand curve for the input. A demand curve must indicate the quantity demanded at each price; and it has been shown that the quantity of the input demanded by such a firm will be whatever quantity makes the input's price (and, hence, its marginal resource cost) equal to marginal revenue product.

The same profit-maximizing concept that underlies the demand curves of individual firms for the resource can be extended to all firms hiring a given resource to create a market demand curve for that resource. The resulting curve, like those of the individual firms, is a derived demand curve. As we have seen, the

FIGURE 13.3	PROFIT MAXIMIZATION FOR A PRICE-TAKING FIRM

(a)

Quantity of Input (1)	Marginal Revenue Product (2)	Marginal Input Cost (3)	Total Variable Cost (4)	Fixed Costs (5)	Total Revenue (6)	Total Profit (7)
1			$5	$100	$20	−$85
	$19	$5				
2			10	100	39	−71
	18	5				
3			15	100	57	−58
	17	5				
4			20	100	74	−46
	16	5				
5			25	100	90	−35
	15	5				
6			30	100	105	−25
	14	5				
7			35	100	119	−16
	13	5				
8			40	100	132	−8
	12	5				
9			45	100	144	−1
	11	5				
10			50	100	155	5
	10	5				
11			55	100	165	10
	9	5				
12			60	100	174	14
	8	5				
13			65	100	182	17
	7	5				
14			70	100	189	19
	6	5				
15			75	100	195	20
	5	5				
16			80	100	200	20
	4	5				
17			85	100	204	19
	3	5				
18			90	100	207	17
	2	5				
19			95	100	209	14
	1	5				
20			100	100	210	10

(b)

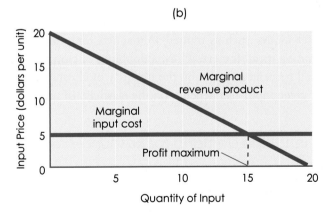

Maximizing profits requires that a firm buy just enough of each resource input to equalize marginal revenue product and marginal resource cost. Here it is assumed that the firm is a price taker in the market where it sells its output and that the product price is $1 per unit. The point of profit maximization falls between 15 and 16 units of input.

demand for any input ultimately does not stem from the usefulness of the input itself but, rather, from the demand for the products the input is used to produce. The market demand for farmland is derived from the market demand for food, the market demand for typographical workers from the market demand for books, and so on.

Like the demand for outputs, the demand for inputs changes in response to changes in economic conditions. A change in the market price of that input will cause the quantity of the resource demanded to change; a movement along the demand curve represents this. Changes in economic conditions other than a change in the input's price can cause a change in the demand for that input; this is shown by a *shift* in the demand curve.

The price elasticity of demand for a resource, as for any other good, is the ratio of the percentage change in the quantity demanded of the resource to a given percentage change in its price, other things being equal. The degree of price elasticity of demand for a resource is influenced by several circumstances.

Because the demand for any input is derived from the demand for the product it is used to produce, elasticity of demand for an input depends on the elasticity of demand for the product. Suppose, for example, that the demand for taxi services is elastic. If taxi fares are forced up as a result of an increase in drivers' wages, the quantity of taxi service demanded will fall sharply and there will be a correspondingly large effect on the quantity of drivers demanded.

A change in the price of an input will have a greater effect on the demand for it the greater its share of total costs, other things being equal. For example, the cost of coal represents a large share of the cost of generating electricity. Doubling the price of coal, therefore, will have a big percentage impact on the price of electricity and a correspondingly large effect on the quantity of electricity demanded. The resulting drop in the quantity of electricity demanded will, in turn, cause a substantial drop in the quantity of coal demanded.

Other things being equal, the demand for an input will be more elastic the more easily other inputs can be substituted for it. For example, clowns are an essential part of circus entertainment. If clowns' wages rise, a circus can substitute other inputs, such as trained animal acts, only to a limited degree without disappointing its customers. Thus, a doubling of clowns' wages would have a relatively small percentage effect on the quantity of clowns demanded. Elasticity of demand for given input also depends on the elasticity of supply of substitute inputs.

Changes in Demand for Resources

Three kinds of changes are capable of causing shifts in the demand curve for inputs of any productive resource.

A CHANGE IN DEMAND FOR OUTPUT In the case of shifts in the resource demand curve, as in the case of movements along the curve, the principle of derived demand plays a key role. In particular, a change in demand for the product produced by an input (that is, a shift in the product demand curve) will cause a change in demand for the input. The source of changes in product demand can be either microeconomic or macroeconomic in nature. A microeconomic example is the increase in demand for the labor of poultry workers as a result of a shift in consumer tastes from beef to chicken. A macroeconomic example is the rise and fall of the demand for labor as the economy experiences expansions and recessions over the course of the business cycle. Expansion brings tight labor markets and increased overtime work; recessions bring layoffs and unemployment.

A CHANGE IN THE PRICE OF ANOTHER INPUT   A second source of shifts in the demand curve for an input is a change in the price of some other input. The notions of *substitutes and complements*, which were introduced in an earlier chapter, are applicable here. For example, consider labor and farm machinery, both of which are used to grow corn. In Mexico, where labor is relatively cheap, relatively little machinery is used per bushel of corn produced; more machinery is used in the United States, where labor is relatively expensive. Labor and machinery, thus, can be viewed as substitutes in the production of corn. On the other hand, consider diesel fuel and the labor of drivers, both of which are used to produce truck transportation. A drop in the price of fuel will lower total costs, increasing the quantity of transportation services demanded. As a result, the number of drivers hired will increase. Thus, labor and fuel are complements in the production of truck transportation.

CHANGES IN TECHNOLOGY   Changes in technology are a third condition that affects the demand for inputs. As improving technology shifts firms' cost curves downward, the quantity of inputs needed to produce a *given* quantity of output is affected. Sometimes technology will cause the demand for one input to rise while the demand for another input falls. For example, the introduction of improved crop varieties in developing countries as part of the so-called green revolution has led to a decrease in the amount of land needed per unit of crop yield, but it has required an increase in the amount of chemical fertilizers required per unit of crop yield. Frequently, however, a new technology reduces the quantities of *all* inputs needed to produce a given unit of output. For example, the introduction of e-mail dramatically shortened the time needed to produce and circulate a memo to colleagues working on a project within a firm. As a result, an office could produce a given number of memos using both fewer labor hours and less specialized printing and copying equipment than before.

Over time, however, an increase in demand for the product, itself sometimes stimulated by improvements in technology, may more than offset the reduced quantity of an input used per unit of output. The end result of the whole process of technological change and growth may be an increased quantity demanded of a given resource. Consider the relationship between clerical workers and office equipment. In the eighteenth century, firms employed clerks to copy documents laboriously by hand. In the nineteenth century, the typewriter replaced pen and ink. In the twentieth century, word processors and photocopiers became available; these, in turn, were supplanted by e-mail. Each technological innovation vastly reduced the number of clerical-worker hours needed to process a given volume of documents. At the same time, the quantity of document processing demanded grew dramatically, with the result that the clerical labor force is larger now than at any time in the past.

The Labor Market

Up to this point, we have discussed marginal productivity and demand for input in general terms. When we turn to the supply side of resource markets, however, we cannot be so general because the considerations affecting supply are different for various factors of production. In this section, we will discuss the supply curve for labor and then see how demand and supply together determine equilibrium in the labor market. The following chapter will take up markets for capital and natural resources.

The Labor Supply Curve

The same individuals and households whose role as consumers was analyzed in Chapter 5 supply labor. A similar approach can be applied here. We begin with the labor supply decision for an individual worker; we then turn to market labor supply curves.

LABOR SUPPLY FOR AN INDIVIDUAL   Previously we showed that all consumer choices involve trade-offs. Individuals' decisions regarding how much labor to supply can be analyzed in terms of a trade-off between two "goods": leisure and purchased consumer goods. Leisure is valued for relaxation, recreation, and the completion of household tasks. Time spent at leisure is time taken away from work, however; and hence it is time diverted from earning income that could be used to buy consumer goods. In making the choice between the two, consumers are faced with two key constraints: (1) the limit of a 24-hour day to be divided between income-earning work and leisure, and (2) the wage rate that determines the purchasing power earned per hour of work.

The hourly wage rate can be thought of as the opportunity cost of leisure in that it represents the dollar equivalent of the goods and services that must be sacrificed in order to enjoy an added hour of leisure. As the wage rate increases, the work-versus-leisure decision is affected in two ways:

1. There is a *substitution effect* as the increased wage rate raises the opportunity cost of leisure, providing an incentive to substitute work (and the goods bought with the resulting income) for leisure.

2. The increase in the wage rate has an *income effect* that tends to reduce the number of hours worked. The higher wage rate—assuming that the prices of goods and services remain unchanged—increases workers' real incomes. With higher real incomes, workers tend to consume larger amounts of normal goods and smaller amounts of inferior goods. Leisure is a normal good. Other things being equal, people generally seek more leisure, in the form of shorter working hours and longer vacations, as their incomes rise. Taken by itself, then, the income effect of a wage increase is a reduction in the amount of labor supplied by workers.

As illustrated in Figure 13.4, the net effect of an increase in the wage rate depends on the relative strengths of the substitution and income effects. It is generally believed that for very low wages the substitution effect predominates; therefore, the quantity of labor supplied by an individual initially increases as the wage rises. As the wage rises still more, however, the income effect becomes stronger. People seem to treat leisure as a normal good; after they have assured themselves of a certain material standard of living,

FIGURE 13.4 AN INDIVIDUAL'S LABOR SUPPLY CURVE

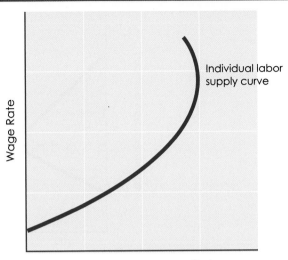

Individual labor supply curve

Wage Rate

Quantity of Labor Supplied
(worker-hours per year)

On the one hand, a higher wage tends to increase the amount of work that a person is willing to do, because the extra income compensates for time taken away from leisure pursuits. On the other hand, a higher wage allows a person to take more time off from work and still enjoy a high standard of living. Taken together, the two effects tend to give the individual labor supply curve the backward-bending shape shown here.

they begin to consider "spending" any further wage increases on more time off from work. If such a pattern prevails, the labor supply curve for an individual will have a backward-bending shape like the one shown in Figure 13.4. Over the positively sloped low-wage section, the substitution effect of wage changes predominates; over the negatively sloped high-wage section, the income effect prevails.

MARKET LABOR SUPPLY CURVES Although the labor supply curves for individual workers may bend backward, at least over some range of wages, the supply curve for any given type of labor as a whole is likely to be positively sloped throughout. Consider, for example, the supply of electrical engineers in New York, of clerical workers in Chicago, or of farm laborers in Texas. Beyond some point, each individual engineer, clerical worker, or laborer might respond to a wage increase by cutting back on the number of hours worked. For the market as a whole, however, this tendency would be more than offset by the entry of new workers from other occupations or areas. Thus, other things being equal, if the wage rate for electrical engineers in New York rose, more engineering students would take up that specialty; if the wage rate for clerical workers in Chicago rose, more people would go into such work instead of, say, becoming hotel workers; and if the wage rate for farm laborers in Texas rose, workers would be drawn in from Arizona, Florida, and Mexico. As a result, for any discussion of the market for a particular category of labor at a specific time and place, it is reasonable to draw the labor supply curve with the usual positive slope regardless of the shape of the individual labor supply curves underlying it.

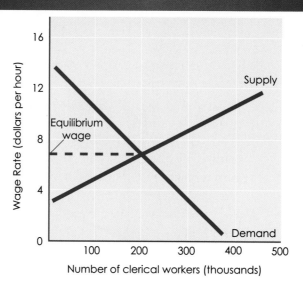

FIGURE 13.5   DETERMINATION OF THE EQUILIBRIUM WAGE IN A COMPETITIVE LABOR MARKET

Although each individual worker may have a backward-bending supply curve, the supply curve for clerical workers in any local market will have the usual positive slope. As the wage rises, people will be drawn into this occupation from other kinds of work or other localities. When both employers and workers are price takers in the labor market, the point of equilibrium is found where the supply and demand curves intersect. Here the equilibrium wage rate is $7 an hour, and the equilibrium quantity of labor is 200,000 workers.

Competitive Equilibrium

Determining the wage rate in a labor market that is perfectly competitive on both sides is a simple matter of supply-and-demand analysis. Figure 13.5, for example, shows supply and demand curves for the labor market for clerical workers in Chicago. It assumes that a large number of workers compete for jobs and a large number of employers compete for them so that both are price takers. The market supply curve has a positive slope, and the market demand curve for clerical workers is derived from the demand curves for individual firms.

Equilibrium in this market requires a wage rate of $7 an hour, with 200,000 workers employed. If the wage rate were lower, there would be a shortage of clerical workers. Some firms, unable to fill all their job openings, would offer premium wages to workers from other occupations or regions. The wage rate would thus be driven up to the equilibrium level. If, on the other hand, the wage rate were above $7 an hour, there would be a surplus of clerical workers. Many people would be looking for such jobs and not finding them. After a sufficiently long search, some would be willing to accept work at lower-than-desired wages, thereby pushing the wage rate down toward equilibrium; others would move into other occupations or regions.

In a labor market such as this one—in which both employers and employees are price takers—the equilibrium wage rate equals the marginal revenue product of labor. In the special case in which all employers are price takers (perfect competitors) in the market where they sell their output as well as in the market where they purchase inputs, the equilibrium wage rate also equals the value of marginal product.

The Marginal Productivity Theory of Distribution

Marginal productivity theory of distribution

A theory of income distribution in which each input of production receives a payment equal to its marginal revenue product

Supply and demand determine how much each worker earns as well as how much labor will be used in making each product. When employers are price takers in the markets in which they buy inputs, profit maximization requires that each resource be used up to the point at which its marginal revenue product will equal its price. This reasoning suggests that each unit of each resource receives a reward equal to the contribution it makes to the firm's revenue. The idea that resources are rewarded according to their marginal productivity is known as the **marginal productivity theory of distribution**.

In an economy in which all markets—output as well as input—are perfectly competitive, the marginal productivity theory applies even more directly. In this case marginal revenue product equals output price times marginal physical product. In such an economy the reward that each unit of each input receives is equal to the value of marginal product. If an extra hour spent pulling weeds in a cabbage patch increases production by 20 pounds and cabbage sells for $.50 per pound, the equilibrium wage rate must be $10 an hour—no more, no less.

The marginal productivity theory of distribution as we have defined it is a proposition of positive economics. However, some people find this principle of distribution appealing in a normative sense as well, in terms of both efficiency and fairness. Under the marginal productivity principle, the reward of every worker is exactly equal to that worker's contribution to the productive process. If a worker or other resource owner withholds a unit of productive services from the market, that person will suffer a loss of earnings exactly equal to the value of production that is lost to the economy as a whole. The normative version of the marginal productivity theory is, in effect, the old idea of "from each according to ability, to each according to work" restated in the language of neoclassical economics.

Monopsony

Monopsony

A situation in which there is only a single buyer in a market; more generally, any situation in which a firm is a price searcher in a market in which it is a buyer

Not every input market meets the conditions required for the marginal productivity theory of distribution to apply. In particular, there are cases in which firms are price searchers rather than price takers in input markets. In labor markets, this will tend to occur when one or a few employers dominate the market in a particular location or for a particular skill. It can also happen when workers vary in their perceptions of non-wage characteristics of jobs with different employers. Some people might work for Acme because it is close to their neighborhood; some might prefer Zeus Company because the managers there are friendlier; and so on. Whatever the reason, the employer cannot hire unlimited numbers of workers at a constant wage. The labor supply curve faced by the individual employer is not horizontal as it is in a perfectly competitive labor market.

The extreme case, in which a single employer accounts for 100 percent of the demand in a resource market, is termed **monopsony**. In ancient Greek, from which these terms are derived, *monopsony* means "one buyer" just as *monopoly* means "one seller." In principle, we could also identify the resource market structures of *oligopsony* (a few buyers) and *monopsonistic competition* (many buyers perceived as different by sellers). However, it is common, although not very precise, to apply the term monopsony to all markets in which buyers are price searchers.

In a monopsony labor market, then, the wage rate is not a given. Instead, the employer must choose among a set of wage-quantity combinations lying along a positively sloped labor supply curve. As an example, compare the situation of a retail store in Los Angeles that wants to hire a few security guards with the situation of the U.S. government, which wants to hire soldiers for the army. The retail store is a price taker in the market for security guards. If the going wage for such guards is, say, $40,000 a year, it can call an agency or put an ad in the paper and get as many guards as it wants at that price. The situation of the government as the employer of volunteer soldiers is very different. Experience has shown that the number of soldiers that can be recruited depends on the level of military pay. When the need for recruits increases, the military services offer more by way of monthly pay, benefits, and enlistment bonuses.

The Marginal Resource Cost Curve

In discussing monopoly we distinguished between price-discriminating monopoly and simple monopoly. The latter sells all units at the same price, whereas the former sells to different customers at different prices. The same distinction applies in the labor market. In this chapter we consider only the simple case in which an employer pays the same wage to all workers who do the same job. In Chapter 15, we will briefly consider some of the complications of paying different wages to different workers for the same work.

Figure 13.6 shows the market situation for a hypothetical simple monopsonist—say, a large insurance company that employs most of the clerical workers in a small town. The supply schedule for these workers shows that no one will work in this occupation at a wage rate of $3 an hour or less. Above the $3 wage, each extra $.02 per hour will attract one more worker.

Consider in detail what happens to the monopsonist's total labor cost each time it hires an additional worker. No one will work at $3 per hour, so the first worker must be paid at least $3.02. The wage would have to be raised to $3.04 to hire a second worker. Because all workers are paid the same, the first worker would get a raise of $.02 per hour when the second worker was hired, making the marginal resource cost $3.06 ($3.04 + .02). Similarly, hiring 150 workers costs $6.00 per hour but hiring 151 requires a wage of $6.02 an hour. Moving from 150 to 151 workers raises total labor cost from $900 per hour to $909.02 per hour. The marginal resource cost at this point is thus $9.02. Whatever the chosen starting point, the monopsonist's marginal resource cost exceeds the resource price (in this case, the wage rate).

Part (b) of Figure 13.6 shows a marginal resource cost curve based on the marginal resource cost column of the table in part (a). This curve lies above the supply curve at every point. The horizontal distance from the vertical axis to the marginal resource cost curve is, at every wage rate, exactly half the distance from the vertical axis to the supply curve.

Monopsony Profit Maximization

The monopsonist's marginal resource cost curve together with its marginal revenue product curve determines the quantity of labor that results in the maximum profit.

FIGURE 13.6   MARGINAL RESOURCE COST UNDER MONOPSONY

(a)

Quantity of Labor Supplied (Number of Workers) (1)	Wage Rate (Dollars per Hour) (2)	Total Resource Cost (Dollars per Hour) (3)	Marginal Resource Cost (Dollars per Hour) (4)
1	$3.02	$3.02	
2	3.04	6.08	$3.06
3	3.06	9.18	3.10
150	6.00	900.00	
151	6.02	909.02	9.02
152	6.04	918.08	9.06
200	7.00	1,400.00	
201	7.02	1,411.02	11.02
203	7.04	1,422.08	11.06

(b)

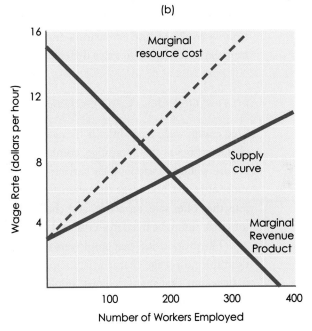

Under monopsony, marginal resource cost exceeds factor price. Consider an increase in quantity from 150 to 151 units of labor. The wage rate must be raised from $6 to $6.02 not just for the 151st employee but for all the previous 150 as well. Marginal resource cost in this range thus is $9.02 rather than $6.02 an hour. Profit is maximized where the marginal revenue product curve intersects the marginal resource cost curve. At the point, 150 workers are hired.

Following the general rule that profit is maximized at the quantity of labor for which marginal resource cost equals marginal revenue product, the monopsonist will hire 150 clerical workers at a wage rate of $6 an hour.

When a labor market is in monopsony equilibrium, the wage rate is lower than both the marginal resource cost and the marginal revenue product of labor. In the example just given, the equilibrium wage rate is $6 an hour (which is equal to the height of the labor supply curve), although the marginal revenue product is $9 an hour at the point at which the marginal revenue product and marginal resource cost curves intersect. Despite the gap between the wage rate and the marginal revenue product, adding to the amount of labor hired would not raise revenue enough to offset higher labor costs. The reason is that the cost of hiring another worker is not just the $6.02 an hour that must be paid to the 151st worker; instead, it is that sum plus the extra $.02 per hour by which the wages of all 150 previously hired workers must be raised. The complete marginal resource cost for the 151st worker thus is $6.02 + $3.00, or $9.02 an hour.

Why Wage Rates Differ

According to a widely shared concept of justice, all people are created equal. But if that is so, why do people's earnings in labor markets differ so widely? Why do different people receive different wages within a given labor market, and why do the wage structures of some markets differ markedly from those of others? In this section we look at some extensions of conventional marginal productivity theory that help explain why wage rates differ.

Non-Wage Job Characteristics

One reason wage rates differ is that jobs differ in ways other than wages, including such characteristics as safety, prestige, comfort, and challenge. Other things being equal, workers are willing to supply their services at lower wages to employers that offer jobs with more attractive non-wage characteristics. Knowing this, many employers try to make the jobs they offer safe, attractive, and challenging. Employers who must attract workers to jobs that cannot be freed from risk and discomfort often have to pay higher wages.

The proposition that employers must pay more to attract workers to jobs with less desirable non-wage characteristics applies only when *other things are equal*. In practice, it turns out that many tedious, unpleasant, and even dangerous jobs pay low wages, while the high-salaried occupants of the executive suite work in air-conditioned comfort and eat lunches served on fine china in special dining rooms. How can this seeming paradox be explained in terms of labor market theory?

Economists see nothing paradoxical in the contrast between the heat and noise of the factory floor and the cool calm of the executive suite. They simply interpret the observed pattern as evidence that comfort on the job is a *normal good*. As people's incomes rise, they want more comfort. An employer must take this into account when offering a package of wage and working conditions to various employees. Suppose that a firm offered a warehouse worker a cut in pay from $7 an hour to $6 an hour ($2,000 a year) in return for which it would replace the vinyl tile in the warehouse coffee room with wool carpet and replace the cheap posters on the wall with original artwork. Would it be surprising if the warehouse worker turned down the offer? Suppose the same firm offered its president a raise from $500,000 a year to $502,000 a year, in exchange for which the carpet in the president's office would be ripped out and its oil paintings replaced with cheap posters. Would it be surprising if the president turned down the offer?

This principle applies on an international scale, as well. Major U.S. multinationals with plants in developing countries are very often regarded as local leaders in terms of the wages and working conditions they offer. Their factories are, more often than not, cleaner, better lit, and safer than those of their small, local competitors. Yet when these overseas plants are compared in terms of working conditions with factories in the United States, they often are denounced as "sweatshops." What is the truth? Are multinational corporations ruthlessly exploiting foreign workers? Are those workers, who are just making the first steps out of dismal poverty, less willing to trade off hard cash wages for improvements in workplace amenities? There is often no unambiguous answer to such questions.

Human Capital

Differences in the non-wage characteristics of jobs do not fully explain why wages differ. Ability also counts. If the supply of abilities needed for the job of corporate president were as abundant as the supply of abilities needed for the job of warehouse worker, we would not expect labor markets to give rise to such a big difference in pay to the two occupations.

Some people are born with special abilities, or at least with unusual potential for developing them. The enormous salaries of professional ballplayers, first-rate opera singers, and other superstars are a direct result of the scarcity of those abilities. The abilities people are born with are only part of the story, however. Training and education are at least as important as innate ability for most occupations, from lawyers and accountants to glassblowers and hairdressers.

Economists view the costs of training and education as a form of investment. Taking courses to become an accountant, in this view, is much like buying a dump truck in order to go into the gravel-hauling business. In both cases one makes an expenditure now to acquire something that will increase one's future earning power. The main difference is that the dump truck operator acquires capital in the form of a machine, whereas the accountant acquires **human capital**—capital in the form of learned abilities.

According to human-capital theory, the earnings of each occupation that requires special training must be high enough to make up for

Human capital

Capital in the form of learned abilities that have been acquired through formal training or education or through on-the-job experience

First rate opera singers and other superstars draw enormous salaries due to the scarcity of people with those abilities.

the opportunity cost of getting the training. In the case of a person going to college to acquire a degree in accounting, the opportunity cost includes both the costs of getting the degree (tuition, books, and so on) and the income that could have been earned if the college years had been spent working in an occupation that required no college degree. Other things being equal, we would expect occupations that require longer or more expensive training to pay more than those that require less. Thus, we would expect doctors to earn more than lawyers, lawyers to earn more than hairdressers, and so on—and that is in fact the case.[1]

Of course, the non-wage characteristics of jobs may play a role in people's willingness to invest in various kinds of human capital. If certain occupations are more exciting or prestigious than others, people may be willing to enter them even if the pay alone is not enough to justify the investment in training. For example, the training required to become a ballet dancer may be as long and rigorous as that needed to become, say, an orthodontist, but dancers, on the average, earn less than orthodontists. The difference in pay presumably has something to do with the value placed by would-be dancers on the opportunity for artistic expression.

Formal education is by no means the only way to invest in human capital. On-the-job training is also important. In total, employers may spend as much for on-the-job training as is spent on formal education at all levels. Both employers and employees benefit from this vast investment in human capital. Employers benefit from the ability to fine-tune the skills of their work forces to the physical capital in which they have invested. In that sense, physical capital and human capital are often complementary inputs. At the same time, employees benefit not only from immediate promotions and higher pay but also because training may broaden their options in the labor market.

Efficiency Wage Theory

Efficiency wage theory

The theory that wages above the minimum necessary to attract qualified workers can raise productivity by enough to increase profit

Human-capital theory suggests that the ability to perform a job better results in an increase in the wage rate of a worker or group of workers. Another theory suggests that the opposite may also be true—higher pay may itself lead to better on-the-job performance. This line of reasoning is referred to as **efficiency wage theory**.

Efficiency wage theory poses the following question: Why do many firms pay a wage that is higher than necessary to attract workers with the desired minimum qualifications? Anyone who has ever looked for a job has probably had the experience of hearing about an employer who offers a high wage for particular skills and working conditions, only to learn that the employer has hundreds of applications on file and a low turnover rate. According to the simple supply-and-demand model, the profit-maximizing strategy for such a firm would be to lower the wage rate, allowing the backlog of job applications to shrink to just the number necessary to cover turnover. Yet employers do not always do this.

The explanation offered by efficiency wage theory is that the high wage stimulates productivity. Several reasons have been suggested, including improved morale, lower absenteeism, and lower employee turnover. Also, workers at a high-wage firm are likely to be less willing to risk losing their jobs because of poor performance and, therefore, may work to the best of their abilities with less supervision and monitoring.

Efficiency wages are not a new idea. In 1914, Henry Ford used efficiency wages when he cut turnover and increased productivity by raising his workers' pay to the unheard of level of $5 a day. *Applying Economic Ideas 13.1* gives a contemporary example.

Taking all things together, we see that there are many reasons why wage rates differ. The principles of labor markets covered in this chapter will provide useful background for even broader questions that will be discussed in Chapters 15 and 16, which cover problems of labor market policy, discrimination, income distribution, and poverty.

Applying Economic Ideas 13.1
COSTCO VERSUS SAM'S CLUB IN THE LABOR MARKET

Costco Wholesale store in Tacoma, WA

Sam's Club warehouse in Reno, NV

Costco versus Sam's Club is one of the hottest rivalries in U.S. retail trade. Both companies follow the philosophy of "pile 'em high and sell 'em cheap." Both feature huge stores with rock-bottom prices for a wide range of merchandise, much of it top-of-the-line brand names.

However, in the labor market, where they compete for workers, the two companies take different approaches. Costco pays its full-time U.S. employees an average of $17.41 per hour, well above the industry average. An experienced cashier can make $40,000. Sam's Club is a division of Wal-Mart, which pays its employees an average of just $12 per hour, on the low end of the industry scale.

Benefits as well as wages differ at the two companies. According to the *Wall Street Journal*, 82 percent of Costco's employees are covered by insurance, compared with 44 percent for Wal-Mart. Costco pays 92 percent of insured workers' premiums, compared to 66 percent at Wal-Mart.

Costco also has a different attitude toward labor unions. Wal-Mart resists unionization vigorously. Costco

does not actively encourage unionization, but it accepts workers' rights to unionize if they think doing so will improve their lot. About 20 percent of Costco's U.S. employees are unionized.

The result of these differences in policy is a dramatic difference in employee loyalty. According to the *Financial Times*, Costco has an annual labor turnover of just 17 percent. Wal-Mart's is near the industry average of 44 percent.

"Paying good wages is not in opposition to good productivity," says Costco Chief Executive Officer and President, Jim Sinegal, speaking to a reporter from *Business Week*. "If you hire good people, give them good jobs, and pay them good wages, generally something good is going to happen."

SOURCES: "James Sinegal, Costco: The Bargain Hunter," *Business Week* Sept. 23, 2002; "Costco's Dilemma: Is Treating Employees Well Unacceptable for a Public Corporation?" *Wall Street Journal*, March 26, 2004; "Pile High, Sell Cheap, and Pay Well," *Financial Times*, July 11, 2005.

Capital and Interest

Capital, in the broadest sense, refers to all means of production that are made by people. Some capital takes discrete, tangible forms, such as shovels and crushers used by a mining company. Improvements to land are another form of capital; for a mining company, they might include excavations that permit access to mineral deposits and access roads to carry out the product. In addition, as we saw in the previous section, skills like those of a mining engineer, achieved through education and enhanced by experience, are examples of human capital. In this section, we look at some features that are shared by all forms of capital.

Capital and Roundabout Production

A fundamental feature that is shared by all forms of capital is a trade-off between the present and the future. To accumulate capital it is necessary to bear opportunity costs now in order to reap a return later. Suppose, for example, that you want to catch fish from a well-stocked pond. You might be able to catch a few fish by wading in and grabbing them with your bare hands. That way you would have some fish today, although not many; but you could also spend the day weaving string into a net and cutting a branch to use as a handle for the net. You would go hungry today; but tomorrow you would be able to catch lots of fish, many more than you could catch with your bare hands. The opportunity cost in the form of forgone meals that you endured to accumulate capital in the form of the net would be repaid by future benefits.

The example of the fishing net shows why economists sometimes refer to production using capital as *roundabout* production. Many other examples could be given. Making cars in an automated factory uses more capital than making them one by one using hand tools. A great quantity of labor and other resources has to go into building the factory before cars start to come off the line; but when they do, more of them are produced at a lower cost per unit. Digging a ditch to lead water to a field is a roundabout method of irrigation compared with carrying water to the field in buckets. Writing a specialized computer program to calculate a company's payroll is a roundabout method compared with working out the numbers each week on general-purpose spreadsheet program, but the time taken to write the program pays off in time saved later.

The Rate of Return on Capital

The use of capital as a productive input can be analyzed using a variant on the marginal product technique employed in the preceding chapter. Because capital created today is typically employed over a long period in the future, its marginal product is commonly expressed as a percentage—the **rate of return on capital**. For example, if we say that the rate of return on capital in a certain application is 10 percent per year, this means that adding one dollar to the capital stock will increase output by about $.10 each year in the future. The law of diminishing returns acts to reduce the marginal physical product of capital as more capital is applied to a production process,

Rate of return on capital

The marginal product of capital expressed as an annual percentage rate holding other inputs constant. Consequently, the demand curve for capital, like the demand curves for other resources, has a negative slope.

The supply curve of capital, on the other hand, can be analyzed in terms of the principle of diminishing marginal utility. To acquire more capital, more present goods must be forgone, raising the marginal utility of the increasingly scarce present goods that remain. At the same time, acquiring more capital makes future goods more abundant, so their marginal utility falls. Thus, the marginal resource cost, or opportunity cost, of capital—the ratio of the marginal utility of present goods forgone to the marginal utility of future goods gained—rises as the quantity of capital invested increases. (In the fishing example, spending more hours on net building means catching fewer fish today. As a result, the increasingly hungry net builder becomes more and more reluctant to make an additional present sacrifice in return for an even larger feast tomorrow.) The rising marginal opportunity cost of capital gives rise to a positively sloped supply curve.

Time Preference

Time preference

The tendency to prefer goods now to goods in the future, other things being equal

Other things being equal, people prefer goods now to goods in the future. This tendency is referred to as **time preference**. Time preference is revealed in a thousand familiar aspects of human behavior. Young children "can't wait" to open their birthday presents; without time preference, they would attach no more utility to a new bicycle today than to a new bicycle next week. Similarly, teenagers "can't wait" to get a driver's license, grandparents "can't wait" for their first chance to hold their new grandchild, and so on.

Time preference does not mean it is never worth waiting, however, because "other things" are not equal. Although we do not want to postpone something now to get something equally good later, we may be persuaded to postpone something good now to get something even better later. Suppose that in our fishing example, a person would be willing to forgo having 10 fish today in order to have 11 fish tomorrow. The *rate of time preference*, expressed in percentage terms per unit of time, would then be 10 percent per day.

If time preference and the marginal productivity of capital are both expressed in percentage terms, a simple relationship emerges: In an equilibrium state in which the optimal quantity of capital is employed, the rate of return on capital and the rate of time preference will be equal.

Interest and the Market for Loanable Funds

Up to this point, the discussion has proceeded entirely in terms of physical units. Our next step—which takes us from the world of an imaginary fisher to that of Wall Street—is to introduce money. Money is a means of payment for goods and services; it is also a store of value that can be used to buy things either now or later. It makes possible another class of transactions involving time: borrowing and lending.

Consider two individuals, A and B. A finds it advantageous to borrow from B whenever A's rate of time preference is higher than B's. The terms of the loan will be mutually beneficial at any interest rate that is higher than B's rate of time preference and lower than A's. For many reasons, rates of time preference differ in such a way that loans are mutually advantageous. Consider some examples:

- One person may simply be more impatient than another. Bill is so eager to go skiing this year that he is willing to borrow the funds, with interest, from Jane. Jane, who is less impatient, thinks the interest she will earn is a sufficient inducement to put off skiing until next year.

- People may borrow and lend to smooth out consumption over time. Al, who is just entering the job market, borrows to buy a car. Jose, who has already worked for several years, is saving for retirement. Jose will have even more money after he retires if he lends part of his savings to Al at a good rate of interest.

- One person sees better opportunities to use capital than another. Jill thinks that buying a greenhouse in order to start a cut-flower business will result in a rate of return of at least 20 percent. Mike thinks investing to expand his cookie store would result in a return of only 5 percent. It would thus be advantageous for Mike to lend funds to Jill, rather than to invest in his own business, at any interest rate over 5 percent; and it would be advantageous for Jill to borrow, rather than to forgo the business opportunity, at any interest rate less than 20 percent.

Loanable funds market

A general term for the set of markets in which people borrow and lend, for whatever reason

All people who borrow and lend, for whatever reason, are participating in a set of markets that economists call the **loanable funds market**. That market is shown in Figure 13.7. The demand curve for loanable funds indicates that, other things being equal, people will borrow more for both investment and consumption if the interest

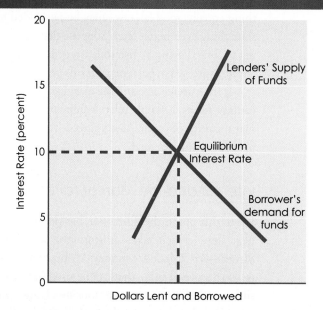

FIGURE 13.7   THE MARKET FOR LOANABLE FUNDS

All people who borrow and lend, for whatever reason, are participants in the market for loanable funds. The demand curve in this market reflects that, other things being equal, people will borrow more for both investment and consumption purposes as the interest rate falls. The supply curve for loanable funds reflects that, other things being equal, people will be more willing to make loans at higher rates of interest. The equilibrium interest rate is determined by the intersection of the two curves.

rate is lower. The supply curve for loanable funds indicates that, other things being equal, the higher the rate of interest, the greater a person's willingness to make a loan. The equilibrium interest rate is determined by the intersection of the supply and demand curves for loanable funds. Behind those curves, in turn, stand the rate of return on capital and the rate of time preference, which will be equal at the margin when the loanable funds market is in equilibrium.

Markets for Natural Resources

We turn now from markets for capital to markets for natural resources. Natural resources arise from land, and not all land is alike. Location and physical attributes, such as elevation and climate, make any individual piece of land more suitable for some activities than for others. Some land can be used to grow corn, some is suitable for building houses, some land is rich with mineral deposits, and still other land is best preserved as wildlife habitat or for recreation.

Pure Economic Rent

In an earlier chapter, we defined *economic rent* as any income received for a factor of production that is greater than its opportunity cost. The theory of rent goes back to the days of the classical economists two centuries ago.

The classical economists thought of land in terms of the natural productive powers of the earth and the location advantages of particular sites. They considered the supply of land, in this sense, to be perfectly inelastic. No matter how high its rental price, the amount of land is fixed; and no matter how low the price, the land is always there. The income earned by a factor of production whose supply is perfectly inelastic in the long run is referred to as **pure economic rent**. Note that artificial improvements to land or reclamation of land count are capital. To the extent that they raise the value a parcel of land, the added income counts as return on the capital invested, not as rent.

The market price paid for land can be expressed either in terms of an annual rental payment, or when land is bought outright by the user rather than rented, a purchase price. There is a relationship between the value of a piece of land expressed as an annual rent and the price at which that parcel can be sold in the market. The market price of a piece of land is said to be the **capitalized value of a rent**—the present value of all future rents the land is expected to earn.[2]

Differential Rent

The theory of pure economic rent is concerned with land as an abstraction. It implicitly assumes that all land is alike and that it is interchangeable in all uses. In practice, land differs in terms of its fertility, its climate, and its location advantages. Land in Kansas has a comparative advantage in producing wheat, land in Cuba for producing sugar cane, and land in France's Rhone valley for growing wine grapes. For that reason, as economists since David Ricardo have recognized, not all land earns the same rent in a competitive market.

Consider Figure 13.8, which shows the marginal cost and average total cost of producing wheat on three different farms with different qualities of land. The costs

Pure economic rent

The income earned by any resource whose supply is perfectly inelastic with respect to its price

Capitalized value of a rent

The present value of all future rents that a piece of land or other resource is expected to earn

FIGURE 13.8   DIFFERENTIAL RENT

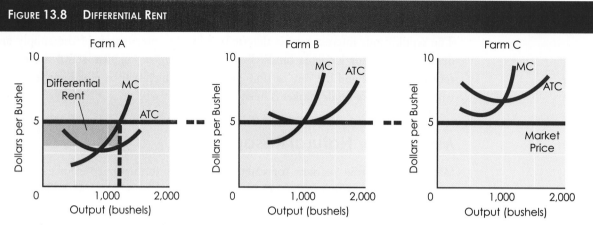

The theory of pure economic rent implicitly assumes that all land is alike. In practice, different pieces of land have different degrees of productivity in various uses. Those differences will affect the rent earned in a particular use. This figure shows marginal and average total cost curves for three wheat farms that differ only in terms of the quality of their land. Given a market price of $5 a bushel for wheat, Farm A earns a differential rent of $2 per bushel, equal to the difference between the cost of production on its highly productive land and the market rental on land. Farm B just breaks even at $5 per bushel and earns no economic rent, and Farm C does not produce at that price. If the price rose to $7, Farm C would enter the market, Farm B would begin to earn a differential rent, and Farm A would earn an even larger differential rent.

include all outlays for labor, machinery, fertilizer, and other inputs except the land itself. At a market price of $5 per bushel, Farm A will produce 1,200 bushels per year, Farm B will produce 1,000 bushels per year, and Farm C will not find it worthwhile to grow wheat at all.

Given that market price and those outputs, Farm A receives total revenue of $5 per bushel and incurs average total costs of $3 per bushel. The $2 excess of revenue over cost is associated with the superior productivity of the land on Farm A. It is a special example of rent that is called **differential rent**.

Differential rent

The rents earned by superior units of a resource in a situation in which units of a resource differ in productivity

At a market price of $5 a bushel for wheat, Farm B just breaks even on its total costs and earns no differential rent. What if the market price were to rise to $7 per bushel? In that case, Farm C would find it worthwhile to enter the market. Farm B would step up its output to 1,200 bushels per year and earn a differential rent equal to a little under $2 per bushel; and Farm A would increase its output to 1,400 bushels, causing its differential rent to rise to $3.50 per bushel.

Differential rents are not unique to land as a factor of production. They can arise in the case of any input that is not homogeneous. Examples can be found in markets for many specialized kinds of labor. For example, in the preceding chapter, the fact that lawyers earn more on the average than truck drivers was attributed to their greater investment in human capital; but strictly speaking, that applies only to the earnings of a lawyer without special aptitudes. Some lawyers have not only the needed education but also a special ability to bewitch jurors and charm judges. Those lawyers earn differential rents over and above the opportunity costs of acquiring their education.

Inframarginal Rents

Differential rents arise in markets in which some units of a resource are more productive than others. Another kind of rent can arise in markets in which units are equally productive but differ in terms of the willingness with which they are supplied.

Consider Figure 13.9, which shows hypothetical supply and demand curves for the market for nurses. For the sake of discussion, it is assumed that all nurses, once they have the needed training, are equally productive. However, not everyone is equally willing to be a nurse. In the figure, the first few people would be willing to enter the profession at a wage rate as low as $5 per hour. An increase to $7.50 per hour would attract 500,000 people to the profession, and further increases would draw in even more, as is shown by the supply curve. Given the demand curve, the equilibrium wage rate is $10 per hour, enough to attract one million people to the profession.

Why is it that some people are willing to enter the nursing profession at a lower wage than others are? Like other economic choices, a worker's decision regarding whether to enter the nursing profession depends in part on their objectives or preferences. For example, some people may be willing to enter the nursing profession at a relatively low wage because they value the work itself positively. They find that nursing suits their preferences

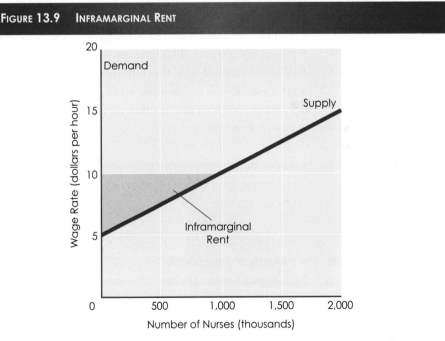

FIGURE 13.9   INFRAMARGINAL RENT

In some markets, units of a resource are equally productive but differ in terms of the willingness with which they are supplied. This figure shows supply and demand curves for nurses. Some people would be willing to work as a nurse for as little as $5 per hour. As the supply curve shows, increasingly higher wage rates must be offered to draw more people into the market. At the equilibrium wage rate of $10 per hour, only the marginal nurse is paid just the wage needed to work in this market. The others earn an inframarginal rent equal to the difference between the equilibrium wage rate and the minimum they would accept rather than pursue other alternatives.

in terms of flexible hours, opportunities to serve people in need, and so on. A higher wage rate is needed to attract people who dislike the non-wage characteristics of nursing. In part, differential rent also depends on the constraints people face, especially their other job opportunities. The better a person's job opportunities in other professions, other things being equal, the higher the wage required to draw the person into nursing.

Whether it is looked at from the viewpoint of objectives or constraints, or both together, the positive slope of the supply curve for labor in a particular profession can be understood as reflecting the differing opportunity costs faced by different workers. In a competitive labor market equilibrium, then, where all workers receive the same wage, all but the marginal worker—the one who is just barely attracted to the profession at the equilibrium wage rate—are paid a wage that is higher than their opportunity costs. In economic terminology, they earn **inframarginal rents** equal to the difference between the equilibrium wage and the minimum they would accept rather than pursue other opportunities.

Inframarginal rents are helpful in understanding why so many people are so strongly attached to the job they currently hold. News reports commonly treat a major layoff or plant closing as a disaster for the workers involved. People often perceive the loss of a job as a trauma comparable to a hurricane, a divorce, or a major illness. Why? For a person "on the margin," whose job pays just enough in terms of wages and non-wage satisfaction to make them willing to do that work rather than the next best available to them, losing a job would be no big problem. The next-best job would be about as good. The majority of workers in any given occupation are not at the margin, however. They occupy jobs that pay a significant inframarginal rent. If they have to change jobs, that inframarginal rent, whether it is monetary or has a non-wage form like job satisfaction, prestige, or location advantage, will be lost. No wonder such people lament a layoff or plant closing!

Inframarginal rents

The difference between the payment made to a unit of resource and the minimum required for that resource to be willingly supplied in a situation in which units of a resource differ in terms of the willingness with which they are supplied

---

Summary

1. **What circumstances determine demand for productive inputs?** For a firm that is a price taker in its output market, the *marginal revenue product* of any input is equal to the input's *value of marginal product*—that is, marginal physical product times the product's price. For a firm that is a price searcher in the output market, it is equal to marginal physical product times marginal revenue and thus is less than the value of marginal product. In both cases the firm makes the maximum profit by buying each input up to the point at which marginal revenue product equals *marginal resource cost*. Hence, the marginal revenue product curve is the resource demand curve for any firm that is a price taker in its input market. The demand for a resource is said to be derived from the demand for the goods it is used to produce.

2. **What circumstances determine the supply curve for labor?** Labor supply curves depend on the trade-off that people make between leisure and the goods and services they can buy with income earned in the labor market. The labor supply curve for an individual worker, and perhaps for the economy as a whole, may bend backward above a certain wage rate. However, the supply curve for a single labor market is positively sloped throughout its length.

3. **What are the characteristics of equilibrium in a competitive labor market?** In a labor market in which employers are price takers, the equilibrium wage rate will be equal to the marginal revenue product of labor, a proposition known as the *marginal productivity theory of distribution*. If employers are also price takers in the output market, the equilibrium wage rate also will be equal to the value of the marginal product.

4. **What are the characteristics of labor market equilibrium with only one or a few employers?** *Monopsony* refers to a situation in which employers are price searchers in the market in which they buy inputs. The marginal resource cost curve for such a firm lies above the supply curve for labor. The equilibrium input is established at the intersection of the marginal resource cost curve and the marginal revenue product curve. In such a market the equilibrium wage is below the marginal revenue product.

5. **Why are wages not the same for all labor markets and for all individuals within a labor market?** Wages differ among markets and among individuals for a variety of reasons. Some wage differences stem from differences in the non-wage characteristics of jobs or from differences in the *human capital* possessed by individuals. According to *efficiency wage theory* some employers pay more than the going wage because doing so results in higher productivity.

6. **How do markets determine the rate of return on capital?** The use of capital as a productive resource involves a trade-off between the present and the future. Reducing consumption now makes possible the accumulation of capital, which will increase output in the future. The marginal product of capital, expressed in percentage terms per unit of time, is called the *rate of return on capital*. In a market economy, capital accumulation tends toward an equilibrium rate at which the rate of return on capital just offsets the *time preference*—the tendency to prefer goods now to goods in the future, other things being equal. People differ in

terms of their time preference and the investment opportunities they perceive. Their differing preferences and perceptions are accommodated through borrowing and lending in loanable funds markets. The equilibrium rate of interest in loanable funds markets tends toward equality with the rate of return on capital and the rate of time preference.

7. **How do supply and demand determine rents for land?** *Pure economic rent* is the income earned by any factor of production whose supply is completely inelastic. Land is the classic example of a factor that earns a pure economic rent. The *capitalized value of a rent* determines the market price of land. Other factors whose supply is perfectly inelastic, such as the special talents of athletes or performing artists, can also earn rent. Other kinds of rent are possible in markets in which land or other resources are not subject to perfectly inelastic supply. Where various units of a factor differ in terms of productivity, the more productive units are said to earn *differential rents*. Where they differ in terms of the willingness with which they are supplied, those that would be supplied willingly at prices below the equilibrium price are said to earn *inframarginal rents*.

Key Terms

Problems and Topics for Discussion

1. **Outsourcing**   How might increased outsourcing affect the quality of the U.S. labor force? If regulations preventing outsourcing were successful, how would this affect U.S. companies? What about consumers buying goods and services from these producers?

2. **Households as buyers in resource markets**   This chapter discusses only resource markets in which the buyers are firms. Are households ever direct buyers of the basic factors of production? For example, would you be the direct buyer of a factor of production if you hired someone to tutor you in mathematics? How would the theory of resource markets have to be modified to take into account cases in which the buyers of resources are households rather than firms?

3. **A case of backward-bending labor demand**   In his historical novel *Chesapeake*, James Michener describes the unsuccessful efforts of early European colonists to run their plantations using hired Native American labor. Among the many factors that led to the breakdown of relationships between the planters and local inhabitants were economic problems. For example, Michener reports the frustration of a planter who finds that an offer of higher wages does not keep Native American workers from quitting their jobs in the fields after a few weeks of work; in fact, the workers seem to quit sooner when their pay is raised. Does what you have learned in this chapter shed any light on this situation? Discuss.

4. **Monopsony and monopoly**   Is a monopsonist always a monopolist, and vice versa? Try to imagine a firm that is a monopsonist in its factor market but a perfect competitor in its product market. Then try to visualize a firm that is a monopolist but not a monopsonist.

5. **The relationship between "how" and "or whom"**   Discuss the following statement: "It is a good idea to let resource markets determine how things are produced; but the matter of for whom things are produced should be handled according to need, not according to supply and demand." Is it possible to separate the "how" and "for whom" functions of resource markets?

6. **Trends in the pay of men and women**   The wage gap between men and women has narrowed somewhat in the past ten years and is expected to narrow further. Do you think the narrowing of the wage gap has anything to do with the facts that (a) women are more than proportionately represented in service occupations and (b) demand for services is growing faster than demand for goods? Discuss.

7. **Wages and working conditions in the newly industrialized countries**   Evaluate the following statement: "We probably can't do much about the fact that workers in Bangladesh, Vietnam, and other newly industrialized countries are paid less than U.S. workers doing similar jobs. However, we should not tolerate the fact that those workers are forced to work under conditions that fall far short of U.S. standards for health, safety, comfort, and hours of work. We should either insist on better working conditions or stop importing goods made by workers who are exploited in that way." How would this proposal affect workers in the newly industrialized countries (a) if the threat to cut off trade worked and labor conditions in those countries were brought up to U.S. standards, and (b) if the threat failed and trade with the countries in question were cut off?

8. **Two ways to make bricks**   Suppose that there are two ways to make bricks. One is to form them by hand out of clay scooped from the ground and then bake them over an open fire. Using that method, you can make 100 bricks a month. Another way is to use a whole month's output of bricks to build a kiln in which bricks can be baked. When the kiln is complete, the hotter fire and lower fuel consumption make it possible to make 120 bricks per month with the same labor that was previously used to make 100. Is the kiln

an example of capital? Why or why not? If so, what is the rate of return on the investment in the kiln, stated as a percentage per month? Under what circumstances of time preference would it be worth your while to build the kiln?

Case for Discussion

The Great American Nursing Shortage

Jose Pineda, a doctor in the Philippines, went back to school—to be a nurse. At age 41, Pineda gave up his private practice in 2003 and moved to the United States. "I am not planning for myself anymore," said Pineda. "I am planning for my kids." Pineda makes $50,000 a year as a nurse at St. Mary Medical Center in Long Beach, California—four times what his physician's salary was in the Philippines. Thousands are making the career switch from doctor in the Philippines to nurse in the United States.

Nurses are in such short supply in the United States that hospitals are looking abroad to fill the gap—offering record salaries and signing bonuses. To satisfy the need for more nurses, the U.S. federal government promises priority immigration status. In the Philippines, economic and political uncertainties have many professionals planning to leave.

In this country, Pineda doesn't deliver babies or cure patients. He works in the telemetry ward at St. Mary's, monitoring seriously ill patients. Dr. Alex Leung is one of the few people at St. Mary's who knows his history. "When I talk to Jose, I talk to him like he's a doctor," Leung said. "I tell him, 'Don't call me doctor.' Because he knows more than I do."

One study surveyed 113 nursing students in 2003. Only 6 percent considered nursing an interesting career, and 59 percent said it was degrading to become a nurse. More than three-fourths said money had driven their decisions. "We feel a lot of shame," said 29-year-old Alberto del Pilar, who works the night shift at Western Medical Center in Anaheim, California for $26.22 an hour. "I never imagined myself changing someone's diapers," he said. "It is a real adjustment

draining the urine from the urine bags, scratching their backs. Lots of patients like to be scratched."

"Which am I going to choose: to be an RN in America or a surgeon in my own country?" del Pilar asked his father, an engineer. He said, "Son, the opportunity is in America, not here in the Philippines."

Del Pilar plans to make another career switch—to being a doctor again. He spends most afternoons at Starbucks, keeping himself awake with double espressos while studying for the U.S. medical board exams in the hope of eventually practicing medicine in his new country. Many new arrivals come with the same dream, though nursing has proved so lucrative—and the path back to medicine so arduous—that few have time or resources to reinvest in medicine.

Some visas allow foreign physicians to enroll in U.S. medical residency programs, but there are many barriers to entering them. In addition, U.S. physicians have pushed to keep foreign doctors out of practice in America.

A recent federal study estimated that the United States would be 800,000 nurses short of its needs by 2020. Recruitment of nurses abroad has become big business, particularly in California, where nearly a fourth of nurses have received their training overseas; and a new state law mandates higher staffing levels, increasing the demand. Media ads in the Philippines promise high salaries, visa sponsorship, flights to Guam to take the U.S. nursing exams, and moving expenses. The process takes two years.

While paying as much as $10,000 per recruit, American hospitals have discovered that, once recruited, the doctors often save on training costs. For example, it typically takes three months to prepare a nurse for the operating room. "But if you get a surgeon, training is shorter," said Manuel Atienza, a Philippine doctor who runs a nurse recruiting business in Las Vegas.

The nursing shortage in the United States may lead to a doctor shortage in the Philippines. The country produces too many nurses and has long been the biggest supplier of foreign-born nurses to the United States. This raises concerns that the country will eventually face a shortage of doctors, especially in rural areas. In the Philippines, it is precisely rural doctors who are most likely to turn to nursing in the United States. The supply of doctors countrywide is already low.

SOURCE: Alan Zarembo, "Physician, Remake Thyself," *Los Angeles Times*, January 10, 2004.

QUESTIONS

1. Analyze the U.S. nursing shortage in terms of supply and demand. Has the demand curve shifted? If so, why? Has the supply curve shifted? If so, why? Do you think market forces will eventually eliminate the shortage? Why or why not?

2. From the point of view of a hospital, one effect of the "prospective payment" system is to raise the opportunity cost of using doctors' labor to provide health care since the hospital can no longer be certain of reimbursement for unlimited doctors' fees. Why would this cause an increase in demand for nurses' labor? Does the example suggest that doctors' and nurses' labor are substitutes or complements in the production of health care?

3. Jose Pineda says that he quit medicine in the Philippines because of the prospect of higher pay as a nurse in the United States. Would the nursing shortage make hospitals more likely to improve nurses' working conditions? How will the influx of nurses from abroad affect the treatment of existing nurses in the United States? Explain your answer in terms of the theory presented in this chapter.

4. How is the situation in U.S. nursing related to the outsourcing issue in the lead-off case for this chapter? Why might customer service jobs leave the United States, while nursing jobs have remained?

End Notes

1. Human-capital theory implies that workers with more education tend to be paid more than workers with less education because the knowledge they acquire makes them more productive on the job. This theory has been challenged by some economists, who think that the primary function of education is to help employers screen job candidates for certain desirable traits, such as intelligence and self-discipline, that are not themselves acquired through education.

2. Applying the method of discounting, introduced in the Appendix to Chapter 6, will give a fuller understanding of the relationship between the purchase price of a piece of land and its annual rental value.

CHAPTER 14

The Economics of Information and Uncertainty

INFORMATION IS AMONG the most valuable of all of the world's scarce resources. Economists have long recognized the importance of information in determining how resources are used to meet people's wants. More than forty years ago Friedrich von Hayek maintained that efficient use of knowledge is the central economic problem facing society (see *Who Said It? Who Did It? 14.1*). Hayek concluded that the success of markets as an economic institution can be traced to the effectiveness of market prices as a mechanism for creating and transmitting information.

In previous chapters we have encountered several applications of the concept of transaction costs, which include the costs of acquiring and exchanging information. The exchange of information is often hampered by the fact that potential buyers and sellers may opportunistically hide what they know as they maneuver to gain an advantage. When people are not in possession of complete information, they must make decisions under conditions of uncertainty and increased risk. This chapter addresses a number of problems in economics that have, as

Who Said It? Who Did It? 14.1
FRIEDRICH VON HAYEK ON MARKETS AND INFORMATION

Friedrich von Hayek, a recipient of the Nobel Memorial Prize for economics, was a pioneer in monetary theory and made fundamental contributions to many other branches of economics as well. Born and educated in Vienna, he is considered a key contributor to the approach to economics known as the *Austrian school*. With such books as *The Road to Serfdom* and *The Constitution of Liberty*, he also gained a reputation as a political philosopher.

A distinguishing feature of the Austrian school is its focus on the process through which markets adjust to changing circumstances. In Hayek's view, the role of markets as creators and transmitters of information is a key to understanding the market process. In 1945, Hayek presented his views on this matter in a classic article, "The Use of Knowledge in Society."

Suppose, says Hayek, that a major new use for tin arises. It may be in manufacturing, electronics, medicine—it does not matter. The exact nature of the new use does not matter, either. All the users of tin really need to know is that the opportunity cost of using tin has gone up; that is, some of the tin they used previously can now be used more profitably elsewhere—and, as a consequence, they must economize on tin. The great majority of them need not know what the new use is. They need only know that there is some new, more urgent use. If only some of them know the nature of the new use and switch resources over to it, they will create a gap between the quantities supplied and demanded at the originally prevailing price. People who are aware of the resulting gap will fill it with new supplies, and the effect will spread rapidly. It will influence the uses not only of tin but also of its substitutes and of substitutes for the substitutes. It will affect the supply of all things made of tin, the supply of all things made of its substitutes, and so on. All of this will happen with the great

majority of those involved unaware of the exact cause of the original disturbance.

How will people be notified of the change in the tin market? The means of communication that Hayek has in mind are not television, newspapers, or government directives but the market price of tin. It is a rise in the price of tin that will notify each user that a more urgent use has arisen elsewhere.

Prices are an efficient means of communicating this information because they allow each user to concentrate on the details of the particular work for which tin is needed in each case. No one needs to know about all uses of tin. Prices give just enough information about opportunity costs to guide decisions in the right direction. As Hayek puts it, "The whole acts as one market, not because any of its members survey the whole field, but because their limited individual fields of vision sufficiently overlap so that through many intermediaries the relevant information is communicated to all."

In recent years there has been a resurgence of interest in the economics of information. A common theme in the literature of this topic is the need to understand that markets are more than curves crossing on a graph. They are the nerve fibers along which messages pass from one part of the economic organism to another, thereby allowing the whole to adapt to a constantly changing environment. Hayek's 1945 article is frequently cited as a seminal contribution to the economics of information.

Friedrich von Hayek receiving the Nobel Memorial Prize in Economics from the Swedish king Carl Gustaf.

SOURCE: *Friedrich von Hayek on Markets and Information* adapted from F. A. von Hayek, "The Use of Knowledge in Society," *American Economic Review* (September 1945): 519–530. Reprinted by permission of the *American Economic Review*.

their common elements, the treatment of uncertainty as a barrier to efficient resource use and the treatment of information as a scarce resource. The first section of the chapter uses the insurance industry to introduce a number of important concepts related to risk and uncertainty. The second section discusses speculation and its role in financial markets. The final sections deals with auctions as a pricing strategy to deal with certain situations in which normal supply and demand mechanisms fail to supply all the information that buyers and sellers need for efficient resource allocation.

Insurance and Risk Pooling

One aspect of imperfect information is lack of knowledge about what the future will bring. Will there be enough rain for the corn crop? How good a job offer will I get if I major in economics instead of accounting? Whenever people do not know what will happen in the future, we say that they face risk.[1]

Attitudes Toward Risk

Expected value

For a set of possible outcomes, the sum of the probability of each outcome multiplied by the value of that outcome

People's attitudes toward risk vary according to their personalities and the circumstances in which they find themselves. Suppose, for example, that I owe you a dollar; and instead of simply paying, I offer you double-or-nothing on the flip of a coin. Heads, I pay you $2; tails, I pay you nothing. What I offer you is a fair gamble because the **expected value** of the outcome is the same as the $1 I owe you to begin with. (Expected value is calculated as the sum of the values of each outcome times the probability of that outcome. See *Applying Economic Ideas 14.1*.)

Applying Economic Ideas 14.1
EXPECTED VALUE

The expected value of a set of possible outcomes is equal to the sum of the probability of each outcome multiplied by the value of each outcome. This concept has numerous applications in economics, statistics, games, and elsewhere.

Suppose, for example, that you hold one of 50 tickets in a lottery. The winner of the lottery will receive a prize worth $100. The expected value of a ticket is calculated as follows:

Winning numbers on a lottery ticket

Probability of winning: .02
Value of winning outcome: $100
Probability of not winning: .98
Value of non-winning outcome: 0
Expected value: (.02 x $100) + (.98 x 0) = $2.00

Sometimes, some of the outcomes in the set under consideration have negative values. For example, suppose that you have a bright idea for a new Christmas toy. You

will have to invest $100,000 to bring the toy to market. If it is successful you will recover the $100,000 you have invested and earn a profit of $500,000 besides. If the toy is a flop, you will lose your entire investment. Your experience in the toy business tells you that your idea has about one chance in five of succeeding. You calculate the expected value of your investment as follows:

Probability of failure: .8
Loss in case of failure: $100,000
Probability of success: .2
Profit in case of success: $500,000
Expected value of project:
(.8 x –$100,000) + (.2 x $500,000)
= –$80,000 + $100,000
= +20,000

Conclusion: Although bringing out the new toy is a risky venture, it does have a positive expected value.

Risk aversion

A preference for a certain outcome with a given value over a set of risky outcomes with the same expected value

Risk preference

A preference for a set of risky outcomes with a given expected value over a certain outcome with the same expected value

Risk neutrality

Indifference between a certain outcome with a given value and a set of risky outcomes with the same expected value

Will you take the offer of double-or-nothing? If you prefer a risk-free outcome with a certain value rather than a set of risky outcomes with the same expected value, you are said to display **risk aversion**. A risk-averse person would turn down the double-or-nothing offer. If you prefer the risky outcome with the same expected value as the risk-free outcome, you are said to display positive **risk preference**. A person with risk preference would accept the double-or-nothing offer. If you are indifferent between risky and risk-free outcomes with the same expected value, you are said to display **risk neutrality**.

There is a good reason, grounded in the theory of consumer behavior, to expect most people to be risk averse most of the time. This can be explained with the aid of the concept of utility. As explained in Chapter 5, it is sometimes useful to imagine that utility can be measured in units called "utils," even though in practice it is impossible to measure *utility*. If you were able to measure the utility, not of just one good, but of a person's total wealth in utils, you could draw a graph similar to the one in Figure 14.1. The graph shows that starting from zero, adding $1,000 to your total wealth would give you 200 utils. Another $1,000 would add 100 more utils, a third $1,000 would add 40 more, and a fourth $1,000 would add just 20 more.

The fact that each equal addition to your wealth increases your utility by less than the previous addition reflects the principle of *diminishing marginal utility*. On a total utility graph, such as that in Figure 14.1, the marginal utility of wealth is equal to the slope of the

FIGURE **14.1** RISK AVERSION, UTILITY, AND WEALTH

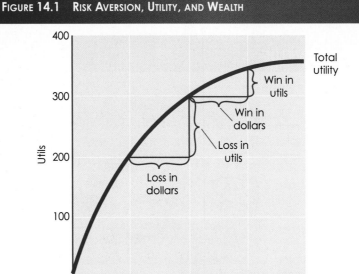

The total utility curve shown here is drawn on the assumption that utility can be measured in units called "utils." As you acquire more wealth, your total utility increases; but each added $1,000 adds less to total utility than the previous $1,000—an example of the principle of diminishing marginal utility. Suppose that you initially have a total wealth of $2,000, equivalent to 300 utils on the arbitrary utility scale. A decrease in wealth of $1,000 would decrease your utility by 100 utils, but an increase in wealth of $1,000 would increase your utility by just 40 utils. That being the case, you would not find it attractive to wager $1,000 on the flip of a coin. The wager would have an expected value of –30 stated in utils, even though it would be a fair wager (zero expected value) in terms of dollars. This reasoning shows that a person who is subject to diminishing marginal utility of wealth will tend to be *risk averse*.

total utility curve. Thus, as wealth increases, the slope of the total utility curve decreases, indicating a diminishing increment to utility for each equal increment of wealth.

To see the link between risk aversion and diminishing marginal utility, suppose you start with a total wealth of $2,000, and I offer to bet you $1,000 on the flip of a coin. Heads, I pay you $1,000; tails, you pay me $1,000. If you win, your total wealth will rise to $3,000. If you lose, you will be down to $1,000. In terms of money, it is a fair bet. Your expected value is zero because the probability of a $1,000 gain is equal to that of a $1,000 loss, but in terms of utility the bet does not look so attractive. If you lose, your utility level will drop by 100 utils, from 300 to 200. If you win, it will rise by just 40 utils, from 300 to 340. The expected value in utils of flipping the coin is $(-100 \times 0.5) + (40 \times 0.5) = -30$. Your *expected utility* drops by 30 utils if you accept the coin toss. You, therefore, decide to keep your $2,000 rather than flip the coin. Diminishing marginal utility makes you risk averse.[2]

The Principle of Risk Pooling

Risk pooling

A technique in which the risk of loss is shared among many people so that the impact of a loss on any one of them is small

Risk is part of life. No amount of human ingenuity can eliminate it. However, there are ways to soften the effects of risk. One way to do so is to share risks among several people so that the impact of an undesirable outcome on any one of them is small. This technique is called **risk pooling**.

Many examples of risk pooling can be found in financial markets. Suppose, for example, that you have $5,000 that you would like to invest in the stock market. Because stock is usually sold in units of 100 shares, with only $5,000 to invest, you would probably end up putting all your eggs in one basket. Over time the average return on stocks of major U.S. corporations has been very good, but any company can run into trouble. If you were unlucky, a drop in the price of your chosen stock could wipe out a big chunk of your $5,000.

Risk pooling offers a solution to this problem for small investors. Suppose that you put your $5,000 together with similar amounts that 1,000 other people want to invest. This would give you a pool of $5 million, which you could invest in the stock of dozens or hundreds of different companies. You and your fellow investors would share equally in the profits and losses earned on stocks in the pool. Your pool would be called a *mutual fund*.

Now and then one of the companies represented in the pool of stocks would have a run of bad luck, but that would very likely be offset by the unusual good fortune of another company. Your investment in the mutual fund would be largely shielded against fluctuations in value caused by changes in the fortunes of individual companies. Of course, a problem such as a recession or severe inflation in the economy as a whole could affect all companies at once and could still cause a loss for the fund. Pooling cannot eliminate all risk, but it can help.

Application of Risk Pooling to Insurance

Financial risks such as changes in stock prices are not the only ones that people face. There are many risks in everyday life as well, such as the risks of being in an automobile accident, being robbed, or becoming ill. People can protect themselves against the consequences of these risks through risk pooling in the form of *insurance.*

Suppose, for example, that you live in a house valued at $100,000. There is one chance in a thousand that your house will burn down in any given year. The expected dollar value of your loss from a fire is $100 per year. However, your expected loss in utility from a fire is much greater than the marginal utility of $100 cash because, although a fire is not likely, if one happened it would push you far down along the steep portion of your utility curve. What should you do?

One solution is to join with a group of your neighbors to form a mutual insurance fund. Suppose there are 1,000 members in the group. Each time a member's house burned down, that person would be compensated with $100,000 from the fund, and the members would kick in $100 each to cover the expense. On the average, you would have to pay just one claim for loss each year. If no houses burned down, you would pay nothing; if two burned down, you would pay $200; and so on. By adding more members—tens of thousands or even millions—the risk of variation in your annual contribution would become very small, so that an annual contribution very close to $100 would be a virtual certainty.

By forming the mutual insurance society, you and your neighbors convert a small risk of a catastrophic loss into a highly likely small loss. Risk pooling through insurance does not change the expected value of loss in dollar terms, but for risk-averse people it produces a big benefit in terms of expected utility. This is the fundamental principle underlying all forms of insurance.

Asymmetrical Information, Opportunism, and Transaction Costs of Insurance

In the real world, policyholders must pay premiums that exceed the expected value of claims because their premiums have to cover the costs of organizing and operating the insurance companies as well as the cost of claims. Costs other than claims can account for as much as a quarter of each premium dollar for property insurers, somewhat less for life insurers. Such costs include the clerical costs of keeping the books and mailing out bills. In addition, they include some special transaction costs that arise because not everyone has access to the same information. To use the term favored by economists, insurance companies face a situation of **information asymmetry**.

Information asymmetry

A situation in which some parties to a transaction possess relevant information that other parties do not possess

Adverse selection

The tendency of people facing the greatest risk of loss to be most likely to seek insurance

Whenever information asymmetry exists, there is a danger that people who have information that their trading partners lack will behave opportunistically. *Applying Economic Ideas 14.2* gives a vivid noneconomic example of opportunistic behavior based on information uncertainty. In the business world, the insurance industry faces two particular problems arising from information uncertainty, known as *adverse selection* and *moral hazard.*

ADVERSE SELECTION   **Adverse selection** refers to the tendency of people who face the greatest risk of loss to be most likely to seek insurance. The people closest to a river are most likely to buy flood insurance, those who live in bad neighborhoods are most likely to buy burglary insurance, and so on.

Applying Economic Ideas 14.2
THE HUSTLER

The poolroom hustler makes his living by betting against his opponents in different types of pool or billiard games; and as part of the playing and betting process, he engages in various deceitful practices. The terms "hustler" for such a person and "hustling" for his occupation have been in poolroom argot for decades, antedating their application to prostitutes. ...

The structure of a gambling game determines what methods of deception, if any, may be used in it. In many games (dice, cards, etc.) one can deceive opponents by various cheating techniques. Pool and billiard games are so structured that this method is virtually impossible. Every move is completely visible, easily watched by opponents and by spectators; it is not possible to achieve anything via tampering with the equipment.

However, one structural feature of pool or billiards readily lends itself to deceit: On each shot, the difference between success and failure is a matter of a small fraction of an inch. In pool or billiards it is peculiarly easy, even for the average player, to miss one's shot deliberately and still look good. The hustler exploits this fact so as to deceive his opponent as to his (the hustler's) true level of skill (true "speed").

As the foregoing indicates, the hustler's cardinal rule is, *don't show your real speed.* ... It might be thought that once a hustler has engaged an opponent, a bet has been agreed upon, the stake money put up, and the

The poolroom hustler is the best known hustling occupation.

game has started, the hustler might safely let out all the stops. This would be terribly shortsighted.

In the first place, the typical non-hustler bets only a small amount on the game. The hustler's only hope of making real money, therefore, is to extend the first game into a series of games, entice his opponent into doubling up when he is behind, etc. If the hustler does this well, the opponent will hang on for a long time, may even come back after the first session to play him on another day and turn into a real "fish" (the poolroom term for an inferior opponent who doesn't catch on that he's outclassed and keeps coming back for more).

Secondly, there are spectators to take into account. Some of them are potential opponents.

The sooner everyone in the poolroom knows the hustler's true speed, the sooner he exhausts the real hustling possibilities among the room's regular players. Such a situation constitutes one of the career crises that every hustler has to face. When it occurs, either he must move on to a poolroom where he's less known; or if he stays in the room, he has to take games he shouldn't or else restrict his pickings to strangers who wander in.

SOURCE: Excerpted from Ned Polsky, *Hustlers, Beats, and Others* (Garden City, N.Y.: Doubleday Anchor Books, 1969), Ch. 1. Originally published by Aldine, 1967.

If measures are not taken to control adverse selection, insurance can become unavailable to many people. Suppose, for example, that there are two neighborhoods in a city, one of which is closer to a river than the other. Residents in the Riverside neighborhood face an expected loss from flood of $10,000 per year. Those in the Highlands neighborhood face an expected loss of just $1,000 per year.

If equal numbers of people from each neighborhood sign up for flood insurance, the average expected loss will be $5,500 per year. A premium set at that level (plus an allowance for clerical costs and other overhead costs) would just allow the company to break even over time. However, residents of Highlands would quickly recognize that it is not worth their while to sign up. Seeing that the premium far outweighs the expected loss, they would start dropping out. As they did so, the average expected loss of those remaining in the insurance plan would rise, as would the premium required for the company to break even. Eventually all the Highlanders would drop out, the premium would rise to $10,000 per year, and only the Riversiders would purchase insurance.

To generalize, if adverse selection is not controlled, insurance will be available only at rates corresponding to the worst risk category. People with low, but not zero, risk would like to buy insurance; but they cannot practically do so because premiums are too high relative to the probability of loss they face. To control this tendency, firms employ *underwriters* whose job is to select and classify applicants into risk groups so that the company can calculate an appropriate premium for each group.

In the flood insurance example, the underwriter's job would be easy. Residents of Highlands are placed in a low-risk class and pay a premium of $1,000 per year (plus an allowance for overhead costs), and residents of Riverside are placed in a high-risk class and pay a premium of a little over $10,000. It is not always so easy to classify applicants into risk groups, however, because some of the relevant information may be known only to the insured.

Take life insurance, for example. Insurance companies ask life insurance applicants a lot of questions to try to classify them into risk groups. How old are they? Do they smoke? Are they overweight? What is the family's health history? Even so, the companies do not learn everything they need to know.

For one thing, some applicants may opportunistically conceal information to try to qualify for a lower premium. They may lie about their drinking habits. They may "forget" to mention that Uncle Fred died of a heart attack at age thirty-five. By slipping through the underwriting process, such people gain an advantage at the expense of other policyholders, whose premiums are pushed up accordingly.

In addition, legal or ethical restraints limit the kinds of information that insurance underwriters can take into account. Information about race is one example. In the past, life insurance companies took race into account in their underwriting. They then charged blacks more than whites for equivalent policies for the statistically well-founded reason that life expectancy is lower in the black population than in the white population. Today, even though it remains true that life expectancy is lower for the black population than for the white population, it is no longer ethically (or legally) acceptable to use race as a factor in setting insurance premiums.

Although insurance was the first in which the problem was clearly recognized, it is not the only area of business in which adverse selection occurs. Adverse selection can occur any time that sellers are unable to classify customers according to the cost of serving them. Adverse selection can also occur when buyers are unable to distinguish among sellers offering different qualities of service (see *Applying Economic Ideas 14.3*). In short, adverse selection must be counted as a pervasive phenomenon that boosts transaction costs in a world in which information is not universally available or willingly disclosed by those who possess it.

Moral hazard

Behavior that increases the risk of loss and, yet is undertaken in the knowledge that losses will be covered by insurance

MORAL HAZARD   The term **moral hazard** refers to behavior that increases the risk of loss yet is undertaken in the knowledge that losses will be covered by insurance. Sometimes a simple lack of care is involved. For example, a driver whose car is insured against theft might be less careful about locking it when it is parked. In

Applying Economic Ideas 14.3
THE ECONOMICS OF "LEMONS"

In 1970 George A. Akerlof caused a minor sensation in the economics profession with an article entitled "The Market for Lemons." The subject of the article was the market for used cars—more specifically, the market for bad used cars, or "lemons." The article drew attention to a potential source of market failure that had previously received little attention. This article, and related work, was later to win Akerlof the 2001 Nobel Prize in economics.

Akerlof's argument can be restated as follows. Suppose that there are two kinds of used 1995 Honda Civics. Some have been maintained lovingly and driven carefully. Owners would not part with them for less than $2,000, and potential buyers would be willing to pay up to $2,400 for them. The other 1995 Civics have been hot-rodded around, have never had their oil changed, and cannot be counted on for reliable service. They are lemons.

Buyers take their chances when buying a used car.

Owners would be happy to unload them for anything over $1,000; and buyers, if they knew what they were getting, would not pay more than $1,200.

If there were separate markets for good cars and lemons, there would be no problem; but, says Akerlof, there is a catch: Sellers know whether or not a car is a lemon, but buyers have no way to tell. Sellers of lemons will opportunistically misrepresent the quality of the cars, and the true quality of the cars cannot be observed.

Asymmetrical information strikes again. Not knowing which cars are which, buyers have to take their chances. If equal numbers of good cars and lemons were sold, buyers would have a 50-50 chance of getting one or the other. The maximum they would pay for a Civic of unknown quality would be $1,800, the average of the value to them of the two types of cars. However, owners of good cars would not sell them for $1,800. They would rather go on driving

them. That would leave only lemons on the market. Buyers would pay up to $1,200 for a lemon, a price at which owners would willingly sell. In the end, lemons would drive good cars out of the market altogether even though potential buyers value the good cars more than sellers do. That would be a clear case of market failure.

As economists discussed the issue, it became clear that the lemons problem was not a completely new form of market failure but rather the old problem of adverse selection in a new guise. The tendency of lemons to drive good cars out of the market is much the same as the tendency of bad risks to drive good risks out of the insurance market. The difference is that the insurance example involves adverse selection among buyers, whereas the lemons problem involves adverse selection among sellers.

When the problem is recognized as one of adverse selection, the path to resolving it is clear. Buyers must find some way to penetrate the information asymmetry. In the case of cars, they have several options. They can ask to see service records. They can (for a fee) take the car to an expert mechanic who may be able to detect signs of mistreatment; or they can buy used cars only through reputable dealers who hope to get repeat business from satisfied customers and those customers' friends. The process will never be perfect. A few lemons will slip through (just as a few people with weak hearts may slip through the qualifying procedures for life insurance). But if buyers can form at least a rough idea of the quality of used cars, it will be possible to maintain a market in both good and bad cars.

SOURCE: George A. Akerlof, "The Market for Lemons: Qualitative Uncertainty and the Market Mechanism," *Quarterly Journal of Economics* (August 1970): 488–500. Copyright 1970 The MIT Press. Reprinted by permission.

other cases there is actual dishonesty—for example, if a landlord sets fire to a building to collect the insurance.[3]

Insurance companies take whatever measures they can to control moral hazard. Sometimes they insist on certain precautions as a condition for insurance. Thus, a hotel might be required to install a sprinkler system to qualify for fire insurance. To protect against fraud, insurance companies hire specialists to investigate the circumstances of suspicious claims. Finally, insurance companies try to prevent people from over-insuring. Selling someone $10,000 of theft insurance on a car that is worth only $5,000 is an invitation to a real or faked theft.

However, like efforts to control adverse selection, efforts to control moral hazard are never completely successful. Again, information asymmetry is a reason. The insurer simply cannot observe many kinds of opportunistic behavior. As a result, moral hazard makes insurance premiums higher than they would otherwise be, and the careless and dishonest benefit at the expense of the careful and upright.

Speculation and Its Role in the Economy

Speculation

Buying something at a low price in the hope of selling it later at a higher price

The whole point of insurance is to avoid risk, but there are occasions when people voluntarily take on risk. **Speculation**—the activity of buying something at a low price in the hope of selling it later at a higher price—is an important example. Speculators can be found in many markets, including those for stocks, bonds, agricultural commodities, precious metals, foreign currency, and real estate, to name just a few.

Speculation and Risk

Speculation is inherently risky. Suppose I buy stock in ExxonMobil at $40 a share in the hope that rising world oil prices will boost the firm's profits, allowing me to sell the stock for $60 a share next year. Instead, the discovery of huge new oil reserves in Kazakhstan sends world oil prices tumbling, and ExxonMobil stock falls to $20. *C'est la vie;* it is all in a day's work for a speculator.

Why would I want to take such a risk? One explanation would be that unlike the majority of people, who are risk adverse, I have positive risk preference. Economists like to avoid explaining behavior in terms of preferences alone when other explanations are available, however. In this case there is such an explanation. Even though I am risk averse and would not speculate on ExxonMobil stock if I thought there was an equal chance that its price would rise or fall, I might do it if I thought there was a greater chance of an increase than of a decrease. For example, suppose that I think there were a 75 percent chance of an increase to $60 a share and just a 25 percent chance of a fall to $20 a share. In that case, the expected value of the stock a year from now would be $50 ([.75 × $50] + [.25 × $20] = $50). If I bought the stock now at $40, my expected gain would be $10 a share. That expected gain could well be enough to overcome my aversion to risk.

This account of speculation raises another question. If the expected value of the stock next year were $50, why would anyone sell it for $40 today? There are two possible answers. One is that other people are even more risk averse than I am. The 25 percent chance of a loss so terrifies them that they will pass up the expected $10-per-share gain. The other answer is information asymmetry: Other people have not yet discovered the information I have that leads me to think world oil prices are significantly more likely to rise than to fall.

In practice, both factors may be at work. A smaller-than-normal degree of risk aversion probably explains why some people become professional speculators. Their success as speculators depends on being the first to learn new information, whether through organized research or simply by keeping their ears to the ground.

Futures Contracts and Options

In the preceding example, speculation took the form of buying ExxonMobil stock today and holding it for resale a year from now. Two other methods of speculation involve *futures contracts* and *options*.

A **futures contract** is an agreement to exchange something at a specified future date at a price that is agreed on now. Suppose that I find another trader who expects the *spot price* for ExxonMobil stock a year from now to be $40, the same as today's spot price. (The **spot price** is the price at which a good is offered for immediate sale at any given time.) I could enter into a futures contract with that trader under which I would agree today to buy 10,000 shares of ExxonMobil stock a year from now at $40. If the spot price rises to $60 by then (as I think there is a 75 percent probability that it will), I will make a killing because I can immediately resell the shares for $20 more than I paid for them under the terms of the futures contract. Of course, there is a risk (which I put at 25 percent) that the spot price will fall to $20. In that case I am still bound by the futures contract to purchase the stock at $40 a share, $20 over its spot price at that time.

Win or lose, from my point of view as a speculator the futures contract has an advantage over buying the stock at today's spot price and holding it for a year. The advantage is that I do not have to tie up my own funds by actually holding the stock. All the buying and selling is done a year from now on the date specified by the contract.

Options are a variation on the idea of agreeing now on the terms of a transaction to be completed later. If I enter into an options contract to buy ExxonMobil stock from you at $40 a share a year from now, you have the obligation to sell the stock to me at that price if I still want it; but if I change my mind, I have the right not to exercise the option. If the spot price goes up to $60, I make the purchase and profit from it. If the spot price falls below $20, I say, "Thanks but no thanks." Of course, you would not enter into such a "heads I win, tails I break even" deal unless there was some compensation to you. The compensation is in the form of an up-front fee (called a premium) of, say, $2 a share for accepting the options contract. If I exercise the options contract at a loss to you, the $2 fee helps you offset the loss. If I do not exercise the option, the $2 is a profit for you.

The kind of option just described, which gives me the right to buy from you at an agreed price, is called a *call option*. Another kind of option gives me the right, but not the obligation, to *sell* stock to you at some time in the future at a price we agree on now. Such a contract is called a *put option*. Call options and put options are commonly used not just for shares of stock, but also for bonds and commodities like wheat or oil.

The Social Usefulness of Speculation

In terms of popularity and social respect, speculators rank about as high as poolroom hustlers. In fact, though, speculators perform a number of socially useful functions.

HEDGING   Although speculation itself involves the calculated acceptance of risks, speculators also make it possible for other traders to avoid risk. This is done through **hedging**, an operation that uses futures or options markets to offset one risk with another.

Futures contract

An agreement to exchange something at a specified date in the future at a price that is agreed upon now

Spot price

The price at which a good is offered for immediate sale

Options

Contracts under which one party obtains the right (but not the obligation) to buy something at a specified date in the future at a price that is agreed upon now

Hedging

An operation in which futures markets or options markets are used to offset one risk with another

Suppose, for example, that you are a baker. You enter into a contract to sell 10 million loaves of bread to the Army at $.50 a loaf over the course of the next year. Your bid is based on the current price of flour that, in turn, depends on the price of wheat. The price of wheat is currently $6 per bushel and is expected to stay at that level over the next year, but no one is sure what will actually happen. If the price of wheat unexpectedly goes up during the year, flour will become more expensive; that would wipe out your profit on the bread contract. What can you do to avoid this risk?

The answer is that you can enter into a futures contract at $6 a bushel to buy a quantity of wheat equivalent to the flour needed to make the bread. If the spot price of wheat rises, you will make a profit on your wheat futures contract that will offset the impact of a higher wheat price on your bread profits. If the spot price of wheat falls, you will make a loss on the wheat futures contract, but cheaper flour will allow you to make a greater profit than you expected on the bread contract. Through hedging you have shifted the risk of gain or loss on wheat prices to a speculator. You can tend to your own specialty, which is baking bread.

TRANSMISSION OF INFORMATION   A second socially useful function of speculation is transmission to the general public of information about future economic outlooks. This might seem paradoxical at first. Speculators clearly have an incentive to acquire information. They, therefore, acquaint themselves with the details of a business, hire research staffs, construct computer models, and so on. Our earlier example showed that speculators' profits depend on knowing information that other people do not know, however. Why would they share the results of their research with others?

The answer is that they cannot help doing so. Consider the example of oil prices and the prices of oil-company stocks. If my research indicates that the price of oil is likely to rise, I can profit by buying oil-company stock today (or trading in futures contracts or options, which amounts to the same thing). As soon as my fellow speculators and I start buying the stock, however, we bid up its market price. Other people look at the movement of the stock's price and say to themselves, "Somebody must think oil prices are going to rise. In fact, they must be sure enough of it to put their money on their information." The secret is out.

SPECULATION AND CONSERVATION   A final socially useful function of speculation is to promote conservation by smoothing out trends in the use of scarce resources over time. Suppose that something—say, natural gas—will become increasingly scarce in the future as reserves are depleted. Optimal use of the resource over time requires that conservation efforts begin now; but the lower the current spot price, the less incentive there will be to conserve gas.

Enter the speculator. Anticipating future shortages, speculators buy up gas wells and cap them, hoping to sell later when the price is higher. By doing so they reduce the flow of gas to the market today, thereby driving up the current price. This is the signal that is needed to spur conservation.

Of course, speculators also make mistakes. When they do so, they may destabilize prices and send false signals of scarcity to other market participants. Whether that causes significant problems for the operation of the market depends, in part, on whether the speculators who make mistakes suffer losses as a result. If the speculators who make mistakes bear the losses, a process of market selection will tend to favor the speculators who are most skilled at their job of discovering new information and putting it to use. However, sometimes people are able to speculate with other people's money. They then share the winnings from correct guesses while shifting the losses to others. For example, everyone has heard stories of "rogue traders" at securities firms who earn bonuses for a while by making lucky guesses on the direction of stock or commodity prices, but eventually lose millions or even billions of dollars of shareholders' money when they run out of luck. If shareholders and executives do not implement proper controls and appropriate bonus policies, they may encourage forms of speculation that destabilize, rather than stabilize markets.

The Economics of Auctions

In most of the markets we have discussed up to this point, sellers inform buyers in advance of the prices they will charge.[4] Buyers are offered the opportunity to buy as much or as little of the good as they want at that price, or not to buy at all.

For some goods, however, it is not feasible to announce prices in advance. Instead, the price is established at the actual moment when the transaction takes place. Several examples come to mind. One is markets for unique items that are bought and sold only rarely, such as works of art. Another is markets for perishable goods like cut flowers in which inventories cannot be stored; prices change from moment to moment in such markets to keep quantities supplied and demanded closely in balance. Markets for such goods as racehorses or tobacco, which vary greatly in quality from one unit to the next, are still another example.

When a price is not established until a transaction actually takes place, how do buyers and sellers get the information and incentives they need to use resources efficiently? How can the market ensure that scarce resources will move to their most highly valued uses? Auctions are one institution used to deal with these issues. This section examines the economics of auctions, providing special emphasis on the way they handle information.

Types of Auctions

Reservation price

The maximum price that a buyer is willing to pay for a good or the minimum price at which a seller is willing to offer it

An auction always begins from a situation of asymmetric information. Suppose I want to sell a painting. I know my **reservation price** (the minimum I would accept to part with the painting), but I do not know the reservation prices of potential buyers (the maximum that they are willing to pay). Information is asymmetric on the buyers' side, too. Buyers know their own reservation prices, but they do not know that of the seller or those of other buyers. Needless to say, both buyers and sellers in an auction expect others to behave opportunistically. Each side seeks to gain an advantage while revealing as little as possible about its own reservation price.

The preceding paragraph describes an auction that is organized and conducted by the seller, who accepts bids from buyers. We can call these *sellers' auctions*. In other cases, a buyer, who solicits bids from a number of potential sellers, organizes the auction. We can call these *buyers' auctions.* For example, I might seek bids from a number of construction contractors to build a house. In such a case I know my reservation price (the maximum I am willing to pay) but not the reservation price (the minimum acceptable bid) of potential contractors. Also, the contractors do not know the minimum acceptable bids of other contractors.

Three types of auctions are common. The sellers' versions are described here, but buyers' versions of each also exist.

English auction

An auction in which bidding starts low and proceeds until the good is sold to the highest bidder

1. In an **English auction**, the bidding starts low and competing buyers successively call out higher bids until only one buyer is left. The object is then sold to the high bidder.

Dutch auction

An auction that begins with a high bid, which is lowered until a buyer is found

2. In a **Dutch auction**, the bidding starts high and the auctioneer calls out successively lower bids until one is accepted. In this case, the object is sold to the first buyer who accepts a bid.

Sealed-bid auction

An auction in which all buyers submit bids at the same time, and the item is sold to the highest bidder (or bought from the lowest bidder)

3. In a **sealed-bid auction**, all buyers submit bids simultaneously, and the object is sold to the highest bidder.

English auctions are probably the most familiar type. They are frequently used for artwork, livestock, and charity fundraisers. Sealed-bid auctions are most often seen in the buyer's version, in which competing contractors submit bids to build houses, pave roads, develop weapons systems, and so on. The U.S. Treasury also sells some kinds of securities through sealed-bid auctions. Formal Dutch auctions are not as common, although they are used in the Netherlands to sell fresh flowers. An informal version of the Dutch auction is often used to sell houses, used cars, and other items. The item is first advertised at a price that reflects the seller's most optimistic hopes. If there is no response, the price is gradually lowered until a buyer is found.

The Revenue-Equivalence Theorem

Which type of auction works best? Which will yield the highest price to the seller when there are many buyers? Which will elicit the lowest bid for the buyer when there are many sellers? The surprising answer is that under certain broad conditions the three types of auctions can be expected to produce very nearly the same results on the average. This is known as the **revenue-equivalence theorem**.

Revenue-equivalence theorem

The proposition that under certain general circumstances English, Dutch, and sealed-bid auctions can be expected to produce approximately the same winning bid

The essence of the revenue-equivalence theorem can be understood by means of an example. Suppose that I am selling a 1998 Honda Civic at a wholesale auction to a group of experienced used-car dealers who plan to offer the car for resale. On the basis of an estimate of the resale value, each buyer mentally sets a reservation price for the car—a price at which the resale transaction would just break even. Because the buyers are uncertain exactly how much they can get for the car, the reservation prices for a given car will differ from one buyer to another.

To begin with the simplest case, suppose that I use an English auction. The bidding starts at $1,000 and quickly moves to a point at which only two bidders, Janet and George, are left. Janet bids $2,400, and George answers with $2,450. Finally Janet bids $2,500 and

George does not respond. Sold, to Janet, for $2,500. What have I learned? I have learned that George's reservation price was a little less than $2,500, while Janet's reservation price is at least $2,500. To generalize, an English auction will result in a sale at a price a little higher than the *second-highest* reservation price among the competing buyers.

Now consider the Dutch auction. I start the auction at $5,000, expecting no immediate takers, and there are none. At $3,000 I hit Janet's reservation price. Will Janet immediately jump in? No, because at $3,000 she would be buying the car for exactly the amount she thinks she will get when she resells it. There would be no profit. So Janet puts on a poker face and keeps quiet. Behind the poker face, she is putting all her experience to work to estimate the reservation price of the *second-highest* bidder at such an auction. She guesses that it will be somewhere near $2,500. Just as the bid drops close to that level, Janet raises her hand and buys the car. Sometimes Janet will guess wrong, and George or someone else will get the car before she has a chance to bid. However, all the buyers are professionals. Their guesses will tend to be correct on the average. As a result, the average selling price at a Dutch auction will again be close to the reservation price of the second-highest bidder.

Finally, suppose that the auction is conducted by means of sealed bids. Janet's reasoning will be almost the same as in the Dutch auction. She certainly will not bid her reservation price of $3,000—that would guarantee that she would not make a profit. Her profit-maximizing strategy in a sealed-bid auction such as this one is to submit a bid close to her estimate of the reservation price of the second-highest bidder. With this strategy, she stands a good chance of getting the car for $2,500.

Under certain general conditions, then, the expected winning bid will be about the same for all three types of auction: close to the second-highest reservation price among the bidders. There are exceptions, however. Sometimes special characteristics of the product or the information available to buyers or sellers will make one type of auction work better than another. Presumably, buyers and sellers in various markets develop a feel for such things over time, so that when a particular type of auction would make a difference, that type is chosen.

All in all, auctions are a reasonably efficient solution to the problem of pricing unique goods under conditions of asymmetric information and opportunism. In sellers' auctions, goods tend to end up in the hands of those who value them most; in buyers' auctions, the winners tend to be those who can supply the goods at the lowest cost. Adequate incentives are maintained in both types of auctions to call forth a supply of the goods and services that are demanded.

The Winner's Curse

Winner's curse

The tendency for winners of an auction to pay more for a good or service than it is worth (or to offer to sell at a price below the cost of providing the good or service)

Despite a generally favorable assessment of auctions, a number of observers have identified a potential market failure known as the **winner's curse**. This term refers to an alleged tendency for the winners of auctions to pay more than the item is worth or, in the case of buyers' auctions, to bid less than the cost of supplying the item.

The winner's curse is associated with a certain class of auctions known as *common-value* auctions. In such auctions, the item to be sold has the same actual value to all buyers, but the buyers do not know the exact value of the item when they submit bids. In a classic classroom demonstration, students are asked to bid on a jar of coins. Their bids are based on a guess regarding how many coins are in the jar. Bidding for oil drilling rights on government land is a real-world example. No one knows how much oil will be found on a given tract until a well is drilled, so bids must be based on estimates derived from indirect geological information.

Suppose that in a common-value auction each bidder's estimate is based on a method that, on average, accurately reflects the actual value of the item. For example, bids on a jar containing $10 worth of coins might range from $5 to $15, centered on an average value of $10. Under these conditions the winner of the auction will be the bidder who had the bad luck to most overestimate the value of the item being sold. Someone will end up paying $15, or close to it, for $10 in coins, or $15 million for drilling rights worth $10 million, or whatever. In a buyers' auction the curse would take the form of a winning bid to supply an item that failed to cover the supplier's costs, for example, a bid of $250,000 to pave a stretch of road that cannot be completed for less than $300,000.

Various writers have claimed to observe the winner's curse at work. Oil companies have been said to overpay for the value of offshore drilling rights. Publishers have been said to overpay for the rights to best sellers. Nevertheless, many economists doubt that the curse is widespread. They reason that people would not participate in auctions year after year knowing that the auctions were cursed. Instead, they think that bidders learn how to protect themselves by submitting bids that are lower than their reservation prices—lower, that is, than their actual estimates of the value of the item.[5]

Summary

1. **How does insurance help protect people from the consequences of risk?** Most people are risk averse, meaning that they would prefer a certain outcome with a given value to a set of risky outcomes with the same expected value. Risk-averse individuals can protect themselves through risk pooling, a technique in which losses are shared among the members of a large group so that each faces the certainty of a small loss rather than a small risk of a large loss. Mutual funds and insurance are examples of risk pooling.

2. **What information problems are faced by the insurance business?** The insurance business faces two problems arising from *asymmetrical information*. The first, *adverse selection*, refers to the tendency of individuals facing the greatest risk to be most likely to seek insurance. The second problem, *moral hazard*, refers to behavior that increases the risk of loss, yet is undertaken in the knowledge that

losses will be covered by insurance. Adverse selection and moral hazard, and efforts to control them, raise the transaction costs of providing insurance.

3. **Why do speculators willingly accept risk?** *Speculation*, the activity of buying at a low price in the hope of reselling at a higher price, is inherently risky. Risk-averse people will find speculation attractive only if they think they possess better information about future market conditions than other market participants do. Speculation can take the form of buying something in the *spot market*, holding it, and reselling in the spot market at a later date. Alternatively, speculators can use *futures contracts* or *options* to profit from expected changes in prices of goods that they do not currently own.

4. **What socially useful purposes are served by speculation?** Speculators make it possible for others to avoid risk by *hedging*—an operation that uses futures markets or options to offset one risk with another. A second socially useful function is the

transmission of information about future economic developments via price changes that take place when speculators trade in spot, futures, or options markets. A third socially useful function of speculation is to promote conservation by smoothing out trends in the use of scarce resources over time.

5. **What is the role of auctions in the economy?** Auctions are a method of trading in markets in which prices are subject to variation with every transaction. Auctions are possible with one seller and many buyers, one buyer and many sellers, or sometimes many of each. In the *English auction*, bidding starts low and proceeds until one high bidder remains. A *Dutch auction* begins with a high bid, which is lowered until a buyer is found. In a *sealed-bid auction*, all buyers submit bids at the same time. The *revenue-equivalence theorem* states that under certain general conditions the expected winning bid is the same for all three types of auctions, although special circumstances may make one type work better than others for some purposes. An auction is said to be subject to a *winner's curse* if the winning bidder typically pays more than the item is worth (or bids less than the cost of supplying it, in a buyer's auction).

Key Terms

Problems and Topics for Discussion

1. **Hustlers and lemons**   Evaluate the following argument: "The ordinary pool player of average skills wants to play for even odds against another player of equal skill or against a slightly better player at odds that make the game a fair match. Hustlers thwart this desire. They disguise themselves as average players and, in order to get games, offer odds that are more attractive than ordinary players can afford to give. The result is an equilibrium in which hustlers drive ordinary players from the poolroom, leaving only hustlers and 'fish' at the tables."

   What parallels do you see between this argument and the "lemons" problem discussed in *Applying Economic Ideas 14.2?* What conditions are necessary for ordinary players to survive in the poolroom and successfully enter into games with one another?

2. **Expected value**   You are offered a chance to invest $5,000 in the production of a Broadway play. There is one chance in ten that the play will be a success. If it is a success, your share of the profit will be $50,000. If the play is a flop, you will get nothing back on your investment. What is the expected value of the investment? Bonus question: Under what conditions, if any, would you be willing to make the investment?

3. **Nuclear war insurance**   Home insurance policies often exclude coverage for damage caused by nuclear war. Why does the principle of risk pooling not work in the case of nuclear war? Can you think of any similar examples?

4. **Speculation**   The Black Knight has laid siege to Fairie Towne. As soon as he hears the news,

Trader Sharp runs to the market in Fairie Towne and begins to buy all the wheat, corn, and potatoes he can get his hands on. Other citizens complain to the sheriff that Sharp is driving up the price of foodstuffs. The sheriff arrests Sharp and issues a decree that no merchant is allowed to raise the price of wheat, corn, or potatoes above the price that prevailed on the day before the siege.

Which person's actions contribute more to helping Fairie Towne survive the siege as long as possible—Sharp's or the sheriff's? Discuss.

5. **Silent auctions**   St. John's Church decides to hold a "silent auction" to raise funds for new choir robes. Parishioners contribute quilts, jars of jam, and other items to be auctioned. The goods are put on display with a box beside each item. People put slips of paper into the boxes with their names and the amounts they bid for various items. At the end of the evening, the winning bids are read off and the winning bidders pay for the items. All the proceeds go to the choir fund. In several cases, the winning bidder turns out to be the person who donated the item in the first place. Some people think this is cheating. Next time, they say, there should be a rule that people should not be allowed to bid on their own contributions. Other people think that no such rule is needed but that people were stupid to buy their own items. If they were going to do that, why not simply contribute cash to the choir fund? What do you think?

6. **The winner's curse**   Fill some jars of different shapes and sizes with coins and auction them off by the sealed-bid method in your economics class. Do the results show evidence of a winner's curse? Discuss the results.

Case for Discussion

Insurance and the Crisis in Health Care

A widespread perception has developed that the U.S. system for financing health care is in crisis.

In part the perception of a crisis comes from the rapid growth in the percentage of gross national product devoted to health care. In the 1950s, health care expenditures amounted to 5.3 percent of U.S. spending. By the 2008, that share had risen to over 16 percent. Several countries that spend less on health care have better health statistics, as measured by such indicators as life expectancy and infant mortality.

Some economists see overly generous insurance coverage as one reason for high health-care spending. People who have "first dollar" coverage, that is, who pay nothing to see a doctor or enter the hospital, are more likely to seek medical help for relatively trivial problems. Those whose policies include a "coinsurance" clause, under which they have to pay a set percentage of their medical bills, spend less. A study by economist Willard C. Manning indicated that people with first-dollar coverage spend 40 to 50 percent more on health care than those with a 33 percent coinsurance rate. Yet U.S. tax law, which makes employer-provided health insurance fully tax deductible, encourages big companies to provide first-dollar coverage.

What is more, there is a perception that health care has become not only increasingly expensive but also less equitably distributed. For the most part, people working for the government and large corporations still receive full health insurance coverage; but some 45 million people have no health insurance. Those who are uninsured include not just the poor but also millions of self-employed people and employees of small businesses.

Part of the problem stems from the reluctance of health insurance companies to insure those who need insurance the most. Instead, the companies try to estimate each person's likelihood of becoming ill and set their premiums accordingly. People who have suffered illnesses in the past, or who are genetically predisposed to illness, may find it altogether impossible to buy private insurance.

Small employers are disproportionately hit. Large firms can obtain low premiums by spreading the risk of illness among hundreds or thousands of employees. However, a small firm that hires even one employee in a high-risk group may see its health insurance premiums jump to prohibitive levels. As methods for early detection of illness are perfected, the problem becomes more and more severe.

During the 2008 Presidential election, candidates from both parties promised to do something about the health insurance crisis. Details of their plans differed, but they had certain elements in common: reducing administrative costs, encouraging greater risk-spreading, and making health insurance universally accessible.

Given the widespread agreement as to the need for change, it is likely that major changes in the U.S. health-insurance system lie ahead.

SOURCES: Williard G. Manning, et al., "Health Insurance and the Demand for Medical Care: Evidence from a Randomized Experiment," *American Economic Review* (June 1987): 251–277; Joseph P. Newhouse, "Medical Care Costs: How Much Welfare Loss?" *Journal of Economic Perspectives* (Summer 1992): 3–21; Kathleen Day, "Health Insurer's Catch 22: The Ill Need Not Apply," *The Washington Post,* October 4, 1992, H1; *Health Insurance Coverage: 2002,* Current Population Survey, U.S. Census Bureau, September 30, 2003; and *National Product and Income Accounts,* Bureau of Economic Analysis, January 2004.

QUESTIONS

1. Does this case provide any evidence that a problem of moral hazard lies behind the health insurance crisis, at least in part? What about a problem of adverse selection?

2. Why does traditional insurance coverage tend to break down in cases of illnesses that can be predicted far in advance—such as illnesses with genetic causes or those, like AIDS, for which infection precedes actual illness by a long period?

3. Review recent news stories for health-care proposals put forward in Congress or by the White House. What aspects of the insurance crisis do these proposals appear designed to address?

End Notes

1. Sometimes a distinction is made between *uncertainty,* meaning lack of information about the probabilities of future events, and *risk,* meaning a situation in which people do not know exactly what will happen but do know the mathematical probability of various possible outcomes. In this introductory discussion, however, we use the terms *risk* and *uncertainty* interchangeably.

2. If diminishing marginal utility implies risk aversion, why do people ever gamble? Economists have puzzled over this question for years. One hypothesis is that some people experience increasing marginal utility over some ranges of their utility function. (Imagine a utility graph that has several humps in it, like a playground slide.) A second hypothesis is that people overestimate the likelihood of winning. (That is what the poolroom hustler counts on.) A third hypothesis is that people get pleasure out of the act of gambling itself. (That seems to fit people who play poker for small stakes but would be bored playing for matches.) Take your pick.

3. Some insurance experts distinguish between *moral hazard,* meaning dishonest behavior on the part of the insured, and *morale hazard,* meaning merely careless behavior. Economists usually combine both types of behavior under the heading of moral hazard.

4. This section draws on an excellent review of the literature on auctions by R. Preston McAfee and John McMillan, "Auctions and Bidding," *Journal of Economic Literature* (June 1987): 699–738. For a shorter summary, see Paul Milgrom, "Auctions and Bidding: A Primer," *Journal of Economic Perspectives* (Summer 1989): 3–22.

5. For an excellent discussion of the winner's curse, see Richard H. Thaler, "The Winner's Curse," *Journal of Economic Perspectives* (Winter 1988): 191–202.

CHAPTER 15

Labor Markets, Discrimination, and Public Policy

After reading this chapter, you will understand the following:

1. Whether unions can be viewed as economic maximizers
2. What unions do in addition to bargaining over wages and benefits
3. How discrimination and anti-discrimination policies affect wages and employment of various groups
4. The economics of equal or unequal pay for men and women

Before reading this chapter, make sure you know the meaning of the concepts:

1. Monopsony
2. Human capital
3. Efficiency wage theory
4. Inframarginal rent
5. Transaction costs
6. Opportunism
7. Asymmetric information
8. Median voter model
9. Self-regarding and other-regarding preferences

THE DISCUSSION OF labor markets in Chapter 13 emphasized maximizing behavior while giving little attention to labor market institutions. This chapter looks beyond supply and demand to examine other considerations that affect labor market outcomes for individuals and groups of workers. The first section examines the role of labor unions in the economy, the second section takes up the issue of discrimination, and the final section looks at the issue of equal or unequal pay for men and women.

Labor Unions

Labor unions have played a role in the U.S. economy for more than 200 years. *Applying Economic Ideas 15.1* gives a brief history of labor unions in the United States. Just what role have unions played in the economy over this long period, and what role do they play today? There seems to be no simple answer to this question. Unions do many things, and not all unions do the same things.

Applying Economic Ideas 15.1
LABOR UNIONS IN THE UNITED STATES: A BRIEF HISTORY

The first labor unions began to appear in the United States in the late eighteenth century. These were craft unions, that is, organizations of skilled workers practicing the same trade. None of them grew large or lasted long. The first large-scale union—the Nobel and Holy Order of the Knights of Labor—emerged after the Civil War, reaching a peak membership of 700,000 in 1886. Unlike the earliest unions, the Knights of Labor offered membership to anyone who worked for a living, not just skilled workers, but also miners, unskilled laborers, even farmers. Its economic impact was limited, however; and it faded away almost as quickly as it had emerged.

Unions were created to improve wages and working conditions.

Meanwhile, craft unionism emerged in a new, more vigorous form under the leadership of Samuel Gompers, who founded the American Federation of Labor in 1881. Gompers had a narrowly economic view of unions as organizations that would enhance the bargaining power of skilled workers who, if they stood together, could not easily be replaced. The AFL viewed organization of unskilled workers or grand political goals as a waste of time.

Although unions had been recognized as legal as early as 1842, they continued to have their difficulties in court. In the early part of the twentieth centuries, the **Sherman Antitrust Act** was applied to restrict union activities on the grounds that they were conspiracies in restraint of trade. Membership decreased during the 1920s.

The Great Depression of the first large-scale industrial unions emerged in the 1930s. Unions won an important political victory with the passage of the **Norris-La Guardia Act of 1932**, which gave workers the right to strike and picket. The **Wagner Act** that formally recognized the right of collective bargaining followed in 1935.

Protected by the **Wagner Act**, the first large-scale *industrial unions* emerged in the 1930s. These, unlike craft unions, brought skilled and unskilled workers in industries like steel and automobiles together in economically powerful organizations. By the end of the 1930s, 30 percent of nonagricultural workers were unionized; and in 1945, union membership hit an all-time peak at just over a third of the labor force.

After the war, the pendulum began to swing back again. The **Taft Hartley Act of 1947** added a list of unfair union labor practices to balance the **Wagner Act's** list of unfair employer practices. Spurred by corruption scandals, the **Landrum Griffin Act of 1959** put the government in the business of policing the internal affairs of unions. Attempts to organize workers in the South and West fell short of their goals. Neither did unionism ever become as popular among the growing ranks of service workers as it had been among industrial workers. Today, unions represent only about 12 percent of workers, an all-time low, in the United States.

Unions, Wages, and Jobs

One approach to labor unions is to look at them in terms of objectives, constraints, and rational choices, as economists do when they look at firms and households. This approach emphasizes the monopoly power that union members achieve by presenting employers with a united front. Consider, for example, the case of a union that was formed in a competitive market and now seeks higher wages through the threat of a strike.

Figure 15.1 shows a labor market in which the competitive equilibrium wage rate is $8 an hour and the equilibrium level of employment is 300,000 worker-hours per year (point E_1). Now suppose that the newly organized workers tell employers that they want $10 an hour or else they will go on strike. The strike threat is shown in the graph by a change in the shape of the supply curve. Initially the supply curve had the usual positively sloped shape. After the strike threat, employers face a supply curve that contains a kink. The horizontal left-hand branch of the kinked supply curve shows that if the employers do not pay at least $10 an hour, no workers will be available. Up to 400,000 worker-hours will be supplied at $10 an hour. To hire more labor than that, the employers would have to raise the wage above what the union is demanding.

If the employers accept the union's demand, they will react by shifting to a new equilibrium at point E_2, where the demand curve and the horizontal part of the new supply

---

FIGURE 15.1   EFFECT OF UNIONIZATION IN A COMPETITIVE LABOR MARKET

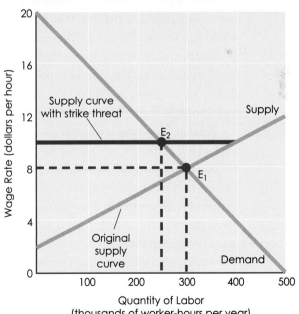

A union formed in a competitive labor market can use a strike threat to bargain for higher wages. Here, the union threatens to strike unless the wage is raised from its competitive level of $8 an hour ($E_1$) to $10 an hour. At that point, the supply curve for labor becomes horizontal at $10 an hour up to 400,000 worker-hours per year. A new equilibrium is reached at E_2, where the new supply curve intersects the demand curve. The wage is higher than before, but the quantity of labor employed is smaller.

curve intersect. There they will hire 250,000 worker-hours per year at $10 an hour. The union will have succeeded in raising its members' wages, but only at the cost of reducing the amount of work available from 300,000 to 250,000 worker-hours per year.

In this example the union can win a higher wage rate, but only at the expense of jobs for its members. How far up the demand curve should a union try to move in attempting to serve its members' interests? As of 2008, union workers in the United States earned about 14 percent more than their non-union counterparts, according to calculations by the Economic Policy Institute. At the same time, union membership was close to a record low that year, at just over 12 percent of the labor force. Does this trade-off between wages and jobs represent some kind of rational maximizing behavior? The answer is not at all obvious.

At one extreme, suppose that a union tried to maximize the number of jobs open to its members. In Figure 15.1, that would require a wage of $8 an hour, as shown by the intersection of the supply and demand curves. At that wage, 300,000 worker-hours per year will be employed. At any higher wage, employers will be unwilling to use so much labor. At any lower wage, not enough workers would apply for work to meet employers' demand. However, $8 an hour is the same as the wage that would prevail in a competitive market without a union. Thus, an employment-maximizing union might represent workers politically or might provide social benefits, but it would not affect the wage rate. The situation would be different in a market where the employer was a monopsonist.[1] Up to the point where the labor supply and demand curves intersect, a union facing a monopsonistic employer could, in principle, achieve gains in both employment and the wage rate compared with the monopsonistic equilibrium. Beyond that point (a wage of $8 per hour in Figure 15.1), it would face the same trade-off between jobs and wages as in a competitive market.

Another possible goal for a union would be to bargain for the greatest total wages for all its members. That would happen at point where the labor demand curve is unit elastic, its midpoint, when the demand curve is a straight line. The wage of $10 per hour shown in Figure 15.1 maximizes total wages.

A union that attempted to maximize total wages would face a dilemma, however. The wage of $10 per hour creates an excess supply of labor. Workers will be willing to supply 400,000 hours per year, but only 250,000 will be required. The union can simply allow workers to compete for jobs on a first-come, first-served basis and not worry about who can get a job. Alternatively, it can try to divide up the available work among all the workers who want jobs in the industry. Each worker will be able to put in only a limited number of hours. Whatever route is taken, the union must be able to prevent nonunion workers from undercutting it by offering their services at a wage lower than the union rates.

Unions as Political Entities

Models of unions as rational maximizers treat them as single-mindedly pursuing some objective just as a firm pursues the objective of profits. The reason these models fail to give clear answers to the questions of what unions maximize lies in a crucial difference between labor unions and business firms: Union members have no common interest that unites them in the way that profits unite a firm's owners.

Consider a corporation that is trying to decide whether an increase in its price will increase its profit. It compares marginal cost with marginal revenue. If the comparison is favorable, the firm will increase its price and the resulting increase in profit will be distributed among all shareholders. If all shareholders are certain that the calculations are correct, they will agree unanimously on the price increase.

The situation of a union bargaining for an increase in the wage rate is fundamentally different. If the labor demand curve is inelastic at the current wage rate, raising the wage will increase total wages received by workers, but the gain will not necessarily be shared among all union members. Instead, as the employer is forced up and to the left along the labor demand curve, some workers are likely to lose their jobs while those who remain on the job will reap all the gains. Theoretically, the union could share the gains among everyone by keeping all workers on the payroll and reducing hours per worker; however, that is not the usual practice.

If some workers gain and others lose their jobs when the wage goes up, it follows that each worker's "maximizing" wage is different from that of every other worker. Whether a given worker will favor a given wage increase will depend on whether he or she fears being laid off as a result. If, as is often the case, layoffs are made in reverse order of seniority, more senior workers will favor relatively higher wages.

THE MEDIAN WORKER MODEL   Faced with the diversity of interests among union members, some labor economists have borrowed concepts from public choice theory to analyze union behavior. For example, Bruce E. Kaufman has suggested using a variant of the median voter model. If union leadership is responsive to the wishes of a majority of members, he says, the target wage rate will correspond to the interests of the *median worker*—the one in the middle of the seniority scale. The idea is that the median worker plus all more-senior workers form a majority-voting bloc within the union. When workers vote on a contract that will increase wages at the expense of some job losses, the bloc of more-senior workers can, in principle, override the interests of less-senior workers, who are most threatened by layoffs.[2]

However, as Kaufman and others who take this approach recognize, the median worker model has some curious implications. Taken at face value, it suggests that 50 percent of the union plus one member would force through a wage increase that would get the rest of the membership laid off; the next year, half of those left would force through another such wage increase; and so on, until only one worker remained on the payroll. The fact that this does not happen suggests that the median worker model by itself does not give a full explanation of union behavior.

OTHER FACTORS   In practice, other factors offset the tendency for unions to shrink to the vanishing point, as would happen in the pure form of the median worker model. One is the fact that union members, like other people, are motivated, in part, by other-regarding as well as self-regarding preferences. Union members have a sense of solidarity that is best satisfied when all members of the group they care about have steady work at fair wages. Sometimes strong economic pressures can undermine that solidarity. For example, in recent years, the United Auto Workers union has reluctantly accepted wage contracts that pay newly hired workers less for doing the same work—an arrangement that goes against the grain of union traditions. Despite such exceptions, a model of union behavior that ignores other-regarding preferences, like feelings of worker solidarity, cannot be complete.

In addition, theories must take into account the fact that unions are complex representative structures that are influenced by the interests, including the self-regarding interests of their leaders as well as those of the rank and file. Union leaders have an interest in keeping the union membership large to enhance their own power, income, and prestige. They may also be subject to pressures from community leaders, such as city council members and newspaper editors, to behave in a "responsible" manner. If so, union leaders will balance the interests of their members against those of local government officials, merchants, and others who do not want labor-management conflict to threaten the survival of the employer.

Whatever the specifics, no neoclassical maximizing model analogous to the profit-maximizing model of the firm can do justice to the process of collective bargaining. Rather, like governments, unions must be treated as instruments for reconciling the divergent interests of their members. As in the case of government, there can be no guarantee that the outcome will optimize or maximize any particular definition of those interests.

What Else Unions Do

To focus entirely on unions' effects on wages would be misleading; unions do many other things besides bargain over wages. This has been true from the earliest days of unionism, when the Knights of Labor campaigned for worker education and self-improvement, to the present, when unions provide social activities, help members with personal and family problems, and serve as a channel for participation in national politics. Some of the things that unions do reach beyond the scope of economics; but, even on the economic level, unions affect more than wages.

THE UNION VOICE IN THE WORKPLACE   Most important, unions give workers a voice in how the workplace is run. They bargain with employers over health and safety conditions in the workplace. They help settle workers' grievances in matters ranging from job assignments to company policy to conflicts with supervisors. They bargain over issues of fairness, such as the role of seniority in layoffs and recalls. In many plants, unions and management also cooperate to elicit ideas from the work force that can lead to improvements in production processes and product design.

Unions help bargain with employers over health and safety issues.

The role of unions within the firm reflects the more general role of firms in the market economy. Firms exist because they reduce the cost of organizing complex transactions, especially those in which the parties must make a long-term commitment of specialized resources. Through their internal governing structures, firms facilitate coordination, control tendencies toward opportunistic behavior, and adapt to changes in the business environment. Unions contribute to the accomplishment of these tasks. Consider the following points in particular:

1. Workers often make commitments of specialized resources, such as acquiring firm-specific job skills or moving to a location where few alternative jobs are available. Those commitments bind the firm and the workers to each other and make separations more costly for both sides. Unions can potentially reduce the transaction costs of managing such long-term relationships.

2. Both workers and managers face temptations to behave opportunistically. Supervisors and line managers are needed to prevent shirking by workers. At the same time, union shop stewards and grievance procedures are needed to prevent arbitrary behavior by supervisors, increases in workload beyond the agreed-upon level, and so on. Without a framework for resolving such problems, worker morale would drop and turnover would rise. Unions are one way of providing such a framework.

3. Circumstances may change unexpectedly for better or worse. If a firm prospers, workers will want to claim a share of the rewards. If it falters, workers may have to share hardships to ensure the firm's survival. New technologies may sharply change working conditions and require new skills. Collective bargaining often provides a way of making the necessary adjustments to change.

FIRMS WITHOUT UNIONS   It is fair to ask, if unions are so helpful in facilitating coordination and cutting transaction costs, why has union membership been falling for nearly half a century? Three answers can be given.

First, some researchers think that U.S. unions have simply priced themselves out of the market. During the 1950s and 1960s, unions gained wage differentials some 20–25 percent above labor market rates for nonunion workers. Economists David Blanchflower and Richard Freeman conclude that such differentials were "probably economically justified when the United States was the clear world economic leader;" but today, in a more competitive world economy, they have become "a major liability to the development of unionism in the country." They note that differentials over market rates earned by workers in other countries are significantly smaller, which may explain the fact that union membership has not declined elsewhere as it has in the United States.[3]

Second, although unions are sometimes partners with management in improving quality and raising productivity, there is a darker side to unions' voices in company affairs. There have been episodes in union history when they fought new technologies that they feared would eliminate jobs; they have sometimes tried to prevent women, members of minority groups, and immigrants from gaining access to jobs that were traditionally reserved for white males; they sometimes stirred up worker hostility to make themselves seem more needed; and they have sometimes battled competition from nonunion workers with threats and violence. These aspects of unionism reduce labor-management cooperation and economic efficiency.

Third, managers have discovered that harmonious and productive labor relations can be achieved without unions. In the earlier part of the century, workers were often treated as robots. Management attitudes of that period created a fertile climate for the growth of unions. Today, top nonunion firms often go out of their way to give workers a voice in company affairs. *Applying Economic Ideas 15.2* contrasts

Applying Economic Ideas 15.2
LABOR-MANAGEMENT RELATIONS

Bob Stinson knew what labor-management relations were like in the automobile industry before the advent of unions.

"I started working at Fisher Body in 1917 and retired in 1962, with 45 and 8/10 years service," he told an interviewer. "Until 1933, no unions, no rules: You were at the mercy of your foreman.

I left the plants so many nights hostile. If I were a fella big and strong, I think I'd a picked a fight with the first fella I met on the corner. It was lousy. Degraded. You might call yourself a man if you was on the street; but as soon as you went through the door and punched your card, you was nothing more or less than a robot. Do this; go there, do that. You'd do it."

Today the "do this, go there, do that" style of management is out at top U.S. nonunion companies. Two generations after Bob Stinson started work at Fisher Body, Fred. K. Foulkes made a study of management practices at several top U.S. firms. He concluded that such firms see the main advantage of operating in a nonunion environment as higher productivity, not lower wages. The higher productivity comes partly from lower employee turnover and less absenteeism, partly from greater worker loyalty, and partly from wider acceptance of new technology.

Foulkes found that managers of the companies he studied made special efforts to give workers a voice in company affairs and to improve the quality of work life. For example:

• Managers work hard to create a sense of equality. Executive status symbols, such as exclusive dining rooms, and country clubs, are avoided. In many firms, managers and workers park in the same parking lots and eat in the same cafeterias.
• Many firms do everything they can to avoid layoffs. Instead, they handle slack periods by reducing hours or producing goods to be stored for later sale. They respond to peak demands by employing part-time or recently retired workers rather than hiring workers who would have to be laid off when the peak had passed.

Managers of nonunion companies tend to give their workers a voice in company affairs.

• The firms tend to promote from within. They post notices of job openings in their plants and offer training to workers who want to upgrade their skills.
• Many firms offer wages and fringe benefits that are competitive with those in unionized firms. (Exceptions can be found in such industries as steel, airlines, and trucking, where union wage scales are unusually high.) They also tend to pay blue-collar workers monthly salaries rather than hourly wages.
• Managers are good listeners and keep their office doors open. They are very careful about the handling of grievances and pay attention to workers' suggestions as well as complaints.

Should these practices be viewed as evidence that unions are not really necessary in a well-managed firm? Should they be considered evidence that the threat of unionization causes nonunion firms to treat their workers better? You be the judge.

SOURCES: The Stinson quotes are from an interview in Studs Terkel, *Hard Times: An Oral History of the Great Depression* (New York: Pantheon Books, 1970), 129. The material on management practices today is based on Fred K. Foulkes, "How Top Nonunion Companies manage Employees," *Harvard Business Review* (September–October 1981): 90–96.

management practices then and now. The fact that some top nonunion firms are willing to pay high wages to a highly productive work force is consistent with efficiency wage theory as discussed in an earlier chapter.

Minorities and Women in the Labor Force

As we have seen, workers have been attracted to unions not just by the hope of higher wages but also by the ideals of justice and equality in the workplace. However, neither unions nor market forces have succeeded in eliminating inequality and perceived injustices.

Persistent differences in earnings between ethnic groups and between men and women are a particular focus of concern. As of 2008, average weekly earnings of full-time black or African American workers were only 79 percent of what white men earned.[4] Hispanic or Latino workers averaged only 72 percent of white workers, while Asian workers earned 116 percent of whites. Full time women workers earned, on average, about 79 percent as much as men. The gender gap was wider for whites and Asians than for blacks and Hispanics. The overall gender gap for the United States is about average for high-income countries, among which women's wages range from a low of about 61 percent of men's in Japan to over 90 percent in Belgium. As Figure 15.2 indicates, the gender gap in the United States has narrowed substantially in recent years.

In part, the wage gaps can be explained by the different human-capital endowments of men, women, and minorities. Among these are differences in years of formal education,

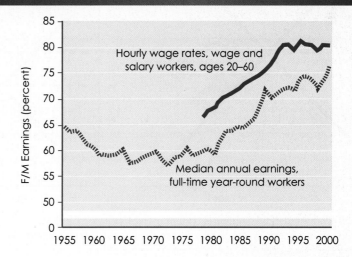

| FIGURE 15.2 | RATIO OF WOMEN'S TO MEN'S PAY IN THE UNITED STATES, 1955–2000 |

As this chart shows, although women in the United States earn less on average than men, the gap has narrowed over time. The gap is narrower for hourly wages than for annual earnings because women, on average, work fewer hours per year than men.

SOURCE: June O'Neil, "The Gender Gap in Wages, Circa 2000," *American Economic Review*, Papers and Proceedings (May 2003) Figure 1.

years of job experience, amount of on-the-job training, and time spent out of the labor force after completion of schooling. Some of those differences may or may not reflect discrimination that takes place outside the labor market, and some may reflect cultural differences or differences in preferences. Such indexes of human capital are estimated to account for about half of the wage gap; the exact numbers vary from one group to another and from one study to another. The remaining half cannot be explained in terms of human capital or other easily observable economic factors. This section is concerned with this unexplained part of the wage gap, which may be a result of discrimination in labor markets, and with policies designed to correct the effects of discrimination.

An Economic Model of Discrimination

Employers can be said to practice **labor market discrimination** against a group of workers if they are unwilling to hire members of that group at the same wage rate that they pay to equally productive members of a more favored group.

Figure 15.3 shows the effects of discrimination by employers. Part (a) shows the supply and demand curves for workers in the favored group. This demand curve, as usual, is the marginal revenue product curve. Part (b) shows the supply and demand

Labor market discrimination

A situation in which employers are unwilling to hire members of a disfavored group at the same wage rate that they pay to equally productive members of a more favored group

---

FIGURE 15.3   EFFECTS OF DISCRIMINATION ON WAGE RATES AND HOURS WORKED

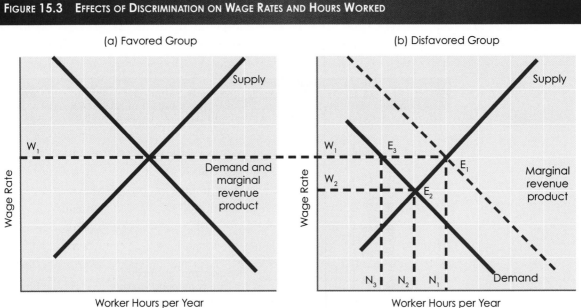

This figure shows the effect of discrimination in a labor market that can be divided into a group of workers who are favored by employers and a group of workers who are disfavored. The two groups are assumed to be equal in terms of productivity, but the demand curve for the disfavored group is shifted to the left of the corresponding marginal revenue product curve. If there are no equal-pay laws, the disfavored group's pay will fall to W_2, below the level of W_1 received by members of the favored group. If the law requires equal pay, both groups will receive wage W_1, but fewer members of the disfavored group will be employed. Many members of the disfavored group who would be willing to work in this occupation at wage W_1 will be forced into other, less attractive sectors of the job market or into unemployment. With or without the equal-pay law, then, discrimination is harmful to the disfavored group.

curves for workers in the disfavored group. In this market the demand curve is shifted to the left relative to the marginal revenue product curve. This indicates that employers will hire members of the disfavored group only if they are more productive than members of the favored group or if they are equally productive but will work for less.

EQUILIBRIUM UNDER DISCRIMINATION   Two types of equilibrium are possible under discrimination. First, let us assume that there are no legal restrictions on discrimination. In this case, the wage rate for the disfavored group will fall to W_2 compared with a rate of W_1 for the favored group. Workers from the two groups will then work side by side, doing the same job, but will receive different pay. All members of the disfavored group who want to work at wage W_2 will be able to find jobs in this market. In the second case, we assume that the law prohibits paying different wages to members of different groups for doing the same work. In this case, employers must pay wage W_1 to members of both the favored and the disfavored groups. As a result, they will employ only N_3 worker-hours per year from the disfavored group.

The effect of the equal-pay law on members of the disfavored group is mixed. On the one hand, members of that group who remain employed in this market are paid more than they would be without the law. On the other hand, fewer workers from the disfavored group get jobs at wage W_1. Those who do not get jobs in this market either remain unemployed or are crowded into some other sector of the labor market, possibly one in which employers do not discriminate. However, whether employers in those markets discriminate or not, wages there will be pushed down by the increased supply of workers who are unable to find jobs in the market. In the end, then, discrimination lowers the average wage of members of the disfavored group even when the law requires equal pay for all workers doing a given job and when there are some markets in which employers do not discriminate.

COMPETITION AND DISCRIMINATION   Now that we have examined the effects of discrimination on workers, we turn to the effect on employers. At first it might seem that employers gain from discrimination in that it pushes down the wages of members of disfavored groups. However, this is true only to the extent that employers are united in their desire to discriminate. Looking at the matter from the viewpoint of a single employer, there is an incentive not to discriminate.

Consider the case in which there is no equal-pay law. In that situation the wage rate for workers from the disfavored group is lower than that for workers from the favored group. Employers who set aside their prejudices and hire only workers from the disfavored group will have a cost advantage over employers who discriminate. This cost advantage potentially allows them to undercut their competitors' prices, either driving them out of the market or forcing them to change their hiring practices. In the long run, competition will tend to erode both the practice of discrimination and the pay gap.

All in all, the situation of discrimination in the labor market is somewhat like that of a cartel. Discriminating employers or cartel members can gain as long as they are united, but in practice each has an incentive to cheat on the system. Just as cartel members are pulled by the profit motive to undercut their fellow members, so are employers pulled by the profit motive to abandon established patterns of discrimination. *Applying Economic Ideas 15.3* looks at these forces in the South during

Applying Economic Ideas 15.3
DISCRIMINATION AND THE LAW IN THE JIM CROW SOUTH

In the southern United States during the Jim Crow era (the 1890s through the early 1950s), there was no lack of discrimination against black workers. Especially in the early part of the period, the economy was dominated by white plantation owners who employed large numbers of blacks As a group, they had an interest in holding down the wages of black farmworkers, both to boost their own profits and to maintain the dominant position of the white race in social and political life.

There was one problem, however. The greed of many white employers overcame racial solidarity. Despite warnings in newspapers that "white men must stick together," the employers competed for black labor. Black workers often left their jobs for higher-paying ones, especially at harvest time, when labor was in short supply. In addition, labor recruiters from the North would appear in the South to entice black workers to come to work in the North's growing industries at wages that, while low by today's standards, were nonetheless better than those paid by the southern planters. Something had to be done to protect the traditional system of exploitation against erosion by market forces. The solution was a set of labor laws, which were passed in most southern states between 1890 and 1910, including the following:

- *Enticement laws* made it a crime for white employers to "entice" a worker who had a contract with another employer. The aim was to prevent competition for workers that might bid up wages.
- *Contract enforcement laws* made it a crime for a black worker to break a labor contract with a white employer in order to seek work elsewhere. The standard contract period was one year. The aim was to prevent competition at harvest time when the demand for labor was strongest.
- *Vagrancy laws* made it a crime for any person who was able to work to "wander or stroll in idleness." The aim was to keep black workers in the labor force and to prevent them from spending time between jobs shopping around for the best wage offer.

Headquarters for workers favoring approval of Kansas City's Public Accommodation ordinance in an election April 7, 1964

- *Emigrant-agent laws* curbed the activities of labor recruiters from other states or even other counties. For example, a law passed by the city of Montgomery, Alabama, imposed a $100 fine or six months in jail on anyone who printed, published, wrote, delivered, posted, or distributed any advertisement that tried to persuade people to leave the city to seek work elsewhere.
- *The convict lease system* allowed black prisoners, including those who had been imprisoned for violating contract or vagrancy laws, to be leased to private employers. Being on the chain gang was worse than being a slave. Since the lease was short term, the employer, unlike a slave owner, did not even have an interest in preserving the worker's health.

In a study of the Jim Crow labor laws, economist Jennifer Roback finds that they were effective in keeping wages down and limiting migration. She concludes that without the laws, competition would, over time, have undermined racial exploitation of workers.

SOURCE: Jennifer Roback, "Exploitation in the Jim Crow South: The Market or the Law?" *Regulation* (September–December 1984): 37–44. A longer version of the article appears in the *University of Chicago Law Review* (Fall 1984).

the Jim Crow era. In that case, competition and the profit motive threatened to undermine discrimination to such an extent that states passed laws fostering employer discrimination.

SOME QUALIFICATIONS   Although competition is a force that tends to break down labor market discrimination, it cannot be counted on to eliminate discrimination altogether. One possible case is that of employers that are monopsonists in the markets in which they hire labor. An employer that faces a positively sloped supply curve in the labor market can be compared with a seller that faces a negatively sloped demand curve in the product market. It is profitable for a seller to practice price discrimination, provided that the market can be divided into two or more segments with different price elasticities of demand. A higher price is then charged in the market in which the elasticity of demand is lower. In labor markets, a monopsonistic employer can discriminate if groups can be identified according to their elasticity of supply. The profit-maximizing strategy is to pay a lower wage to the groups with the least elastic supply. Those will be the groups that have the least attractive alternative employment opportunities—namely, women and minorities.

In other cases, competition may fail to eliminate discrimination because the discrimination originates with customers or fellow employees rather than with the employer. If customers do not want to be served by members of a minority group, they will take their business to employers who do not hire minority-group members. The discriminating employers may then be at a competitive advantage overall even if they have to pay somewhat higher wages, as the theory set forth earlier indicates that they will. On the other hand, workers from dominant groups may not want to work side by side with minority-group members. In that case, an employer who wants to hire a mixed labor force may have to pay higher wages to members of the dominant group than one who hires only members of the dominant group. Again, this could give the discriminating employer an advantage over the nondiscriminating employer, despite the considerations discussed earlier.

Finally, there are cases in which employers are not responsive at all to market forces. Government employers are an example. It is no accident that some of the early targets of the drive for equal pay for women were city and state governments. In addition, some economists have argued that managers of large corporations do not always share their shareholders' interest in maximum profits. If the white male managers of such a corporation like to hire only other white males even when more highly qualified women or minority candidates are available, they may be able to get away with doing so, at least for a time, even if the firm's profits suffer as a result.

Discrimination and Asymmetrical Information

The preceding discussion assumes that someone *wants* to discriminate—that employers, fellow workers, or customers prefer not to deal on an equal basis with members of the other gender or other racial groups. It is possible, however, that discrimination can occur even when, other things being equal, all parties would prefer not to discriminate. This can happen when employers wrongly ascribe to an individual member of a certain group characteristics that may be statistically valid for the group as a whole but are not true of that individual—a phenomenon sometimes termed *statistical discrimination*.

One commonly cited example concerns the tendency of women, on the average, to spend more time out of the labor force than men. It is not disputed that the number of years a person spends in the labor force has a positive effect on productivity and wages. Given these circumstances, suppose that I am an employer looking for entry-level workers to train for career positions, and that I am convinced that women and men who spend equal years with my firm will turn out to be equally productive in their jobs. I have just interviewed two young, unmarried candidates who are alike in all respects except that one is a woman. Which do I hire?

If I am a rational profit maximizer (and if I am constrained to offer the same wage to both candidates), I hire the man. I have no way of knowing how many years each candidate will remain in the job, but the statistical probability is that the man will stay longer. Suppose, though, that you are the woman who is passed over for the job. *You know* that you are career bound, and that you, unlike many women, will not drop out of the labor force to raise children. *You know* that you will, therefore, be just as productive as the male candidate. You feel discriminated against, and you are right to feel that way.

The problem here is one of asymmetric information: I do not know as much about your future employment plans as you do, and I have no way of finding out. Can I ask? No. First of all, it is illegal for me to do so; even to ask about your family intentions is considered evidence of discrimination. Moreover, it would be pointless to ask. You might currently intend to stay with the job but later change your mind. Even if you intended to drop out of the labor force the minute you got married, there would be no reason for you to tell the truth. Asymmetric information and opportunism compound each other. In this case, they prevent me, the employer, from learning what I would like to know about you, the employee, in order to make a decision that is in all ways fair and efficient.

Now, the story just told contains some implicit assumptions that make it a worst-case scenario. In many cases, there are other sources of information available to an employer who is not lazy or prejudiced. For example, if a job requires math skills, it would be ridiculous for an employer to exclude women on the basis of a belief that "women are not good at math." The generalization is not valid to begin with and even an employer who wrongly believed it to be true could determine an individual candidate's math skills by testing, looking at high school and college transcripts, and so on.

Also, the story assumes that employers cannot arrange contracts in a way that protects them against employees who leave their jobs before the employer reaps the full benefits of their on-the-job training. Seniority-based salary scales, bonus systems, and deferred compensation in the form of pensions and other devices can protect the employer against excessive turnover among employees of either gender.

Empirical studies suggest that the problem of asymmetric information does not always prevent employers from rewarding women and men equally when they are equal in terms of labor force attachment. One study showed, for example, that men who never marry and women who never marry have comparable labor force histories, whereas married women spend fewer than half as many years in the labor force as never-married women. Within the category of never-marrieds, women earn 99 percent as much as men, even though married women earn substantially less than married men. Another study focusing on college professors showed that never-married women actually did better in terms of salary and promotions than never-married men.[5]

Such studies suggest that labor markets—like markets for other goods and services—find ways of at least partially overcoming the problem of asymmetric information. Nevertheless, it is likely that at least some cases of perceived labor market discrimination are due to information asymmetry.

Federal Antidiscrimination Policies

Since the 1960s, the federal government has instituted a number of policies designed to combat discrimination in the labor market. The first of these was the Equal Pay Act of 1963. As explained earlier, however, mandating equal pay for members of different groups within the labor force is not enough by itself to protect disfavored groups against the effects of discrimination. In the face of employer discrimination, an equal-pay requirement alone may only reduce the number of workers hired from the disfavored group.

The Civil Rights Act of 1964 made a more direct attack on employment discrimination. Title VII of that act outlaws discrimination of any kind based on race, color, religion, sex, or national origin. The law applies to firms with fifteen or more employees and also to labor unions. In the years since passage of the act, there has been much debate and litigation about what constitutes discrimination. The current interpretation is that any practice is suspect if it has a "disparate impact" on various groups. A practice with a disparate impact can be justified only if an employer proves that it is related to job performance. Thus, the requirement of a minimum height for employees holding a certain job could be challenged on the ground that it has a disparate effect on women. The requirement would be upheld if the employer could prove, say, that only a person over the minimum height could safely operate a certain piece of equipment.

A third important federal policy is Executive Order 11246, which was signed by President Johnson in 1965. This order sets antidiscrimination standards for all companies doing business with the federal government; it, therefore, covers most major firms. A key feature of the executive order is that major federal contractors must file *affirmative-action programs*. Under an affirmative-action program, a firm pledges to do more than simply not discriminate: it conducts a statistical analysis of its work force and takes concrete steps, through recruitment, training programs, and the like, to hire women and members of minority groups for jobs in which those groups are currently underrepresented. Federal law explicitly forbids the establishment of numerical quotas for hiring on the ground that they constitute discrimination against white males. However, affirmative-action measures are often criticized as constituting de facto quotas.

A number of empirical studies have attempted to determine the effectiveness of federal antidiscrimination policy. They have focused on reductions in the wage gaps among various groups before and after passage of the key civil rights acts. These studies have found federal policy to have a modest, but measurable, favorable impact on the earnings of minority men. They appear to have had a strong effect in helping to close the wage gap between black and white women. Their effects on the earnings of white women have been negligible, however. In some cases affirmative action has caused white women to be displaced by minority-group members of both genders.[6]

Occupational Segregation and Gender Inequality

In many respects, theory and policy issues having to do with discrimination by race and gender are similar, but there are some notable differences. One of the differences concerns segregation by occupation. Occupational segregation by gender is much stronger than segregation by race. For example, there are black and white truck drivers and black and white secretaries, but the truck drivers, whatever their race, tend to be men, whereas the secretaries tend to be women.

Duncan index of dissimilarity

For a set of occupations in which both men and women are employed, the percentage of men (or women) who would have to change occupations to equalize the numbers of men and women in each occupation

MEASURING OCCUPATION SEGREGATION   A common measure of occupational segregation is the **Duncan index of dissimilarity**. This measures the percentage of either group alone that would have to change occupations to equalize the numbers of men and women in each occupation. The index is 100 if occupations are completely segregated and 0 if each group is equally represented in each occupation. For example, suppose that the labor force consists of 100 men and 100 women. Of the women, 75 are secretaries and 25 are truck drivers, while 25 of the men are secretaries and 75 are truck drivers. The Duncan index in this case would be 50. Occupational segregation could be eliminated if 50 of the male truck drivers (half of all male workers) became secretaries, or if 50 of the female secretaries (half of all female workers) became truck drivers.[7]

The Duncan index of gender segregation for the U.S. labor force was 57 in 1980. This implies that more than half of all men (or women) would have to change jobs to equalize representation by occupation. By contrast, the Duncan index for occupational segregation by race was 33 for men and just 28 for women. Moreover, occupational segregation by gender is changing less rapidly than segregation by race. Between 1960 and 1980 the index of occupational segregation by race fell by 17 points for men and by 28 points for women. Over the same period the index of gender dissimilarity fell by 14 points for blacks and by just 5 points for whites. The index of occupational segregation by gender is over 50 for all age groups; this is also true for all educational groups except people with graduate degrees, for whom it is 43.[8]

The occupational segregation of men and women would be of little consequence if the occupations dominated by women were paid as well as those dominated by men, but that is not the case. Instead, occupations dominated by women have significantly lower average pay levels than those dominated by men.

Occupational differences in pay contribute strongly to the gender gap in earnings. As we saw earlier, about half of that gap can be explained by differences in human capital. Nearly all of the remaining half can be explained by occupation. To put it in more concrete terms, male and female truck drivers with equal training and experience get paid about the same. So do male and female receptionists with equal training and experience. The average pay of all truck drivers, most of whom are men, however, is higher than that of all receptionists, most of whom are women.

The policy implications of this situation are substantial. In the case of race, where there is relatively little occupational segregation, ensuring that blacks and whites are placed on the same pay scales and have equal opportunities for promotion within their occupation can make much progress toward equality. Those are the chief goals of the major civil rights legislation of the 1960s. In the case of gender, where there is much more occupational segregation, those measures will not by themselves equalize pay without either a change in the relative pay of various occupations or a major shift of genders among occupations.

ORIGINS OF OCCUPATIONAL SEGREGATION   The source of occupational segregation by gender is one of the most controversial topics in labor market economics. There are two very different views on this matter.

According to one view, occupational segregation reflects choices made by women, choices that have both cultural and economic origins. Cultural factors might lead women into nurturing occupations such as teaching and nursing and men into more physical occupations such as construction or mining. As cultural images change, occupational choices change, too. For example, the idea of women as doctors and lawyers seemed strange to many people a generation ago, but today, very close to half of medical and law students are women.

According to the opposite view, occupational segregation reflects choices made by men. In this model, men choose first. They decide which occupations they would like, leaving the rest for women. Economist Barbara Bergman conjectures that the earmarking of jobs by sex has its origin in social systems that decree that women are and should be inferior in status to men. The result is that men feel uncomfortable when working side by side with women as equals, and even more so when working under the supervision of women. To avoid this discomfort, men confine women to a limited set of job categories.[9]

In both views, wages are set by supply and demand within each occupation, and it is supply and demand that determines the pay gap. The disagreement is over why the supply of women in certain occupations is as great as it is despite low pay. In the one view, women choose those occupations voluntarily because they have attractive nonwage characteristics. In the other view, men leave women no other place to go.

THE COMPARABLE-WORK REMEDY   The different views on the origins of occupational segregation by gender have very different policy implications. Those who see occupational segregation as a product of women's choices see no need for any remedy beyond those already on the books. Those measures prohibit paying different wages to men and women doing the same work and, through affirmative action, grant women access to nontraditional occupations. Those who see occupational segregation as male dominance of labor markets want more, however. They want equal pay for women now, without waiting for massive cultural and occupational shifts to occur.

One suggested way to do this is to institute equal pay for work of *comparable worth*. Under this approach, various statistical job evaluation techniques would be used to measure the worth of work in different occupations, such as those of secretary and truck driver. Each job would be assigned points for traits like physical demand, initiative, and responsibility. The results would be plugged into a formula that can be used to arrive at a pay recommendation. Skeptics see the concept of equal pay for comparable work not only as unnecessary (because they assume that current wage differences reflect voluntary choice) but also as actively harmful, for several reasons.

First, they say, job evaluations fail to take supply and demand into account. Suppose that petroleum engineers and lawyers receive equal job evaluation points and hence are assigned equal pay. Then, during a boom in the oil industry, firms would have no way of bidding up wages to attract the extra engineers they need; and positions would go unfilled. During a downturn in the industry, petroleum engineers would have to be laid off rather than be offered the option of continued employment at reduced pay.

Second, job evaluation techniques are inherently subjective. Different point scales and different evaluators produce different relative values for the same pair of jobs. For these reasons, private firms that already use such scales as part of their human resources management use them only as one factor among many in setting wages.

Finally, the critics point out that raising wages in traditionally female-dominated jobs would cause firms to cut back on employment in those occupations. Hospitals would use more automated monitoring equipment in order to economize on nurses. Insurance companies would substitute computers for clerical workers. The reduced employment opportunities would offset the wage gains for women in the affected occupations.

Advocates of comparable worth acknowledge that job evaluation techniques are imperfect. They agree that assigning every wage decision in the country to a computer would be a bad idea, and they deny that this is their intention. Rather, they claim that intelligently applied, job evaluations and other comparable-worth policies can make a contribution to a more just and productive labor market.

Summary

1. **Can unions be viewed as economic maximizers?** In a competitive labor market, any increase in the wage brought about by unionization tends to reduce employment. Some models of unionization emphasize maximization of employment or the wage bill. Other models view unions as political structures, applying concepts like the *median worker model* that are borrowed from public choice theory.

2. **What do unions do in addition to bargaining over wages and benefits?** Besides affecting wages, unions give workers a voice in how the workplace is run. In this regard, unions can be viewed as part of the mechanisms by which firms coordinate complex transactions under conditions of long-term commitment of specialized resources, opportunism, and change. Managers of top nonunion firms recognize that productivity is enhanced when workers are allowed a voice in company affairs.

3. **How do discrimination and anti-discrimination policies affect wages and employment of** various groups? A firm is said to practice *labor market discrimination* against a group of workers if it is unwilling to hire members of that group at the same wage rate that is paid to equally productive members of a more favored group. Discrimination by employers will reduce the wages of members of the disfavored group if there are no legal restrictions, and it will reduce employment of members of the disfavored group even if the law requires equal pay for equal work. Competition tends to erode discrimination by employers but not discrimination by customers or fellow workers. Where there is asymmetric information about worker characteristics, discrimination can occur even though employers would prefer not to discriminate, other things being equal.

4. **What are the economics of equal or unequal pay for men and women?** The degree of occupational segregation is much greater by gender than by race, and occupations that have traditionally been dominated by women are less well paid than those that have traditionally been dominated by

men. To correct this situation, some have proposed that the equal-pay principle be extended so that workers performing jobs of comparable worth receive equal pay.

Key Terms

Problems and Topics for Discussion

1. **Unions and monopsony**   Turn to Figure 13.6, which shows supply, demand, and marginal resource cost curves for a monopsonist, in the preceding chapter. The equilibrium wage under monopsony is $6 per hour. Suppose now that the workers threaten to go on strike unless they are paid at least $8 per hour, and the employer is forced to accept this demand. What happens to the supply curve of labor, given the union's wage demand? What happens to the marginal resource cost curve? Compared with the initial equilibrium, what happens to the wage rate? To the number of workers? Is there a limit to how high this union can raise wages without sacrificing the jobs of members? If so, what is the limit?

2. **Unionization on campus**   Are the non-teaching staff of your university unionized? Is the teaching faculty unionized? Are any efforts under way to unionize either of these groups? Interview one member of the non-teaching staff and one member of the faculty to learn their attitudes toward unionization.

3. **Labor unions and cartels**   Review the section on cartels in Chapter 11. In what ways do unions resemble cartels? How do they differ from cartels? Do you think that public policy should treat unions and producer cartels differently? Discuss.

4. **Labor unions in the news**   Search the Internet for news about labor unions and collective bargaining. Have recent rounds of bargaining centered on issues of wages and benefits or on such matters as job security and productivity? Give examples.

5. **Discrimination at Hertz**   In 1981 two women who had worked as automobile rental agents at Hertz Corporation filed a suit saying that they had been discriminated against when they had applied repeatedly for jobs as station manager and had been passed over in favor of male candidates. Although most rental agents were women, few had ever been promoted to the position of station manager. Hertz's city manager in the city where the women worked had told them that a woman should not be given the job of station manager because she cannot go away for training and because, in the manager's view, "a woman's place is in the kitchen." The judge in the case decided in favor of the women. Do you think that the judge's decision was a proper one? Would it have been better to wait for competition to eliminate the discrimination, or do you think there was no real discrimination? Discuss.

6. **The Duncan index of dissimilarity**   A company employs 200 men and 200 women as clerks and managers. Of the managers, 160 are men and 40 are women. Of the clerks, 40 are men and 160 are women. What is the Duncan index of occupational dissimilarity by gender for this firm?

Case for Discussion

Wal-Mart Faces Class Action Suit by Women Employees

In February 2007, the United States Court of Appeals for the Ninth Circuit permitted a group of female Wal-Mart employees to proceed with a mammoth class-action suit. At least 1.5 million current and former Wal-Mart employees would potentially be affected.

In a 2-to-1 split decision, the court's majority concluded that "Plaintiffs' expert opinions, factual evidence, statistical evidence, and anecdotal evidence present significant proof of a corporate policy of discrimination and support plaintiffs' contention that female employees nationwide were subject of a common pattern and practice of discrimination."

Wal-Mart's lead attorney disagreed. "Wal-Mart has a strong antidiscrimination policy," he said.

The lawsuit alleges that women were discriminated against both in pay and promotion. According to the plaintiffs, female managers at Wal-Mart earn $89,280 on average, while men make $105,682. Female hourly workers earn $17,459 compared with $18,609 for male hourly workers. Women hold only 34 to 40 percent of managerial jobs at Wal-Mart.

The February 2007 decision did not conclusively resolve the issue of discrimination. It only allowed the plaintiffs to move ahead toward trial of their case. In late 2008, Wal-Mart settled a number of smaller class-action discrimination suits, paying workers up to $640 million. However, the main suit discussed here remains under appeal and has not yet come to trial.

SOURCES: Based in part on Christopher Caldwell, "Licensed to Curb a Retail Leviathan," *The Financial Times*, February 11, 2007, and Steven Greenhouse, "Court Approves Class-Action Suit Against Wal-Mart," *The New York Times*, February 7, 2007

QUESTIONS

1. In a dissenting opinion, Court of Appeals Judge Andrew J. Kleinfeld wrote that it was unrealistic to conclude that illegal discrimination was the sole cause of Wal-Mart's female employees failing to advance to better jobs. What other factors might play a role? Which of these factors, in your view, represent "choices made by men," and which would be "choices made by women?"

2. Data presented by the plaintiffs suggest that Wal-Mart is able to attract qualified female managers at wages less than those paid to equally qualified males for comparable jobs. If so, could Wal-Mart further increase its profits by replacing some of its higher-priced male managers with equally competent, but less expensive, women? Why do

you think Wal-Mart has not done so? Do you think economic or non-economic motivations lie behind the under-representation of women in managerial jobs?

3. Data cited earlier in the chapter suggest that across all occupations, women in the United States earn about 81 percent as much as men. At Wal-Mart, according to data submitted by plaintiffs in this lawsuit, women managers earn about 85 percent as much as men and women hourly workers about 94 percent as much as men. These numbers suggest that Wal-Mart, although not perfect, is doing better than the average for all U.S. businesses in providing equal compensation for its female and male employees. Do you think this should have a bearing on the way the case is decided? Discuss.

End Notes

1. See Chapter 13, for an explanation of monopsony in labor markets.
2. Bruce E. Kaufman, *The Economics of Labor Markets and Labor Relations* (Hinsdale, IL: Dryden Press, 1986), 461–463.
3. David Blanchflower and Richard Freeman, "Going Different Ways: Unionism in the United States and Other Advanced OECD Countries," NBER Working Paper No. 3342, 1992.
4. Bureau of Labor Statistics, New Release USDL 08-1460, October 17, 2008. According to data provided by the Economic Policy Institute in *State of Working America*, 2008, unions appear to narrow the gap between minority workers and white workers, as indicated by a larger "union premium" for minority workers. However, the union premium for women is smaller than for men.
5. These and other studies are discussed in Walter Williams, *Explaining the Economic Gender Gap* (Dallas: National Center for Policy Analysis, 1983).
6. For a brief summary of the empirical literature, see Kaufman, Economics of Labor Markets, 392–393.
7. Mathematically, the Duncan index is found by summing across occupations the absolute value of the differences between the percentages of the two groups employed in each occupation and dividing that sum by two. If M_i is

the percentage of one group in occupation i and N_i is the percentage of the other group in occupation i, then the index, D, is found by the formula

$$\sum_i \frac{|M_i - N_i|}{2}$$

8. See Victor R. Fuchs, "Women's Quest for Equality," *Journal of Economic Perspectives* (Winter 1989), Table 1.

9. See Barbara Bergman, "Does the Marker for Women's Labor Need Fixing?" *Journal of Economic Perspectives* (Winter 1989): 43–60.

CHAPTER *16*

Income Distribution and Poverty

After reading this chapter, you will understand the following:

1. How income distribution can be measured
2. How poverty differs from inequality and how it is measured
3. What are the effects of labor market policies intended to alleviate poverty
4. How transfer payments can be used to alleviate poverty and how design of transfer programs can be improved

Before reading this chapter, make sure you know the meaning of the concepts:

1. Income and substitution effects
2. Human capital
3. Public choice theory
4. Economics of discrimination

THIS CHAPTER EXAMINES the problems of income distribution and poverty. These subjects are an extension of the theory of resource markets. As we saw in Chapter 13, workers and owners of capital and natural resources are rewarded according to the productivity of the factors of production they contribute. Entrepreneurs earn profits or losses according to their degree of success in finding and taking advantage of new opportunities, but not everyone starts from the same position when entering the labor market. People are born with different skills and talents. They grow up in different countries and different regions or school districts within a country. They control different amounts of capital and natural resources, and encounter different prejudices. These differences by themselves are enough to cause incomes to vary. As people go through life, the decisions they make, including those that affect their human capital, and the entrepreneurial risks they take, cause incomes to vary still more. As a result, some earn little or nothing, while others earn millions of dollars a year.

In addition to what people earn in factor markets, public policies also influence the distribution of income. Transfer payments like unemployment compensation and Temporary Assistance for Needy Families (TANF) are intended to raise the incomes of poor families, while tax systems in most countries affect income distribution by taxing the poor comparatively less than the wealthy.

This chapter will take a comprehensive look at the sources of income inequality and poverty and at public policies that are intended to alleviate them.

Measuring Inequality and Poverty

Inequality in the United States and Around the World

Lorenz curve

A graph that represents the degree of income inequality in an economy

Figure 16.1 provides a good place to begin a discussion of how inequality is measured. The diagram shows a **Lorenz curve**—a visual picture of income distribution. It is drawn as a square with the horizontal axis representing a percentage of the population and the vertical axis a percentage of income earned by those at or below each population percentile. Reading this particular Lorenz curve, we see that about 7 percent of

---

FIGURE 16.1   A LORENZ CURVE FOR THE U.S. ECONOMY

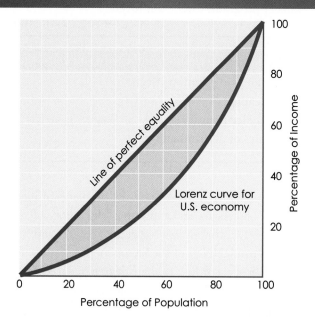

A Lorenz curve can be used to represent the degree of inequality in an economy. Such a diagram is drawn in a square, with the horizontal axis representing the percentage of the population and the vertical axis the percentage of all income earned by those at or below each population percentile. In an economy in which income was distributed equally, the poorest 20 percent of the population would earn 20 percent of all income, the poorest 40 percent would earn 40 percent of all income, and so on. In that case, the Lorenz curve would be a straight line from one corner of the box to the other. In the U.S. economy, where the poorest 20 percent of the population earns just 3.5 percent of all income and the richest 20 percent earns 50.1 percent, the Lorenz curve sags toward the lower right-hand corner of the box. The degree of inequality can be measured by the Gini coefficient—the ratio of the shaded area between the Lorenz curve and the line of perfect equality to the area of the whole triangle beneath the line of equality.

all income is earned by the poorest 20 percent of the population, about 25 percent by the poorest 50 percent of the population, and so on.

If income were distributed equally among all members of the population, the Lorenz curve would be a straight line, labeled as the line of perfect equality in the diagram. Twenty percent of the population would account for 20 percent of the income, 50 percent of the population for 50 percent of the income, and so on. The more unequal the distribution, the more the Lorenz curve sags below the line of equality. In a society where one person earned all the income and no one else had anything at all, the Lorenz curve would hug the axes, having a reverse-L shape.

The fact that the Lorenz curve sags more and more as inequality increases provides a simple way to reduce the concept of inequality to a single number. The **Gini coefficient**, invented in 1912 by the Italian statistician Corrado Gini, is the ratio between the shaded area lying between the Lorenz curve and the line of equality to the whole triangle lying beneath the line of equality. If income is distributed perfectly equally, the Gini coefficient

Gini coefficient

A measure of inequality of income equal to zero under conditions of perfect equality and to one under perfect inequality

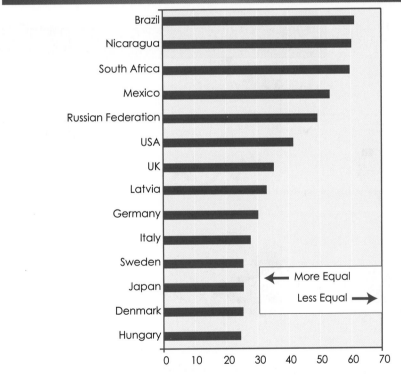

FIGURE 16.2   GINI COEFFICIENTS OF INCOME INEQUALITY FOR SELECTED COUNTRIES

The Gini index is a measure of inequality that has a value of 0 under conditions of perfect equality and 100 under perfect inequality. As this figure indicates, the United States is near the middle of the range of world countries in terms of inequality. A world bank study estimates the Gini Index for the whole world, throwing together the poorest people in poor countries and the wealthiest people in the richest countries, as about 66—more unequal than the in-country distribution for the least equal individual countries.

SOURCE: World Bank

Gini index

The Gini coefficient expressed as a percentage

is zero. If one person has all the income, the Gini coefficient is 1. The Gini coefficient multiplied by 100 is called the **Gini index**.

Figure 16.2 provides data on income inequality in selected countries. As can be seen, inequality varies greatly around the world. Latin America and some African countries stand out as regions of the greatest inequality. The high-income countries of Europe and some high-income Asian countries are among the most equal. The United States is about in the middle with regard to income inequality as measured by the Gini index. A World Bank study estimates the Gini Index for the whole world, throwing together the poorest people in poor countries and the wealthiest people in the richest countries, as about 66—more unequal than the in-country distribution for the least equal individual countries.[1]

Earnings, Taxes, and Inequality in the United States

Income inequality differs not only from country to country but also over time within any given country. Figure 16.3 uses the shares of the lowest-income 20 percent, the highest 20 percent, and the highest 5 percent of households to show how inequality of before-tax income in the United States changed over the second half of the twentieth century.

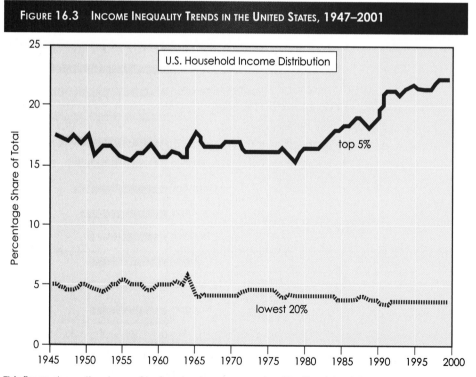

FIGURE 16.3   INCOME INEQUALITY TRENDS IN THE UNITED STATES, 1947–2001

This figure shows the share of before-tax income received by the richest 5 percent and the poorest 20 percent of U.S. households. The distribution of income reached its historically most equal values in the period between the mid-1950s and the late 1970s. Since 1980, the distribution of income has become steadily less equal.

SOURCE: U.S. Bureau of the Census

The figure shows that after reaching its historically most equal point from the mid-1950s to the late 1970s, U.S. income distribution has become steadily less equal since 1980. A number of factors lie behind this trend.

DEMOGRAPHIC CHANGES The distribution of income by individuals is somewhat less unequal than the distribution by households since the lowest-income households are, on average, smaller than those at the top of the income distribution. The poorest 20 percent of households include only about 15 percent of the population, whereas the richest 20 percent include nearly a quarter of the population. Demographic changes appear to be of increasing importance. For example, in 2006, for the first time fewer than half of American women were married. The rate of unmarried women is greater and increasing more rapidly for low-income than for high-income households, which reinforces the disparity in family size.

Furthermore, there appears to be a tendency for an increased number of marriages among partners of similar income levels. At the risk of using an overly stylized illustration, we might imagine that in the past, male doctors married wives who did not enter the labor force while male laborers married female grocery clerks. Today, the male doctors are marrying female lawyers while both the male laborers and female grocery clerks are marrying later, if at all. Such changing patterns of marriage would have the effect of increasing income inequality among households even if the degree of income equality among all male and female individuals were to remain unchanged.

CHANGES IN RELATIVE WAGES OF SKILLED AND UNSKILLED WORKERS   Some of the most dramatic changes in income inequality occurred within the category of wage and salary income. During the 1980s, there was a sharp increase in the earnings of college-educated workers relative to those with a high-school education or less. This change continued although at a slower rate, during the 1990s. Because college-educated workers already earned more than the less educated to begin with, this change added to overall inequality. Several explanations have been offered for this trend:

- *Skill-biased technological change*   One common explanation of the increased return to education is skill-biased technological change. Computerization of both manufacturing and services may have increased the demand for college-educated workers more rapidly than they increased as a percentage of the labor force.

- *Immigration and trade*   Another possible explanation of the relative increase in pay of more educated workers lies in immigration and trade. If immigrants, including illegal immigrants, were less skilled than the average U.S.-born labor force, the relative supply of low-skill workers would have increased at the same time the relative demand for low-skill workers was falling. If instead of "importing" workers, U.S.-based firms "exported jobs" by moving low-skill production processes abroad, the effect on relative demand and supply for low-skilled workers would have been much the same.

- *Decline of unionization*   Some observers believe that the decline of labor unions in the United States, a process that began earlier but continued during the 1980s and after, may also have contributed to inequality. The reason for thinking this is that unionized manufacturing jobs were traditionally among the best-paying alternatives for workers with a high-school education or less.

The above explanations are not mutually exclusive. It is likely that each of them has played some role in the trend toward greater inequality of income in the United States over the past quarter century. Although many studies have been undertaken, there does not appear to be a firm consensus as to which of the causes is the most important.

TAXES As the distribution of before-tax income changed over time, the distribution of taxes by income group has changed as well. In particular, income tax rates in the United States have fallen substantially since the late 1960s, when the maximum rate was as high as 90 percent, while payroll taxes (Social Security and Medicare contributions) have risen. Federal corporate and inheritance tax rates have also changed although these taxes account for a smaller share of total revenue. As shown in Figure 16.4, on balance, federal tax rates have decreased for both the lowest and highest income groups since 1960, while tax rates have increased for middle-income families.

A tax system is said to be *progressive* if the distribution of after-tax income is more equal than that of before-tax income, and *regressive* if the opposite is true. Personal

---

FIGURE 16.4 FEDERAL TAX RATES IN THE UNITED STATES, 2004 AND 1960

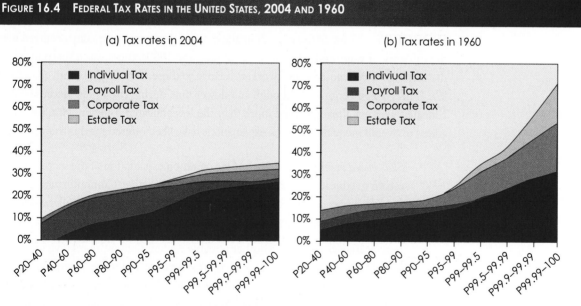

These figures show federal tax rates by income group for the United States in 1960 and 2004. The labels on the horizontal axis show income groups by percentiles. For example, "P20–40" includes those whose incomes fall in the range above the poorest 20 percent of the population, but below the richest 60 percent. The group "P99–99.5" shows rates for households whose incomes are in the top 1 percent, but below the top 0.5 percent, and so on. Comparing the two figures, we see that tax rates were higher in 1960 both for the lowest- and highest-income groups. By 2004, tax rates were lower for both the very poor and very rich, while middle-class tax rates had increased significantly.

SOURCE: Thomas Pikkety and Emmanuel Saez, "How Progressive is the U.S. Tax System?" *Journal of Economic Perspectives* (Winter 2007) 3:24.

income taxes are an example of a progressive tax, while sales taxes and payroll taxes are regressive. On balance, the U.S. tax system, like that of other countries, is progressive. At the low-end of the income scale, the federal tax system has become more progressive over time as shown in Figure 16.4. This is

Tax distribution and percentages have changed over time.

especially true with regard to income taxes. In fact, as a result of the Earned Income Tax Credit (discussed further below), the average tax rate for families with incomes below the fortieth percentile is negative—they get more back from the credit than they pay.

At the top end of the income scale, the picture is very different. In 1960, the average federal tax rate for the top 0.1 percent of the population was over 50 percent whereas by 2004, it had fallen to about 34 percent. In 1960, the top 0.1 percent of households accounted for about 3 percent of all income before taxes, but only about 1.5 percent after taxes. By 2004, the top 0.1 percent accounted for almost 7 percent of before-tax income and about 5.5 percent of after-tax.

Interestingly, although tax rates on top income earners have fallen, the total share of all taxes paid by that group has increased. In 1960, the richest one-tenth of one percent of the population paid about 8 percent of all federal taxes. By 2004, that total had risen to about 12 percent. In part, this may have happened because tax cuts for high earners encourage them to make greater efforts to earn more, although not many economists think that effect is large. Perhaps more likely, lower tax rates may have increased income *reported* by higher earners because tax cuts decreased incentives to participate in legal tax shelters and illegal tax.

It also appears likely that the high share of income earned and taxes paid by the highest-earners in 2004 was due in part to the growth over time of executive compensation and bonuses. According to calculations by the Economic Policy Institute, average executive compensation rose from about 25 times that of the average worker in 1965 to an astonishing 275 times that of the average work in 2007. The trend was especially pronounced in the financial services industry.

Measuring Poverty

Poverty and inequality are related concepts, but the relationship is not a simple one. Inequality is a statistical concept, whereas poverty is a sociological one. Poverty implies a lack of means to provide for basic material needs. As discussed in *Applying Economic Ideas 16.1*, there are countries in the world where almost everyone is poor and others where almost no one is poor, even though income is nowhere distributed equally.

Applying Economic Ideas 16.1
POVERTY IN THE UNITED STATES AND AROUND THE GLOBE

Poverty in the United States is undeniably a problem that merits serious attention by economists and policymakers. Nonetheless, to place things in perspective, it is worth keeping in mind that even low-income families in the United States are incomparably richer than the poor in many regions of the world.

The World Bank uses an income of $1.25 per day as a measure of extreme poverty. Some 1.4 billion people, or more than a quarter of the world population, fall below this level. This is an improvement over the count of 1.9 billion extremely poor people in 1981, but the improvement has been uneven. While economic growth and globalization

More than a quarter of the world population falls below the level of extreme poverty or income below $1.25 a day.

have lifted hundreds of millions of people out of poverty in China and India, more than half of the population of Sub-Saharan Africa continues to experience extreme poverty. In the poorest countries, like Ethiopia, four out of five people fall below this threshold. By comparison, an income of $1.25 per day, or $1,825 per year for a family of four, is just 8 percent of the U.S. government's official poverty threshold. In the United States, almost no one qualifies as extremely poor by the World Bank's standards.

People in the United States and other high-income countries may have a hard time understanding what it means to live on less than $1.25 per day. Numbers alone fail to paint a clear picture. To help understand the nature of global poverty, try answering yes or no to the following questions:

1. *Yes/No: Do you own more than one change of underwear?*

2. *Yes/No: Do you own a pair of shoes?*

3. *Yes/No: Do you have access to transportation other than walking (e.g., car, bicycle, or public transportation system)?*

4. *Yes/No: Do you have more than one choice of food for your dinner tonight?*

If you answer, "yes" to all of these questions, you are among the world's wealthy. Many people in the World Bank's "extremely poor" category can answer yes to none of them.

Since the 1960s, the U.S. government has followed an official definition of poverty based on an estimate of the income needed to provide a minimum standard of living. The definition starts from an economy food plan devised by the Department of Agriculture. The plan is supposed to provide a balanced diet at the lowest possible cost given prevailing market prices. By itself, a total income equal to the cost of the economy food plan is not enough to keep a family out of poverty. To take other needs into account, the government sets the poverty threshold—the dividing line between the poor and the nonpoor—at three times the cost of the economy food plan. In 2007 the low-income level was $21,203 for a family of four, about 30 percent of the median income for such families. Below that level, it is assumed that the pressure of a family's needs for shelter, clothing, and other necessities tends to become so great that the family will forgo the needed food to get other things.[3]

As shown in Figure 16.5, 12.5 percent of the U.S. population was officially considered poor as of 2007. Although the poverty rate tends to rise during recessions and fall during expansions, it has remained within a range of about 12 to 15 percent since the 1970s. The fact that the rise in income inequality since 1980 has not resulted in a

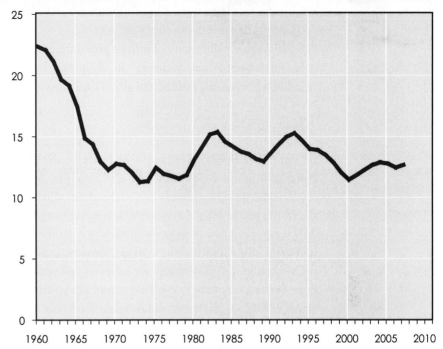

FIGURE 16.5 OFFICIAL POVERTY IN THE UNITED STATES, 1960-2005

According to the official definition, about 12.5 percent of the U.S. population was poor as of 2007. This percentage has varied within a narrow range from about 12 percent to about 15 percent since the 1970s.

SOURCE: U.S. Bureau of the Census

corresponding increase in poverty serves to underline the difference between the two concepts. The increase in income inequality has taken place against the background of a doubling of real gross domestic product in the past twenty-five years. High earners have captured most of this increase. While the rich have gotten richer, not much has happened to the poor, one way or the other, at least as measured by official statistics.

Since its introduction, the official poverty definition has been subject to criticism. One set of criticisms stems from the way it defines income. The official definition includes income before taxes plus the value of cash transfers, such as TANF, unemployment compensation, and disability payments. In a sense, by including transfers intended to alleviate poverty, the official definition understates the magnitude of the underlying problem. A measure of *pre-transfer poverty* would be based on a family's income before receiving government aid. Such an adjustment would be substantial. In a 1999 study, when the official poverty rate was 11.9 percent of the population, the Census Bureau estimated pre-transfer poverty to be 18.4 percent.

On the other hand, if the intention is to measure how many people remain poor *after* government programs have done their work, a different adjustment needs to be made. This would be to include the money value of noncash income. The most important sources of noncash income are noncash transfer payments like food stamps, medical benefits provided either by government or by private employers, and changes in the equity value of homes owned by poor families. In addition, after-tax rather than before-tax income should be used. These adjustments would have lowered the poverty rate in 2007 from 12.5 percent to about 9 percent.

Although the different definitions give different absolute numbers of poor people, it is worth noting that changing the definition has very little effect on long-term trends. Over time, the official and alternative definitions move up and down together.

Persistence of Poverty

A final important measurement issue concerns the persistence of poverty. The image that comes to mind when one thinks of a poor person is one without income, without assets, without skills, without a job, and without much hope for positive change in any of the above; yet the official measure of low income captures many people whose income is only temporarily low. A person's income may be low because he or she is between two high-paid jobs. Construction workers, farmers, actors, writers, stock speculators, even professional poker players may experience good years and bad years but still have adequate income on average. What we would like to know is how many people experience extended periods of poverty, and how many are poor only for short spells.

The data reported in Figure 16.6 attempt to address this question for the years 1993 and 1994. The years are representative in that neither was a year of unusually high nor low poverty, and in that the overall rate changed little from the first year to the second. As the figure shows, many more people experienced short spells of low income than

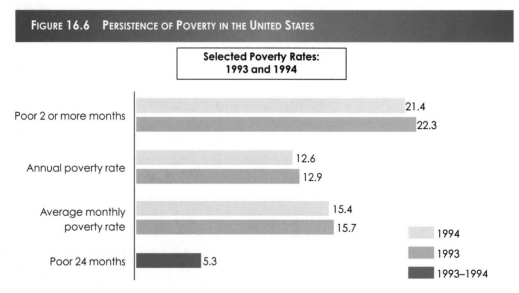

FIGURE 16.6   PERSISTENCE OF POVERTY IN THE UNITED STATES

Selected Poverty Rates:
1993 and 1994

Poor 2 or more months — 21.4 (1994), 22.3 (1993)
Annual poverty rate — 12.6 (1994), 12.9 (1993)
Average monthly poverty rate — 15.4 (1994), 15.7 (1993)
Poor 24 months — 5.3 (1993–1994)

1994
1993
1993–1994

The data presented above come from a study that attempts to distinguish long-term, chronic poverty from short spells of low income. In 1993 and 1994, about 22 percent of the population had incomes below the poverty threshold in at least two months of a calendar year; yet just 5.3 percent of the population were poor for the entire 24-month period.

SOURCE: Bureau of the Census, Current Population Report P70-63, July 1998.

experienced persistent poverty. By the official measure, which asks whether a person's total annual income is below the poverty threshold, just less than 13 percent of the population was poor in each year. Looking at periods shorter than a year, the figure shows that, in any given month, more than 15 percent were poor if poverty is defined as a monthly income less than one-twelfth of the annual poverty threshold. Furthermore, more than 22 percent of the population had two or more low-income months in each year. However, when people were followed from the beginning of 1993 through the end of 1994, only 5.3 percent of the population was poor in every month of the two-year period. Is poverty a long-term trap or a revolving door? A little of both, it seems.

Policies to Fight Poverty

At one time, responsibility to support low-income individuals was thought to lie with families, local communities, and private charities. In some countries this remains true to this day. In the United States and other high-income countries, however, national governments have long made the alleviation of poverty a major focus of policy. In many European countries in the mid-twentieth century, governments led by Labor or Social Democratic parties instituted comprehensive "welfare state" policies. In the United States, the 1930s saw the advent of Social Security to combat poverty among the elderly. Today, the elderly have lower poverty rates than those of the working-age population. In the 1964, President Lyndon Johnson declared a "War on Poverty." By the end of that decade, poverty had declined to its present rate of 12 to 15 percent from rates higher than 20 percent in the 1950s. In the 1990s, a major legislative effort, led by President Bill Clinton and receiving broad bi-partisan backing in Congress, resulted in extensive reform of antipoverty policy. This section briefly summarizes the main types of policy used to fight poverty in high-income countries.

Labor Market Policies

Without a doubt, work is the most effective of all antipoverty programs, at least in high-income countries. In the United States, the poverty rate for families with at least one full-time worker is about a fifth of that for families with no workers. Not surprisingly, then, governments have tried to combat poverty by improving wages and job prospects of people who might otherwise fall into poverty.

In the broadest sense, a whole range of public policies help to alleviate poverty by improving work prospects. Take education, for example. In the United States, the poverty rate for people without a high-school diploma is nearly double the national average, while the poverty rate for college graduates is less than a quarter of the average. Public health policies also combat poverty since poor health is something that cuts many people off from the labor market. Important though such policies are, however, this section will focus on a narrower group of labor market policies that aim to ensure that those who do work will not fall into poverty.

MINIMUM WAGE POLICIES   Although those who work are less likely to be poor than those who do not, it remains true that even in the United States, one of the world's highest income countries, almost 6 percent of people in families with a full-time worker have incomes below the poverty threshold. If wages were higher, it would be easier for a full time worker to raise a family out of poverty. That is the intention of minimum wage laws. The first federal minimum-wage law was passed in 1938 and required employers to pay $.25 per hour. Since then the federal minimum wage has been raised several times. In 2007, Congress enacted a schedule of increases raising the minimum wage to $7.25 per hour as of 2009. That is enough to raise a single full-time worker above the poverty threshold. However, even at the increased minimum wage, it would require two minimum-wage workers to keep a family of four out of poverty; and even that might not be enough if work-related expenses were taken into account. Several states and a few cities mandate a wage above the federal rate.

Some economists warn that minimum wage laws have unintended consequences that undermine their effectiveness as an antipoverty program. Although raising the minimum wage does make some low-skilled workers better off, it reduces the quantity of such workers demanded. Each increase in the minimum wage therefore means that some people lose their jobs—restaurants remain open fewer hours, automated gates replace parking lot attendants, and so on. During periods like the early 2000s, when the minimum wage was low compared to average wages, these effects appear to have been small. As the minimum wage rises closer to the median wage, employment effects would be expected to become larger.

An additional limitation of a minimum wage as antipoverty policy is that not all low-wage workers are poor. In the United States, it is estimated that something like half of all workers with minimum wage jobs come from households in the top half of the national income distribution. These workers include students working part time and living with their families, low-paid spouses in households in which both husband and wife work, and so on. At the same time, a minimum wage does little or nothing to help the three-quarters of poor families in which no one holds a full-time job. Rather than relying on wages, these families support themselves with income from pensions, disability payments, welfare, and other nonwage sources.

UNEMPLOYMENT COMPENSATION   As discussed earlier, many people who are not chronically poor experience periods of poverty. One reason for such episodic poverty is unemployment. Unemployment compensation temporarily replaces the lost income of unemployed persons and keeps them out of poverty until they can find a new job.

Like minimum wages, however, unemployment compensation has unintended consequences. The principal such consequence is to lengthen the time workers take until they find a new job. Up to a point, this is not all bad. It takes time and careful search to match workers to the jobs for which they are best suited; and if people had no choice but to take the first job that came along, the labor market might operate less smoothly. Still, excessively generous unemployment compensation leads to higher unemployment and, over all, a less productive economy.

Among high-income countries, there is somewhat of a divide between policies in the United States, paralleled to some degree by some other English-speaking countries, and the approach of continental European countries. The U.S. model emphasizes a time limit on unemployment payments. It tends to use payments high enough to keep the unemployed out of poverty without necessarily replacing the full income of their last jobs. Also, it tends to require those receiving unemployment benefits to participate actively in training and job-search programs, including placement in jobs that may pay less than those previously lost. The continental model tends to be more generous in terms of time limits, compensation levels, and retraining requirements. A cross-country comparison by Stephen Nickell found that countries with higher benefits and longer duration of benefits tend to have significantly higher unemployment rates and, also, more long-term unemployment as a share of total unemployment.[4] France, Germany, Italy, and some other European countries have attempted to reform unemployment policies although reform efforts are in their early stages and meeting much political resistance.

ANTI-DISCRIMINATION AND JOB SECURITY POLICIES   As discussed in Chapter 15, the United States has a comprehensive range of policies to combat labor market discrimination against women and minority groups. Other high-income countries have similar policies. To the extent women and minority groups historically have higher poverty rates than white men, there is an antipoverty component to antidiscrimination policies. It is likely that these policies have contributed to the increase in earnings of women and minorities relative to white men. These gains have been a factor slowing the growth of income inequality for the population as a whole. As discussed in the last chapter, there are circumstances under which these programs, too, might have perverse unintended consequences; but they are considered so important for the sake of social justice that few people propose discarding them on the grounds that they undermine labor market efficiency.

In continental Europe, many countries have gone much further in protecting workers' job security than is the case in the United States. These policies tend to make it difficult for employers to dismiss workers. Often they also place strict limits on use of part-time workers and overtime work, with the intention of increasing the number of full-time jobs. France has one of the strictest policies, limiting almost all workers to a 35-hour workweek. These policies, like generous unemployment schemes, are the subject of intense debate because of their perceived unintended consequences. Although intended to protect job security for employed persons, they make it more expensive for employers to create new jobs. The study by Nickell, mentioned earlier, found that these policies, too, contribute to high European unemployment rates.

In sum, labor market interventions definitely have their limitations as tools for combating inequality and poverty. In many respects, they are more realistically seen as furthering the interests of middle-income workers who already have strong labor market attachment at the expense of marginal workers with low skills and weak labor market attachment.

Transfer Programs

The principal alternatives to policies intended to improve the labor market prospects of poor people are programs that give them cash or in-kind benefits. We refer to these as *transfer programs*. From 1935 to 1996, the best-known cash transfer program was Aid to Families with Dependent Children, now replaced by Temporary

The new debit card is replacing the paper food stamps. Food stamps are one of the best known in-kind transfer programs.

Assistance for Needy Families. The best-known in-kind transfer programs are food stamps and Medicaid. This section examines the intended and unintended consequences of such programs and reforms to U.S. transfer programs in the 1990s.

INCENTIVE EFFECTS OF TRANSFER PROGRAMS

Transfer programs, like policies centered on the job market, have the intended consequence of raising the incomes of people who would otherwise be poor. Both types of programs also have unintended consequences. For transfer programs, the unintended consequences that have attracted the most attention are changes in work incentives. Figure 16.7 demonstrates the incentive effects of income transfer programs.

Suppose that the poverty threshold P for a certain family is determined to be $10,000, and suppose that the family's earned income is Y. We call the difference between P and Y the *poverty gap* for the family. One way to ensure that the family will not be poor would be to give them a cash grant equal to the poverty gap. For example, a family with no earned income would get a grant of $10,000; one with $3,000 of earned income would get $7,000; and families with earned income over $10,000 would get no grant.

Under such a program, the total disposable income for various families would follow the line PQRS. The program would be completely successful in terms of its intended effect of keeping the family out of poverty. Unfortunately, it would have a severe unintended effect on work incentives. The family would get no financial benefit whatsoever from earnings up to $10,000. Taking into account the effort of holding a job, not to mention job-related expenses like transportation, clothing, and childcare, many families might prefer not to work even if they were offered a job paying somewhat more than $10,000.

Benefit reduction rate

The amount which reduces transfer benefits for each added dollar of earned income

Alternatively, payments to the family could be linked to earned income. A family with no income would still receive $10,000, but the amount would be reduced only by part of a dollar for each dollar of earned income—the **benefit reduction rate**. Graphically, the benefit reduction rate is represented by the ratio of line ab to line bc.

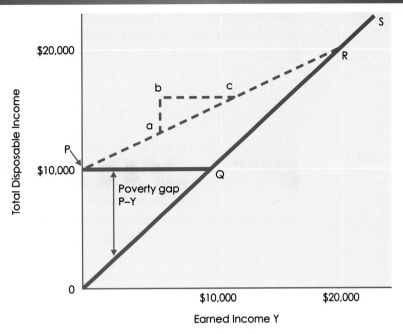

FIGURE 16.7   WORK INCENTIVES AND TRANSFER PROGRAMS

In this figure, the poverty threshold is P ($10,000 in this example) and earned income is Y. The poverty gap is the difference between P and Y. If a family is paid exactly what is needed to fill the poverty gap, its total disposable income follows the path PQRS as earned income increases. In that case, work incentives are 0 up to point Q. If the program is modified to include a benefit reduction rate of 50 percent (the ratio ab/bc), total disposable income follows the path PRS. Work incentives are increased, but now some payments are made to families whose earned income is already above the poverty threshold.

If the benefit reduction rate were 50 percent, the family's total disposable income would follow the path PRS in Figure 16.7. Compared with the program described in the previous paragraph, this would have the advantage of providing a substantial work incentive. However, reducing the benefit reduction rate has the further effect that some families now receive transfers even though their earned income is greater than the poverty threshold. For example, a family with $12,000 earned income, previously ineligible for assistance, would receive a grant of $4,000 under a program with a basic benefit equal to $10,000 and a benefit reduction rate of 50 percent. Whether such a program would cost less overall depends on how people respond to work incentives and how many families there are, to begin with, at various income levels.

The situation gets even more complex if earned income is subject to an income or payroll tax. If so, the amount by which total disposable income increases for each dollar earned depends on both the tax rate and the benefit reduction rate. The sum of the two is called the **net marginal tax rate**. Suppose, for example, that all earned income, starting at zero, is taxed at a 20 percent rate. If we add this tax to the previously described program, the result is a net marginal tax rate of 70 percent for income up to $20,000 and a net marginal tax rate of 20 percent above that level.

Net marginal tax rate

The sum of the benefit reduction rate and the rate of income tax

Negative income tax

An antipoverty program under which low-income people receive grants from the government and high-income people pay taxes, subject to a net marginal tax rate of less than 100 percent for everyone

WELFARE REFORMS OF THE 1990S   In 1962, University of Chicago economist Milton Friedman proposed that all antipoverty programs be integrated with the income tax system. He called the scheme a **negative income tax.** Under this scheme, low-income families would receive payments from the government and higher income families would make payments to it, with the net marginal tax rate held low enough for everyone to provide adequate work incentive.

Friedman's proposal was made at a time when most welfare programs had very high net marginal tax rates, sometimes more than 100 percent. Such high rates occurred because the benefit reduction rates and tax rates of various programs are additive. For example, if a family received an AFDC grant with a benefit reduction rate of 67 percent, a food-stamp grant with a benefit reduction rate of 50 percent, and paid Social Security payroll taxes of 14 percent, its net marginal tax rate would be 131 percent. For each $100 earned, the family would end up $31 poorer in terms of total disposable income. *Applying Economic Ideas 16.2* provides details of an actual example of high net marginal tax rates during the 1980s.

Friedman's ideas helped focus the attention of economists and policy makers on the inefficiencies, not to say the injustices, of existing antipoverty programs. More and more, people came to perceive AFDC, food stamps, and similar programs as "paying people to be poor." In response to these criticisms, many experiments in welfare reform took place during the 1970s and 1980s. Some of these were small-scale experiments with negative income taxes that aimed to measure the response of poor families to changes in benefit reduction rates. Others took the form of changes in the way antipoverty programs were implemented in different states. Many of these experiments showed promising results. In the 1990s, they culminated in major reforms of the welfare system at the national level. The reforms were championed by President Bill Clinton and received unusually wide bi-partisan support in Congress.

One major reform, enacted in 1993, was the expansion of a previously small federal program known as the Earned Income Tax Credit (EITC). Under the EITC, families with very low earned incomes receive a federal tax credit for each dollar earned. For example, as of 2000, a family with two children received a credit of $.40 for each dollar of earned income up to an income of $11,790. At that point, the tax credit reached a maximum of $4,716 and continued at that level up to an earned income of $15,399. After that point, the credit was reduced by approximately $.21 for each additional dollar of earned income until the credit fell to zero at an income of $37,782. The EITC operates on top of other existing federal taxes. For very low incomes, the EITC exceeds taxes due on earned income, so taxpayers receive a check from the government. For higher incomes, the EITC may be less than taxes due; but nevertheless, they reduce tax owed. The net marginal tax rate is the sum of the EITC rate and applicable rate of other income and payroll taxes.

The EITC is a variant on the negative income tax concept, but one that contains even more potent work incentives for the lowest-income workers than did Friedman's original proposal. The reason is that up to the maximum EITC threshold, payments actually rise rather than fall when earned income increases. Another way to put it is to say that the benefit reduction rate in this income tax range is not just low but negative.

The other major set of reforms was implemented in 1996 under the clumsy title Personal Responsibility and Work Opportunity Reconciliation Act (PRWORA). The PRWORA reforms are difficult to summarize because, although they establish certain

Applying Economic Ideas 16.2
NET MARGINAL TAX RATES FOR A LOS ANGELES FAMILY

Before the welfare reforms of the 1990s, poor families were often subject to an extremely high net marginal tax rate. The table provides a real-world example based on taxes and reductions in benefits for an inner-city family of four in Los Angeles in the 1980s. The column "monthly gross wages" includes wages paid plus employer and employee contributions to Social Security. The data on disposable income reflect all payroll and income taxes and assume that the family makes use of the maximum city, county, state, and federal welfare benefits to which it is entitled.

The net marginal tax rate is the sum of the marginal tax rates and benefit reduction rates to which the family was subject. The disincentive effects of benefit reductions and taxes reached a peak just above and below the poverty threshold, which was $833 a month for a family of four at the time. Note that as a family's gross wages increased from $700 a month to $1,200 a month, its disposable income would fall from $1,423 to $1,215. This reflects the loss of $385 in welfare benefits, the loss of $9 in food stamps, a reduction of $23 in the family's housing subsidy, an estimated reduction of $130 in the value of its medical benefits, an $8 increase in state income and disability insurance taxes, $68 in payroll taxes, and $85 in federal income taxes.

SOURCE, Arthur Laffer, "The Tightening Grip of the Poverty Trap,"Cato Institute Policy Analysis No. 41, August 30, 1984. Reprinted with permission.

Monthly Gross Wages (Dollars)	Monthly Family Disposable Income (Dollars)	Change in Disposable Income (Dollars)	Net Marginal Tax Rate (Percent)
0	1,261	NA	NA
100	1,304	43	57
200	1,341	37	63
300	1,366	25	75
400	1,391	25	75
500	1,419	28	72
600	1,429	10	90
700	1,423	−5	105
800	1,418	−5	105
900	1,420	2	98
1,000	1,432	12	89
1,100	1,253	−178	278
1,200	1,215	−39	139
1,300	1,217	2	98
1,400	1,296	39	61
1,500	1,294	38	62
1,600	1,330	37	63

federal guidelines, they are implemented at the state level. In practice, state programs vary greatly. Without examining all the variants, the main features of PRWORA were as follows:

- Aid to Families with Dependent Children (AFDC), previously the main welfare program, was replaced by Temporary Assistance for Needy Families (TANF).

- A complex set of training programs and work incentives was implemented. These included mandatory participation either in employment or training for most families, plus incentives like expanded child care grants for working parents.

- A time limit was established for TANF payments beyond which recipients were required to make the transition to self-sufficient employment.

The response to PRWORA was dramatic. In the late 1990s, welfare roles, measured as the number of families receiving AFDC or TANF, decreased sharply (Figure 16.8a); and labor force participation rates increased—especially for the key group, single women with children. As discussed earlier in the chapter, the 1990s

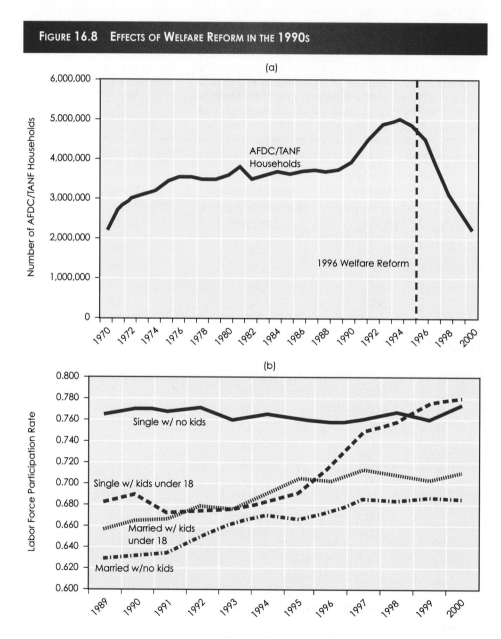

FIGURE 16.8   EFFECTS OF WELFARE REFORM IN THE 1990S

After passage of reforms in the 1990s, the number of families receiving AFDC or TANF fell sharply; and the labor force participation rate of women with children increased significantly.

SOURCE: Rebecca M. Blanc, "Evaluating Welfare Reform in the United States," *Journal of Economic Literature*, Vol. XL, No. 2, December 2002, Figures 3 and 4.

did not bring a permanent reduction in the overall poverty rate for the United States. However, for single women with children, the poverty rate declined significantly, from over 35 percent in 1992 to under 25 percent by 2000.

A large amount of research has attempted to explain just why welfare roles fell and labor force participation increased in the late 1990s. All of it seems to agree that, in combination, the EITC and PRWORA reforms made a helpful contribution to these trends. However, it remains difficult to determine exactly which parts of the reforms worked and how well. One reason is that the reforms took place against the background of a booming labor market that would have reduced welfare roles and increased employment even if there had been no reforms. Another reason is that many reforms were implemented at once. Furthermore, the reforms were implemented differently from state to state, a fact that sometimes helps researchers by providing contrasting state-level cases, and sometimes frustrates them by complicating the analysis of national trends. Many observers fear that reformed welfare systems, which performed well in times of prosperity, will encounter serious difficulties as unemployment rises and incomes fall during the recession that began in 2007.

Whatever the final outcome of the academic analysis, the U.S. reforms have attracted interest from many other countries. It remains safe to say that few people would prefer to return to the welfare system of the 1980s and before.

Summary

1. **How can income inequality be measured?** Inequality is most often measured using the Gini coefficient or Gini index. The Gini coefficient is 0 under conditions of perfect equality and 1 under conditions of perfect inequality. The Gini index converts this to a percentage by multiplying by 100. The United States has a Gini index of about 40 for personal income before tax—about average for countries of the world. The income distribution in the United States reached its historically most equal point in the 1960s and 1970s. Since that time inequality has steadily increased.

2. **How does poverty differ from inequality, and how can it be measured?** Poverty implies a lack of ability to meet basic needs. In the United States, poverty is officially measured by a threshold equal to three times the cost of buying a minimum adequate diet for a family. Since the 1970s, the percentage of households in poverty in the United States has usually ranged from about 12 to 15 percent, with no strong trend one way or the other. On a global scale, poverty is often measured by a threshold of $1 or $2 per person per day. This is much lower than the U.S. poverty threshold.

3. **What are the effects of labor market policies intended to alleviate poverty?** One way to raise people out of poverty is to improve their prospects in the job market. Indirectly, policies supporting education and public health are helpful in this regard. Direct efforts to improve earnings and job security include minimum wages, unemployment compensation, and measures to discourage layoffs, part-time work, and overtime. All of these policies may improve the income of the employed but have the unintended consequence of raising the unemployment rate.

4. **How can transfer payments be used to alleviate poverty, and how can design of transfer programs be improved?** Transfer programs are

intended to eliminate poverty by making up the gap between the poverty threshold and earned income. Their most troublesome unintended effect is to discourage work effort. Work incentives can be improved by keeping benefit reduction rates and net marginal tax rates low. The negative income tax is one proposal for maintaining work incentives. Welfare reforms in the United States in the 1980s incorporated some aspects of the negative income tax and also added direct incentives to participate in work or training.

Key Terms

	Page #
Lorenz curve	388
Gini coefficient	389
Gini index	389
Negative income tax	400
Net marginal tax rate	400
Benefit reduction rate	400

Problems and Topics for Discussion

1. **Poverty versus inequality** "It is a mistake to think of poverty in terms of absolute needs. The best way to measure poverty would simply be to consider the bottom fifth of the income distribution in each country to be 'poor' and the rest to be 'nonpoor.' Do you agree, disagree, or agree in part? Is this approach applicable to very rich countries? To very poor countries?

2. **Cash versus in-kind transfers** What are the relative merits of cash and in-kind transfers? Review Chapter 5, paying particular attention to the concepts of marginal utility and consumer equilibrium. Suppose that program A gives a family a $1,000 cash benefit and program B gives it $1,000 worth of goods in kind, but in proportions that are not chosen by the family itself. Which program would be likely to give the family greater utility? *Bonus question:* If you read the appendix to Chapter 5, illustrate these two programs for the case of an economy in which there are just two consumer goods: food and clothing.

3. **Social insurance** Suppose that an effective negative income tax was in force and poverty, as defined by the Bureau of the Census, had been eliminated. Would you then be willing to see social-insurance programs such as social security and Medicare abolished? Why or why not?

4. **Transfer payments and the nonpoor** Discussions of "waste" in poverty programs often focus on the fact that some benefits go to families whose incomes are above the poverty line. After reading this chapter, do you agree that it is wasteful to pay benefits to some nonpoor families? Would you favor a program that cut off all benefits when the poverty line was reached? In what ways might such a program itself be wasteful? Discuss.

5. **Fight Poverty—Get a Job!** A popular bumper sticker reads "Fight Poverty—Get a Job!" This slogan is presumably intended to do more than call attention to the fact that those who work are less likely to be poor. Rather, its purpose seems to be to evoke a set of normative judgments related to "deserving" versus "undeserving" poor, willingness to work versus opportunity as reasons for not working, and so on. What is your position on these issues? Discuss.

Case for Discussion

Two Steps Forward, One Step Back

The Sacramento City Council adopted a "living wage" ordinance that took effect on January 1, 2004. "This is a great day," said Chris Jones, chairman of the Sacramento chapter of the Association of Community Organizations for Reform Now. Jones added, however, that it is "just the beginning" of city efforts to improve pay for the region's low-wage workers.

The ordinance will increase wages to $9.00 an hour for private employees on city contracts, if the company provides health benefits. If the company does not provide benefits, the hourly wage will be $10.50 an hour. The living wage rises to $9.50 in 2005 and to $10 in 2006, with an additional $1.50 for companies that don't provide health coverage.

All that glitters is not gold, though. According to a city-funded report, when low-wage workers earn higher income, they no longer qualify for the same federal and state public assistance and social insurance benefits. For instance, a single parent with two children would receive $2,533.20 in annual food stamps if he/she earned minimum wage. With a living wage of $8.50/hr., that benefit falls to $1,273.20. Living-wage workers also receive less from the federal Earned Income Tax Credit and the state disability insurance fund, and they pay more in federal and state taxes.

Even with reduced federal- and state-funded aid, the living wage does improve disposable income for prior minimum-wage workers. For households with two children, disposable annual income including transfer payments would rise by $1,553.65 with a $8.50/hr. living wage, and by roughly $2,700 with a $10.00/hr. living wage.

Who pays the bill? City government, taxpayers, and employers will share the cost of the living wage. With higher wages, employers will not only pay more to their workers, but to social security taxes as well. Also, if the $9.00 living wage chases away potential contractors for the City of Sacramento, the remaining vendors may be able to bargain for more costly contracts to offset higher labor cost.

SOURCE: Suzanne O'Keefe and Stephen Perez, "A Living Wage for Sacramento," CSUS Regional Development Initiative, September 2002; Andy Furillo, "City Living-Wage Plan Gets Final Approval," *Sacramento Bee*, December 10, 2003.

QUESTIONS

1. What do you think is the motivation for the additional $1.50 per hour to be paid to workers who do not receive health benefits? Which is better, health benefits or the extra money? How would you know? Would the answer be the same for all workers?

2. How does the living wage help to reduce poverty? Suppose a household with two children earns an additional $2,000 per year in annual gross income as a result of Sacramento's living wage. Will this household take home $2,000 in additional disposable income? Why or why not?

3. How does the living wage change the nature of public assistance in Sacramento? Who bears the cost of helping the poor now that the city has imposed the living wage? Who bore this cost before?

End Notes

1. Research by the World Bank's Branco Milanovic summarized in Robert Wade, "Winners and Losers," *The Economist* (April 26, 2001).

2. A thorough discussion of the problems of using tax return data to track changes in inequality can be found in Alan Reynolds, "Has U.S. Income Inequality Really Increased?," Policy Analysis No. 586, Cato Institute, January 8, 2007.

3. The government's 3-to-1 ratio was based on a study done in 1961. More recent surveys suggest that poor families typically spend less than a quarter of their income on food. Thus, some have suggested that the poverty "multiplier" should be raised to 4 or even to 5.

4. Stephen Nickell, "Unemployment and Labor Market Rigidities: Europe vs. North America," *Journal of Economic Perspectives* (Summer 1997): 55–74.

Glossary

Absolute advantage   The ability of a country to produce a good at a lower cost, in terms of quantity of factor inputs, than the cost at which trading partners can produce the good

Access fee   The part of a two-part pricing strategy paid for the right to become a customer

Accounting profit   Total revenue minus explicit costs

Adverse selection   The tendency of people facing the greatest risk of loss to be most likely to seek insurance

Aggregate concentration   The degree to which the economy as a whole is dominated by the largest firms

Antitrust laws   A set of laws, including the Sherman Act and the Clayton Act, which regulate market structure and the competitive behavior of firms

Barrier to entry   Any circumstance that prevents a new firm in a market from competing on an equal footing with existing ones

Benefit reduction rate   The amount which reduces transfer benefits for each added dollar of earned income

Bounded rationality   The assumption that people intend to make choices that best serve their objectives, but have limited ability to acquire and process information

Budget line   A line showing the various combinations of goods and services that can be purchased at given prices with a given budget

Capital   All means of production that are created by people—including tools, industrial equipment, and structures

Capitalized value of a rent   The present value of all future rents that a piece of land or other resource is expected to earn

Cartel   A group of producers that jointly maximize profits by fixing prices and limiting output

Change in demand   A change in the quantity of a good that buyers are willing and able to purchase that results from a change in some condition other than the price of that good; shown by a shift in the demand curve

Change in quantity demanded   A change in the quantity of a good that buyers are willing and able to purchase that results from a change in the good's price, other things being equal; shown by a movement from one point to another along a demand curve

Change in quantity supplied   A change in the quantity of a good that suppliers are willing and able to sell that results from a change in the good's price, other things being equal; shown by a movement along a supply curve

Change in supply   A change in the quantity of a good that suppliers are willing and able to sell that results from a change in some condition other than the good's price; shown by a shift in the supply curve

Closed monopoly   A monopoly that is protected by legal restrictions on competition

Coase theorem   The proposition that problems of externalities will be resolved efficiently through private exchange, regardless of the initial assignment of property rights, provided that there are no transaction costs

Comparative advantage   The ability to produce a good or service at a relatively lower opportunity cost than someone else

Complementary goods   A pair of goods for which an increase in the price of one results in a decrease in demand for the other

Concentration ratio   The percentage of all sales that is accounted for by the four or eight largest firms in a market

Conditional forecast   A prediction of future economic events in the form "If A, then B, other things being equal"

Conglomerate mergers   Mergers of firms in unrelated markets

Constant returns to scale   A situation in which there are neither economies nor diseconomies of scale

Consumer equilibrium   A state of affairs in which a consumer cannot increase the total utility gained from a given budget by spending less on one good and more on another

Consumer surplus   The difference between the maximum that a consumer would be willing to pay for a unit of a good and the amount that he or she actually pays

Contestable market   A market in which barriers to entry and exit are low

Cross-elasticity of demand   The ratio of the percentage change in the quantity of a good demanded to a given percentage change in the price of some other good, other things being equal

Deadweight loss   A loss of consumer or producer surplus that is not balanced by a gain to someone else

Demand   The willingness and ability of buyers to purchase goods

Demand curve   A graphical representation of the relationship between the price of a good and the quantity of that good that buyers demand

Derived demand   Demand for a productive input that stems from the demand for the product the input is used to produce

Differential rent   The rents earned by superior units of a resource in a situation in which units of a resource differ in productivity

Direct relationship   A relationship between two variables in which an increase in the value of one variable is associated with an increase in the value of the other

Diseconomies of scale   A situation in which long-run average cost increases as output increases

Duncan index of dissimilarity   For a set of occupations in which both men and women are employed, the percentage of men (or women) who would have to change occupations to equalize the numbers of men and women in each occupation

Dutch auction   An auction that begins with a high bid, which is lowered until a buyer is found

Dynamic efficiency   The ability of an economy to increase consumer satisfaction through innovation and technological change

Econometrics   The statistical analysis of empirical economic data

Economic efficiency   A state of affairs in which it is impossible to make any change that satisfies one person's wants more fully without causing some other person's wants to be satisfied less fully

Economic rent   Any payment to a factor of production in excess of its opportunity cost

Economics   The social science that seeks to understand the choices people make in using scarce resources to meet their wants

Economies of scale   A situation in which long-run average cost decreases as output increases

Efficiency in distribution   A situation in which it is not possible, by redistributing existing supplies of goods, to satisfy one person's wants more fully without causing some other person's wants to be satisfied less fully

Efficiency in production A situation in which it is not possible, given available knowledge and productive resources, to produce more of one good without forgoing the opportunity to produce some of another good

Efficiency wage theory The theory that wages above the minimum necessary to attract qualified workers can raise productivity by enough to increase profit

Elastic demand A situation in which quantity demanded changes by a larger percentage than price, so that total revenue increases as price decreases

Elasticity A measure of the response of one variable to a change in another, stated as a ratio of the percentage change in one variable to the associated percentage change in another variable

Empirical Based on experience or observation

English auction An auction in which bidding starts low and proceeds until the good is sold to the highest bidder

Entrepreneurship The process of looking for new possibilities—making use of new ways of doing things, being alert to new opportunities, and overcoming old limits

Equilibrium A condition in which buyers' and sellers' plans exactly mesh in the marketplace, so that the quantity supplied exactly equals the quantity demanded at a given price

Excess burden of the tax The part of the economic burden of a tax that takes the form of consumer and producer surplus that is lost because the tax reduces the equilibrium quantity sold

Excess quantity demanded (shortage) A condition in which the quantity of a good demanded at a given price exceeds the quantity supplied

Excess quantity supplied (surplus) A condition in which the quantity of a good supplied at a given price exceeds the quantity demanded

Expansion path A line on an isoquant diagram showing the least-cost combinations of inputs used to produce various levels of output, for given input prices

Expected value For a set of possible outcomes, the sum of the probability of each outcome multiplied by the value of that outcome

Explicit costs Opportunity costs that take the form of explicit payments to suppliers of factors of production and intermediate goods

Externalities The effects of producing or consuming a good whose impact on third parties other than buyers and sellers of the good is not reflected in the good's price

Factors of production The basic inputs of labor, capital, and natural resources used in producing all goods and services

Fixed costs The explicit and implicit opportunity costs associated with providing fixed inputs

Fixed inputs Inputs that cannot be increased or decreased in a short time in order to increase or decrease output

Full rationality The assumption that people make full use of all available information in calculating how best to meet their objectives

Futures contract An agreement to exchange something at a specified date in the future at a price that is agreed upon now

Giffen good An inferior good accounting for a large share of a consumer's budget that has a positively sloped demand curve because the income effect of a price change outweighs the substitution effect

Gini coefficient A measure of inequality of income equal to zero under conditions of perfect equality and to one under perfect inequality

Gini index The Gini coefficient expressed as a percentage

Government failure   A situation in which a government policy causes inefficient use of resources

Heckscher-Ohlin theorem   The proposition that countries tend to export goods that make intensive use of the factors of production that the country possesses in relative abundance

Hedging   An operation in which futures markets or options markets are used to offset one risk with another

Herfindahl-Hirschmann index (HHI)   An index of market concentration that is calculated by squaring the percentage market shares of all firms in an industry then summing the squared-values

Hierarchy   A way of achieving coordination in which individual actions are guided by instructions from a central authority

Horizontal mergers   Mergers of firms that compete in the same market

Human capital   Capital in the form of learned abilities that have been acquired through formal training or education or through on-the-job experience

Implicit costs   Opportunity costs of using resources contributed by the firm's owners (or owned by the firm itself as a legal entity) that are not obtained in exchange for explicit payments

Import quotas   A limit on the quantity of a good that can be imported over a given period

Income effect   The part of the change in quantity demanded of a good whose price has fallen that is caused by the increase in real income resulting from the price change

Income elasticity of demand   The ratio of the percentage change in the quantity of a good demanded to a given percentage change in consumer incomes, other things being equal

Indifference curve   A graphical representation of an indifference set

Indifference map   A selection of indifference curves for a single consumer and pair of goods

Indifference set   A set of consumption choices, each of which yields the same utility so that no member of the set is preferred to any other

Inelastic demand   A situation in which quantity demanded changes by a smaller percentage than price, so that total revenue decreases as price decreases

Inferior good   A good for which an increase in consumer incomes results in a decrease in demand

Information asymmetry   A situation in which some parties to a transaction possess relevant information that other parties do not possess

Inframarginal rents   The difference between the payment made to a unit of resource and the minimum required for that resource to be willingly supplied in a situation in which units of a resource differ in terms of the willingness with which they are supplied

Inventory   A stock of a finished good awaiting sale or use

Inverse relationship   A relationship between two variables in which an increase in the value of one variable is associated with a decrease in the value of the other

Investment   The act of increasing the economy's stock of capital—that is, its supply of means of production made by people

Isoquantity line (isoquant)   A line showing the various combinations of inputs with which a given quantity of output can be produced

Labor   The contributions to production made by people working with their minds and muscles

Labor market discrimination   A situation in which employers are unwilling to hire members of a disfavored group at the same wage rate that they pay to equally productive members of a more favored group

Law of demand   The principle that an inverse relationship exists between the price of a good and the quantity of that good that buyers demand, other things being equal

Law of diminishing returns The principle that as one variable input is increased while all others remain fixed, a point will be reached beyond which the marginal physical product of the variable input will begin to decrease

Limit pricing A strategy in which the dominant firm in a market charges less than the short-run profit maximizing price in order to limit the likelihood of entry by new competitors

Loanable funds market A general term for the set of markets in which people borrow and lend, for whatever reason

Logrolling The practice of trading votes among members of a legislative body

Long run A time horizon that is long enough to permit changes in both fixed and variable inputs

Lorenz curve A graph that represents the degree of income inequality in an economy

Macroeconomics The branch of economics that studies large-scale economic phenomena, particularly inflation, unemployment, and economic growth

Marginal cost The increase in cost required to raise the output of some good or service by one unit

Marginal cost of abatement The cost of reducing waste discharged into the environment by one unit

Marginal external cost The total of the additional costs borne by all members of society as the result of an added unit of pollution

Marginal physical product The increase in output, expressed in physical units, produced by each added unit of one variable input, other things being equal

Marginal productivity theory of distribution A theory of income distribution in which each input of production receives a payment equal to its marginal revenue product

Marginal rate of substitution The rate at which one good can be substituted for another with no gain or loss in satisfaction

Marginal resource cost The amount by which a firm's total resource cost must increase for the firm to obtain an additional unit of that resource

Marginal revenue The amount by which total revenue changes as a result of a one-unit increase in quantity sold

Marginal revenue product The change in revenue that results from the sale of the output produced by one additional unit of an input

Marginal utility The amount of added utility gained from a one-unit increase in consumption of a good, other things being equal

Marginal-average rule The rule that marginal cost must equal average cost when average cost is at its minimum

Market Any arrangement people have for trading with one another

Market concentration The degree to which a market is dominated by a few large firms

Market failure A situation in which a market fails to coordinate choices in a way that achieves efficient use of resources

Market performance The degree to which markets work efficiently in providing arrangements for mutually beneficial trade

Market structure The key traits of a market, including the number and size of firms, the extent to which the products of various firms are different or similar, ease of entry and exit, and availability of information

Median voter model A model showing that there is a tendency for decisions in a democracy to reflect the interests of voters whose preferences lie near the middle of the scale

Microeconomics The branch of economics that studies the choices of individual units—including households, business firms, and government agencies

Minimum efficient scale The output level at which economies of scale cease

Model A synonym for theory; in economics, often applied to theories that are stated in graphical or mathematical form

Monopolistic competition A market structure in which there are many small firms, a differentiated product, and easy entry and exit

Monopoly A situation in which there is only a single seller of a good or service

Monopsony A situation in which there is only a single buyer in a market; more generally, any situation in which a firm is a price searcher in a market in which it is a buyer

Moral hazard Behavior that increases the risk of loss and, yet is undertaken in the knowledge that losses will be covered by insurance

Nash equilibrium An equilibrium solution to a game in which each player's strategy is optimal given the other players' choice of strategy

Natural monopoly An industry in which long-run average cost is minimized when only one firm serves the market

Natural resources Anything that can be used as a productive input in its natural state, such as farmland, building sites, forests, and mineral deposits

Negative income tax An antipoverty program under which low-income people receive grants from the government and high-income people pay taxes, subject to a net marginal tax rate of less than 100 percent for everyone

Negative slope A slope having a value less than zero

Net marginal tax rate The sum of the benefit reduction rate and the rate of income tax

Normal good A good for which an increase in consumer income results in an increase in demand

Normal profit (normal return on capital) The implicit opportunity cost of capital contributed by the firm's owners (equity capital)

Normative economics The area of economics that is devoted to judgments about whether economic policies or conditions are good or bad

Ockham's razor The principle that simpler theories are to be preferred to more complex ones when both are consistent with given observations

Oligopolistic interdependence The need to pay close attention to the actions of rival firms in an oligopolistic market when making price or production decision

Oligopoly A market structure in which there are only a few firms, at least some of which are large in relation to the size of the market

Open monopoly A monopoly in which one firm is, at least for a time, the sole supplier of a product but has no special protection from competition

Opportunity cost The cost of a good or service measured in terms of the forgone opportunity to pursue the best possible alternative activity with the same time or resources

Options Contracts under which one party obtains the right (but not the obligation) to buy something at a specified date in the future at a price that is agreed upon now

Other-regarding preferences A set of objectives that includes not only the material welfare of the decision maker, but also the material welfare of others and their attitudes toward the decision maker

Perfect competition A market structure that is characterized by a large number of small firms, a homogeneous product, freedom of entry and exit, and equal access to information

Perfectly elastic demand A situation in which the demand curve is a horizontal line

Perfectly inelastic demand A situation in which the demand curve is a vertical line

Political rent seeking (rent seeking) The process of seeking and defending economic rents through the political process

Positive economics The area of economics that is concerned with facts and the relationships among them

Positive slope A slope having a value greater than zero

Present value The value today of a sum payable in the future (In mathematical terms, the present value of a sum Vp, payable t years in the future, discounted at r percent interest, would grow to the value Vt in t years; the present value formula is Vp = Vt/(1 + r)t.

Price discrimination The practice of charging different prices for various units of a single product when the price differences are not justified by differences in cost

Price elasticity of demand The ratio of the percentage change in the quantity of a good demanded to a given percentage change in its price, other things being equal

Price elasticity of supply The ratio of the percentage change in the quantity of a good supplied to a given percentage change in its price, other things being equal

Price fixing Attempt by two or more firms to cooperate in setting prices

Price leadership A situation in which price increases or decreases by a dominant firm in an oligopoly, known as the price leader, are matched by all or most of the other firms in the market

Price searcher Any firm that faces a negatively sloped demand curve for its product

Price taker A firm that sells its output at prices that are determined by forces beyond its control

Principle of diminishing marginal utility The principle that the greater the consumption of some good, the smaller the increase in utility from a one-unit increase in consumption of that good

Producer surplus The difference between what producers receive for a unit of a good and the minimum they would be willing to accept

Production possibility frontier A graph that shows possible combinations of goods that can be produced by an economy given available knowledge and factors of production

Property rights Legal rules that establish what things a person may use or control, and the conditions under which such use or control may be exercised

Protectionism Any policy that is intended to shield domestic industries from import competition

Public choice theory The branch of economics that studies how people use the institutions of government in pursuit of their own interests

Public goods Goods that (1) cannot be provided for one person without also being provided for others and (2) when provided for one person can be provided for others at zero additional sum

Pure economic profit The sum that remains when both explicit and implicit costs are subtracted from total revenue

Pure economic rent The income earned by any resource whose supply is perfectly inelastic with respect to its price

Rate of return A firm's accounting profit expressed as a percentage of its net worth

Rate of return on capital The marginal product of capital expressed as an annual percentage rate

Rationality Acting purposefully to achieve an objective, given constraints on the opportunities that are available

Reservation price The maximum price that a buyer is willing to pay for a good or the minimum price at which a seller is willing to offer it

Revenue Price times quantity sold

Revenue-equivalence theorem The proposition that under certain general circumstances English, Dutch, and sealed-bid auctions can be expected to produce approximately the same winning bid

Risk aversion A preference for a certain outcome with a given value over a set of risky outcomes with the same expected value

Risk neutrality Indifference between a certain outcome with a given value and a set of risky outcomes with the same expected value

Risk pooling A technique in which the risk of loss is shared among many people so that the impact of a loss on any one of them is small

Risk preference A preference for a set of risky outcomes with a given expected value over a certain outcome with the same expected value

Scarcity A situation in which there is not enough of a resource to meet all of everyone's wants

Sealed-bid auction   An auction in which all buyers submit bids at the same time, and the item is sold to the highest bidder (or bought from the lowest bidder)

Self-regarding preferences   A set of objectives that depend only on the material welfare of the decision maker

Short run   A time horizon within which output can be adjusted only by changing the amounts of variable inputs used while fixed inputs remain unchanged

Simple monopoly   A monopoly that offers its output at a single price that is uniform for all customers and allows all buyers to purchase as much or as little as they want at that price

Slope   For a straight line, the ratio of the change in the y value to the change in the x value between any two points on the line

Speculation   Buying something at a low price in the hope of selling it later at a higher price

Spontaneous order   A way of achieving coordination in which individuals adjust their actions in response to cues from their immediate environment

Spot price   The price at which a good is offered for immediate sale

Static efficiency   The ability of an economy to get the greatest degree of consumer satisfaction from given amounts of resources and technology

Substitute goods   A pair of goods for which an increase in the price of one causes an increase in demand for the other

Substitution effect   The part of the increase in quantity demanded of a good whose price has fallen that is caused by substitution of that good for others that are now relatively more costly

Sunk costs   Once-and-for-all costs that, once incurred, cannot be recovered

Supply   The willingness and ability of sellers to provide goods for sale in a market

Supply curve   A graphical representation of the relationship between the price of a good and the quantity of that good that sellers are willing to supply

Tangent   A straight line that touches a curve at a given point without intersecting it

Tariff   A tax on imported goods

Tax incidence   The distribution of the economic burden of a tax

Theory   A representation of the way in which facts are related to one another

Time preference   The tendency to prefer goods now to goods in the future, other things being equal

Total physical product   The total output of a firm, measured in physical units

Transaction costs   The costs, other than production costs, of carrying out a transaction

Transitivity   The principle that if A is preferred to B and B is preferred to C, A must be preferred to C

Two-part pricing   A pricing strategy in which people must pay for the right to become a buyer before choosing how much to buy at a given price

Unit elastic demand   A situation in which price and quantity demanded change by the same percentage, so that total revenue remains unchanged as price changes

User charge   The per-unit price offered in a two-part pricing strategy to qualified customers who have paid the access charge

Utility   The pleasure, satisfaction, or need fulfillment that people obtain from the consumption of goods and services

Value of marginal product   Marginal physical product times the product's per-unit price

Variable costs   The explicit and implicit costs of providing variable inputs

Variable inputs   Inputs that can be varied within a short time in order to increase or decrease output

Vertical mergers   Mergers of firms with a supplier-purchaser relationship

Winner's curse   The tendency for winners of an auction to pay more for a good or service than it is worth (or to offer to sell at a price below the cost of providing the good or service)

Photo Credits

Chapter 1: iStockphoto, 3; iStockphoto, 6; iStockphoto, 7; iStockphoto, 11; iStockphoto, 17.

Chapter 2: iStockphoto, 41; iStockphoto, 42; AP Wide World Photos, 58; iStockphoto, 60.

Chapter 3: Shutterstock, 71; AP Wide World Photos, 78; iStockphoto, 83; iStockphoto, 87.

Chapter 4: Fotosearch, 97; iStockphoto, 98; iStockphoto, 103; iStockphoto, 109; iStockphoto, 110; iStockphoto, 112.

Chapter 5: iStockphoto, 119; iStockphoto, 121; iStockphoto, 127; iStockphoto, 128; AP Wide World Photos, 129.

Chapter 6: iStockphoto, 147; iStockphoto, 148; AP Wide World Photos, 157; iStockphoto, 165; iStockphoto, 167.

Chapter 7: iStockphoto, 175; iStockphoto, 177 (left); iStockphoto, 177 (right); iStockphoto, 186; iStockphoto, 188; iStockphoto, 189.

Chapter 8: iStockphoto, 199; iStockphoto, 205; AP Wide World Photos, 217 (top); AP Wide World Photos, 217 (bottom); iStockphoto, 220.

Chapter 9: iStockphoto, 231; Shutterstock Photo, 241.

Chapter 10: AP Wide World Photos, 257; iStockphoto, 265; iStockphoto, 267 (left); iStockphoto, 267 (right).

Chapter 11: iStockphoto, 283; AP Wide World Photos, 284; iStockphoto, 288; AP Wide World Photos, 295; AP Wide World Photos, 296.

Chapter 12: AP Wide World Photos, 311; Library of Congress, 312; AP Wide World Photos, 313; AP Wide World Photos, 315.

Chapter 13: iStockphoto, 331; iStockphoto, 347; AP Wide World Photos, 349 (left); AP Wide World Photos, 349 (right).

Chapter 14: iStockphoto, 361; AP Wide World Photos, 362; iStockphoto, 363; iStockphoto, 367; Shutterstock Photo, 369.

Chapter 15: AP Wide World Photos, 381; AP Wide World Photos, 382; iStockphoto, 386; AP World Wide Photo, 388; AP World Wide Photo, 392.

Chapter 16: iStockphoto, 403; iStockphoto, 409; iStockphoto, 410; AP Wide World Photo, 416.

Index

W